The
Lively
Arts

The
Lively
Arts

Gilbert Seldes and the
Transformation of Cultural Criticism
in the United States

MICHAEL KAMMEN

New York   Oxford
OXFORD UNIVERSITY PRESS
1996

Oxford University Press

Oxford   New York
Athens   Auckland   Bangkok   Bombay
Calcutta   Cape Town   Dar es Salaam   Delhi
Florence   Hong Kong   Istanbul   Karachi
Kuala Lumpur   Madras   Madrid   Melbourne
Mexico City   Nairobi   Paris   Singapore
Taipei   Tokyo   Toronto

and associated companies in
Berlin   Ibadan

Published by Oxford University Press, Inc.,
198 Madison Avenue, New York, New York 10016

Oxford is a registered trademark of Oxford University Press

Library of Congress Cataloging-in-Publication Data
Kammen, Michael G.
The lively arts : Gilbert Seldes and the transformation of
cultural criticism in the United States / Michael Kammen.
p. cm.   Includes bibliographical references and index.
ISBN 0-19-509868-4
1. Seldes, Gilbert.   2. Art critics—United States—Biography.
3. Seldes, Gilbert—Influence.   4. Arts and society—United States—
History—20th century.   5. Popular culture—United States.
I. Title.
N7483.S38K36   1996
700'.92—dc20
[B]   95-12446

1 3 5 7 9 8 6 4 2

Printed in the United States of America
on acid-free paper

For

Mary Kelley and Michael J. Hogan

Arnita A. Jones

and

Robert C. Ritchie

With deep appreciation
for their friendship, support,
and superb professionalism

Contents

Illustrations

To live over people's lives is nothing unless we live over their perceptions, live over the growth, the change, the varying intensity of the same — since it was *by* these things they themselves lived.

— HENRY JAMES

It will be the function of the critic to transmute the experience which the American people will obtain in the pursuit of their national purpose into socially formative knowledge.

— HERBERT CROLY

It is the tragic story of the cultural crusader in a mass society that he cannot win, but that we would be lost without him.

— PAUL F. LAZARSFELD

Gilbert Seldes as he appeared on the cover of the *Saturday Review of Literature,* vol. 17 (Jan. 15, 1938).

Introduction

I n one of the very last essays that Gilbert Seldes wrote, in 1966, he made the following assertion and deliberately cast it entirely in italics: *"In my own lifetime I have witnessed more changes in the modes of communication than occurred in all recorded history before."* That observation is noteworthy not only because it is true, but because Seldes' persistent emphasis upon the constancy of change in American culture characterized his entire career as a critic and historian. As early as 1926 he called attention to "the speed in America, that uncertainty and restlessness, the incapacity to attach itself for a long time to one pleasure and refine it, or to one discipline and master it. . . . "[1]

During the 1950s he frequently noted the vast transformation in popular culture that had occurred since he first wrote about aspects of the phenomenon in 1922–23. He acknowledged that the emergence of various electronic media had been at the heart of this transformation and expressed concern about the impact of mass-produced mediocrity via television, radio, and especially film. In May 1963, when Seldes gave his last lecture as Dean of the Annenberg School of Communications at the University of Pennsylvania, he told the audience that his favorite topic, the lively arts, had changed so fast that he could barely keep up with it. "The subject never stood still," he remarked. And referring to the communications revolution in general, he commented wistfully yet gratefully that he had lived through the very heart of it and had made a career

Fig. 1. Stuart Davis, *Study for the History of Communications Mural* (1939), the design of Davis' gigantic mural created for the Hall of Communication at the New York World's Fair in 1939. Courtesy of the Minnesota Museum of Art, St. Paul, Minnesota.

as a public observer/critic of that major transformation.[2] (See Fig. 1.)

Much of what Seldes said in this candid farewell monologue he expanded upon in the numerous pieces of his unpublished memoirs. Writing a twelve-page segment in 1964, for example, he made a fast-forward shift from the 1920s to the '60s but expressed an apprehensive concern that the two decades really could be connected. "I am not a hyphen between two different worlds," he remarked, referring to popular culture in its prime and to the recently impressive impact of technology in the realm of entertainment. "As I lived, they developed their own connection and (another part of my great good fortune) I moved back and forth." Elsewhere in that same declaration, however, he made an invidious comparison between the lively arts of his youth, which he recalled with great affection and, "like a dark shadow," the current dominance of mass media.[3]

Hyphen or not, there is a genuine sense in which Seldes *was* a man who lived engagingly between two historically distinct eras. During his youth the Progressives had measured social improvement and reform in moralistic terms. By the 1950s and '60s, his final decades, such critics as Lionel Trilling, Reinhold Niebuhr, and James Agee once again measured cultural values in terms of moral concern and intensity. By contrast, during Seldes' own distinctive "moment," roughly 1920 to 1950, the democratization of culture mattered considerably more than assessing the quality of humanistic matters in moralistic terms. For Seldes and most of his contemporary critics, nationalistic and populistic concerns attracted far more attention than moral intensity. That is partially why, during his later years, he found himself less on the leading edge of intellectual life in the United States.

The likes of Walter Lippmann, Randolph Bourne, Van Wyck Brooks, and Gilbert Seldes came of age at a time when aspiring critics confronted a decline of traditional cultural authority. A major portion of their success and prominence, in fact, resulted from the diverse ways in which they responded to that waning of cultural authority—exemplified by the dissipated genteel tradition—as an opportunity to reformulate the nature and thrust of expository criticism. Note that in 1929 Waldo Frank looked back to the creation of *The New Republic* fifteen years earlier as the genesis of a "new critical era," one that provided a foundation for a "democratic nation" offering a meaningful role for artists and intellectuals.

Seldes' career as a critic did coincide with an astonishing series of innovations in popular and mass culture: the transition from silent film to sound; radio; television; and through it all, the proliferation of middlebrow journalism in such venues as the *Saturday Evening Post, Esquire,* and the *Saturday Review of Literature.* He not only speculated continuously about the future prospects for all of those media, but became a participant as well: writing and adapting plays, preparing scripts for lengthy series of radio programs, becoming the first Director of Television for CBS, participating in discussion programs on radio and television, serving as an adviser to Hollywood film studios, and so forth. Seldes was never an "ivory tower" critic.

He invariably identified his vocation simply as critic. Although he rarely used cultural as a modifier, he did use various other modifiers, such as professional critic, claiming on one occasion that he sought to offer constructive criticism, and denying on another that he was "merely a destructive critic."[4] During the mid- and later 1920s, when Seldes first donned his professional mantle, he wrote essays lamenting that Americans did not respect their cultural critics yet also acknowledging that too many critics carped unfairly and tended to be extremist in their views. By the late 1930s, when Seldes became intensely concerned about the rise of totalitarianism, he liked to insist that he was a citizen first and a critic second.[5]

Seldes' career is instructive because he belonged to a new generation of critics who came of age immediately after World War I. Unlike their predecessors, who tended to specialize in literary criticism (William Crary Brownell, the foremost American disciple of Matthew Arnold), music (James Gibbons Huneker), art (Royal Cortissoz), or architecture (Montgomery Schuyler), Seldes' cohort was courageously versatile and wrote about virtually anything and everything. In Seldes' case, like his contemporaries Edmund Wilson and Lewis Mumford, he also tried his hand at social history and fiction—each in its way offered as an indirect form of cultural criticism.[6]

For Seldes, especially, writing history and writing cultural criticism were not compartmentalized activities. They connected. Between 1910 and 1917 the prominent anthropologist Alfred L. Kroeber wrote extensively in order to explain his concept of culture, which he preferred to call "history." From Kroeber's perspective, altered circumstances over time, along with the values of a society, could interchangeably be designated as culture or history. Seldes complained, on occasion, when he felt that social groups or critics conceived of culture in needlessly narrow terms.[7]

Although Seldes was neither as complex nor as profound a thinker as Wilson and Mumford, he displayed the very considerable virtue that he challenged intellectuals *and* the informed public as well to reconsider phenomena that they took for granted as normative. He significantly expanded the targets of inquiry and the criteria that cultural critics applied. Even more, he broadened the role and definition of what it meant to be a critic. As he declared in 1925, "the significance of a critic is measured by the problems he puts to us. . . ."[8] Although Seldes cannot be designated as *the* representative critic of his time—no single individual could serve in that capacity—he was representative of the dominant course that cultural criticism followed in the decades after the 1920s: toward enhanced interest in the lively arts and popular culture. It is ironic, perhaps, that Seldes is best known for his earlier writings, when his views were more commonly contested, and less likely to be remembered for what he wrote after 1945 when he was not often challenged and was invariably referred to as Gilbert Seldes, "the distinguished critic."

By that time the scope of criticism as a vocation had expanded in several important respects. Film criticism, for instance, developed rather slowly as a respectable genre and even encountered resistance during the 1920s and '30s. (When Nunnally Johnson proposed to Harold Ross that he contribute film reviews to *The New Yorker,* Ross replied scornfully that "movies are for old ladies and fairies.") Radio reviews and criticism required a while to develop, too, but a substantial coterie of critics did eventually emerge. Television criticism became regular fare much more swiftly, in part because of an early concern by parents that violence and crime received disproportionate program time, but also because of high expectations for television as an entertainment and informational phenomenon.

If cultural criticism truly came of age as a vocation during the 1920s, its maturation was assisted by the proliferation of journals and magazines, highbrow as well as middlebrow, during the early and middle decades of the twentieth century. Between *The New Republic, The Masses, The Seven Arts, The Nation, The Dial, Vanity Fair, The American Mercury, Theater Arts Monthly, The Saturday Review, Esquire, Partisan Review,* and many others, outlets for critics abounded. Who could keep up with all of these essays and reviews, especially when some of them tended to pontificate or nitpick? Mary McCarthy, who contributed her own share of criticism, referred sardonically to the insights of such critics as "the sacred droppings of holy birds."[9]

Although Seldes directed prickly barbs at some of his fellow critics on occasion, he much preferred to point out instances when prominent people in public life totally misjudged the future of some medium or form of entertainment. He didn't find these ironic so much as amusing because his own gaffes prompted the realization that new art forms could be highly unpredictable. Seldes loved to recall, for instance, that Thomas A. Edison had objected to showing moving pictures on a screen. If pictures were presented in a room where several hundred people could see them at the same time, Edison warned, the appeal of the pictures would swiftly be exhausted and film entrepreneurs would go bankrupt. It didn't turn out that way, of course; and Seldes also delighted in reminding readers that Herbert Hoover had predicted the American people would not tolerate advertisements on the radio. Seldes chuckled at skeptics who insisted that the advent of television would absolutely kill the film industry. That briefly threatened to happen during the early 1950s, partly because of television's novelty and partly because those in charge of the film industry did not initially take TV seriously. Their ostrich-like posture ended by the mid-1950s, however, and the prophets turned out to be false ones for a full generation, at least.[10]

I would not claim that Seldes was infinitely wiser or more prescient than his contemporary critics. But two aspects of his career might have made him more of a visionary and less likely to make imprudent predictions: first, his "hands on" experience as a practitioner directly involved with most of the popular arts that he wrote about; and second, his truly remarkable versatility as an editor, free-lance writer on every conceivable subject, historian, novelist, playwright, film-maker, script writer for radio, program director for CBS Television, and founding dean of the Annenberg School of Communications. Seldes deserves to be remembered as one of the earliest serious film critics; and, in a very real sense, he can properly be regarded as a progenitor of the discipline known today as cultural studies—a mixture of communications theory, film and television analysis, historical and literary investigation.[11]

In addition to his versatility, Seldes is also conspicuous among his contemporaries because of his abiding commitment to the democratization of culture. Unlike William Crary Brownell, who spoke for the genteel critics in holding up the "aristocratic democrat" as an American ideal, and unlike Dwight Macdonald who scorned both mass and middlebrow culture as being vulgar beyond redemption, Seldes genuinely believed the taste level of ordinary Americans was not inevitably contemptible, and that, in any case, taste levels could be elevated. That was not an elitist point of view. Seldes felt certain that ordinary men and women *wanted* and deserved better than the fare they were being offered by those who controlled the media.* "Even now," he observed in 1936, "we are only beginning to understand what democracy means in connection with education, entertainment, and the arts."[12]

Writing in 1961 for a mass audience, he posed the rhetorical question: "Are Critics Necessary?" He responded that "the critic is the only true believer in democracy," and added that as a critic committed to democratic values he wanted to assist in creating "a nation of critics." In his very last book, *The New Mass Media* (1957), Seldes reaffirmed his belief that the media could and should play an instrumental role in the enhancement of cultural democracy.[13]

It is significant that the first chapter of that book is devoted to "The Mass Media and the Individual" because Seldes had always prized what he called "the independent thinking individual." Recognizing that the communications revolution threatened to diminish autonomous thought and individualism, Seldes sought to reconcile mass culture with his long-cherished Emersonian ideal of individualism as a mandate both for American identity *and* for resistance to external authority, ranging from group pressure to the State.[14]

---

*In 1937 Seldes addressed himself to "the whole question of the relations of the worker in the arts and those to whom he is communicating any important or trifling thing he has to say. The priests of the church are willing to talk to the common man, but the priests of art deliver themselves in obscure terms and go into an unpriestly rage when interlopers translate their message and vulgarize it and perhaps corrupt it, and make themselves understood." GS, "The People and the Arts," *Scribner's* 101 (April 1937): 60.

That dualism—admiring individualism both for its yea-saying *and* for its dissident qualities—brings us to several others that characterized Seldes. He had an impulse to cut against the grain, and he tended to advocate whatever it was currently fashionable to attack. If he defended American culture during the later 1920s and '30s when H. L. Mencken made it trendy to mock the mediocrity of American culture, Seldes could also be quite critical, subsequently, when the national mood mindlessly reaffirmed the whole of American culture. With the passage of time he increasingly became a moderate with a strong distaste for extremist positions. He once idealized Bing Crosby because he was so American and because he seemed so normal. "He is that amazing product of the Far West—the Cosmopolitan American. He is also that odd American freak, a gifted artist without temperament, with all the normal instincts and the average reactions, the reasonably good citizen, the *homme moyen sensuel* [man of normal human instincts]."[15]

Looking back near the end of his life, when Seldes labored on a long autobiographical memoir, he saw himself as a mediator and as a man disposed to transcend conventional boundaries or the compartmentalization of human endeavor and culture. Contemplating his own work-in-progress in 1965, he offered this self-reflection to a confidant.

> I find that my whole book is a record of crossing—crossing what were to me artificial lines on a map—between the fine and the popular arts, between Jews and non-Jews, between the academic or scholarly and the technological practical (as in the mass media) and my strongest interest now, between the fine arts and the sciences so that both are recognized as parts of the humanities.[16]

An intermediary, a moderate, a man who admired judiciousness—those attributes might have made for blandness. On the contrary, however, the qualities that Seldes admired most in the arts were high spirits (he loved to laugh and sing with his family), fantasy, gayety, but above all, *intensity*. Al Jolson and Fanny Brice, two of his great favorites, had intensity, and he cherished them on that account. "Intensity" emerged early on as a high compliment in his lexicon; and in his later years when admiring contemporaries sought to describe Seldes, they commonly included the word "intense."[17]

Moreover, Seldes' antagonists in clashes over serious matters—H. L. Mencken, Ernest Hemingway, Ernest Boyd, Norman Bel Geddes, Alexander Woollcott, George Jean Nathan, Dwight Macdonald, Edward R.

Murrow, John Crosby, James Marston Fitch, and Walter Annenberg—considered their adversary anything but bland. Because Seldes had principles and defended them vigorously, his professional quarrels are interesting, symptomatic, and significant. His warm friendships and the activities they generated are also important.

Starting around 1950 Seldes and his wife began to rent a house in Wellfleet or Truro, on Cape Cod, for a month or so each summer. After her death Seldes went to the Cape every summer and stayed until Labor Day. He always gave a very large party on the Fourth of July, and, according to his daughter, it seemed as though "the entire literary population attended."[18] Although Seldes always enjoyed going to Europe, he firmly believed that an artistic or creative American could fulfill himself (or herself) without going abroad. Seldes was genuinely grateful to be an American. He found the country and its culture endlessly fascinating and distinctive—even when his critical impulses prompted him to write in a negative way about his native land. Seldes stayed more in tune with the cultural nationalism of the 1920s and '30s than with the internationalism that became trendy among New York intellectuals and artistic performers following World War II.

Ultimately, his customary judiciousness, integrity, and fairness made him an exemplary cultural critic. A collection or selection of his writings —which he never made—might very well be designated the *non*-partisan review, an approach he internalized as a young man when he served as managing editor of *The Dial*.

That same passion for balance and moderation kept him committed to the belief that popular culture could be both democratic *and* distinguished. Seldes simultaneously wanted to elevate the cultural awareness and self-confidence of ordinary people, yet he never lost sight of the need for critics to take more seriously the cultural enthusiasms and expectations of ordinary Americans. He basically became a bourgeois who proudly identified with the middle class. During his mature years he never pretended otherwise.

Seldes was also a learned intellectual, however, who always scorned pretentious highbrows. Unlike most of the highbrows that he scorned, Seldes loved what he called the lively arts (in 1924) and later the public arts (in 1956). Unlike Van Wyck Brooks, he never ceased to believe that high culture and popular culture could beneficially converge. Their interaction or reconciliation would vastly improve the quality of life for all. Seldes declared in 1951: "If I have any private tradition, any commitment to an idea, it is that the popular arts and the great arts can support and enrich one another, and that this cross-fertilization will come about naturally if the two are not kept apart."[19]

Despite these (and various other) categorical assertions, ambiguities emerge when we take an overview of Seldes' long career: ambivalence about being a highbrow himself while demeaning others who displayed some of the less attractive qualities of that genus, and ambivalence about condemning others as aesthetes while recognizing that he did not altogether lack some of the attributes commonly ascribed to aesthetes.

His views concerning a genuinely democratic culture were not fully and consistently elaborated either, especially when we take note of positions that his contemporaries held on that matter. Seldes' belief that Everyman could be a competent critic, for example, would seem to preclude any commitment to uphold objective cultural "standards." Yet some of Seldes' contemporaries, such as Henry Seidel Canby, insisted that in a democracy people are *entitled* to learn about "the best" by having easy access to cultural authorities. In sum, Seldes made defining statements about a democratic culture without entirely coming to terms with what significant others had to say about such a problematic goal.[20]

The reader ought not to anticipate wondrous consistency from any cultural critic, least of all one who pursued that vocation for close to half a century. Personal ambivalence provides merely one explanation: at times he found himself genuinely torn between conflicting possibilities. More important, however—and this affected all of Seldes' contemporaries as well—there were highly significant, unanticipated changes in the very nature of the public arts themselves—and in their swiftly expanding audiences between the 1920s and the 1960s.

A third source of inconsistency can be found in Seldes' passion for fairness and his contempt for extremism. In the decade following World War II, for example, when he felt most disheartened because the producers of mass and popular culture seemed satisfied with mediocrity, he nonetheless hated to succor those archly elitist critics who were absolutely negative about anything and everything middlebrow or popular. Hence the shift in his tone from rather harsh in *The Great Audience* (1950) to more hopeful in *The Public Arts* (1956).

Fourth, Seldes admittedly vacillated in his views concerning government support for culture in general and the arts in particular. He did so primarily between the later 1930s, when private sector funds to support cultural endeavors were in desperately short supply, and the later 1940s when economic recovery made it appear that the public arts could survive without government funds and might thrive more independently without intervention by bureaucratic agencies. Governmental support was not a matter of principle for Seldes. It was a necessary expedient in hard times.

When Seldes felt perplexed on occasion during his final decades it was because swift changes in the social and economic context of entertainment and broadcasting were themselves genuinely perplexing. He saw no simple solutions, an abundance of cultural contradictions, and consequently offered no easy answers. Moreover, what cultural critics had to say seemed to make a difference during the 1920s and '30s, but much less so after World War II when the lively arts were increasingly controlled by big commercial entities rather than accountable individuals, by corporate sponsors rather than independent publishers and producers who operated on a human scale. Hence the growing frustration during the 1950s of critics as different as Seldes, Dwight Macdonald, Clement Greenberg, Edmund Wilson, Theodor Adorno, and Lewis Mumford.

Ultimately, Seldes' career is so instructive because both as a citizen and as a critic he connected with all taste levels. Although he frequently made fun of highbrows, he acknowledged to confidants like Arthur M. Schlesinger, Jr., that by virtue of education and cerebration he was one. Nevertheless, like many other highbrows, such as Virginia Woolf, he had a predilection—indeed, an enthusiasm—for types of entertainers and pleasures that were customarily stereotyped as lowbrow. Seldes shared Charlie Chaplin's sense that he was (without anomaly) a "high lowbrow."

Even so, as he entered middle age Seldes identified increasingly with the middle class and recognized that he nurtured bourgeois values. He understood that in the United States commerce and culture could not be dichotomized. In his later years he also realized that commerce inevitably shaped culture because it was inseparable from it. As early as the 1920s he defended ordinary Americans, even American businessmen, against savage attacks from such as Sinclair Lewis and H. L. Mencken.

Like other critics who accommodated middlebrow taste during the interwar years, he happily wrote for the *Saturday Evening Post,* and then for *Esquire,* and still later for the *Saturday Review.* He wrote mystery stories, popularized Aristophanes' *Lysistrata,* and adapted a musical rendition of a Shakespearian comedy. He appeared as a guest on middlebrow radio talk programs and, for a while, hosted his own. It caused him neither distress nor embarrassment to write a daily column for the New York *Evening Journal* and, eventually, even for *TV Guide.*

Certainly no snob, Seldes the man and critic was a cultural democrat. Although he genuinely wished to elevate taste levels, he respected the diversity that he encountered among cultural preferences. He found excellence, and mediocrity, at *all* levels. Duke Ellington's favorite phrase conveying praise, "beyond category," surely applies to Seldes and his criteria as a critic. He transcended categories because, at heart, he found categories confining and arbitrary rather than constructively meaningful.

During the 1920s, when critics thrived on the application of categories and labels, Seldes was unusual simply because his enthusiasms erased boundaries. By the 1960s, when Seldes stepped down from the public rostrum, it had become the norm for critics to scorn boundaries and to blur or conflate taste levels. Above all, it had become doctrinally sound—almost an article of faith—that critics and their audiences should support, above all else, the democratization of culture. What had not been normative in 1925 had virtually emerged as a creed by 1965.

Gilbert Seldes did more than participate in that transformation. He did much to make it happen. His career illuminates the transformation of American culture—and of cultural criticism, during the middle third of the twentieth century.

Clearly, the history of cultural criticism in the United States is not now ready for a meta-narrative because we do not, as yet, have a basic descriptive narrative—as we do in so many other sub-fields. I will feel content if the chapters that follow make a contribution to the essential narrative of cultural criticism in modern American life. A broader overview, perhaps one verging upon meta-narrative, will follow in due course.

1

A Portrait of the Critic
As a Young Man

The first quarter-century of Seldes' life is fascinating for a range of instructive reasons. First, perhaps predictably, because the shaping of Seldes as a mature writer can so clearly be seen in his adolescence, his college experience, and his initial years as journalist and critic—covering World War I in particular. Even so, some striking shifts in his temperament and values must also be noted. Seldes' life did not run along a smoothly guided monorail. For instance, the self-described cultural elitist at Harvard College (1910–14) became, within a decade, the most vocal American champion of popular culture. For the remainder of his entire career, Seldes would be widely recognized as a pioneering advocate for what he called the "lively" or popular arts.

Second, a close look at these formative decades helps to prepare us for a pattern of discrepancies between the life Seldes actually lived and his imperfect memories of it in old age. A man of notable integrity, he would not deliberately dissemble about his episodic life. Seldes' inconsistencies and lapses of memory are those of Everyman. His might be somewhat more problematic, though, because connections between history and memory held special importance for him. He devoted much of his last decade to a memoir that he never completed. The richly textured documentation that he compiled, however, demonstrates both his desire to make history and memory converge as well as the difficulties he faced in seeking to fulfill that passion. Which merely says that Seldes was human and hence fallible. What he had to say in retrospect about his experiences at Harvard, for example, does not altogether accord with what he wrote about the college while he was there. The importance of that lapse lies not so much in ascertaining precise details of Seldes' life as it does in lessons about the human condition. A few people actually invent, or even falsify, themselves. Many people misrepresent themselves, usually in minor ways, at one time or another. Not many men and women make the strenuous effort that Seldes did to be veracious. Not lacking an ego—and being occasionally erratic—he did not always succeed.

His early years are also instructive because they help to explain his life-long penchant for "individuality." The unusual circumstances of Seldes' childhood, family relations, and formal education all reinforced his enduring antipathy toward "going along" in order to "get along." Both Gilbert and his older brother, George, felt a personal compunction to speak their minds, heedless of the consequences. Each of them, but especially Gilbert, would eventually estrange not only people they disliked, but some admired friends as well. That compulsion to be candid persistently undermined the attractive ideal of community. Although Seldes had many close friends, his temperament precluded membership in any kind of ongoing coterie.

Finally, by way of introducing this chapter, the particular years when Seldes came of age, roughly 1910 to 1918, help to clarify some notable differences between two chronological cohorts that have commonly been conflated. One group, born in the 1870s and 1880s, included such political and literary radicals as Max Eastman and Emma Goldman, Floyd Dell and John Sloan, Upton Sinclair, and Charlotte Perkins Gilman, John Reed and Hutchins Hapgood, Claude McKay and Susan Glaspell. The journal that we associate with some of them, *The Masses,* flourished between 1911 and 1917. For the sake of convenience, I call them the generation of 1906–10.[1]

Seldes belonged to a cohort that was a decade younger, born in the 1890s, that I call, once again for convenience, the "generation" of 1915–19, a group that included Harold Stearns, John Peale Bishop, Edmund Wilson, F. Scott Fitzgerald, E. E. Cummings, John Dos Passos, and others whom we shall encounter. They tended to be less intensely political than those roughly ten years older, less concerned with social causes, and more literary in their preoccupations. Individual exceptions come to mind, of course, but they are largely situational. Upton Sinclair, obviously, was a literary man, and Seldes, at certain times, could be a semipolitical man. Nevertheless, as I hope to show, there are subtle yet clear distinctions to be noticed between these two cohorts.[2]

It seems significant, moreover, that Seldes rarely encountered, or even mentioned, members of the "generation" that directly preceded his own. There are a few important exceptions here also, such as H. L. Mencken and Van Wyck Brooks; but even they would ultimately concern him less than writers and artists a decade and more younger than himself. Seldes appears very much a man of the post-World War I era. Although he cared deeply about history, his dialogues were invariably with contemporaries rather than with his predecessors. He pursued the past because it helped him understand and explain the present. Engagement and enjoyment occurred in the here and now. The autobiographical volume that remained embryonic at the time of his death in 1970 he always called "As in My Time." Therein lies a lesson about the man and his sense of context.

I

Gilbert Seldes was born on January 3, 1893, in Alliance, New Jersey, a small community in the southwestern portion of the state, due west of Atlantic City. He attended elementary school not far away in Vineland. More to the point, however, he grew up in a utopian farm colony consisting of about three hundred homes. His parents and grandparents were of Russian origin, non-observant (indeed utterly secular) Jews; and his father, the moving force in this utopian colony, professed an ardent commitment to philosophical radicalism. Both Gilbert and his older brother, George, left vivid recollections of their father, in part because he so clearly was a strong-willed and opinionated man, and in part because their mother died in 1896 when both boys were still quite young (see Fig. 2). Their father, George Sergius Seldes, who remarried but later left his second wife, lived until 1931.

His impact upon the two precocious sons was profound, especially when it came to books. George emphasized in his autobiography that their father

> insisted that we not waste our time reading Alger and Henty and rags-to-riches "boys' books" and popular novels, but read books of some value, frequently a little beyond our understanding. We were told to begin making a library as soon as we were able to buy books, or to suggest good books

Fig. 2. Gilbert Seldes' parents, George Sergius Seldes and Anna
Verna Seldes (ca. 1888–89).

to relatives who sent birthday presents. Father would say, "Don't waste
time reading a book that you will never look at again. Read books that you
will reread—and that you will never outgrow. When you are older you
will not hesitate to underline lines, whole chapters, you believe to be the
most important ideas or thoughts in these books—do not be afraid to write
in the margins. All this world's civilization is to be found between the
covers of books."[3]

Looking back in 1935, both proudly *and* ruefully it would seem,
Gilbert recalled that in 1900 his father allowed the brothers "such freedom of choice, threw so many decisions upon us, left us too independent,

that the enlightened parent of the 1930s seems to us barely to be catching up to him. He actually was to such an extent a philosophical anarchist that he never tried to make philosophical anarchists out of his children." George and Gilbert were denied the secret pleasure (and vice) of reading forbidden books "because no books were forbidden."[4]

The father always remained a "devout" freethinker: devout because he resented being called a heretic, an agnostic, or even an atheist. He passionately opposed the inculcation of any religion in children too young to understand it. When they reached an age of intellectual understanding they might study all of the great religions and feel free to make a choice. Both brothers opted to remain freethinkers, always, and on occasion young Gilbert delivered pronouncements that sound utterly pompous until we recall that he was, at the time, spellbound by Ralph Waldo Emerson. Under the circumstances he seems more derivatively Emersonian than derisively arrogant.* In 1910, for example, while a senior at Philadelphia's Central High School, he wrote to Judith Randorf, a beloved cousin who fortunately preserved all of his letters spanning more than fifteen years, beginning in 1908:

My belief in myself transcends all beliefs in Divinity. I am a Divinity to myself. Were I not, then were the world not—as far as I knew. The very facts of existence are brought to us only thru ourselves. Let us make thoseselves fit to receive them.[5]

Seldes' social and political relationship to Judaism was paradoxical if not ironic. In an article published in 1921 he rejected Zionism because a Jewish state would diminish the "internationalism" of the Jewish people. (Cosmopolitanism, in every sense, remained extremely important to Seldes.) On rare occasions he seemed to acknowledge a disproportionately heightened potential for creativity among Jews. Early in 1923, for example, he wrote the following from France: "Picasso approves of his picture in my book and says that all great men are Jews so I ought to be lucky or great or some-thing. . . ."[6]

Much more common, however, are the snide anti-Semitic remarks made about Seldes (usually in private) by such contemporaries as Ezra Pound, Ernest Hemingway, Archibald MacLeish, and others. Those derisive comments persisted but with diminished frequency following

---

*For his debt to Emersonian individualism, see any edition of "The American Scholar" (1837): e.g., "Each man shall feel that the World is his, and man shall treat with man as a sovereign state with a sovereign state. . . . "

his marriage in 1924 to Alice Wadhams Hall, an upper-class Episco-
palian. Although a lot of the entertainers that Seldes most admired were
Jewish, a great many others were not. He liked Al Jolson and Jimmy
Durante, Jack Benny and Bob Hope.

Late in the 1960s, when Edmund Wilson became deeply immersed in
a careful study of the Dead Sea Scrolls (even pausing to learn Hebrew),
Seldes sent his old friend a hilarious letter because some people mis-
takenly seemed to assume that Wilson must be Jewish.

> You know, of course, how anti-Semitic I am, but I think you should have
> told me. . . . To me the only chosen people are those of Korea and I even
> resent the implication that (being partially white) I am not a Soul [i.e.,
> Seoul]. But for you to go brisking about concealing the fact that your real
> interest in the The Dead Sea Scrolls were that they were in your native
> tongue strikes me as. . . . etc.[7]

The range of Seldes' intellectual interests would always be engagingly
eclectic and ecumenical, but religion remained conspicuously absent. The
conventional distinction between sacred and profane did not play a pur-
poseful role in Seldes' cosmology or his cultural criticism. Rather than
the sacred and the profane, this totally secular, assimilated Jew thought
in terms of a different dualism: the aesthetically creative versus the
culturally mundane. Seldes, in fact, admired much that we (and his
contemporaries) would consider profane, like vaudeville. Profane conveyed no pejorative connotations, but mundane did. Achieving artistic
excellence served Gilbert Seldes as a surrogate for conventional notions
of the sacred.

The legacy of childhood lived in a utopian farm colony involved more
than a rejection of institutional religion and orthodox belief. In several
important respects Seldes would repudiate the lifestyle and the circumstances of his youth. Growing up on a farm, for instance, meant hoeing
and digging potatoes, and picking strawberries at the rate of one cent per
quart. In autumn the brothers picked grapes which their grandfather
sold to a man named Charlie Welch, the inventor of an alcohol-free wine
that he cleverly called grape juice. Seldes would become an urban creature with little trace of nostalgia for agriculture or the pastoral. Even so,
as late as 1916 he could not imagine that New York City would be his
destination and cultural destiny for most of the half-century from 1920
until his death. In 1916 he wrote from London to his cousin in Philadelphia that he was homesick, and speculated about where he might live

when he returned after the war. He had enjoyed Philadelphia (where he wrote concert reviews for a local newspaper) after graduation from Harvard in 1914. "And though I might choose Boston," he remarked, "I shouldn't choose New York unless something quite big, like the NYWorld or the New Republic demanded my presence."[8] This is an early example of Seldes' erratic career as a seer. Personal prophecy did not turn out to be his greatest strength.

Perhaps Seldes' distaste for rural life owed something to the primitive circumstances of his father's problematic colony. The sandy and unfertile farms had no amenities—none. Electric lines and telephone wires were unknown. The colony did not have a single indoor bathroom. No one had running water. What it *did* have, Seldes recalled many years later, "was an incompetent lot of stingy farmers," anarchists, and cranks. It seemed, in retrospect, that Seldes had spent his childhood in "constant communication" with impractical, poorly educated, self-isolated dreamers and seekers. During his mature years, he never shed an aversion to all such types, preferring moderate reformers. Growing up in an unworkable utopia left Seldes with a penchant for moderation, a mistrust of wild-eyed idealism, and an appreciation for what he later called "humane capitalism." Unlike many of his generation, socialism never attracted Seldes.[9]

His mother, regarded by the colonists in Alliance as a "good woman, the kindest woman they had known," died when the boys were six and three respectively. Their father persuaded his sister, Bertha, the head nurse at a small Philadelphia hospital, to give up her career, come to Alliance, and raise the boys there until 1906 when Gilbert went to Philadelphia to attend prestigious Central High School. The widowed father, meanwhile, recognizing that his agrarian colony was rapidly becoming a dyspeptic, non-viable distopia, took himself to Philadelphia where he worked in a drugstore as a pharmacist and studied law at night. Eventually, with the help of friendly physicians, he obtained mortgages and ran his own drugstore, at first in Philadelphia and later in Pittsburgh. Curiously, though, he became a shareholder in a semi-utopian colony located near Peekskill, New York.[10] To paraphrase Dr. Johnson, that investment represented a triumph of hope over experience.

Meanwhile George Sergius Seldes occasionally visited his sons in Alliance and they saw him in Philadelphia. He later joined them in London during 1916–17 when both young men covered the war as journalists. Their relationship remained congenial and Gilbert subtly pumped his father for pieces of information about family history and the quirky saga of Alliance as a failed, infertile Garden of Eden.

Much of that information, as well as a portrait of his father's idealism and integrity, appear in Seldes' best work of fiction, *The Wings of the Eagle* (1929). A finely drawn sketch of "Unity," a farming community that failed, Seldes sets up a striking contrast between Stephen Lodor, the naive idealist with unrealistic expectations about human relations, and Arthur Gordon, a more worldly, practical, and realistic "survivor" who manages to bring the colony shop-work, modernity, and a modicum of prosperity by accepting such human imperfections as lust, greed, and personal aggrandizement at the expense of communal harmony. Despite a tragic and somewhat improbable ending, *Wings of the Eagle* is an utterly engrossing exploration of complex interpersonal relations and profound psychological contrasts within a small community of Polish Catholic and Jewish immigrants at the turn of the century.

Given the book's sensitive and compelling narrative, it is hard to understand why Seldes stopped writing fiction. Perhaps he felt that he had exhausted his mine of autobiographical treasure. Perhaps, after three novels in as many years, he looked to more lucrative ways of supporting a wife and two children. (Although his novels were reasonably well received by reviewers, they did not supply a significant source of income.) Most likely, however, he felt more attracted by the prospect of writing for and about theater, film, and current affairs, as we shall see.

Although Seldes' trajectory would differ from his father's in many ways, vocational and ideological—note for purposes of contrast that so many radicals who wrote for *The Masses* had fathers who were idealistic, principled dreamers, hostile to the status quo, and chose to follow in their footsteps[11]—his father's legacy was incalculable albeit elusive. It included a love of good books, rock-solid integrity, and an astonishing array of contacts that ranged from W. W. ("Big Bill") Haywood and Emma Goldman to Maxim Gorki and the acclaimed actress Alla Nazimova.[12]

The most elusive aspect of "Pa's" legacy involves the formal ideas and literature that young Gilbert imbibed. In 1939, for example, a correspondent at Antioch College asked Seldes whether he had been influenced by Edward Bellamy's utopian novel *Looking Backward* (1888). Seldes answered that he knew the book before he even learned to read. "All my people spoke of it," he replied; and yet, "although I was brought up in a community which was established originally for a kind of salvation seeking, I do not recall that the spiritual values of the book were very much emphasized." Seldes even acknowledged that he did not actually read *Looking Backward* until the late 1920s, perhaps when he composed *The Wings of the Eagle*.[13]

His father also admired Henry George and supported his unsuccessful mayoral aspirations in New York in 1886. *Progress and Poverty* (1879) would have been yet another text that Seldes most likely internalized before he actually read it. Despite the emphasis in Bellamy and George on social co-operation and collective well-being, however, both Gilbert and George Seldes recalled, more than once, that from their earliest childhood they were "indoctrinated with the idea of individualization." Their father's philosophy of individualism caused him to regard conformity as a "criminal act," a betrayal of the self and consequently of society. Gilbert felt that his experience at Harvard College strongly reinforced that penchant for "individuality" and this became a cherished value throughout his mature years.[14]

The emergence of mass media and mass society during Seldes' lifetime brought subtle yet significant shifts in the ways that he invoked individualism. In 1940, for example, he viewed society as a covenanted network of individuals—a relationship recognized by the abstract whole as well as by particular persons. Hence he would quote these lines from Walt Whitman:

> I swear nothing is good to me
> now that ignores individuals,
> The American compact is altogether
> with individuals.

Near the close of his career, however, in his very last book, Seldes worried that "as a member of a huge, undifferentiated audience, the individual loses importance. As a communicator, too, the individual has lost influence." He suspected that the mass media did not care about the individual, whereas Seldes proclaimed that "the individual is not only our central concern; we say that he is the central concern of the free society. This centrality of the individual is what we wish to preserve." On that issue, especially, Gilbert Seldes was very much his father's son.[15]

By the time he became a senior in high school Seldes had learned to negotiate a middle way between the role of autonomous loner and an other-directed identity designed to please and succeed. Late in 1909 he also quoted Walt Whitman, but this time referring pejoratively to the poet's wish to live among the cattle because they have no politics and no bureaucrats. The seventeen-year old commented that the loneliness of his [Whitman's] exalted place would be intolerable. *I want to live among men*—despising them perhaps but beating them at their own wretched game. I have learnt, too early, perhaps, that *this world is not a place to dream dreams about but a stern school to work deeds in.* We may dream—but we must make our beds first. Don't think tho' that I am becoming practical. I *hate* the *commercialism of today*—I hope some day to better the world a little by having lived in it—but I am going to live in it.[16]

If the young man's tone sounds altogether arch, mistrustful, and moralistic, let us bear in mind the perceptive observation made by Henry F. May that at that time American intellectuals regarded the bond between moralism and progress as both firm and inevitable. Seldes and his cohort would not perpetuate that connection when they came of age in the 1920s and '30s; but in 1910 it illuminated their universe and informed their ambitions. In April 1910, Seldes wrote an essay for his high school's annual oratorical contest. Titled "Public Morals," it is mundanely about morals and progress. Modernism and the lively arts lay a decade ahead.[17]

Despite a vital capacity for friendship and a personality best described as socially gregarious, particularly while in his twenties, thirties, and forties, Seldes was not a joiner; and for reasons of temperament he tended to remain an outsider. He did not become a part of H. L. Mencken's "smart set" and he did not participate in the famed Algonquin circle despite his physical proximity to its 44th Street "clubhouse" and his familiarity with its members. He didn't care for most of them. In the spring of his freshman year at Harvard, Seldes literally forced himself to compete for the debate team because he felt that he ought to associate himself with some cultural endeavor. The young achiever acknowledged to his cousin in Philadelphia that he hoped to "make a name" in one way or another. "I ought to affiliate myself with something here," he explained, and lamented that he hadn't done the requisite scut work for the dramatic club ("and thereby delayed my chances of election"), nor had he submitted anything to the student papers. Writing came relatively easy to Seldes. Joining did not.[18]

By the time he reached Central High School's upper classes in 1908–10, Seldes had become a voracious reader, especially of such classic American authors as Emerson, Thoreau, and Whitman. Although he was sufficiently outstanding to win a scholarship to Harvard, the intense young *érudit* could also be didactic, pedantic, and a bit of a prig. During his senior year he wrote these two sentences to a female cousin: "I am going to write you an essay on *Books and Reading. You must not forget, my dear, that tho I am an embryo philosopher I am also litterateur* and that, if you want a list of books as literature I can cast aside my filosofy [*sic*] long enough to make one."[19] Never again would Seldes sound so insufferable. For a while in the 1920s hyperbole became something of a personal trademark, but he left pomposity behind at the age of seventeen—sooner than many.

He pursued the prescribed general course of study at Harvard, which he did not find difficult, and concentrated on English literature. By 1913 he was entranced by the vogue of Arthur Machen (1863–1951), a Welsh writer of "atmospheric" tales of terror, most notably *The House of Souls* (1906) and *The Hill of Dreams* (1907). It is not clear whether Machen's American cult owed more to his evocations of the grotesque and the supernatural or to his satire of puritanical intolerance of all art devoid of any moral purpose. Machen's contempt for Puritanism in general, and America in particular, suited the young Harvard literati at that time.[20] Seldes would soon outgrow such anti-American stances, but the belief that art required no moral purpose remained with him. Decades later one of Seldes' major contentions would still be: don't corrupt the lively arts with moral purpose. Their principal objective is to entertain.

He also became enchanted at Harvard by the fiction of Compton Mackenzie (1883–1972), particularly *Carnival* (1912), an immensely popular and critically acclaimed melodrama about a female dancer who falls in love with a young male dilettante who deserts her when she will not become his mistress. In despair she first allows herself to be seduced by an old lecher, and then collapses into a disastrous marriage with a Cornish farmer who kills her in a fit of jealousy when the dilettante reappears on the scene. Seldes published a review of *Carnival* in *The Harvard Monthly,* a new literary magazine, wrote to Mackenzie offering to be his guide at "our Oxford" when the novelist made his American tour late in 1912, and indicated that Mackenzie's work served as an inspiration for an aspiring writer, age nineteen. They eventually met in 1916 at Mackenzie's London club when Seldes served as a journalist in Britain during the war.[21]

In the course of his junior and senior years Seldes became more involved with fiction by American authors, or at least Anglo-American writers like Henry James. After deep immersion in James' novels, he later mused, he felt "sure that I knew all that needed to be known about the technique of fiction." Seldes' years at Harvard provided him with a solid grounding in serious literature and philosophy. (He did not think much of Hugo Münsterburg; but in 1912 he took the last course that

George Santayana offered before resigning, on aesthetics—and loved it.)[22] Ten years later, when Seldes became disenchanted with high culture and championed the lively arts instead, he knew exactly what he was rejecting. It should be understood, however, that he did not repudiate the best of high culture. He simply rejected highbrow snobs and insisted that popular culture deserved and required serious critical scrutiny.

Henry F. May has written that Harvard College before World War I offered a blend of morality and genteel taste, but also the prospect of rebellion. Some, like T. S. Eliot, opted for the first two, while others, like Van Wyck Brooks and John Reed, chose rebellion. Still others, like Walter Lippmann and Gilbert Seldes, not yet set in their sense of identity, managed to internalize the whole contradictory package.[23]

Initially, however, the potential for rebellion remained quiescent in comparison with his voracious desire for erudition. Early in 1912, while Seldes was a sophomore, he wrote a remarkable letter to his brother George, who had gone directly from high school into journalism. Gilbert successfully persuaded George to attend classes at Harvard that fall as a non-degree candidate. Two extracts from this long letter make it very clear that Seldes' sense of self was consciously elitist rather than socially rebellious.

> Some of the best things which I have got from college: a sort of pedantry; a devotion to style and manner; a distrust of mere honesty and good-nature as sufficient to make a man desirable as acquaintance; a sort of snobbishness, to be sure, but I do not deny it. . . . Do you remember Walt [Whitman]?: "Whatever is cheapest, commonest, easiest—that is I. . . . By God I will have nothing which the next man may not have on the same terms." I say nothing against the view except that it is not mine, and if it is yours, as with the journalistic training it may well be, then the modification it will undergo up here will be a bitter pill, but believe me, a good one.[24]

Four months following his graduation from Harvard in June 1914, Seldes published an essay about Harvard in which he confessed to feeling ambivalence yet came down on the side of tradition. "I cling, in spite of successive disillusions, to the belief that *the function of the college is to create a tradition of culture.*"[25] Rebellion awaited him almost a decade ahead.

Eight years later, when H. L. Mencken commissioned a series of essays on colleges for *The Smart Set* magazine, called "The Higher Learning in America," Seldes wrote the piece about Harvard.[26] He felt, in retrospect, that "the only important thing to me about Harvard is that it actually encourages an interest in the activities of civilized human beings." He noted his familiarity with members of the Dramatic Club as well as members of the Socialist Club (and their chief enemies). He added that "our widest and deepest friendships were with upper classmen and all of us feel that we profited mightily by knowing all the best men in a cycle of college years instead of in our own year alone."[27]

Just for the record, and to note the social profile at Harvard, Seldes' 1914 classmates included James Bryant Conant, who became president of the university in 1933; James Phinney Baxter III, historian of American foreign relations and later president of Williams College; Leverett Saltonstall, who became governor of Massachusetts and then U.S. Senator; Sumner Welles, a diplomat; Junius Spencer Morgan, who became a banker; Bernhard Knollenberg, who became the librarian of Yale University; and, closest in his interests to Seldes (eventually), Laurence Schwab, who left Harvard in 1912, went from vaudeville to the legitimate theatre to producing films, mainly in Hollywood.

As Seldes noted, however, the closest contacts commonly developed with men in other classes, such as Scofield Thayer and James Sibley Watson, Jr., classes of 1913 and 1915, who subsequently became the "angels" who underwrote *The Dial* during the 1920s; Harold Stearns, '13; E. E. Cummings, '15; and John Dos Passos, '16. Although Seldes and Dos Passos corresponded on friendly terms until they both died in 1970, Dos Passos' rightward turn to a curious Jeffersonian conservatism following World War II left Seldes puzzled and a bit put off. Nonetheless, their mutual respect never waned. Above all, Seldes and Cummings enjoyed an affectionate, unbroken rapport until the poet-artist died in 1962. Seldes was deeply distressed by Cummings' death. (For Cummings' sketch of Seldes at *The Dial,* see Fig. 5, p. 78.) The Princeton trio, consisting of Edmund Wilson, F. Scott Fitzgerald, and John Peale Bishop, entered that college in 1912 (Wilson) and 1913 and met Seldes through Bishop. Edmund Wilson told Seldes years later that he had admired Seldes' essays and fiction in *The Harvard Monthly* during Wilson's first years at college.[28]

We need to take note of one other college contemporary. Gilbert's older brother, George, had gone directly into journalism following his graduation from Vineland High School in 1907. During Gilbert's sophomore year he besieged his reporter brother with letters insisting that he "would be an ignoramus" for life unless he went to college. So George took a leave from the Pittsburgh *Post,* enrolled at Harvard in 1912 as a special student for one academic year, and took the same five courses that his precocious brother was attending. The most interesting, perhaps, was English 12, a creative writing course taught by the famous, idiosyncratic Charles Townsend Copeland. The opportunity to write under Copeland's tutelage had been the chief attraction for George in coming to Harvard.

Copeland praised George's realistic narratives and spoke pejoratively about aesthetes who described their ecstatic responses to a sunset. Seventy-five years later, in 1987, George recalled a whimsical, telling episode that occurred one day in "Copey's" class:

> Although my brother was not an esthete, he belonged to the top literary group. He was an editor of the *Harvard Monthly* in its great days. One afternoon, for some reason, Copey leaned toward him over his desk and, pointing a finger, said in a tense voice: "I do *not* like you, Mr. Gilbert *Vivian* Seldes, I like your brother, George Henry Seldes." I do not know for whom Gilbert was named—it was probably for one of Mother's romantic book heroes—but Gilbert never again in his lifetime used his middle name. Nor was he offended by being singled out by Copeland. We had all been warned by seniors, and we got what we expected from Copey: severe criticism, ironic remarks, and perhaps even a little rudeness. We had been told that Copey was a "character," and we found he lived up to his reputation.[29]

So far as I am able to tell (and based upon a personal interview with George in 1991 when he was 101 and very sound in mind), the brothers really were not rivals and remained good friends even though they did not see one another very often after Gilbert married and returned to the United States in 1924. George remained in Europe for many years and achieved fame as the correspondent there for Colonel McCormick's Chicago *Tribune*. (The cranky publisher got along with his radical reporter because more than 4000 miles separated them.) George had immense respect for Gilbert's intellect, and Gilbert admired his brother's professional ingenuity, feisty temperament, and perhaps envied the international range of his contacts. At one time or another George interviewed most of the famous figures in twentieth-century Western history.[30]

In 1929, in fact, after Gilbert published *The Stammering Century,* a newspaper invited George to write a character sketch of his literary brother. George's piece, filled with affectionate barbs, was syndicated in assorted papers for more than a year. Two extracts from that sketch are engagingly illuminating.

Gilbert was for books; I was for bloodshed. He studied his humanity in cloistered aloofness; I preferred mine in man at his worst. And what did it all lead to? I got Gilbert to come to Pittsburgh and do newspaper work, and he got me up to Harvard. . . . He has been amazed for years by my participation in all the wars and rebellions and mass violences which an unsatisfactory peace made inevitable in Europe. He thinks I have had something to do with these events, he thinks I like being in the midst of battle, murder, and sudden death. He refuses to believe that I hate them and am scared by them. He thinks I am a fearless fellow.[31]

Beneath the good-natured banter lay a very large kernel of truth. George's grand passions concerned international politics, freedom of the press, governmental secrecy, and the public's right to be fully informed. He was, in every sense, a political man. Although Gilbert later cared very much about the problem of censorship, and shared George's concern for social justice (the Sacco and Vanzetti travesty ultimately enraged Gilbert, for example), he was, at heart, not a political activist. Gilbert's grand passion involved artistic creativity in general and the lively (or popular) arts in particular. According to an essay that appeared in the *New Masses* in 1933, the generation that came of age around 1910 felt certain that "art and politics were closely related."[32] Although that seems valid, in general, the Seldes brothers divided art and politics between them, each one quite content with his portion.

In 1914, when both men turned to journalism as a vocation, Gilbert and George collaborated on an essay titled "The Press and the Reporter." They wrote in response to an unkind essay, published in *The Forum,* that spoke harshly about reporters and "our dirty little profession." The aspirant siblings expressed outrage. "The hard, cynical, degraded reporter of public fancy," they declared, "is still sentimental enough to believe that his profession, that of the *news-writer,* is clean, and his life is usually a bitter, and often successful, struggle to keep that profession clean." Yet another comment made it clear that their very own *amour-propre* had been sullied. So they quoted an unnamed city editor who had met "hundreds of men in his experience." According to that authority, *"the reporter, and especially the young reporter, is the saving grace of the news-paper."*[33]

This brief collaboration by the Seldes brothers, the only one that I have found, is interesting for two related reasons. First, because it makes a strong appeal for integrity in journalism—at all levels of authority—a position that both men would abide by throughout their long, distinguished, and divergent careers. And second, because it condemns censorship, manipulation, and conspiracies of silence by the press—anticipating issues that both men would later be outspoken about. Because of their very junior positions in journalism, they closed with a hierarchical distinction that is a bit hyperbolic, or at least overstated, yet symptomatic of their critical outlook in 1914: "*News is suppressed by interested persons in authority: the city-staff, reporters and city editor, are not interested and have no authority.*"[34]

Soon after Gilbert's graduation from Harvard in 1914 he published an essay critical of changes that had been occurring there for several years. The piece is significant because it reveals Seldes' understanding of culture at that time—which would change within seven or eight years—and his specific discontents with the decline of college life as he contemplated it in ideal form. It distressed Seldes that President Lowell had abandoned Eliot's free elective system and now required the equivalent of a major. On that account he pontificated that "College should not spoil a man for life; it should enable him to appreciate life, make him 'able and active in distinguishing the great from the petty.' That is what culture means; and that is precisely what Harvard has decided not to do."[35]

Seldes then launched a litany of woes that he dated from 1911, less than two years after Lowell began his long reign as president:

Within the past three years the degeneration of every cultural activity has been persistently rapid. *The Lampoon* alone resists, and it is marked by its satire on all the new movements. The Socialist Club was founded in 1909. Its boast that it included the active intelligence of the college was always a gross exaggeration, but it was in itself active and intelligent. This year it is practically dead; free, incisive thinking has gone out of fashion. The Dramatic Club started at about the same time with high ideals and even higher achievement. Its record for the past two years has been one of protracted failure. . . . Even more disastrous has been the career of the *The Harvard Monthly*—*The Atlantic Monthly* of the colleges—which was founded about thirty years ago and has had on its boards such men as George Santayana, Professor George P. Baker, Robert Herrick, Norman Hapgood, and a host of other distinguished men. It always lacked popular appeal, but there were always enough men at Harvard to produce a superior magazine and almost enough readers to make the production worth while. Within the last few years it has been found almost impossible to keep the *Monthly* going, and its dissolution is imminent.[36]

As for culture, Seldes believed that the "tradition of culture" had prospered at Eliot's Harvard because it was "fulfilling the great mission of *cultural* institutions in helping each man to a ripening of his powers, to enlargement of his interests, and to widening of his sympathies." The poisonous enemies of those unexceptionable qualities? Scrapping the free elective system, "contempt for dilettantism, [and] the emergence of the scholar."[37] On the surface Seldes simply sounds anti-modern, a smug lover of the status quo. Although there is a touch of that, to be sure, we are also seeing anticipations of Seldes' astonishing range of interests ("dilettantism") and his versatility as a critic along with antipathy toward the academy ("scholars") so characteristic of independent intellectuals in his generation.[38] During the last twelve years of his life that hostility would wane. Seldes became a dean, corresponded cordially with scholars, and occasionally even deferred to them.

II

Young Gilbert started going to the theatre at the age of seven. As a senior in high school, enchanted with works by Ibsen and Shaw, he announced to a friend that he had chosen play-writing as his profession. During his sophomore year at Harvard, Seldes went regularly to Boston in order to see the Irish Players perform and reported that they showed him the immense possibilities of brilliant tragedy and truly great acting. He became an ardent fan of John Millington Synge and undertook a major project on Frank Wedekind (1864–1918), the German dramatist regarded by many as a forerunner of the expressionists. In January 1912, Seldes told his cousin that he was bored with his studies and felt a great urge to escape to some quiet coastal town and write a play. He did, in fact, write a one-act play that has since disappeared.[39]

During the 1920s Seldes wrote two plays of no particular distinction and during the 1930s he collaborated on two of considerable importance. But from the autumn of 1914 until the end of 1919, more than five years, his destiny lay with journalism. In 1914–15 he served as music critic for the Philadelphia *Evening Ledger,*[40] and after he went to London in 1916 the *Ledger* not only printed articles about the war that he dispatched, but syndicated many of them without bothering to tell Seldes or to pay him a supplemental sum. He also wrote for the Boston *Evening Transcript,* for *The Forum,* and for *The New Statesman* in London. Although he made several trips to the front as a war correspondent, his ostensible assignment was to examine and report on social conditions in England. In the fall of 1916, however, he complained that his task was difficult because "you can't interview the middle class—and officials are not to be trusted as psychologists."[41]

Most of his work in 1916 and 1917 was not as bifurcated as it might at first sound: simultaneously explaining the war to American readers and United States policies and attitudes to British readers. Because the brothers supported the Allied cause so fully, a certain petulance crept into their utterances. Gilbert wrote a two-part essay for a Boston journal, *The Living Age,* in which he described the American attitude to a world at war as "one of indifference based upon ignorance" because Americans were so preoccupied with their own affairs. Seldes supported Wilson's proposal for a League of Nations and declared that to achieve a successful peace after the war the United States needed "only to think, but she is blessed (or cursed) among the nations because she has had, in her years, no need of thinking." If that smacks of alienation, withhold judgment for just a moment: Seldes was then, and always would be, a staunch patriot. In the same piece he also attacked socialism and Marxism— interesting because in a public letter written in 1964 Seldes remarked that in 1914 "we were all en route to being socialist."[42] Curious contradictions of that sort occur with surprising frequency. Perhaps he only used an editorial "we" to describe *other* young intellectuals in the mid-1910s. More likely his memory fished up notions of the way things must have been, or ought to have been, back then.

On the very day the United States entered the war, April 6, 1917, Allen and Unwin published in London Seldes' first (and least remembered) book, *The United States and the War.* It was well received, in part, perhaps, because the British so gladly welcomed American intervention. George Seldes recalled the frustration of wanting to serve but waiting endlessly for the U.S. military to get its act together. Following the declaration, George remembered that

Gilbert and I who had been devoted to the cause of the Allies, went to call on Ambassador Page and volunteer for active service. He advised us to wait for a draft. We waited for a physical examination but none was announced as the months went by; at the end of the year Gilbert, tired of waiting, went home to volunteer again, and became a machinegunner at Camp Lee; and I went to Paris, where Floyd Gibbons arranged for me to work on the Army Edition of the *Chicago Tribune* until my draft notice arrived. It never did.[43]

Gilbert Seldes' military service occurred in the deep South. In a class report years later for Harvard College he claims to have participated in the "battle of Spartanburg" and received a promotion to sergeant. He then managed to get to Washington where he became political correspondent in the United States for *L'Echo de Paris*.

Two aspects of Gilbert's experience in the years 1916–18 are especially noteworthy. Although in 1932 he recalled having been "an enthusiast for everything English," at the time he actually discovered startling depths of chauvinism. "I have become a frightful patriot," he wrote home early in 1917. "I can't stay abroad very long because I feel myself drifting away from any sympathy with the U.S. That's fatal." That is also ambiguous, but in March he expressed vexation to his cousin in Philadelphia because he had received no mail for a month. "*I,* who live on knowing about America, received not one word. . . ."[44]

Seldes would, in fact, soon make a career out of knowing and writing about America; and by the close of 1917 he felt homesick and anxious to return. He even tried to plan his own "welcome home" reception by friends and family in New York City and Philadelphia. "I shall weep at the sight of the Statue of Liberty," he warned, "and break down at the vision of New York if we come in at night."[45]

Seldes' growing awareness of his American identity during the years 1916–18 is directly related to his becoming a writer and defining what kind of writer he wished to be. Although his books and essays would primarily focus on some aspect of the contemporary scene, usually cultural, a developmental or historical perspective mattered vitally to him. Late in 1916, for example, while finishing his first book, he explained to his cousin that "I am trying to analyse the feelings of the U.S., to trace them back to their sources in the history and habits of the country, and to explain why things are as they are, how they can become different, in the way of alliances and sichlike [*sic*]."[46] That emphasis fundamentally describes the approach taken in two of Seldes' most important books, *The Stammering Century* (1928) and *Mainland* (1936).

He had already established his credentials as a cosmopolitan. By the spring of his sophomore year at Harvard, Seldes was writing reviews of serious books on diverse topics. His versatility and range as a critic had begun to be apparent. In the spring of his senior year he indicated that he had been offered a "paper" when he felt ready to take "complete editorial control—I probably won't be ready until 1920—but the offer, with finances, will be just as good then." Although that would seem to describe, exactly, his trajectory to *The Dial,* where he became an editor in 1920, it is difficult to imagine that his Harvard friends, Thayer and Watson, had made such a commitment in 1914. By the time he left Harvard, Seldes had written literary, historical, and philosophical essays, editorials, verse, and worked on a novel.[47]

Yet his letters from 1916 through 1918 reveal a great deal of hesitation and uncertainty. His authorial impulses did not flow evenly at first: "The good stuff is only beginning to come" (1916); "Slowly I am getting back the trick of writing—it fell off dreadfully at first" (early 1917); "I feel another book—two in fact—coming over me. One on England in wartime, for America and the other a novelette on the War—or rather on a war-theme. That's for money chiefly. But the main thing is to want to write again and to feel that it is going to be good." By the summer of 1917, age twenty-four, despite many mood swings, Seldes essentially determined to support himself as an independent writer: with non-fiction foremost and fiction as a second string to his bow, primarily for its potential economic rewards.[48]

A lesser reason for his progress by fits and starts arose from not beginning to keep a diary until early April 1917. As he explained to his cousin the previous autumn, "Up to now I have had to keep working desperately, digging out stories, writing them, sending them off in the hope of acceptance. Presently, you see, I shall have all that regularized. And since I dont diary, I dont note down all details. . . ."[49]

The more important reason for his fitful progress, I believe, is that the exigencies of wartime caused him to feel obliged to write about public affairs rather than about cultural matters in fiction and non-fiction—his destined métier. International relations, politics, and even issues of social reform were not his primary interest; but being in London in 1916–17 they were inescapable. During that winter he explained his profound distress at the world situation and lamented that he had "to think so much of politics and economics, not to mention industry." That same season he spelled out his dilemma at greater length:

I am writing a book, what Graham Wallas refers to as a damned book, which will be about the United States and why it is such a stand-offish nation and what can be done to it to make it stir about and be human and take an interest in Czechs and hunkies and Slovaks. Also, big secret, I am developing what you might call a social consciousness, but no uplift, and I am in deadly fear every day that the undeveloped powers I may have had as a humorist or novelist or whatever I wanted to be will be swept away forevernever [*sic*] by the preoccupation with affairs. Thus the war blights noble young lives. Seriously, I am thrown about spiritually, cant understand the placidity of living, as I did, for two years, right on the edge of what is going on here.

In June he summed up succinctly: Seldes "didn't feel that writing novels was worth while in a world where there is war."[50]

A few months later Seldes acknowledged his aspiration for fame along with his pleasure at finding a way to write about a society under siege rather than about international relations and war itself. "I suppose I want recognition as much as anyone," he confessed. "I certainly bask in it, even if it comes from those of the least discrimination. But I have cared a lot too much for what comes with it." Seldes then explained that he had a series of articles in progress. "All of them will be about civilians in war time, and I mean to work out the basics of a study of the psychology of the stay-at-home in war time. I'm very hot about it just now and the articles are shaping up beautifully."[51]

Although Seldes welcomed the war's end like everyone else, for more than a year (1918–19) he went through a transitional period during which he became as much of a bookman as a writer. In addition to newspaper pieces for *L'Echo de Paris* and occasional reviews for *The Dial* (still based in Chicago), he became an associate editor at *Collier's Weekly* and launched a minor crusade to enhance the distribution of books to ordinary Americans. He observed that in 1917–18 the American Library Association successfully collected money and books for distribution to soldiers. Although the war had popularized reading for pleasure, in his view men seemed to lose the habit when they came home in 1918–19. Seldes urged that books should travel, as he phrased it: they ought to be more readily in circulation.[52] That concern for the democratization of culture can be viewed as a significant harbinger of the much broader message that he began to disseminate in 1922–23.

As for less bookish concerns, prior to 1927–28 Seldes wrote only occasionally about such matters as sexuality, either his own or else intimate relations in their social context. In 1914 he published a short story about free love. It concerned a woman and two men who not only vie for her affections but present contrasting views on the question of free love versus monogamous relationships. All three characters end up unhappy.

When Paul, the man with bourgeois morals, rejects his wife, Evelyn begs Godfrey, her erstwhile lover, "don't you send me away now—I couldn't stand it."[53] A close variation on that theme is central to Seldes' 1929 novel, *The Wings of the Eagle*. Perhaps some sort of unusual lovers' triangle occurred at the farm colony in Alliance, or else subsequently in Philadelphia after Seldes' father became a widower and remarried.

At a more personal level, Gilbert included this paragraph in a 1917 letter written from London to his cousin in Philadelphia:

> I had my flight. Went up in the finest and newest type of aeroplane and, like everyone else who goes up, feel that nothing can ever be the same again. It is the greatest sensation in the world bar *none*. It resembles some of the more violent forms of the second greatest.[54]

Within six or seven months Seldes became romantically involved with a beautiful and clever American reporter raised in Georgia and later in Yuma, Arizona, following her mother's death in 1903. Her hardnosed father had become the sheriff there after deserting his wife. Jane Anderson began to publish journalistic pieces in *Harper's Weekly* as early as 1910 when she was only seventeen. After attending Kidd-Key College in Sherman, Texas, she migrated to New York City in 1914 in search of a publisher. There she met the prominent musicologist and composer Deems Taylor, and married him in a "non-binding" way. A year later, however, she arrived in England and France alone as a war correspondent. An aspiring novelist also, she greatly admired Joseph Conrad and managed to meet him in April 1916. She promptly proceeded to insinuate herself into the Conrads' domestic situation at Capel House. At the very least she and Conrad carried on an intense flirtation—he described her as "quite yum-yum"—thereby enraging Mrs. Conrad, who weighed more than two hundred pounds and was something less than yum-yum. When their son, Borys, met Jane Anderson in Paris in the spring of 1917, he became infatuated with her as well.[55]*

Early in 1918 Anderson met Seldes and returned with him to the United States aboard the *Rochambeau*. Their intense affair had a curious literary interlude when Jane asked a college classmate, who in turn invited her friend, Katherine Anne Porter, to join them during the summer of 1918 at a lodge on Cheyenne Mountain near Colorado

*Jozef H. Retinger, a friend of Conrad who had an affair with Anderson, wrote that she "turned the heads of many conspicuous and famous men both in Europe and in her own country. Exceptionally gifted, a good newspaperwoman and a short-story writer of more than average talent, she had a marvelous capacity for listening and understanding."

Springs. Anderson and Seldes did not get along well with Porter because they regarded her as poorly educated and unworldly. To make matters worse, however, Porter always beat them at cards, which became a bore. The upshot was that Jane Anderson is not only immortalized in some of Joseph Conrad's later fiction, but mercilessly caricatured in Katherine Anne Porter's earlier stories and in *Ship of Fools* (as La Condesa).[56]

Jane Anderson was, quite literally, a scheming adventuress, and European adventures (especially at the front) seem to have destabilized her emotionally by 1918. The summer of love with Seldes in the Colorado Rockies turned out to be one wild and unpredictable fling. Anderson could be wonderfully amusing but also morbid, hypersensitive, and easily unnerved. Instead of working at the writing for which she had contracted, Jane devoted most of her sober hours to Gilbert. According to one reliable account she "spent the first hours in his bed each night and afterward returned to her own bed, took barbiturates for her 'war nerves,' and remained sedated until noon the next day." Because Seldes and Anderson consumed a considerable amount of liquor, one wonders about the combined effect upon Anderson of barbiturates and alcohol.[57]

Whatever the answer to that speculation, the couple drifted apart in 1919. Perhaps it had been too wildly intense to endure. But perhaps Anderson's contempt for American culture eventually irritated Seldes; for as we shall see, he had little sympathy for the nation-bashing so fondly indulged in during the 1920s by H. L. Mencken and the expatriates. In one of Porter's essays there is a thinly veiled description of Jane:

> She talked constantly of Europe, of the drama, the art, the society, the traditions and rich backgrounds of culture abounding there. She contrasted this with America and its uncouth ways. She never failed to use the word "crude" when describing us. No matter what the subject in hand might be, it invariably came back to the manners of this country, and its crude state as regards all that made the life of this lady worth living.[58]

Although I cannot say what Seldes thought of Katherine Anne Porter, we do know that he found the cultural self-hatred of anti-Americans distasteful. In addition, Anderson seemed to be falling apart just when Seldes was finding himself, quite literally, as an emerging man of letters.

Anderson continued to practice political journalism during the 1920s, carried on numerous love affairs, became an ardent anti-communist, and is believed at one point to have conspired in a plot to assassinate Lenin. In

1934 or so she married a Spanish nobleman and subsequently became a loyal supporter of the Franco regime. Following a strange tour of the United States in 1937–38 when she made vitriolic attacks on Franklin Roosevelt's New Deal *and* the USSR, she returned to Spain where she did propaganda work for Franco in 1939 and '40. Joseph Goebbels was so impressed that he invited her to Germany where she identified totally with National Socialism. Between April 1941 and March 1942 she made numerous anti-American radio broadcasts from Berlin—known as the "Georgia Peach." Following the war she was arrested in Salzburg in 1947; but the Department of Justice which brought an indictment against her in 1943, declined to prosecute her for treason and she returned to Spain, where she died in obscurity.[59]

Seldes remained an intense patriot throughout the 1930s and World War II. I suspect that his affair with Anderson almost a quarter of a century earlier had long since become an embarrassment. Given the absence of references to her in his papers, it almost appears as though that once fierce amour gave way to forced amnesia.

Other kinds of intensity burned brightly between 1915 and 1919, each of them historically more important than Seldes' love affair with Anderson. The call for a new, revitalized American culture pervaded the so-called little magazines in 1915–17. In 1915 Van Wyck Brooks published his influential manifesto, *America's Coming-of-Age,* which called attention to the problem of cultural stratification in the United States. That same year young Randolph Bourne rejected both "lowbrow" culture as well as the "stale culture of the aristocrat," a criticism that anticipated Seldes' more sustained analysis of the same question nearly nine years later.

In 1917, James Oppenheim founded the *Seven Arts,* a short-lived but seminal journal that resulted from conversations in 1916 between Oppenheim, the novelist and critic Waldo Frank, and the music critic Paul Rosenfeld. They resented the creation of *The New Republic* in 1914, a "journal of opinion," because the "real thing" needed was a "journal of art." Although Gilbert Seldes later contributed many essays to *The New Republic,* that distinction between "opinion" (public affairs) and art would differentiate and separate Seldes' circle from Walter Lippmann's, which was only five or six years older. The circular that announced *Seven Arts* explained its principal aim: "to become a channel . . . an expression of our American arts that shall be fundamentally an expression of our

American life." Because Oppenheim and his pals opposed United States involvement in World War I, they alienated their angel and the magazine died in 1917. Oppenheim's retrospective explanation of failure in 1930 ignored the harsh polarization caused by international relations. "That we should have thought that the arts and the criticisms could rule business appears so ludicrous now as to be beyond laughter."[60]

The creation in 1916–17 of a new, lively magazine devoted to criticism and the arts helped to provide Seldes, and many others, with a vocational compass. They were a bit younger than the dashing and self-romanticizing generation of journalists like Richard Harding Davis and John Reed. Seldes was attracted to a less melodramatic form of journalism—not in the genteel tradition, by any means, but less drawn to flashy situations and spectacular events. Seldes preferred to write about books, theatre especially, music, and the arts. Although he was much less ideological than those who wrote for *The Masses* (1911–17), he also rejected pure aestheticism and the tired notion of art for art's own sake. Although he certainly lacked a vision of art in the service of revolutionary change, he was nonetheless receptive to proposals for political and social reform.

Among his contemporaries there were many with similar origins and parallel careers, though some who might logically have been his friends turned out to be bitter enemies. Alexander Woollcott, for example, also came from an unconventional family with roots in an upstate New York Fourierite community. He, too, was interested in journalism and theatre. In 1914 Woollcott became the *New York Times'* drama critic and played a vigorous role as a theatre critic during the 1920s. In the '30s he became a book reviewer and cultural critic on the radio, attracting the largest radio audience of any critic in history. Like Seldes, Woollcott would help to loosen the moorings of genteel culture, and like Seldes the range of his enthusiasms was considerable. Unlike Seldes, however, Woollcott became a genuine celebrity, a household name, because his taste (and droll manner of presentation) was more middlebrow and less cerebral than Seldes'.[61]

Jealousy or resentment may have played a part, but Seldes had serious ideological and cultural axes to grind with Woollcott. Woollcott, of course, epitomized the Algonquin circle that Seldes deemed precious. They were not friends during the interwar years, and became overt enemies during the later 1930s because Seldes regarded Woollcott as myopic about the nature of U.S. participation in World War I and said so in print.[62] Thus all of the young journalists who became cultural critics, even when they sprang from utopian seeds, did not end up as peas from a single pod. The differences among them in temperament and approach rivaled the similarities.[63]

One more anticipation of what lay ahead. In many ways H. L. Mencken would dominate cultural criticism in the United States during the 1920s. He would not dominate Gilbert Seldes, however, because Seldes grew weary of Mencken's penchant for poisonous comments about American culture. Perhaps Seldes also took umbrage in 1920 when Mencken called Philadelphia "a cultural slum."[64] Seldes had flourished there at a first-rate high school and began his career in journalism by covering the Philadelphia symphony and other musical events. In 1920, Seldes had not yet become an addicted New Yorker.

2

On Being an Editor
and Becoming a Critic

E arly in 1919 a friend found Seldes a job writing editorials for *Collier's* shortly before the Crowell publishing firm took over that weekly magazine from the Whitney family. At *Collier's* he met Finley Peter Dunne, who came to the office once a week to drop off the latest folk wisdom of Mr. Dooley. Writing his memoirs in the mid-1960s, Seldes believed that "the Crowell people kept me on, reluctantly, as a symbol of continuity, perhaps, with the old regime; I am sure they would have fired me shortly—but the offer from *The Dial* intervened and I was saved." He referred to the pre-eminent journal of literature and art published in the United States during the 1920s.

One of Seldes' college friends, Scofield Thayer (Harvard, 1913), essentially bought the magazine in 1919, moved it from Chicago to New York City, and along with Dr. James Sibley Watson, Jr., a slightly younger Harvard man, sustained this distinguished monthly for a decade with funds from their family fortunes. They hired Seldes early in 1920 as an editor. He swiftly became the managing editor, a title he continued to hold for more than a year after he left for France early in 1923 in order to write his best-known book, *The 7 Lively Arts* (1924).

In many respects the three years from early 1920 through the end of 1922 were the most exciting in *The Dial*'s history, years as exuberant and bold as any in the entire span of literary magazines in the United States. The exhilarating headiness of those years is vividly conveyed in a letter that Gilbert sent to his brother George, by then a journalist in Europe, late in 1921—a letter that reads like a breathless telegram that might have been composed by Seldes' close friend, E. E. Cummings:

> Quite a lot of nice people giving parties newyork where am rapidly becoming famous young editor stop now [that Scofield] thayers away i do social end, even to making a speech week from today mygod! . . . i work violently andhard many hours daily and am writing very well indeed. . . . am carrying on a lone and vicious battle against the following: algonquin crowd (so named after hotel where they eat . . . 2) Chicago gang, now here, running magazines and writing books: see my attack on ben hecht last month, the best in a long time; 3) nyevepost lit sup gang including christopher morley, the benet tribe (see same review) and others; 4) the bookman gang; 5) the theatres generally. i have made about twenty new enemies this half year and it is magnificent. also a few friends, very close indeed. also carrying on affairs, how shall i say not so public, i add this so that you may not think of me as being too utterly unliving in a living world stop[1]

Seldes suddenly became involved in regular contacts with William Butler Yeats, Picasso, H. G. Wells, D. H. Lawrence, Ezra Pound, T. S. Eliot, and other famous or soon-to-be famous literati. He helped the magazine instrumentally as a conduit, and in the process found himself personally connected to all sorts of fascinating figures—but also gradually embroiled in numerous controversies, some of them major, some of them quite trivial, and a few of them (involving people like Hemingway, Woollcott, Mencken, and others) for the rest of his and their lives.

In 1932, when Seldes published a critique of *The Liberation of American Literature* by the Marxist critic V. F. Calverton, it annoyed him that Calverton had curiously omitted any mention of *The Dial,* despite the crucial role it had played in the liberation of American literature. Although *The Dial* was trans-national and cosmopolitan by design, it did have an editorial policy that favored and promoted the careers of such younger American writers as E. E. Cummings, Marianne Moore, and William Carlos Williams. So Seldes concluded his review with this paragraph:

> However I have read myself out of the record: I cannot criticize any proletarianate book because I have petty bourgeois ideology in my blood. This doesn't prevent me from knowing that I'm a Fool is probably the best single story Sherwood Anderson ever wrote and that it hasn't any more economic significance than a fly has; and that it was published in a magazine called The Dial which had more to do with the liberation of Ameri-

can writers than nine-tenths of the magazines Mr. Calverton mentions. But it was petty bourgeois; so Mr. Calverton has discreetly omitted it from his history altogether.[2]

Seldes would forgive critics of *The Dial* and of his role as managing editor, but not those who utterly ignored the journal for ideological or unhistorical reasons.

There appears to be a consensus among cultural and literary historians that the "take-off" years for modernism occurred between 1910 and the mid-1920s.[3] *The Dial* played an instrumental and highly influential part in that take-off, a fact that many people noted in response to the single most illustrious issue of *The Dial,* November 1922, the one that featured the first American printing of "The Waste Land" by T. S. Eliot. Although Seldes himself, as a writer, did not radically experiment with language or form and had little use for fancy literary theory or the arcane language of insiders, he nonetheless played a key role in facilitating and promoting modernism. In 1927 he complained in an essay that "critics are few who understand the new terms which artists use." During his years at *The Dial* he worked doggedly to make those terms accessible and meaningful.[4] Before he was done, Seldes had found his own voice and métier. By 1923 he knew what kind of cultural critic he wanted to be. His voice, in fact, would adjust somewhat over the years, along with his views. But not his primary vocation as a critic.

I

Although *The Dial*'s name endured, its ownership and mission changed over a span of almost four generations. Ralph Waldo Emerson and Margaret Fuller had created a literary, philosophical and polemical *Dial* back in 1840–44. That *Dial* helped to immortalize the Transcendentalists, and surely they, in turn, did as much for the journal. In 1880 Francis F. Browne, a transplanted Vermonter, northern Democrat, and Union veteran, founded a new *Dial* in Chicago. Up until his death in 1913 Browne published it twice a month and made it the leading critical review in the Middle West. Considered liberal and literary at the time, it attracted essays from the likes of political scientist Woodrow Wilson and from Supreme Court Chief Justice Melville W. Fuller. After Browne's death William Dean Howells eulogized him for those "spiritual, intellectual, and moral qualities which in their peculiar concord rendered him unique in his time and place."[5]

Following several years of transitory and uncertain direction, a young decorator from the East named Martyn Johnson bought *The Dial* and emerged in 1916 as its new publisher. Perhaps because he had cut his editorial teeth on the fledgling *New Republic,* Johnson's *Dial* highlighted radical politics along with literature and the arts. He attracted a number of notable contributors, including Randolph Bourne, Padraic Colum, Horace Kallen, John Dewey, and even the young journeyman Gilbert Seldes, whose first piece appeared on January 25, 1917.[6] In 1918–19 Thorstein Veblen published a series of essays in *The Dial* that later appeared in book form as *The Vested Interests and the State of the Industrial Arts.* During his mature years Seldes devoted occasional essays to the state of the industrial arts. It seems certain that his inspiration for that topic's viability and importance owed more than a little to Veblen's pieces in the "old" *Dial,* when Seldes' career was still embryonic.

In 1918–19 a series of circumstances converged that undermined Johnson's new project: a serious falling out between Bourne and Dewey over U.S. intervention in the war; Bourne's tragic death from influenza; and conflicts between Johnson and Thayer, a principal financial backer, over policy matters. Paradoxically, the extremely wealthy Thayer was a committed socialist, and shared that orientation with other prominent writers and members of *The Dial*'s editorial board. Thayer believed, however, that *The Liberator, The New Republic,* and *The Nation* adequately handled issues of public policy and foreign relations. Therefore Thayer wanted *The Dial* to devote itself exclusively to literature and art; and so in 1919, after a series of convoluted, on-again, off-again negotiations, Thayer, Watson, and a few friends bought *The Dial* from Johnson, moved it to New York, and converted it from a lively fortnightly publication to an elegant, meticulously planned monthly.[7]

From the very outset Thayer defined policy to a greater degree than anyone else, even his congenial partner, Watson; and those guidelines remained dominant after Thayer went to Europe in 1925 and withdrew from his engaged role as editor-in-chief. They persisted until *The Dial* ceased publication in 1929. The essence of those guidelines? An aversion to partisanship, ideology, and above all to any particular aesthetic theory or set of standards. As Thayer wrote in his 1925 valedictory, he and Watson intended to establish in the United States a magazine which should be devoted exclusively, and in the most general sense, to art and letters. Not only did we have in mind no literary or artistic propaganda, no desire to urge, for example, the advantages of free verse as opposed to regular (or of regular as opposed to free), but also we depended upon no aesthetic system either of our own or of another to guide us in selecting what should be the contents of *The Dial*. We did not, and do not deem that it is feasible, in aesthetic matters, to judge by reference to any detailed theoretic code.[8]

The Dial deliberately pursued a policy of being a "marketplace of ideas," of listening to both sides of an issue. Thayer loved to play off George Santayana against Bertrand Russell, the two prominent philosophers, by asking each one to review books by the other. They differed on just about everything, and their disagreements were not particularly cordial. Such intense conflicts helped to make *The Dial* exceedingly lively—indeed, exciting. In the most amusing illustration of this policy, perhaps, the January 1921 issue gave space to John S. Sumner's prudish essay on "The Truth about 'Literary Lynching,'" in which the head of New York's Society for the Suppression of Vice defended the prosecution it undertook against *The Little Review* for publishing extracts from *Ulysses*. Immediately following that essay, in the same issue, Thayer and Seldes placed reproductions of three female nudes by Gaston Lachaise, one of them exceedingly voluptuous.[9]

It is abundantly clear that Gilbert Seldes internalized this ideal of judicious balance along with Thayer's antipathy toward zealous theorizing. In 1932 Seldes praised the MacDowell colony in Peterborough, New Hampshire, a place he dearly loved because it always rejuvenated him: "It is not a place where any theory of art is promulgated; nor is it a permanent community as far as the artists are concerned."[10] More than twenty years later Seldes engaged in a harrowing conflict with Edward R. Murrow, a man he admired immensely, because Murrow's famous telecast about Senator Joseph McCarthy seemed utterly one-sided to Seldes, a violation of the "fairness doctrine" that he had learned at *The Dial* in 1920–21. It was perfectly acceptable to take sides; Seldes did that all the time. But one at least had to acknowledge the existence of alternative perspectives and perhaps even try to understand why they appealed to certain people.

Thayer's long-term impact upon Seldes can be seen in other important ways. As editor, for instance, Thayer made the necessity for extreme individualism a frequent theme in *The Dial.* He found it perfectly acceptable, and perhaps inevitable, that the "imaginative individual" would invariably be the "marooned individual." Individualism as an imperative would recur throughout Seldes' career as a writer. The most distinctive attribute that people ascribed to Thayer was intensity, a quality that he very much admired and desired in creative work.[11] Seldes did, too, and his own cerebral intensity remained readily apparent right through the 1960s—both in his writing and in his television appearances as a panelist or cultural commentator.

Thayer's intensity was especially evident in his relentless pursuit of excellence and the perfection he expected in performance by his staff. After each issue appeared, Thayer combed through it for gaffes involving typography or the placement of illustrations or the sequencing of fiction, non-fiction, poetry, and art. Seldes received Thayer's wrath more than once, and felt that he functioned on a fairly short leash as managing editor. Most decisions of any consequence had to be cleared with Thayer and/or Watson, along with some decisions that seem in retrospect rather minor. Much as Seldes learned and grew because of his role at *The Dial,* his decision to resign in 1924, and thereafter contribute mainly the "Theatre" column, resulted from his desire for greater autonomy. As he lamented to Amy Lowell in 1922, "I am still without plenary powers."[12]

Thayer's intensity in pursuit of excellence certainly had its positive side. He recruited an astonishing array of writers to provide cosmopolitan reports concerning the arts outside of the United States. Thus Thomas Mann wrote the German Letter, Maxim Gorki the Russian, Ezra Pound reported from Paris until Thayer sacked him in 1923 (an action for which Pound forever blamed Seldes!), and T. S. Eliot wrote the London Letter until he begged off in 1922 and was replaced by Raymond Mortimer for years thereafter. Responsibility for the Dublin Letter shifted from Ernest Boyd (whose dislike for Seldes was cordially reciprocated) to W. K. Magee. Thayer's intensity could be capricious, however. In 1922 he aimed harsh scorn at Sherwood Anderson, the first recipient (in 1921) of the coveted *Dial* award. For an example of intensity rewarded, however, in 1924 Thayer finally persuaded Thomas Mann to let *The Dial* publish "Death in Venice," a terrific coup.[13]

Thayer's considerable wealth and disdain for his family's mercantile origins in Worcester, Massachusetts, may or may not have prompted Seldes' often bemused observations about the world of commerce in general and relations between business and the arts in particular. In 1932, for instance, Seldes commented in a newspaper column that Americans *do* tend to talk about business. Whereas foreign observers found that a fault, Seldes declared that "talking about business is quite proper: that is what makes artists so interesting, that they never talk about anything else—only it is their own business, which in the end may make them tiresome." There is an element of ambiguity here because it is not altogether clear whether "business" meant the vocation of being an artist or how they were actually doing financially.[14] In any case, with the passage of time Seldes, unlike Thayer, became more interested in business as a public phenomenon, especially advertising and social responses to it. Seldes' personal finances would forever be riding a kind of roller coaster, however, with highs in the early 1930s and lows in the 1940s. He lived entirely by his pen—no easy business—and that required a mercurial mix of skill and serendipity.

II

Thayer and Watson hired Seldes at the beginning of 1920 as their second associate editor. After six months he became the managing editor. Thereafter he would be assisted by Kenneth Burke, a young and feisty literary critic, and Sophia Wittenberg, a bright and attractive young woman who soon married Lewis Mumford. (Mumford had been fired not long before Seldes joined the staff on the grounds that he was too "sociological"; Seldes' being more literary suited *The Dial*'s new orientation.) Late in 1992, Sophia Mumford recalled for me her work at *The Dial* seventy years earlier:

> Gilbert was lighthearted and easy to get along with. Though he was serious about his work, which he seemed to enjoy, I would not say he was intellectually intense. He was rather keenly interested in and alert to trends of the times. I would not call him pompous or domineering [in contrast to Thayer?]. The Dial in its early days, and I was there in one capacity or another from the start, was conducted in the office along rather informal lines with a general camaraderie, and Gilbert did much to foster that. I think he thoroughly enjoyed his work.[15]

The editorial offices were located in a handsome, spacious three-story home at 152 West 13th Street, and Seldes lived within walking distance on East 19th. Such proximity would always be important to Seldes because he never (well hardly ever) drove an automobile. He eventually learned how, but because he was so intently cerebral, conversations would distract him, cause him to lose concentration and become a hazard on the road to himself and others. The life of the mind genuinely mattered to Seldes, even to the point where it might endanger life itself.

His editorial work at *The Dial* clearly matches a pattern so characteristic of his cohort. Edmund Wilson, for example, worked as an editor at *Vanity Fair* in 1920–21 and 1922–23. In between those stints, when their mutual friend John Peale Bishop ran *Vanity Fair,* Wilson served as managing editor of *The New Republic,* and during that phase Wilson and Seldes developed a cordial relationship, social as well as intellectual, that became extremely close in their later years when both men vacationed on Cape Cod. From 1920 until 1924 Van Wyck Brooks held the position of literary editor at *The Freeman.* He and Seldes were moving in opposite directions, of course, because Brooks felt increasingly unfriendly to modernism while Seldes became steadily more supportive of it. To complicate matters in a manner so typical of the time, *The Dial* gave Brooks its much coveted annual award in 1923. A few years later, writing his *Sketches in Criticism,* Brooks expressed impatience with the formal aestheticism that he felt was dominant at *The Dial.* "A strange, brittle, cerebral aristocratism has succeeded the robust faith of the last age," he wrote in *The Freeman.* "Today the 'triumph of abstract thought' and of an art divorced from humanity is very evident in the literary world."[16]

Criticism of *The Dial* seemed to increase in direct proportion to its visibility and success. Moreover, the barbs came from diverse quarters, some of them surprising because they really did not involve direct competitors. *Time* magazine, for instance, launched its career on March 3, 1923, with a jibe at *The Dial:*

> There is a new kind of literature abroad in the land, whose only obvious fault is that no one can understand it. . . . *The Dial* has awarded its $2,000 prize for the best poem of 1922 to an opus entitled *The Waste Land,* by T. S. Eliot. Burton Rascoe, of *The New York Tribune,* hails it as incomparably great. Edmund Wilson, Jr., of *Vanity Fair,* is no less enthusiastic in praise of it. So is J. Middleton Murry, British critic.

> Here are the last eight lines of *The Waste Land:*
> > "London Bridge is falling
> > down falling down falling down
> > Poi s'accose nel foco che gli affina
> > Quando flam ceu chelidon—O swallow swallow
> > Le Prince d'Aquitaine a la tour abolie
> > These fragments I have shored against my ruins

> Why then Ile fit you. Hieronymo's mad againe.
> Datta. Dayadham. Damyata.
>   "Shantih Shantih Shantih"

The case for the defense, as presented by the admirers of Messrs. Eliot, Joyce, et al., runs something like this:

> Literature is self-expression. It is up to the reader to extract the meaning, not up to the writer to offer it. If the author writes everything that pops into his head—or that is supposed to pop into the head of a given character—that is all that should be asked. Lucidity is no part of the auctorial task.

It is rumored that *The Waste Land* was written as a hoax. Several of its supporters explain that that is immaterial, literature being concerned not with intentions but results.

In 1922 two recent graduates of Yale, Brit Hadden and Henry Luce, went to visit H. L. Mencken (then the co-editor of *Smart Set* and about to launch his *American Mercury*) in order to use him as a sounding board for the unprecedented weekly newsmagazine that they envisioned. Mencken listened quietly and gave the earnest young journalists his acerbic, un-equivocal judgment: "It will never work. Nobody will read it." He was dead wrong, of course; but even more important, though barely remembered now, the early success of *Time* owed a great deal to its section designated "Back of the Book," which helped to popularize culture in middle America. As one correspondent recalled, "Luce had a profound effect on Americans by telling them that a symphony orchestra in your town is a good thing for business. And so is an art museum. The Back of the Book made that magazine."[17]

Even though *The Dial* deliberately aspired to be a highbrow publication and *Time* swiftly became, perhaps, the ultimate middlebrow magazine, Hadden and Luce just had to include a lead-off hit against their prestigious non-competitor. Perhaps those former editors of the *Yale Daily News* couldn't resist taunting those former editors of the *Harvard Monthly*, Thayer and Seldes. Whatever the provocation may have been, Seldes didn't forget *Time*'s desire to tarnish *The Dial* when both were very young. Three decades later, when Seldes lashed out at Luce, he did so privately and on a matter much more important than that 1923 snideness. (See Chapter Ten, pp. 365–66 below.)

In 1922 a literary critic named Gorham B. Munson created a rebellious literary magazine, titled *Secession,* on a shoe-string budget with its "temporary editorial office" located in Vienna and its actual headquarters based in Brooklyn. The very first issue included an intemperate fusillade jealously aimed at its well-heeled rival and by then pre-eminent leader in the field of serious literature. Munson called his three-page diatribe Exposé No. 1:

> The *Dial* is, I suppose, generally considered to be America's leading magazine of literary expression. One critic has even called it the recognized organ of the young generation! True, there is not much competition for these honors, and the career of the *Little Review* has been sufficiently obscure for the *réclame* brought by size, money, circulation and famous names to over-shadow it in public esteem. What then, is our "leader" like?
>
> It boasts: "We have freed ourselves from commercialism and manifestos, from schoolmen and little schools, from a little nationalism and a snobbish cosmopolitanism." That is, it has freed itself from a fixed point for judging. . . . It has liberated itself from a definite direction. It feels no obligation to homogeneity. Naturally, its chief effect is one of diffuseness. It is late Victorian, Yellow Book, philosophic, naturalistic, professorial, dadaistic, traditional, experimental, wise, silly, international and nationalistically concerned in a developing literature. . . . It features a wallowing ox of a stylist who retails each month acres of vague impressionistic excrement on music, painting, and books. Still, his uncouth attempts at new sentence rhythms, word coinage, and telling inversions give more hilarity than pain. . . . It would be less compromising to go one way or the other. Stay on dry land like the *Atlantic Monthly* or leap headfirst into the contemporary stream. If you wish a good swim, take off your life-belt!
>
> I should not like to see the *Dial* annihilated but I should enjoy seeing its pretences abandoned. Vulgarization is a legitimate business. Some large American publisher might well bring out the *Dial* as Émile Paul Frères publishes *Les Écrits Nouveaux*. That would be a frank undertaking.
>
> The existence of this *Yale-Review*-in-a-Harvard-blazer is one of the bitter necessities calling for *Secession*.[18]

It is not clear whether Munson meant to single out Seldes when he referred to a "wallowing ox of a stylist," but he surely knew that his canard splattered not one but three critics. Paul Rosenfeld served as *The Dial*'s music critic; Henry McBride (as well as Thayer) wrote about art; and Seldes provided a lot, but by no means all of the book reviews. In any case, *Secession* scarcely crested many waves, and Seldes' magnanimous response was representative of his customary behavior, throughout his career, when attacked. A letter from Kenneth Burke, editorial assistant to Seldes, to his pal Malcolm Cowley, a contributor to and supporter of *Secession,* is engagingly revealing:

News on the *Dial:* They are a bit huffed about the first number of *Secession.* And as I prophesied, they ruffled somewhat about your sponsorship. Indeed, I had made no mention of *Secession,* was talking about you and me (gently blurbing), when Seldes suddenly says, "Cowley seems to be pretty much the sponsor for *Secession.*" The discussion then fell upon the anti-*Dial* stuff. I assured him that you had had nothing to do with that phase of the magazine. I told him that Munson's idea was eventually to make a board of editors, of which he was director, but that up to now his editorial policy was independent of the other contributors. Then Seldes, "Well, we are not going to do anything to our youngsters. In fact, I believe magazines like that are a good thing."[19]

As petty as these squabbles might seem, they involved much more than mere resentment directed by those with aspirations against those who had already achieved inspiration. Cowley, and to a lesser degree Burke, felt strongly that genuine contemporary creativity in the arts required absolute rather than half-hearted or merely judicious support. They also believed in the necessary development of a distinctly American mode of cultural and literary criticism. The people running *The Dial* did not feel so compelled at that time. After a while those in charge as well as loyal former associates, like Seldes, simply assumed that harsh attacks were the inevitable cost that success commanded. When *The New Republic* accused *The Dial* in January 1927 of not being open to new writers, Seldes responded with alacrity even though he had not, in reality, been a member of *The Dial* staff for almost four years. He observed that, as an outsider, he noticed three to seven names on each month's contents page, not only new to *The Dial* but unknown to him. A dialogue between *The New Republic* and anonymous spokesmen for *The Dial* (Marianne Moore and James Sibley Watson, Jr.) lingered throughout 1927, not quite a civil war among friends but a less than civil discourse among cultural warriors.[20]

Sometimes the contentiousness that passed between this hot-blooded bunch of young authors and editors owed much to their free-lance situation as writers. When they had a piece accepted, more often than not they needed to be paid and found the slightest delay vexing. That tension could be compounded when significant intellectual or ideological differences existed between them. Seldes, for example, detested Albert Jay Nock, Van Wyck Brooks' literary assistant at the *The Freeman,* and wrote an enraged letter when Nock delayed publication of Seldes' review of *The Enormous Room* by E. E. Cummings: "Apart from indicating your contempt for me and for the normal courtesies of correspondence I do not see what you gained by delaying to answer my letter."[21]

Substantive disagreements with journals more radical or modernist than *The Dial,* like *Secession,* were balanced by quarrels with mainstream publications more cautious or conservative than *The Dial.* Late in 1922, for instance, after Seldes' notable review of *Ulysses* appeared in *The Nation,* he had words (publicly as well as privately) with Henry Seidel Canby, influential editor of the "Literary Review" of the New York *Evening Post,* "a weekly magazine for book-lovers." From Canby's perspective, Seldes and other admirers of *Ulysses* were so enamoured of its innovations that they could not even acknowledge its indecencies and the "rather obvious and probably pathological weaknesses of its author." Canby speculated that he might need "to erect a statue for you of that Athenian who went always seeking for new things!"[22]

Slings and arrows did not fly constantly. Good-natured high jinx also characterized and occurred among many of these critics. Much of it seemed to focus on *Vanity Fair,* a lively monthly less aggressively intellectual and more fashionably middlebrow. In 1922–23, when Seldes wrote for almost every issue and sometimes even twice per issue, *Vanity Fair* enjoyed a circulation of approximately 92,000 whereas *The Dial* might have exceeded half that number at its peak in the mid-1920s. *Vanity Fair* received many contributions from British writers, and that mattered in those years of ardent cultural anglophilia. Clive Bell, the English writer and art critic, appeared regularly. He and Seldes, who emerged as fast friends when Seldes went to Europe to write in 1923, became known as the "twin gilded bantams" ruling Frank Crowninshield's roost at *Vanity Fair.*[23]

In 1922, when Edmund Wilson returned to *Vanity Fair* as managing editor, Seldes sent him a spoof letter of submission to accompany a "satirical romance" that might have been written by Maxwell Bodenheim, the imagist poet and cynical novelist who became part of the bohemian scene in Greenwich Village at that time. (Bodenheim and his third wife were murdered by a psychopath in 1954.) "Permit me to say," Seldes/Bodenheim wrote, "that I do not expect you to take it. Three editors of Vanity Fair before you have collaborated in a conspiracy of hate against this work or against me. I do not know which, and I see no reason from your published work to assume that you are more intelligent or more indulgent to those who differ from you."

To make it easier for you I will remind you that your immediate prede-
cessor, Mr. John Peale Bishop, jr., (it begins to look as if one must be a jr. to
be managing editor of your jejune magazine) informed me without blush-
ing that God is considered even more irreproachable in America than
Warren G. Harding. I need hardly say that this attitude is what is stran-
gling American letters.

It is also perhaps superfluous to call to your attention the fact that the
attitude taken by Vanity Fair to my own work has nearly driven me to
despair. Your rejection of the enclosed will simply be another drop in a
bucket long over-flowing with gall and bitterness.[24]

Although we cannot quantify the number of *authentic* letters of that
sort received by Seldes, Wilson, Bishop, Moore, Brooks, Nock, Munson,
and their fellow editors of the early and mid-1920s, there must have been
many. A few, involving the likes of Ernest Hemingway, would cause
Seldes intermittent torment for the rest of his days. Sometime in 1922 or
1923, Hemingway submitted short stories and vignettes to *The Dial* that
later appeared in his book *in our time*. Scofield Thayer (and later, perhaps, Marianne Moore) rejected Hemingway's work. But Dorothy Parker and Louis Sobol, who did not like Seldes, spread a rumor that Seldes
personally had not only rejected Hemingway's short pieces but had even,
gratuitously, told Hemingway that he should stick to newspaper work
and harbor no illusions about becoming a serious writer. To complicate
matters, Seldes' successor as managing editor of *The Dial,* Alyse Gregory,
altered the title of Edmund Wilson's review of *in our time* for *The Dial* to
"Mr. Hemingway's Dry-Points." The allusion involved—to Goya's medium for his *Tauromachia* (1815–16), an etching with aquatint—was
meant to be complimentary, just as Wilson intended his review to be
highly positive. But because Goya's technique owed much to Rembrandt,
the inference was conveyed that Hemingway's book was derivative, following a well-established tradition. So once again *The Dial* wounded
Hemingway's very considerable *amour-propre.*[25]

Finally, to aggravate matters even more, Seldes wrote a rave review of
Fitzgerald's *The Great Gatsby* for the August 1925 issue of *The Dial.* But
in the process Seldes made unkind comparisons with Fitzgerald's earlier
novels, a tack that seems to have annoyed Hemingway far more than it
bothered Fitzgerald. Perhaps, also, because Seldes went on to say that
Fitzgerald had "more than matured; he has mastered his talents and
gone soaring in a beautiful flight, leaving behind him everything dubious

and tricky in his earlier work, and leaving even farther behind all the men of his own generation and most of his elders." That conveyed more of a put-down than the fiercely competitive Hemingway could bear, even if F. Scott Fitzgerald was his good friend.[26]

Seldes' review of *Gatsby* commended Fitzgerald's command of irony and pity in depicting a small section of life with consuming passion. Hemingway responded by including in *The Sun Also Rises* (1926) a discussion during a fishing expedition in Spain that turns into a slur upon New York-based critics and the New York literary establishment in general. Without actually citing Seldes, of course, there is an excessively long, mocking conversation about irony and pity in literature. All the insiders on the scene knew perfectly well that Hemingway had aimed a sharp arrow at Seldes.[27]

Hemingway also took a snide swipe at Seldes in the *transatlantic* for July 1925, then engaged in a pro and con cannonade with Seldes in *Esquire* (September and November 1934 and January 1935); and left a subtle parting shot against his old nemesis in *A Moveable Feast,* published posthumously in 1964. In private correspondence Hemingway remained vicious and vulgar. Early in 1924 he informed Ezra Pound that Seldes, "his sphincter muscle no doubt having lost its attractive tautness, has left the Dial. An aged virgin [Alyse Gregory, who remained as managing editor until 1925 when Marianne Moore took over] has his place. There is no doubt a similarity." Until his death in 1961, Hemingway would caricature Seldes as asexual or impotent, and the bisexual Thayer was ridiculed as a "perennial bugger."[28]

Hemingway always insisted that he had received an inept, insulting letter from Seldes rejecting his poems in 1923. Dorothy Parker, writing in *The New Yorker* in 1930, referred to a "young gentleman who once occupied the editorial chair of a now defunct magazine of culture" who once read some of Hemingway's work, rejected it and said, "I hear he has been a reporter—tell him to go on reporting and not try to write." Ruminating from Key West to a confidant in 1934, Hemingway crowed that

I've had him [Seldes] worried about that letter for a very long time now and I'm going to keep him worried. Don't say I mentioned it anymore. I've got it locked up with my papers in Paris and no matter how his critical career comes out this makes a bum of him in the end. I've written all the facts about Gertrude [Stein] so they'll be on tap if anything happens to me but I don't like to slam the old bitch around when she's here [on a U.S. tour] having a wonderful time.[29]

The putative letter has never been found and authorities on Hemingway's career do not believe that it ever existed. That includes Nicholas Joost, who wrote two meticulous books about *The Dial* and one on Hemingway's relationship with literary magazines, as well as Carlos Baker, Hemingway's first thorough biographer and the editor of his letters, and William Wasserstrom, another expert on *The Dial*'s controversial career.[30]

It is noteworthy that Seldes not only sought no revenge, but consistently praised Hemingway, often lavishly, throughout his life. In 1926 Seldes mentioned *The Sun Also Rises* to Marianne Moore with considerable enthusiasm. In 1929 he reviewed *A Farewell to Arms* for the New York *Graphic:*

> There is no question that the current center of interest justifies the excitement it has created. Hemingway's *A Farewell to Arms* is not only more interesting than most books of the average season, but interesting in more ways. It is a tragic love story written by a member of that generation which is supposed not to believe in love and not to be capable of tragedy; it is beautifully written by a man who has always given the impression that he is doing his best to avoid beautiful writing; it includes a supremely fine rendering of the physical impact of the war and it lets all the moral effects rise out of the story of their own necessity. In its weaker moments it still is a melodrama of considerable excitement. Best of all, you have the sense, when you are reading it, that you will continue to read Hemingway, because he is going to go on, changing and developing and being always an individual you have to reckon with. The way he has impressed himself upon the intelligent world is formidable.[31]

In 1932 Seldes devoted one of his daily columns in the New York *Evening Journal* to *Death in the Afternoon,* which he considered "exceptional in every way." Seldes noted the "rude" references to novelist and critic Waldo Frank, also of Jewish extraction, but uttered no complaint. Near the end of his life Seldes remarked that "the reference to me in *A Moveable Feast* (in connection with Gatsby) doesn't endear EH to me, but it is brilliant."[32] The last sentences that Seldes ever composed about his old nemesis appear in notes that he dictated two years before his death, notes toward a memoir of the 1920s and '30s. Seldes would have titled that memoir "As in My Time," an ironic if not quixotic echo of Hemingway's first book, *in our time.* "I am essentially not concerned with anything personal about H." Seldes said at the end,

> I am thinking of him in connection with the other writers of his early years and of his report on the America of that time. . . . I do not think I ever felt that H was an expatriate in the sense that others were. When I first knew him he was on assignment from a newspaper, as my brother was and many others—and these foreign correspondents were the most resolutely American of all Americans abroad.

Thayer and Watson often left New York City for Europe and elsewhere, sometimes for months at a time, leaving Seldes in charge with much responsibility but little ultimate authority. In 1922, with Watson in Paris, Seldes wrote him urgently: "Please hurry back because I am no longer able to stand the attacks against me in the public prints." It is not clear whether he composed those words in mock fear or with genuine anxiety. A blend of both, I suspect. He stood up to Hemingway astonishingly well for decades—even beyond the novelist's gory death, and transcended the vituperative barrage of buckshot in seeking a better understanding of literary nationalism in the 1920s.[33]

It is tempting, yet problematic, to ascribe Seldes' enmities to anti-Semitism. He dressed the part of a dandy in those days and, as a critic, Seldes called them as he saw them (see Fig. 3). Hence some contemporaries viewed him as opinionated and self-indulgent—qualities that could be applied to most of his friends and foes alike. Lawrence Langner, an international patent attorney and playwright who helped to organize the Theatre Guild in 1918–19, remembered Seldes as "an argumentative young aesthete with a time sense which led him in easy steps from literature to television." Literary friends seem to have been conscious of his Jewish origins and invited him to review books on cultural or literary subjects involving Judaism. Unlike the literary historian and novelist Ludwig Lewisohn, Seldes was never publicly rejected for institutional employment because of his Jewish heritage, nor were his books ever reviewed negatively simply because of Seldes' religious origins. In 1933, for example, Dorothea Brande remarked in a review of Lewisohn's *Expression in America* (1932) that it "cannot be denied" that modern critical imbecilities "come to us oftenest and in their most extreme form from Jewish writers."[34]

Even when Seldes' fellow writers referred to his Jewishness, they often

Fig. 3. Gilbert Seldes (ca. 1922).

did so in a complimentary way, however convoluted. Sherwood Anderson, for example, described the literary crowd in New York as "superficial men . . . book-made men." After that his ambivalence surfaced. "Then there are the Jews—Gilbert Seldes, Paul Rosenfeld, Alfred Stieglitz—intense men, not sour, very fine, in contrast to the men like [Waldo] Frank who have . . . something of the Jewish prophet spirit in them, preachers really and by just that much corrupt." Following a big reception during the summer of 1924 Archibald MacLeish penned a less ambiguous letter to Seldes' good friend John Peale Bishop. (MacLeish, like Bishop, lived in France during the mid-1920s in order to write and have a convenient base for travel.) "There is something queer about Seldes. I fancy its the fact that, in spite of erudition & surprising power of evoking affection, he *is* a kike (how does that write itself) and a pithy one."[35]

Although the language and sentiments expressed are unattractive, we must be careful not to judge the 1920s according to criteria that became normative two generations later. Seldes himself, a man of unusual tolerance, as we shall see, occasionally used words like pansy, queer, and Japs. Moreover, his early comments about African Americans sound as condescending to us as those made by MacLeish, Pound, and many others about Jews. In a signed essay published in 1921 Seldes offered a tendentious explanation of "Why the Jew is never merely a cosmopolite and why the Negro is not international; because the one has his unity and the other, with no other identity so far than that of color, is insufficiently grounded in himself to resist the inroads of cosmopolitanism." Robert C. Benchley, a contemporary and friend of Seldes, offered the same sort of strangely ambiguous (to us) comments in one of his drama columns for 1922 called "The Negro Revues." Although Seldes' logic made little sense and seems embarrassingly ill-informed, he grew and changed. From the 1930s onward he became an ardent advocate of African Americans in what had emerged as his special field of cultural criticism, the lively arts.[36]

Although anti-Semitism may have augmented Ezra Pound's distaste for Seldes, the principal cause was Thayer's dismissal of Pound as *The Dial*'s Paris correspondent in 1923, for which Pound, like Hemingway, managed to hold Seldes personally responsible. As early as 1920, however, when Pound so urgently tried to find a job for T. S. Eliot that would liberate him from banking to full-time literary pursuits, he sent John Quinn a letter scarred by anti-Semitism and asked: "I wonder if Dial would guarantee him [Eliot] a three years editorial post in N.Y. in place perhaps of Seldes or extra [an add-on position]. I have no [rancour?] against Seldes." Late in 1922, after *The Dial* had published "The Waste Land," Seldes wrote a letter published by *The Literary Review*. "A great many people," he declared, "do not realize why Mr. Ezra Pound is so refreshing." Seldes never, to my knowledge, spoke ill of Ezra Pound.[37]

Seldes' relationship with T. S. Eliot, by comparison, continued to be benign on both sides despite complexities involving *The Dial* and a dispute concerning the publication history of "The Waste Land" that lingered into the 1970s, half a century after the event. Let's consider the personal first, and then the professional. Although Eliot would write publicly about the need for racial homogeneity and avoiding "any large number of free thinking Jews" (which Seldes was) along with any "spirit of excessive tolerance," his correspondence with Seldes always remained cordial. They had met briefly at Harvard in the fall of 1912 when Seldes was an undergraduate and Eliot returned from Europe as a graduate student in philosophy. After the complex and sensitive negotiations for *The Dial*'s publication of "The Waste Land" had been completed, Eliot told Pound that Seldes and Watson had been very kind, a view that he conveyed directly to Seldes after the famous poem first appeared in *The Dial*'s November 1922 issue. A few weeks earlier, moreover, Eliot sent Seldes very strong praise after his lengthy review of *Ulysses* was published in *The Nation*.[38]

Although the professional contretemps became a subject of speculation and disagreement for decades, the recent publication of Eliot's correspondence by his second wife helps to clarify the matter considerably. In 1921 Thayer created the *Dial* award, an annual sum of $2000 for outstanding service to American letters rendered by a contributor to the journal. Sherwood Anderson was the first recipient in 1921, followed in successive years by Eliot, Van Wyck Brooks, Marianne Moore, E. E. Cummings, William Carlos Williams, and Kenneth Burke. All of them, along with many other aspiring independent writers, needed the money, some of them rather desperately, and the prestige associated with this award was immense. Needless to say, considerable resentment often occurred when wistful aspirants were passed over.[39]

The most heated controversy has hinged on the question: did Eliot receive the award in 1922 as a quid pro quo for permitting *The Dial* to be the initial American publisher (almost simultaneous with Eliot's own *Criterion,* a quarterly review in England) of "The Waste Land," without its notes, prior to publication in book form? Nicholas Joost, the leading authority on *The Dial,* has answered with a categorical yes. In 1965, after Joost's detailed study of *Scofield Thayer and the Dial* appeared, Seldes insisted to several people, ranging from very old friends like Edmund Wilson to such scholars as Richard Poirier, that Joost was incorrect. I am persuaded that Seldes' memory failed him on this matter, but his sincere recollection deserves to be heard, especially because Seldes' honor and integrity are not at stake here, whatever the truth may be. He flatly told Wilson in 1965 that literary historians were wrong to believe that "in order to get The Waste Land we promised TSE the Dial award. So far as I knew, we intended to give it to him that year in any case—and he knew we had a fixed rate for poetry, anyhow."[40]

Then what, in essence, actually happened? First, it should be mentioned that T. S. Eliot had known Scofield Thayer when they were both students at Milton Academy and at Harvard College. Even so, Eliot initially felt skeptical about *The Dial* because it looked as though it might be a weak imitation of *The Atlantic Monthly*. Nevertheless, early in 1922 Eliot offered "The Waste Land" to Thayer for publication. He remarked that it had taken him a year to compose his "biggest work" and wanted to know what *The Dial* would pay. When Thayer proposed $150, the journal's standard sum for a poem of that length, Eliot expressed annoyance and asked for $856! A kind of paralysis ensued in their relations.[41]

The poem's reputation as an extraordinary work had been rumored for quite some time, and those responsible for *The Dial* believed, correctly as it turned out, that publishing the poem would provide a boost in the journal's circulation. Finally, in August, John Quinn, the notable lawyer, collector, and patron, invited Seldes and Horace Liveright to his office where they reached a swift agreement: *The Dial* would publish the poem without notes and would purchase 350 copies of the book. In return Liveright would permit prior publication. Eliot would receive *The Dial*'s customary rate for poetry along with the $2000 *Dial* award for 1922. In October Eliot told Pound that Seldes and Watson "have behaved extremely nicely . . . ." No one seemed to doubt, least of all Seldes and Eliot, that "The Waste Land" was destined to become a literary landmark.[42]

One immediate piece of fall-out is worth noting. The December issue of *The Dial* announced Eliot's award and included an effusive essay in praise of Eliot by Edmund Wilson. This encomium displeased Eliot. He explained why to Seldes and wanted Wilson to know. Seldes had recently published his own positive appraisal of "The Waste Land" in *The Nation*:

> I can say without flattery that I prefer your remarks about "The Waste Land" to those of Mr. Wilson which are somewhat more sensational in tone. I do not mean that I do not like his article, but the whole thing was just a little too highly coloured. . . . There is one point in Mr. Wilson's article to which I must strongly take exception. I do very much object to be made use of by anyone for the purpose of disparaging the work of Ezra Pound. I am infinitely in his debt as a poet, as well as a personal friend, and I do resent being praised at his expense. Besides, what Mr. Wilson said of him was most unfair. I sincerely consider Ezra Pound the most important living poet in the English language. And you will see that in view of my great debt to him in literature it is most painful to me to have such comments made.[43]

When Seldes wrote to Richard Poirier in 1965 to explain that no "deal" had been made with Eliot guaranteeing him the *Dial* award,

Seldes insisted that Eliot had been "in the running, if not among the two leaders, in 1921." Therefore, Eliot's selection in 1922 should, in retrospect, come as no surprise.

Supporting evidence for Seldes' sincerity on this point will be found in two letters, hitherto unknown (or else ignored) that Seldes sent to Sibley Watson in 1966 and 1968. In the first Seldes attempts to reconstruct the deliberations that accompanied the first two awards. He recalls that he and Thayer considered Eliot very seriously in 1921 but "decided (intelligently) to give it to an American who had not left these shores." The loyal American turned out to be Sherwood Anderson, and Seldes observed in 1968 that he received preference "not on the grounds of greater service to letters, but that it wouldn't have seemed proper for us to have given the first one to an expatriate."[44]

The Dial's relationship with Anderson, and more particularly Seldes', are indicative of the highs and lows of literary reputation along with the notable capacity those people had to separate professional judgments from personal friendships. Just because the former went sour, that didn't prevent the latter from remaining amiable. On October 26, 1921, Seldes officially notified Anderson that he would be honored as the first recipient of the *Dial* award. Almost immediately the grateful author sent Seldes the manuscript of a story called "A Testament" to be considered for publication. No one at *The Dial* liked it and poor Seldes had to write an awkward letter of explanation epitomized by one critical sentence: "I do not think that you have got what you are after." The story was not rejected outright until March 16, 1922, however. One week earlier, perhaps to soften the blow, Seldes wrote Anderson the following:

> This is a quaint magazine we run. I don't suppose that we have ever told anybody what sort of thing to write for us, but oh man, if you can write another in the vein of I'm a Fool some day when you are feeling good, I will not be displeased.[45]

At the close of the letter that Seldes reluctantly sent as his initial response to "A Testament" he added: "I beg you, for Heaven's sake, to remember that I am a [*sic*] individual human being, an intense admirer of your work." How often have editors felt obliged to say such things? And in this instance, Seldes meant every word. He admired "I'm a Fool" extravagantly. With the passage of time, however, his feelings about Anderson's work would lose their intensity and wane. Late in the 1960s Seldes dictated a fascinating twelve-page memoir about Sherwood Anderson and his attitude toward the man and his work. As for the work, this is what Seldes had to say about Anderson's best-known book at the time of *The Dial* award in 1921:

> I've gone back and read WINESBURG, OHIO once in the past five years or so and find myself virtually unable to read it. I had completely forgotten the stories, and had no interest in finishing more of them. The whole book struck me as being peculiarly unreal, and not in the sense of created people but half-created people, who had possibly little relevance to the people that Sherwood actually knew. I thought that the whole thing,—and this is the oddest thing to say about anyone so transparently honest as Sherwood Anderson was—I thought it was an intellectual fake. I thought that the agonizings of the characters were over-done and in a sense applied to the characters from the outside. I recognized little depth of understanding, and perhaps I recognized too many current intellectual fads. It is quite possible that Sherwood wrote the book without being aware of the fads, but it seems to me incredible now that anyone should have thought that WINESBURG, OHIO was a new beginning in American literature.[46]

Sic transit gloria Anderson. And Seldes was neither mean-spirited nor hypercritical. Many other critics shared those sentiments well before Anderson died in 1941. As for their personal relationship, however, it stands in marked contrast to the professional, a common pattern at that time. Seldes recalled:

> It was an instant friendship, and it was definite and quite deep in spite of the fact that we met perhaps only three or four times. I remember once coming to see him during a trip through Chicago, and saying to him "Sherwood, I have been married, since I saw you last," and he roared with laughter and said "I've been divorced and married since I saw you last."[47]

Despite Anderson's prominence in 1921, quite a few critics and writers resented his being the recipient of the *Dial* award because of his age, forty-five. Many felt that younger, less established authors should receive the recognition (and the much needed cash). By mid- and later 1922, in fact, an intergenerational ruckus arose among critics that was highly symptomatic of intense feelings shared by Seldes and his cohort that their time had now come.

The fuse for this explosion, however, was not Anderson's award but an essay by an older critic, Joel E. Spingarn, titled "The Younger Generation: A New Manifesto." He acknowledged that a group of critics and writers called *les jeunes* felt agitated and age-conscious, but declared that "I, who once called upon young men for rebellion and doubt, now call upon them for thought and faith." What did he mean by such an admonition? First, he reaffirmed the grounds for his own rebellion more than a decade earlier, criteria that he wanted to see carried forward by his legatees. "There is only one real division to-day that has any reality, and that is the division between an old-fashioned materialism and a new idealism." It had been necessary, he reminded readers in 1922, to destroy the sterile forms that critics and writers once used rather than social realities. But now that Spingarn and his allies had been so successful, the newcomers should nurture their talents and build upon the controlled iconoclasm of their seniors. "Judgment is maturity," Spingarn proclaimed, "and this is why it is impossible to expect . . . criticism from those who have not attained the spiritual state of maturity."[48]

Although Edmund Wilson and many others felt quite vexed by Spingarn's arch defense of the status quo in criticism, Seldes found himself in an awkward position because Spingarn had personally and publicly praised Seldes' first signed editorial in *The Dial.* So Seldes, momentarily torn between gratitude and a strident position of innovation that he would begin to articulate later in 1923, wrote Spingarn a private and stuffily deferential letter six weeks after the "new manifesto" appeared: "I think that all the stages of the controversy after your original pronouncement have become progressively more tedious and more vulgar intellectually, and I think that is more of a pity, since your manifesto required and gave basis for clear thinking."[49]

If the *New York Times* was correct in its assessment that *The Dial* was Spingarn's ultimate target, then perhaps Seldes should have been more aggressive and even confrontational. One reason for his apparent quiescence, quite uncharacteristic of his behavior after he left *The Dial,* may well have been that Thayer and Watson wanted their journal to be open to outstanding writers *of all* generations, did not want to be identified with any particular cohort or ideological perspective, and did not care much for polemics. It became commonplace to say that *The Dial* was *The Seven Arts* without politics, and during the 1930s critics referred to the "solipsistic aestheticism of the *Dial* school and the inane eclecticism of the liberal and individualistic critics."[50]

Early in the 1920s Van Wyck Brooks declared that "the editors of *The Dial* were aesthetic or nothing," a term of derision that he reiterated years later in his autobiography. In the case of Scofield Thayer, aesthete seems to have been a thinly disguised euphemism for homosexual or bisexual. Looking back to the years 1921–22 from 1933, Edmund Wilson recorded in his journal that Dr. Albert Barnes, the affluent and opinionated Philadelphia art collector, persecuted Thayer on sexual grounds for purposes of artistic control. Seldes told Wilson that Barnes would "burst in" on Thayer and Seldes, "perhaps hoping to catch them *in flagrante delicto* (he was always scenting homosexuality) in a hotel room in Paris and did what amounted to serving notice on Thayer that he must drop McBride and Rosenfeld, so that Barnes could direct the artistic policy of *The Dial,* and hence of America."[51]

In 1924 an Irish-American critic named Ernest Boyd enhanced "aesthete" as a term of disdain by publishing a satirical essay titled "Aesthete: Model 1924." After being dropped as *The Dial*'s Dublin correspondent, Boyd became an unrelenting critic of that journal, and he based his composite portrait of the aesthete on Seldes, Burke, Wilson, and Matthew Josephson, "with touches borrowed," according to Malcolm Cowley, from Dos Passos, Cummings, Gorham Munson, John Farrar, and Cowley himself. "The resulting hero," Cowley recalled with some mockery of his own, "a spraddling, disproportionate creature, was endowed by his author with a name, a history and several pansylike gestures."[52]

Predictably, perhaps, Boyd became convinced that the objects of his ridicule were literally out to get him. Walking along the street one day, according to Cowley,

> he encountered Gilbert Seldes, a writer whose features were included in the portrait of the imaginary Aesthete. Seldes harbored no grudge and raised his walking stick in friendly greeting. Mr. Boyd, however, interpreted this gesture as a threat and walked hurriedly away. Seldes followed him, having a message to deliver. Mr. Boyd walked faster. Seldes shouted and quickened his pace. It is easy to imagine the spectacle of these two prominent critics, both of them sedentary and peaceful by disposition, one fleeing with terror dogging his footsteps, the other pursuing with an uplifted cane and the most amicable intentions.[53]

Late in the 1960s, ruminating on Santayana's profound influence upon him, Seldes mused that it had not been the philosopher's fault that "in common with many of his students I would become, temporarily, the kind of aesthete which came in—and had I but known it, went out— with *The Yellow Book*. I was for art because the vulgar were not, it was a sign of my superiority."[54] Despite those mellow words, dictated late in the 1960s, Seldes did hold a grudge. From time to time Boyd became the butt of snide remarks by Seldes; and for most of his remaining life he regarded the word "aesthete" as an epithet.

III

In mid-July 1922 Seldes sent Sibley Watson (in Europe) an updated inventory of material then available for publication in *The Dial*. In terms of genuine quality, the cupboard seemed bare; so Seldes implored his "boss," who was in fact searching for first-rate writing and art: "Please send me a poem or something. The literary life is very hectic." When Thayer and Watson were away from the office, a common occurrence, Seldes supervised the regular monthly departments, assigned book reviews and evaluated them when they arrived, wrote his own book reviews along with the monthly "Theatre" column, and composed "Comment," the closing editorial essay in quite a few issues. Invariably, however, he deferred to Thayer and Watson whenever time and proximity permitted. As Seldes explained to Edmund Wilson in 1965: "In 1920 and 1921 Thayer was here and during the early part of his analysis with Freud he was very active. When he was away, Sibley Watson acted. . . .* No poem or picture, no major work of fiction, ever got into the magazine entirely on my say so. When Alyse Gregory and Marianne Moore took over, the conditions were changed. They were editors. I was managing editor and did a good job."[55]

Despite occasional chiding from Thayer, Seldes did work effectively under difficult circumstances. During the winter of 1921–22 he undertook a lot of promotional work for *The Dial*, much of it almost anonymously. Sometimes he served as an intermediary between Thayer and Watson, at other times as a conduit between prominent writers and one or both of the two owners. In corresponding with Amy Lowell in 1921–22 he handled that formidable woman so graciously that he won her praise repeatedly. "Your August number was the *ne plus ultra* of what a magazine should be," she told him in 1921.[56]

In some issues, such as the famous one of November 1922, Seldes had as many as four contributions: one under his own name, others under such pseudonyms as Vivian Shaw and Sebastien Cauliflower, and still

---

*In June 1922 Watson wrote to Thayer from Paris: "Why don't you come? Is Freud treating you for Syphilis? Other conjectures in N.Y. are less charitable. . . ."

others anonymously. Often he might write a review of a volume (poetry, fiction, or non-fiction) that appealed to him; but if someone else turned in a thoughtful essay on the very same book, Seldes would suppress his or else publish it in another journal. He made arrangements with Max Beerbohm, the eccentric British caricaturist, to everyone's satisfaction; and he negotiated with authors who wanted permission to reprint their works elsewhere. It was an understatement when Seldes told Raymond Mortimer, who followed Eliot as London correspondent, that "I am particularly concerned with the technical work of getting the magazine through the press." He did all of that and more—acquiring in the process a complete education in publishing a literary magazine and coping with enlarged egos.[57]

Somehow Seldes also made time to read and work steadily on his own material. In April 1922 someone on *The Dial*'s staff told Sibley Watson that "Gilbert has gone into retreat for the writing of reviews and comments." His book reviews could, at times, be arch and cutting. But the young critic was fearless. He wrote boldly about new works by Edith Wharton, Willa Cather, Joseph Hergesheimer, F. Scott Fitzgerald, Heywood Broun, and Robert Benchley. He could be disparaging toward Stephen Vincent Benét (just starting out) and harsh on Ben Hecht, who became a lifelong foe as a result. He also wrote about a diverse group of British and Anglo-Irish authors: George Bernard Shaw and G. K. Chesterton, whom he admired greatly; John Maynard Keynes, despite Seldes' lack of expertise in political economy (a topic he often returned to in his 1930s journalism); and, beyond the grave, Henry James for his acute perceptions concerning the novel, and Nietzsche's letters. Seldes' cohort in college had been, almost to a man, fascinated by Nietzsche, substance and style.[58]

In a 1922 review of Willa Cather's new novel *One of Ours*, Seldes made a carefully reasoned distinction between the work of a reviewer and the critic's vocation:

> The reviewer can guide the reader and buyer of books; but the critic, having his centre of interest in the art which is being practised, and the centre of influence in the public taste, with more than a slight concern for the creative process, looks to something a little more serious than the signpost for his symbol. He has to think, when he considers a novel, of what the novel has been and can be; he has to remember how books are read as well as what books; he has to want, however presumptuously to assist the

creative power by giving it a wider appreciation as well as by indicating its present lapses and its possible achievements.[59]

When Seldes composed the "American Letter" (pseudonymously as Sebastien Cauliflower) for *The Dial's* November 1922 issue, he managed to touch base with such recent works as *Contemporary American Novelists* by Carl Van Doren, *On Contemporary Literature* by Stuart Pratt Sherman, and *Definitions* by Henry Seidel Canby, along with *Letters and Leadership* by Van Wyck Brooks, *The Sacred Wood* by T. S. Eliot, and *Rousseau and Romanticism* by Irving Babbitt, which had all appeared a few years earlier. Ultimately, however, Seldes' "Letter" was not a review of these books but an intensely focused lament that recent cultural criticism seemed to illuminate "nearly everything except letters."

He went on to observe that most were "critics not of literature, but of economics, sociology, psychoanalysis, morality—and so on." He acknowledged that technical criticism of non-fiction, novels, and poetry did appear, but "it is not exactly technical criticism we want. It is, I suppose, aesthetic criticism." (Perhaps Ernest Boyd's satirical essay in January 1924 had some foundation in fact.) The final paragraph of this mini-manifesto is interesting because it is clear and judicious yet unexceptionable, neither distinctive nor innovative. Seldes was less than a year away from finding his "own voice," the one that would convey his special identity for the rest of his days. In 1922 his perspective as a critic could not be so readily distinguished from that of several others. Everyman might not be a cultural critic, but Seldes soon spoke as a critic for Everyman.

> For many of us the use of literature as a means to an economic end has become tiresome. We do want to know the relevance of a book to life, of course; but we want our critics to tell us just how well the "criticism of life" is managed in a novel, for instance, and then to go on and make our enjoyment greater by referring us to the artistic harmonies which the novel may possess, to let us share a little the rapture of the creator. . . . If our modern novelists are creating beautiful things, let our critics define for us their beauty or at least make it possible for us to see it, instead of trying to make us believe that the chief interest in a man like Lawrence is in his "sexology"—a word we do not use here. We are, as foreigners have observed, eager for culture, but we are a little afraid that our critics are giving us something else. Mr. Eliot says that the important critic is absorbed in the present problems of art and wishes to bring the forces of the past to bear

upon the solution of these problems. Perhaps that is the kind of importance we are looking for.[60]

Moreover, Seldes remained every bit the highbrow, a vocational and cultural identity that he would abjure in 1924 and after. In his "Theatre" columns for November and December 1921 in *The Dial,* Seldes issued a clarion call to "destroy the audience," a variation on Gordon Craig's plea to destroy the theatre. What did Seldes mean? Simply that the expansion of vulgar middlebrow attendance and the democratization of theatre tempted serious writers to water down the content of their drama. Somerset Maugham, for instance, began with fine comedy but "steadily wrote it down and down, so that the lowest intelligence could not fail to see every point." Nevertheless, more often than not, stupid and vulgar audiences did not seem to comprehend what a serious play was really about. Here is Seldes' infuriated report on the opening of "Anna Christie" by Eugene O'Neill:

> In Anna Christie Mr. O'Neill sets before you a young girl whose father believes her to be incomparably virginal and innocent. Actually she has been a prostitute. I find nothing laughable in this situation. Yet every time Anna Christie spoke the vicious racy ugly slang of her past, every word of which should have fallen like sleet upon our stricken hearts, the audience of which I was a part gathered itself with refreshment and laughed. It was a second night audience, at least part of it came by invitation; I do not dare to think of the nights that followed. In The Circle the blame was shared by the author and the two actors who made the scene at the bridge table meanly humorous; in this case I absolve Mr. O'Neill and his producer, both. The audience must go.[61]

Such bold and pungent words had impact. Other prominent drama critics took notice and explicitly echoed Seldes. Robert C. Benchley, for one, the regular drama writer for *Life* (not Henry Luce's photographic weekly, which began in 1936), promptly acknowledged the power of Seldes' point late in December 1921:

> It needed, however, the intrepid terseness of Mr. Gilbert Seldes, writing in *The Dial,* to formulate a slogan which we should have been afraid to be the first to utter but to which we subscribe with all the vigor that is left in these old bones after a series of devitalizing defeats. "Destroy the audience!" rings out the voice of Cato Seldes. "Every-thing else will follow."[62]

By the beginning of 1924 Seldes felt sufficiently confident in his reputation and work that he openly speared the theatre criticism being written by Alexander Woollcott and Heywood Broun. They belonged to the
Algonquin circle, of course, and Seldes kept his distance from that
crowd. By 1922 he wrote a "New York Theatrical Letter" for the *Public
Ledger* and other papers served by the Ledger syndicate. He also wrote at
least one (and sometimes two) articles each month for *Vanity Fair,* and
occasional pieces for *The Freeman* and *The New Republic.* All of which
provided a livelihood and, equally important to the aspiring critic, recognition and responses. As he wrote to his brother George, in Europe,
telegram style: "General impression of getting on and some nice come-
backs from here and abroad. Business of keeping alive paying off debts
and etcetera will be presently accomodated [*sic*] but business of keeping
health while working million hours daily is too much."[63]

Seldes' most challenging assignment for a publication other than *The
Dial* during these years involved his extended review of James Joyce's
Ulysses for *The Nation,* one of the (if not the very) first notices to appear
in the United States. During the autumn and winter of 1921 the imminent publication of *Ulysses* stirred immense excitement among literati.
First came the scramble to transport review copies from permissive Paris
to prudish America. As Seldes informed Sylvia Beach at Shakespeare
and Company in December, "a disagreeable rumour has reached me—to
the effect that our smut-hounds are going to try to keep the book out of
America by holding it up in the mail." Although Seldes asked Beach to
send him a copy in an "unmarked cover" by American Express, he
apparently got one when Dorothy Schiff, the heiress, soon-to-be publisher of the New York *Post,* and sooner-to-be Seldes' sister-in-law (1924),
smuggled in a copy on her return from a visit to France.[64]

The prospect of reviewing such an innovative book elated Seldes but
also seems to have challenged him on grounds of inappropriate ethnicity.
When he told Mary Maguire Colum (the wife of Padraic) about this
assignment, he acknowledged her warning that "none but und Irisher
could [properly do it]—but think of my special qualities for Bloom." He
told Carl Van Doren that *Ulysses* offered "exceptional interest in five or
six different ways . . . . I shall certainly skirt the problem of the Irishness
of Joyce's work. I am more competent to discuss the Jewishness of his
principal character [Leopold Bloom]." Seldes devoted the better part of
twelve weeks to the project, and when he completed it confessed to
Henry Seidel Canby that the final product gave him great pleasure.[65]

It should have because it was exceedingly lucid in presentation, well balanced considering spatial constraints (he stressed neither Jewishness nor Irishness), and ardently appreciative. In my view it is the best writing that Seldes had yet done, and perhaps one of the finest essay reviews he ever wrote—and they number in the hundreds, at least. He believed that Joyce had now become "possibly the most interesting and the most formidable writer of our time." He felt that Joyce had brought the novel as developed by Flaubert and James "to its culmination; he has, it seems likely, indicated the turn the novel will take into a new form." After an astonishingly clear description of what occurs in the novel and its relationship to Homer's narrative, Seldes devoted the second half to an assessment of the book's achievements:

> If it is true, as Mr. Yeats has said, that the poet creates the mask of his opposite, we have in "Ulysses" the dual mask—Bloom and Stephen—of James Joyce, and in it we have, if I am not mistaken, the mask of a generation: the broken poet turning to sympathy with the outward-going scientific mind.

Seldes concluded by explaining why he had called Joyce formidable: "The innovations in method and the developments in structure which he has used with a skill approaching perfection are going to have an incalculable effect upon the writers of the future; he is formidable because his imitators will make use of his freedom without imposing upon themselves the duties and disciplines he has suffered."[66] There is more, and Seldes proved to be a good prophet as well as an astute critic. The praise that he received from people like T. S. Eliot meant a great deal to him, and in 1923, when he went to Paris to write what turned out to be his own best-known book, he corresponded with Joyce and soon met him.[67]

IV

More than half a year before that review appeared, however, Seldes seems to have "arrived" as a cultural critic. *Vanity Fair* invited ten of the "modern critics of America" to "substitute new laurels for old." The publisher and editor, Crowninshield and Bishop, explained in their introduction that "a great Transvaluation of Values . . . has recently taken place in America." Therefore the purpose of this fascinating (and fun) exercise was to "orient the American public among the newer critical standards. The chart presents an abstract of the opinions of ten of our younger critics, and, also, a composite picture of the new critical mind, as a whole." So H. L. Mencken, George Jean Nathan, Heywood Broun, Deems Taylor, Edmund Wilson, Seldes, and four others were asked to give numerical evaluations from plus 25 to minus 25 to an immense list of people ranging from Abelard and Henry Adams to William Butler Yeats and Flo Ziegfeld![68]

Seldes, who had not yet read *Ulysses,* gave James Joyce 20. (Only Burton Rascoe ranked Joyce higher at 25. Nathan gave him 2 and Wilson 13.) Who did Seldes put at the very top? Charlie Chaplin, Henry James, and Friedrich Nietzsche were the only ones to warrant 25. George Bernard Shaw (23), Aristotle and Voltaire (21), and Dickens (20) placed next. Irving Berlin followed with 18, T. S. Eliot and Cezanne with 17, Ezra Pound and Oscar Wilde with 16. Seldes gave H. L. Mencken only 5 (for reasons that will emerge in Chapter Five),[69] Freud got 15 and Karl Marx didn't even make the list, although Lenin did with 8.

Seldes' minus list is moderately amusing. Benjamin Franklin and Henry Ford got −22, James Huneker (a prominent critic from the period 1890–1920) got −17, and F. Scott Fitzgerald −20. Seldes did not think well of his early work, and *Gatsby,* which Seldes admired, lay three years in the future. Fitzgerald obviously forgave that −20 because the two men became mutually supportive and fast friends after 1925. Ring Lardner, whose stories Seldes soon grew to love, got only a 4. Seldes' taste and criteria would change significantly in the decade ahead; but so did the quality and visibility of some of the younger "artists" on the list, like Fitzgerald.

The fact that Seldes gave President Warren G. Harding 0, nothing negative and 22 points higher than Franklin, does not indicate wretched judgment so much as it does Seldes' apolitical aspect, especially during the 1920s. Recall the sweeping assertion that Fitzgerald made in 1931: "It was characteristic of the Jazz Age that it had no interest in politics at all." Eight months later Seldes commented in his daily column that "as a matter of custom, almost a matter of habit, I shall miss [not attend] the national conventions; I always do." He frankly found them tedious, and predicted that there would be only trivial differences between the two party platforms.[70] For more than a decade, from 1935 until the end of World War II, Seldes became more of a political person than at any other time in his life. Yet never enough to satisfy his brother, George, to whom politics and international relations mattered much more than the arts, highbrow or popular.

From January 1920, when Gilbert Seldes joined *The Dial* as an editor and published a book review titled "A Competent Critic," he considered himself a cultural critic. During the next half-century, however, when some occasion required him to supply a professional identity, a public sense of self, he simply used critic, as we shall see.[71] That was not unusual, nor is it exceptionable; but from 1914 onward he was a journalist: he wrote a daily column for the New York *Evening Journal* during the 1930s, and served as a regular columnist for *Esquire* and the *Saturday Review of Literature* (1930s through the 1950s), as a volunteer essayist for the *Village Voice* in the later 1950s, and a regular writer for *TV Guide* in the early 1960s. Was there higher status associated with the identity of "critic" than with being a mere "journalist"? The answer depends on which writer you consult.

In 1916 a very nasty brouhaha flared up between H. G. Wells and the aging Henry James. When Wells attacked, James responded with a lofty discourse about "art" providing life with interest and importance. To which Wells retorted: "I had rather be a journalist." So just when Seldes and his cohort came of age, Wells and others whom they admired found value and luster in sound journalism. As late as 1943, writing an autobiographical essay, Edmund Wilson was pleased to call himself a journalist because he earned his living mainly by writing for periodicals. As late as the 1960s, when everyone regarded Wilson as America's most distinguished man of letters, he still referred to himself as a journalist.[72]

Be that as it may, several prominent figures who were a full generation older than Wilson and Seldes saw themselves as critics, by which they really meant cultural critics. (See Fig. 4.) William Crary Brownell (1851–1928), the most important American disciple of Matthew Arnold, provides one example; and James Gibbons Huneker, who wrote primarily but not exclusively about many forms of music, provides another. Huneker is particularly interesting because, on occasion, he wrote self-consciously about the critic's craft and what it meant to be a critic. In response to Brownell's maxim that criticism is an art, Huneker suggested that "a little humility in a critic is a wise attitude. Humbly to follow and register his emotions aroused by the masterpiece is his function. There must be standards, but the two greatest are sympathy and its half-sister, sincerity." With music, drama, and books foremost in mind, Huneker observed that "the happy mean between swashbuckling criticism and the pompous, academic attitude, dull but dignified, seems difficult of attainment. But it exists. A critic must not be narrow in his outlook on the world. . . . He should be cosmopolitan in his sympathies, else his standards are insufficient."[73]

One of Seldes' first (and not so frequent) forays into explicit discourse

Fig. 4. *The Critic* (Francis J. Ziegler) by Thomas Eakins (ca. 1890). Ziegler was a drama critic and translator who lived in Philadelphia. Courtesy of the Fogg Art Museum, Harvard University Art Museums. Bequest of Grenville L. Winthrop.

about the nature and practice of criticism occurred when he wrote an appreciative essay about T. S. Eliot as poet and critic. It appeared in *The Nation* just when *The Dial* announced its award to Eliot. Seldes asserted that literary criticism should be directed at the ideas expressed *and* the artistic qualities conveyed by a work. Criticism for Eliot, he observed, requires a "statement of the structures in which our perceptions, when we face a work of art, form themselves." Seldes then quoted a sentence from Eliot that many writers would invoke, one way and another, for more than a generation: "The important critic is the person who is absorbed in the present problems of art, and who wishes to bring the forces of the past to bear upon the solution of these problems." The good critic, Seldes concluded, is concerned with "the aesthetic problem" in a work but will also recognize the "place" of ideas in a work of art.[74] Achieving such an equilibrium would always engage Seldes. What changed in little more than a year, for him, was his increasingly inclusive notion of what qualified as a work of art.

Seldes wrote in earnest about Eliot, and criticism, yet the trendy thing to do at that time was to write about the critic's vocation, if one did so at all, in a flippant or mock-serious manner. Huneker had warned back in 1916 that "iconoclasm in criticism is all the rage." Within half-a-dozen years iconoclasm had been spun into self-spoof, preferably with an outrageous tone. In 1922 the old *Life* ran an interview with Mr. Sharpley Harpoon, dramatic editor of *The Hardware Era*. The interviewer observed how much things had changed since the "old days when it was the delight of a critic to find himself completely flabbergasted":

> Flabbergasted! That is the one thing we must guard against. Why, we might write the most intelligible sort of stuff if we became flabbergasted. Where would our literary inhibitions be? Why we might even drop from cleverness to coherency. We might fall even into the horribly passé thing of letting the play speak through us to the public. Flabbergasted! Why, that's what was the matter with the old-time critics. They were *moved* one way or the other by the plays they saw. My God! I couldn't think of allowing myself to become so impressionable![75]

When George Jean Nathan carried this mood to its ne plus ultra in "The Code of a Critic" (1923), he proclaimed that, to him, the theatre was a toy and that he cared only about the "surface" of life: "life's music and color, its charm and ease, its humor and loveliness. The great problems of the world—social, political, economic and theological—do not concern me in the slightest. I care not who writes the laws of a country so long as I may listen to its songs." Nathan ended this devil-may-care declaration, often anthologized because it seems to catch the mood of that moment, with an arch statement of self:

> I am merely a man gifted, as I see it, with an admirable practicability: one who believes that the highest happiness in life comes from doing one's job in the world as thoroughly well as one knows how, from viewing the world as a charming, serio-comic, childish circus, from having a few good, moderately witty friends, from avoiding indignation, irritation and homely women, and from letting the rest—the uplift, the downlift, the whole kit and caboodle—go hang. Selfish? To be sure. What of it?[76]

Editors of *The Dial,* especially when Thayer, Watson, and Seldes manned the watch, not only had more gravitas but they connected their thoughts about cultural criticism to a growing concern about their journal's stance toward the United States. *The Dial* almost seemed to please European readers more than those at home. In September 1920 Scofield Thayer told Ezra Pound that "we are considered un-American." So he promptly published some poems by Amy Lowell along with Indian songs in order to be (or appear) more American. Such anxieties prompted leaders of this new generation of editors and critics to articulate an enhanced role for the American critic: without losing his or her essential cosmopolitanism, he must help to create a congenial intellectual setting and an informed audience for the American artist. Early in 1922 *The Dial* published an anonymous editorial, most likely written by Seldes, that offered this explanation. "What has happened in America over and over again is this: the potential artist has stopped halfway because no critic and certainly no public demanded of him the last item of his strength as artist. The American critic has hit soft and the American writer has gone soft."[77]

By 1927–28, as we shall see in Chapter Four, Seldes had become an affirmative observer of American culture, and a decade after that he would emerge as an outright chauvinist—suggesting the Pilgrim's Progress of an exceedingly secular true believer, more so than most of his contemporaries, in fact.* But in 1922 tough-minded skepticism was still the dominant mood. He closed an erudite review of Lillian Eichler's *Book of Etiquette,* for instance, with a loosely connected coda critical of the perceived need in the United States to be guided by the hand toward good manners and middlebrow culture. "Is this civilization?" he asked, with more than a touch of hyperbolic rhetoric.

> Or, directly, does not one see in this, in five-foot shelves, in manuals and guides, in advertisements and life extensions, the strange vacuity of our healthy American lives? They reach out, aware at odd uncomfortable moments, that they have not come to grips with life, that something mysterious is being kept from them. It is the habit of their minds to find everything outside; romantics we Americans shall be to the last, and like all romantics shall dream our Golden Age. It is only the horrid laid on gilt [glitter, falseness?] of that age as we conceive it which makes us pause and consider.[78]

*Seldes surely recalled this sentence from Emerson's "American Scholar": "We have listened too long to the courtly muses of Europe."

Seldes sounded like a more polite, less caustic alter ego of H. L. Mencken. Seldes would change his tune, however, whereas Mencken and his fans would not. Even as Seldes wrote, though, a new and now forgotten little magazine, *Broom,* began to appear and conveyed to a much smaller readership than the one reached by *The Dial* upbeat messages about aspects of American culture. In June 1922, for example, Matthew Josephson anticipated some of the central themes of Seldes' brief book, *The Movies Come from America* (1937), which had a preface written by Charlie Chaplin. "It would surely be a strange surrender of our prerogatives to imitate Europe," Josephson asserted, "or Paris, for that matter. The fundamental attitude of aggression, humor, unequivocal affirmation which they pose, comes most naturally from America." He continued chauvinistically:

> The high speed and tension of American life may have been exported in quantity to Europe. But we are still richest in material. Our preposterous naive [*sic*] profound film will never be surpassed by artistic or literary German cinemas. . . . Reacting to purely American sources, to the at once bewildering and astounding American panorama, which only Chaplin and a few earnest unsung film-directors have mirrored, we may yet amass a new folk-lore out of the domesticated miracles of our time.

By the autumn of 1923 even a French contributor to *Broom* acknowledged that Chaplin had given an "extraordinary vigor, an incredible superiority, to the American movies," and closed with a proleptic plea: "at the present time we can only ask Los Angeles to continue to be the city of singular dreams and of tormenting realities."[79]

Despite *Broom*'s public position that *The Dial* seemed cosmopolitan at the expense of American achievements, in 1922 Seldes exchanged complimentary notes with Harold Loeb, the publisher of *Broom.* Meanwhile, gradual shifts in orientation became evident at *The Dial.* It published Malcolm Cowley's "Two American Poets," a review of Conrad Aiken and Carl Sandburg in which Cowley sought to explain what "American" meant as a modifier when applied to poets. Cowley's commitment to the notion of American exceptionalism actually antedated Seldes'.[80]

V

Throughout 1922 Seldes published frequent, enthusiastic essays about aspects of popular culture, mainly in *Vanity Fair* with a few in *The Dial* and *The Freeman*. He swiftly sensed that he was investing himself in a subject that might give him a distinctive identity as a critic, and he yearned for free time at the MacDowell Colony in Peterborough, New Hampshire, an association "for the purpose of giving creative workers in the seven arts a practical workshop in a favorable environment." He hoped to spend time there during the summer of 1922, but because he could not get away from *The Dial* his brief sojourn was delayed until mid-September. Once there he wrote a long and revealing letter to his good friend John Peale Bishop, then the outgoing editor of *Vanity Fair* but soon, like Seldes, destined to sail for Europe:

> i am three hundred miles away from the degrading and cynical life of a magazine editor and the effects of the short year in which you witnessed my rise and fall are all too evident. my brain is tired. . . . [He writes at length, excitedly, about *Ulysses* and "The Waste Land."] my activities you certainly know about from reading dial and vanity fair . . . you started me on a career of vice with yr suggestion about slapstick, as there seems to be no end to the vulgarities in which i find pleasure and about which [Frank Crowninshield] and Edmund [Wilson] are willing to have me write. . . . and oh the difference to me. . . .
>
> [These last three sets of ellipses are Seldes'. He then describes his new-found skill at mixing good cocktails.] the divine amanda [his future wife] having been like myself in town during the summer, and no one else having been so of her companions, she has testified on occasion to the poisonous skill of these mixtures.[81]

In October Seldes made plans to sail for a nine-month stay in Europe where he would transform his well-received essays on popular culture into a book; solicit fresh material for *The Dial* (especially art) and thereby remain on the payroll; receive money from the recently formed Theatre Guild to scout European theatres for plays that might be brought to the United States; and finally, "in order to rest and particularly to rest the Bean which in association with the Nerves is very wobbly, I am trying to settle my mind."[82] As he explained to his brother George, then based in Berlin as the European correspondent for the *Chicago Tribune:* "The purpose of this voyage is a four months trip of rest, frivolity, and impressions to be followed, if arrangements here are agreeable, by about six months of an already arranged for solitude to be spent in writing a couple of books." On December 23 Seldes invited close friends and professional associates to drop by his apartment on 19th Street between 10 p.m. and 2 a.m. "It is not a farewell party," he told them, "only a sort

Fig. 5. Gilbert Seldes, pencil drawing by E. E. Cummings (ca. 1922–23).
From Cummings, *CIOPW* (New York: Covici, Friede, 1931), by permission
of the Houghton Library, Harvard University.

of rising vote of gratitude on my part to a few fellow creatures who have
been indulgent with me and entertained me during the last year or so."[83]

Seldes sailed in January as planned; but instead of living in Berlin with
George he lived in the Paris apartment (on the Ile St. Louis) of Lewis
Galantière who was in Italy for a spell; and there in a span of four intense
months Seldes wrote his best-known book, *The 7 Lively Arts,* the subject
of the next chapter.

Seldes did find time for a social life, however. He met Gertrude Stein, saw James Joyce twice ("a terrific experience"), started a warm friendship with Pablo Picasso, and caroused with such old college friends as E. E. Cummings and John Dos Passos. (See Fig. 5.) One of their nightly revels ended with Cummings in jail for relieving himself in a public place—an episode that caused Cummings and Seldes considerable anxiety at the time and much hilarity for decades to come whenever the three companions tried to reconstruct exactly what had happened—who had been heroic and who had been out of control. Cummings' own clipped account, written barely three months after the incident is the most succinct, and is essentially reliable:

Should it interest yourself & H.C. to know the basis of aforementioned apocalyptic i beg to mention

    a. that Dos, Seldes and self had a party

    b. E. E. Cummings was lugged to the rue des Grands Augustins police station for having pissed opposite the Calvados Joint of rue Gît Le Coeur (time 3 AM)

    c. that Dos accompanied me; & even entered the station—only to be thrown out protesting

    d. that Seldes, despite great tipsiness, followed Dos

    e. that next day i presented self at station (alone) & was given a kind of 3rd degree for not having reported change of address on carte d'identité—also threatened with expulsion from France, etc. etc. etc.

    f. that Seldes immediately visited m. Paul Morand, Quai d'Orsay

    g. that P. M. (so far as we now know) squelched both charges against me; & wrote Seldes a very pleasant promise that "C. will have no ennui."—[84]

In late May, Seldes notified George from Paris that "i want to write another book. I've just sent off all but 15 uncopied pages of The Seven Lively Arts [to Canby for Harper's]. Its a whale of a book. Clive Bell [the English art critic who had taken Seldes to meet Picasso at his studio] says it ought to be the book of the epoch. . . ." Seldes celebrated by going to London to visit with Bell and Raymond Mortimer, *The Dial* correspondent, and hopefully to lunch with John Maynard Keynes and Lytton Strachey (the luncheon didn't occur). Then off to see H. G. Wells and Bertrand Russell, both contributors to *The Dial*.[85]

From June until early September Seldes traveled and ran significant errands for *The Dial* and for the Theatre Guild. During his absence

Edmund Wilson wrote *The Dial*'s "Theatre" column and Kenneth Burke served (without title) as managing editor. Although Seldes resigned his editorial position at *The Dial* in December, he resumed responsibility for the monthly "Theatre" pieces and continued to do them, faithfully, until *The Dial* ceased publication in 1929. He also wrote occasional essays and reviews, especially in 1924–25 while in transition to a new and (for him) different approach to free-lance writing. Waiting for his book to appear (in April 1924) became an anxious time. He missed Europe but he did *not* miss the daily grind of office routine. Could he "quit all work, and live by the PEN"? He didn't know, but he hoped so. To John Peale Bishop, now enviably married and living in France, Seldes wrote: "tsquite possible that i'll earn enough out of my book to sail other seas. prey for me in that hope."[86]

As the close of 1923 drew near, however, he clearly recognized that he had found his own theme and voice. Seldes mentioned *The 7 Lively Arts* to John Quinn and explained to that lawyer-collector-patron of contemporary arts the book's central message: "that the minor arts, those frequently called 'lowbrow' are not hostile to the major arts, and that both the minor and the major arts have their chief enemy in the second rate bogus arts." He also felt confident that he was achieving a professionally viable degree of versatility. He explained to a staff member at Harper's, his new publisher, that he was "a critic of literature, music and the theatre." Asked to epitomize his book, he observed, "I apply to ragtime and popular songs and musical comedy and vaudeville and the vulgar arts generally, the same kind of criticism as I give to the workers in the major arts."[87] Seldes' distinctive subject and signature had emerged.

VI

The Dial has attracted more commentary and analysis than any other American literary/cultural publication of the twentieth century. It enjoyed its greatest visibility and prestige in the years 1920–23, while Seldes served as managing editor. Some of the art, essays, stories, and poems that appeared after his departure in December 1922 had also been procured by him. The importance of *The Dial* owed much to its concern for top-notch criticism and its emphasis upon the highest standards in book reviewing—criteria that crystallized new assumptions about literature and its place in the social environment. No other contemporary review was as consistent or as influential as a medium of cultural criticism.[88]

In terms of Seldes' personal transition in 1922–23, noted above, we need to understand how an acknowledged aesthete, *érudit,* and highbrow in 1920–21 became a cultural populist with a passion for the popular arts. The dominant figures at *The Dial* were James Sibley Watson, Jr., a pro-Pound modernist, and Scofield Thayer, who always sought excellence but with unease if not disdain for modernism in the arts. Seldes had to negotiate tactfully between those two positions, and, in the process, doing so helped him to reconsider his own taste levels and criteria as a critic.

His years at *The Dial* provided him with far more than positions to redefine or react against, however. Because *The Dial* did not give preference either to experimental *or* established writers, and because it published European *and* American authors and artists, it achieved a degree of balance and cosmopolitanism found in no other journal. The pages of *The Dial* were open, by design, to opposing points of view. We need only note that its coveted award went to Sherwood Anderson in 1921, T. S. Eliot in 1922, and Van Wyck Brooks in 1923: a proclamation of commitment to diversity *and* excellence. In a very real sense, Seldes' apprenticeship stressed balance, fairness, and the need for openness to opposing views —qualities and desiderata that he would carry forward for decades.[89]

When T. S. Eliot founded *The Criterion,* an English counterpart to *The Dial,* he invited Seldes to be its American correspondent. In his "New York Chronicle" for 1926 Seldes summarized, and implicitly responded to, the main lines of complaint that had been directed at *The Dial:*

> From *The Little Review*, that it is a de-alcoholized *Little Review*; from the intellectual bourgeoisie, that it is too radical; from Mr. Ernest Boyd, that it pretends to be contemporary, yet published the work of Thomas Mann and Anatole France, and appoints its foreign correspondents without the approval of Mr. Boyd. *The Dial* is generally supposed to be run by a clique, to the non-existence of which I can testify. Indeed, the more intelligent criticism is that there is not enough cohesion between the writers, certainly not enough specific direction in the work it publishes.[90]

Twenty-five years later, in a monthly column that Seldes wrote for *Park East* magazine early in the 1950s, he explained why *Dial* loyalists tended to shun the Algonquin wits and literati. Because *The Dial* had been losing some $50,000 each year on a meager circulation of 20,000 or so, the staff wondered "whether so much [Algonquin] wit and prestige and influence had to be at the service of the trivial while all we worked for was neglected. We didn't see dancing in the streets when 'The Waste Land' was published."[91]

From the mid-1950s to the mid-1960s, when literary scholars became intensely fixated on the 1920s, Seldes responded to numerous queries and his letters shed even more light on how *The Dial* looked in retrospect.[92] We will return to that problematic yet symptomatic phase of retrospection and elusive memories in the final chapter. It is appropriate here, however, to provide a few extracts from the brief memoir of *Dial* days prepared by Kenneth Burke after Seldes' death in September 1970. Born in 1897, Burke was four years younger than Seldes.

> My memory of him in those days is of a highly companionable fellow who never gave the slightest impression of bossiness. Each of us had his work to do. And since neither Scofield Thayer nor Sibley Watson was regularly in the office, Gilbert was in command. I recall that his ways of being in command were both gracious and vivacious. It was really good fun to work with Gilbert and to share his bright metropolitan interest in the daily vicissitudes of the literary marketplace. . . .
>
> I realize: I spontaneously came to expect of him a kind of ebullience as unsinkable as a cork on the waves, if ebullience can properly be called unsinkable. And there was always the brisk interlude when, each afternoon, he got the Hearst edition with the latest Krazy Kat cartoons, and we took time off to admire Herriman's civilized ingenuities. We all believed in this lore as much as he did. But he was to be the one who made the first Grand Presentation of those cartoons and of the many exhibits in line with his prophetic exhortings as regards the "lively arts." . . .
>
> Yes, Gilbert was a charming colleague to work with. Already he was building up the kind of material that he was later to be best known by. Yet at the same time he was quite at home in the heavier stuff. And I was particularly impressed by his professionalism as manifested many times on the day when we made up the magazine. If we found out, for instance, that a review of a certain length was still called for, Gilbert would go into the back office, close the door, you'd hear the typewriter clicking almost without hesitation—and after a fitting interval he would emerge with a copy of the exact amount needed. Gilbert was indeed a pro. . . .[93]

The adjective "ebullient" would recur repeatedly and cling to Seldes, like an ineffable personal scent, for the rest of his life.

3

The Lively Arts and
Cultural Criticism Revitalized

The astonishing vitality that we customarily associate with American culture during the 1920s sprang primarily from the popular arts. Theatrical productions and musical revues on Broadway, but elsewhere as well, blended the exuberant energies of new music, lyrics, comedy routines, and interpretive dance. Although such entertainments were deemed unworthy of careful assessment by serious critics at the time, a few among the newer cohort did pay attention (and generally applauded) what was happening on stage, in film, in nightclubs, and on occasion, in public spaces for celebratory or civic purposes. George Jean Nathan, Matthew Josephson, Marsden Hartley, and Gilbert Seldes come promptly to mind.

Nathan observed that if drama was art because it helped us to understand life, then musical shows and revues also qualified as art because they taught us to enjoy life. Josephson found in the "vulgar music-hall comedies the germs of true literature." Hartley viewed vaudeville as a "collection of good drawings." And Seldes saw in the "commoner expressions of the artistic impulse some relief from the unmitigated tedium of the professionally second rate in the arts." This small contingent of enthusiasts did not see eye to eye on everything, though. Early in 1923 George Jean Nathan attacked Seldes' views on theatre expressed in *Vanity Fair*, and Seldes responded in his 1924 book, *The 7 Lively Arts.* Their friendly feud would persist for decades.[1] Considered as an ensemble, however, the unabashed enthusiasm these writers felt for popular culture stimulated the genesis of a transformation that required a full generation to complete.

In the second edition of *The 7 Lively Arts* (1957), Seldes interspersed retrospective comments on the seismic cultural shift that had occurred. He found much to applaud in the impulse toward democratization that began to emerge in the 1920s, but also some cause for concern on account of less attractive aspects and perceptions of change that had become apparent in the 1950s.[2] At the heart of that transformation lay the development of electronic media and the commercialization of entertainment on a scale previously unimagined. As Seldes put it, "the moment radio arrived a revolution began and all the popular arts became much bigger business than they had been before. Perhaps the Twenties were the last flowering of our simple arts." Although radio received an uncritical reception for years, Seldes observed, "by the time television arrived, genuine criticism of all the popular arts had become a regular feature of many newspapers and the exploitation of them was a staple of the large-circulation magazines."[3]

When Seldes moved beyond the emergence and historical development of cultural criticism, however, he transmitted inconsistent (or perhaps genuinely ambivalent) signals about his sense of future prospects for popular culture in a democratic society. At one point in the 1957 edition of *The 7 Lively Arts* he opined, perhaps not altogether puckishly, "that the mass media into which the lively arts turned can still perform reasonably in a democratic society. All they need is some ten million independent-minded people being eternally vigilant about them." On the very last page of the book, though, Seldes pointed to a grave danger—indeed, *the* grave danger: "with the shift of all entertainment into the area of big business, we are being engulfed in a mass-produced mediocrity." On this crucial point the mature Seldes would often vacillate between hopeful projections and gloomy predictions. The cause of his waffling: swiftly changing conditions rather than some fatal flaw of indecision on his part.[4]

This chapter will move from a history of *The 7 Lively Arts,* and responses to it following publication in 1924, to the issue of American culture as perceived by Europeans—and by Americans obsessed with European views of their culture. The two topics were closely connected, especially during the 1920s. As Seldes wrote in *The 7 Lively Arts,* "the circumstance that our popular arts are home-grown, without the prestige of Europe and of the past, had thrown upon them a shadow of vulgarity, as if they were the products of ignorance and intellectual bad manners." Toward the very end of the book, written in June 1923, Seldes sounded a theme on which he would play variations for decades: "What Europeans feel about American art is exactly the opposite of what they feel about American life. Our life is energetic, varied, constantly changing; our art is imitative, anaemic (exceptions in both cases being assumed). The explanation is that few Europeans see our lively arts, which are almost secret to us, like the mysteries of a cult. Here [recall that Seldes wrote this book on the Ile St. Louis in Paris] the energy of America does break out and finds artistic expression for itself. Here a wholly unrealistic, imaginative presentation of the way we think and feel is accomplished [by foreigners]."[5] Correcting such inconsistent perceptions would pre-occupy Seldes through the rest of the 1920s.

I

Thus far we have seen little in Seldes' background that would explain either the substance or the title of his most influential book. According to H. L. Mencken, writing at the end of 1920, avant-garde writers in Paris during the 1870s and 1880s had alluded to the "seven arts." Between 1914 and 1916 James Gibbons Huneker, the prominent cultural critic based in Philadelphia, had called his column in *Puck* "The Seven Arts" and in 1917 he published an essay titled "A Synthesis of the Seven Arts," concerning poetry and acting, painting and sculpture, and so on. When the *Seven Arts* magazine began its brief existence in November 1916, Waldo Frank proclaimed that this new and lively journal "is not a magazine for artists, but an expression of artists for the community."[6]

In 1922 Seldes had a commission from Frank Crowninshield and Edmund Wilson to write an extended series of essays on the popular arts, essays that appeared at the steady pace of one or two each month. Seldes recalled in 1957 that after a number of these pieces had been published he took John Peale Bishop and possibly Edmund Wilson to watch Al Jolson perform:

> We saw one of the last performances of one of his weakest shows, but toward the end, when Jolson, working hard against a cold house, came to his "You ain't heard nothin' yet" the electric spark sprang from him to the audience and as we walked away from the theatre I said I'd use the pieces I was writing as the point of departure for a book which I would call "The

Seven Lively Arts." Bishop pointed to the Spearmint electric sign with its galvanic jumping men, and asked, "Including that?"

Seldes also sought to clarify in his preface to the new edition that the number seven sounded euphonious but was not meant to convey precision.

> One thing should, perhaps, be made clear about the phrase. There were those who thought (correctly) that you couldn't find seven and there were those who felt (stuffily) that the seven were not arts. Lively was for the most part unchallenged. The sacred 7 came from the classics, from "the seven arts" (which was also the name of a magazine recently defunct) and I never tried to categorize the contents of the book to conform to the figure. If you tried you could make seven, counting feature movies and Keystone comedies as one or you could make ten if you counted all the forms of music separately. I never took a position on the matter.[7]

As for the book's substance, it is important to bear in mind that Seldes' years at *The Dial* were not entirely arid in terms of popular culture. Praise could be found in its pages (often written by Seldes, to be sure) for silent film and comic strips, musical comedy, vaudeville, popular music, interpretive dance, and, eventually, radio. Moreover, *The Dial* reviewed openings of the Ziegfeld Follies with as much enthusiasm as it did new plays by Eugene O'Neill. In addition, during 1922–23 several European critics took notice of selected aspects of American popular culture. Seldes surely saw a book by the British theatre critic James Agate, *Alarums and Excursions* (1922), along with works by St. John Ervine, who took an intense interest in film and other popular arts. *The Art of Cineplastics* (1923) by Elie Faure first appeared in *The Freeman*. Seldes quoted Faure's work in *The 7 Lively Arts*.[8]

Seldes might even have been influenced by a seemingly unlikely source, his former teacher George Santayana. In 1927, admittedly several years after the book appeared, Santayana sent Van Wyck Brooks an intriguing letter from Rome which suggests that certain stereotyped views of Santayana as an other-worldly aesthete are highly misleading. "One more little protestation," he concluded:

> A certain degree of sympathy and assimilation with ultra-modern ways in Europe or even Asia may be possible, because young America is simply modernism undiluted: but what Lewis Mumford calls "the pillage of the past" . . . is worse than useless. I therefore think that art, etc. has a better

soil in the ferocious 100% America than in the Intelligentsia of New York. It is veneer, rouge, aestheticism, art museums, new theatres, etc. that make America impotent. The good things are football, kindness, and jazz bands.[9]

Moreover, as Seldes always acknowledged, he did not discover the lively arts singlehandedly; he merely made an impassioned pitch that highbrow critics should be less myopic and expand their vision of artistic creativity as well as suitable subjects for assessment. Such painters as Reginald Marsh created visual images that closely paralleled Seldes' critical concerns: ranging from vaudeville, burlesque, and amusement parks to grand opera. Although Seldes may have been more positive and Marsh more satirical about most of these endeavors, both men determined to chronicle and appraise modes of cultural expression at multiple levels of status and dignity. Also, both men seemed to indicate that the audiences for these multiple levels were not so radically different from one another, nor were the levels themselves. In 1923 *Theatre Arts Magazine* ran an essay insisting that qualities of the venerable *commedia dell'arte* were found not only in vaudeville but in other aspects of commercial theatre as well—musical comedy, farce, burlesque, and in the movies. The author of that piece singled out Charlie Chaplin for praise, just as Seldes recently had in an essay for *Vanity Fair* and soon would do again in *The 7 Lively Arts.*[10] Seldes, it turns out, had a strong predilection for *commedia dell'arte,* invoked it for years in explaining phenomena ranging from movies to clowns, and late in the 1920s wrote a short piece for theatre designed as a modern send-off in the style of *commedia dell'arte.*

Late in 1922 Seldes commented to a correspondent that he hadn't just recently discovered vaudeville but, rather, had long been a fan. Writing in *Vanity Fair* that fall he rebuked Simeon Strunsky, a critic for the New York *Evening Post* who had alluded to "the intellectualist rush to be elemental and almost vulgar, which has recently elevated Krazy Kat and Miss Fanny Brice to very near the top-most rank in American art." Seldes prophesied that "the moment must come in the history of culture when vaudeville can be taken without comparisons for what it is":

Weak-minded intellectuals have always yearned for the abysmal, the vulgar, and the primitive; alert ones have frequently found or tried to find in the commoner expressions of the artistic impulse some relief from the unmitigated tedium of the professionally second rate in the higher arts. They have known that rag-time, circuses, slapstick, burlesque, and the like, whatever their faults may be, are seldom pretentious.

Seldes added, for good measure, that vaudeville was the "only genre I know which can live by burlesquing itself."[11]

A month after that essay appeared Seldes wrote a lengthy description of the book that he envisioned for Henry Seidel Canby, who had commissioned it for Harper's. The first three paragraphs indicate just how clearly Seldes had his project under control, because they succinctly describe the very substantial book that he completed more than seven months later in June 1923:

The idea of my book is a series of essays on The Seven Lively Arts— among them, and the number need not be exactly seven—will be

Slapstick Moving Pictures
Comic Strips
Revues
Musical Comedy
Colyums
Slang Humour
Popular Songs
Vaudeville

and such things. There will also be at least one article on the admittedly "supreme" people, such as Chaplin, Jolson, Brice, in which the quality of supremacy will be analyzed. In each of those I try to characterize the quality of the art and to do something with its more notable practitioners. Some are written or will be written around one outstanding figure, some on the general practice involved.

In addition there will be an essay to be published in the middle or toward the end of the book, showing the relation of the minor or lively arts to the major arts; and further, there will be two or three pieces dealing with the pretentious fake which passes for high art and which I shall distinguish only as bogus art—classical dancing and probably grand opera.

These are the subjects. Behind them is the one general idea to which I propose not to devote an essay, namely an examination of the genteel tradition, as Mr. Santayana calls it, in the way Americans assume that which is serious and pretentious is by nature high art and that which is simple and cheap cannot possibly have any artistic value. That is, I propose the book to have a sound and entirely unobtrusive critical basis.

In appealing for an assortment of illustrations, cartoons, and photographs, Seldes concluded that the book should appear "as removed from the genteel tradition as the subject matter."[12]

It may seem baffling that Seldes actually composed the entire book in less than five months, with very few notes or other helps at hand other than a folio of Krazy Kat comics and a few clippings. As he remarked in the preface to the second edition, the whole thing was written, "in a sense, from memory." Bear in mind that he was remembering, revising, and incorporating as chapters an extended run of essays that had been carefully polished for publication in *Vanity Fair* during 1922, plus briefer pieces (mostly theatre and movie reviews) that he had written for *The Dial* since 1920. He even adapted "An Imaginary Conversation" that he had written for the Boston *Evening Transcript* in 1916. And soon after reaching Berlin in January 1923 he arranged with Edmund Wilson to continue sending home a whole series of essays on the "lively arts" that would appear in *Vanity Fair* through early 1924 and then become segments of *The 7 Lively Arts*. At the close of one piece in that series, Seldes struck a note that would remain part of his manifesto and be central to his vocation as a critic for years to come: "It is on the strange altar of refinement, indeed, that a nation usually reputed vigorous is sacrificing its robust laughter and its hearty cheers. There ought to be a law against it."[13]

What he was alluding to, a mindless preference for second-rate high culture over first-rate popular culture, permeated his published statements from 1924 onward and brings to our attention the intense dialogue that Seldes sparked over how critics should deal with the highbrow/lowbrow issue that Van Wyck Brooks had introduced in widely noticed essays published in 1915 and 1918. What Brooks wrote and its immediate impact have been extensively discussed by others.[14] Before we pursue what Seldes contributed to that conversation, however, we ought to note, at least briefly, a few of the broader forces that made some people more receptive but others less so to Seldes' message.

Starting with the latter, the negative side, many intellectuals in the Progressive era—ranging from Woodrow Wilson to Jane Addams—did not care for popular culture because it looked to be at odds with their reform agenda: it seemed socially degrading rather than morally uplifting, and for the older Progressives, especially, moral uplift remained the key to progress.[15] Because Seldes was not a moralist in the traditional sense, and because he advocated the unembarrassed enjoyment of leisure, he made hesitant headway against the homilies of those intensely serious Progressive reformers.

On the other side, however, there is a curious sense in which the fierce debate over immigration restriction, especially between 1920 and 1924, may have helped to create a more receptive mood, in certain quarters at least, for the core argument of *The 7 Lively Arts*. Many of the artists and entertainers championed by Seldes were Russian Jews (like Al Jolson and Irving Berlin) or else of Italian extraction (like Jimmy Savo and later Jimmy Durante). As one opponent of immigration restriction remarked in 1924, "the country is somewhat fed up on high brow Nordic superiority stuff."[16]

The important point, however, is that for more than a decade intense advocates from both camps had been posting their broadsides, but with no resolution of the conflict anywhere in sight. As early as 1906, for example, Albert Levering drew a "cartoon" for *Puck* in which he belittled the cultural pretensions of Broadway theatre by coupling "Hamlet," an icon of high culture, with the prospect of pop entertainment. The caption for this drawing read:

IF SHAKESPEARE HAD WRITTEN FOR BROADWAY.

Hamlet. — To be-e-e-e, ornottobethatisthequestion!
Chorus of Danish Palace Guards. — Ah, yesss, that is the quest-shun!

Levering made the scene ludicrous by casting Hamlet as a woman wearing a scanty costume, and by adding a chorus line of dancers to the prospective production (Fig. 6).[17]

During the summer of 1922, just when Seldes was conceptualizing his book in defense of popular culture, *Life* (very much a light-hearted middlebrow magazine) ran a full-page ad for the Haldeman-Julius Company which sought to sell books on serious subjects by mail order. "ARE WE A NATION OF LOW-BROWS?" topped the advertisement, followed by: "It is charged that the public is intellectually incompetent. Is this true?" And then, this opening paragraph in defense of the public but not in defense of popular culture:

> The main criticism, as we find it, is that the people support ventures that are unworthy, that represent no cultural standards. The public is fed on low-brow reading matter, low-brow movies, low-brow theatrical productions, low-brow music, low-brow newspapers, low-brow magazines. As for ourselves, we think the criticism is unfair in that it does not recognize the fact that the public is without cultural leadership. Those who have the divine spark get off by themselves. We believe the public has never had a real chance, never had an opportunity to get acquainted with the great and the beautiful things of life. Given half a chance, we think the public will respond.[18]

Fig. 6. Albert Levering, "If Shakespeare Had Written for Broadway," from *Puck*, vol. 60 (Dec. 26, 1906). Courtesy of the Henry E. Huntington Library and Art Gallery.

Seldes is significant in this context because he sought, though not with complete success, to show that the whole issue of highbrow versus lowbrow was much more complex than Van Wyck Brooks and others realized. Here is a representative extract from the close of *The 7 Lively Arts*:

> And now a detour around two of the most disagreeable words in the language: high- and low-brow. Pretense about these words and what they signify makes all understanding of the lively arts impossible. The discomfort and envy which make these words vague, ambiguous, and contemptuous need not concern us; for they represent a real distinction, two separate ways of apprehending the world, as if it were palpable to one and visible to the other. In connexion with the lively arts the distinction is clear and involves the third division, for the lively arts are created and admired chiefly by the class known as lowbrows, are patronized and, to an extent enjoyed, by the highbrows; and are treated as impostors and as contemptible vulgarisms by the middle class, those who invariably are ill at ease in the presence of great art until it has been approved by authority.[19]

It needs to be recognized that throughout his career, Seldes considered himself an intellectual, and that his brother George always regarded him as a highbrow.[20] The essential point, however, is that Seldes disliked the terms highbrow and lowbrow because he felt that they created or conveyed a misleading if not a false dichotomy. As he explained in the closing chapter to *The 7 Lively Arts,* which actually could have been its introduction, Seldes always believed that "there exists no such hostility between the two divisions of the arts which are honest—that the real opposition is between them, allied [i.e., taken together], and the polished fake," which he referred to throughout as the *faux bon.* Seldes insisted that for a civilized person "there need be present no conflict between the great arts and the minor; he will see in the end, that they minister to each other." In Seldes' view the "great arts" were characterized by "high seriousness" while the "essence of the minor arts is high levity which existed in the *commedia dell'arte* and exists in Chaplin, which you find in the music of Berlin and Kern."[21]

At that point Seldes launched a series of propositions that constitute the intellectual core of his book:

> That there is no opposition between the great and the lively arts.
>
> That both are opposed in the spirit to the middle or bogus arts.
>
> That the bogus arts are easier to appreciate, appeal to low and mixed emotions, and jeopardize the purity of both the great and minor arts.
>
> That except in a period when the major arts flourish with exceptional vigour, the lively arts are likely to be the most intelligent phenomena of their day.
>
> That the lively arts as they exist in America to-day are entertaining, interesting, and important.
>
> That with a few exceptions these same arts are more interesting to the adult cultivated intelligence than most of the things which pass for art in cultured society.
>
> That there exists a "genteel tradition" about the arts which has prevented any just appreciation of the popular arts, and that these have therefore missed the corrective criticism given to the serious arts, receiving instead only abuse.
>
> That therefore the pretentious intellectual is as much responsible as any one for what is actually absurd and vulgar in the lively arts.
>
> That the simple practitioners and simple admirers of the lively arts being uncorrupted by the bogus preserve a sure instinct for what is artistic in America.[22]

All of which helps to explain Seldes' immense admiration for Robert C. Benchley, the journalist, drama critic, and humorist, despite his close affiliation with the Algonquin circle. Benchley had graduated from Harvard in 1912, wrote for *Collier's* in 1919, did a column for the New York

World throughout the 1920s (three days each week) on "Books and Other Things," and during the mid-1930s prepared a column (also three times a week) for the King Features Syndicate. Benchley could be characterized (like Seldes) as a "high-spirited highbrow" with tolerance and affection for popular culture. In 1924 Benchley praised Seldes for publicly recognizing the comic virtues of Joe Cook in vaudeville, Ring Lardner as a delightful writer, and George Herriman, creator of Krazy Kat, as the supreme cartoonist. Benchley proposed that some seemingly lowbrow humorists of the nonsense school were actually "Grade-A highbrows" because of their "madness" and their subtle touch. He believed that their work belonged higher up on the critical scale than certain more widely honored forms of traditional comedy.[23]

At that time, however, Seldes did not have many allies like Benchley. Moreover, he frequently differentiated between high and popular culture in qualified ways that appear to be at odds with his desire to minimize distinctions as exemplified by the extracts quoted above. Here is an example of differentiation from *The 7 Lively Arts:*

> The minor arts are, to an extent, an opiate—or rather they trick our hunger for a moment and we are able to sleep. They do not wholly satisfy, but they do not corrupt. And they, too, have their moments of intensity. Our experience of perfection is so limited that even when it occurs in a secondary field we hail its coming. Yet the minor arts are all transient, and these moments have no lasting record, and their creators are unrewarded even by the tribute of a word.

Looking back from the vantage point of 1957, Seldes denied that he had ever been hostile to the "major arts," but then modestly added that he had never been sufficiently cerebral to enjoy a successful career as a highbrow critic.[24]

By 1924, when *The 7 Lively Arts* appeared, people professionally concerned about the production and consumption of culture tended to worry about the brow level they wished to achieve *and* the brow level at which they would be perceived. In May 1924, for example, when Seldes returned to Europe, the publisher of *Vanity Fair* wrote to request that Seldes undertake some tasks for the magazine, particularly in procuring material from prominent European writers. Crowninshield commented that T. S. Eliot had promised to send something soon, "but I am not particularly anxious about this, as he is likely to be a little high brow for us."[25] *Vanity Fair* did not want to be perceived as a highbrow magazine. In a very real sense, it couldn't afford to be so perceived. An upper-middlebrow identity would mean subscription sales well into six figures, whereas a highbrow identity might mean a subscription level of 30,000 copies at best.

II

Before turning to the context of Seldes' book and the critical response it elicited, a few words are appropriate about his activities between January 1923, when he began to write, and early spring 1924, when *The 7 Lively Arts* appeared. First there are the circumstances of composition. Seldes always said that he wrote almost entirely from memory. If that is true, and I have no evidence to the contrary, he pulled off a virtuoso performance. From time to time his text will say, "as I recall," or words to that effect; yet his memory for the descriptive details of films is simply phenomenal (even if he had seen certain favorite movies four or five times). He incorporated whole stanzas from popular songs, and there are lengthy quotations from such writers as Stark Young.[26]

Perhaps Seldes filled in a few blanks, or made some corrections after his return in September 1923. The fact remains that he mailed Harper's a complete manuscript several months before he left Europe for home in the autumn. Everyone associated with Scofield Thayer at *The Dial* recalled the importance of "intensity" to him and the degree to which intensity characterized him. The same applies to Seldes, for whom intensity along with exuberance became appropriate emblems of identity.[27]

To illustrate both, notice how Seldes celebrated the completion of his book. He invited James and Nora Joyce to attend the Russian Ballet in Paris on June 16, the "day of Ulysses," and thereby gathered on that occasion, at the same event, the man he regarded as the greatest writer of his day with the greatest composer, Strawinsky (Seldes always spelled it so), and the greatest painter, Picasso.[28] All of which gave Seldes enormous satisfaction, not because he was a name-dropper but because he genuinely admired excellence in the arts—in this instance highly innovative approaches to them. When Seldes wrote about his beloved lively arts, Joyce and Strawinsky did not figure in the story though Picasso did. Seldes would continue to be engaged by several levels of cultural production. Their common ground was excellence.

On February 10, 1924, according to the *New York Times,* Vincent Lopez conducted a program of "contemporaneous popular music" in New York's Anderson Galleries. Professor Edward Burlingame Hill spoke on the subject of jazz, and Gilbert Seldes "was an interested bystander."[29] His pertinent book was imminent. His mere presence seemed newsworthy. Seldes was becoming a minor cultural celebrity.

In May 1924 Seldes published in *Vanity Fair* an essay that provided an epitome of his book and served notice of its publication. Next to his byline appeared a droll caricature of Seldes wearing a harlequin's diamond-pattern costume, his hairline receding above his temples, his features contorted into a scornful scowl. With one hand on his right hip, Seldes stands ready to do battle with all who disdain the lively arts. "Once we get over our snobbishness about the popular arts and like them without patronizing them," he declared, "the gratifying and surprising thing is to find that, apart from their definite pleasures, they have also an artistic interest." He then played his signature theme, ending with an acknowledgement of difference but also providing a basis for accommodation:

> The real reason for caring for the popular arts will always reside in the qualities that make them popular: their lightness and humour; their simplicity and capriciousness, their broad human touch. But that is no reason why people of taste should not recognize and relish in them the qualities of artistic presentation which they possess. The minor arts do not deal with the great problems of life—why should they? But they do treat their limited material with a precise and calculated technical mastery which is admirable.[30]

At first glance, Seldes' central theme in *The 7 Lively Arts* seems perfectly straightforward. There is no necessary opposition or conflict between the great and the lesser arts. Because they complement one another, a person really isn't culturally alive who fails to appreciate both. The appropriate targets for contempt then? The "bogus arts," by which he meant second-rate grand opera (e.g., Puccini), pretentiously serious, intellectual drama (e.g., Ibsen), pseudo-classic dancing, civic pageants, and "high-toned" movies. The problem, according to Seldes, was that the bogus arts could not harm or prevail against the great arts, but they *could* menace the lively arts. As an example of his reverse snobbery, Seldes compared the customary productions of the Metropolitan Opera unfavorably to a "good revue," such as the Ziegfeld Follies.[31] Seldes' principal shortcoming in this book was his penchant for hyperbole, and at times, for the *reductio ad absurdum*.

Most of the volume, fortunately, concentrated on particular modes of entertainment and their outstanding performers: in slapstick film, Mack Sennett's Keystone comedies and especially Charlie Chaplin; in popular

song, Irving Berlin and Jerome Kern; in musical composition and entertainment, George Gershwin and George M. Cohan; in comedy and
musical drama, Fanny Brice and Al Jolson; in vaudeville the perfection
of Joe Cook; in burlesque, acrobats and brilliant circus clowns in France,
such as Grock and the brothers Fratellini; and finally the most "despised" of all the lively arts, the cartoon strip, brilliantly exemplified by
George Herriman's Krazy Kat.

Seldes explained that he loved the comic strip as a genre because it
connected in meaningful ways to the "average American life." He praised
Krazy Kat so effusively, and so often, that beginning in 1922 Herriman
regularly drew Seldes' Christmas and New Year greeting cards as personalized episodes featuring Ignatz Mouse, Krazy Kat, and Offissa Pupp,
with a message from Seldes (later en famille) to his friends (Fig. 7).[32] He
drew fire from some cartoon fans as early as the summer of 1922,
however, when his initial essay on the comics, published in *Vanity Fair*,
described Mutt and Jeff as the "first of the great hits and still the best
known of the comic strips." That offended Krazy Kat fanatics, which
Seldes was himself; but he always acknowledged the reality that affection
for Krazy Kat required a more sublime sense of humor. It never enjoyed
such wide syndication as some of the better known and less subtle series.
As Seldes explained to the publisher of *Vanity Fair*, who had forwarded
the irate letters, "Mutt and Jeff have put their names and characters
definitely into the language and ideas of the American people."[33]

Seldes felt unabashed enthusiasm for musical comedy and proposed in
The 7 Lively Arts establishing a lyric theater devoted to all forms of "light
musical entertainment," ranging from Mozart and Gilbert and Sullivan
to Franz Lehar and Jerome Kern. By 1923–24, however, he acknowledged that we are now "full in the jazz age." Consequently he felt a sense
of loss and nostalgia because the traditional popular songs were rapidly
becoming passé. Even so, he understood that jazz was a distinctly American mode of music, expressed a pervasive mood of the 1920s, and should
not be neglected by serious critics. "It is our characteristic expression," he
insisted, "the normal development of our resources," and above all it
marked the "arrival of America at a point of creative intensity." Note the
invocation of Seldes' innate quality, intensity.[34]

In August 1923 Seldes published "Toujours Jazz" in *The Dial* as a
response to Clive Bell's harsh attack on jazz—the seeming incomprehen-
sion of an English highbrow. Upon returning to the United States in
early autumn, Seldes found that his essay had had an unanticipated

Fig. 7. George Herriman, creator of "Krazy Kat," drew the Seldes' family greeting card (early 1930s). Courtesy of the Marianne Moore Papers, the Rosenbach Museum & Library, Philadelphia.

impact upon some of the leading jazz composers. He informed Irving Berlin that his "jazz article has raised the roof. I am told that the writers of jazz are getting so high toned that they refuse to use the word any more." That essay became one of the most widely noticed chapters in *The 7 Lively Arts*.[35]

At times Seldes could be enormously witty on the subject of cultural stratification. In 1925, for example, he published a clever, futuristic spoof about the shape of jazz operas that might some day be performed at the Metropolitan. He had George Gershwin putatively working on a jazz opera based on the life of William Ewart Gladstone, and other equally improbable prospects. Seldes also made some observations that he later came to regret, however. In *The 7 Lively Arts* he differentiated between white jazz, which he considered more intellectual and serious, and Negro jazz, which he viewed as intuitive and highly expressive but less cerebral. "In words and music," he wrote in 1923, "the negro side expresses something which underlies a great deal of America—our independence, our carelessness, our frankness, and gaiety. In each of these the negro is more intense than we are, and [actually *but*] we surpass him when we combine a more varied and more intelligent life with his instinctive qualities."[36] Seldes soon realized that he had casually perpetuated racial stereotypes verging upon caricature.

During the 1930s and '40s, as we shall see, Seldes became a cultural Negrophile with such enthusiasm that several productions designed for African-American performers on which he lavished energy were simply too far ahead of public opinion to achieve commercial success. In the 1920s, however, he remained the unliberated prisoner of traditional stereotypes. When the Swedish Ballet came to New York late in 1923 with decor by Fernand Léger, and three French dancers in a "Negro Ballet of the Creation," Seldes' review referred to "the syncopation and the shuffle which the American negro has made characteristic in our music and dance." Seldes obliquely distinguished between authentic Africanisms and the adaptations and permutations of black culture in the United States. Although he was neither hostile nor critical of the latter, it clearly wasn't the real thing and therefore lacked authenticity. Seldes, like Dwight Macdonald, casually used words like "darkies," "high-yaller," and "the real nigger show," and commented that the latter lacked "art" but had "tremendous vitality." He could not bestow enough superlatives on Florence Mills, James Reese Europe, and Eubie Blake, however, and by the 1930s both his language and his general perceptions of African-American entertainment would change significantly.[37]

When praising Jewish artists or entertainers, Seldes rarely identified them (or their work) in ethnic terms; but occasionally an oblique allusion indicated both his pride in their achievements along with his belief that their cultural heritage helped to explain that achievement. After describing Al Jolson and Fanny Brice, for example, he remarked that "these two stars bring something to America which America lacks and loves—they are, I suppose, two of our most popular entertainers—and that both are racially out of the dominant caste. Possibly this accounts for their fine carelessness about our superstitions of politeness and gentility." Because they were outsiders, Jolson and Brice could freely flout genteel constraints. In Seldes' view that became a plus for them, and even more, for American popular culture.[38]

The book also praised the most prolific and successful songwriter in United States history, Irving Berlin, a man from humble Russian Jewish origins, and included a glossy photograph of the young celebrity in a chapter titled "Tearing a Passion to Ragtime." In 1924 Berlin was court-

ing Ellin Mackay, a Roman Catholic whose parents were utterly opposed
to their marriage. Seldes wrote with bemusement and pride in 1957:

> Forbidden the consolation of having the man's photograph in her room,
> she constantly carried a copy of *The 7 Lively Arts* with her, making herself a
> sort of walking advertisement for the book—until her private motive was
> disclosed. Eventually the marriage took place, so did a reconciliation with-
> in the family, my book was placed on a shelf, and all was—and is—well.[39]

Seldes never attempted to separate his admiration for Berlin from his
enduring personal friendships with the songwriter and his wife. (Seldes
himself wed an Episcopalian in 1924, a marriage that did not exactly
thrill her family; so he felt a special bond with Berlin that went beyond
professional esteem and personal compatibility.)

Seldes' relationship with Edmund Wilson was quite different though
highly characteristic. Despite their enduring friendship, each one commented on the other's work with critical detachment. Wilson wrote "The
Theatre" column for *The Dial* while Seldes was in Europe during 1923;
and in November he even described Seldes' enthusiasm for the lively (or
"minor") arts, initially expressed in essays for *Vanity Fair,* as a bit excessive. At just about that time Seldes befriended Wilson (who was "hard
up" financially) by getting him a job as press agent for the Swedish ballet
touring the United States. In April 1924 Seldes sent a newly minted copy
of *The 7 Lively Arts* to Wilson, who proceeded to dispatch to *The Dial* a
laudatory yet somewhat skeptical review—one of the most acutely perceptive reviews published by any critic of the book. The closing paragraph provides a clear sense of Wilson's overall tone:

> In any case, *The Seven Lively Arts* is a genuine contribution to America's
> new orientation in respect to her artistic life which was inaugurated in 1915
> by Brooks's *America's Coming of Age* and two years later more violently
> promoted by Mencken's *A Book of Prefaces.* Mr. Seldes's view of the arts has
> perhaps been a little confused by his evidently quite recent discovery that it
> is possible to appreciate, not only Krazy Kat at the same time as James
> Joyce, but both Krazy Kat and Joyce at the same time as "the Medea of
> Euripides"; but his book contains a brilliant chronicle of the high spots in
> our popular entertainment. If not all these forms of entertainment have
> really quite reached the dignity of arts, Mr. Seldes has succeeded in invent-
> ing them as such: it is he who is the artist here. He has precipitated pure
> crystals of irony from the cheap adulterated compounds in which it is
> usually sold; he has caught the enchanting echoes of our popular gaiety and

melody as they drift in the city air. To read his book is to live again the last ten years of vaudeville and revue, newspapers and moving pictures, but in a purified and concentrated form—tasting nothing but the magic tune, the racy flash of characterization, the moment of mad laughter. As for the trained dogs, the melodramatic playlet and the sentimental soloist, they, too, become entertaining through the wit of our guide's comments. If he were only a little less fanatical about magnifying the importance of the whole affair, he would make the perfect companion.[40]

A mere glance at Wilson's collected pieces in *The American Earthquake* (1958) makes it clear just how much popular culture had interested him during the 1920s. Later, on several occasions, Seldes acknowledged his good fortune that Wilson moved on to writing fiction, literary history, and criticism, thereby leaving the field of cultural criticism in the popular arts to Seldes. He had competition, to be sure, but no one of Wilson's genius. Seldes recognized that Wilson would have been the pre-eminent writer on American popular culture had he chosen to pursue it, and always remained grateful that *Axel's Castle, To the Finland Station,* and other projects diverted "Bunny" as a formidable rival.[41]

Now that Wilson's diaries have been published, we can at least get glimpses of his private feelings toward Seldes and his wife, Alice. In 1925, for example, Wilson commented that Seldes had "unusual abilities." Not long after that Wilson visited the couple at her father's 2500-acre camp near Saranac in the Adirondacks. Wilson mused that "Alice, as she got on in her married life, matured as a lady of that particular sort, as different as possible from Gilbert.—She had that nice frank laugh, which became freer and bolder."[42] I don't believe that that comment was meant to be uncomplimentary to Gilbert Seldes, who also loved to laugh. Aside from Wilson's eye for attractive women, the point is that Seldes could be intense while his wife was more relaxed.

In 1926 Wilson pulled a stunt that should have strained his relations with Seldes, but it is difficult to be sure. Wilson published anonymously in *The New Republic* for June 30 a long essay, called "the All-Star Literary Vaudeville," that lamented the decline of literary and cultural criticism in recent years. Part of the problem seemed to be an excess of mutual back-scratching, and part derived from an excess of literary nationalism:

> The present writers on American literature all have interests in one phase or another of it: either the authors know one another personally or they owe one another debts of gratitude or they are bound together by their

loyalty to some stimulating common cause. And almost all forget critical standards in their devotion to the great common causes: the cause of an American national literature in independence of English literature, and the cause of contemporary American ideas as against the ideas of the last generation.[43]

Wilson then proceeded to weave his way through novelists and dramatists, skewering many yet praising a few. Before moving on to a lengthy consideration of poets, he paused among the critics to deflate Mencken and laud Paul Rosenfeld and, briefly, George Jean Nathan. Lewis Mumford, receiving half a sentence, "gives the impression of some one perhaps about to be." The treatment of Seldes was neither quite so short nor quite so anticipatory:

> Gilbert Seldes, through his activities as an editor of the *Dial* and his cultivation of the popular arts, has filled a role of considerable importance; but his principal literary quality is a kind of undisciplined wit which figures too often in his writings at the expense of lucidity and taste. He has lately become addicted to aesthetic editorial writing, a department for which his alert and vivid but glancing and volatile mind, is perhaps not very well adapted. In my opinion, he is seen at his best in passages of straight description of some movie or vaudeville act which has aroused his imagination.[44]

Seldes received a copy of *The New Republic* in July near Cannes on the Riviera and promptly wrote a private letter to Wilson and a public letter to the editors of *The New Republic,* one of whom was Wilson. The intimate letter only referred to the "deliberate unfairness of the writer" and then moved on to personal matters, including the (to me) astonishing news that Hemingway was then staying with the Seldeses at their villa high above the sea. Did Seldes know, or have a shrewd guess, concerning the identity of the poison-pen polemicist? Perhaps, but it is hard to tell from his public letter (never printed), which mainly complained that the author had very oddly made no mention of Edmund Wilson!

> Mr. Wilson is in all probability the most erudite of our younger critics, and wears his erudition well; he can, as has been pointed out, quote twenty-seven names on one page—but he writes entertainingly and his allusions have point. It is true that he often leaves the field of literature in which he is at his best to stray in greener pastures and to frisk his heels; but there is always a grave charm about his caprices. He has been honoured with the opening essay in the Atlantic and in The Dial; he has nobly filled many of

your own pages. He is an excellent reporter as you know who published his report of a murder trial. If unsympathetic readers find him a little cantankerous, I would say that that is precisely the quality needed among our critics at present; and if frivolous people find him dull, I would say that he is precisely the sort of critic they need.

But Mr. Wilson's qualities and defects are really beside the point. At least in comparison with the defects of your anonymous contributor who shows himself singularly incapable of picking out important critics and makes up for this by devoting too much attention to insignificant ones. Is it possible that your writer has a grudge against Mr. Wilson? Or is he, as would be only just, preparing to treat the subject in a separate essay?[45]

Had Seldes been snookered? Or was he being droll almost to the point of overkill? If he really did not realize that Wilson had been the harpoonist, when did he learn? I don't know, and Wilson did not reprint the audacious piece in one of his collected volumes until 1952. It all makes for a minor but bizarre and intriguing moment in the anti-social history of American cultural criticism.

III

Overall, the critical response to *The 7 Lively Arts* could hardly have been more positive, at least at first. On April 27 Herbert S. Gorman gave it a rave review in the *New York Times* and Hendrik Willem van Loon waxed euphoric in the *Tribune:* "On the first of April of the year of grace 1924 (just 415 years and five months after the outbreak of the great spiritual revolution) Gilbert Martin Seldes Luther bravely left the sheltering portals of the Monasterium Algonquinensis and boldly hammered his defiant theses on the doors of the solemn edifice which our ancestors have erected to the noble idea of civic gentility." Clive Bell praised it extravagantly, not once but twice, in *The New Republic* and at home in the *Nation and Athenaeum.* So did Walter Prichard Eaton in *The Atlantic,* and an anonymous reviewer in *The Outlook.* Bell struck a note that Seldes himself would subsequently echo: because these lively arts, in particular, "are generally recognized as America's contribution [to] Western civilization [this book] must be of interest to all students of the present and future on both sides of the Atlantic."[46]

A few mixed notices appeared in such places as the New York *Evening Post* and the Springfield *Republican,* along with Wilson's supportive yet critical review in *The Dial.* Ernest Boyd provided *The Independent* with a scathing but pointless and altogether predictable attack. Promptly incorporated into a book of his essays, Boyd's piece bemoaned that "the clowning of Charlie Chaplin, the humors of Joe Cook and Fanny Brice must now be bathed in the vapors of aesthetic mysticism."[47]

I suspect that some of the reviews that mattered most to Seldes, which appeared in comparatively obscure, highbrow journals, mattered simply because Seldes respected the judgment of their editors and reviewers alike. It looked at first as though T. S. Eliot would review it in Britain for his own publication, *The Criterion*. Eliot praised the book in a letter to Seldes, though it is not at all clear that he had really read the entire work. Eliot wrote as though *The 7 Lively Arts* was primarily about comedians. In any case, Eliot got Conrad Aiken (Harvard, 1911), better known as a poet but actually a very shrewd critic, to do the job. Aiken found the book entertaining and Seldes remarkably well informed. He quibbled a bit about emphases and the distribution of kudos, but acknowledged overall that Seldes selected "his heroes with excellent judgment, and writes of them amusingly and discriminatingly." Then Aiken dropped the other shoe, so to speak:

> It is when Mr. Seldes indulges in theory and propaganda that one wants to take one's leave; it is when he rides his hobby of the "vulgar" versus the "genteel" that one gladly permits him to ride out of sight. Like a good many contemporary critics, he is obsessed with the horribleness of what he calls the faux bon, or "bogus," in art. The bogus, or faux bon, appears to Mr. Seldes to be a dreadful menace—a kind of monster which must be slain; he seems to know exactly and shudderingly what it is; but what it is he never makes quite clear. One suspects him, here, of over-simplification; and one suspects him also of having, towards his "bogus" or "pretentious" or faux bon art, what a psychiatrist would describe as an "over-determined" feeling: for some reason, this vague nightmare excites him too much.

There is more in that long paragraph, and another harsh one followed. Then came Aiken's crushing finale:

> The trouble is that Mr. Seldes is a little too arbitrary and self-conscious and perverse in his theorising (perhaps influenced by the contemporary French admiration for American liveliness), and also he is very superficial. He has not been at sufficient pains in grasping the psychological factors of the relation of artist to art, or art to audience. To maintain that the "bogus" arts spring from "longing, weakness and depression," while the "major" and "lively" arts spring from "gaiety" and "strength," strikes one as remarkably

naive. In its false contrasts, its failure of understanding, and its ignorance of facts, it suggests a critical bankruptcy almost complete.[48]

Seldes surely felt grateful that *The Criterion* was still too new to be well known in the United States, and at its peak had only 800 subscribers.

He fared better in the *transatlantic review,* an equally new cultural magazine, in part, perhaps, because the assessment came from Lewis Galantière, in whose Paris apartment Seldes had written most of the book! Galantière did go on about the catchy title and correctly forecast that it would become common parlance. He called the title "delectable, irresistibly bright." Although much of the argument made sense, it bothered Galantière that Seldes so cavalierly elevated Irving Berlin above Puccini, and George Gershwin above Mozart. "To preach the destruction of the *faux bon* is excellent," he declared, but to raise in its place, even by implication, the ephemeral and merely amusing was not so wise. Galantière also feared that Seldes had developed a thesis "which will assuredly be seized upon by the ignorant as a lever."[49]

The same issue contained an unsigned editorial, written by Ernest Hemingway, that aimed a cheap shot at Seldes and his new enthusiasms. How pleasant it is to appear to know, to really know, Hemingway mused,

> languages other than our own and how difficult it is to do so, and what really profound admiration we have for Americans who really do know French and how tired we get of others who pretend to, and how very much better dadas the American dadas, who do not know they are dadas, unless, of course, Mr. Seldes has told them. . . .[50]

On and on, gratuitous and rather pointless.

How did young Hemingway happen to be writing this particular editorial, anyway? Earlier in 1924 he had gone from New York to Paris where he met Ford Madox Ford through Ezra Pound. Ford had recently started the *transatlantic review* and chose Hemingway as his sub-editor. Already a cantankerous iconoclast, Hemingway decided to make his maiden editorial a satirical piece that would impugn the skills and artistic interests of Tristan Tzara, Jean Cocteau, and Gilbert Seldes. Since Seldes had only a tenuous connection with Tzara, Cocteau, and dada, the assault was especially gratuitous. What really seems to have agitated Hemingway was his notion that Seldes' roles at *The Dial,* indirectly at *Vanity Fair,* and now with his widely noticed book would make him *the* arbiter of new cultural trends for American readers.[51]

Hemingway may also have known that Seldes felt skepticism toward the American expatriates. He published the following, for example, two months after *The 7 Lively Arts* appeared and little more than a month before Hemingway's dada crack:

> I am the last one to suggest that being an American automatically implies a severance from the cultural tradition of Europe. But it does imply—it fairly necessitates acceptance of our American world. . . . It was not in a reality, but in a falsity of the past that the maladjusted American found refuge.[52]

Much of this essay also took (polite) aim at early criticisms of *The 7 Lively Arts,* even in predominantly favorable reviews by such men as Clive Bell. Seldes saved his serious ire for Ernest Boyd and wrote a lengthy response to his nasty review for *The Independent.* Seldes accused Boyd of gross ignorance, adding that "the former British consular representative in Baltimore has no more right to be ignorant than the most industrious of our book-reviewers to read books carelessly." Seldes concluded his letter by giving as good as he got:

> Mr. Boyd also says that the implication of my title, The Seven Lively Arts, is that the other arts are excessively dull. May I say that although he has said this ever since last January, it remains not my implication, but his own, and that I cannot cope with a reviewer who misquotes, misreads, and finally imputes to me silly and obnoxious opinions which are exactly contrary to the slender, but explicit, ideas in my book.[53]

Looking back from the perspective of 1956, Seldes felt that his principal foes in 1924 had really been American expatriates and highbrow snobs. His harsh critics, he believed, were neither college professors nor pedants—perhaps the foes he most feared before the book appeared. Rather, his shrillest dissenters were bright young people "ready to accept any novelty in the arts provided it was not native to America and not popular among the lowbrows."[54]

Be that as it may, Seldes soon became so visible as a critic that he served, quite literally, as a moving target for writers jealous of his sudden prominence on the cultural scene. F. Scott Fitzgerald wrote from Paris to Maxwell Perkins of Scribner's in 1925 that "the reviews I have seen of [Ring Lardner's] *What of It?* were sorry imitations of Seldes' stuff and all of them went out of their way to stab Seldes in the back. God, cheap reviewers are low-swine—but one must live."[55]

No one stabbed Seldes more often or more viciously than Ernest

Hemingway. Early in May 1924 he sent Ezra Pound a truly ugly letter. First he reported that Lincoln Steffens had gone to Italy with a twenty-two-year-old "Jewine." Next that E. E. Cummings had married Scofield "Buggaring" Thayer's former wife (presumably a relief to both of the Thayers). And then this: "George Washington Seldes, the man who discovered Burlesque shows were funny, marrying and enroute to Yar-rup [Europe]. Let us hope the marriage will be consummated."[56]

Hemingway clearly meant Gilbert because brother George did not marry until 1932 and Gilbert married Alice Wadhams Hall in Paris on June 21, 1924. They met one year earlier at the wedding of John Peale Bishop because Alice Hall and Margaret Bishop had been classmates at the Brearly School in New York City (see Fig. 8). For a while during the

Fig. 8. Alice Wadhams Hall before her marriage to Gilbert Seldes in 1924.

Fig. 9. Pablo Picasso, drawing presented by the artist to Alice and Gilbert Seldes on the occasion of their wedding in June 1924 in France.

spring it looked as though the Seldes wedding would have to be postponed because of the complexities and formalities of French law. The anxious period of waiting for a go-ahead was made easier by the congeniality of Seldes' new friendships. As he wrote to a cousin, "some very nice things have happened—nicest of all the warmth of our reception here—Picasso embraced me publicly and [Clive] Bell flirted charmingly with Amanda."[57] Seldes considered the name Alice too bland and always called his beloved Amanda.

They had a civil ceremony followed by a gala wedding party in the Bois de Boulogne, at which Picasso presented the couple with a drawing (see Fig. 9). Gilbert and his Amanda remained compatible and mutually devoted until her death in Florida early in 1954 (see Fig. 10). From time to time Seldes took up the topic of marriage as a social institution in his informal journalism. In 1932 he observed that "of all human inventions marriage has had the worst press." As the product of an anarchist utopia in which many members were committed to the practice of free love, Seldes had undergone a total turnabout. "To be against marriage," he observed, "has been, since 1900 at least, the sign of forward-looking and high thinking, whether marriage was considered as a holy sacrament or

Fig. 10. Gilbert and "Amanda" Seldes (mid-1930s).

an economic arrangement." Seldes thereupon launched into one of his cleverest (though quite earnest) columns. Here is an extract:

> I have been hearing at the movies and in the theatres about the usual number of jokes about marriage, and, being more than usually depressed by their staleness, made the discovery that the jokes are stale because they are allusions to something that has been dead for generations; that is, the circumstances of ordinary marriage. Long ago I heard the familiar objection—think of seeing the same face every day at the breakfast table; and it occurred to me that seeing a different face at the breakfast table every day would be an unimaginable horror. But that complaint at least pointed to one of the ancient embarrassments of marriage–that people in pioneering days lived isolated and were thrown so exclusively on each

other's company that they found pleasure only in making catalogues of each other's faults.[58]

The Seldeses spent part of their honeymoon at the Riviera home of Zelda and F. Scott Fitzgerald, a couple whose marriage turned out to be considerably more complicated and less serene than the Seldeses'. Here once again, as with Edmund Wilson and others, we have an example of people compartmentalizing the professional and the personal. Seldes and Fitzgerald became good friends despite Seldes' critical review of Fitzgerald's early fiction, especially his "deplorable" short stories and *The Beautiful and Damned* (1922). In 1923 Seldes had Christmas dinner with the Wilsons and Dos Passos at the Fitzgeralds' home in Great Neck on Long Island. The friendship would be considerably strengthened, however, when Seldes wrote a rave review of *The Great Gatsby* for *The Dial* in 1925. Although he once again minimized the quality of previous work—"I cannot find in the earlier Fitzgerald the artistic integrity and the passionate feeling which this book possesses"—Seldes said that "the technical virtuosity is extraordinary" and proclaimed *Gatsby* "one of the finest of contemporary novels."[59]

Fitzgerald knew that it was coming. Early in June, John Peale Bishop wrote from the States to say that he had dinner with Van Wyck Brooks and Seldes on the 8th. Seldes loved the book and ranked it above anything by Sinclair Lewis or Willa Cather. Then Seldes reviewed it lavishly in *The Criterion,* prompting Fitzgerald to tell Max Perkins: "Quite a bit from Gilbert who only likes Ring, Edith Wharton, Joyce and Charlie Chaplin." After *The Dial* review appeared Fitzgerald thanked Seldes effusively, of course, but more interesting, perhaps, is an earlier letter that Fitzgerald wrote Seldes from France while waiting for the paean of praise to arrive. According to a pejorative assessment by Burton Rascoe, Fitzgerald said, *The Great Gatsby* "is just Robert Chambers [a popular novelist of mediocre melodramas] with overtones of *Nedra* [an English novel by George Barr McCutcheon, 1906]. So I think I'll write a 'serious' novel about the Great Struggle the Great American Peasant has with the soil. Everyone else seems to be doing it."[60]

Following the stunning triumph of *Gatsby,* the remainder of Fitzgerald's career seemed, in several respects, a troubled anti-climax. Many people speculated why, but two explanations are particularly interesting. Decades later an interviewer asked Malcom Cowley whether success could be harmful. Cowley responded this way:

> It was always said that Gilbert Seldes's review of *The Great Gatsby* which
> was ecstatic, probably damaged Scott Fitzgerald. The trouble is that after
> something like that, every word has to count . . . every word has to live up
> to this marvelous praise. The poor author gets stage fright.

In 1951 Seldes himself tried to make sense of Fitzgerald's decline and
observed that during the early and mid-1930s Fitzgerald drifted away
from his "literary conscience," Edmund Wilson, and tried to rely upon
Seldes for counsel. "It wasn't a success," Seldes wrote, "because I couldn't
give him what he wanted and he didn't respect me enough. I was not
essentially a [literary] critic and couldn't make him feel, as Wilson could,
that he was part of the great body of world literature."[61]

Although Hemingway persisted as a daemonic force, he could not
disrupt the genuine rapport between Seldes and Fitzgerald. Hemingway
wrote to Maxwell Perkins from Key West that "critics like Seldes etc. are
poison for him." In 1929 Hemingway offered praise in order to cajole
Fitzgerald into finishing *Tender Is the Night.* He referred to "that review
of Seldes's in the Dial. After that you became self conscious about it and
knew you must write a masterpiece. Nobody but Fairies can write Masterpieces. . . . You'd have written two damned good books by now if it
hadn't been for that Seldes review." Yet another snide reference is followed by a touch of anti-Semitic sarcasm: "This should be enough from
Jeremiah Hemingstein the great Jewish Prophet."[62]

It surely did not help that in 1926 Seldes wrote a piece from Seville
conveying *his* impressions of bull fighting. He called it a "big game hunt
with ritual and rules," and found its only redeeming qualities to be the
grace and perfection with which large animals are killed. That brief but
sardonic dig surely did not escape Hemingway's notice.[63]

IV

Late in 1958, when Seldes had begun work on the memoir he never
completed, he dictated the following: "our expatriates were colossally
ignorant. They thought of America as something that had come into
existence with the passage of the 18th Amendment." Although he had
three extended periods in Europe during 1923, 1924, and 1926, by the
summer of 1924 Seldes had begun to clarify his views about Americans
abroad. He started with tourism by making fun of those who derived
snob-value from foreign travel. In December 1924 his lead essay in *Vanity*

Fair praised the distinctiveness of American culture but criticized Van Wyck Brooks for a "peculiar form" of artistic chauvinism. Seldes then fired his *7 Lively Arts* salvo. Advocates of American culture, he asserted, should demand and help to produce "such works as America creates more satisfactorily than any other country—the arts of popular entertainment, of vaudeville, of the comic strip, of the fantastic and farcical movie, of musical shows, and of jazz."[64]

In a curious way, however, Waldo Frank provoked a dialogue with Seldes in the middle of 1925 by misrepresenting him. Frank opened an essay in *The New Republic* by announcing that "Gilbert Seldes has revived what might be called the classic debate of American culture: Should an American artist stay at home? Mr. Seldes holds that the artist is at home wherever he chooses to settle. And he cites instances in favor of his contention." Frank proceeded to acknowledge that Henry James, Ezra Pound, T. S. Eliot, and their ilk did well to live and work wherever they felt most creative. "But the artist who is tempted to the task of forging new organic life from chaos may bless his stars if America is his home. For in all the world there is no symbol of this chaos so potent and so pregnant as our American jungle."[65]

Seldes quite properly dispatched a letter insisting that he had been misrepresented because he had not advocated a need for American artists to go abroad, and acknowledged that, like Frank actually, he had fudged his response to the issue and stated that a creative artist's "capacity to work depends largely upon his nerves, as they are touched by [an] alien or native civilization."[66]

Meanwhile, from the fall of 1925 onward, Seldes initiated a new emphasis that would become a staple of his journalistic (i.e., magazine and newspaper) criticism, namely, that Europeans too commonly misunderstood American culture or else failed to take it seriously. The French, above all, displayed "enthusiasm for the jazz side of America" but failed to react to more serious or traditional artistic pursuits in the United States. If Americans accepted the validity of such views they would miss the totality of their heritage. He criticized the British for failing to appreciate the distinctive style of the American musical revue, and then devoted an essay to French hostility directed at American tourists, goods, and especially American industrial innovations and methods.[67]

As early as December 1924 Seldes started to assert that the American contribution to art, broadly conceived, would occur most notably in the realm of industrial design. The United States, in fact, would develop such totally new "arts" as the art of the motor car body, the art of the advertising poster, and of the electric sign. Two years later he discussed clocks, dynamos, and especially refrigerators as symbols of American progress because they manifested precision, neatness, and mastery. Seldes hoped that America would expand its innovations in the industrial arts and move beyond making ice cubes to higher aesthetic pleasures.[68] When the Deutsches Museum of History and Science opened in Munich on the eve of World War I, it promptly had a very broad impact and stimulated writers like Thorstein Veblen to discuss industrial design as a manifestation of changes wrought by technological growth. On this subject Seldes had clearly received a stimulus from Veblen.

Despite Seldes' upbeat view of industrial design and its social implications, his essays in 1925–26 were less sanguine about the temperament and values of American business and advertising. He blasted Bruce Barton's best-seller, *The Man Nobody Knows,* for explicating the life of Jesus as a positive parable for contemporary businessmen. Unfortunately, in Seldes' view, when Americans achieved a service mentality, they did so only in order to make money. He mocked the recently constructed Broadway Temple because of its call for "a 5 percent investment in your Fellow Man's Salvation." And he initiated his enduring interest in advertising by lamenting the loss of the "brief, informative" ad which says very little about the product itself and too much about the kinds of people who buy it. Although Seldes regarded ads as a viable litmus of American impulses, they did not qualify as art, even by his inclusive criteria.[69]

He blasted Henry Ford because that quixotic industrialist had proposed banning all foreign languages from the United States on grounds that they hindered "science and invention and commerce" just as they also hindered "world peace and understanding." Similarly, in Ford's view cultural and artistic pursuits were inconsequential because they retarded industrial progress. Although Seldes too was a self-made man, he could nonetheless be critical of popular literature that glorified self-made men like Ford and former President James Garfield. *From Log Cabin to White House,* a homiletic biography of Garfield, annoyed Seldes because it seemed "tasteless; it might almost be a symbolic record of success in America, devoid of interest in detail and fated to futility in the end." Seldes had little sympathy for the "legend of opportunity" in the United States: excessively beguiling and utterly devoid of artistic merit in its pseudo-literary manifestations.[70]

Who or what, then, did Seldes *admire* in American writing? From 1924 onward he remained a loyal fan of Ring Lardner, and for reasons completely consistent with the central argument of *The 7 Lively Arts* but also because Lardner's achievement stood as a refutation of Van Wyck Brooks' insistence that high culture and popular culture never converged in the United States. Seldes observed in *Vanity Fair* that Lardner had become "one of the most popular of our humorists, with a weekly syndicated article, a comic strip, and an inexhaustible market for 'pieces' of any description. But he is, at the same time, admired by the cognoscenti for whom, in his long life as a writer, he has apparently never cared a snap of his fingers."[71]

Seldes' enthusiasm for Lardner also provides a clue to his own shift from aesthetic cosmopolitanism to a growing fascination with the meaning of America. Seldes identified Lardner's two great qualities as "his clear-eyed observation of America and his gift of the fantastic." He saw in Lardner "a boundless imagination—an American quality—and an apparently inexhaustible energy." When Seldes asked why Lardner was achieving such acclaim, the explanation appeared obvious, at least in part: "the new interest in purely American artistic phenomena which has developed since the war." Lardner would always remain "purely American," and not once but twice in the decades ahead, Seldes would edit anthologies of Lardner's prose.[72]

Seldes' effusive support for George M. Cohan commented that "The Song-and-Dance Man," a legitimate comedy drama, made use of "the American language with a moving eloquence approaching close to poetic utterance." In the cadence of speech used "it is the American language, elliptical, swift, clear, and poignant." In a 1925 essay called "Jazz and Ballad," Seldes stressed that ragtime and its progeny, jazz, were important manifestations of American culture, "a musical counterpart to some of our physical and perhaps some of our mental, or spiritual rhythms." Returning to the subject of popular music in 1926, Seldes featured Jerome Kern because the key to his genius, in Seldes' view, was simplicity —a quality that Seldes regarded as essential for success in any of the popular arts.[73]

Consistent with the widely noticed appeal of *The 7 Lively Arts,* Seldes became a missionary not merely for popular culture but, on more than one occasion, an apologist for the "vulgar" arts when they had the salutary effect of evoking "robust laughter and hearty cheers." He criticized the producers of musical revues, even Florenz Ziegfeld and John Murray Anderson, because they had fallen "under the spell of the small, polite smile . . . . They would rather have their comedies called dull than vulgar." Seldes blasted his fellow critics for failing to protest against this "wasteful gesture of respect to the idea of good taste."[74]

Predictably, perhaps, he preferred ordinary nightclubs to exclusive social clubs because at nightclubs the music is good, the patrons are not hypercritical but involved, enchanted in fact—by the crowd, by the dance floor, and by the rhythm of the music. Businessmen preferred exclusive clubs to nightclubs and dance clubs because the latter epitomized everything that they despise: "leisure and laziness and incontinence; carelessness of time and money; what seems to be an impertinent indifference to getting on." Precisely because industrialization had robbed the United States of leisure, the country desperately needed social institutions that could compensate with recreational opportunities for "loafing" and play. Similarly, Seldes expressed enthusiasm for the Charleston because it added excitement to the American stage and provided greater opportunities for individual expression in social dancing. When praising comedians and clowns Seldes singled out Harpo Marx because he shared Chaplin's "escape from reality" without imitating Chaplin as so many others did.[75]

Meanwhile, Seldes also turned his hand to several aspects (or levels) of theatrical entertainment in 1925—without any significant popular success, but providing a preview of important developments that would alter his vocational trajectory during the 1930s. First, in collaboration with his father Seldes translated some Russian plays into English and Brentano's published them. He also wrote "The Wisecrackers," a comedy in three acts produced by the Fifth Avenue Theatre in December 1925. Intended as a satirical fling at the social life of New York's literati, Seldes devised a young couple separated by their "wisecracking" friends (Algonquin types, perhaps?), but ultimately reconciled by the prospect of parenthood. (The Seldeses' first child, Timothy, was born in December 1926.)[76]

The play bombed, an echo of which we hear in a note that Seldes received from Scott Fitzgerald in Europe: "Ring sent me a clipping about your play—I know how it feels to see one go pop before your eyes and I deeply sympathize with you." Seldes' financial resources had run very thin by then, but his sister-in-law gave the couple a trip to Europe as a Christmas present in 1925. The cost of living was much lower in Europe; and Seldes borrowed $1000 from Fitzgerald, his near neighbor at Juan-les-Pins on the Riviera. Seldes recalled, long after, that "the last night we were there, Scott gave me 1000 francs to gamble with at the casino at J-le-P and I won a huge amount which we divided."[77]

Following eight months of intense writing for magazines and equally intense playing, mainly in the south of France, with brother George nearby in late summer, the Seldes sailed for home on the *Caronia* early in October. A varied career as a "colyumist" awaited him in New York. The newspaper and magazine column, joined with a distinctive personality, had just begun to achieve popularity early in the 1920s. Seldes devoted a chapter of *The 7 Lively Arts* to this cultural phenomenon and claimed that "the most sophisticated of the minor arts in America is that of the colyumist. It is, except for occasional lapses into the usually journalistic disrespect for privacy, a decent art. . . . The colyumist is, to begin with, a newspaper humorist, and there are times, when questions of art and letters are discussed, when one wishes he had remained one. . . . His usual manner is to take a notable or obscure item of news and play with it, in the manner of Mark Twain."[78] That is exactly what Seldes did during his years writing a daily column for the New York *Evening Journal,* 1931–37. From the end of 1926 until 1930, however, his career as social historian, critic, and "colyumist" was even more diverse. In addition to three novels and three books of non-fiction, he continued to do the "Theatre" review for *The Dial,* write columns on assorted subjects (especially drama) for the New York *Graphic,* and serve as a contributing editor to *The New Republic* (November 1925 until June 1932). It was a hectic life, highly social yet infused with a love of learning. Seldes enjoyed it immensely.[79]

V

Before moving on to the later 1920s, however, we want to know what subsequently happened to the word-concept as well as the actual marrow of the seven lively arts. To begin, Seldes elaborated at first but later modified a few of his views (regretted that he hadn't been more generous to Eddie Cantor, apologized for his insistence that pop song be accepted as folk art, and in 1968 even wondered whether his fanaticism for Krazy Kat had been excessive), yet always remained associated in people's minds as *the* "distinguished critic of the lively arts."

During the later 1920s he embellished. Writing in 1927 for the *Saturday Evening Post,* for instance, he insisted that highbrows had gained the most from "their recent contact with the lowbrow arts." If only the highbrows would restrain themselves and not "try to uplift the lively arts, these arts may develop freely and create, in their sum, a real American art." Moreover, the true "lover of the popular arts takes them as he finds them." On the other hand, "if the idea of uplifting the lively arts is nauseating, the idea of never criticizing them is silly." Some of these issues would recur frequently in Seldes' newspaper columns, in the department that he wrote every month for *Esquire* (called "the lively arts") from its founding in 1933 through 1946, and in his big book on American national style, *Mainland* (1936).[80]

It should be no surprise that *The 7 Lively Arts* helped many people feel that their "low" tastes ought not to be embarrassing. Considerably more startling is Seldes' apparent impact on some highly prominent critics from the generation prior to his own. William Crary Brownell (1851–1928) had been Matthew Arnold's most important American disciple and, without question, in book after book, a genteel highbrow. In his very last work, however, *Democratic Distinction in America* (1927), Brownell turned his attention not only to popular culture, but to the comic strip! "As a social force," he wrote, "education is the great leveler—inevitably also leveling up, not down." Yet another old-timer, Percy Holmes Boynton (1875–1946), produced an essay in 1927 titled "Democracy and Public Taste," an essay filled with uncanny echoes of Seldes' by then famous book. Boynton preferred movies to opera, like Seldes, and emphasized the cultural importance of Paul Whiteman's jazz concerts. No one who had read Boynton's earlier essays and books could have predicted his newly generous view of the public arts and popular taste.[81]

From the later 1930s onward, Seldes' emphases and priorities would be appropriated by others without so much as a nod of the head, a footnote, or a bibliographical acknowledgment.[82] In 1938, when Kurt London published *The Seven Soviet Arts,* he devoted part three to music, literature, theatre, opera, ballet, the beaux arts, applied arts, fashion, and architecture. Part four considered film, radio, and the gramophone. The author spent 1936–37 in London and New York. He very clearly looked back, over his shoulder, to Seldes' 1924 book.[83]

Billy Rose appropriated the title of *The 7 Lively Arts* for an extravagant musical review that opened on Broadway in December 1944 to huge promotional ballyhoo. Despite songs by Cole Porter, ballet music by Igor Stravinsky, sketches and monologues written by Moss Hart, George S. Kaufman, and Ben Hecht, plus Beatrice Lillie, Bert Lahr, Benny Goodman, Alicia Markova, and Dolores Gray as performers, it had no direct relationship to Seldes' book and disappointed critics and the general public alike. The show closed after a little more than twenty weeks, a massive bust. In 1966 Jack Warner sold his interest in Warner Brothers to a holding company called Seven Arts, Limited, for $32 million.[84]

Recognition came in desultory but increasingly gratifying ways. A philosopher at Columbia University wrote in 1951 that he recalled "the day a generation ago when your work *The Seven Lively Arts* was required reading for all the young intellectuals." Cleveland Amory praised the second edition in the *New York Times Book Review* (1957). Writing about "The Discovery of the Popular Culture" in 1961, Reuel Denney called Seldes' book "then and now the classic in its field."[85] An English edition published in 1960 received warm notices. Eric Larrabee wrote Seldes in 1965 and called himself a "quondam practitioner in the field you invented." In his introduction to a shrewd collection of essays concerning American popular culture (1987), Paul Buhle observed that "for more than thirty years, critic Gilbert Seldes's *The Seven Lively Arts* (1924) stood alone as a sympathetic treatment of popular culture, recognized but not taken particularly seriously."[86]

In his last years, recalling and narrating shards of his life for "As in My Time," Seldes often returned to his motives and his achievement in writing *The 7 Lively Arts*. His "discovery," he declared, was that the popular arts were worthy of "intelligent criticism." Later, in February 1968, he explained that "I wasn't against the fine arts, I was only against 'high-class-trash' as, indeed, I was against low-class trash."[87]

In 1967, responding to a woman writing an M.A. thesis about his most famous book, Seldes speculated that "as no one else was writing about popular arts, I had a free field. It was good luck." At the very close of a seventeen-page transcript that Seldes dictated near the end of his life, he observed that what began with him as the "lively arts" in 1923–24 became the "mass media" within a decade. How fortunate he was, he reiterated, because he could remain engaged with the whole subject, and its transformation, throughout his entire professional life.[88]

It should also be noted that Seldes began to practice a particular mode of retrospection, as a critical tactic, as early as 1924. Seldes never explicitly discussed it as a professional strategy, so I call what he did "looking back a decade." He loved to compare things as they are with the way they had been ten years earlier. Writing "The Great Theatre Hoax of 1914," he commented that those were not the "happy days." Rather, the things most savored in the theatre in 1924 were just about to blossom a decade before.[89] That is one of the few occasions when Seldes employed this tactic without nostalgia.

Three months later, once again for *Vanity Fair*, Seldes compared the jazz band of ten years before with its modern counterpart, to the complete disadvantage of the latter. Jazz was becoming excessively regularized. "If the process continues," he asked, "what will become of the characteristically joyful and frivolous thing we know as Jazz?" He noticed a silver lining, however, if one looked beyond jazz aficionados. Arrangers prided themselves on their classicism, and that had mixed implications:

> In the process of conversion, some of the old snap is bound to be lost—the Negro band will preserve it longest. . . . The discoveries which jazz has made, the freshness of tones—the American noises, in short—will be snapped up by composers in and out of the jazz movement. It is the musical world at large which will ultimately gain by the coming of jazz. . . .[90]

Little more than a year later he prepared a piece for *The New Republic* looking back to the impact that reading Nietzsche had upon him ten years earlier. In 1932, on the twentieth anniversary of the marriage of George McManus' Jiggs and Maggie, Seldes recalled that a decade earlier he had taken issue with Harold E. Stearns concerning the quality of this popular cartoon. So he rehashed the merits of the case.[91]

In June of 1932 he began one of his daily columns by observing that "It is now ten years since—by a happy accident—I hit upon a series of subjects which made writing a pleasure, paid me rather well, and got me into trouble which I would hardly say will follow me to the end of my days, but which still crops up from time to time. . . ."

> My real discovery of ten years ago was that no one was writing about a lot of people who were tremendously entertaining, and that while pretty poor actresses and worse dramatists had books and magazine articles devoted to them, men of the first order, in another class, were popular with millions of people and neglected by the intellectuals alone. This neglect I attempted to end, out of gratitude to those who had given me pleasure and out of a lively sense of needing more money than I was earning.

After a reprise of his favorites, from Krazy Kat to jazz, Seldes noted: "It seems incredible, now, that the first point of the book should have been missed. The point was that all the people whom I admired were tremendously popular. With one or two exceptions, each was the acknowledged master in his or her field."[92]

He then declared that his major differences with critics had resulted from a misunderstanding for which he took responsibility:

Certainly I gave the impression to dozens of critics that I was pretending to be the actual discoverer of Chaplin and Joe Cook and Gershwin and Irene Castle and George MacManus; at least that was the complaint I heard, and it wasn't until five years had passed that I found the right answer. It was that, for myself, at least, I was uncovering (not discovering) qualities in these artists which had not been noticed. Probably I was wrong a good many times; but they gave pleasure and most of them still do.

Looking back from 1932, however, Seldes proclaimed victory: "the battle is won":

The odd habit of admiring an artist because he hangs in the Metropolitan Museum, and despising him because he appears in a daily newspaper had not entirely disappeared; but the trick isn't so often played. Twenty years ago, no first line critic went to a musical show (however resplendent) if a legitimate show (however trivial) opened the same night. I am not responsible for the change. With worse and worse plays and better and better musicals, the critics finally had to give way. . . . It is long since I have had a propagandist's enthusiasm for what I carelessly called "the lively arts." I can take them or leave them alone. Yet I still find more pleasure in a good farce than in a bad tragedy, more in a good piece of jazz than in a pretentious opera, more in a good comic strip than in an imitation of Picasso by a talentless painter.[93]

Seldes felt upbeat about his distinctive project and good about himself. Why not? For more than a decade he had been on a roll, and by 1932 had achieved recognition as a prominent critic with a particular angle of vision: the appeal of popular culture at its best.

"It Was a Good Time
for Magazine Writers"

Although Seldes discovered his distinctive medium and fashioned his own stylistic voice during the years from 1923 until 1926, the next phase of his career (1927–30) would be rather different in terms of its focus, output, and above all, the clarification and ripening of his views as a cultural critic. In *The 7 Lively Arts,* for example, he had written, "Faced with the vast myths of the American pasts, our poets simply haven't found the medium for projecting them." That remark resonates with observations that Van Wyck Brooks had been making for a decade, and might well have been written by Brooks. Seven months later, however, Seldes noticed strong tendencies toward "artistic chauvinism" in Brooks, and more important still, observed that Brooks needed to resolve an ambivalence that Seldes himself had just begun to sort out. "He is perpetually between Scylla and Charybdis: it grieves him to note that America fails to supply its artists a proper background, and it grieves him to note that, when they seek that background abroad, Europe corrupts them. He would like the great arts to develop *à l'americaine.*"[1]

In 1927, while Brooks was still mired in his prolonged mental breakdown, but well before Brooks began his unequivocal affirmation of American culture, Seldes observed with satisfaction that "in the past generation writers and painters have begun to work more independently of Europe; in the past decade composers have made fresh discoveries on American soil." A few months later, while preparing *The Stammering*

Century, a critical look at American society in the nineteenth century, Seldes ascribed substantial blame to routinely praised sources of American thought and culture: "A considerable proportion of the fallacies to which the American mind has been partial, a like proportion of the bad taste and bad judgment of which it stands accused, are directly to be ascribed to Europe." Although Europe sent some wonderful stimuli to the United States, he concluded, it had also "foisted on us feeble ideas, questionable taste, quackeries and crazes."[2]

The final four years of the '20s would be highly significant for Seldes (and for the critic's vocation in the United States) for numerous reasons: he took a position and came to terms with anti-Americanism, whether it arose from the expatriates, from such people as H. L. Mencken, or from foreigners; he developed a more broadly affirmative view of art and culture in the United States; although he continued to emphasize some of the themes that were central to his widely recognized book, the lively arts and popular culture gave way to a more middlebrow orientation that mediated between his highbrow/lowbrow divided loyalties of the years 1920–26; he added a responsible (rather than a reckless) use of satire to his craft; and above all, perhaps, he also pursued and called particular attention to the cultural importance of *historical* knowledge and understanding. By 1928–29 Seldes received recognition as a serious student of American history.

In addition to becoming more versatile as a writer and critic in these years—owing in part to his broadening interests and in part to the kinds of publishers who supported him—major developments also occurred at a more personal, though still professional level. Seldes tried his hand at fiction but then rather abruptly stopped. He was quite competent, though not stellar, and he knew it. He also acknowledged, with some regret, how comparatively apolitical, even politically inert he had been, though he made only sporadic efforts during the 1930s to rectify that aspect of his behavior and temperament.

There are noteworthy parallels, in several respects, between Seldes' career and that of Bernard DeVoto (1897–1955), the opinionated writer, critic, and from 1935 until his death the incumbent of the "Easy Chair," a monthly column in *Harper's* that was, in fact, the most enduring feature in American journalism, dating back to 1850. Both men loved to write about the American past because they believed that it contained lessons for those living in the present. Both wrote fiction under a pseudonym because they produced novels primarily for money and regarded the fiction they wrote as "infra dig" stuff. Both wrote extensively for the

Saturday Evening Post because it paid so well and reached a vast audience. Both men viewed the cocktail hour as sacred, scorned Prohibition, and wrote devastating critiques of it.[3]

Both men preferred writing prose to poetry, and both enjoyed serious conversation and gossip almost equally. DeVoto very much admired Seldes' two major works on the historical determinants of American values and culture, *The Stammering Century* (1928) and *Mainland* (1936). DeVoto's prominent review of *Mainland,* in fact, became an encomium deeply prized by Seldes. Above all, both men were feisty critics who resolutely refused to pull their punches and, as a consequence, ran afoul of friends as well as foes. More than a few folks regarded both of them as brilliant minds but fairly difficult curmudgeons.[4]

I

These later years of the '20s happen to have been a halcyon phase for free-lance journalism. Seldes, DeVoto, Wilson, and many others thrived under the circumstances. As swiftly as they could produce, their type-scripts appeared in print. That is partly what Lewis Mumford had in mind when he reminisced to Van Wyck Brooks in 1956: "One of the things that impresses me about the literary life of the twenties was how easy it was to get things done." He recalled, particularly, the proliferation of bold young publishers and the speed with which his first book, *The Story of Utopias* (1922), went through production. Nevertheless, his comment has a broader applicability and validity.[5]

Steven Biel has observed that "free-lancing changed journalism into a kind of anti-career for intellectuals, characterized by frequent movement, a sense of autonomy and integrity, resistance to specialization and professionalization, and an unwillingness to conform to commercial demands." Except for the last point, and some instances of compromised integrity, those generalizations are very much on target.[6]

The frequent movement that Biel alludes to derived in part from restlessness among writers and in part from shifting relationships between publishers and editors, on the one side, and authors on the other. Yet another factor involved the rise and fall of reputations in the magazine and newspaper worlds, which helped to make the allegiances of writers rather capricious at times. The New York *World,* which had been the most vibrant and readable newspaper in the United States, and at one time the most influential, gradually declined during the later 1920s and died in 1931. Meanwhile the New York *Herald Tribune* began a steady ascent, capturing one fine columnist after another; and by 1920 the *New York Times* matched Herbert Bayard Swope's *World* in circulation, exceeded it in advertising, and started to surpass it in reputation.

Early in the 1920s, however, Swope made some dramatic innovations that did much to delay his paper's senescence. He essentially created what we now call the Op-Ed page by setting aside the page opposite the main editorial page to display the skills of such newly acquired columnists as Heywood Broun and Franklin P. Adams' humorous "Conning Tower." Alexander Woollcott became the drama critic, Deems Taylor the music critic, and starting in 1922 Swope hired widely admired Walter Lippmann to run the editorial page. The *World* enjoyed some heady years before it fell.[7]

As early as 1924 Seldes wrote a column about the mortality of metropolitan newspapers; it appears to have been incredibly prescient, though not so much in terms of the years immediately ahead in the 1920s as in terms of newspaper demographics since Seldes' death in 1970. Clearly, a problem that seems so contemporary to us had its genesis more than two full generations ago. Writing mainly with reference to New York City papers, Seldes lamented their "inevitable loss in variety." Just why the process seemed inevitable to him is not clear, but he bemoaned the prospect "for the journalist who still holds to the old-fashioned ideals of his profession." Seldes regretted the incessant consolidation and crass commercialism of New York's newspapers and expressed the hope that publishers would carry on, despite the regard for papers as "properties to be bought and sold," into a golden age when they would become institutions of integrity once again.[8]

It should come as no surprise that even the most prestigious journalists regarded theirs as a precarious profession. George Seldes, for instance, led an utterly fascinating, vital, and successful life. Nonetheless, he viewed journalism as ephemeral work, and more than once considered quitting in order to "attempt writing of more lasting value." Edmund Wilson customarily called himself a journalist (rather than a critic), and his working definition of what it was all about for him closes with the delicate balancing act that Wilson, Seldes, and so many others like them faced: how to write about the subjects of your choice and not merely manage to get paid, but actually support a family.

When I speak of myself as a journalist, I do not of course mean that I have always dealt with current events or that I have not put into my books something more than can be found in my articles; I mean that I have made my living mainly by writing in periodicals. There is a serious profession of journalism, and it involves its own special problems. To write what you are interested in writing and to succeed in getting editors to pay for it, is a feat that may require pretty close calculation and a good deal of ingenuity.[9]

Gilbert Seldes seems to have felt quite comfortable writing ephemeral pieces, such as "reports" on what had happened in the arts in New York City during the previous season. Unlike Wilson, he did not mind writing the kinds of journalistic essays, easily dated, that could not possibly be collected into book form. Nor did he find it difficult or degrading to adapt himself to the idiosyncratic format of particular magazines, such as the *Saturday Evening Post,* which became his principal meal ticket for more than four years. In 1965 he recalled how that relationship came about.

Seldes and his wife returned from Europe late in the summer of 1926 "without money and without prospects. . . . I had less than $20 when I got off the boat and my father met me and gave me $40." Seldes took the draft of something that he had written, "a negligible thing and out of my line," and showed it to his agent, Brandt and Brandt. Nannine Joseph there asked why he didn't submit something to the *Saturday Evening Post.* When Seldes answered that he didn't think they would be interested, "she reminded me that I had had a book published (The 7LA) in the past year or so and 'had a name.'" So he outlined an article on the European prophets of doom (such as Spengler), called it "The Cassandras of Europe," and the *Post* promptly commissioned it for publication. "With this," Seldes recalled, "began some five years during which the Post was my major source of income. I look back at some of the work I did with grave doubts; but the Post itself was irreproachable. I always submitted an outline of major articles. If the outline was approved, the Post never changed nor asked me to change a word of the text."[10]

Throughout the interwar years many other serious writers also felt grateful that the *Post*'s huge circulation (well over two million) enabled the magazine to pay extremely well and thereby subsidized more serious creative or critical efforts that might not otherwise enjoy broad appeal and bring big bucks. Stephen Vincent Benét told Archibald MacLeish that the *Post* would pay him $1,750 for a short story. That seemed wildly extravagant to Benét, "but it means that I can make a living and have a certain amount of time off for my own work. On the other hand, I am getting a little sick of New York and of having to interrupt the poem all the time to do other things." The work of an independent writer tended to be punctuated by a series of interruptions—however essential they may have been to keeping body and soul together.[11]

Looking back from the perspective of the mid-1960s, Seldes commented that "it was a good time for magazine writers, and I suppose, for book writers of all kinds. New houses were coming into existence and some of them were not conservative: Viking and Liveright and presently The Dial Press. As well as Knopf and presently Random. . . . These houses went after writers. I'd known Guy Holt and when he became editor of John Day Co. he wanted a book—and got The Stammering Century. There wasn't then any difficulty in getting published."[12]

In addition to the *Saturday Evening Post,* Seldes joined the staff of *The New Republic* in November 1925 as a contributing editor, an association that endured until June 1932. He became drama critic for the New York *Evening Graphic* in 1929, and for seven years starting in 1931 he had a daily column, "True to Type," in the New York *Evening Journal.* In 1927–28, while working on *The Stammering Century,* his social history of American evangelists, utopian seekers, and fanatical reformers, Seldes published quite a few trial balloons in magazines and had more professional impact than he could possibly have known at the time.[13]

Many years later, for example, J. C. Furnas, a widely read social historian of the United States, recalled going to New York during the later 1920s to look for a career as an independent critic and writer. He read Samuel Eliot Morison's *Oxford History of the United States* and saw that it was possible for a "learned, intelligent, and urbane scholar to make American history march and sing. I was hooked. Most unmethodically I began to widen that opening, learned hand over fist, and was helped by the examples of such as Gilbert Seldes and Gerald Johnson to see that responsible journalism could be good training for the non-academic handling of history."[14]

Seldes would surely have been gratified by the compliment, and most likely would have agreed, I believe, that he had always sought to be "responsible," knowing full well, at times, that doing so might mean trouble. Nevertheless, his own estimation of his work when it was all done—an appraisal he never published—rings true. It seems almost excessively modest yet largely accurate. Although written in 1964, it relates primarily to the work he did between 1924 and 1930. He begins by referring to his role in writing about the popular arts, but has in mind his work on American history as well:

This is an exercise in the use of my own critical faculties which, when applied to subjects I know something about, I consider very close to first rate. When I say I should have been of the second order in criticizing the fine arts, I mean that I haven't the bent, the steadiness, for study. . . . I am nothing of a scholar. I haven't ever, consciously, written to suggest that I knew much of an intricate subject when I hadn't studied it. But I've been content to be superficial. So that in this double way my sheer pleasure in the arts of entertainment and the chance I saw to communicate that pleasure as a critic, were happy for me. I got out of doing work in which I would have been pretentious and dissatisfied—and my field was left virtually unoccupied.[15]

Seldes had boundless admiration for Edmund Wilson's intellect, for his descriptive and explanatory abilities in relation to a work of art, and for his sensibility as a critic. Writing in 1928, however, Wilson himself had a rather negative view of criticism as a vocation in the United States. Although he had reference in the following extract primarily to literary critics, I feel confident that his remarks reflected his assessment of cultural criticism generally. After enumerating and evaluating the likes of H. L. Mencken, Van Wyck Brooks, Lewis Mumford, Joseph Wood Krutch, and others, Wilson concluded that, overall, "they do not communicate with one another; their opinions do not really circulate. It is astonishing to observe, in America, in spite of our floods of literary journalism, to what extent the literary atmosphere is a non-conductor of criticism."

When one considers the number of reviews [journals], the immense amount of literary journalism that is now being published in New York, one asks oneself how it is possible for our reviewing to remain so puerile. Works on history are commonly reviewed by historians, and books on physics by physicists; but when a new book of American poetry or a novel or other work of belles lettres appears, one gets the impression that it is simply given to almost any well-intentioned (and not even necessarily literate) person who happens to present himself; and this person then describes in a review his emotions upon reading the book. . . . A work of art is not a set of ideas or an exercise of technique, or even a combination of both. But I am strongly disposed to believe that our contemporary writing would benefit by a genuine literary criticism that should deal expertly with ideas and art, not merely tell us whether the reviewer "let out a whoop" for the book or threw it out the window. In a sense, it can probably be said that no such creature exists as a full-time literary critic—that is, a writer who is at once first-rate and nothing but a literary critic.[16]

During the later 1920s quite a few writers produced essays evaluating the condition of cultural history and criticism in the United States. The diversity of what they wrote would seem to confirm Wilson's lament about the lack of dialogue or even communication. The *dramatis personae* discussed seemed to remain pretty much the same, yet the judgments rendered turned out to be quite variable. Percy Holmes Boynton, for instance, provided an overview in 1927 that coincided in important ways with Seldes' views, though less stridently expressed. As for members of his own generation (1875–1946) who admired Old World culture excessively, Boynton courteously observed,

> Oddly they have never been concerned with the relation between European culture and European chaos, though they have been unremitting in their assault on the relation between American culture and American commercialism. The resulting controversy—since at last the day dawned of healthy controversy—has not been evenly balanced.

Fortunately and happily, to Boynton's mind, "a critical interest has been aroused in young America, and a critical objective has been defined." Despite agreement upon the objective, however, Boynton perceived fierce partisanship on such issues as quality, origins, and future prospects:

> No doubt the critics who are of the American world as well as in it are all concerned both with future possibilities and present conditions; but in point of emphasis they are markedly and sometimes violently in disagreement. They apply to themselves and to each other various tags and epithets which are more or less disingenuous; and, with certain rare and honorable exceptions, they incline in the heat of argument toward personalities which testify to nothing but the unpertinence of impertinence in debate. By and large they fall into two main groups: the critics who are chiefly occupied in showing how, from dubious beginnings, America has fallen into the lowest of low estates, and how the worst in American life and art is due to its culture and the best is a miraculous bloom from no known seed and with no perceivable promise; and the critics who are chiefly concerned with showing that there have been some virtues in the past and that there is some hope for the future provided the current corrupting tendencies can be checked and overcome.

It should be no surprise, then, that in 1931 T. S. Eliot noted the need for a leader to emerge on behalf of the newer generation of humanists, "and in these days of dog-eat-dog in the criticism of literature and life, that is no small promise [i.e., desideratum]."[17]

More explicitly than most observers of the cultural scene, Gorham B. Munson made a careful distinction between the cohort that had been young in 1916 ("our elder cousins") and those who came of age after 1920, such men as Kenneth Burke, Yvor Winters, Allen Tate, and Gilbert Seldes—"we younger critics." After being perversely unfair to Edmund Wilson, whom Munson curiously placed with "our elder cousins" because "there is something unpronounced about the quality of his work that lets it blur in with the main critical chorus," he proceeded to praise Seldes extravagantly, but quite correctly, I believe, categorized him as an independent:

> Of Gilbert Seldes I make an exception. The heavily serious and the pretentiously frivolous seem to join in being unjust to his gifts. He is light and agile, and the serious-minded therefore put him down as superficial. He is sharply intelligent, and this appears to alienate the mere "cleverists." Actually, he is a roving critic, brightly independent, very well informed, and expert in making discriminations in the arts of levity and diversion, so much less charted and therefore so much more risky to the critical taste than the serious arts. I would not say that he assimilates very well with the kind of thing that Mencken represents, but on the other hand he was never in the forefront of the contributors to *The Little Review.* An independent.[18]

More than most of his contemporaries—perhaps more than any— Seldes contemplated the impact of criticism upon the object of critical attention, and not merely upon the critic's audience. Consequently in a laudatory essay about Irving Berlin, Seldes offered an observation that might easily have been subjectively autobiographical: Berlin "has needed criticism not to make him do what others wanted him to do, but to reassure him that what he himself wanted to do was preeminently worth doing."[19]

Most of the creative writers and artists were quite sensitive to what critics wrote, and could be spurred on by praise or paralyzed by negative assessments. Hence the imaginative writers themselves commonly raised the morale of their comrades—partly as an act of friendship but mainly as a means to foster productivity. Thus F. Scott Fitzgerald told his Princeton friend, John Peale Bishop, in 1929 that "no one in our language possibly excepting Wilder has your talent for 'the world,' your culture and acuteness of social criticism as upheld by the story." But then there was always Hemingway, who not only gave the impression that he personally felt oblivious to criticism, but that the genus "critic" must necessarily be an inferior form of life. "For every writer produced in America," he pontificated in 1924, "there are produced eleven critics. . . . As I have always regarded critics as the eunuchs of literature . . . But there is no use finishing that sentence."[20]

II

Early in 1929 F. O. Matthiessen issued a call for a broad, more inclusive approach to the history of American culture. His emphasis upon the need for attention to communication and travel, the movies and cartoons, the Ford car and the radio revealed the reach of Seldes' influence. Matthiessen lamented that scholars and independent writers had obscured "the two interrelating factors essential to any real comprehension of our literature: the implications of American life, and the organic relation of our thought to that of Europe." Edmund Wilson would echo such sentiments a few months later in a private letter to Allen Tate in which he wondered whether the time had not arrived "for the intellectuals, etc. to identify themselves a little more with the general life of the country."[21]

What men like Matthiessen and Wilson seemed to be looking for in 1929 Seldes had actually been crusading for since 1927, soon after returning from his third visit to Europe in four years. He began with the observation that for almost a century the arts in America had been imitative, derivative from Europe. During the past generation, however (exact duration undefined), writers and painters had begun to work more independently of Europe, and since World War I composers had made "fresh discoveries on American soil." From there Seldes shifted to praise for American design, broadly conceived, especially in architecture, but also in automobiles and even in engines. "In a thousand ways," Seldes insisted, writing historically about the very recent past, "the life of America became sharply distinct from the life of any other country. A few artists saw it and got excited about it."[22]

A few months later he returned to this theme in another format. He began by decrying the destructiveness of those American intellectuals who demeaned their own culture. "Anyone who has followed the literature of attacks on America, particularly that portion of it composed by Americans, is aware of the wide universality of criticism: America is too materialistic and America is given to callow idealism." He then moved on to a more specific charge, namely, that Americans are peculiarly susceptible to frauds, quacks, bad taste, and poor judgment. Seldes proceeded to enumerate a catalogue of corruptions that had been carried to the United States from abroad, however, and closed with an ironic proof of wisdom or common sense emanating from native grounds. "Americans picked out of mesmerism," he noted, "the one element which has since proved fruitful—its work with the hypnotic trance; whereas Europe was particularly concerned with the other important element—cures by magnetism—which has proved utterly worthless."[23]

The perpetuation of foreign stereotypes about the United States enraged Seldes for several reasons. First of all, having read a lot of literature written by visitors, Seldes became convinced that outsiders are "so mercilessly prepared to see those things and no others" and then mindlessly replicated or reiterated the old travel books. Second, he stressed that a century of change had undermined the familiar, glib generalizations. Because western Europe was well established, an old civilization, it followed that "if the national character of France or of England was correctly reported a century ago, that report may still serve as a rough guide to France or England today." However, he continued,

> To the point of terrifying European observers, we are perpetually changing. . . . The fact that we are always changing is one of the few unchangeable things in our national make-up. And that is the tragedy of the foreign observer. He knows that we have changed, but his own report on us changes hardly at all.[24]

It is no coincidence that Seldes was writing *The Stammering Century* at the time, a social history that emphasized discontinuities, for example, between Jonathan Edwards and the post-Calvinist evangelicals of the early and mid-nineteenth century. His stress upon change helped to validate his growing enthusiasm for the necessity of historical knowledge and perspective. Ever since 1924 Seldes had tried to think in terms of a comprehensive history of culture in the United States, and it is undeniably true that his best-known books trace transformations that occurred in the popular arts, and subsequently in modes of communication and related technologies. Nonetheless, there remains an anomaly in Seldes' outlook because near the beginning of *The Stammering Century* he not only acknowledged but really insisted upon calling attention to "continuity in our mental habits." The unattractive faddists and kooky reformers of the 1910s and 1920s had their roots firmly planted in American culture and experimentalism during the nineteenth century.[25]

How are we to explain this apparent inconsistency? Not so easily; but it helps if we recognize that Seldes was temperamentally attracted to judicious, moderate positions. If he did not think well of European prophets of gloom and decay (like Spengler), he condemned even more strenuously extremist self-derision at home. He believed that a "great deal of the criticism of America by Americans is consciously or unconsciously inspired by European standards." It astonished and saddened Seldes that in the United States the "philosophical critics have exaggerated the country's weaknesses and the country has let them do it without bitterness."[26]

Even as Seldes had denounced the "literary klanners" in 1924 for their hyper-Americanism, he excoriated arch expatriates for caricaturing and denouncing the ill manners of American tourists abroad. The issue of boorishness, he believed, actually connected with the need for historical knowledge; and so Seldes accused others, such as Henry James, Henry Adams, and their hyper-sensitive heirs, of snobbish inconsistencies: "It is just as well to remember that Americans have always been accused of lacking a historical sense. Yet the people who make this accusation are also the ones who want Americans, when they come abroad, not to pay tribute to everything history has left visible."[27]

Throughout the later 1920s Seldes sustained his relentless attack upon the expatriates and their snide attitudes. The *Saturday Evening Post,* staunchly chauvinist, situated one such attack as its lead story on New Year's Day 1927. Expatriate Americans, Seldes insisted, "having failed to get on in America, revenge themselves by belittling everything American." To compound matters, he proclaimed "the one universal law of expatriatism—that Americans living abroad usually hate all other Americans living abroad." Expatriates were invariably maladjusted people who lacked "the capacity to make the best of their world." In contrast, Seldes had highly positive things to say about European expatriates in the United States—though the same rationale could certainly be applied to Americans in France from Josephine Baker to James Baldwin—namely, that such great artists as Gaston Lachaise, the French sculptor, come to the United States "not to make money but because they feel a sympathetic atmosphere."[28]

Seldes had never been sympathetic to the belief that only an outsider could achieve great genius, and he rejected the notion of some necessary nexus existing between the condition of expatriates and creativity in the arts. He therefore repudiated the long accepted notion that America's lack of a past, or insufficient "background," provided unfertile ground for authors and artists to sow their creative seeds. Instead he blamed the apparent lack of "background" on the "wilful neglect of ourselves which artists and critics have practiced." Whereas the French had not allowed themselves to forget Descartes, he commented, Americans had already eclipsed William James, their most distinguished philosopher. Americans, he lamented, had not "bothered to develop a national memory." The most successful writers in the United States, according to Seldes, did not actively seek an American past anyway, but seemed content instead to write about "objects in the immediate foreground."[29]

Seldes also prepared a closely related essay for *The New Republic,* prompted by a piece that Edmund Wilson published on Henry James two weeks earlier. (The brief lead time required by magazine journalism in those days could also be quite gratifying. One did not have to wait very long to see print, and that fact facilitated genuine public dialogues.) Seldes began by noting that Wilson had accepted one of Van Wyck Brooks' major and well-known premises, namely "that an artist gains by immersion in the experience of his own country, and loses, seriously, by exile."

> Mr. Brooks's description of the vicious circle is that America fails to encourage its artists, places obstacles in their paths, and nowhere offers them adequate nourishment (Mark Twain); and that when they leave America, to seek scenes more propitious, they become anaemic and irrelevant because they are breathing an alien air (Henry James). The significance of a critic is measured by the problems he puts to us, and Mr. Brooks's dilemma is of the first order.

Seldes then proceeded to examine Brooks' assumption, and started by citing an unidentified expatriate artist (in fact, his friend Picasso) who

> startled me once with the assertion that Lincoln and Jack Johnson owed their eminence to the fact that they were both racial outcasts. He insisted, in fact, that they were both Jews. But this fanciful beginning led to a serious thesis: that the great man, and especially the artist, *must* be an outsider in the country in which he works—alien by nationality, by religion, or by a spiritual hostility to his place and time.
>
> It is not necessary to accept this categorical must; but there are enough facts to make this position a good corrective to that of Mr. Brooks. At the present moment five men, each so eminent in his field as to be held great,

are working on alien soil: Picasso, Strawinsky, Joyce, Santayana, and Charlie Chaplin—Santayana having characteristically departed from two native
shores.[30]

After considering an array of particular cases, ranging from André
Gide to James Joyce, Seldes proceeded to raise a series of sensible issues:

> When we say that an artist ought to stay at home and write about his own
> people we are really begging a number of questions. What, for example, is
> the kind of saturation we want a novelist to have? Do we want him to
> know "facts" or motives? Who, in America, are his own people? And what
> kind of work are we unconsciously dictating to him? Novels of local color?
> Or the great American novel? Or a great novel which can be read in Russia
> as War and Peace is read here? What is it that the local air gives which is so
> precious: the material for the artist's work? or the sense of security, of
> belonging, of being wanted and doing something worth doing?[31]

Ultimately, however, Seldes seemed fairly empathetic to Picasso's argument for the necessity of expatriation, yet took an agnostic position—
let's wait and see—that concluded with an implicit affirmation of his
thesis in *The 7 Lively Arts:*

> If I were urging all potential novelists to go abroad, I might add that the
> early maturing of judgment, through comparison of civilizations, is invalu-
> able to the modern novelist who must so master (not flee from) his data as
> to be able to omit nearly all of it from his work and transmute the rest to
> his purpose as a writer of fiction. To some artists this fundamental brain-
> work is superfluous and some cannot bear the shock of violently contrast-
> ing impressions. But I feel that a Marin would paint his Maine as well after
> five years on the Riviera, and that Dreiser's sense of the disorderliness of
> American life would be more poignantly expressed if he had had any
> experience of the discipline and comeliness of the pre-war social structure
> in Europe.
>
> There are many other questions which these involve, and far too many
> indecisive examples: the Bret Hartes who perish abroad, and the Goethes
> who flourish at home, the Turgenievs and the Tolstois; and the medi-
> ocrities who never desert their doorsteps. We know, in fact, almost nothing
> of the "favorable environment" until an artist occurs and teaches us. We do
> not even know whether a "favorable" environment may not be the worst of
> all because of its lack of resistance to the artist's nature. As for America, we
> might observe it a little longer and if it still refuses to produce artists we
> can decide that the situation is really unpropitious, and wonder whether it

will not be wholly outside the line of the major arts that we will make our contribution to history.

Now that was written in May 1925. As we have seen, within the next few years Seldes became increasingly an American cultural chauvinist, an American exceptionalist, and an acerbic critic of the American expatriates. (If Spaniards wanted to be expatriates in Paris, that was fine. Seldes never challenged Picasso.) By 1933 Seldes articulated a position that he would adhere to for the rest of his life: "America has always been rather lucky in one respect: that few of its citizens have succumbed to the temptation, made famous by Gilbert and Sullivan, to belong to another nation, and of those few, hardly any were wanted by their native land. . . . It was one of the grand things about being an American twenty or thirty years ago that we knew all the time of hundreds of thousands of foreigners who wanted nothing so much in the world as to become one of us."[32]

III

Developing alongside that aspect of Seldes' criticism was his growing hostility toward the so-called debunkers, in general, but more particularly the kind of anti-American venom produced by H. L. Mencken, George Jean Nathan, and Sinclair Lewis throughout the 1920s. For the sake of chronological clarity (and etymological originality) it should be noted that as early as 1919 Robert Benchley, responding to a suggestion from the managing editor of *Collier's,* began a series of home-life pieces with himself as the "poor boob." In 1924 Seldes alluded to the "boobery (Mr. Mencken's nice name for us)" and clearly preferred to be identified with the boobery rather than with Mencken.[33] Even so, the very core of Seldes' counterthrust against Mencken occurred in the years 1927 to 1932, and especially 1927 to 1929 in the pages of the *Saturday Evening Post.*

Seldes launched his crusade with a few paragraphs in a salvo directed against the historical debunkers, to which we will return. He observed that philosophical critics in the United States had grossly exaggerated the country's shortcomings, and witless people had let them get away with it. Seldes then departed from his recent affirmations of American exceptionalism in order to assert that no society had a monopoly on mediocrity:

Each month Mr. Mencken brings in the American Mercury several pages of incredible clippings from the newspapers of the country, forming an apocalyptic vision of the dullness and stupidity of American life; in ten days' reading of one London newspaper I collected an equal assortment; and a week's news in the French provincial press will supply such a record of human fatuity, superstition, violence and ignorance—if you pick only the right items—as will make the reader think himself back in the Middle Ages. The sentimental beliefs on which the American is supposed to base his normal life are paralleled throughout the world.[34]

Almost four months later Seldes fired his heaviest ammunition and scored his most direct hits in an essay that he titled "The Boob Haters." Although it is not sharply focused and meanders, it fearlessly defends the American middle classes (*sic*) against attacks that had been launched for a long time by the idol of most American intellectuals and college students. Seldes' essential points are easily summarized. Who are the boob haters? he asks. With a few exceptions, unidentified, they are "only boobs with a superior vocabulary." Toward the end it emerges that the "only distinguishing mark of the man who is not a boob turns out to be that he is a boob hater."[35]

And the objects of their scorn? The "average stupid man . . . the mass known as the booboisie, which has changed our democratic form of government into a boobocracy." On their behalf, however, Seldes indulged in a bit of his own hyperbole, namely that the average middle-class American "fulfills the ancient Greek ideal of avoiding excess—in other words, that the boob is the perfectly balanced man." Moreover, Seldes subsequently declared, the claim that only the boobs "are subject to crowd emotions, the claim that the intelligent body of men are independent thinkers, will not hold." Exactly why is never specified, however, although Seldes (then writing a book about fads and fanatics in United States history) loved to point out that one or another particular fad "took in the educated, the sophisticated, the independent thinkers, before the boobs succumbed to it."[36]

The following summer Seldes devised a delightful spoof, an amazingly long and imaginative litany of what people like Mencken and the Algonquin crowd believed in (and about themselves). Super-Americans assumed that they were altogether free of superstition, that all courtesy is hypocritical, that no one ever does anything except for the worst motives, that intelligent people take no interest in politics, "that nothing essentially fine was ever popular" (a defense of Seldes' special turf), "that if you join a lodge you are a herd man; but if you join a literary group and lunch with the same people every day you are a man of force and originality," and that no great novel could possibly be written in America because "the background is thin, because American social life is not based on class distinctions, and because Americans look down on the arts." In sum, Mencken, Nathan and the super-cynics were arrogant snobs.[37]

For more than half a dozen years Seldes returned to variations on these themes, always taking the side of cultural democracy, diversity, and pricking the pretentions of a self-annointed intellectual elite. Seldes' report on the American scene for Eliot's *Criterion* in 1926 declared, "The *Mercury* remains anti-democratic in a large slapdash way . . . is generally well-informed, and not always significant. Its relation to the arts is too much by way of criticism; the editor is not a lover of poetry and has made few discoveries in fiction." By implication, Seldes and his associates had done better at *The Dial*. Seldes made it a principal theme of *The Stammering Century* that quackeries and fads were first accepted in the United States by "superior people, by men and women of education, intelligence, breeding, wealth, and experience. Only after the upper classes had approved," he insisted, "the masses accepted each new thing." Unfortunately, Seldes could surrender to overstatement almost as easily as Mencken: "the more gifted, the more intelligent, the more experienced classes were the first to accept an absurdity and the last to give it up."[38]

In 1932, writing his daily column for a downscale newspaper owned by the Hearst publishing empire, Seldes returned to the fray with a droll satire directed at a composite critic who mocked the country where "he had made a small fortune":

> "America," said Sinclair Mencken, talking to himself or to Mencken Sinclair, it doesn't matter which, "America, pfui! Could I write a book." "You have written a book," murmured an innocent bystander, but the author thought he was alluding to Arrowsmith, so he made no answer, and went on with the calm good temper and fairness which had always marked his criticisms of the country in which he had made a small fortune and for razzing which he had been proclaimed one of the world's immortals. "A country lacking in taste—that's fundamental. Because a country which had a tradition, a sense of decency, could never vulgarize its heroes as America does."

From there Seldes launched into an explanation of why the American celebration of the bicentennial of George Washington's birth was more felicitously done than Germany's commemoration of the hundredth anniversary of Goethe's death. Less than four months later, writing from Sweden where he toured extensively, Seldes insisted that American intellectuals—he scornfully called them the civilized minority—were in fact easily gulled by phony art and ephemeral trendiness. "I came seriously to doubt," he scoffed, "whether the readers and writers of the *American Mercury* were essentially more intelligent than the people they despised; and nothing has happened to persuade me that they are. They are quicker to snap at a new kind of boob-bait; and that is all."[39]

At least once a decade for the rest of his days Seldes revived the old animus. He conflated Mencken and Nathan into a singular critical persona. (George Jean Nathan used to refer to the editors of *The American Mercury* as "Menk and I," which then became in common parlance "Menkneye.") "For a considerable time I made a living by reacting against Menkneye," Seldes informed readers of *Esquire,* "because neither of them could stomach ordinary American conservatism, they left a nice spot open for someone who also disliked loose American radical thought, but found the answer to it in such purely American phenomena as the Populist party." In the 1950s he acknowledged the general consensus that Mencken was "in the 'twenties the most readable of critics, [but] there is some doubt whether his judgments were notably sound . . . and there is an element of surprise at the discovery that Mencken was never a good democrat." In 1968 he recalled for Edmund Wilson getting the sense, many years before, that Mencken must have been

a bit of a fake—he was jeering at his booboisie as if they were still in the depths of the Victorian era. And I pointed to the date—The Great Divide and The House of Mirth occurred in the decade before Menck even got started . . . they were both shocking to Puritan morality and they were both successful.[40]

Beyond Mencken, Nathan, and the intellectual snobs, Seldes also railed against those iconoclasts who rewrote American biography to demonstrate that men enshrined in the pantheon really had feet of clay (or bad morals, or bad teeth), that the Puritans bore responsibility for American self-repression, and that the Founding Fathers were self-interested cads rather than disinterested public servants. Seldes alluded to the debunkers glancingly in 1927, and perhaps minimized their vogue. "Obstinately the American has refused to be upset. He has bought the books and magazines, has read the horrible revelations, and remained almost wholly unaffected by them. Somewhere or other there is a defect in the logic of the debunkers."[41]

By the autumn of 1928, however, he realized that he had underestimated their pernicious influence. With *The Stammering Century* recently published, Seldes now had a credential in the field of American history and provided the New York *Herald Tribune* Sunday magazine with a two-part series called "Debunking the Debunkers." Declaring that they had little genuine respect for history, Seldes attacked the superficiality of self-styled experts. In his fifteen years of contact with the debunkers, he remarked, he had met exactly two men who had really studied relativity, possibly six who had read Darwin, four with any genuine knowledge of American history, and so forth. Attacks on the quality of small-town life were cheap shots, according to Seldes (who had fled from the small town of his childhood and lived in large cities ever after), and criticism of business was unfair because "the debunkers have almost invariably applied European standards of culture to an American product." It would be more sensible, he argued, to apply American standards to the American businessman, "to treat him as an end in himself, and not as a thwarted European." A constructive critique of business would not begin with its faults "(which are largely hangovers from the past) nor with its pretentions (which merely indicate a natural uneasiness in unfamiliar circumstances) but with the positive good already indicated." In 1932, the two hundredth anniversary of George Washington's birth, Seldes proclaimed the debunkers to be failures: "we have been bored by the people who think the destruction of myths will destroy the real things which the myths represent."[42]

Seldes and the debunkers, especially Mencken, managed to agree on only one issue: that Prohibition was stupid in principle and that federal regulation of alcohol consumption was a violation of personal liberty. After publishing a lively essay about a "strange new type," the wet who dries up in rebellion against the social tyranny that makes drinking compulsory, Seldes brought out a lively little book titled *The Future of Drinking,* accompanied by droll drawings by Don Herold. With chapters called "The Romance of the Speakeasy," "The Art of Drinking," and "The Religion of Drinking," it took a typical Seldes stance: opposed to extremes or excess. As a reviewer for *The Outlook* magazine observed, "certainly those of us who find drunkenness as revolting and vulgar as we find prohibition unintelligent and blind ought to be pleased with the book." A reviewer for the *New York Times,* H. I. Brock, described Seldes as using provocative levity and having a "sprightly Alexandrine fling. It is a manner much in vogue with our intelligentsia which is often as effective as it is annoying. In Mr. Seldes's cases it is both."[43]

I doubt whether it pleased Seldes to be lumped with Mencken and his disciples, or with the wits of the Algonquin circle. The fact remains that he, too, could be a stylish writer, especially when he engaged in satire. Writing under the pseudonym of Lucien Bluphocks in 1925, he spun an engagingly witty satire to show that neither the putative "man in the street" nor the "woman in Des Moines" really existed. In 1927 he even devoted an essay to the absence of satire as a pure literary form in the United States. (He designated Will Rogers a political humorist "upon whom satire has been thrust.") His reviews of films that he did not like could be wickedly satirical.[44]

IV

In one of his critical essays aimed at the debunkers, Seldes commented upon a development of the recent past that seemed exceedingly salutary to him: "We looked within and discovered a great many things; but perhaps the greatest discovery of all was that we had a past. It had been so insistently drummed into us that we were a new country that the idea of having a past, good or bad, was a novelty." During the winter of 1926–27, following his return from Europe, Seldes himself became part of that phenomenon. His motives had as much to do with personal liberty as with any professional or nationalistic challenge. Having transcended his own utopian origins, he wanted to explain the historical roots of American cults and fanaticisms; and he wanted to clarify the differences between Russian and American communism. "The communism of the American past was pacific and idealistic; the communism of the international present is fierce, direct and realistic." In his first journalistic piece anticipating the big book, Seldes remarked that utopian leaders in the nineteenth century had been prophets without honor and remained so "in the verdict of time. In America, at least, time has given its approval to very few leaders who swam always against the stream, and it is an extraordinary fact that of these few the great majority have been women."[45]

As the project developed Seldes kept *The Dial* and Edmund Wilson, then an editor at *The New Republic,* abreast of his progress. He offered to review books related to his subject, especially the "individuals whom one might call Apostles, Prophets, or Leaders, true or false; cranks, faddists, leaders of cults." By the summer's end in 1927 he had completed a draft at Amanda's family camp on Saranac Lake. By August 1928, when *The Stammering Century* appeared, Seldes hoped that Wilson would have it reviewed in *The New Republic* by Charles Beard, an historian for whom he felt great admiration.[46] Beard did not, but Robert Morss Lovett, a non-professional historian like Seldes, praised it, as did Constance Rourke in the New York *Herald Tribune*. "The virtue of the book," Rourke wrote, "is that it temperately describes strange people and bizarre movements with an acute discernment as to human character and a stimulating range of observation."[47]

Most other reviews were equally positive, in newspapers as well as journals of opinion. Seldes must have been especially gratified by the approval of James Truslow Adams, the most prominent non-academic historian in the United States at that time; by Merle Curti's admission that "scholars have largely neglected this stream of thought, and they should be grateful that so talented and clever a journalist as Mr. Seldes has turned their eyes to these fascinating if minor eddies"; and by Woodbridge Riley's comparison with the *American Mercury*'s level of discourse: "Unlike Mencken he does not content himself with counting the boils on the body politic, but goes below the symptoms to the causes."[48]

Seldes, always aware of his Jewish origins, may have been bemused by "A.N.W." (Alfred North Whitehead?) who observed in *The Outlook* that "in contrast to all these vagaries [cults, fads, sectarian fanaticism, etc.] one prizes his essential intelligence and sanity. In contrast with their false optimism one welcomes the Christian realism in contemplating the world. . . ." Only two reviewers struck sour notes. Writing for *The Nation*, Herbert Solow was simply unfair in saying that "the thinking is inconsequential, the writing is generally dull, and the puns are simply horrendous." But a prominent full-page assessment in the *New York Times* stands out both because it was atypically critical and because it raised, at an unexpected time, the issue of American exceptionalism that would not be widely or thoughtfully contested until the 1980s:

The fact is, however, that these things are neither characteristically American nor characteristically of the nineteenth century. Mr. Seldes, or anyone else, can write the same history and draw the same conclusions by taking not America in the nineteenth century, but England in the seventeenth century, Germany in the sixteenth, France in the eighteenth or Rome in any of several centuries. People behaved in all those times and places exactly as they did on the American prairies; and Mr. Seldes's history shows nothing whatever about the American mind, as distinguished from the universal mind.

Even so, the reviewer conceded that "it is a good history. If one divests himself . . . of Mr. Seldes's assumption that he is probing into some peculiarly American neurosis, he will find plenty in it to excite his interest and stimulate his reflective powers."[49]

In 1964, when Collier Books issued a paperback edition of this highly readable volume, with a new preface prepared by Arthur M. Schlesinger, Jr., Seldes told his good friend that the book had originally been "badly received . . . . I can't remember an enthusiastic notice." What a strange lapse of memory considering that positive reviews outnumbered negative ones by about four or five to one. A few months earlier Seldes told Schlesinger that he had tried to connect the eccentrics of nineteenth-century America with what he took to be the "eccentrics of our time."[50]

That whiggish emphasis upon continuity between then and "now" is somewhat problematic in several respects. First, because the author's presentist concerns about Tennessee legislators (in the Scopes evolutionism trial) and "the sour figure of the modern Prohibitionist" created some forced connections. Seldes saw the roots of the "prohibitory-reformer" of the 1920s in the "radical reformer" of the 1840s. Whereas national Prohibition was supposed to be enforced by "embittered bureaucrats," however, the persistent nineteenth-century temperance movement was guided by individuals and voluntary associations at the grass roots. Important differences and changes got blurred because of Seldes' commitment to a model of continuity.[51]

To complicate matters, Seldes began with a chapter devoted to Jonathan Edwards as an evangelical revivalist. He acknowledged that Edwards' theology was elitist and reactionary—the crucifixion only made salvation possible for *some* saints, a predestined elect—and consequently it was utterly *dis*continuous with the inclusive evangelism of Finney, Moody, and other prominent proselytizers later. In their view, *anyone* could come forward and make a decision for Christ. Edwards' highly constrained notions concerning freedom of the will were totally jettisoned by his nineteenth-century successors. For this and many other reasons, it made no sense for Seldes to say that "if we want to understand the peculiar complex of activities which made the next hundred years so notably and so absurdly a century of reforms, we must begin with the solitary eminence of Edwards' spirit." Seldes very nearly held Edwards' theology culpable for subsequent fanaticisms in the same way that some ideologues later blamed Nietzsche for Naziism. It's just too reductive.[52]

In this volume, as in his occasional essays throughout the 1920s, Seldes eschewed the use of psychoanalytic theory as an explanatory tool.[53] "The belief in psychoanalysis," he wrote, "marks the intellectual cultish mind of to-day." Yet having said so, here and there he did use raw slices of psychoanalytic theory rather casually and unsystematically, most often at the expense of fanatics, radicals, and do-gooders ("cranks") whose sanctimonious self-assurance irritated Seldes.[54]

His explicit mistrust of single-minded reformers, his detestation of "fanatical radicals," and his concluding assessment that "the history of radicalism suggests only that to live sanely one must avoid cults," prompt one to ask, once again, to what extent was Seldes basically an apolitical person? In 1956, after Arthur Schlesinger, Jr., had read *The Public Arts,* he sent the author an effusive congratulatory note, but added, "I only wish you had included some analysis of the relationship between the public arts . . . and politics." That wistful query might well have been applied to much that Seldes wrote.[55]

He considered himself a liberal, and from time to time attempted to define and explain what that meant—in general rather than personally. Precisely because liberalism was in transition during the 1920s, some of his essays may very well have been efforts at self-knowledge and self-definition. In 1924 he acknowledged the transition but in such a detached manner that he almost seemed to be above it all. "In America there has been a change of a somewhat peculiar order," he observed, "one involving a change even in the meanings of the labels we apply to different groups in politics." Because "reformers" in the 1920s seemed to be people who did not mind impinging upon the liberties of others, Seldes commented that the customary connection between liberal and reformer had been severed. The dominant mood in public life seemed to be indifference.[56]

In 1928 and '29 he returned to the issue, though in a half-hearted way. What do liberals want? The greatest possible freedom for the individual and the least possible restraint upon his activities. Liberals would limit the police power of the State and keep the statute books clean of all laws that interfered with private habits. Liberals favored equal opportunity (and, sometimes, even the more equitable distribution of wealth), competition, small farms, and handiwork. Liberals mistrusted courts and kings, standardization rather than diversity, trusts and other large economic combinations. By 1930 Seldes' essays on this subject had become opaque and meandering. It was not coincidental that the concept itself required significant reformulation in public discourse. Not being a political philosopher, or even a particularly political man, Seldes was not the one to undertake such a project.[57]

When we peer ahead into the 1930s and '40s, we find (with some key exceptions) even less concern in Seldes' work with connections between culture and politics and no anticipation whatever of the "keywords" that Lionel Trilling would use in contemplating liberalism during the 1940s: moral realism and moral imagination. Writing a reprise of the 1937 season on stage and in film, however, Seldes warned that "so long as dramatists think of liberalism as something to talk about, and not as a principle of action (which it is)," their plays on the subject will be merely loquacious and their plots will not sustain the theme. By the time he reached maturity, as Seldes himself phrased it in 1965, he preferred a "flexible ordered society." Not rigidly ordered, but not flexible to the point of chaos either. He was a moderate liberal and a patriot, as we shall see.[58]

Seldes wrote an intriguing, candid postscript that is pertinent to his apolitical persona during the 1920s. Working on his memoirs in 1968 he recalled that he only learned about the notorious Sacco-Vanzetti case from a Frenchman in Paris in 1926! Rather belated, by his own admission. He admired the outraged protest made by Felix Frankfurter and others in 1927 and after. Nevertheless, he continued in a dictated statement,

> nothing in public affairs has caused me so much regret as my failure to join them. I can make many excuses—the only one that seems even faintly valid to myself is that I wasn't, by nature, a joiner of movements. Particularly after the appointment of the committee headed by Abbott Lawrence Lowell, I should have joined the protest. I think I am right in saying that the thought of protesting never occurred to me and I also think it right to say that my chief source of income was *The Saturday Evening Post*. (The others were *The Dial* and *The New Republic*.) I can't be sure of my political state of mind at the time. It was probably a mixture of my version of philosophical anarchism and indifference; groups with which my father was associated had been mentioned by the unspeakable Lusk committee— on the other hand the reports from the Bolshevist ("and it works") were now become critical. I was then writing *The Stammering Century* which plunged me into American history without plunging me even into Populism; and I was (for an anarchist) leading a remarkably bourgeois existence:

I was happily married, I had a son, and we spent the summer of 1927 on an island in the Saranac River, where my wife and her sister and brothers had spent their childhood and the guide who taught me to use an outboard motor had taught them to swim and to paddle a canoe. In a sense, this absorption into a life I had never anticipated and the prosperity I enjoyed, could make me indifferent to public causes. But the Sacco-Vanzetti case was a special one and it still seems to me that I had committed the sin of withdrawal.[59]

Strange as it may be, that withdrawal haunted Seldes throughout his life. In 1939, when called upon to write the usual autobiographical statement for his twenty-fifth Harvard College class report, he did something highly unusual, especially for Seldes, because it was radical and political. He made a proposal to his classmates that went un-heard—in fact, it was flat out ignored. That so rankled Seldes that he recapitulated the episode in his fiftieth anniversary report many years later:

I proposed to my classmates that we establish a scholarship or an award or a prize for the best essay written by an undergraduate on the theme of the relation between the process of justice and the contemporary socio-economic situation. It seemed to me a reasonable subject. Were men (or women) hanged in year X who might have been merely fined a hundred years later because what they said or did was less dangerous to society as a whole? Having myself been the beneficiary of various grants from Harvard, I wanted to add another. Also, knowing what happens to fixed awards, I suggested that the principal sum should revert to the general scholarship fund after five or ten years.

One classmate responded—exactly one—and he wrote, truthfully or not, that he had been in jail. Robert Benchley (of another year) was enthusiastic and he told me, his friend John P. Marquand, was interested.

Other things intervened—none of them as significant. I didn't push the matter because a number of other things I wanted to do came up and were easier to accomplish. The name of the award, scholarship, or prize was the *Sacco-Vanzetti* (award, etc.).

I am, in 1963, profoundly ashamed of my failure. I envy those who, years before the execution of these men, tried to save them. I probably contrib-uted money to their defense. At the critical time, I was busy with earning a living and other secondary interests. I could have done more. And when nothing could be done except expiate the sin of not having done what had to be done—even then, I let the matter drop.

Almost everyone who made the final decisions that sent Sacco and Vanzetti to death was a Harvard man. Few of them—if that is a consolation—from the Class of 1914.[60]

It seems mete, perhaps, that a man who found out about the Sacco-Vanzetti case belatedly, but highlighted the value of historical knowledge in 1927–28, eventually saw the case in historical perspective and even engaged in polemics with those who defended the integrity of Judge Thayer, President Lowell, and the criminal justice system in Massachusetts. In 1927, while working on *The Stammering Century,* Seldes recognized that what it meant to be a "radical" changed over time, that radicalism is a protean concept that must be understood in historical context. Eighteen months later he declared in somewhat disillusioned but realistic phrasing that "our conception of the history of America . . . remains at the eighth-grade level. . . . The reality of American history, it happens, is profoundly interesting. . . . A record of tremendous achievement and failure, of glorious things done and things a patriot would wish undone."[61]

In a 1932 column harshly critical of the publishing industry in the United States, Seldes said that its only achievement in the past decade had been "the publication of important works of history, biography and science . . . ." Four years later he made manifest his belief that history was a powerful determinant of what could and could not, what would and would not happen in the future for the United States. Although he did not write a great deal about history thereafter, he never lost sight of the lessons he learned between 1927 and 1936 concerning the importance of history.[62]

V

Because he became a regular contributor to the *Saturday Evening Post* after 1926, and because he held the editor, George Horace Lorimer, in high esteem, we need to know more about Seldes' relationship to the *Post,* particularly the sorts of topics that he chose and that Lorimer wanted. The *Post* did enjoy, after all, the largest circulation of any magazine in the world, nearly three million by 1929. With an article each month for almost four years, and intermittent ones thereafter until 1937, Seldes soon became a notable name, at least in middle- and upper-income homes. Not a name like Babe Ruth or Rudolph Valentino, to be sure, but a widely read, well-known name nonetheless.

In a memoir of his association with the *Post* that Seldes composed in 1965, he recalled no constraints—only an astonishingly generous amount of freedom, in the realm of both substance and style. Although what Seldes wrote "was not always in accord with its editorial policy," Lorimer never pressured him and, in retrospect, Seldes admired Lorimer's shrewd judgment in rejecting a novel that Seldes submitted for consideration as a serial. Lorimer knew immediately that it was mediocre; the author took a little longer to reach the same conclusion.[63]

Because we know that Seldes' memory was quite fallible during the 1960s—too often at odds with documents that he wrote in the 1920s and '30s—we are entitled to second guess some aspects of his sanguine recollection. Surely he submitted himself to a house style in certain respects. Many of his pieces begin with such a long and airy amount of throat-clearing that we often cannot guess what the intended subject is going to be. It must not be merely fortuitous that there is such a clear pattern, and that one finds it in the essays of other writers as well. It seems to have been a stylistic tic of the *Post* that leisurely beginnings—indeed, meanderings—were not merely acceptable but desirable. And then there is the matter of titles. I cannot imagine that Seldes, or anyone else, perhaps, was permitted to select the titles for his own pieces. They invariably tended to be fey, frothy, and usually meaningless. Rarely did they give more than a clue to the actual contents of the essay. Titles were catchy and cute, kind of a tease to pique the reader's interest.[64]

In his memoir of the interwar years Seldes also recalled an important turning point, accurate in every respect except the last sentence because his work continued to appear in the *Post,* at irregular intervals, until 1937. The story is useful because it conveys some sense of what it must have been like to work in such a precarious profession, and because it suggests the enormous impact that the Great Depression had on popular as well as literary publishing in general.

> In midsummer 1929 I wrote a parody of Mencken's American Credo—some fifty clichés of the MencknI gang. The SEP took it—paid me at the highest rate I'd reached which was, I think, $850. A few weeks later the crash came in Wall Street—the Post had five or six articles of mine "in the vault." The size of the magazine diminished (it seemed) over night. I think I never sold them anything else.[65]

What, then, did Seldes write about during the later 1920s when his subject wasn't debunking the debunkers, or potential chapters for *The Stammering Century,* or Americans who felt they could find their creative souls only if they went abroad? The answer to that is cultural criticism, but almost exclusively involving the lively arts, his personal métier (and daemonic drive) ever since 1923. In one way or another, many of the pieces that Seldes now wrote were really codas to *The 7 Lively Arts.* In 1927, for example, he noted with satisfaction the growing enthusiasm for jazz, for not only reading but collecting comic strips (as future works of art), and the belief by some critics and producers that the future of American drama lay in careful attention to the entertainment techniques of burlesque and vaudeville. He concluded that a transformation had started to occur in the position of the popular arts in the United States: "They have begun to be appreciated by the critical minority, to be taken with some degree of serious consideration."[66]

Seldes also devoted numerous columns in *The New Republic* to such subjects, heaping "exhubilant" praise on comedians like Jimmy Durante and a comic strip artist named Tad who, in addition to being a superb draftsman, provided strips that were candid and often "poetic." On occasion Seldes had upbeat things to say about the new musical revues by Florenz Ziegfeld and Earl Carroll, especially when they featured such performers as Durante and Ruby Keeler.[67]

By the end of 1929, however, Seldes seemed increasingly disenchanted with New York's musical productions. There is no indication that his overall mood had been darkened (yet) by the economic crash. Rather, Hollywood and the Metropolitan Opera appeared to converge in having adverse effects upon composers, writers, and directors. He felt that live entertainment in the United States was being threatened, perhaps paradoxically, on two fronts: "by a lack of sophistication in the big musicals and by a violent effort to be smart in the smaller ones." He also disapproved of a new kind of sentimental song becoming common in musical shows, songs that pandered to the taste level of the "lower classes." He felt that the emotions invoked were too strong for the medium to sustain, and concluded that "only the very greatest works of art are, therefore, entitled to use the more serious of our emotions." A small-scale revival of burlesque in 1931–32 prompted Seldes to complain that the quality of music, comedy, and dance was generally poor. By way of compensation, however, these ribald rivals of vaudeville at least helped to sustain such old line comic stereotypes as the stage Jew and Irish Mick, or the grafting policeman. Seldes felt a certain sentimental affection for these caricatures. In general, however, Seldes' critical stance toward the lively arts was more detached by 1930–32 than it had been in 1923–24.[68]

During the later 1920s Seldes also turned increasing attention to two topics, seemingly unrelated, that he managed to connect: why did Americans in general feel defensive about their inadequate knowledge of art, and how could the American businessman become more hospitable toward art? Here we have, obviously, a variation on his anti-Mencken defense of the New World philistine. Seldes declared that, historically considered, art had not been appreciated by ordinary folks in the United States because it "was offered to the American man as something dead," accompanied by excessive mystery and mummery. The businessman felt so little sympathy for artists because ever since the early nineteenth century the artist had isolated himself and stopped saying anything of interest to the businessman. "For about a century," Seldes declared, "art has had, for the successful man, a faint odor of the sick room."[69]

Seldes ascribed much of the credit for changing all this to the emergence of the "new woman," a person who happily "went in for sport instead of maladies, and for business, who was self-reliant and created a life of her own . . . whether she remained at home or went to an office." When art ceased to be regarded as the special domain of neurasthenic women, it achieved liberation. "As art drew closer to life," Seldes concluded, "the man of affairs drew closer to art." Lithographs of prize fighters and steel mills somehow made fine art an acceptable object of interest for businessmen. Although it might have been less trendy to say so, Seldes could have given just as much credit to the new breed of public relations man as to the new woman.[70]

Barely a month before the Great Crash in 1929, Seldes brought out a piece in the *Post* that took the following question as its point of departure: "Whether the fiction writer has ever delivered a faithful account of the businessman or has, instead, rigged up a lifelike dummy. My suspicion is that the American novelist has for a long time been shadow boxing—mistaking his own shadow for the business-man bogeyman." Seldes suspected that most novelists really knew very little about the actual habits and character of the businessman as a social type. "His intelligence and his breeding and his morality are all debunked, and he is shown as the enemy of decency, the destroyer of beauty, the man who reduces all lovely things to the terms of money."[71]

It is not all that clear what prompted this passing apologia for the American businessman, but I suspect that it owed a great deal to Seldes' impulse to go against the grain of whatever was currently trendy among the intelligentsia. If the debunkers and Sinclair Lewis said black, Seldes was bound to say white. They provoked him to stake out an alternative position. One suspects, too, that George Horace Lorimer and readers of the *Post* heartily approved of Seldes' reverse snobbery.

The same impulse also prompted him to attack the new moralistic tyranny that he called the "cult of health" in the United States. Outspoken Americans felt compelled to eat only what was good for them. Perhaps his memories of dining well in France remained vivid. "Without a tradition of the pleasures of the table, America fell easily under the domination of the new dietitians—the slenderizers."[72]

At a time when more and more cultural critics were beginning to concern themselves with negative aspects of a "machine civilization"— Ralph Borsodi, Horace Kallen, Lewis Mumford, and Charles Sheeler come to mind—Seldes' response to this issue was notably judicious and much less engaged than usual in taking a distinctive position against the grain. In a serious essay prepared for the *Post,* which really preferred light and semi-whimsical pieces, Seldes weighed the pros and cons of new technology and applied science. He believed that "the machine" would give Americans more leisure time and stimulate more varied interests. Thinking democratically, moreover, these benefits need not be limited to a select few. Ultimately, he argued, "the machine can give freedom, and if it seems for the moment to contract the limits of our lives, it is still the only force which can cure its own abuses."[73]

For someone whose lifestyle had become increasingly urban, and whose chosen specialty virtually required the vivacity of New York's richly varied nightlife (from theatre to musicals to jazz clubs, and so forth), Seldes' essays on the subject of provincialism and the supposed virtues of urban life are somewhat surprising yet consistently interesting. In 1925 he pleaded for the preservation of geo-cultural diversity in the United States. "What people want [and need] in their home town is a cultivated grace," he warned, and so he detested those who abandoned "that which is native and characteristic" in order to imitate New York. Why this disturbing excess of imitation? "The reason is that everybody is afraid of being provincial—the deep-rooted affection for places is being overcome by an eager desire to be sophisticated and New Yorkish."[74]

By 1930, however, returning to the same subject, Seldes suggested that the comforts of city life had declined while the quality of country life had improved. Whereas he saw a "morbid terror of loneliness" in urban America, "the man in the hinterland is enjoying himself not only as much as, but sometimes at the expense of, his city brother." More partic-

Fig. 11. Strawberry Hill, the Seldes country home in Croton Falls, New York (1939).

ularly, entertainment was being adapted to the tastes of those who did not dwell in big cities.[75] This was not a characteristic contrast for Seldes to make, and his adult experience of rural or small-town America was surely minimal in 1930. Yet he clearly felt an increasing need to escape the intense pace of big-city life. In the later 1930s he bought a grey stone home in Croton Falls (near Brewster) to which he liked to escape on weekends and for longer stretches when he could. He called it Strawberry Hill (Fig. 11).[76]

By the close of the decade Seldes had become such a versatile journalist that he could knock out "colyums" on anything and everything— ranging from why people change their names (mocking the socially pretentious), to an appreciation of the recently deceased Serge Diaghileff along with speculation about the future of the Russian ballet, to an essay on the Dutch tulip craze (as an investment opportunity) during the 1630s—even though most of these diluted his distinctive role not merely as a cultural critic but as *the* authority on popular culture in America. The common denominator of such miscellaneous pieces, however, and perhaps a genuine justification for doing them, was their descriptive qualities. Seldes told a story well, especially the exotic social or cultural bagatelle.[77]

VI

Precisely because he *could* tell a story well, Seldes' brief career as a semi-successful novelist needs to be noted and perhaps explained. By 1927 he had become sufficiently intrigued by murder mysteries and detective stories to write an omnibus review of the latest crop for *The Bookman*. In the process he produced a small theory concerning the genre: "The detective story does not need body," he declared; "it is a geometrical arrangement, a point extended until it is a line, a line extended until it is a square, and so on. Its single obligation is to be interesting, and it ought, ideally, to appeal to a single faculty, the logical one, through the single instinct of curiosity."[78]

By the time that essay appeared Seldes had, in fact, recently published his first murder mystery under the pseudonym Foster Johns. It sparked sufficient speculation about the author's true identity—with several fingers pointing to Seldes—that his little discourse on the genre even paused to deny that he had, in fact, written *The Victory Murders*. The publisher's announcement, clearly written by Seldes, revealed that "as a child he won $20 for an essay on municipal government, a subject in which he was, and still is, profoundly uninterested." The so-called child was Seldes as a senior at Central High School; but few if any of his professional peers knew that.[79]

Drawing upon his experience as a journalist in World War I, Seldes created an engaging and plausible story that utilized his cosmopolitanism effectively: his knowledge of British and French personalities, of Paris and London, of air raids in England and at the French front. The character of Robert Lee, who works for a New York paper, is at least partially Seldes, and there is also Mr. Bonte of the Philadelphia *Public Ledger*. November 11, Armistice Day in 1918 and 1919, becomes a day of death, destiny, and mystery. There are numerous suspects and surprises, but the eventually revealed murderer turns out to be a Spaniard mad as

Don Quixote "but turned to evil instead of to good." And he doesn't kill for money, but to revenge thwarted love.[80]

It is quite a good novel and received effusive praise in the *New York Times* and in the *World*. Robert Benchley, who most likely saw through the secret, noted the "unobtrusive evidence that the author knows his Paris, his music halls, his business, and his ABC's." Only Dashiell Hammett, not yet famous for *The Maltese Falcon* (1930), struck a sour note: "All its gadgets—including the quick-acting poison of which you may have heard previous mention—are second-hand, and as the story progresses it becomes unnecessarily complicated and not altogether plausible. Nevertheless it is far above the average prevalent in its field—an entertaining history of the deaths of charming ladies, of intrigue, deceit, and blithe violence in Marseilles, London, Paris, and New York with a villain whose guilt is adequately concealed."[81]

The Square Emerald also drew upon geography and prototypes familiar to Seldes. Most of the action takes place in lower Manhattan; there is considerable specificity about the financial district; the murder victim is a financier embroiled with a mistress; and the denouement takes place near Saranac Lake in the Adirondacks, where Seldes' in-laws, the Hall family, owned an extensive camp. The novel anticipates several characteristics that would become standard fare during the 1930s: a criminal gang whose behavior seems bizarre because the reader doesn't have sufficient information, and conflicts between a private detective and the police. The *Herald Tribune*'s reviewer liked it well enough, but the Boston *Transcript* gave a fair summation: "In spite of a confused method of narration this is a good detective story of the conventional and uninspired type. It starts off slowly, but gathers momentum as it goes on until it reaches an unexpectedly exciting climax. It is written well and contains some excellent though stereotyped characterization."[82]

The following year, 1929, Seldes shifted from murder mysteries to fiction based upon his knowledge of unsuccessful utopian experiments, mainly his father's, of course. In June and July the *Saturday Evening Post* serialized Seldes' "Back from Utopia" in four installments. A semifictional accompaniment to *The Stammering Century,* it concerns a young man "looking for a way out of radicalism" who goes far enough to complete in a foreign country the process that he began at home—"the Americanization of an American." Eventually the young man wishes to take over his father's shoe factory. When asked why, he replies: "I thought it would help me to find out what America is about. . . . " Seldes would devote much of his writing during the 1930s, like so many other writers, to a quest for the meaning of America. A thinly veiled *Bildungsroman,* the *Post* serial never appeared in book form.[83]

The Wings of the Eagle, discussed earlier in Chapter One, offered in fiction Seldes' parting shot at the flawed nature of utopia and the internal tensions that make its demise virtually inevitable. Absolute idealism does battle with compromising realism, and the tragic loser turns out to be the woman who loves, not wisely but poignantly, a self-destructive idealist, based in part, but only in part, on Seldes' father George. Reviews were mixed at best, and the dominant objection seems to have been lack of subtlety. The novel verged too close to homily. As the *New York Times* put it, *The Wings of the Eagle* "bears resemblance at times to a long and elaborate tract which, if it points out no definite moral, at least deals with a subject in which there is a moral issue . . . . The reader is often overawed by Mr. Seldes's purposefulness. A little more fiction and a little less theme would not be unwelcome."[84]

Seldes had reviewed enough fiction—excellent, good, bad, and indifferent—to know perfectly well the desired criteria in any given genre, from mystery to history to moral saga. His swan song as a novelist took the form of a brief and inconclusive essay published simultaneously with *The Wings of the Eagle.* After reading and quoting the views of so many people concerning the novel, he conceded, "I can hardly make up my mind." A great novel must have purpose and a deliberate pattern. That's how much he apparently had learned.[85] It was time to move on to other modes of writing, and he very shortly did so with astonishing success on the stage. Before that occurred, however, Seldes enjoyed a taste of controversy caused by the most notorious theatrical composed by his modernist friend, E. E. Cummings.

In 1926 Cummings wrote an unusual (to say the least) play called *him.* *The Dial* printed portions of it and then Boni and Liveright published the whole script in book form even though it still had found no producer by 1927. Meanwhile the Provincetown Playhouse wanted to find a new talent to replace Eugene O'Neill, who had moved up to Broadway. Despite many difficulties—a large cast, quite a long play (21 scenes), a tiny theater at 133 MacDougal Street—*him* opened on April 18, 1928, to a bewildered but enthusiastic audience. Expecting the worst, Cummings had a "Warning" printed on the handbill/program which advised:

Relax and give the play a chance to strut its stuff—relax, stop wondering what it's all "about"—like many strange and familiar things, Life included, this Play isn't "about", it simply is. . . . Don't try to enjoy it, let it try to enjoy you. DON'T TRY TO UNDERSTAND IT, LET IT TRY TO UNDERSTAND YOU.

Although all of the critics detested the play, audiences responded well to the burlesque sketches, vaudeville skits, Dada nonsense, verbal pyrotechnics, and sets designed by Ben Shahn. It ran to full houses through twenty-seven performances.[86] Meanwhile, during the run the board of the Playhouse printed a pamphlet titled *him and the critics,* contrasting extracts from the harsh reviews (introduced by withering sarcasm) with the views of assorted intellectuals including Conrad Aiken, William Rose Benét, Waldo Frank, Paul Rosenfeld, John Sloan, Edmund Wilson, and Stark Young. Gilbert Seldes wrote an introduction, not so much because of his warm friendship with Cummings but because what Cummings had tried to do, and the way he tried to do it, so resonated with Seldes' personal mission in *The 7 Lively Arts.*

From Seldes' vantage point the play was not obscure at all:

It is a tragic fantasy. This is by way of being a novelty, for fantasies are generally comic or satiric; but novelty or not, the author states his theme and reiterates it throughout the play. The conflict is announced at the very beginning, when the girl says, "Why should we pretend to love each other?" and the man says that his life is based on three things—that he is a man, an artist, and a failure.

Later, in an exceptionally lucid and attractive discussion, Seldes concluded that

There is one other element which may be mentioned—a philosophical one. The title of the play, the names of the principal characters and some of the action all point to the author's consuming interest in the problem of identity. What is the essential thing I call myself? Am I myself or am I the image I see in the mirror—the mirror itself being a variable thing? Am I in love with you or am I in love with the self which you create? It is an entirely legitimate theme in connection with the others.[87]

In his "Theatre" column for *The Dial* in July 1928, Seldes defended *him* against all the critics who had savaged the play. He quoted Aristotle to support his point that the reviewers—only George Jean Nathan was singled out by name—had abused the play as "mad and sophomoric and dirty; they put adjectives to it—not nouns or verbs; they . . . talked about Mr. Cummings' typography, his poetry, his prose. But they gave no clue to the perfectly apparent character and nature of the play itself."[88] Seldes and Nathan would cross swords several times again during the next twenty years.

VII

By the end of the '20s a cluster of themes had emerged in Seldes' prolific journalism that would become even more prominent in his criticism— books, essays, reviews, and even plays—during the 1930s. He wanted to say, most of all, that the United States of America had a meaning that needed to be defined, and that the U.S. deserved a national culture that should not be neglected by the schools. In modified but unabashed ways, Seldes believed in national character in general and American exceptionalism in particular.[89]

Next, and more particularly, he worried about tyrannies, large and small, that could harass the individual citizen. The social tyranny of the crowd (à la Tocqueville) provided one example; censorship of books and films by private organizations provided yet another; and governmental regulation of personal liberty revealed still another. Any form of regimentation was abhorrent; even the income tax "is in some way an attack on our privacy, an unwarranted intrusion of government." Although Seldes acknowledged that "the ideal of the utmost possible freedom of the individual has always been forced to compromise with the necessities of the state," history nonetheless taught that a century earlier, in the Jacksonian era where *The Stammering Century* really started, power had been more equitably distributed. "If the liberal did not exist . . . to protest and fight against encroachments, the sheer weight of power would crunch us at once."[90]

William Crary Brownell, a critic from the preceding generation, continued quite confident in 1927 that "socially we remain very much a nation of individuals." But Seldes' friend Edmund Wilson shared his less sanguine concerns, and voiced them to Allen Tate in 1929.

> The American social revolutionaries who look forward to a clean sweep of American bourgeois civilization seem to me in the same class as the peoples whose eyes are turned toward the past, because they are looking forward to something which seems to be extremely unlikely, if not impossible. . . . The only thing possible in the present situation is for the individual to save his own integrity. . . . But I begin to wonder whether the time hasn't

arrived for the intellectuals etc. to identify themselves a little more with the general life of the country.[91]

During the very last years of the 1920s, Seldes and his wife were especially close, socially, to Wilson and the Fitzgeralds. When Wilson began to fall apart emotionally and psychologically in 1929, Seldes pleaded with him to join them in Bermuda where Seldes had taken a cottage to combine quiet, scenic beauty, and productive writing; but Wilson chose to remain in New York, do his writing there, and later that year suffered a nervous breakdown.[92]

Years later, in 1952, Wilson wrote an engaging memoir of a wild weekend spent with the Seldeses, Thornton Wilder, and others at "Ellerslie," a country estate near Wilmington, Delaware, that the Fitzgeralds rented for two years. "In a conversation with Seldes and me," Wilson recalled, "Scott somehow got around to inviting us frankly to criticize his character. Gilbert told him that if he had a fault, it was making life seem rather dull; and this quite put him out of countenance till we both began to laugh." If that sounds like a bizarre conversation, it should be kept in mind that a considerable amount of alcohol got consumed on these occasions.[93]

Wilson also recalled some bibulous exchanges at this "revel" about an Ellerslie ghost. Fitzgerald awakened during the night and decided that he really hadn't done justice to the "possibilities" of the resident ghost in an earlier pantomime. So Fitzgerald draped himself in a sheet and "invaded the Seldeses' room. Standing beside their bed, he began to groan. . . . But Gilbert started up from his sleep and gave a swipe with his arm at the sheet, which caught fire from a cigarette that the ghost was smoking inside his shroud [not too shrewd]. In the turmoil, something else caught fire, and everybody was rather alarmed."[94]

According to Seldes, writing right after the incident, Fitzgerald unwisely carried a candle to guide his ghostly way. "I struck him (being scared stiff) and threw a cigarette on the counterpane, so that the ghost business was ended in an effort to prevent the sparks from setting us on fire." Once the genuine potential for tragedy had been averted, the whole episode seemed quite hilarious. It certainly did nothing to damage the friendship between Seldes and Fitzgerald, which remained especially close during the next six or seven years. In 1933 Fitzgerald urged Ring Lardner's son, John, to select Seldes as the editor of a selection of his father's stories. The phrasing of Fitzgerald's recommendation is revealing and instructive: "Gilbert is one of the very first journalists in America and if anyone can make an interesting and consecutive narrative of it he can do it, and, to repeat, he is interested in the idea. When a Jew is interested he has the strong sense of the track that we other races don't even know the sprinting time of."[95]

Apropos of Seldes' recognized penchant for making books attractive to a general audience, we must note one other characteristic of his persona as a critic that emerged at the start of the 1930s: an anti-academic bent that verged, at times, on becoming a curious mode of anti-intellectualism. Seldes developed the conviction that art (and especially entertainment art) should be kept uncluttered by excessively cerebral baggage. In his daily column for the New York *Evening Journal,* Seldes commonly struck a tone hostile to highbrows. In one, for instance, he warned that reading books "can dull the edge of a man's brain, can contract his interests instead of expanding them, and may be a nuisance in his apprehension of the world." Later in 1932 he commented on the current tendency of American novelists "to grow sociological, as though they no longer respected the art of fiction and felt that unless they did something in economics they weren't fulfilling their duty."[96]

That complaint arose from Seldes' conviction that Marxist ideology and good fiction simply didn't mix. Simultaneously, however, he also pleaded that musical revues and other forms of theatrical entertainment should not be burdened with didactic or strategic and homiletic messages. One of Seldes' persistent appeals throughout the 1930s and 1940s would assert: let entertainment be entertainment, unshackled by ideology or moralism. When Seldes began his monthly "department" in *Esquire* late in 1933, that message became, in fact, his principal leitmotif.[97]

5

Accessible Culture for Depressed Times

A ccording to the conventional view, American intellectuals generally moved to the left during the Great Depression—and cultural critics did so especially. That supplies us with not one but two orthodoxies that require some modification. There is more than a kernel of truth to both views, of course, and the evidence supporting them is not trifling.[1] In recent years, however, the shrewdest interpretations of American culture during the 1930s emphasize the "complexities and contradictions" of that decade along with the confusions caused by flux and change. More specifically, they find a startling degree of acquiescence in the social and political status quo, an unexpectedly modest degree of radicalism, and a widely shared willingness to be patient.[2]

If these latter historians are correct, and I believe that they are, then Gilbert Seldes emerges as a fairly representative figure, very much in the mainstream of political culture in the United States during the Depression. He felt dissatisfied for many reasons, as we shall see, and offered all sorts of criticisms. Nevertheless, he was no revolutionary and he wanted to improve economic circumstances rather than scrap the entire system and begin anew. He remained *relatively* apolitical, most notably from 1930 until 1936, and refused to be diverted from his primary concerns: live entertainment and lively topical journalism.

One of his characteristic and persistent themes, of course, reiterated that American intellectuals tended to be excessively partial toward European culture and needlessly defensive about the apparent mediocrity of American culture. To compound this foolish inversion of preferences, Seldes also felt that native critics lacked sufficient empathy for the taste levels of ordinary Americans and, in too many instances, held elitist cultural values that they barely bothered to conceal. "Highbrow" now became a term of genuine derision in Seldes' vocabulary, and his persona as a critic, increasingly, became that of the cultural democrat, avoiding extremes and upholding the popular arts most enjoyed by ordinary men and women. During the 1930s Seldes had much less to say about the quest for excellence, irrespective of cultural strata, than at any other time in his career as a critic.[3]

That does not mean, however, that Seldes abdicated his standards or his customary stance as a judicious yet tough-minded critic. He peppered Glenway Westcott, the novelist, for writing a boring, overly generalized work of non-fiction dealing with national identity in Europe, the international economic crisis, and the peril of war. And he carped about *Titans of Literature,* a new work published in 1932 by fellow critic Burton Rascoe, who seemed pretentious and wrong-headed to Seldes. About all that Seldes would concede was that Rascoe could usually "generate excitement of some sort." Seldes sometimes damned by parceling out the faintest of praise.[4]

He could also be exceedingly generous, however, especially when an author or performer suited or reinforced his predilection for the popular arts. He warmly welcomed, for example, the appearance of new volumes in Mark Sullivan's series titled *Our Times.* Although Seldes noted curious errors involving art and the influence of Freud in America, he declared that Sullivan "is infinitely better on the things which came out so well in his other books—changes in fashion, dancing and popular songs, what happened to the newspapers, the political scene and the whole mixed and unconsciously happy life of the years before the war." Seldes particularly admired Sullivan's ability to find and mobilize meaningful trivia: for example, the fact that as late as 1913 Henry Ford still did not appear in *Who's Who* and was "known only to the public as the trade name of a motor car." Seldes also admired the carefully chosen illustrations: "there are pictures of Vernon and Irene Castle looking astonishingly awkward, and there is the story of Irving Berlin and the emergence of the word 'highbrow' as a term of contempt." The last point intrigued Seldes especially.[5]

(The swiftness with which Van Wyck Brooks' neon phrase from 1915, highbrow, was noticed and flashed back at him as a personal epithet is noteworthy. In 1927 Upton Sinclair published a little-known collection of brief essays that looked at literary studies in the United States from "the economic point of view." In chapter 27, "The Critic-Caste," Sinclair proclaimed that critics are "parasites . . . who live by telling the public what the artist means, and how and why he is great." As for Van Wyck Brooks himself, who had written unkind remarks about Sinclair's work ever since 1921, the novelist described Brooks as "a perfect example of the highbrow school, fastidious and aloof."[6])

Seldes praised the existence of major awards, such as the Nobel and Pulitzer prizes, because the publicity that accompanied those honors made people think that "writing books or discovering a germ may be an important activity in the world, as important perhaps as being brave under fire or working twenty-five years for one company." Oddly enough it bothered him, however, that the Pulitzer prizes "definitely announce one work in each field as the best of the lot, which is a misfortune. They ought to be given for work of merit, without implying comparisons." (More in the spirit of *The Dial*'s annual award, perhaps?) As for the particular selections made in 1932, Seldes had effusive praise for Archibald MacLeish's poem "Conquistador" and Maxwell Anderson's controversial play *Both Your Houses*. Although Seldes had long admired (and cited without any modification) the work of Frederick Jackson Turner, he lamented the posthumous award in history to Turner for *The Significance of Sections in American History* because the prize really ought to go to a living author. Seldes' choice would have been John Chamberlain's *Farewell to Reform: Being a History of the Rise, Life and Decay of the Progressive Mind in America*. "At the moment," Seldes felt, "when Americans are undergoing violent changes because reforms were not carried through fifteen years ago and more, Mr. Chamberlain's book is of absorbing interest."[7]

Even more important than his attraction to historical works that helped to explain the present, however, was Seldes' abiding interest in theatrical productions of all kinds. That fascination was perhaps the most enduring of his entire career. Although he had many competitors in the line of theatre criticism (George Jean Nathan above all), Seldes could be quite generous, most notably to younger critics just starting out. In 1932, for instance, he had lavish praise for the theatre criticism being written for *Hound & Horn* by Lincoln Kirstein, a recent graduate of Harvard College where this modernist and earnest magazine had its genesis. Seldes also seized the occasion of that particular column, however, to voice his strongly felt disquietude with the state of American theatre during the early 1930s. Part of the problem, from his perspective, he labeled "the total bankruptcy of realism." A larger part, perhaps, the stage shared with a fairly new phenomenon, talking films:

> Looking backward over the last few years and forward to some of the promised productions, I think I can see a reason why the stage has to fight so hard to hold on. It is getting a little too special—and the talkies are, as usual, falling into the same rut. I mean that the stage is dramatizing crooners and gossip writers and newspaper reporters, and the talkies are doing night nurses and cab drivers, and neither of them remembers that what people are interested in is people.[8]

With those complaints in view, Seldes decided toward the end of 1929 to try his own hand at a theatrical production. Although his previous efforts had failed, this time he hit the jackpot.

I

Seldes chose to prepare an adaptation (not a new translation) of *Lysistrata* by Aristophanes, a comedy set near the close of the persistent Peloponnesian War late in the fifth century. The women decide to withhold conjugal privileges from their warrior husbands until the latter (notably from Athens, Sparta, Thebes, and Corinth) arrived at a peace settlement. Although the play opened in Philadelphia on April 28, 1930, under the auspices of the Philadelphia Theatre Association, it is important to note at the outset just how much this bawdy, almost slapstick new rendition owed to cultural currents of the 1920s: disillusionment with war; the sexual revolution in general, but war between the sexes as a comic subject in particular; and the jealous divisiveness of small city states, a form of provincialism that social critics tended to loathe during the 1920s. Because the full impact of the Depression had not yet begun to be felt, audiences continued to be amused by familiar social issues and themes. They loved *Lysistrata* and it enjoyed a considerable run after it moved to Broadway in late May (252 performances), appeared in book form, was subsequently taken to other cities by alternative casts, and made considerable money for Seldes. Measured purely in financial terms, it ranks as the most successful project—book, play, or radio series—that Seldes ever undertook.

Seldes acknowledged in his preface to the book version that he had interpolated some scenes not found in the original. He insisted, nonetheless, that this rendering approximated what Aristophanes "might have done if he were alive today . . . . The original play would have run some forty minutes and a great part of this would have been taken up by lengthy choruses for which our ears are no longer grateful, and by secondary scenes which had meanings to the Greeks twenty centuries ago, but have none for us."

Seldes then went on to indicate why this type of entertainment not only appealed to him, but seemed like such a logical project for the author of *The 7 Lively Arts:* "Scholars assure us that the Greek comedy had little in common with what we call comedy now. It was closer to farce and burlesque; it used choral voices and music; it had movement and dance. It is as farce then—but as farce with a sound and credible intellectual basis that *Lysistrata* has to be taken."[9] The objective of combining farce with a sound intellectual foundation was, and always would be, a prominent characteristic of Seldes' approach to art, entertainment, and even criticism.

Norman Bel Geddes designed and directed the production, and during the first week of its try-out in Philadelphia there were some tense moments because Seldes suggested a variety of changes.[10] Brooks Atkinson promptly praised both men along with the production in an influential review for the *New York Times,* and so this *succès fou* was well launched. He called it an "accommodating adaptation . . . in the modern spirit." That meant the production was "frankly bawdy. It does not wink at the facts of life. It ogles them with goat-song relish. . . . When this 'Lysistrata' is dull and heavy, it is arguing the strategy of anti-war propaganda. When it is lively, which is three-quarters of the time, it is treating of men and women with the freedom they still cultivate on a democratic rooftop at Second Avenue and Houston Street." All in all the play made "as sound an evening of entertainment, both subtle and gross, as you are likely to encounter in this dwindling theatrical season."[11]

John Mason Brown cited the "sprightly and colloquial adaptation that Gilbert Seldes has made." The New York *Sun* warned (with delight) that "you will blush, probably, at the daring nearness of Mr. Seldes's approach to Aristophanic license." The young Grecian women "wear fewer clothes than at first blush . . . . You will not want to take those of very tender years. . . . The comic spectacle of life. It is open; a gusty wind sweeps it. It is not for the prurient any more than it is for the moralistic." A week before the production moved to the Forty-fourth Street Theatre in Manhattan, a critic for the Boston *Evening Transcript* praised Seldes' wit, observed that he is "unafraid of salty humor; uses words patly [a compliment, I think]; happens to be a practising journalist—all in degree Aristophanic attributes." And Brooks Atkinson, in a pre-Broadway preview, declared that "on the whole" *Lysistrata* is, "technically and textually, one of the most interesting ventures the American stage has made in several years."[12]

Five days later Atkinson observed that the New York performance seemed slightly toned down (i.e., less risqué) and Norman Bel Geddes (already famous for his lavish set designs) had contrived a magnificent panorama, "imaginative, free, sculptural and colorful, and the concluding bacchanal, when viewed from the rear of the auditorium, is a memorable flow of color and motion." As for Seldes' role, he had provided an adaptation "colloquial enough to be relished, and the sheer artlessness of the slapstick episodes makes them palatable and enjoyable even for the sciolists of Broadway." Writing for the *Herald-Tribune,* Percy Hammond praised the adaptation and added, "It is said that Mr. Seldes so adores the works of Aristophanes that, like St. Chrysostom, he sleeps with them under his pillow."[13]

Atkinson's review called attention to one aspect of the New York production that anticipated trouble ahead in less liberal venues and intensified Seldes' life-long hatred of censorship in any form. What he referred to as the "Comstock gang," the New York Society for the Suppression of Vice, had prodded the police to take notice. According to Atkinson's account of opening night, "members of the constabulary were present . . . to safeguard the morals of Broadway art patrons. Although the police listened to some of the raciest conversation to be heard outside the marts of commerce, they will be relieved to know that it is tamer than what members of the Philadelphia Theatre Association heard when *Lysistrata* opened in that well-bred metropolis." The production thrived and endured in Manhattan, despite threats from the "Comstock gang"; but in January 1932 authorities in the City of Los Angeles arrested the entire 53-member cast and shut down the local production of *Lysistrata* as obscene and indecent. Small comfort to the backers and performers that Captain Deighton MacDougall Jones, commander of the Police Morals Squad, served a sentence of fifty days in the county jail for contempt of court (he zealously defied a restraining order). One rumor circulated that the L.A.P.D. scoured the city in search of one Arthur Aristophanes, the alleged author of this scandalous play. They failed in that endeavor but succeeded in keeping *Lysistrata* dark. As one article covering the case concluded, Los Angeles could consider itself "Lawless but Pure!"[14]

By then the Seldes–Bel Geddes production had run for almost a year in New York, six months in Chicago, eighteen weeks all told in Philadelphia, and briefer periods of time in numerous cities across the United States. No community protest or police action occurred anywhere else in the country. By July of 1930 the frenzied openings in Philadelphia and New York had so exhausted Seldes that he and Amanda sailed for Paris in July to gain a respite from celebrity and intensity. Seldes told F. Scott Fitzgerald at the time that despite the usual "theatrical gyppery which stole about two thirds of my royalties," he was making a "killing." In 1932, after the dust had settled on the Los Angeles debacle, he brought T. S. Eliot up to date on his doings since they last met late in the '20s. Seldes referred somewhat defensively to his "vulgarization of Lysistrata," which had at least been profitable; and then added a sentence that largely characterized his professional activities from 1930 to 1936: "I am writing almost no criticism now, spending my time partly on a daily column of more or less intellectual comment for the Hearst press and in writing plays."[15]

II

Seldes' *Lysistrata* had a pre-history and a postscript worthy of mention. In 1925 Gilbert and his father collaborated on a translation of *Lysistrata* from Russian in a volume of plays from the Moscow Art Theatre that turned no profit for anyone. The point is simply that an American adaptation of Aristophanes' antiwar comedy germinated in Seldes' mind for almost five years. As for the post-script, in 1946 Seldes' adaptation received a revival in New York with an all-black cast. It received mixed reviews and closed after four performances.[16] The production is notable not only because Seldes had by then become such a Negrophile in the arts, but because this failure followed a rather massive one late in 1939 when Seldes prepared an adaptation of *A Midsummer Night's Dream* for a spectacular cast that included Louis Armstrong as Bottom and many other black stars. More on that at the end of this chapter.

When Seldes wrote to Eliot in April 1932 he explained his lapse in submitting "New York Chronicles" for Eliot's *Criterion* by confessing that ever since 1929 he had felt himself "lacking in communication with pure letters." Although communication had not yet been "completely re-established," Seldes suggested that if Eliot wanted a Chronicle for the summer issue, he could provide something "interesting or entertaining, or possibly both." To Scott Fitzgerald, when *Lysistrata* was surpassing all expectations in 1930, Seldes said that he wanted to try "a few more adaptations and perhaps an original play." He did just that, though he never remotely approximated his huge success with *Lysistrata*.[17]

In 1925–26 Seldes began to prepare an adaptation of Carlo Gozzi's scenario for the *Love of Three Oranges,* a Venetian Harlequin play from the late Renaissance that had also been made into an opera. It was commissioned by Robert Edmond Jones, Eugene O'Neill, and Kenneth Macgowan. They accepted Seldes' script and fully intended to produce it, but then their theatre folded. Consequently its only production was an amateur one in 1926 by the Harvard Dramatic Club—well received by the Boston *Evening Transcript* and the *Christian Science Monitor.* The Theatre Guild looked at the text and, along with George S. Kaufman, encouraged Seldes to proceed with revisions and expansion, but made no commitment. That worried him because without some assurance of production, he did not want to devote a lot of time to it. In 1931 he proposed it to the Philadelphia Theatre Association, original sponsors of *Lysistrata,* because it "falls in the tradition of *Lysistrata* . . . . That is, it brings to life one of the masterpieces of comedy."[18]

Although this *commedia dell'arte* inspiration, which Seldes always referred to as the "Orange Comedy," never did get off the ground, it is interesting for what it reveals about Seldes' desire to negotiate modern adaptations of comic classics as pure amusement with respectable roots (not a phrase that Seldes would ever have used). He incorporated into his script "some of the most famous stunts from other authors of the time ranging from Goldoni to Molière, and the thing should be done in the technique of a vaudeville show or a burlesque." He recognized the difficulties involved in what he wanted to do because, on the one hand, "it is full of the eternal horse-play of the theatre . . . and should be put on as slapstick. But through Gozzi," on the other hand, "there runs a pretty powerful vein of intellectual satire as well." Cerebral satire and slapstick were not so easily joined.[19]

Moreover, just to complicate matters, Seldes wanted to include modern allusions but in a manner that would be faithful to Gozzi's time and place. Hence "all the references to modern times are indirect—that is, I have used only such things as had parallels in the time of the original play. A scene in a dentist chair and a halitosis scene, for example, are specifically of the period, and the correspondence to our own time is secondary in every case to the value of the original comedy." In the explanatory notes that Seldes sent to Philadelphia he insisted that *The Love of Three Oranges* "is NOT a play; it is a SHOW. . . . It is a harlequinade, an extravaganza; it requires production in the tempo and style, more or less, of vaudeville and burlesque. Most of it is to be played with or through music." He wanted to achieve "a fantasia of satirical fun." Then came the clearest link between this project and Seldes' enthusiasms ever since *The 7 Lively Arts.* "The essential things are the scenes played by the Masks of the commedia. Some of these are directly taken from the old texts and reports; some are invented and have more bearing on modern times. I see Harlequin, Sganarelle, Pantaloon, etc. as the Chaplins and Jolsons of their time, and I think to be played in this way."[20]

The dramatis personae had potential even though it is difficult to see, in some instances, how Seldes expected to avoid anachronism successfully. The Queen of Hearts personified everything negative. She prohibited books, cards, consumption of alcohol, and so forth, in her kingdom. "She issues a proclamation to keep the earth flat when she hears that people are beginning to say it is round." Above all she hates laughter. Smeraldina, by contrast, a Moorish maid, wears blackface and talks like a woman in a minstrel show with a black, lower-class accent. The Captain wears a Ku Klux Klan mask, mobilizes his company (grotesque Klan caricatures), and puts them through a military drill.[21]

Because the prince is ill, the king has summoned all of the most learned doctors to discover what ails him. Then a soothsayer arrives who can interpret the meaning of dreams, the great dottore Sigismondo of Vienna. All of the doctors agree that this outsider is a fakir, but the king invites him in anyway. Dressed to suggest Sigmund Freud, the visitor proceeds with a burlesque of psychoanalysis and dream interpretation.

Throughout the play, Seldes utilized the form and traditional characters of *commedia dell'arte* to satirize current trends in popular theatre, song, entertainment, and fads. Near the end, Harlequin invites the entire court to attend a show. At that point the satire becomes entirely contemporary. As Seldes explained, "the scenes will have to be written just before rehearsals begin" so that the spoofs would be entirely *au courant.* At the end of each number, Seldes noted, the prince informs Harlequin that he is not amused. Whereupon Harlequin launches into an imitation of Al Jolson singing an Italian version of a Mammy song. When that fails to please, Harlequin starts up a cabaret act with Texas Guinan effects. Two or three swift parodies of current hits follow—to be written only when the hits of the season are clearly known—still, nothing pleases the prince.

Finally, as Seldes envisioned it, Harlequin puts on a typical "naked girl number" in the manner of a Ziegfeld Ben Ali Haggin tableau. At that point the enraged queen sweeps down upon Harlequin and banishes him from the court. As she rushes toward him, however, Harlequin sticks out his foot, trips the queen, and she goes sprawling—exposing her buttocks. In the terrified silence that follows, the prince bursts into gales of laughter. Thereupon the gloomy scene is transformed. Splendid dresses and outfits are illuminated by bright lights. Music and dancing commence, and shouts of joy make it clear that the prince is cured. "The enchantment is over."

Perhaps it is not surprising that no takers, or backers, emerged, and the "Orange Comedy" languished. Seldes did not attempt another adaptation until 1939. Instead he devoted considerable attention in his daily column for the New York *Evening Journal* to all aspects of the stage and to theatre criticism. Having complained, for example, that "certain playwrights have nothing to say," some who took exception accused him of starting a school of dramatic criticism and asked rhetorically "what a certain critic turned dramatist had to say in his adaptation entitled 'Lysistrata'?" Seldes offered a ready response:

I took good care that I injected nothing into the play because an old dead man named Aristophanes had put into that play more than enough for one play to carry. He had said something of vital importance about a war and something interesting about sex. He had chosen the two subjects on which nearly all the world is either too prejudiced or too sentimental to think clearly, and he had thought clearly.[22]

By the end of 1932, with the Great Depression fully three years old, Seldes' perception of the popular arts underwent an important shift. Rather than valuing entertainment purely for its own sake, as he customarily had, he began to urge that the theatre take into account grim realities then gripping millions of Americans. He wished that "the depression would hit the theatre and hit it hard." He didn't mean the box office or the owners of theatre buildings. Rather, he had in mind those who

write for the theatre and those who produce plays. My idea is that it might be a good thing for the theatre to become aware of the fact that 125 million people are thinking now thoughts which they did not think three years ago, and are perhaps a little impatient of hangovers from the past. I do not mean that all the plays ought to be concerned with the farmers' strike in Iowa and the bread lines in New York, although I do not see why at least a few of the plays do not deal with these subjects. It is possible to be aware of what has happened in these three years and make your awareness felt even in a light comedy. In fact, light comedy and operetta need only be good to escape reproach; it is the serious play which becomes tiresome when it lags behind the spirit of events.[23]

He offered very strong praise, however, for the Jewish Art Theatre in general and particularly for its production during the winter of 1932–33 of *Yoshe Kalb,* one of the most interesting events in many a theatrical season. It is the story of a studious young man "who sins, swept away from honor and righteousness by the passion of a young, unhappily married woman." Then comes his expiation when, falsely accused of a different crime, the young man refuses to defend himself and "is finally cast out to wander the world like a banished spirit." Seldes especially admired the ending, "a masterly meeting of the sanhedrin to decide the question not of guilt or innocence, but of identity—to determine who this man is."[24]

He also wrote with enthusiasm about George Bernard Shaw as a superb drama critic as well as playwright. Seldes denounced the cynical complaint that American theatre was dominated by Jewish playwrights and, with withering sarcasm, called attention to "those two notable Hebrew patriarchs, George Bernard Shaw and Eugene O'Neill." Seldes sang the praises of Oscar Hammerstein, a German-Jewish impresario, real estate developer, and inspired master of vaudeville who created meaningful competition for the moribund Metropolitan Opera—so much so that the Met had to buy him off. Seldes' profile of Florenz Ziegfeld for *The New Yorker,* a classic in that genre, was appreciative though not altogether admiring. When Dwight Deere Wiman, a theatrical producer, had four smash hits between 1936 and 1938, Seldes observed that Wiman didn't receive the recognition he deserved because his productions were in a "light vein," which Seldes admired nonetheless. And Seldes offered the loudest applause for George Balanchine, who created in *Slaughter on Tenth Avenue* "the best American ballet presented so far."[25]

Seldes could also be acerbic in his criticism, however, and felt perfectly comfortable flouting popular opinion. When the George S. Kaufman–Ira Gershwin musical *Of Thee I Sing* pleased virtually everyone in 1931–32, and received a Pulitzer for its book and lyrics, he felt that doing so gave the "accolade of propriety to a vicious attack on the shabbiness and stupidity of politics in America." Seldes had ambivalent feelings about political satire in musical shows that seemed excessively unpatriotic. It didn't help, perhaps, that *Of Thee I Sing* was a direct competitor of *As Thousands Cheer,* written by Seldes' good friend Irving Berlin, and that Berlin's was a more conventional musical revue whereas its rival provided major innovations by having a story to integrate the song and dance routines.[26]

Although Seldes achieved fame as an advocate for the popular arts, he could be severely critical of mediocrity or innovations that left him unmoved, such as sentimental torch songs. Sometimes he complained that the emotions they conveyed were too strong for their flimsy medium to sustain. A small-scale revival of burlesque in New York during 1931–32 annoyed him because the music, comedy, and dance that accompanied were so dull and poor. He bemoaned the declining quality of a particular kind of act in musical revues, the short sketch with a trick ending on which the lights were doused and the curtain drawn—mostly episodes about sexual improprieties, more often than not adulterous. By 1936 Seldes had really soured on the state of theatrical standards in New York. "The producers go merrily on as if unaware of new competition," he wrote, referring to the rapid rise of film. Seldes declared that between two-thirds and three-fourths of the plays produced each year were "the worst enemies of the theatre. Just how to prevent their appearance, I don't know," he lamented. "Contraception is against the law."[27]

There is an ironic aspect to that last remark because one of Seldes' enduring crusades concerned censorship. When the Los Angeles police closed down *Lysistrata,* Seldes' response was actually rather mild. In March and April 1933, however, he expressed outrage on several occasions in his daily column on account of censorship affecting public statuary, books, and even certain films because of scandal associated with the private lives of the actors, rather than the actual content of the movies themselves. Seldes gave testimony in lawsuits involving censorship, and his memories of the United States government keeping James Joyce's *Ulysses* on the contraband list remained vivid. He could be remarkably judicious, however, in recognizing why an impasse so commonly occurred:

> I have not only failed to make out a case complete and final, against the censorship as an institution, but haven't even found such a case in all the books and articles written on the subject. One reason is, of course, that

those who favor and those who detest censorship are both moralists. . . . Both are, or pretend to be anxious for the moral health of the community, and if one works on the psychology of fifty years ago and the other on the psychology of the year after next, neither has anything like proof.

Referring to the situation of film, in particular, Seldes added that "the weakness of the censors, at present, is that few of them are intelligent and that the great image of authority inflates the censor's idea of his own duties and powers."[28]

A few weeks later the provocation was precipitated by unclothed statues of Eve in such a public place as Radio City in midtown Manhattan. Seldes ended a serious discourse on a semi-whimsical note. He wanted to know who had really been offended or corrupted. He therefore proposed passing out slips to the audience. The first question would be, "Did you notice the statues?" And then, "for purposes of comparison, the next should be, 'Were you a moral man or woman when you entered?'" By the spring of 1933 Seldes had achieved sufficient visibility as a champion of tolerance that several book publishers sought his assistance, presumably by means of his widely read column, in combating potential censorship. One of the books, *God's Little Acre* by Erskine Caldwell, deserved support in Seldes' view, but the other did not. That discrepancy provided him with an opportunity to expound upon the libertarian's dilemma—which was less complex than the critic's dilemma:

The out-and-out opponents of censorship are not at liberty to choose between these two books. They have to defend the one they despise as heartily as they defend the one they admire. Their good argument is that a victory for Mr. Sumner [head of the N.Y. Society for the Suppression of Vice] over the cheap and trivial book will give him encouragement to march against the serious and intelligent one. This is true because Mr. Sumner is unfit to exercise censorship, especially in a society which has not made up its mind about the proper limitations and the proper functions of censorship. Having met Mr. Sumner in full magistrate's court and knowing his mind and his methods, I see the advantage of defeating him all down the line; so that I regret giving him any aid whatever.

The practical problem, however, is to preserve the freedom of those who are capable of using freedom. It may be a good thing in theory to abolish all limiting laws, and for that purpose it may be useful to defend the printer of pornographic postcards; in practice I would sacrifice a thousand purveyors of willful dirt if I could allow the works of Mr. James Joyce to enter our ports openly and Mr. Erskine Caldwell to publish "God's Little Acre" without running the risk of prosecution. I have heard often enough that freedom must be absolute freedom, and that if I set up my standard of latitude I have no right to protest against Mr. Sumner doing the same. But I am not fighting a literary Scottsboro case; I am not even much interested in abstract justice.[29]

In the months and years that followed, Seldes' crusade extended to the mistreatment of movies starring Fatty Arbuckle even though a jury had found him innocent of the death of a young woman following a wild party at which both had been present. Women's clubs all over the United States made it virtually impossible to show or see an Arbuckle film. Seldes also attacked the proscribing of so-called suggestive songs from radio. In his view, "the radio has never needed a moral czar or a censor because it has censored itself almost out of existence." He subsequently moved on to efforts aimed at preventing children from reading "trash." While he acknowledged getting into trouble from time to time for recommending Rabelais for children, he insisted that the entire crusade against "bad books for children" was in reality "something of a racket." Although Seldes had long since scrapped his youthful exposure to philosophical anarchism, he did invoke it as a principle in permitting children to read whatever they pleased. In his view, the whole process of locating and reading good literature should be left to natural selection. Besides, the great enemy of children's reading was really the seductive radio; so Seldes urged that good literature (expurgated if necessary) be read on the radio for youngsters.[30]

On the subject of sex in entertainment, and particularly in the popular arts, Seldes' perspective was complex and critically interesting. In general, he complained when entertainment relied excessively upon sex, but also when films and other forms of entertainment ignored passion (and sex) as a human reality. Looking at American theatre in 1932, Seldes remarked that contemporary playwrights were missing an opportunity by assuming that they must "put a lot of sin into their plays to make them interesting. I simply do not believe," he continued, "that sin is so interesting (or even so much fun) as virtue." Consequently Seldes saw an impoverishment of modern drama. Because sin was usually short-lived or monotonous, he wished that playwrights would hunt for the excitement to be found in virtue, "which I take to be the sustained effort to achieve real values," because virtue was "both long-spanned and exciting."[31]

The contrasting circumstances of sex on stage and in film fascinated

Seldes, especially because he perceived a paradox in the contrast: "while the pictures remain one hundred per cent pure—even illicit love is made abstract and decent—the stage shows are often as shady and nudging as you would find in the usually rough revue. What is more, the audience loves the stage show as much as it does the picture." Was it possible, Seldes wondered, wishing to resolve the paradox at least partially, that the stage shows were too licentious, or that the movies were too cautious? He liked to insist, however, that Rin-Tin-Tin movies were superior to Clara Bow ("It") films, and that Mary Pickford became Queen of the Movies without ever exploiting sex. Just a few months later Seldes reported very favorably on a new symposium, "Sex in the Arts," and especially an essay by Struthers Burt that criticized films for constantly promising (or at least suggesting) far more than they were prepared to deliver. Burt noted the "salacious names which are always attached to innocent pictures, and that we get neither voluptuousness nor serious thought about sex in them."[32]

Seldes' divergent responses to Mae West's movies and Noel Coward's plays are altogether consistent with his preference for honest, broad humor over pretentious sophistication. Over the years he published quite a few admiring pieces about West. In contrast to Hollywood's promotion of "It," associated, "of all things, with a hoydenish little girl," West established her fame by a "vigorous, downright, honest exploitation of the commodity which in her splendid simplicity, she has made her own [i.e., robust femme fatale sexuality]." Seldes asserted that West was not vulgar despite her explicit suggestion that sex should be pleasurable for both liberated women and men. In Seldes' view, Mae West's message served to liberate women from certain familiar worn-out stereotypes about themselves.[33]

By contrast, Seldes acknowledged that Noel Coward had written the most brilliant comedy in years, *Private Lives*. Otherwise, however, Coward's theatrical writings were "almost entirely negligible"; therefore Seldes wished to explore his reputation for sophistication. When Coward spoke of "an unpremeditated roll in the hay" in *Design for Living*, Seldes wrote, "he gratified all those who wanted a new name for fornication and in the rest of the play treated the relation between the sexes, and the usual expression thereof, as not to be compared with the pleasure of good company." From the perspective of 1937 Seldes felt that Coward's work remained period pieces, vintage 1921–25, a phase when the breakdown of morals and the intake of liquor were not ascribed to the natural human desire to get drunk and commit adultery. Rather, "they were 'dignified' by the profound disillusion of the peace that embittered the war." From all of that, alas, "sprang the noble notion that to chatter brightly was the only proper aim of man, because the chatter covered the broken heart." Seldes then proclaimed the irrelevance of such facile sophistication. "The world has grown too interesting and its problems have become too pressing." Polite comedy had reached a dead end because it could only grow more polished and had ceased to divert the mind—its only legitimate function. Seldes ended with praise that damned more than faintly. Sometimes Noel Coward dazzled like a magician, he acknowledged: his plays could do the impossible. But by 1937, "doing the possible has become more exciting."[34]

Practicality and realism about human relations emerged as more prominent motifs in Seldes' essays during the 1930s. Based upon a joint survey taken among students at Columbia College and Barnard, for example, he predicted a high divorce rate early in the 1940s because young men and women seemed to have naive expectations about what they sought in a mate. The men wanted a clever, sensitive woman of culture "whose conversation mingles gentleness and wit in gracious proportions." Young women gave top priority to "culture, good looks, money and a sense of humor." Perhaps tongue-in-cheek, though I am not entirely sure, Seldes anticipated emotional disturbances because *none* of the eight qualities that were enumerated offered the slightest suggestion that "sex is a factor in marriage."[35]

From time to time Seldes used the issue of marriage being a problematic institution as an attention-getter in his journalism. Queries such as this one, for example: "If simply by pressing a button you could dissolve your marriage, would you press the button or not?" In an equally outrageous and speculative piece, Seldes applauded the way that repeal of Prohibition and related social trends had combined to liberate men from female domination—Prohibition having been invented by women and foisted upon men. Hence the "revival of interest in natural foods with their coarser tastes and textures has marched with the revival of hearty eating at speakeasies." Innovations in domestic architecture, affecting kitchens and bathrooms in particular, had somehow made the American home more amenable to men's needs. (Hitherto everything had been arranged to suit the woman's convenience.) As a consequence, Seldes believed, or at least he declared, that ever since the 1920s American men had been re-asserting themselves against the "aggressive and powerful female."[36]

Sometimes Seldes succeeded in being so droll that readers could not be sure whether he was serious. We know that he enjoyed hearty comedy and loved to laugh, especially at ludicrous topics and situations. In 1932 he was intrigued by one author's explanation for the immense contemporary popularity of humorous writers, artists, and comedians—"by suggesting that we are ill-at-ease in the world, worried and self-conscious . . . [so] we give anything for a laugh. I do not know whether this is true, but it is interesting, and for those of us who are not intentionally funny it is a consolation." A few days later, also in his daily column, Seldes noted an intriguing historical reversal. Sixty or seventy years earlier American humorous writers were, or pretended to be, "simple, uneducated guys, who looked up at the intellectuals and the 'right people' and laughed at them." Ever since the Great War, however, much of American humor had been written by "people who stand on top, or think they do, and look down at the unintelligent mob and laugh at them."[37]

Similarly, Seldes explained in 1933 that burlesque was dying, almost finished in fact, because it had become "only a rowdier version of the usual musical show." What had kept burlesque vital for so long was a "genuine comic spirit." Its comedians were masters of makeup and gesture, "and the reason they could be dirty—and they were—is that when the character was established as a grotesque and unreal one, the dirt did not matter too much." With burlesque declining, he wondered where the next great batch of comedians and dancers would come from. He saw at least one silver lining in this dark cloud, however. "By absorbing burlesque, the musical stage saved itself from becoming mincing and polite and damnably intellectual."[38]

That last epithet calls to our attention one of Seldes' most frequent refrains during the 1930s and through much of the '40s—seemingly a curious manifestation of anti-intellectualism. Writing in admiration of P. G. Wodehouse characters, and cartoon figures like them, Seldes declared: "In men as in dogs, I do not like too much intelligence." Taken at face value, that could be misleading because Seldes actually admired intelligence very much indeed. What he did insist upon, however, was that entertainment should not be weighted down with an excess of cerebral or moral messages. He disliked musical shows, for example, designed to convey the political perspectives of *The Nation* or *The New Republic*. "Usually I have found that ideas in the legitimate theatre are pretty tedious fare," he explained. "The great thing about the old style musical was that it satisfied the native human desire to think about nothing at all."[39]

It annoyed Seldes that highbrows tried to minimize Chaplin's overt funniness. Intellectuals tended to assert that Chaplin's primary virtues were "the poignance of emotion, the cosmic, as opposed to the comic, implications of his work." In Seldes' eyes Chaplin was "primarily and essentially funny," and his genius was outrageous comedy. Similarly he wondered why writers willingly ruined detective stories with "lectures" on art, archaeology, physics, and love. Because of S. S. Van Dine (Philo Vance), Dorothy Sayers, and Frances Iles, people were beginning to believe that the highest possible praise for a detective story was to say that it is "more than a detective story." Seldes announced in 1938 that he had given up mystery stories because they failed to keep him awake![40]

He took consistent positions in writing about jazz when it became too genteel or refined and semi-popular music like Gershwin's when it was composed only to be heard rather than sung. Seldes admired George Gershwin immensely, yet his attractive simplicity "doesn't come out in his work which gets more complicated and interesting and brittle and un-melodious with every year." Seldes, who did not much care for opera, was not a fan of *Porgy and Bess;* and it almost came as a left-handed compliment when he observed that no American composer was "brighter, more generally aware, more likely to give you a mental satisfaction than Gershwin."[41]

Unlike Gershwin, whom Seldes genuinely admired, Cole Porter received grudging praise because he was so versatile, adaptable, and above all popular. Seldes would acknowledge that Porter had great talent and virtually flawless technique, but his sentiments were sometimes pleasantly cynical, "sometimes a little smeared with smut." Seldes added that Porter's career seemed to pass through phases: when he discovered the facts of life and zoology at the same time, for example, he became the great leader of the "habits-of-rabbits" school of popular song. Ultimately, responding to Porter's new hit, "You're the Top," Seldes concluded that Cole Porter had "almost unerring taste for the second rate." That would not be Seldes' last attack on Porter.[42]

In the mid-1930s, while contemplating changes that had occurred during the previous decade in types of music and their performance, Seldes noticed what I regard as one of the most important characteristics in the transition from popular to mass culture: namely, active participation giving way to passive observation or listening. Writing about George Gershwin in 1934, as noted, Seldes asserted that Gershwin "now composes to be heard, not to be sung. He is lucky because we are becoming a nation of listeners, thanks to the radio." Two years later Seldes observed a comparable change in jazz. Coming out of ragtime, he commented, jazz was meant for dancing. Yet the popularization of jazz among the "respectable" elements, and the development of jazz as music appropriate for the concert hall, had the effect of making it, too, a source of passive rather than active pleasure. As Seldes explained,

> Somewhere in the twenties both the composers and the band leaders became so expert at their work that jazz could be listened to, at least for a brief time, without movement. When Paul Whiteman, after a concert at Carnegie Hall, took his orchestra across the country and played to people seated in auditoriums, instead of people getting up from night-club tables to dance, he was actually preparing the way for the radio.[43]

Without conceptually articulating the transition as such, Seldes perceived symptomatic aspects of the emergence of mass culture, a gradual process that began only in the '20s, accelerated in the 1930s with the advent of radio, and reached high gear during the 1950s when television came of age.*

III

Throughout those decades Seldes had ample incentive to observe and opportunities to comment upon cultural change. In addition to ad hoc assignments for miscellaneous magazines and his topical books, Seldes wrote a daily column for the New York *Evening Journal* (1931–37), a monthly department for *Esquire* called "The Lively Arts" from the moment of its founding in 1933 until 1946 (he never missed an issue), and a biweekly column on film, radio, television, and books for the *Saturday Review of Literature* during the 1950s.

His situation with the *Evening Journal* was somewhat paradoxical because, as a Hearst paper, it tended to emphasize foibles of the rich and famous, sports, somewhat sensationalized accounts of the news, and anything that smacked of society gossip or scandal. Yet it welcomed Seldes publicly by announcing to readers "that he is a highbrow, a man of amazing cerebral altitude."

---

*Although cultural critics in recent years, such as Michel de Certeau and John Fiske, have insisted that mass culture continues to be interactive and participatory, Seldes and his contemporary critics, along with such diverse social scientists as Harold Innis and Paul Lazarsfeld, all feared the growing cultural passivity caused by the advent of electronic mass media.

Surely that would not have been a strong incentive for most readers of the *Journal;* but, as it happened, Seldes wrote about everything under the sun in these columns though not very much that could be considered "highbrow." His typical columns did include a fair number of casual (rather than in-depth) book reviews, but also such topics as: a raid on a speakeasy, why Hollywood continually miscast Greta Garbo, why the Americans and the French fail to understand one another, new kitchen gadgets and utensils, science, travel, and "You can tell a nation by the zoos it keeps," along with letters from workers, students, and others who wanted to agree or disagree with Seldes' point of view. He wrote more about contemporary politics and politicians in the *Journal* than anywhere else (or any other time in his career). He candidly confessed in 1933 that "to be a political prophet requires a special knack which happens never to have come to me, so that when I make a guess in politics, and it comes out right, I put it down to accident." Seldes could be refreshingly candid, and in this instance he was dead right. In 1933, for example, he found Adolf Hitler unimpressive "as a candidate for dictatorship but he may be better and more responsible when he gets into his stride. The threat of a three-day revenge, meaning slaughter of Jews and Communists, will probably not come off. . . . "44*

Seldes offered the same concession concerning prophecy in the realm of culture, but there he had greater expertise, shrewder instincts, and did far better. His predictions about the future of talking films and radio were often quite prescient. To those who complained about the apparent homogenization and "standardization" of American culture, Seldes shrewdly pointed to ongoing signs of diversity. He liked to meet with college students and took the measure of their assumptions and aspirations quite accurately. At his best he could be provocatively perceptive about matters unrelated to his specialty, the popular arts. "For generations we have been told to rejoice that we have no classes in America," he observed. "It isn't precisely true; but it is true in one unfortunate way. The classes are so shifting and variable that we have no solid bulk of a middle class. . . . If we have a forgotten man, it is only because we never knew him well enough to get his features in our memories. He changed right before our eyes."45**

*For a comparable example of myopia in 1935 by a young man who became a distinguished scholar of recent European history, and especially of ideologies, see *Gentleman Rebel: The Memoirs of H. Stuart Hughes* (1990), 100–101.
**In 1936 and 1938 Seldes would address two major books to an American middle class that seems to have rapidly congealed. See Chapter Eight below.

From time to time Seldes and others among his contemporary critics commented on the strain involved in producing daily or weekly columns on a tight schedule. Van Wyck Brooks commiserated with Lewis Mumford during the mid-1930s when his obligations to *The New Yorker* and other journals kept him on a very short leash.[46] In reality, of course, it was not easy to maintain consistent quality when churning out "colyums" on such a routinized basis. In Seldes' case, aside from problems with political judgment, he sometimes failed to make any clear point at all, or else ended so inconclusively that readers could not have been sure just what message he wanted to convey. Often his column in the *Journal* would comprise a miscellany of two or three unconnected items, and his monthly essay for *Esquire* might begin with one topic but then meander to another that was loosely related. It has to be said on Seldes' behalf that none of these "lapses" was peculiar to him. Many other writers did exactly the same thing, so much so that the absence of tight focus certainly does not seem to have been a cardinal sin during the 1930s and '40s. On the other hand, when Seldes chastised rival critic Alexander Woollcott for being dead wrong in his negative assessment of *Mourning Becomes Electra,* he surely had an obligation to the reader to say *why* Woollcott was dead wrong, but didn't.[47]

On other subjects Seldes was simply his idiosyncratic self, not necessarily wrong but potentially controversial, which, in a sense, must have been an expected part of his job. In 1932, for example, he argued that Amelia Earhart's achievements in aviation didn't demonstrate equality between men and women. It only showed this particular woman's great courage and ability. Therefore we should applaud her as an individual, and not on behalf of her sex. Seldes then castigated men for asserting their superiority to women. Charles Lindbergh hadn't performed his solo feat in order to demonstrate male superiority and Earhart hadn't followed suit in order to disprove it. Writing for *Esquire* in 1934, however, Seldes served up lavish praise for W. C. Fields as a great pantomime artist in silent films who made a successful transition to sound films with no loss of effectiveness. Women could be entertaining, Seldes acknowledged, but with the singular exception of Fanny Brice, rarely really funny. (And Seldes didn't much like it when Brice played Baby Snooks on the radio.) Perhaps women didn't believe in the belly laugh, he speculated, possibly because they felt that it lacked refinement. Not all male comics are truly funny, Seldes conceded, but men were much likelier than women to be hilarious entertainers.[48]

Seldes could be clear and salutary on the value of historical knowledge, a topic that he took up from time to time. He felt that the greatest shortcoming of his education at Harvard had been that "it failed to give me a mature and complete view of the history of my own country. . . . It was possible (and I suspect it is still possible) to go through a great American college with no more knowledge of American history than you got in the eighth grade of grammar school." The problem transcended simple neglect, however. Seldes warned that Americans needed to "stop being haters of history. When we declared our independence of England," he observed, "we also declared ourselves outside the influence of the past":

> History meant to us the history of bad old Europe, with its dynasties and its wars and its poverty and cruelty; we wanted no part of that. History was against the American experiment, and we set ourselves to teach history a lesson. We succeeded for a long time. Perhaps history is now about to have its revenge.[49]

Seldes' enthusiasm for Americana in general continued to expand. When Americana Week occurred in March 1933 he urged readers to look at volume two of James Truslow Adams' *The March of Democracy,* especially because of the freshness of the illustrations. He then made a revealing distinction, given Seldes' notoriety for preferring the popular over the cerebral—a distinction that would, in fact, become increasingly important to him. He commented that the episodic and illustrative material in Adams' *March of Democracy* constituted the material "on which the same author based his more thoughtful" *Epic of America,* published a year earlier. Seldes did not necessarily salute or embrace mass circulation material. Moreover, he concluded with a mild criticism of the closing portion of *The March of Democracy:*

> I was a little disappointed to find that in dealing with the final years of his story Mr. Adams had changed from the calm, cool, philosophical historian into a more bustling, more personal recorder and commentator. I do not hold with those who say that "it is too soon" to write about the events of the last few years. Columnists and editorial writers discuss events of the last few years.[50]

Those observations prompt a comparison of Seldes with Frederick Lewis Allen, columnist, influential editor of *Harper's Magazine* (1931–54), and author of numerous works of contemporary U.S. history. Like Seldes, Allen shared a commitment to the "average American" and disliked Mencken, Sinclair Lewis, and the anti-American elitists who developed a following during the 1920s by being cynical about the common man. Like Seldes, Allen pleaded for the need to debunk the debunkers, and like Seldes, also, Allen tended to be politically inert. He did nothing to protest against the treatment of Sacco and Vanzetti, yet subsequently regretted it. After his highly successful book *Only Yesterday* appeared (1931), a social history of the '20s, Allen liked to call himself a "retrospective journalist." During the 1930s Allen preferred to write about those aspects of popular culture in the United States complementary to the ones highlighted by Seldes, namely: best-seller lists, record-breaking performances in sports (especially track and field), and off-beat personalities. Allen celebrated the democratization of taste and culture, and his next big success, *Since Yesterday: The Nineteen-Thirties in America* (1940) paid considerable attention to popular culture. Like Seldes, also, he considered himself an anti-Marxist liberal, and the book project that Allen set aside in 1941 when he became editor-in-chief of *Harper's,* a work prospectively called "The Americans," would have been remarkably comparable to Seldes' *Mainland* (1936).[51]

Like Seldes, also, Allen was critical of Herbert Hoover's deliberate inaction during 1930–31, and both observers wrote engagingly about the cultural impact of the Great Depression. In 1932 Seldes devoted a column explicitly to the question: "if these bad times continue, what is to become of culture?" He had no facile answers to offer and expressed genuine concern about the future of book publishing, the decline in live drama because producers lacked funds, the hazards to concert orchestras as well as to great artists who earned their living giving recitals. "Are we faced with a world without beauty," he wondered, "without books or pictures, without arts of any form, with no escape from actual drab existence to the realms of imagination, of forgetfulness?" Hence he singled out for praise those plays that offered a genuine "emotional response to the depression," such as J. P. McEvoy's *Americana.*[52]

On more than one occasion—before the WPA projects for writers and artists got under way—Seldes produced semi-serious spoofs aimed at federal neglect of economic support for people engaged in the production and transmission of culture. Seldes clearly believed that government could do more, much more, for the arts, broadly conceived:

> Nothing has been said so far about rationing the output of writers and painters and nothing about putting adagio dancers and acrobats on a thirty-hour week. Apparently we artists are too unimportant to be con-

trolled by the great white chiefs in Washington: for the first time I begin to feel a resentment against the administration. For it is obvious that railroads and button-hole manufacturers who have behaved badly are now going to be saved; whereas artists whose only crime is that they never could make much of a living, are going to be neglected, as usual, and allowed to starve. In the program of industrial reconstruction every industry is allowed to regulate itself; the big companies will not produce so much that the little fellow will be crushed to the wall; there will be no unfair competition. Why not the same thing for novelists and tenors? The former have several trades unions which could serve as governing bodies and against tenors any legislation would be all right. Or they could be allowed to defy the anti-trust laws and merge with the crooners.[53]

By 1936 the grim persistence of adverse economic conditions had diminished Seldes' appetite for satire, his longstanding commitment to individualism, and especially his belief that success surely came to the conscientious and skillful. He devoted an *Esquire* column to a fierce critique of *Wake Up and Live* by Dorothea Brande. Seldes mocked her admonition to the American people ("Act as if it were impossible to fail") and urged the need to undermine unquenchable self-confidence as unrealistic. Because the "idea of individual success runs against the collective spirit of the age," he pleaded for a "shot of pessimism." Seldes did not ordinarily assume the mantle of disillusioned skeptic, but he had no use for false optimism or naive positive thinking.[54]

How did Seldes (and his fellow critics) feel about meeting so many deadlines? About needing to be so versatile, and producing so many words on subjects that were bound to be ephemeral? And in Seldes' case, writing for a newspaper published by Hearst that ranked just a few cuts above a scandal sheet? As for the last issue, Seldes could point to some interesting precedents. Back in 1917, for example, Seldes had written the following to Vincent Starrett of the Chicago *Daily News* about a Welsh novelist both men admired immensely: Arthur Machen. Machen had acknowledged in a preface that he did evening journalism on the London *Evening News,* which Seldes called a "callous, lowdown, scandalous sheet of the Northcliffe aggregation. On it, occasionally on its precious first page, A.M. strews jewels and sometimes writes very bad stories. Usually on the edit page he writes a simple article—a trip to Whitby, or a discussion of what soldiers mean when they say 'Gone

West' for 'Killed.' . . ." So much for maintaining consistent quality, and so much for the company a journalist keeps. One had to be realistic, especially if one wasn't prosperous, which Machen decidedly was not; and Seldes was much less so once his earnings from *Lysistrata* had been dissipated.[55]

Some journalists were snootier than others about the assignments they would accept; some could *afford* to be snootier; and some shifted from ambivalence to disillusionment. In 1933, not long before Seldes made a long-term commitment to *Esquire* for a monthly column on the lively arts, Frederick Lewis Allen declined a very attractive offer from the *Ladies' Home Journal* to write a monthly column interpreting current events. Allen had money flowing in at the time, of course, from *Only Yesterday*. In November 1935, on the other hand, Bernard DeVoto took over the "Easy Chair" editorial column for *Harper's*, a prestigious pulpit but not an especially lucrative one. DeVoto had contributed essays to *Harper's* since 1927. His "Easy Chair" assignment became his very own for life as it turned out. E. B. White, on the other hand, wrote "One Man's Meat" for *Harper's* from 1938 until 1943 when he simply quit because the commitment had become a burden.[56]

While Seldes worked for the *Evening Journal* he was not permitted to write for any other newspaper. Magazine submissions—even regular relationships—could be considerably more "promiscuous" even though George Horace Lorimer of the *Saturday Evening Post* did not approve and reminded a regular contributor in the 1920s that there was too much overlap in the lists of contributors to prominent magazines. Lorimer believed in loyalty and tried to foster it by paying very well.[57] In 1932, just when Seldes' relationship to the *Post* began to cool, he started contributing to *Scribner's*. Five years later he became a regular in the "People and Arts" section of that magazine and began writing the "Screen and Radio" section on a regular basis. In 1936 Seldes' work also first appeared in *The Atlantic,* which meant added visibility along with prestige, and in the *Saturday Review of Literature,* a bond that became quite firm during the 1950s.

Seldes' relationship with the *Evening Journal* seems to have been amicable and flexible, at least at first. When he wished to be away for several weeks—to England, Sweden, or Bermuda, for instance—friends and colleagues usually supplied replacement columns for him, though sometimes his spot simply remained vacant while he traveled. Although he made complimentary references to William Randolph Hearst in 1933 in his book titled *Years of the Locust,* and although his columns concerning politics and economics (more frequent than at any other time in his career) supported governmental efforts to prevent, as he put it, "the collapse of the capitalist system," some sort of falling-out occurred that contributed to Seldes' departure from the *Journal* in 1937. Within a decade Seldes would also endure a falling-out with CBS and with Paramount Pictures. He was no stranger to job insecurity, though that misfortune happened to affect him later than it did the customary employment victim of the Great Depression. When Seldes had a falling-out, temperament was more likely the provocation rather than how the economic pendulum was swinging.[58]

He did have a relationship as an "editorial associate," which terminated rather mysteriously, with a short-lived, whacky, semi-pictorial monthly titled *Americana* that appeared for eighteen issues starting in February 1932. Edited by Alexander King, it specialized in political, social, and literary satire. A full-page editorial explained why "we" were not Republicans, Democrats, Socialists, or Communists. A plague on all of their houses. "We are Americans who believe that our civilization exudes a miasmic stench and that we had better prepare to give it a decent but rapid burial." Its editorial stance opposed Franklin Delano Roosevelt and modern art, and contained satirical shots at such prominent literati as Heywood Broun, Franklin P. Adams, George S. Kaufman, Alexander Woollcott, and Harold Ross (emphasizing their decadence), as well as some nasty cartoons that caricatured Negroes. Its writers included Nathanael West, E. E. Cummings, S. J. Perelman, George Grosz, and Seldes. Their objective seemed to be a wickedly caustic tone with absolutely nothing held sacred.[59]

In November 1932 Seldes contributed an amusing two-page "Short History of a Depression." Here are four sample entries in his chronology:

May 17, 1930. Prosperity fails to keep date with President Hoover. Reported eaten by bears.

June 3, 1930. Inasmuch as nothing was lost (except paper profits) the condition of America is sound. The sound is hollow.

May 2, 1931. Red Cross proves God superior to Man by providing for victims of drought and flood, but not of strikes. Rugged individualism begins to be considered a typographical error.

September 2, 1931. Wages defy wishes of administration and go down. Solution of depression found in economy, balanced budgets, and huge building program to employ two thousand men alternate Tuesdays and Thursdays, preferably without pay. [pp. 10, 20]

In his full-page editorials Seldes acknowledged that the illustrations in *Americana,* as well as its general tone, were "sadistic"; that everyone regarded the presidential election of 1932 with cynicism and the outcome as scant basis for hope; that a proposed investigation by the U.S. Senate of the causes of the Depression would have banal and negligible consequences— "the Senate will turn up a series of villains, and we are all in the mood for finding a scapegoat." For once Seldes actually blamed the "system," which seems to have meant speculative finance rather than industrial capitalism in general.[60]

Seldes wished to modify but not fundamentally challenge the free enterprise system. From 1932 until 1946, for instance, Selden Rodman edited a lively journal titled *Common Sense.* Its opening editorial announced the principal contributors' belief that a "system based on competition for private profit can no longer serve the general welfare." Those contributors included Stuart Chase, Ernest Boyd, John Dos Passos, A. J. Muste, V. F. Calverton, John Chamberlain, and George Soule—but not Gilbert Seldes. He was a liberal in transition from laissez-faire to limited governmental intervention. Socialism had no seductive appeal for him.

IV

Over an extended period of time, but most intensively in the years 1932–38, Seldes rejected communism as a viable option for the United States. His reasons owed as much to his sense of political reality as they did to his prognosis for economic viability. The notion of a communist party seemed ridiculous to him. "That they should be an organization is reasonable enough; that they should appeal for votes, like capitalist Republicans and bourgeois Democrats, is nonsense." Why? Because in Seldes' view communism was part of a world movement that despised the democratic system of the ballot. And precisely because some prominent communists had denied that their credo was really tantamount to a religion, Seldes believed that adherents ought to acknowledge that theirs was like a universal church. "No other political faith," he wrote, "covers so much ground . . . none asks for such a complete self-dedication."[61]

Seldes seriously doubted whether many American Marxists had actually read *Kapital;* and when he published a twenty-seven-page pamphlet titled *Against Revolution* in 1932, he asserted as part of a litany of fourteen points that "what was inevitable for Russia may not be even desirable for America." Moreover, he added,

We have not gone through the hard labor of dissociating the revolutionary method from a hundred generous impulses and a thousand noble objectives, which can be much more economically attained without revolution. In theory we are all in favor of the abolition of poverty and we are ashamed to say that we are against revolution, because it implies that we are in favor of starvation.

Seldes firmly believed that one could be opposed to revolution without defending the status quo. He insisted, in fact, that anyone opposed to revolution "must be willing to change the present system." From his historical perspective, "the profit system cannot be given up in a day; it can only be modified. What can be given up are the excesses of the system: its excess pressure and its excess yield. The profit system is the one which works for profit regardless of the general good. . . ."* He then launched into a devastating critique of the contemporary system and concluded that advocates of investment finance capitalism had sought to defend "practical business by teaching us Horatio Alger myths, and it has gone on believing that human sacrifices to the glory of protective tariff were admired throughout the country." Thoroughgoing reform rather than revolution had to be the best answer.[62]

The pamphlet struck a nerve and elicited positive responses. Many people seem to have shared Seldes' views. The managing editor of *Scribner's* regretted that the piece hadn't appeared first in his magazine but encouraged Seldes to prepare a kind of sequel because people returning from Europe "are surprised at the pessimism and the amount of squawking which they hear over here where conditions are immeasurably better than they are almost anywhere else." The two men met for lunch and Seldes' response to the question swiftly look shape, though it seems to have become a somewhat curious shape. He chose to say, first, that "the real panic was the terror people had before the crash—the terror of selling out below the top, of not making quite so much money as they might." His second point: "that Europe has a tradition of patient suffering which we have not."

Both of these points suggest a sort of defense of the American people in the present situation, but that is a little bit deceptive. I am not going to

---

*Seldes' appeal for a more humane capitalism was not at all unusual at that time. John Strachey "preached" the very same doctrine in *The Coming Struggle for Power* (1933), a treatise that influenced young radicals like Richard Hofstadter, a student in Buffalo at the time.

minimize the tendency of Americans to complain. I think it desirable to point out that the prosperous and the wealthy have been guilty of an unmanly whimpering. But I think that the real loss of nerve, the true spirit of panic expresses itself in paralysis. On one side there are the subjugated unemployed who do not even riot and at the opposite extreme there is a real mental paralysis among statesmen and great industrialists.[63]

In the essay Seldes certainly spoke for himself as well as many others when he observed that Americans were not very political nor disposed to be insurrectionists. He then declared that conditions were really not so bad, and that the worst fears the Americans had were unjustified. Echoing a recent speech by Justice Louis D. Brandeis, Seldes bemoaned the "timidity which has prevented all our responsible leaders from cutting themselves loose from traditions to offer a bold economy for the future." Ultimately the blame could be evenly distributed. "The economic ignorance of our legislators, the corruption of our cities, the selfishness of industrialists and the arrogance of financiers, have left us apathetic."[64]

All the while Seldes worked on his next major book, *The Years of the Locust,* a history of the United States, mainly public policy, during the Hoover era. If anything, he was so judicious in this work that he became strangely generous (though by no means uncritical) to Hoover. Other political leaders and prominent figures in the world of finance got blasted, however, for their inaction and selfishness. Seldes was masterful at incorporating ironic items of detail, such as: late in 1930 the American Federation of Labor rejected the concept of unemployment insurance as un-American! (Within a year the A. F. of L. had softened that hard-nosed stance and committed itself to *some* form of unemployment compensation.)[65]

Although Seldes really did not conceive of the book as cultural criticism, a fair amount inevitably crept in. Looking back to the 1920s, he noted the shift away from "natural needs" to "created demands," and to the wasteful reality that products were increasingly made to be thrown away. Seldes quite successfully showed how Americans managed to distance themselves from historical mistakes that they had made only three or four years earlier. In the very last chapter Seldes commented on the impact of the Depression upon intellectuals, driving many to the left, and conveyed his resentment toward leftist journals in whose view "every writer who had not gone over to Communism was considered not only a renegade to the freedom of the mind, but a paid slave of capitalism." It annoyed him that, according to Marxist gospel, the arts "subconsciously" served the economic system. Quite the contrary, from Seldes' perspective. Ever since 1912–13 the American capitalist "had witnessed a fermentation of intellect and a growth of criticism which colored books and plays, and even popular newspapers; but it had never occurred to him that these things might be a danger to the source of his wealth. . . . Nine out of ten plays exhibiting a business man made fun of him. . . . Everywhere intellectuals were at work sapping. When the crisis came, the capitalist was cold and friendless." American entrepreneurs, in Seldes' view, had no idea that they could be so vulnerable to assaults by cultural critics, and, in any case, the arts had scarcely been a propagandistic "mouthpiece" for capitalism.[66]

The overall configuration of reviews for his book showed a mixture of strong praise and disappointment. John Chamberlain, who became the daily book critic for the *New York Times* in 1932, felt that Seldes' tentativeness in dealing with Hoover—sometimes sympathetic, at other times quite critical—caused the work to be dramatically ineffective. When history had rendered a clearer verdict on Hoover, Seldes' "intelligent distillation of the day's news will save the [future] author much agony," much clipping, reading, and work. "As it is, it is an excellent running commentary to have around the house."[67] Reviewers for magazines of opinion tended to be more positive than those for daily newspapers, and Christopher Morley, a founder and editor of the *Saturday Review of Literature* (1924–40), gave it a terrific send-off for the Book-of-the-Month Club.[68]

Most amusing of all, however, at least as an historical footnote, Franklin Delano Roosevelt explicitly responded to the book in the fourth paragraph of his Inaugural Address on March 4! Raymond Moley had liked *The Years of the Locust* and recommend it to FDR just when the president-elect was preparing for his first inaugural. Because FDR wanted to strike an upbeat note and persuade Americans that there were no systemic problems utterly beyond repair, he felt that Seldes' overall critique (moderate though it may seem to us) was premature. So Roosevelt's third paragraph ended by acknowledging the twin problems of unemployment and low wages for those with work. Then came these three sentences: "Yet our distress comes from no failure of substance. We are stricken by no plague of locusts. Compared with the perils which our forefathers conquered because they believed and were not afraid, we have still much to be thankful for." Thirty-four years later Seldes recalled his reaction at the time as a "trauma . . . . I thought that my own assessment was judicious—but what the hell? The inaugural address was an event."[69]

V

In the process of writing an autobiographical essay in 1943, Edmund Wilson looked back at the adjustments that his coterie of writers had to make as the 1920s gave way to the very different mood of the '30s, and as a new cohort of critics came of age. "A kind of demoralization set in," he observed, and the conditions for writers—topical and economic— became quite different. "The new 'classes' of intellectuals—it was a feature of the post-Boom period that they tended to think of themselves as 'intellectuals' rather than as 'writers'—were in general sober and poor, and they applied the analysis of Marxism to the scene of wreckage they faced." There is abundant affirmation from others that the newer group of writers regarded themselves as intellectuals.[70] For Seldes, however, the meaningful (and problematic) distinctions were between genuine intellectuals (well read and insightful) and highbrows (pretentious and tolerant of mediocrity so long as it was "arty"), between creative people who were personally agreeable and those who were not, between New Yorkers (now the navel of the cultural universe) and regionalists.[71]

In 1935, just after Seldes published a provocative essay that anticipated his big book *Mainland* (1936) by calling for recognition of American traditions, he received a warm and intense letter of approbation from a southern writer he had not previously met: Allen Tate. Assuming that Seldes shared his hostility to communism, Tate proceeded to explain what the anti-industrial views of the agrarians were all about, and welcomed Seldes as a potential contributor to a new weekly magazine that would be published "*away from New York* . . . in the real United States, outside the region where the illusion of a proletarian revolution is the foundation of a literary career." Tate then offered his own addendum to Seldes' article:

> To make your program good, you have got to distinguish between finance-capitalism and the American tradition, although the former has grown up upon the latter. In other words, we have got to be as thorough-going in our criticism of capitalism as the Communists are, just in order to restore the true capitalism, which is widely diffused ownership of the means of production.[72]

A curious correspondence then ensued in which Tate and Seldes schemed for the latter to write an explication of agrarianism for a kind of proselytizing purpose in the *Saturday Evening Post*. Lorimer would have loved the anti-communism but frowned upon the peculiar spin placed upon capitalism ("distribution"). Although nothing whatever came of it, the intense exchange between Seldes and Tate concerning issues of political economy became heady, highly engaged, and nourished a life-long friendship.[73]

By the mid-1930s Seldes had achieved sufficient prominence in the publishing world that all sorts of people sought his help in getting their views into print. Seldes being a moderate liberal or, as he preferred to call himself, an independent, requests came to him from all points along the ideological spectrum. Along with Tate on behalf of the conservative agrarians, for instance, Seldes received imploring letters from the anarchist Emma Goldman, a friendship inherited from his father:

> The fact is dear Gilbert I must earn some money. *Living My Life* [1931] though bringing me much glory will evidently not bring me worldly goods. . . . I am nearly broke, hence forced to turn to something that would keep the wolf from the door. I might have looked for a job as a cook. It is really much more useful work than writing. However, times are too hard for people to afford the luxury of good cooking. That means I must try to earn my keep by my pen. You see my situation is desperate. That's why I am turning to you for some help and suggestions. Can you think of any publication that would take my stuff? If so, please write me as soon as possible.[74]

Seldes does not seem to have been able to help Goldman any more than he could become a publicist for the agrarians, although his feelings were sympathetic toward both. By 1935, while working on *Mainland*, he positioned himself so much in the mainstream that he became more of a cultural chauvinist than ever before. Referring to his 1935 essay for the *Saturday Evening Post*, Seldes conceded to Allen Tate: "You are quite right in saying that I give comfort to the enemies of all art by attacking the kind of art which I considered unsuitable to our own country, and did not speak of any other type."[75]

In 1936 Seldes smacked all artists, at least satirically, in a spoof for *Esquire* that began as follows: "I don't suppose there is any question now that people having to do with the arts are the worst people in the world, and all that remains is to establish a rank, a sort of hierarchy of offensiveness among them." He then proceeded to do exactly that in an essay, one presumes, he hoped his musical, literary, and artistic friends would never see. At one point he explained the "social impossibility of all artists" by remarking that "they are so absorbed in themselves (not in their work) as to become boorish and uninteresting companions." The tongue-in-cheek character of this essay became fully evident as he approached his finale:

> I have met as many businessmen as I have artists, and never found one of the former as absorbed in business as all artists are in art. Why? Because the businessman assumes, perhaps incorrectly, that he is doing a desirable thing and the artist knows in his heart that he isn't. So the artist has to build up a vast secret vocabulary, a series of technical devices, and a sort of mystery about his work which no baseball player or aviation-mechanic requires.[76]

Seldes might have been pandering to his personal stereotype of the typical *Esquire* subscriber. Perhaps, in fact, his opinion of most people in the arts *had* declined during the tough times of the Depression. (Actually, he was considerably more acerbic toward non-American artists in that essay.) But whatever the provocation for this singular piece of whimsical savagery, Seldes never repeated it. He criticized individual artists from time to time, or even the current health of a particular field of endeavor, such as ballet, but never again these sweeping generalizations about the artist's temperament as a function of his or her vocation.

He does seem to have passed through a nostalgic phase during the mid-1930s, yearning for the superiority of popular arts when they had been at once simpler and more compelling. In 1934 he expressed such regrets about the comic strip, suggesting that modern techniques failed to achieve real humor. Popeye was the lone exception because Popeye managed to escape the gentility that afflicted most of the other comics: "He still fights and curses and is a man's man." Seldes also distinguished between the New York school of comic artists and the western (or Chicago *Tribune*) group: the Gumps, Moon Mullins, Gasoline Alley, and others concerned with domestic and business life. In Seldes' view "the creators have given up the effort to make home or business seem comic, in which they may be wise enough." Similarly, Seldes insisted that musical entertainment had been far better in 1925. Except for one or two Negro bands, he said, jazz was not as "hot" in 1935 as it used to be. And grand opera "has been so snooty, so social, and fundamentally so dull" that Seldes couldn't even be bothered to take it seriously. He concluded that his cultural Rip Van Winkle might very well want to go back to sleep for another ten years. He hadn't missed much.[77]

VI

The passage of time, however, only increased Seldes' high opinion of Ring Lardner. By the summer of 1933 Lardner's health was in decline and he suffered from emotional depression. His son John felt that publication of a collection of Ring's more autobiographical pieces from the *Saturday Evening Post,* mainly non-fiction, would provide an ideal "tonic"; so he proposed to his friend F. Scott Fitzgerald that he take on the task of selection and preparation for publication. Fitzgerald, however, then stalled in his own writing, and drinking heavily from time to time, discussed the project with Seldes and urged John to offer it to his friend.[78]

A few weeks later Fitzgerald solidified the project by urging Maxwell Perkins, his editor at Scribner's, to take it under his wing and commission Seldes "to go through *everything* which is not fiction and make a sort of story out of it." Perkins and Seldes each responded with enthusiasm, partially because Ring died on September 25, 1933. The timing of the editorial project could not have been more appropriate, as it turned out. Neither Seldes nor Perkins realized, at first, just how extensive Lardner's non-fiction work had been, and how fugitive so many of the essays were, ranging from newspaper and magazine pieces to the scripts of engaging radio reports. Born in Niles, Michigan, in 1885, Lardner had established himself as a baseball writer by the age of twenty-five, swiftly expanded the range of his subjects, and worked for several Chicago newspapers, but most notably the *Tribune* from 1913 to 1919, the paper that also employed George Seldes as its European correspondent for several decades starting in 1917. George met Ring in Paris after the war and Ring loved to tell people that the irascible Colonel Robert McCormick had sent Seldes to France "to write the comic side of the World War."[79]

Lardner himself, of course, was the true comic, and that quality most attracted Gilbert Seldes to his writing and to this now posthumous project. By mid-January Seldes had made a selection and wrote to Perkins describing his rationale for it:

> I think from this outline you will see that the book should be a companion volume in non-fiction to Round Up [Lardner's collected short stories]. As Lardner never tried to be an essayist, you will not find in this book anything of the highest artistic interest. On the other hand, the book will indicate, perhaps more clearly than Round Up could, Lardner's range; it will include burlesque of considerable savagery and it will be, I think, a

funnier book. It may, in fact, restore the balance a little bit in the critical estimate of Lardner—since so many people have been impressed by one side of him and have forgotten that he was professionally a humorous writer.

Perkins had long admired Lardner's column, "In the Wake of the News," a "steady, easy stream of inspired paragraphs, skits, and verses." He also wanted an example of Lardner's annual coverage of the World Series (titled "A World's Serious"). He got both, along with Lardner on a major prize fight (Dempsey versus Firpo), on a yacht race, on political party conventions, on disarmament, and on radio. Some transcripts of his radio work were included as well as "Symptoms of Being 35" and "The Young Immigrunts."[80]

Seldes never thought well of sports journalism, but enjoyed Lardner's because, unlike most, it wasn't sentimental. "I have the oddest reason," he wrote in 1937, "for disliking the magnification of sport by sentiment. The stuff is silly, but you can find the same thing in the dramatic pages with their guff about the good old troupers who go through with the show even if they're tired or have a bad cold." Seldes complained that bogus sentimentality "gives a false importance to sport, and the next step is toward, if not into, sport as a State function."[81] Seldes might have been startled to consider that, in addition to Lardner, Heywood Broun, Westbrook Pegler, and James Reston all began their journalistic careers as sports columnists.

In February 1934 Seldes considered not only editing but staging Ring Lardner's short plays. He regarded them as "an attack of sheer lunacy," which appealed to him; but that gambit never went forward, in part, perhaps, because (in Scott Fitzgerald's words) "so much of the nonsense is embodied in the stage directions." In any case Lardner's *First and Last* appeared late in the spring of 1934 with a brief preface by Seldes. Some of his central points about Lardner might easily have applied to Seldes himself. He had sought from Lardner's early and later writings

> those pieces which were not entirely transient and to group them in such a way as to give them the cohesion which, in the case of a writer of daily and weekly articles is sometimes lost because of the variety of subjects and changes of treatment. In Lardner's case the central thing was the temper of his mind. Except for a few pieces written under pressure, everything he wrote expressed that temper perfectly. . . . The flexibility of his newspaper writing, compared with his fiction, gave room for some minor excursions, and some of these have been included.[82]

As Lardner's best biographer has concluded, much of his finest journalism "might have gone unresurrected for years had Seldes not applied such diligence to this assignment; and much of the Lardner material that later found its way into various . . . collections and anthologies was first collected between hard covers in this book."[83] In 1945, more than a decade after that labor of love, Seldes edited for Viking *The Portable Ring Lardner* (1946). Along with a predictably sympathetic twenty-page introduction, Seldes included most of *First and Last* along with the full texts of two popular novels, *You Know Me Al* (1916) and *The Big Town* (1921) plus a selection of eleven short stories.

By the time of his death in 1933 Lardner's books barely sold any longer, and Seldes' compilation did little to spark a revival even though Lardner's reputation grew steadily in the years that followed. What Seldes did achieve, to his dismay, was reactivation of Hemingway's bile. During the early and mid-1920s Hemingway admired Lardner to the point of imitating his style, at times. In September 1934, however, he devoted a mean-spirited, long-winded piece in *Esquire* to an explanation of why Lardner wasn't a great writer: because he must have felt superior to that part of the human race he knew best. He wouldn't use in print the off-color words that folks commonly used. Since Lardner didn't seem earthy enough to Hemingway, he must have been a prude. Given the timing of all this (Seldes had devoted a praise-piece to Lardner in the July *Esquire*), Hemingway slapped Seldes by diminishing Lardner. Two men of trivial talents.[84]

Seldes replied, of course, although in a notably civil tone. Lardner *did* use dirty words, on occasion, but that seemed beside the point. "What Mr. Lardner knew perfectly and Mr. Hemingway doesn't know at all is that these words, except in moments of peculiar stress, have ceased to possess any meaning whatever, least of all a dirty meaning. They are counters, slipped in with the regular coins of conversation, for makeweight." As for Hemingway's implication that there cannot be great literature without the use of words not permitted in polite society, Seldes felt that nothing need be said. "It happens that the hairy-he words were used for a long time in English literature and that that period offers little of consequence."[85]

Not content merely to be defensive, however, Seldes then took to the offensive. After noting Hemingway's fondness for prize-fighting, Seldes pointed out that Lardner observed boxers much less romantically than Hemingway looked at a sailfish or a bull. Because Hemingway was such a romantic writer, he presented the world with a series of "unreal ideal characters" on whom we are expected to hang the trappings of greatness. Lardner's characters, by contrast, aren't better than life. "They are horribly like ourselves." That conveyed a very high compliment, of course; and, for good measure, Seldes devoted his December essay to suggesting that the public had grown weary of hype and hysteria for the heroes of sports.[86]

Hemingway retaliated with the lead essay in January, this time pairing his sarcastic attack on Seldes with a spearing of William Saroyan:

> The magazine [*Esquire*], it seems, is coming out early: a break for all of us who can not wait a whole long month to get another shot of Gilbert Seldes. (It's a vice with me. I tried to break it off. They said all it would bring was blindness, insanity and death but I said no, I'd paid the fifty cents. I could take it or I could leave it alone. Besides I knew his brother George and he was a damn fine newspaper man. Go on. Leave me alone. Let me read Seldes if I want to. It's no worse than a bad cold and if you get it at the start you can knock it with this stuff I'm going to give you. No man need fear Seldes any more. Come on out from under those wheel chairs. Throw away your crutches. There's no danger, men, as long as old Doc Hemingstein is in the magazine. Just take it in your stride.)

Was the "Hemingstein" usage meant to be an anti-Semitic crack at Seldes? Perhaps, but at last the dust then settled for almost three decades, until Hemingway stirred it up once again with a kick from the grave in *A Moveable Feast* (1964). As late as 1969, however, Gilbert had brother George checking his files for information that might explain Hemingway's harsh animus during the 1930s. Gilbert hoped to have the last word in his own memoir.[87]

Late in 1935 Edmund Wilson bashed Hemingway in *The New Republic,* but did so in a way that didn't exactly cover Seldes with glory either because Seldes also wrote on a regular basis for *Esquire.* Discussing *Green Hills of Africa,* Wilson lamented that "the self-dramatized Hemingway we get has the look of having been inspired by some idea of what his public must expect after reading his rubbishy articles in the men's-wear magazine, *Esquire.*" Seldes, however, did not take offense at criticism of his current medium so long as Wilson did not fire at his actual message. Three weeks after Wilson's essay appeared, Seldes' wife sent Wilson a holiday invitation: "Dear Bunny—Please come in for cocktails Friday, January third [GS' birthday]—Love, Amanda."[88]

Fig. 12. Gaston Lachaise, *Gilbert Seldes* (1931), plaster, cast in bronze in 1958. Seldes greatly admired Lachaise.

VII

By the mid-1930s Seldes' financial windfall from *Lysistrata* had been almost entirely used up, expended on busts of himself and his family made by Gaston Lachaise, a sculptor much admired by Seldes (see Fig. 12), and other condiments of the good life. (Lachaise sorely needed the commission at that time.) Early in 1935 he published in *Harper's* a little

Fig. 13. In 1934, the first year following the end of Prohibition, Seldes posed for a liquor advertisement. He received $300 and was nearly fired as a daily columnist for the New York *Evening Journal*. In 1930 he had published *The Future of Drinking*.

parable about "the last American who wanted simply to have a good time and who bought things because he enjoyed them." Although Seldes was really not a self-indulgent consumer, a subjective element clearly pervaded that parable.[89]

One consequence of his straitened circumstances was a willingness to lend himself to purely commercial projects—though it should be noted that he selected them carefully in relation to his personal enthusiasms (see Fig. 13). In 1934, for example, he collaborated with the photographer Leigh Irwin to produce what amounted to a souvenir book for tourists visiting New York City. Titled *This Is New York: The First Modern Photographic Book of New York*, it highlighted more recent structures, such as skyscrapers, though the buildings tended to be oddly anonymous. For that reason it appeared more as an art book than a guide book. Photographic art books were just beginning to come into their own: notice, for example, *Metropolis: An American City in Photographs* by Agnes and Frederick Lewis Allen, images of one day in the life of New York, from dawn to midnight.[90]

Ventures of this sort, along with Seldes' production of a documentary

film, *This Is America* (1933), based upon selections from the most important newsreels of the previous two decades, suggest that the changing
circumstances of his life dictated changes in his vocational priorities. In
1932 he wrote a scornful review of a new book edited by Will Durant,
On the Meaning of Life. Seldes rejected the work because it seemed both
pretentious and middlebrow. Not only would his own work, however,
verge on the middlebrow taste level from time to time, but Seldes repeatedly identified with and defended the middle class. He had a particular
fondness for that phrase *l'homme moyen sensuel,* an idiom literally meaning the man of normal instincts. He first used it in *The 7 Lively Arts* to
explain the special virtues of Mr. Dooley, Finley Peter Dunne's sensible
and tough-minded Irishman of indeterminate social status (lower middle
class?). But it achieved increasing prominence in Seldes' vocabulary of
values and criticism after 1934, when he became a more vocal advocate
for middle-class values.[91]

In 1935 Seldes sent a curious letter to Professor George Sarton, a
famous historian of science at Harvard, requesting assistance: "I am
looking for instances of invention or discovery or the solution of problems specifically made in response to prizes offered." Money as an incentive for creativity! Six months later he published an essay in the *Post*
asserting that creative people needed money in order to survive and that
many marvelous deeds had been accomplished because of the desire for
wealth. Columbus, for example, wanted a 10 percent cut on the precious
things he might find. Ultimately Seldes wished to repudiate the notion
that true art and remuneration were incompatible. "We have very few
records of civilized society," he declared, "in which money was not
important. It would, therefore, be hardly worth saying that these artists
worked for money, if it were not for the continual assumption that
money is the enemy of true art, just as true art is the enemy of money."
What did it all mean? People with great minds had indeed done things
for money, they did them well, "and the world is a better place for it."[92]

During the course of his career Seldes became increasingly intrigued
by interconnections between commerce, culture, and the arts. Much later,
starting in the 1950s, he fully intended to write a book about advertising,
but never got farther than a few insightful essays. The point that needs to
be made here is that his fascination with advertising as a social phenomenon originated during the Great Depression. In 1932, for instance, he
noticed that Bertrand Russell had observed that in times of domestic
retrenchment people were most likely to dispense with necessities but
continue purchasing things that provided them with standing in the

community. That provided an ideal point of departure for a tongue-in-cheek "colyum":

> There ought to be a moral for American manufacturers in this thought. Perhaps they have been wrong in advertising their motor cars and their radios as necessities since our luxuries give us prestige and we cling to them to the end. The ideal commodity, for a depression, ought to be something entirely useless and comparatively expensive, something chic and saleable on the installment plan. And showy.[93]

By 1935 Seldes once again started devoting essays to a topic of growing interest for him: the American passion for attractive industrial design. He called it the "most spectacular artistic triumph of the American people" and claimed they insisted that "certain familiar objects made for and by them should be well designed and handsome." He surveyed the work of a dozen first-rank industrial designers—an exercise he would repeat from time to time—and concluded that designers had contributed notably to the "attractiveness of every-day life by making more and more of the objects we handle and use suit their purpose and please our eye." Seldes especially admired the work of Walter Dorwin Teague, a prominent designer who "remade" Kodak cameras, glassware, and business machines; prepared the Ford exhibits for the San Diego Fair in 1935 and for New York's futuristic World of Tomorrow exposition in 1939; and wrote *Design This Day: The Technique of Order in the Machine Age* (1940).[94]

In 1936 Seldes developed a long and rambling essay to proclaim that, like it or not, commerce and art had been irrevocably united in American culture. Here is how he began, a catchy attention-getter: "When Bing Crosby spoke the name of Marcel Proust into the microphone on the night of August 6, 1936, more or less in honor of Miracle Whip, the long uneasy, half-scandalous affair between commerce and the arts was at last acknowledged." Seldes then remarked, partially aiming to shock his readers, that "the chief producers of works of art" in America during the previous six months included:

> in the field of design: *the New York Central*
> in the theatre: *The Works Progress Administration*
> in light literature: *the Bristol-Myers Company*
> in music: *Henry Ford* and *General Motors*
> in classic drama: *Warner Brothers* and *M-G-M*.[95]

What did it all mean? "The arts have been taken over either by private enterprise or by government and for the first time in history they run the risk of becoming popular." What could explain such a strange trend? The fine arts now seemed increasingly remote. They failed to communicate. They lacked contact with the common man. Consequently, "seeing a vast field for exploitation, business and the government both step in, one for profit, the other to compensate for the defects of the profit system, but both fairly insistent on popularity." Did Seldes have any misgivings or regrets about this state of affairs? Only one, and that fairly predictable for him by 1936:

> A considerable part of the work sponsored by the Government, especially in the theatre and in murals, has had an intellectual-proletarian overtone, which is a pity only in this way: that it has somewhat alienated the body of citizens who still feel they have a stake in the present form of society, the people of the middle class who are so hastily abandoned by radicals that they become an easy prey for demagogues and fascists. For these people, the great commercial enterprises produce works of art, and they do it with a sincerity and passion which sets these productions far ahead of the mincing intellectual works still provided by those who hold art to be a small exclusive property to be enjoyed, like a restricted bathing beach, by the few.[96]

There is a personal coda to Seldes' growing interest in the nexus between commerce and art. Hard times lay ahead, at intervals, because his royalties never kept pace with his readily expanding reputation as a "distinguished critic." In 1969 he typed up on a single sheet what he called "my own adventures with money." It is anecdotal, whimsical, and poignant. Seldes liked to live well, but that would not really be possible after the income from *Lysistrata* ran out. The last item on his list read: "Instances of real indifference—Muriel Draper to poverty and Gerald Murphy to real wealth." Seldes never knew either extreme, but he was hard-up on occasion, and he was not indifferent to deprivation. It annoyed him.[97]

VIII

In that same 1936 essay about commerce and art—actually a sweeping review of all the popular arts during the preceding year—Seldes commented in passing on the mixed qualities of a recent Warner Brothers

Fig. 14. Louis Armstrong as Bottom in *Swingin' the Dream* (Dec. 1939). Courtesy of the Theatre Collection, the New York Public Library for the Performing Arts, Lincoln Center, New York.

film version of Shakespeare's *A Midsummer Night's Dream,* directed by Max Reinhardt. The movie must have planted a seed that germinated in his mind for several years, leading eventually to his own adaptation of that play, a musical extravaganza on which he collaborated with Erik Charell, using music by Felix Mendelssohn, Benny Goodman, and others, scenery following cartoons designed by Walt Disney, and choreogra-

Fig. 15. Butterfly McQueen as Puck, Maxine Sullivan as Titania, and Louis Armstrong as Bottom in *Swingin' the Dream* (Dec. 1939). Courtesy of the Theatre Collection, the New York Public Library for the Performing Arts, Lincoln Center, New York.

phy by Agnes de Mille. Although the show folded after only thirteen performances at the immense Center Theatre in midtown Manhattan, it was most notable—and should have been memorable—not merely because the cast was racially mixed, but because the African-American performers included an astonishing array of stars: Louis Armstrong as Bottom (see Figs. 14 and 15), Jackie ("Moms") Mabley as Quince, Butterfly McQueen as Puck, Dorothy Dandridge and her two sisters as the pixies, Maxine Sullivan as Titania, and Bill Bailey dancing as Cupid.

Although Seldes was not always a 100 percent enthusiast, he had long been intrigued by black jazz. In 1936 he recalled that a dozen years earlier he customarily carried around with him a recording of the "Livery Stable Blues" to use at his public lectures as contrast to Paul Whiteman's soft and smooth rendering of "A Stairway to Paradise." All-black musical revues achieved considerable popularity during the 1920s, and did well in northern cities, above all in New York. Writing for *Esquire* in 1937 Seldes remarked that "the native steps of the Negro have got themselves incorporated into American dancing in both popular and tap dancing."[98]

In 1932 Seldes heard Paul Robeson sing at a private gathering and then enjoyed an extended conversation with him. Seldes asked Robeson how he felt about "Ol' Man River," his only vocal contribution—though a real show-stopper—to *Show Boat.* Robeson explained, according to Seldes' newspaper report, "that musically it is a complete miracle, the creation of the tone of the Negro spiritual by an alien to the Negro's traditions. The proof is that he can sing it between two spirituals and it is not a false note, there is no change in the emotional response of the audience." Seldes then observed what a peculiar and difficult problem Robeson had to face as an ambitious African-American performer who did not want to compromise his integrity or his identity:

> As a concert singer, Robeson had a pretty problem to solve. As a Negro he could make his greatest success by singing spirituals, but as a singer he had a range far beyond that required by the Negro's songs. He determined, he says, to sing other songs, but never to sing songs which could spoil his singing of spirituals by forcing him to adopt a style foreign to him. Italianate arias and at least half of the sentimental German songs, he had to rule out, and only recently, learning Russian as if by instinct, he has uncovered a new and sympathetic repertory of songs for himself.[99]

Seldes clearly felt considerable enthusiasm for blacks as performers and for African-American musical rhythms, dance, and style. What remained to be determined were the vehicle, the medium, and the necessary production support. In 1937 he prepared an adaptation of *The Taming of the Shrew* for the Columbia Shakespearian Cycle, broadcast over CBS during July and August. In 1938 a WPA Federal Theatre project brought *The Swing Mikado,* an all-black, lively adaptation from Chicago (where it played for five months) to New York. The setting was shifted to a South Sea island, and the idiom was redolent of "hot" Harlem night spots. Seldes now had all the inspiration he needed to cut loose, and he got not only the monetary backing but the largest theatre in New York, at Radio City.

Seldes' musical rendition of *Swingin' the Dream* was set in New Orleans in 1890. He used white performers to portray aristocrats and blacks to portray Shakespeare's humble folk, clowns, and fairies. The off-stage music by Benny Goodman was so sensational that it outshone the actors (see Figs. 16 and 17). Brooks Atkinson loved Goodman's sextet but only tolerated "a whole regiment of Negro jitterbugs gyrating through the

THE · CENTER · THEATRE

Fig. 16. Al Hirschfeld, cartoon for *Swingin' the Dream* (late 1939).
© 1939 Al Hirschfeld. Drawing reproduced by special arrangement with Hirschfeld's exclusive representative, the Margo Feiden
Galleries Ltd., New York.

background." Otherwise he called it an "uneven show indifferently ex-
ploited." A reviewer for the *Herald Tribune* felt that despite a lot of
activity and energy "a curious air of the desultory hangs over the proceedings. . . . [It] proves in the end to be just a series of good night-club
turns, tossed rather carelessly together and brought to no good end."
Several reviewers complained that Seldes and Charell were too deferential to the bard, became tedious as a result, and silenced both Goodman
and Armstrong for too long at a stretch. As the *Daily Mirror* put it, the
production was swell when it "loses the book and shags and jives"; but
that didn't happen often enough. John Anderson of the *Journal American*

Fig. 17. Al Hirschfeld, the cast of *Swingin' the Dream* (late 1939). © Al Hirschfeld. Drawing reproduced by special arrangement with Hirschfeld's exclusive representative, the Margo Feiden Galleries Ltd., New York.

said almost the opposite, however. He found the show "riotous in color, superb in its trucking, giddy, gaudy, and cockeyed. My only complaint is that there is too much of a good thing. It wore me down."[100]

All of those reviews appeared on November 30, following opening night. They spelled doom for the production, and subsequent notices were not much kinder. According to *Variety, Swingin' the Dream* was "more Cotton Club than the Bard" and the whites tended to be verbose in their libretto. *Time* called it a "lavish jitterbug extravaganza," but as a show "it falls flat as a pancake. It is overcrowded, over-elaborate, too much of a good thing. . . . The authors seem to feel that if they have less than 50 people on the stage the audience will imagine it is intermission." To complicate matters, the four distinct plots of *A Midsummer Night's Dream,* "which clog it plenty as a play, virtually wreck it as a musical." (Other reviewers only counted three "interweaving" plots.) A reviewer for the *Catholic World* provided the most particular reasons for disaster:

As for the fairies, Maxine Sullivan from the radio, is Titania. She enters in a World's Fair taxi and goes to sleep in a Murphy bed that pops out of a tree. As her voice is not suited to the vast distances of the Center stage, microphones in the shape of caterpillars or snails shoot up in front of her whenever she begins to sing.

Rosamond Gilder wrote an obituary six weeks after the show had died of natural causes: "Showmanship was not there, nor any ingenuity in direction or planning which would have made of a collection of brilliant ideas a functioning whole."[101]

Perhaps Seldes had some small premonition of how the decade might end for him—with a huge let-down—when he opened one of his daily columns this way in 1933:

> It occurs to me that the business of reviewing books ought to be taken away from book-reviewers just as the business of criticizing plays ought to be taken away from dramatic critics. I can say this with freedom, at the moment, because I am under the guns of neither of these enemies of royalty statements, and I might add that I held the same opinion when I was reviewing both books and plays.

The reason, however, turned out to be considerably less interesting than the assertion. The actual reason, according to Seldes,

> is that reviewers of books and plays are under moral obligation to read books and to see plays. Things have come to such a pass that a reviewer feels bound to tell, openly, at what page or what act he gave up the effort to follow an author. This duty coupled with the fact that reviewers get books and plays free, makes them uncertain guides. On one side they are influenced by the normal man's dislike of doing what he has to do; on the other side they are advising us to pay for a thing which they are valuing without paying for it.[102]

He seemed to be saying that sometimes reviewers and critics are simply non-rational curmudgeons. Although that is true, such a negative consensus about *Swingin' the Dream* suggests that candor rather than mean spirits were at work in December 1939. In any case, Seldes never wrote or adapted another production for the stage, though he did go to Hollywood several times after World War II to try his hand at film scripts for Paramount. Those ventures did not turn out very well either.

Regarding critics and audiences alike, Seldes might have recalled the closing sentence of a letter that he received from T. S. Eliot in 1924 (and carefully saved): "Yes, one can never strike the popular fancy, I'm afraid: all one can do is avoid writing for intellectualsintelligenzzia [*sic*] by aiming at what OUGHT to be the popular fancy if there was a People (and in these days of democracy there isn't any people) and if it had a fancy."[103] There would have been limited solace for Seldes in that warning, however, because unlike Eliot he happened to believe that there *was* a "people" and he felt committed to cultural democracy.

Seldes' problem, it seems to me, both as a critic and as a creator of culture, was that he did not belong either with the pure populists and Marxists or with the high-culture elitists. Although a genuine intellectual and modernist, he truly happened to enjoy what he labeled *Lysistrata* when writing to Eliot in 1932: "vulgarization." In sum, Seldes liked both the avant-garde and kitsch, an unusual combination.

In 1939, concidentally, the influential critic Clement Greenberg published an essay that subsequently became quite famous, called "Avant-Garde and Kitsch." From Greenberg's perspective, of course, the two impulses were mutually exclusive rather than compatible. He believed that avant-garde initiatives in the arts had emerged almost simultaneously with kitsch, which he defined as popular (indeed vulgar) commercialized art and literature. (That simultaneity, by the way, just happened to coincide with the start of Seldes' career as an editor, author, and critic.) By 1939, Greenberg believed, kitsch had been taken for granted for much too long. Kitsch occurred at several different levels, he felt, some of them "high enough" to be dangerous to the cultural health of people who were naive or ill-informed.[104] Whereas Greenberg scorned kitsch, however, Seldes had far more ambivalent feelings about the phenomenon, liking some manifestations but not others. Moreover, to paraphrase E. B. White's famous line, one man's kitsch could be another man's prized possession.

In a very real sense, the year 1930 marked the beginning of a new chapter in American cultural history. It was highly symptomatic, for example, that *The Dial* terminated its existence in 1929, even before the great crash, and the seminal Provincetown Playhouse closed in December 1929. The new decade began for Seldes with his huge success in *Lysistrata* but closed with a costly, colossal flop, *Swingin' the Dream*. The decade did not end conclusively, however, because Seldes moved increasingly toward middlebrow culture during the 1930s. He made a documentary film and achieved prominence as a film critic, made radio programs and appeared as a guest on talk shows—as we shall see in Chapters Six and Seven. He also became the first director of television for CBS. All of that, added to his daily newspaper column and his monthly essays in *Esquire* and elsewhere, meant that his career had become inextricably intertwined with diverse modes of communication.

In consequence, Seldes' role as a critic involved him, more and more, as someone deeply concerned with all those agencies of communication, new and old. Some years before, Frederick Lewis Allen had argued that American magazines had great potential power, should be taken very seriously, and warranted close critical attention.[105] While others were more responsive to Allen's particular appeal, Seldes chose to concentrate his scrutinizing analyses on film and radio, but also the popular arts with which his reputation as a critic had begun.[106] Moreover 1939 was not exactly a year of closure for him because in 1935–36 he began a preoccupation with Americana and Americanism that persisted with intensity for a decade. Even though his relationship with the *Saturday Evening Post* ended in 1936–37, Seldes seemed to take upon himself, as a personal challenge, the *Post*'s self-imposed mission to "interpret America to itself." More on all of that in Chapter Eight.

6

"The Movies Come from America"

S eldes wrote film criticism along with essays about the movie industry for almost four decades, from the early 1920s until the later
1950s. Because his basic views and criteria remained constant, in
many respects, I have chosen to look at responses to silent and sound film
in a single chapter that ranges across all but the last years of that span,
when he became much less sanguine about what he saw. He regarded
American-made films as a fairly distinctive species, for better and for
worse, though he did not emphasize that point unduly. The message he
did reiterate with great frequency concerned the need to recognize that
stage and screen were absolutely separate media, that the theatre had
contributed virtually nothing to movies, and that film-makers should not
attempt to borrow any characteristics or techniques from the stage. Consequently he criticized movie actors who performed as though they were
still on stage. When the "talkie" emerged in 1927–29, he carried the
distinction a step farther and insisted upon the importance of recognizing differences in appropriate techniques between stage, silent film, and
"talkies."[1]

One effective way to make his point was to contrast what happened
when a good play, such as Eugene O'Neill's *Strange Interlude,* became a
first-rate film. In O'Neill's original version, for example, the secret
thoughts of characters would be spoken aloud while other people on
stage at the time behaved as though they heard nothing. It couldn't be

done that way on the screen, of course, so clever devices were developed to communicate private sentiments to the audience though not to other participants. Seldes also believed that with movies, little things were more likely to be noticed or remembered. "When you see a tragedy or a musical show," he observed, "you are inclined to think of it as a whole; you liked it or you didn't; you liked some parts but not others. . . . Whereas in the movies, you are constantly picking out little bits."[2]

Closely linked to his belief in film as a unique form of entertainment was Seldes' emphasis upon the uses of motion and the rhythm of movement as the screen's most distinctive attribute. As he wrote in 1929, all good pictures "are based on a single principle, which is the use of motion. Motion includes the flow of images as well as a race with motor cars; it takes in rhythm as the governing principle of the whole picture as well as gait and pace in the movement of a single player across the screen." Hence D. W. Griffith successfully conceived of "his crowd as a combination of movements," and Seldes worried that certain inevitable attributes of costume (i.e., historical) drama would inhibit the appropriate flow of motion on film. In fact, when the talkies emerged late in the 1920s he feared for a while that even speech might impede or interfere with motion.[3]

Although Seldes wished to make particular observations about many individual films, and developed an array of general points about trends as well, a cluster of central themes is readily apparent in his work. From the late 1890s, when highbrows began to attack the earliest movies as vulgar, on through the contempt expressed by George Jean Nathan and H. L. Mencken twenty-five years later, the dominant impulse was for intellectuals to scorn film as an art form that did not deserve attention from serious or cerebral people. As Wolcott Gibbs wrote in *The New Yorker,* movies were aimed at an audience "incapable of reading without moving its lips."[4]

Seldes rejected such snobbery, and in the process he advocated the democratization of popular taste by means of film, but also the democratization of criticism itself. He insisted that "our habitual dismay at the low taste of the public is thoroughly illogical," and by the mid-1930s he acknowledged that the emergence of a mass medium required a reorientation of critical standards. "In fiction and the theatre," he wrote, "neither of which has ever been directed to the great public, the taste of the public does not coincide with the judgment of the critics; but in an art or entertainment, like the movies, specifically intended for the vast majority, the popular judgment is backed by critical opinion." Although he referred to the movies positively as "mass entertainment," he certainly did not approve of all that Hollywood produced, nor did he believe that it required approval. Rather, he seemed to feel that Hollywood owed much of its success to serendipity. For months on end, he complained, the movies produce the "kind of drip which makes enthusiasts like myself speechless for the defense. Then they drop any attempt to achieve actuality and go back to their business, which is to provide mass entertainment (above the level of social harm); and then they turn out dozens of topnotch entertainments, the intellectual and artistic quality of which are quite as high as that of current plays and novels."[5]

By the end of the '20s Seldes also achieved historical perspective on the emergence of film criticism itself, a sub-genre that he had been noticing for more than a decade. He broke it down into four categories: what appeared in professional journals, "which is merely a by-product of paid advertising and is entirely negligible"; what appeared in "independent professional journals, directed to the exhibitor and offering for the most part criticism of the box-office value of films"; what appeared in the daily press, "which was for a long time in the hands of gushing girls or cub reporters, [and] is still ridden by those pests, but is emerging into decent criticism varying only with the intelligence and the independence of the critics"; and finally, the work of "unattached aesthetes of the film" who had, unfortunately, "recorded some extraordinary errors." If that sounds like unmitigated cynicism (and sexism) directed at all film critics, Seldes nonetheless looked back to those he called the "theoretical critics" and lauded them for telling the producers that "they were not using their own material to best advantage and that the secret of good movies lay in the camera. They said that the camera could be made to express more things, more clearly, more effectively, more rapidly."[6]

Seldes concurred and the key to what he meant can be found in his constantly reiterated emphasis upon movement as the distinctive quality of film. In the motion picture, he declared,

America actually discovered a form of artistic expression which corresponded to the way America had lived for a century and will live: because the essence of the movie is exactly what you think: movement, and that happens to be the one dominant characteristic of all American history. And the moment the movie appeared the aesthetes shrank back to whatever was motionless and still.

Despite his strong admiration for Walker Evans, Seldes did not regard still photography as a high or serious art. He found it pretentious, much touted by aesthetes, static and lacking in "rude energy" by comparison with movies. It bothered Seldes that the still camera could be brutal: "it always catches people with their mouths open or, in a sense, with their pants down." He also disliked the contrived angles so common in still photography at that time.[7]

Any form of contrivance, in fact, irritated Seldes. Consequently he complained in 1940 that the "Face-Job" made all women look alike on the screen, it removed their individuality and humanity and substituted a "degraded tendency to present men in movies as 'worms,' that is, as gangsters or war-makers." In his view men were being degraded in films because they did not appear as the intelligent equals of women.[8]

Above all, however, Seldes' most common concern—aimed at producers, directors, and critics alike—involved their failure to acknowledge and act upon film as a singular medium. As he wrote in 1927: "The conception of the movie as having standards of its own, laws and compulsions which it must follow, and possibilities for independent existence, has not yet become an accepted part of the critical equipment." What he disliked so stridently in Cecil B. De Mille's *King of Kings* was connected to his distaste for still photography. Because the picture moved so ponderously, he argued, a series of still paintings would have been equally effective. Consequently the "success of such a picture sets back the art of the movie by a decade."[9]

Seldes wrote that particular review, of course, during the difficult period of transition from "movies" to "talkies," a shift that virtually all critics worried might not prove viable. In 1928, for example, he speculated about the potential impact of sound upon film: Would it simply be used as an accompaniment, or would it become a basic and integral element in film? More pointedly, given Seldes' theoretical emphases, would the introduction of speech inhibit freedom of movement in film? Would the delightful attributes of pantomime be lost? Perhaps movies would come to resemble filmed stage plays once sound was fully introduced—an outcome feared by Seldes. Because he had not been satisfied with the overall quality of silent film during the mid-1920s, Seldes also worried that directors would regard the advent of speech as a "godsend, for it offers a novelty and again postpones the day when their feeble intelligence and atrophied imagination will be driven out of the movies."[10]

If Seldes seems excessively concerned and lacking in vision at the advent of sound in film, we must remember that he hardly stood alone at that juncture. His fears appear to have been highly representative. Graham Greene, for instance, although much better known as a novelist, wrote a great deal of film criticism for *The Spectator* between 1935 and 1940. The advent of sound horrified him, Greene recalled: "It seemed like the end of film as an art form."[11]

I

If we start with Seldes' first phase as a film critic, 1923–28, we discover that his immense enthusiasm for Mack Sennett, Charlie Chaplin, D. W. Griffith, and a few other major figures of the early years did not carry over to the industry or the medium as a whole. Writing one of his earliest ten-year retrospective pieces (in 1924), Seldes remarked that "in ten years, the movie as we know it, was created; in the last five it was very nearly ruined." Although in the next sentence he expressed strong hope for its future, he remained sharply critical in most of his work on film until the end of the decade.[12] He reiterated his basic complaints with regularity: too many worthless epics and "spectacle" movies, poor direction, failure to treat film as a distinct genre quite different from live productions on the stage, and an unwillingness to recognize that plot per se did not matter nearly as much as "the treatment by which the plot is realized."[13]

Another point that Seldes insisted upon at this time arose from his persuasion that film could be an artistic success and still achieve popularity with the "nickel and dime patrons." He refused to believe that high culture and popular culture were irrevocably cruising along separate tracks. In 1925, when the International Film Art Guild asked Seldes to suggest a list of ten movies to be shown as part of a special program of films that would otherwise be forgotten, he took pains to explain why his list was a "mixture of sacred and profane." He declared that efforts to keep alive the popular film were just as important as sustaining the "arty" film. (That to an organization devoted to the perpetuation of art films!) Lest such a declaration sound like an acknowledgment of bi-level culture tracks, Seldes argued repeatedly during the 1920s (and later) that artistic integrity or quality need not make a film "arty" or restrict its potential audience. He firmly believed that superb technique would result in better movies and not scare away any segment of their potential clientele.[14]

One other theme recurrent in Seldes' essays on film during the 1920s concerned the differences between those produced in the United States and those made elsewhere. German films, for example, despite their technical limitations, "had definitely something to teach us." Producers there had, perhaps intuitively but possibly "by long study, learned something about the responses of the human eye; they had used architectural devices; they had used space in relation to crowds instead of depending wholly upon movement in relation to crowds." And in 1921 the Germans had exported *The Cabinet of Dr. Caligari,* a serious, enigmatic, expressionist, and innovative film. The sheer intelligence of such films intrigued Seldes, and he also noticed that foreign movies (especially English, French, and German ones) had a far more delicate sense of tempo than most American films. "We have all seen climaxes played without a single variation of pace, and [the fact] that emotional intensity can be projected by contrast of pace, rather than by mere increase, has not yet been shown on our screen."[15]

When it came to substance, however, Seldes revealed by 1925 an ambivalence that he never really resolved. On the one hand, he observed, foreign directors had injected a distinctly new element. "Accustomed to the free play of ideas in the drama, they have supplied texture and body by inserting ideas into the film." Lest that sound altogether complimentary, however, Seldes also felt a strong predilection for melodrama, westerns, and thrilling chase scenes. He even expressed grave reservations about overly serious movies, such as lengthy explorations of "the philosophy of the battle of the sexes." Nevertheless, when Hollywood languished in prolonged periods of drought or utter banality, Seldes would decry that tendency and declare that "the old formulas are stale."[16] In 1936, for example, he began one of his most important essays about the American film industry (and its critics) with sharp words for the industry and a droll, emblematic story:

> The permanent situation in Hollywood is this: every producer says, seriously and with the greatest sincerity, that the pictures he will offer next year will be in every way superior to those he has made this year; but it is an offense against the current morality to suggest that any of this year's pictures are in any way short of perfection. To hint a fault or hesitate dislike is not only bad manners; it brings you, directly or indirectly, to the final argument, that the picture you have criticized has made, or will

make, a million and a half at the box office, with the implied rebuke that any improvement you have mentioned would have cut down the excellent figure.

The error of criticism so far has been that the critics accepted the producers' finances and disagreed with them about art. I propose, instead, to take the cue dropped by Bernard Shaw many years ago, in one of the most famous, and probably most authentic, of all the stories about Samuel Goldwyn. Haggling over prices for the plays, Mr. Shaw was assured by Mr. Goldwyn that the movies made out of the plays would be in every way loyal to the original intent of the author and, as productions, incomparable. "You are a business man, Mr. Goldwyn," said Shaw, "and interested only in art; I am an artist, and interested only in money."[17]

By 1927 Seldes had become a regular film critic for *The New Republic,* which meant writing about particular films, reviewing books about film as art and industry, but above all assessing movies in general as a cultural phenomenon. He commented astutely, for instance, on the social composition of movie audiences in the early decades. It is now the conventional wisdom to mention, in passing, that movie-going had special appeal for immigrants and the working class; but in 1929 Seldes specified why:

> The moving picture attracted those people for whom no fixed form of entertainment existed; people without knowledge of the language, barred from the theatre, the library, the light magazine, even the burlesque show; those without the slight discipline of mind necessary to follow a play; those too poor to afford vaudeville or the cheap melodrama.

His emphasis upon ethnicity, class, and educational level reinforced his ongoing hostility to highbrows—in this instance because they regarded the Keystone comedies as vulgar and unrefined, whereas Seldes found them delightful. As cultural critics, he declared, highbrows had been "ineffective on the course of the movies," and he liked to point out that ordinary movie-goers appreciated Charlie Chaplin before the "aesthetes knew of his existence."[18]

In the same slim book containing these observations, a book that established Seldes permanently as a pre-eminent film critic, he argued most emphatically for the distinctiveness of film as a social and cultural experience. Only with movies, he observed, and in no other art form, did people arrive in the middle and depart in the middle. Only with this particular medium, moreover, did people first make the decision to go to the movies and subsequently determine what film to see in particular.

For many it really didn't matter. What counted was the sociable and distracting experience of going to *some* movie, almost any movie. Whether or not it was a good or an important film seemed to be quite secondary.[19]

In this same volume, also, Seldes first developed for American readers his emphasis upon the centrality of movement as the very essence of film as an art form. Influenced by his reading of Elie Faure's *The Art of Cineplastics* (1923) and several works by Alexander Bakshy, he quoted Faure's comment that "the interpenetration, the crossing and the association of movement and cadences already give us the impression that even the most mediocre films unroll in musical space."[20] *An Hour with the Movies and the Talkies* received very positive reviews at the time and remained a standard work. Hence Seldes' annoyance in 1965 when drama critic Robert Gessner announced as a kind of personal discovery the important role of movement in film. As early as 1924, in *The 7 Lively Arts,* Seldes had explained the essence of motion pictures as *"movement governed by light,"* a concept that he elaborated in 1929.[21]

With a mixture of petulance and poignancy, Seldes wrote Gessner that "many years ago I decided that priority in the announcement of an idea or principle was relatively unimportant. But I am, frankly, dismayed by your failure to mention the few people who did anticipate yourself in seeing that *motion* was of the essence in the cinema. . . ." This would neither be the first nor the last occasion when Seldes was ahead of his time among American critics yet received little or only partial credit for his prescience.

II

During the course of his career as a cultural critic Seldes wrote innumerable essays in which he speculated about the future of vaudeville and burlesque, silent films and talkies, radio and television—and above all, the impact of one medium's emergence and development upon another. What would an older medium have to do in order to improve, or survive, or remain competitive? Seldes became a kind of cultural diagnostician, prognosticator, and sometime polemicist. Re-reading his scattered and uncollected essays about film, we are able to recapture the uncertainties, false starts, and ambiguities in his (any many others') responses to the transition from silent movies to sound. It was a complicated shift, and what observers had to say at the time is important not because of their profundity—they often speculated incorrectly—but because the history of hesitation, uncertainty, even confusion, deserves a more prominent place in our cultural assessments than it has hitherto received.

When talkies began to emerge in 1928, Seldes felt that the film industry faced a crisis. How could it best handle the technology as a completely new art form rather than as an add-on? He believed that each type of film would develop in its own distinctive way, but that silent film still had a great artistic future. He was wrong on both counts. "The film with full dialogue," he wrote, "will become a separate form of entertainment, drawing to itself nearly everything tawdry and vulgar in the silent film and leaving the silent film in the hands of people, mostly foreigners and amateurs, able to appreciate its values." Seldes feared that talkies would have a "minimum of illusion and will make a minimum appeal to the imagination." Silent film seemed superior because it retained so much room for viewer imagination. Others who were positioned even closer to the movie world shared these views and communicated them to Seldes. Charlie Chaplin, who favored sound effects but not dialogue, remarked that "motion pictures need dialogue as much as Beethoven symphonies need lyrics."[22]

In 1929, when Seldes discussed this issue in several essays and a book, his uncertainty became more evident. He recognized that a transition was in progress, accurately calling it "the awkward age." On the one hand, he acknowledged the inevitability of sound and speech, "not as an accident, not as a toy, not as an additional attraction, but something demanded by the nature of the whole which they have created." Nevertheless, he did not feel at all sanguine about the inevitable success of talkies, in part because of an inability, thus far, "to find the proper relation between the camera and the microphone." Perhaps what he called the "mobile camera" would supply a solution to utilizing speech without interrupting the continuity and flow of film or hampering its freedom of movement.[23]

By 1930, however, Seldes had ceased making a categorical distinction between movies and talkies as modes of entertainment with separate destinies. He referred, instead, to the "movie-talkie," a hybrid mix that "refuses to take the sanctity of [cinematic] marriage seriously." Although sound had somehow harmed the newsreel, in his opinion, he acknowledged that some comedy worked well with speech and felt assured that the talkie would not destroy Chaplin's career as an entertainer.[24] By 1937–38, moreover, he had ceased to be caustic about talkies, but believed that film had started to "swing back to good principles, in spite of sound, and you can now believe that the fundamental art of the pictures has been modified, but has proved itself superior to change."[25]

Seldes eventually gave the sound screen credit for improving the intelligence level of film and for developing the animated cartoon accompanied by sound. On occasion, however, even as late as 1940, he seemed more than a bit nostalgic in commenting that Hollywood could still learn a lot from the genius of silent film. Observations of that sort drew fire from younger critics who had not grown up so enamored of silent movies. As one of them wrote, "his statement that the things one remembers most vividly out of sound pictures will always be a purely visual impression, such as the silent screen could have given equally well, is pretty suspicious." Basically, however, Seldes was neither romantic nor nostalgic, and his belief that the ultimate impression left by film was primarily visual rather than aural seems sensible.[26]

In a 1942 book defending American culture in general, Seldes acknowledged that movies did not become a truly prodigious cultural force until the 1930s when sound techniques had been mastered. Because that development coincided with radio's coming of age during the 1930s, there is a sense in which Seldes dated the emergence of mass culture, as distinct from popular culture, to the mid- and later 1930s.[27] The success enjoyed by such publications as *Life, Look,* and *Reader's Digest* during the 1930s reinforced that view, along with the democratization of art that resulted from New Deal support for cultural programs.

It comes as no surprise, then, that during the 1930s critics and lay persons alike increasingly thought about cultural transmission in terms of the desirability of documenting ordinary lives as well as newsworthy events. By the later 1920s American producers had begun to dominate the international newsreel business by employing a world-wide network of news-gathering facilities, cameramen, contact men, and reporters. In 1928 Roy E. Larsen of *Time* magazine coined the term "newscasting." He initiated the weekly broadcast of a ten-minute program series of brief news summaries drawn from current issues of *Time*. That program was beamed over thirty-three stations across the United States. Between 1931 and 1945 "The March of Time" became one of radio's most popular programs. It was presented in various formats, often three times each week for fifteen minutes per show, or once a week in a thirty-minute format, sometimes on CBS and sometimes on NBC. Filmed newsreels also enjoyed very broad appeal, especially during the 1930s, though they were never big money-makers for their backers. Coverage and production costs tended to rise along with revenue.[28]

Given Seldes' deep interest in all aspects of film, it should also come as no surprise that from time to time he contemplated a more creative involvement in the process. Although his achievements in this area turned out to be minor, they need to be noted because his first-hand engagement in the process not only made him a more astute critic, it later led him to write an important manual on the nitty-gritty techniques involved in preparing television productions.[29]

As early as 1922 Seldes amused himself, as he explained to G. K. Chesterton, by preparing a film scenario "which was in effect a free fantasia" on a theme in one of Chesterton's stories. Although Seldes sought permission to proceed with production, nothing came of the project. In 1931 Seldes and Edmund Wilson wondered where they might find investors willing to back a film script by Upton Sinclair, another scheme that came to naught. In the meantime Seldes carped about the success of Noel Coward's *Cavalcade,* a film concerning the trials and triumphs of Great Britain since the early twentieth century. From Seldes' perspective Coward's play evoked intense emotions and patriotism, yet remained superficial because it ignored issues of social injustice. Reading Seldes' 1933 review one clearly gets the sense he felt confident that he could do better if only he had the resources.[30]

Seldes soon raised the necessary funds to produce a historical documentary that did emphasize social injustice in the United States, a work called *This Is America* that was well received later in 1933. He simply made a selection of extracts from the most important newsreels of the previous two decades in the United States, "trying to build up a reasonable history of our time as the camera caught it in action." Although the film made Seldes neither rich nor famous as a documentary producer, that experience would prove to be invaluable six years later when Seldes wrote and produced several prize-winning documentaries concerning American history and culture for CBS radio.[31]

In 1933–34, however, circumstances simply were not propitious for Seldes to break into film-making in an influential or sustained manner. When a proposal emerged that a movie be made of *Looking Backward,* Edward Bellamy's utopian novel, Seldes prepared a rough scenario that he believed "would give a tremendous action to the work." But the project was dropped, a typical experience for Seldes but also for many others working on a free-lance basis for the media in economically depressed and unpredictable times. Insufficient funds and disagreements among media executives concerning matters of commercial viability managed to kill off innovative efforts at script-writing.[32]

In 1935 Seldes declared that films not meant to be feature-length, ranging from cartoons to documentaries, had come a long way yet remained underdeveloped as a genre. He singled out for praise the newsreel *The March of Time* because it combined, despite constraints upon length, "the historical retrospective with the flash of current interest." He felt that it had made "steady progress from a weak, but not bad beginning to solidly built episodes, four to each issue, in which good editing is still more notable than good technical handling, but both combine to make a satisfactory unit." It pleased him that less emphasis was being placed upon re-enactments than in the early years of *March of Time* newsreels, although he understood full well that re-enactments became necessary when certain scenes were unavailable on film. He had used re-enactments himself when he made *This Is America* two years earlier.[33]

By 1938, despite his personal lack of success as a director and producer of documentary films, Seldes had become an ardent enthusiast, especially because most of the feature films coming from Hollywood seemed so dismal to him. He proclaimed *The River* by Pare Lorentz to be the most absorbing film released in 1937. It was a documentary, made for the U.S. Department of Agriculture, in which the Mississippi River was the only character. In February 1938 Seldes lectured at the New School for Social Research in a series devoted to "The Documentary Film as History and Journalism." He illustrated his lecture with selections from newsreels made since 1915, emphasizing the development of pictorial records as an important and powerful contribution to journalism.[34]

After Seldes became the first director of television for CBS in 1937 he wrestled once more with making films, but for him the brand-new medium altered conventional priorities. Whereas music was a known quantity, what to show on the grainy black and white screen was not at all self-evident. For several years he searched for the ideal visual materials to accompany the music he wanted to play. As he explained, "if I should attempt to put on the screen a movie of the solemn tramp of feet, just humanity endlessly walking toward a grave, I would have a good or bad visualization of the funeral march of the *Eroica,* depending on how good my picture was."[35] As we have seen, the advent of a new medium prompted Seldes to think anew because he viewed each medium as having distinctive attributes and possibilities. That was surely one of his most engaging qualities as a cultural commentator.

III

As a film critic Seldes had rather decided likes and dislikes, although he did, on occasion, publish essays at about the same time whose messages were not altogether coordinated. Let's look first at his pet peeves—usually developed beneath the rubric "what's wrong with Hollywood?"—and then at his enthusiasms.

In 1932, on the eve of the Century of Progress exposition in Chicago, Seldes remarked that if he were in charge of such a fair he would emphasize "and bring to view the one thing that movies hardly ever touch—the past." Four years later he expanded upon that complaint in writing one of his fiercest indictments: "The American movie is indifferent to space and time: it annihilates both. It sprawls. It is chaotic, uncomposed, fluid, vulgar. In all these things it is more American than anything else." On several occasions Seldes reiterated his own version of Van Wyck Brooks' quest for a usable past. In Seldes' view, there was more at stake than merely finding a useful past as opposed to an inert one. Rather if Americans failed to appropriate and apply the past in meaningful ways, it would become a tyrannical burden.[36]

By 1935 some of Seldes' earlier concerns about film had been resolved or mollified, but new inconsistencies and ambiguities emerged as this rapidly changing medium developed and grew. In comparing the talking picture with silent film, for example, he now acknowledged that the former provided more varied and intelligent entertainment, and it had greater vitality as well. Nevertheless, he felt dissatisfied overall. He declared in a major retrospective assessment of film ever since the advent of sound that Hollywood had not yet produced "a single work of the highest order of importance; it has floundered in ignorance of its own capacities; and at the present moment it is in grave danger of sinking to a level of monotonous, moderately satisfactory production." He also made a point he would continue to reiterate for years: namely, that musical shows on film tended to be banal despite their popular appeal and commercial success.[37]

Seldes' acerbic critique prompted a fair amount of dissent, from fellow critics as well as from the industry itself, a pattern that would persist for two decades. Some accused him, wrongly I believe, of harboring excessive nostalgia for the silent film era, and others complained that Seldes simply had unreasonably high expectations. J. C. Furnas, a free-lance critic and social historian who admired Seldes, disagreed with his lament that "no film has yet approached the kind of significance which we allow to Oedipus and Hamlet." Furnas acknowledged that in absolute terms the screen would suffer from those sorts of comparisons, but believed that in relative terms the film industry could feel proud of its achievements. Furnas then proceeded to offer a judgment that was wide of the mark in both descriptive and predictive terms, a common tendency during the 1930s. "The movies are not yet essential," he declared, though we now recognize in retrospect that socially and culturally they had become highly essential. "And it is my guess," he continued, "that they will become essential or they will fade." Well, they didn't become any more "essential" than they had been, yet they clearly did not fade—though they certainly changed in key respects during the decades ahead.[38]

In the realm of mild inconsistency, or perhaps ambivalence, Seldes conceded in 1935 that the "intellectual content of the pictures, still not too great, has increased." In that essay, clearly, intellectual content appeared to be desirable; but in several others Seldes warned that the primary purpose of film was entertainment rather than instruction. To be too cerebral or message-oriented was not wise. In that same 1935 reprise, Seldes also proclaimed the newsreel a "disaster" that had lost its "prime quality: that it was a record of actuality. . . . Far too many events are rehearsed and taken, or are taken after the actual event, sometimes with 'improvements.'" Elsewhere, however, Seldes spoke much more positively about the newsreel.[39]

By 1938 he felt even more appalled at the declining quality of Hollywood musicals, "all with lots of names, lots of songs, no taste and no style." To make matters worse, he believed that inferior movie musicals were "killing off" lively musical shows on the stage. By contrast Seldes was encouraged by the release of the *Life of Emile Zola,* in which Paul Muni gave a rather long but highly effective speech, thereby demonstrating that films could "project ideas and movement simultaneously." A few years later he lamented what appeared to be a new and unfortunate tendency: movies whose endings were incompatible with the rest of the film.[40]

Despite this array of critical concerns, Seldes developed and retained certain enthusiasms during the 1930s. Writing about them in journals that ranged from *The Nation* to *The New Republic* to *Esquire,* he conveyed the joyous appreciation for first-rate popular entertainment that had characterized his work in 1923–24 when *The 7 Lively Arts* was his central project. He loved every Charlie Chaplin film he ever saw, considered the longer ones masterpieces (*The Kid, The Gold Rush, The Circus, City Lights*) and after viewing *Modern Times* in 1935 prior to its release, proclaimed it a work of genius.[41]

He also admired the early gangster films of the 1930s and came to believe that the genre had "saved" the talkies from their early shortcomings because gangster movies had action (one of Seldes' criteria for "movement") and rescued the talkies from an excess of static dialogue. By the later 1930s he felt twinges of nostalgia for such crime films as *Hell's Angels* (1930), *Little Caesar* (1931), and *Scarface* (1932) because of their unromanticized treatment of evil and utterly absorbing, menacing plots. By 1938, as variations on the genre evolved, Seldes expressed frustration at the advent of second-rate social realism and the injection of politics into a vehicle designed purely for entertainment. Don't moralize unless you can do it supremely well, he warned. "Neither the heroism of human beings in the past nine years, when their daily work was taken from them and their future was blacked out, nor the hell of tyranny elsewhere in the world, has inspired the films to any [meaningful] effort."[42]

Seldes' admiration for the roles played by James Cagney in the best of these gangster movies highlighted yet another aspect of his emphasis on movement as the critical quality in film. "So long as Cagney is allowed to move expressively," he wrote, "you have the groundwork of a good movie; he was born for the movies, because whatever he wants to say, he says by movement." Seldes believed that few other actors could match Cagney in the "variety and range and expressiveness of movement." As an added attraction, so to speak, Cagney had intelligence about people and situations "which shines through all his appearances."[43]

Seldes' initial enthusiasm for Walt Disney owed much to his belief that animated cartoons offered the purest form of movie by utilizing movement and form as their focus and relegating sound to a supporting role. By 1937 his appreciation of Disney increased because Disney's art had expanded and become more complex. His use of color, his brilliantly conceived characters, the sheer hilariousness of his situations, and his skillful blend of pictures with music all combined to draw constant raves from Seldes. He loved the Silly Symphonies, every one of them, and added Mickey Mouse to the pantheon that already enshrined Ignatz Mouse in "Krazy Kat." (One cannot help wondering whether Seldes'

diminutive height, five feet six inches, inclined him to inordinate admiration for shrewd mice with strong characters.) Seldes speculated that
"Popeye" might eventually offer genuine competition to the Disney cartoons, but otherwise saw no serious rivals in Disney's category. He explained why in the conclusion of a lengthy essay for *Esquire:*

> The major differences between Disney and his rivals are creative ones.
> Many times you see a gag, an invention, a new way to show flowers
> dancing or pencil sharpeners turning into machine guns—but these are as
> amusing in the hands of one animator as in the hands of another. But no
> one else has created such interesting characters, no one else has taken the
> word "animation" to mean giving life, no one else has found so agreeable a
> color scheme and no one else has so successfully integrated pictures and
> music. As these are four of the five fundamental things in animated car-
> toons, it is not hard to see why Disney remains so far ahead in the field,
> especially as in the fifth item, which is sheer, downright, unanalyzable fun,
> he is even farther ahead of them than in the others.[44]

Three years later Seldes penned a hymn of praise to Disney that
perhaps exceeded hyperbole: "Disney is actually one of the immor-
tals. . . . And as he is a god, you have the myth come to life: the god out
of the machine." What distinguishes this essay from all of the others by
Seldes on Disney is the emphasis upon innovations in technique. The
occasion, in a sense, was the nearly simultaneous release of *Pinocchio* and
Gone with the Wind. What the latter demonstrated, from the critic's
perspective, was that "you can make a long picture without contributing
anything whatever to the style, technique, art, or even value of the
movies; whereas, with Disney as a witness, you can make a ten-minute
subject and develop half-a-dozen new methods." What Seldes wished to
emphasize here was that film at its very best involved a marriage between art and technology ("the machine"). That intrigued him because
for decades, Seldes believed, aesthetes had contended that "the machine
would create a robot—a subman; the machine would destroy the creative spirit; and Americans, being peculiarly abased before the machine,
would be the first to dry up and wither and vanish."[45]

Seldes went on to observe that machinery had altered and assisted art
in other ways, most notably through the camera and the photograph. But
film remained, in his view, the most profound and pervasive example of
machinery not merely transforming art but facilitating a whole new art
form. He closed with an intriguing speculation about the "uniqueness" of

individual works of art versus the democratization that occurs when multiple copies of an art work are produced at the very outset:

> I think the moving picture would have been more promptly accepted as art, in spite of the machine process, if it had come into being in single copies. Imagine one print only of a Chaplin, an early Griffith, or a Disney; and note how the vanishing prints of the early pictures are being collected by museums and by individuals, precisely as old masters are collected.[46]

Even when Disney and Seldes advanced in age (they were born eight years apart), and new Disney productions disappointed Seldes, he would accentuate the positive. He didn't care for *Alice in Wonderland* and said so, but swiftly followed with the observation that producers involved in animation had restricted themselves to comedy: "The surprise is that Disney has so often dared to inject a note of satire, a touch of sentimental tragedy into his pictures." By 1951, when Seldes felt increasingly uneasy about mass culture, he awarded Disney the highest compliment by calling him the "creator of one of the few things in mass production you can unreservedly call a work of art."[47]

Seldes' personal hall of fame dated back to 1917, at least, when he lavished praise (in a letter from London) on D. W. Griffith and Mack Sennett. With the passage of time his enthusiasms became increasingly eclectic though invariably consistent with his love of the lively arts. He found Abbott and Costello comedies hysterical, and admired Bert Lahr extravagantly. He especially liked Frank Capra among directors and Sam Goldwyn among producers—Goldwyn because of his feisty independence and his engagement with every detail of film production, but above all because Goldwyn was willing to deal with ideas, often controversial ones. Seldes singled out the significance of Goldwyn's career: "He is the living proof that you don't have to cater to the intelligence of the moron."[48]

Running through these short pieces on particular movie-makers and performers, however, we find a consistent concern for the ultimate quality that mattered in a script and in an actor's performance: the creation of character. As he wrote in 1935, "the one matrix in which plot can be safely embedded is human character. If you are interested in a character, your absorption makes you immune to boredom." It distressed Seldes, at that time, that contemporary films seemed largely to ignore character. That would not always be the case, however, and performers like Bette Davis and Ingrid Bergman soon attracted his praise precisely because they *had* character and so successfully created absorbing characters on the screen.[49]

By contrast, emphasis upon personality in the world of entertainment annoyed Seldes because he felt that it diverted attention from the dramatic creation of compelling characters. He second-guessed those who wrong-headedly speculated about the secret of success in show business. If you say that it's hard work, he observed, that's no secret. If you say that it's personality, you are dead wrong, he remarked. Personality alone could not account for success. And the morbid fascination with intimate details of performers' lives, likes and dislikes, infuriated him because it diverted attention from the characters they created. Seldes deeply admired Orson Welles, and believed that he had learned from daytime serials on the radio that "the moment people are concerned with a character they are content to wait [for action to occur]. . . . It is only when characters are not absorbing that we demand action at once."[50]

If a misguided emphasis upon personality bothered Seldes, he hardly had more patience for the prominence given to sex appeal. In 1926 he simply tried to define its presence and its attributes in American film. Three years later he was more outspoken, minimizing the importance of sex appeal in the popular arts and insisting that it contributed little to their success. The themes of the great, enduring films were patriotism, mother love, rising from poverty, justice and injustice, romance, war, religion, courage, even slap-stick comedy—almost anything but sex.[51] If that sounds naive or prudish, his essays on film during the 1930s help to provide some illumination because in them he not only emerged as a great fan of Mae West, but differentiated between sex and love (in several essays), and explained Hollywood's rather tentative treatment of sex in a 1937 book, his second on film. What Seldes had to say on the subject during the 1930s was as complex and nuanced as his 1920s pronouncements seem simplistic.

In *The Movies Come from America* (1937) Seldes did much to clarify the categorical negation that he had offered in 1929. The traditional treatment of sex in American film, he declared, was rooted in the idea that sex was sinful, a notion that dramatists had customarily liked because it helped to heighten the drama in their plays. During the 1920s, Seldes felt, "the moving picture was inhibited by moral standards, which are loosely called Puritanical, from proceeding directly to a realistic treatment of sex." Consequently there were unrealistic presentations featuring assorted types, such as the vamp (Theda Bara), the "It" girl (Clara

Bow), and others. Seldes bemoaned the incapacity of most movie actresses to convey any *genuine* emotion representative of sex or love.[52]

Then, early in the 1930s Mae West appeared on the scene. She had
begun on stage where she achieved notoriety with vigorous, humanly
honest exploitation of sex as something attractive to both partners and
fun if not downright amusing to contemplate. As Seldes put it, "she
destroys the idea that women have no satisfaction in love, and at the
same time the idea that men's lives are ruined by love. The rudeness, the
grossness, the humour are all brought into play in situations where this
complete honesty about sex, personified in Mae West, comes up against
the old false traditions." Seldes found such honesty and earthiness wonderfully refreshing. He only regretted that because she insisted upon
writing her own scripts, West's pictures soon became repetitious.[53]

In 1935 Seldes wrote a clever and amusing comparison of Mae West
and little Shirley Temple, both of whom he admired greatly, in which he
emphasized their similarities as skilled actresses. He then returned to
(and elaborated upon) his 1929 litany, condemning a film orthodoxy
which, "ever since the days of the first vamp pictures has denied that love
exists between those who are married, and equally denied that physical
passion has any part in love." Four years later he returned to this theme
by observing that "sophisticated" people tend to laugh at the presentation
of sincere love on the screen. "The movie audiences are laughing in the
clinches," he remarked, "and that's bad for the movies. Beyond that is the
fact that the great tradition of love as subject matter for fiction, drama,
and even poetry, has been kicked out of the window."[54]

Just as Seldes tried to achieve a judicious balance in his criticism of the
subjects of sex and love in American movies, he did the same regarding
children in film and movies about young people. He perceived an important distinction. Despite his admiration for Shirley Temple, he resented a
pointless "accent on youth" by Hollywood, putting kids into movies for
no valid or apparent reason. Similarly, he hated the presentation of
children on stage as group comedians. Nonetheless, it baffled him that
virtually no meaningful movies had been made about young people and
the American experience. "Consider the remarkable fact," he wrote,
"that the one body of work which is beyond dispute America's contribution to world literature does deal with the very young: I mean *Tom
Sawyer* and *Huckleberry Finn.* Maybe it's time some other Americans got
going." Unfortunately from his perspective, in the years that followed
children were mobilized in entertainment for cloying cuteness rather

than astute social insights. In 1940 Seldes complained that film, the stage, and even radio had been "cashing in on the tots." He lamented that "the Higher Infantilism of Hollywood has carried the day."[55]

In the same year that Seldes bemoaned the absence of important American films about youth (1937), he also observed that native directors had been notably delinquent in developing documentaries. He noticed that in a recently published international list of thirty-five notable directors of documentaries, only one appeared, Robert Flaherty, and he had not made a film under purely American auspices for some years. The documentary film, according to Seldes, could be adapted "remarkably well to two themes which the American fictional picture has never been willing to handle honestly: political history and mass action." He praised the Soviets and the British, especially, for their achievements in these fields.[56]

Regardless of whether his mood was harshly critical or warmly positive, Seldes invariably called attention to the national distinctiveness of American film—ranging from the industry itself, to the character of movies produced, to audience expectations and behavior. His book *The Movies Come from America* was not so singularly shaped by an emphasis upon American exceptionalism as one might expect. Nevertheless, it did call attention to the domination of international markets by American films, to their huge popularity overseas, and to an explanation for their pervasive influence: "they always put action first, whereas foreign movies are always ready to sacrifice action to pictorial beauty, to ideas and to emotions."[57]

Considering all that we have read thus far by Seldes on the subject of film, this last comparison might well have prompted him to praise foreign movies and damn the domestic product. He did that at other times, but on this occasion his motive was descriptive more than judgmental, and for ideological reasons he sided with broadly based democratic inclusiveness. Fine European "art" films did not enjoy wide appeal to the "average man" and that, surely, was Hollywood's major strength. It tried to give the greatest number of people what it believed they wanted. As it happened, the "average man" around the world seemed to want pretty much the same thing, Seldes thought.[58]

The book received very positive notices in Britain as well as the United States. (It was first published in Britain with the less aggressive title *Movies for the Millions*.) Reviewers seemed particularly responsive to it as a democratic work that ordinary movie-goers should read. As the *Times* of London put it, Seldes successfully avoided "over-subtle theorizing" and sought to "bring home to the ordinary intelligent film-goer the power that resides in the cinema."[59] American critics were equally impressed by Seldes' blend of "critical insight and journalistic common sense." Writing in *Theatre Arts Monthly,* moreover, Jay Leyda proclaimed that "a new book by the author of *The Seven Lively Arts* and *An Hour with the Movies and the Talkies* is an event in our national art," and then suggested that *The Movies Come from America* ought to be "required reading by anyone film-minded, in or out of the film in-dustry."[60]

The central theme of Seldes' book would be reiterated and elaborated by others for years to come. In 1948, for instance, Lennox Grey an-nounced that "the movies are America's chief contribution in the arts, for good and bad." But with the passage of time Seldes modified and quali-fied his categorical assessment of U.S. dominance based on quantitative measures as of 1937. By the end of the 1940s the notable success of fine European films such as *Henry V, The Red Shoes, Symphonie Pastorale,* and *Open City,* impressed upon Seldes the belief that cinema should be as-sessed as more than simply a mass medium. The appearance of serious and tragic pictures among the top attractions, he felt, ought to occasion some reconsideration by those who financed American films. The dilem-ma, of course, involved a mass distribution system dependent on mobiliz-ing a goodly number of ordinary movies for ordinary movie-goers. In 1949 Seldes summed up the situation: "The dilemma of Hollywood, if it is to make mature pictures, is therefore serious: it cannot free itself from its system of distribution and it cannot force a different product into its present channels."[61] In the years immediately ahead, the swift advent of television as a rival medium would only complicate this dilemma, as we shall see at the close of this chapter and in the one that follows.

IV

When Seldes composed that essay in 1949 he knew far more than he ever had about the film industry from the inside because in 1946–47 he did what he called "desultory work in Hollywood" as a script writer and adviser for Paramount Pictures. Although his wife enjoyed the parties, celebrities, and glamour of it all, and returned to New York reluctantly in 1947, Seldes did not particularly like Hollywood, perhaps because he was, after all, a cerebral, compulsively candid critic, and not a team player who could readily subsume his identity and integrity into the collaborative work, often radically revised by market-driven directors, of feature film-making.[62]

Seldes had been in Hollywood for a brief but unproductive stint in the middle of 1936, and returned for one more try during the 1950s when his finances became precarious. His negative feelings about Hollywood, accentuated in 1947 when Paramount essentially dismissed him, were shared by many other writers who went West to seek their fortunes and felt like whores whether they succeeded or not. F. Scott Fitzgerald had threatened to go as early as 1925–26, then actually migrated in 1937 and stayed until his death late in 1940. His final novel, *The Last Tycoon* (1941), unfinished when he died of a heart attack, is seen through the eyes of Cecilia Brady, a producer's daughter. In September 1940, little more than three months before his sudden death, Fitzgerald described the lassitude and corruption of Hollywood for his close friend, Gerald Murphy:

> I find, after a long time out here, that one develops new attitudes. It is, for example, such a slack soft place—even its pleasure lacking the fierceness or excitement of Provence—that withdrawal is practically a condition of safety. The sin is to upset anyone else, and much of what is known as "progress" is attained by more or less delicately poling and prodding other people. This is an unhealthy condition of affairs. Except for the stage-struck young girls people come here for negative reasons—all gold rushes are essentially here for negative reasons—all gold rushes are essentially negative—and the young girls soon join the vicious circle. There is no group, however small, interesting as such. Everywhere there is, after a moment, either corruption or indifference. The heroes are the great corruptionists or the supremely indifferent—by whom I mean the spoiled writers, Hecht, Nunnally Johnson, Dotty [Dorothy Parker], Dash Hammet [*sic*] etc.[63]

John Dos Passos first went to Hollywood in 1934, Faulkner in 1935, Seldes in 1936, Fitzgerald in 1937, along with many others. Was their convergence in time no more than serendipity, or did it reflect a desperate need on the part of writers for cash during the depths of Depression times? Although neither consideration is irrelevant, a more significant factor played a critical part. In 1935–36 the major studios became enamored with the idea of converting classic books and plays into films, a concept that seemed to call for the participation of serious writers. The resulting dynamic both intrigued and disturbed Seldes so much that he wrote about it at length in the fall of 1936, following his first visit to the movie capital. Overall, he believed, the industry did a good job of converting classic books for the silver screen, "from which, at the moment, they draw their most successful and most satisfying pictures. So well in fact, that as a lover of the movies, I am perturbed."[64]

Why? First of all, in his view, movies would never achieve their highest level "until they begin to create their own material as well as they have created their own methods." What did Seldes have in mind more particularly? He did not believe that a good film could really be faithful to the original book or play. He cited two reasons in support of that assertion: one having to do with the distinctive character of the medium, and the other having to do with time constraints:

> A good moving picture cannot be a good reproduction of its original in fiction or drama because the essence of the movie, in spite of the use of dialogue, is movement; and the essential element in the originals is the word, to which the theatre adds action, which is something different from movement. . . .

> It is generally assumed that the violence done to the classics is deliberate, because the producers imagine that their public is stupid and everything has to be vulgarized or simplified for them. . . . But in general it is not a question of taste and intelligence, so much as a question of *time*, which determines the method of changing a novel into a movie.[65]

Despite that fairly charitable explanation, Seldes had been on record for at least four years with a less friendly reaction. "The sneers of the intellectuals and the catcalls of the pedants," he wrote, "have not changed Hollywood a bit. In spite of an Academy and awards and a social nobility, it knows that its strength lies in its immediate appeal to the lowest common factor. You may call it vulgarity; but they, properly, call it success."[66]

By 1939 Seldes resumed that hostile tone, but now supported and justified by historical perspective. Why had the film industry turned so assiduously during the mid-1930s to *Little Women, David Copperfield, Les Miserables, Anna Karenina* and several Shakespearian plays? Because the serious threat of censorship as a consequence of some sleazy films intimidated the studio heads. Filming the classics made it possible to conceal sin beneath a veneer of respectability. Even so, Seldes declared, Hollywood inflicts butchery on the classics that it makes into films.[67]

It needs to be noted, however, that Seldes did not single out Hollywood as the distinctive black sheep (or villain) in American popular culture. When he perceived a widespread tendency toward "escapism" in the arts, for example, he found it in books and radio programs as well as in film, and speculated that people were attracted to the "escape mechanism" because they feared the forces of evil. In Seldes' view, clearly rooted in his formal education, his wide range of reading, and his life experiences through age forty-seven, the true literature of escape involved a paradigmatic story of the fugitive from evil.[68]

The principal exception to this ecumenical view of all the arts concerned the central importance of cinema technique in film, a topic to which he returned time and again. In 1926 and 1927 Seldes saw some innovations to praise but even more to criticize. In 1927, for example, he attacked the excessive use and misuse of special camera angles in films. Overworking the device of special camera angles, he believed, irritated spectators. Nevertheless, doing so at least had the advantage of challenging spectator lethargy. Likewise, the appearance of major new equipment encouraged him to feel that the industry was making major strides. He admired *Chang* in 1927, for instance, a movie set in Siam, because it made such effective use of the magnascope to enlarge the picture projected on the screen. Ten months later he wrote an extremely positive review of King Vidor's *The Crowd,* which he regarded as fresh, credible, and creating intense emotions as well as introducing innovative technical effects. By contrast, mechanical problems that arose during the first years of sound annoyed when they did not amuse him. Some of the early recording equipment, for example, didn't reproduce the sound of the letters "s" and "z" very well, with the result that strong men lisped and a young woman would say to her suitor, "You are a puddle to me."[69] In the long run, however, Seldes acknowledged what he called the technical hunger of American movies and the speed with which the industry solved tough mechanical problems.

Although Seldes often commented on matters of cinema technique, and recognized that it grew and evolved swiftly, unlike John Dos Passos and James Agee he never shaped or altered his prose style in order to incorporate or emulate the camera eye. We must always keep in mind Seldes' strong belief that film was an utterly distinctive art form. He may even have felt that if it should not borrow, neither should it lend. Dos Passos and Agee felt otherwise, of course, and Agee's flawed masterpiece *Let Us Now Praise Famous Men* (1941) is redolent with adapted cinematic devices.[70]

From 1941 until 1948 Agee wrote film reviews and criticism for both *Time* and *The Nation*. Like Seldes, Agee had grown up with silent film and the movies were really his great love—much more so even than for Seldes. We know that Agee had read and very much admired Seldes' books and essays on film. When Agee encountered Seldes' daughter, Marian, an actress, he enthused over her father's work. Unfortunately, the two men never met; but in Seldes' papers there is a collection of clippings that he clearly found meaningful and perhaps intended to engage when he wrote "As in My Time." Among those loose, undated, and unorganized clippings there is one from James Agee:

PICTURES VS. BOOKS

If you compare the moving pictures released during a given period with the books published during the same period—or with the pictures painted or the music composed—you may or may not be surprised to find that they stand up rather well. I can think of very few contemporary books that are worth the jackets they are wrapped in; I can think of very few movies, contemporary or otherwise, which fail to show that somebody who has worked on them in front of the camera or in any one of the many places behind it, has real life or energy or intensity or intelligence or talent.

I am not persuaded that Seldes agreed, but clearly he found it provocative and perhaps intended to respond or else elaborate upon Agee's observation.[71]

Both men shared an interest in the composition and nature of film audiences. In Seldes' case that involved two very different kinds of considerations: the physical settings in which films were shown and the age groups to which Hollywood seemed to direct its primary attention. For a full generation, from *The Great Train Robbery* up through *The Jazz Singer*, audiences mainly watched silent films in relatively small, unadorned rooms that were conducive to intimacy and camaraderie. In settings of that sort audiences were likely to burst into applause spontaneously, or shout warnings to vulnerable characters that the villain had evil intentions. The modest halls tended to erase inhibition and audiences became highly participatory. By contrast, Seldes noted, once the large and elaborate "cathedrals and palaces of the talkies" were built, often as lavish Beaux Arts structures, they seemed to subdue audiences, make people aware of the grandeur of their setting, almost as though customers had gone to grand opera. That tended to intimidate audiences, made them less audibly interactive with the characters on the screen, and caused hissing or applause, when they occurred at all, to be polite rather than raucous. Architecture and decor palpably altered the behavior of movie audiences. Glamorous decor elevated decorum.[72]

Seldes also believed that with the passage of time (the 1930s and '40s particularly) grown-ups went to the movies much less often, partially because they were preoccupied with other concerns but mainly because the fare being offered by Hollywood seemed increasingly juvenile. There simply weren't enough "adult" films being offered at a time when adult didn't mean sexually explicit but rather a film that "challenges your own ability to experience the emotion of others." David and Evelyn Riesman responded to that critical perspective with an essay that used Seldes as a point of departure because he was the best-known exponent of the declining-attendance-by-mature-adults theory. They began by citing Seldes' view that older people stayed away from movies because the films were not sufficiently adult and mature. They acknowledged the survey data that showed the "average" moviegoer to be nineteen and that comparatively few people over the age of thirty went to the movies with any frequency.[73]

The Riesmans then suggested, however, that perhaps there was a real sense in which films were too mature and moved too swiftly for older people to catch on. Expanding the scope of their inquiry, the Riesmans went on to speculate that

> the same may be true of other newly-developed media whose conventions and emotional vocabularies the American young have learned as a mother tongue. Possibly realization that the old have to learn the new language of films (or TV) would be a first step toward appreciating some of the ambiguities of communication in which the movies and other media are involved—ambiguities related to the tensions between the generations, between the social classes, and between the character types.

The Riesmans minimized the emphasis placed by Seldes and others on the seductiveness of film as an "escape mechanism," and argued instead for the importance of socialization and Americanization as a magnet in the early decades of film, desiderata that became less significant during the 1930s and '40s as working-class and immigrant adults grew older and felt that they had learned what they needed to know in order to look and act like Americans. Once again the Riesmans had shrewd insights to offer, ones that took social change into account:

In the studies of the movies made under the Payne Fund twenty years ago, much evidence was gathered concerning use of the movies by young people who wanted to learn how to look, dress, and make love. What has changed since then, perhaps, is the kind of enlightenment that is sought. The young people whose reactions were studied by the Payne Fund investigators were often of lower-class origin; in the films they were suddenly brought face to face with sex and splendor, with settings and etiquettes remote from their own experience and observation. Today, however, American audiences are, with the rising standard of living, less remote from splendor, and with the rising standard of education, less remote from etiquette and social know-how generally.[74]

The authors acknowledged that social class-learning still occurred at the movies, but believed that the blend of messages and sources had become more complex. Fads for youngsters were still stimulated in important ways by film, but peer group pressures, interpersonal competence, and other skills also mattered greatly. For middle-class adults, however, the Riesmans observed that "the loss of older certainties, religious and secular," prompted them to "look to their contemporaries for cues as to what in life is worthwhile." Obviously, the Riesmans' perspective skillfully complemented their well-known emphasis upon the rise of "other-directedness" in modern American society. Be that as it may, they offered an alternative way to think about who went to the movies, why, and with what effect in the United States at mid-century.[75]

I am persuaded that taking the second quarter of the twentieth century as a whole, the perspectives of Seldes and the Riesmans are not mutually exclusive because of the sheer size and structural complexity of the American population. Neither perspective, for example, really takes into account the film enthusiasms of rural America, an aspect that we are just beginning to comprehend. *The Farm Journal,* for instance, the most widely read farm magazine in the United States, had a special columnist named C. F. Stevens who reported regularly on movies and related matters. He provided brief summaries and ranked the new films. Despite crowded rural theatres, however, there is abundant evidence that country people went to the movies much less often than urban dwellers. In rural areas of upstate New York, for example, an average of 37 percent among farm families ever went to the movies; and, even earlier than the trend discerned by Seldes, younger people were far more likely to attend movies than their elders.[76] Much remains to be done before we can comfortably generalize about national film audiences in the heyday of Hollywood.

V

By comparison we know a great deal about the history of film censorship in the United States, and that was an issue Seldes cared about quite strenuously. It recurs as a theme throughout his career. In fact, as a serious cultural issue it virtually coincided with his mature years as a critic. In 1915 the Supreme Court held that the motion picture, being "only" entertainment, was not entitled to protection under the First Amendment. For decades thereafter, state boards of censorship flourished and their power would not be crippled until 1952 when, in the case of *The Miracle,* the Court reversed its earlier judgment.[77]

Seldes emerged rather slowly as a foe of censorship. Although he could hardly be considered prudish, his belief in the distinctive nature of film as a medium—in this case its public nature as a shared spectacle— caused him to be judicious if not cautious. The following appeared in his first book about film (in 1929):

> It is not in my province to supply a solution to the censorship problem. I think it desirable that the opponents of the censor should bear always in mind the peculiar circumstances of the moving picture, instead of assuming that the movie resembles in any way a book read in solitude; they should be aware also of the dirty sexual pictures available in secret places in most large cities and be ready to answer when asked whether they want these pictures publicly shown. It seems to me that as soon as the opponents of the censorship have a positive plan, they can do something to undermine the censor's authority, and not before.[78]

In the winter of 1932–33 a heated controversy arose over the showing of a nudist film, *This Naked Age,* in New York, and Seldes accepted restraints because he believed that liberals inconsistently created a special protective category for sex:

> They will read a manuscript and say, It's good, but it ought to be cut. They will object to sculpture because it sprawls, to painting because it is not compact enough, to a play because it lacks concision. On the ground of art, they are all for cutting, except when the subject in hand touches on sex, when they bawl and cry like babies whose candies have been taken away.[79]

If that argument appears thin and unpersuasive, Seldes fundamentally seems to have felt that it was simply a poor film. "It is on the ground of dullness and timorousness that I vote with the censor. The picture is as appropriate to Nudism as a skit. . . ." Timorous in what way? Endless shots of buttocks (both sexes), but breasts only at a great and fuzzy distance. The film had but one end in view, he wrote, "the rear end. Long shot or closeup, that is what you get. You also get a lot of exercises and the impression that when men and women foregather in nakedness, they have a deplorable tendency to do scarf dances, without the scarves."[80]

The mediocre quality of a film is clearly no grounds for censorship; but within a few years, once Will Hays, an elder in the Methodist Church, became President of the Motion Picture Producers and Distributors of America, Hollywood initiated a pattern of self-censorship that infuriated Seldes and led to a burst of treacly costume dramas that risked nothing and (in artistic terms) achieved less. Precisely because Seldes wanted sex and moral issues to be examined in a mature way, he even-handedly blamed both extremes for the sad state of affairs. "The aesthetes and the Puritans on one side and the pornographer on the other made censorship inevitable."[81]

It must have been small consolation, if any, that the situation in Great Britain could be equally silly. In 1939 the British Board of Film Censors gave *The Wizard of Oz* a certificate for adults only, prompting Graham Greene to write: "Surely it is time that this absurd committee of elderly men and spinsters who feared, too, that "Snow White" was unsuitable for those under sixteen, was laughed out of existence?"[82]

After the war Seldes became increasingly outspoken on this issue. It outraged him that sadistic and senseless violence in film was acceptable while the Production Code made "normal" sexual relations taboo. When *Double Indemnity* by James M. Cain became a Hollywood melodrama, Seldes aimed withering sarcasm at a situation where one essential aspect of the novel, "the frightening sexual hold which the woman has over the man, cannot be shown because Will Hays doesn't believe that there is anything in the rumor that men and women love one another."[83] In the five years that followed, however, 1947 to 1952, communism, race relations, and religion supplanted sex as the most controversial targets for censorship.

When Charlie Chaplin's *Monsieur Verdoux* was released in 1947, critic John Mason Brown published an astonishingly snide personal attack on Chaplin in the *Saturday Review* because of his sordid "amatory activities," his failure to be a model citizen during wartime (e.g., by not being helpful at bond rallies, like other celebrities), and so forth. Brown also labeled the movie itself "tedious, spotty, and repetitious," and then "easy, slick, and shallow." Four days later theatre owners in the United States were called upon to boycott the movie. Seldes wrote an angry letter as a result, referring to Brown's "literary lynching." Chaplin later sent an appreciative letter to Seldes, noting that legally there had been no valid reason for quashing his movie. "It had passed the Breen Office and all the various State censorship boards without a 'cut.'" Chaplin correctly blamed the whole episode on bourgeois morality and Cold War hysteria.[84]

The biggest blow-up of all, however, occurred in 1950–51 when Roberto Rossellini released *The Miracle,* a movie (based on an original story by Federico Fellini) profoundly offensive to Roman Catholics, in particular, because it concerned a woman, played superbly by Anna Magnani, who believes that her pregnancy is immaculate and divine. Set in a small Italian town and the surrounding countryside near Salerno, the scene in which the simple-minded goatherd "is taken advantage of" goes on at great length. The confused woman eventually makes her way to a monastery, having been taunted and driven away by students, and delivers her child unassisted.

What engaged Seldes (and many others) in this instance were the legal maneuverings and the cultural power exerted by bureaucrats. In brief, a movie theatre's license was threatened for showing a film that Francis Cardinal Spellman and some others deemed "blasphemous" and "sacrilegious." The movie had been returned to the screen because a court questioned the right of New York's commissioner of licenses to withdraw a theatre's license just because it was showing a controversial but previously approved film. And then the question arose whether a favorable opinion by the Production Board could be reversed or even challenged just because some public opinion ran negative. Catholic organizations picketed the theatre and Roman Catholics in the United States were not allowed to see it. Ironically, when the picture appeared in Italy no outcry occurred and the issue of censorship never arose.[85]

In the realm of substance Seldes shifted from journalist to film critic. He insisted that controversial bits of *The Miracle* had been misrepresented, especially by people who had not even seen the movie. He also declared that it was not sacrilegious because it did not hold "religion up to contempt." Since a film is not required by the code to "be respectful to all tenets of any single sect or church," this one was surely not out of line.

The whole controversy, Seldes argued, threatened the basic principles of artistic freedom; and he believed that it clearly illustrated what can happen when Jefferson's protected minorities apply powerful pressure in sensitive places: "given sufficient organization, minorities can paralyze the general will of the people."[86]

Later that year, while the case moved to the Supreme Court on appeal, Seldes prepared his broadest attack on film censorship. He began by dismissing as marginal those who held that no picture should ever be banned from any theatre. Most people, he believed, accepted the principle that "the way films are shown and the effect they have on people, compel us to limit absolute freedom of expression." The contested questions then became: Who should be the censor and on what grounds are films unfit for public consumption? In practice the Johnston office (formerly the Hays office), advised and pressured by private organizations, responds to both questions. When a picture slips by (perhaps a foreign film or a Hollywood product not covered by the code), police action may be taken. Moreover, in certain states a local board of censorship may give or withhold approval.[87]

The differences among these three levels of control are significant, and elicited varied responses from opponents of censorship. The Johnston office rendered its verdict, based on the code, before a picture was actually made. The state boards of review passed on a picture after a movie was exhibited. Most opponents of censorship, in Seldes' view, accepted the police power: show the picture; if there is a protest, let the case come before a tribunal or a jury, which then can decide whether it really constituted an offense or a public danger. The authority of state boards was challenged because they were subject to pressure from special interest groups and could place an exhibitor in unfair legal difficulties. The Johnston office was resented most of all because the code that it administered was largely written by and represented the ethical views of Roman Catholics, a minority of the population. Even more important, in Seldes' view, the code "either forbids creative artists to create or compels them to work out devious ways of circumventing the Code."[88]

A large majority of those remotely interested in these matters agreed that the code was basically silly. It prohibited jokes about traveling salesmen and farmers' daughters. It stated that "pictures shall not infer that low forms of sex relationship are the accepted or common thing." "What's 'low'?" Seldes asked. "How often does a thing have to happen to be 'common'?" The impact of the code, he observed, was to force films to present love and marriage as peculiarly sexless. Consequently, when writers sought to deal with the full realities of human existence, the code inhibited them. The result, Seldes commented, "is that writers cease to be creative in the true sense; they can neither illuminate life for us nor guide us; they can only divert us; and *divert* has two meanings—to amuse and to lead us off the right road."[89]

The only other significant element in the code, he added, dealt with crime and brutality. Excessive violence was supposedly proscribed. But *that* prohibition, he observed, was so consistently ignored that it made a mockery of the entire system. In *The Great Audience,* Seldes' first major assessment (at book length) of mass culture, he asserted that violence "without meaning is the outstanding characteristic of our film product."[90] The more things change, the more they remain the same.

VI

During the prelude to World War II Seldes became a fierce critic of fascism, and his staunch patriotism throughout the war was manifest in his film criticism. In 1941 he regarded Chaplin's performance in *The Great Dictator,* a satirical slapstick, as "the funniest thing ever created by the mind of man." Basically the story involved a Jewish barber who is mistaken for the anti-Semitic dictator of his country. To complicate matters, a shell-shocked veteran of the Great War recovers, escapes from his hospital, but is then plunged into the hell of a Nazified world. Seldes not only approved of the movie's ideological thrust, but designated Chaplin as "the great mouthpiece for the unfortunate."[91]

In 1943 Seldes undertook an interesting exercise, one that reinforced his strong belief in distinctive national styles in general and American exceptionalism in particular. He took a systematic look at newsreels produced in different nations, mainly Russian, British, Chinese, German, and American. Struck by their diversity, which he designated as "national differences," he also acknowledged the one "essential" element common to them all, "which is the presence of reality, the absence of the studio, the reassertion of the moving picture as the recorder of the *Fact*." This seems an unusual message from a man who had consistently complained about what he called propaganda movies. But World War II prompted Seldes to suspend some of his customary pet peeves, including his prejudice against most manifestations of the propaganda film.[92]

In any case, he singled out the American films for criticism because of their peculiar and highly distinctive degree of restraint: a reluctance to show serious peril, military action, men dying, civilians suffering, and unanticipated disasters occurring. Why, he wondered, were the American newsreels so sanitized?

> An appalling lot of American shots are safe; the Army and Navy and Marines may have great stuff hidden away, but they are releasing men landing on the Solomons just at the moment the Japs weren't looking; they show men shaving and generals jeeping over bumpy roads and soldiers enjoying the sights in all parts of the world and men landing in Australia, but the actuality of battle they are saving for the archives.

Seldes recognized that "naturally one sees a lot of our own product and only the pick of the imported goods. So the Chinese pictures all seem full of pity and terror. . . ." He went on to note that the established Soviet tradition of creating feature films "out of people, not actors, has worked a miracle," because the Russians were making newsreels just as powerful and effective as U.S. feature films that were fictional. "We Americans have left the grimness and the grandeur of war to the studios, which is foolish; the Russians have brought the excitement and the melodrama of war into their newsreels."[93]

In that same essay Seldes bestowed lavish praise on Frank Capra, a highly successful director (*It Happened One Night, Mr. Deeds Goes to Town, Mr. Smith Goes to Washington,* and *Meet John Doe* (1941), acclaimed as the best film ever made on the theme of democracy), even more patriotic, perhaps, than Seldes. A month later he acclaimed *Casablanca,* right after its release, as "one of the most exciting melodramas the screen has ever produced." In this essay, filled with uncharacteristic encomia for the film industry, he singled out Warner Brothers for special acclaim:

> Perhaps it is not a coincidence that even before the war they were making the best propaganda shorts, propaganda for the faith of America, for civil liberty, for freedom. Somehow the passion that lives in a studio is generated from those who in the end pay the salaries, and make the profits. They may make pictures because they want to make money; but they also make the kind of pictures they believe in.[94]

Four months later, however, Seldes devoted an essay to Robert Montgomery, a superb actor he regarded as a courageous patriot because he refused to do Hollywood's bidding. Seldes never provided unqualified praise of the film industry for very long, and after the war, with the commercial advent of television he really turned up the heat on Hollywood.[95]

Believe it or not, Seldes began to speculate about the possible impact of television on film as early as 1931—he was unquestionably *the* pioneer in that respect—though at the time he expressed greater concern that television might lower "the intellectual level of radio." By 1937 he became more astutely prophetic, observing that "the movies, now so much faster than the radio, will have to speed up again to be as fast as a good television programme." In that same book he also anticipated one of the most pervasive laments of our own generation: the decline of literary culture because of the dramatic expansion of visual media.

> Between the radio giving him the news and the moving picture condensing and dramatizing novels, the necessity for reading steadily diminishes. When they coalesce in television and make the average man a spectator of world events wherever they occur, and at the same time afford him an entertainment with such luxury as ancient despots could hardly imagine, the private art of reading may disappear before the new universal art. In the composite of television, the moving picture will have the greater share.[96]

This represented a reversal of the cavalier position he had taken just three years earlier. (See Chapter Seven, p. 249 and note, below.)

In the years 1949 to 1951 Seldes devoted a good deal of time and space to such questions as: Can Hollywood take over television? Will television ruin the movie industry?[97] In so many ways this seems to have been 1928 to 1930 *redivivus,* when Seldes had speculated endlessly about the potential impact of talkies on silent film, an issue of great uncertainty at the time even though its outcome seems so inevitable to us.

The incredibly swift ascent of television as a commercial and cultural phenomenon prompted this kind of disparagement from Seldes in 1951: "Just as five years ago Hollywood pretended that TV didn't exist, now it turns its back on the nasty little newcomer on the old principle that if you pay no attention to an evil, it will go away." The passage of eleven years provided Seldes with an opportunity for some historical perspective, and in effect he added a postscript to the observations on movie-going behavior that he had made in the 1930s. The rise of television during the 1950s, he commented, clearly altered movie-going habits. By 1960 film became what theatre had also become after movies achieved popularity: something to be planned in advance, a kind of special occasion. The customary habit of just going to the movies on the spur of the moment, to take in whatever might be playing at the neighborhood theatre, was broken. Television now filled that casual and spontaneous role.[98]

During a span of about a dozen years, 1950 to 1962, Seldes shifted his emphasis from assessments of culpability and irresponsible behavior in the media to descriptions of the altered relationships between older and newer modes of entertainment and communication. Those matters will be the subject of Chapter Nine below.

Radio and Television

B y the mid-1950s, when Seldes frequently gave guest lectures and mini-courses at colleges and universities, he was invariably identified as a (or as *the*) radio and television critic. That designation customarily appeared also as part of the byline in his free-lance journalism—appropriately so. Early in 1952 Seldes agreed to serve as a director of the National Association for Better Radio and Television, a non-profit corporation based in Los Angeles. That same year he produced a popular Bantam paperback titled *Previews of Entertainment* containing advance information about more than 700 films and television and radio shows, as well as legitimate theatre productions, as a guide for the pleasure-seeking public in the United States. Seldes hoped to achieve for show business what Duncan Hines had done for dining out. Because most people enjoyed three to four hours of leisure each day, and the options were clearly multiplying, how to choose wisely became a major concern. Seldes wanted *Previews of Entertainment* to be a "species of guide for the travels of the mind and emotions in search of pleasant stimulation." His little book received widespread appreciation as a "smart experiment."[1]

Ever since the early 1930s Seldes had been, quite literally, a multi-media critic. Not only did his daily column for the New York *Evening Journal* range in coverage from books to show business to politics, beginning in 1933 his byline regularly announced that Seldes would appear the

Fig. 18. Gilbert Seldes at his apartment on Henderson Place in New York City (1934).

next Thursday on the "Best Idea of the Week" over radio station WINS at 6:30 p.m. (see Fig. 18). He also indicated in one column that he commonly spent the day at the movies and much of the evening listening to the radio. Lest that sound too much like a man being paid for having fun, he reminded the reader that mostly he encountered the "average everyday product of these two vast industries." It annoyed him that those who ran the industries seem to be working only for the immediate present, confident that they can get by today and late tonight, and that something else will turn up by next Wednesday fortnight. That is, for all their enormous investment and programs arranged weeks and months in advance, they are still on a hand-to-mouth, quickie basis when they begin to think of general principles. To criticism, the usual reply is that such and such a type of picture or broadcast is still pulling in results, the catch lying in the word "still."[2]

His report that listening to the radio left him feeling "very glum" was typical of his tone, more often than not, when evaluating radio. As he wrote on December 7, 1933, "the sponsored and sustaining programs I heard on six stations were monotonous and lacking in conviction. The formula was the same in all: puns and music, music and puns. A commentary on the news now and then, lagging several hours behind the newspaper headlines in time and—this may be sheer prejudice—lagging miles behind the newspapers in crispness and pungency of comment." In 1931 his verdict had been: "usually pretty thin stuff." Thirteen months later he lamented the "jumble of programs, each repeating the other," and observed that radio invariably lowered the standard of the arts from which it borrowed. Hence radio singing was inferior to a good minstrel show. In 1934 and '35 he acknowledged the immense popular success that radio broadcasting enjoyed, yet called it "the most annoying, the most inescapable, and the most insufferable racket ever put over on the American public."[3]

At the core of his critique was an emphasis that he had uttered earlier about movies in relation to the live stage and about talkies in relation to silent film: namely, the need for each new medium to be different and to do things distinctively. "With minor exceptions," he said early in 1934, "radio has not yet created anything for itself," a point he continued to insist upon more than a year later. Seldes singled out "The March of Time" as the only program thus far developed entirely as a radio series and not as an imitation of any other form of entertainment. During the 1950s, when he wrote a regular "TV and Radio" column for the *Saturday Review of Literature,* he reiterated that theme once again: his intense desire that television should "create its own works." He very much admired, for example, "The Last Word," a discussion show on CBS hosted by Bergen Evans. The lively, engaging interchanges demonstrated that "if you give intelligent people something to talk about and change the subject often enough you will get a special kind of gaiety."[4]

Another motif that appeared in all of his media criticism during these decades, very much in line with his aversion to "bogus" characteristics in the lively arts, concerned "phoniness"—whether in describing baseball games, natural disasters, advertising, or excessive politeness and decorum on television. The appearance of phoniness indicated an assumption that the listener or viewer utterly lacked discernment and intelligence.[5] Although Seldes had no grievance in principle with advertising on the air—that seemed to him inevitable—he disliked what happened when radio celebrities decided to satirize commercialism. Their impact was to add a tarnish to advertising in which each man "kids the thing he sells," thereby injecting a whole new element of phoniness. After enumerating a variety of cloying and unsubtle devices that irritated him, Seldes concluded that "the fake behind all these methods robs them of the little that could be said for the other type of advertising—that it was frank."[6]

The other concerns that dominated his writing about radio and television involved the social impact of each medium, the relationship of highbrows (and the issue of social stratification) to each medium, the educational potential of each medium, audience profiles for each medium, the appropriate degree of government regulation for each medium, and, as we shall see, the advent of mass culture—for better (democratization) and for worse (degradation of taste). Most of these concerns matter very much to practitioners of what is now called "cultural studies." Consequently, while I would not exactly designate Gilbert Seldes a founder of cultural studies, I feel that he deserves to be called a forerunner.

I

Seldes' earliest essays about radio convey a feeling of open-minded ambivalence toward the medium. He reveled in its freedom and spontaneity, the relative cheapness that swiftly made it a "universal" means of receiving news and entertainment. He worried, however, about the prospects for repetition, propaganda, platitudes, and censorship in the new medium, and in 1927 he revealed his uncertainties by closing with a perplexing rhetorical question: "It remains simply a force; moving at one time in all directions, spreading what?" He kept abreast of trends in broadcasting and maintained a running commentary in his columns. In 1934, for instance, he opposed making radio broadcasts from a theatre with a live audience on the grounds that "the moment you begin to play for the studio audience you defeat the technique of radio—and its purpose, which is to entertain by sound, not by sight."[7]

Seldes' ambivalence was representative of more general opinion shifts that occurred during radio's first decade. By 1922 radio had achieved parity with mah-jongg as a national mania, and by 1926 one-quarter of all households in the United States had a radio. Many optimists believed that radio would bring about notable advances in education and culture. It clearly would expand the appreciation of good music; as one writer put it, "every home has the potentiality of becoming an extension of Carnegie Hall or Harvard University." On the minus side, however, teachers worried about the decline of reading as a result of radio; and journalists warned against the "radio newspaper" as a poor substitute.* For a period, therefore, the Associated Press prohibited the use of any of its material on the air. By the late 1920s, after radio had lost much of its novelty, people began to be disillusioned. The rapid growth of advertising contributed heavily to that, and by 1930 many erstwhile boosters had turned critical. *The New Republic* proclaimed that "radio in America is going to waste," a judgment in which Seldes concurred. Radio tended to reinforce the status quo because it avoided controversy and appealed to the average. Its prospects as a culturally liberating force seemed much less clear.[8]

When the Hoover Committee on Social Trends issued an in-depth report in 1933, the opening paragraph of its section on radio broadcasting raised many of the critical questions that Seldes would wrestle with for years to come:

> The dramatic evolution of the radio within one decade from a mysterious curiosity to a widely diffused and universally accepted instrument of entertainment, business, learning and mass communication, has few if any counterparts in social history. Its rapid development has brought many problems of organization and control which as yet are not definitely settled. How shall broadcasting be supported? How shall the facilities be allocated? Who shall control the programs? How may all interests be conserved? How are legal concepts of property rights affected? These are but a few of many questions awaiting conclusive answers.[9]

---

*In 1934, however, Seldes concluded his daily column with these four breezy sentences. "I have written enough books myself to care a lot for them and to know that an enormous amount of padding and filling goes into most published books. And I have read enough to know that civilization will not perish from the earth if people stop reading books. I wonder whether Plato read as many books in his lifetime as I read in a month. And if he did, what good they did him." "True to Type," NYEJ, May 5, 1934, p. 13. Cf. Chapter Six, p. 242, above.

Seldes read that huge report with considerable care, of course, and noted in his daily newspaper column that it enumerated more than one hundred social effects of radio, "among them being increase of morning exercises among the American people and increase in stock speculation from mid-ocean." Seldes found the former plausible because music dominated the airwaves in the morning, though he really wondered how many people would "interrupt their bouillon on A-deck to buy another thousand shares of good common stock" while crossing the Atlantic. Six weeks later he asserted that the value of radio in education had not yet been demonstrated. "Even as a form of persuasion," he mused, "we know its worth only when we come to a question of selling goods."[10]

Seldes always found delight in reminding his readers that when Herbert Hoover served as Secretary of Commerce he declared that the American people would never stand for advertising over the air "and therefore that no special law limiting plugs in broadcasts need be passed."[11] He also pointed out, years later, that in 1929 the National Association of Broadcasters (then consisting of 147 stations) put the following into its code of practice: "Commercial announcements, as the term is generally understood, shall not be broadcast between seven and eleven p.m." In 1930, moreover, the president of NBC made this good-faith declaration: "We have refused to permit on our system the sponsoring of football games by commercial institutions. . . . I just did not like to see the Yale-Harvard game announced through the courtesy of so-and-so."[12]

Seldes himself seems to have undergone a curious odyssey with respect to broadcast advertising. During the early 1930s he resented it as the phenomenon became more pressurized and occupied more airtime. "Everything is said three times," he noted, "pleadingly, emphatically, imploringly." By 1936, however, he had become more tolerant (perhaps numbed) except when advertisers seemed to target children for their commercials on the assumption that kids would then pressure their parents to buy things. That annoyed him so much that he devoted an essay in *Esquire* to the subject. By 1945 (after more than seven years on the staff at CBS), he wrote a resounding defense of media policies pertaining to commercials, insisting that they were less obtrusive, in better taste, and far more diverse and imaginative then they had once been. He even declared that the public actually "likes a great many commercials and can make itself heard if it doesn't. No indication has ever been found of public disapproval. A few organizations, special groups who are not representative of radio's audience, pass votes of censure, a few critics object; but the public is indifferent to these moves."[13] During the 1950s Seldes became so intrigued by the whole subject that he did considerable work on a book about advertising in general—one that he never completed. He did, however, produce several important essays on the topic and in Chapter Ten we will look more closely at his later views on advertising.

To understand his odyssey between, say, 1930 and 1945, however, we need only notice that in 1935–36 he became a strong defender of a democratized free enterprise system and joined CBS as its first director of television programs in 1937. For reasons that will become evident later in this chapter, Seldes would never be a true "company man"; but clearly the industry's perspective caused him to be very realistic about the need for sponsorship if programs were to appear and new program initiatives be undertaken. During World War II, moreover, Seldes' patriotism heightened his belief that programs about American civic values (such as Norman Corwin's distinguished series on the Founders and the Bill of Rights) had been facilitated by commercial expansion of the listening audience. "For a generation we wept over the commercialism of radio," he wrote in 1942, "and at the end found that commercial radio had created an audience for statesmen and philosophers." By 1950–51 Seldes had achieved a more cautious view of advertising in the media, and called attention to its myopia and less attractive aspects as well as its achievements.[14]

II

During the early days of radio, especially prior to 1928, classical music and serious programming (descriptive, informational, dramatic, and so on) were prominently featured. After the WLS Barn Dance had its first broadcast in 1924 the program came close to being canceled because a Sears vice president enamored of classical music listened and felt appalled by the down-home tunes supplanting the more refined music that he favored and was accustomed to hearing on the air. Despite his plea that the program be stopped, the station received hundreds of approving telegrams, letters, and cards, especially from rural folk. The Barn Dance remained on the air, and the recognition settled in that rural as well as urban sensibilities would have to be accommodated.[15]

The related issue of highbrow versus popular culture programming could not be so readily resolved and generated a fair amount of discussion among critics. On this issue Seldes took somewhat more consistent positions over the years than he did on advertising, though they were complex because he usually sought a middle ground: level up to higher quality without verging upon pedantry, purely academic programming, or hyper-sophistication. In 1933 he criticized the broadcast industry for underestimating the intelligence of Americans. "They think that people without college educations are half wits," he wrote, "which is not true and allows little for the native wit of Americans. . . . They think that the only way to make people forget their trouble is to feed them synthetic fun."[16]

In a paper that Seldes prepared for a 1936 conference on educational broadcasting he suggested that "even now we are only beginning to understand what democracy means in connection with education, entertainment, and the arts." He evoked the democratic ethos in several respects: inclusive access to the medium, pleasing the people as a stimulus to innovation, and freedom of choice as a determinant for success or failure in programming. The new trends, in Seldes' view, displayed both success and failure:

> It is my belief that the commercial use of radio was an extraordinarily desirable thing, at the beginning at least, and is desirable for us now for these reasons: commerce made the radio virtually universal—that is basic; and commerce exhausted the appeal of certain programs very rapidly. Because the sponsors wanted to keep the people interested, they had to discard whatever proved unsatisfactory, and they had continually to go on to novelties. In the search for novelties the good things got their chance, and some of them have lasted very well indeed. A certain freedom and a high degree of variety in American broadcasting are due to a large extent to the same commercial system which must also take credit for a vast amount of stupidity and dulness.[17]

Radio did give ordinary folks what they wanted. In addition to the many popular comedy shows, Seldes observed in 1950 that "the great invention of radio, its single notable contribution to the art of fiction, is the daytime serial [soap operas, etc.]" Despite that recognition, he continued to hope and personally work for an elevation in the quality of fare offered on radio. In 1937, for example, he called particular attention to a poetic drama titled "The Fall of the City," written specifically for radio by Archibald MacLeish. Seldes praised it on several grounds and declared that seldom had the networks produced any program carrying such a clear warning about the contagion of tyranny. Apart from the important political message of this drama, however, it remained special to Seldes for a different reason. In 1964 he looked back with fondness to MacLeish's "recognition of radio as a medium for drama and poetry when most intellectuals were still sniffing." MacLeish shared Seldes' faith in radio's positive potential as a means of mass communication about issues that truly mattered.[18]

With equal persistence, however, Seldes did not believe that radio provided an appropriate medium for formal education. He became utterly disenchanted with the ineptitude of professors on the air. He had never been enthusiastic about academic lectures anyway—hence his hostility to radio as a didactic device, despite his commitment to democratic uplift:

> There are dozens of places to get education and very few to get entertainment. So if we have to smack the radio down, let us do it with a definite purpose: to raise its level of entertainment. To make entertainment so inclusive that everything interesting to the average mind will be in it—so that while we are entertained, something relevant to our own problems may filter through to us. But no lessons, thank you, and no, damn you, no lectures.

More than eleven years later he still reiterated such sentiments. He did not mind that networks and independent stations continued to produce cultural programs because, "by the terms of their contract with the government and people of the United States, they must operate in the public interest." So long as these were informational or discussion programs, Seldes found them useful. He remained skeptical that a classroom learning experience could be replicated on the air. Some critics pleaded throughout the 1930s and '40s that the cultural uses of radio be placed ahead of its commercial uses. From Seldes' perspective, much as he wished to promote traditional "culture" as an uplifting experience, that did not seem to be a realistic way to think about a mass medium.[19]

When Seldes wrote about comedians and comedy shows on the air, mostly from the early 1930s to the later 1940s, he did so with the gusto of the man who wrote *The 7 Lively Arts,* although he felt rather strongly that performers like Ed Wynn, Fred Allen, and Groucho Marx were even funnier live on the stage than invisible on the air—not because they were invisible but because their acts had to be sanitized for the unseen diversity of American taste. Ed Wynn was wonderful because "one fifth of him comes over the air, and one fifth of Wynn is funnier than five-fifths of most other people." The same applied to Allen, Marx, and others because they possessed some elusive quality that "puts a temporary stop to dullness":

> The comedians on the air are better than Amos 'n' Andy and the Rise of the Goldbergs because whatever is short and funny is better than whatever is long and dull. Mr. Cantor is funny because he has a fund of funny stories and Groucho Marx because he can deliver wit, which he is hunting for in places the radio does not often penetrate and Al Jolson because he is impudent and can be a little offside without being definitely offcolor.[20]

In 1937 Seldes proposed a hierarchy, in terms of popularity, among entertainers on the air: crooners, comedians, gagmen, amateurs, personal-history-and-problems characters. Although unenthusiastic about most crooners, Seldes liked Rudy Vallee and Bing Crosby, the latter because he succeeded in being inoffensively cynical. After suggesting a bond between crooners and comedians that seems artificial and unclear to us, Seldes proposed a "memory test" in order to evaluate comedy: "if you can't laugh tomorrow at what you have seen today, the man who made you laugh is not a comedian; he is a comic personality." Once again Seldes condemned the phony creation of "personality" for and by entertainers, when the quality really wanted was character.[21]

Was there any connection between Seldes' pleasure in marvelous comedy and his intermittent sermons on behalf of radio as potential means of mental uplift? The answer is resoundingly yes. He admired Fred Allen immensely and believed that the best performances of Allen's long career had all been parodies, among which perhaps the very best were parodies of radio itself. What endeared Fred Allen to Seldes above all, though, was that Allen assumed "the existence of a mind in his listeners. . . . Allen has an intellect, a brain." Seldes went on to suggest, however, that if people actually knew that Allen was brainy as well as funny, he would be less popular—an implicit indictment of radio impresarios and/or the American people as anti-intellectual. There is an element of inconsistency here, perhaps, with Seldes' customary insistence that the intelligence and perceptiveness of the American people were consistently under-rated.[22]

Seldes also admired Jack Benny and observed in 1946 that Benny "is probably the most artful master of the technique of radio comedy. He knows why he does what he does, has a shrewd critical eye for his own virtues and deficiencies, and achieves his atmosphere of casual ease by instinct and habit as well as hard work." Those remarks followed a highly unusual sequence of events involving interaction between a critic and a radio comedian. Seldes had published an essay in his "lively arts" series in *Esquire* complaining that too much of radio comedy depended upon the actual or pretended human frailties of the comedians and their troupes: jokes about fat and bald men, mean men and nagging women, stupid ignorant people, and so on. Seldes felt that there ought to be more diversified sources of humor and said that this "mild sadism was becoming a bore."[23]

Benny responded to this highly visible challenge—*Esquire* enjoyed a broad readership during the 1940s—by inviting Seldes to appear on his program. The first half was "all in the usual vein": Benny being jealous of Mary Livingstone because she got all of the requests for autographs; she accused him of falling asleep while dancing with her; the announcer was called "obese"; the orchestra looked like dogs, and so on. The second half of the script closely followed Seldes' criticisms. As he described it in a subsequent issue of *Esquire:*

> Then Benny put me on the witness stand, announced my ideas, and offered to play a sweet show, "sort of a Ma Perkins with a band." This part of the program, therefore, consisted of honeyed compliments, excessive gushing, and attempted interruptions on my part, put down severely by Benny, who treated me as an enemy of radio and a threat to his bread and butter and swimming pool. At the end, Rochester phoned to complain that something had gone wrong with his radio—"Don Wilson's got thin, you got hair . . . etc." And Benny asked me which way I thought the program was best, allowing me to reply, "I think it's better when they insult you."
>
> What Benny had done was, of course, the opposite of what he said he was going to do. He had really played his comedy of insult right through, using a different technique and making me the fall guy instead of himself. There was no situation developed in the second half; there was no need for one. It was only necessary to slather compliments around so extravagantly as to appear ridiculous and pretend that this was equivalent to a program idea. But the program was built up skillfully, reaching its climax when the commercial was sung to the melody of the *Spring Song,* in operatic style.
>
> Into this gooey mess, only one acid note was flung—and it was from me. After all the insults to the orchestra in the first half, including references to St. Bernards, the second half developed a series of compliments to the symphonic training of all the men, to their skill as musicians and quality as gentlemen, after which I was made to say, "Then how come they look like

dogs?" Then Benny shouted, "Mr. Seldes, apparently you haven't read your article in Esquire." Breaking me down had finally accomplished the main purpose which wasn't to present my criticism, but to make a funny show which proved Benny right.

Seldes devoted the rest of this essay, along with a reprise of the whole incident a decade later, to an inside look, exceedingly complimentary, at the way a comedy show is constructed, rehearsed, and presented.[24]

III

Although Seldes' guest appearance on Benny's program was a first-time experience for him in comedy, he had begun to participate in "talk" shows in 1933. Between 1937 and 1940 he became more deeply involved with the medium: first as a scriptwriter/adapter, then as an interviewer, and ultimately as a producer/director. The intensity of his engagement during these years supplanted the energies that had gone into his daily column for the New York *Evening Journal.* Although his monthly piece on the lively arts continued for yet another decade in *Esquire,* and he wrote major essays for magazines like *Atlantic* and *Harper's* with some frequency, the primary focus of his attention shifted for a while from cultural criticism in print to attempts at innovative cultural programming on the radio. These efforts not only provided him with an insider's view of the industry, but ultimately caused him to feel disappointment in the electronic media after World War II when network programming, more often than not, tended to level down rather than level up.

In 1937 he prepared for CBS an adaptation of *The Taming of the Shrew,* starring Edward G. Robinson as Petruchio. Although Seldes did not feel excessively reverent toward Shakespeare, neither did he believe that he could take the kinds of liberties that he had with Aristophanes' *Lysistrata* because the rituals of early Greek drama had become meaningless to modern audiences. By contrast, he commented, Shakespeare's lines were so "tight" and his episodes so closely interrelated that cutting seemed extremely difficult. "The essential thing in Shakespeare," he said, "comes through so clearly that it is impossible to adapt his plays without retaining that essential thing."[25]

Later in 1937 Seldes signed on with CBS as its first director of television programs. Because there wasn't much to direct yet, and wouldn't be for a decade, his principal activities took place in educational radio for

CBS where he had responsibility for developing three program series in adult education. The first of these series was called "Americans at Work," and he described its basic dynamic in a letter to William Allen White, the widely respected editor of the *Emporia Gazette* in Kansas, because Seldes intended to devote one of these thirty-minute evening shows to White and his newspaper.[26] Each week, he explained,

> we give a picture of an important occupation. We have done sandhogs and bakers and milkmen, etc. Usually we have a dramatic and informative section in the studio and then take the microphone to a place where work is actually being done and have it described there. One of the subjects we hope to take up is the work of a newspaper man—or more generally of several types of work which all contribute to getting out a paper.

Seldes wanted to record a portion of the broadcast from the actual plant of the *Emporia Gazette* and conveyed his concern to achieve authenticity as opposed to a staged production:

> We make a special point that the picture of Men At Work should be accurate in the sense that the work is actually being done as it is normally being done and the only difference is that from time to time a worker comes up to the microphone and we ask him some questions about his work and perfectly casual questions about himself. We want the tone and background also to be correct in the sense that we are interested in the occupation, in the work being done and in the way it is being done and we do not want a theatrical or moving picture conversation of newspaper work. We would like to get four or five different people to talk about their work on the microphone and we might be able to arrange them in such an order that we would go from the collection of news through editing, typesetting, printing in logical order.[27]

White responded with interest, enthusiasm, and an emphasis upon American exceptionalism. "The country newspaper, that is to say, the daily newspaper in any town from five thousand to a hundred thousand, is an American product. Continental Europe does not know this small town paper. . . . Here it is founded essentially upon the dignity of the human spirit. It emphasizes the individual." Seldes and his colleagues at CBS were so impressed by White's acute discussion of the social role of the country newspaper that they chose to make the entire program at Emporia, with essential background information woven in at appropriate times. Seldes even became a bit didactic in explaining to White what needed to be highlighted:

We must remember right through the program that the subject is essentially the occupation—in this case the half dozen principal occupations which contribute to the creation of a small town newspaper. At the same time, I feel that every worker is entitled to feel that his particular job has a dignity which comes from being socially useful and this applies to the sandhog as much as it does to the doctor. That is why the position of the newspaper and its place in the community should come out as part of the program and that is the part I think which you should expound.[28]

That particular program and the series as a whole went well. Late in November Seldes devoted one of his brief evening solo programs (called "Headlines and Bylines"), really an oral version of the newspaper column that he had written for seven years, to *Puritan in Babylon,* White's new biography of Calvin Coolidge. Seldes loved the book, of course, because he admired White immensely. But he also used the occasion to relate an anecdote about a facetious proposal that White had made when Seldes visited Emporia in August:

In effect he said, "Look here, no one really knows what constitutes libel or slander so why don't we try to find out. So I'm going to publish this biography of Coolidge. You review it on the air and call it all the bad names you can think of. Then I'll sue you for damages. Then after the case gets to the Supreme Court, and you and I are both dead, the law of libel will be clear and established." He then went so far as to suggest certain particular insults. The only thing he didn't offer to do was to pay the lawyers' fees. Well, I'm afraid the test case will have to wait because I haven't anything actionable to say about The Puritan in Babylon.[29]

On April 25, 1938, soon after both men came to work for CBS, Seldes met Norman Corwin, a young writer and director who swiftly achieved immense distinction in the difficult field of special radio productions. In 1992 Corwin recalled his collaboration with Seldes on "Americans at Work":

There were some earnest but always friendly arguments with Gil on some of the first productions, mainly about what he considered my too free use of sound, but after a while we got to know and respect each other, and made a compatible team. . . . Gil had a professorial air. . . . He had a ready laugh, a keen wit and a lively sense of humor, but he was not easily moved from a position. He was less inclined to compromise than I, a stance which I grudgingly admired.[30]

Seldes, in turn, developed deep respect for his younger colleague and friend, writing in 1945 that "in a radio documentary by Corwin you will always find an honest artisan giving forth the true spirit of democracy." Between 1939 and 1942 Corwin prepared and participated in a series of rousing, well-received broadcasts concerning American values in general and the Bill of Rights particularly.[31] They provide an opportunity to note, however, once again, the absence of anything resembling consensus among cultural critics at the time. In 1942, for example, Lewis Mumford disliked a Bill of Rights Day radio program that Corwin had written and told Van Wyck Brooks that a recent award made to Corwin had been a mistake: "his stuff is false and flatulent, and doubly bad because it imitates cadences and lifts thoughts from nobler works." Brooks replied that he had no idea who Corwin was.[32] The point, I believe, is not that Brooks was seven years older than Seldes and 24 years older than Corwin. The point, rather, is that Van Wyck Brooks seems to have been oblivious to middlebrow material coming across the airwaves. Perhaps Gilbert Seldes was not beating a dead horse, after all, when he continued to scold highbrows who scorned popular culture throughout the '40s and '50s.*

Late in 1952 Frederick Lewis Allen and his wife Agnes prepared a radio script for a two-hour history of the Ford Motor Company. Following its successful production in 1953, the fiftieth anniversary of Ford's founding, the Allens frequently received requests from people in broadcasting about how best to present history on the radio.[33] Although Seldes was never besieged in that way, he had actually pioneered such projects in 1938 by producing and directing a weekly series titled "Living History." He recruited Allan Nevins, a prominent professor of American history at Columbia, to introduce and close each segment, and invited "guest lecturers" to speak about subjects on which they had special expertise—people like Kenneth Roberts, the historical novelist, and historians Dixon Ryan Fox and Harry Carman.[34]

Seldes worked closely with Nevins and nurtured the relationship. In the early programs, involving New World conquest and colonization, Seldes apologetically indicated his belief that "we are right at the begin-

---

*Corwin recalls an occasion on May 8, 1942, when he and others were being honored by the American Academy of Arts and Letters. Mumford gave the principal address, argued the need for an intellectual aristocracy, and urged that artistic expression be limited to works that would be worthy of posterity. His absolutism shocked the younger persons present who felt committed to cultural democracy. Conversation with the author, April 2, 1994, supported by unpublished materials from Corwin's journals.

ning to exaggerate perhaps the dramatic element, although this is a hardship to you and may even unbalance the program a bit." Manifestations of Seldes' New Deal sympathies emerged in this schematization of the American past. He told Nevins that they would devote special attention to the Cumberland Road "both because of its historical interest and because it is a pioneer instance of government improvement and service to the people."[35]

The scripts of these fifteen-minute evening programs have survived and reveal a pleasing common touch that apparently attracted laymen from all walks of life. The introduction to the first installment on May 4, 1938, began this way: "You have made history today. The way you live, your work, your pleasures, your sufferings and your triumphs are all portions of history. Your life today is the result of the way men worked and lived and suffered and triumphed in the past." And then at the close, after a clue to next week's topic, "we want these programs to take history out of the text-books and into your lives. Have we done it? Have we made history come alive for you? If we have, write to us and let us know."[36]

Two weeks later the announcer began by emphasizing the importance of looking at U.S. history in an even-handed, unchauvinistic way. Behind each listener's experience as an American "lies a history of courage, devotion, greed, heroism, trickery, a record of many motives—some selfish, some splendid." In planning for the September 14th installment concerning the creation of a national banking system early in the 1790s, Seldes' pre-occupation with the New Deal surfaced once again. He explained to Nevins that he hoped to indicate, somehow, "that regardless of expressed principles, all parties were carried toward centralization, to an extent." He saw the high drama in Hamilton's conflict with Jefferson, yet observed that Jefferson's policies in acquiring the vast Louisiana territory, and in other respects, "extended the powers of the central government as much as Hamilton ever would have dared to."[37]

In closing that letter Seldes revealed how much pleasure his six-month immersion in American history, from colonization to the Missouri crisis over slavery, had given him, but also his recognition that constraints of broadcast time combined with the genuine complexity of the past made it very difficult to "write" revisionist history for the radio. "In reading a lot of history, lately, I have become aware of forgotten bits [that would help to correct false impressions]. . . . Washington was [actually] in favor of temporary alliances. . . . The correction of misconceptions can't be done, I think, in a program which wants to follow the major course of American history; all we can do is not perpetuate them."[38]

Later that year, on November 13, in conjunction with the U.S. Office of Education, the Department of the Interior, and the Service Bureau for Intercultural Education, Seldes launched another, more ambitious series of broadcasts that adapted its title from a widely noted remark that President Roosevelt had made the previous year: "Americans All— Immigrants All." Seldes wrote the scripts and anticipated the notion of "peopling" North America from a multicultural perspective. His topics moved from "Our English Heritage" to "Our Hispanic Heritage." Following a program devoted to the "Upsurge of Democracy" that concentrated on the Jacksonian period, subsequent broadcasts turned to the Irish, two on Slavic immigrant groups, the Chinese and the Japanese, and the Italians. Then came programs about the contributions that immigrants in general had made to social change in the United States, about life in a New England town, and about life in an industrial city.[39]

The last mentioned show selected St. Paul, Minnesota, in order to demonstrate how immigration had "created and formed and changed a great city of the Middle West." Not only did the program have input from African Americans and members of fourteen different ethnic groups, but gender received special attention also, with the voices of Dutch, Austrian, and Russian immigrant women being heard. This particular program took advantage of a Festival of Nations recently held in St. Paul sponsored by the International Institute. Some 35,000 immigrants and descendants of immigrants gathered to "enjoy each other's foods and viewed the arts and industries brought from the homelands." A narrator described St. Paul as the Apostle of Nations. Seldes took special pride in this celebration of multiculturalism.

When the series opened the announcer explained that it would offer "the story of how you, the people of the United States made America— you and your neighbors, your parents and theirs. It is the story of the most spectacular movement of humanity in all recorded time. . . ." The show enjoyed tremendous success. CBS received more than 100,000 enthusiastic letters and the Women's National Radio Committee selected "Americans All" as the most original and informative program of the 1938–39 season, an award announced on April 23, 1939. The closing program on May 7 explained that in response to such a favorable reception CBS would offer yet another educational series, "Democracy in Action."[40]

The programs were collected into a multi-disc record album and marketed by a commercial firm. In 1964 Seldes attached a memorandum to his copy of the user's manual prepared by J. Morris Jones. (It devoted sections to use in school programs, civic assembly programs, a guide for listeners, and "Cultivating More Appreciative Attitudes Among Culture Groups.") In the memo Seldes proudly remarked that the people who made the series felt especially gratified "when 20% of the letters came from other groups than the one we treated that week." He also revealed his integrative orientation as a pluralist by indicating that his personal favorite had been the first program which "dealt with America as a whole, not with any one group."[41]

More than a decade passed before Seldes returned to radio as an active participant, and during the 1950s his role was more as a commentator on the cultural scene than as a director, producer, or writer. For a while in the mid-'50s he had his own fifteen-minute program, called, not surprisingly, "The Lively Arts," that aired on Sunday evenings on WNEW from New York. The announcer explained that Seldes would report whatever seemed fresh and important or amusing and exciting in the field of entertainment: "in the theatre or the movies, in radio or comic strips . . . in night clubs or popular song . . . sooner or later you will get to all of them in The Lively Arts." The subject areas followed the pattern established earlier by his columns in the *Evening Journal* and *Esquire* during the 1930s and '40s. Seldes also appeared from time to time as a guest on a program called "Conversation" hosted by Clifton Fadiman during the 1950s. It was genteel yet lively: well-read men thinking aloud in a spirited, well-mannered way.[42]

IV

On March 11, 1968, Seldes dictated another segment of the book intended to be "As in My Time":

> The coming of radio made my desire for appreciation of other entertainments seem superficial. At every point of contact, radio as it began, differed from the entertainments I had cherished: for the first time in history entertainment entered the home; for the first time, what was offered was virtually free and, because of this, was virtually universal.

From 1927 onward Seldes speculated about the impact and implications of radio as a mass medium—in key respects the first truly mass medium—and he addressed an array of concerns: weren't programs such as the daytime serials "intellectually sub-tabloid"? What about the passivity of so many people listening inertly, a "sad apathetic state of being"? He correctly recognized by 1935 that one important distinction between popular and mass culture had to do with the greater degree of passivity in the latter. Therefore he tentatively welcomed a new craze for pinball machines during the mid-1930s because it at least required a degree of human initiative and agency, thereby suggesting that "the appetite for active participation in entertainment has not been killed by the movies and the radio."[43]

For more than a decade Seldes remained ambivalent toward the impact of radio as mass entertainment. In *Mainland* (1936) he speculated about positive as well as negative implications, wondering especially whether the radio would be used for propaganda purposes by means of mass indoctrination. In distinguishing between popular and mass culture during a transitional decade, the 1940s, he added sheer scale, audience size, to the criteria of active versus passive roles for the consuming public. "The first music popularized by records or radio was popular in itself," he wrote in 1942. "Within fifty years records and radio will have multiplied the audience for the greatest music, popular or sublime, ten thousand fold."[44]

On the positive side of the ledger, Seldes noted increasingly the potential of radio to democratize culture, in terms of both distribution as well as participation. Referring to the radio as a "new instrument of distribution," he really didn't care whether people called it a democratic or a mass instrument; but he struck an upbeat populist note with the assertion that "actually we know almost nothing about mass entertainment and in the little we do know, the comparatively sound taste of the public is striking."[45]

Oddly enough, Seldes felt no enthusiasm for a national radio craze that began in 1934–35, Major Bowes Amateur Hour and the numerous copy-cat programs that tried to cash in on its instantaneous popularity. Nevertheless he held an elevated notion of the value of views shared by "average" men and women. At the very least, opinion leaders and policy makers who claimed to understand what Everyman wanted now had some basis for knowing more precisely. As he wrote late in 1936:

I should like to see the new thing [public opinion conveyed on radio] develop out of the work of the innocent bystander. . . . The forums and the street inquiries do, within limitations, give the common man a chance to speak his mind effectively—and the great question is only whether the right people listen. The thing needs to be developed on a large scale, with some publicity which would make listeners of political managers and all those who so confidently assert their understanding of the American people.[46]

Seldes liked to learn the views of ordinary folks concerning war, capitalism, social credit, and communism along with the choices of the "professional commentators and speakers of the air." Hence his enthusiasm for town meetings of the air that enjoyed special appeal during World War II. As Archibald MacLeish put it to Seldes in 1942, "it is always interesting to me how despite other mediums, the old 'cracker barrel' still remains the most effective." Engaging the face-to-face qualities of an old-fashioned town meeting with the vast audience for radio seemed a fortuitous combination. As Seldes wrote, "the leaders know precious little of what their followers think and feel and would like to say."[47]

Between 1938 and 1950 the role of "professional commentator" emerged and flourished on the radio, stimulated especially by the popular success of such news analysts as H. V. Kaltenborn and Elmer Davis. Cultural critics like Bernard DeVoto, Frederick Lewis Allen, and Seldes agreed that because of the new radio commentators, "interior America is better educated to what is going on than it has ever been before." As DeVoto told Davis in 1940, "I heard you quoted and analyzed everywhere. Shoe drummers, gas station attendants, truck drivers, county farm agents—everybody was listening to you. And your colleagues."[48]

Seldes, along with other critics, shared more ambivalent feelings about their contemporaries active in journalism during the 1920s who became popular radio personalities through the 1930s and '40s.* In the case of Franklin P. Adams, a fine writer of opinion pieces and humor for a series of prominent New York newspapers, his appearances on the radio quiz show "Information Please" between 1938 and 1948 seemed altogether suitable and satisfactory. Alexander Woollcott, who enjoyed great success as radio's "Town Crier," irritated Seldes because he rarely agreed with Woollcott's views and because "Ilex," as he signed himself, seemed so

---

*There exists no systematic treatment of a whole generation of responsible, professional critics of radio broadcasting, a group that would include John Hutchens of the *New York Times,* John Crosby of the New York *Herald Tribune* (widely syndicated), Stanley Anderson of the Cleveland *Plain Dealer,* Mary Little of the Des Moines *Register,* Leonard Carlton of the New York *Post,* Cyrus Fisher of *The Forum,* Saul Carson of *The Nation,* and Edith Isaacs of *Theatre Arts Monthly.*

fatuous. Mary Margaret McBride, on the other hand, who from 1937 to 1960 captivated a nationwide audience for her personal programs, seemed fairly innocuous as she devoted shows to such diverse topics as the Women's National Exposition of Arts and Industries (1937), the Greek War Relief Association (1943), and the Brotherhood Week observance sponsored by the National Conference of Christians and Jews (1950). From 1952 through 1954 the National Association for Better Radio and Television selected her program as the outstanding daytime program of the year, and in 1954 she was designated the "first lady of radio." She had genuine fans among the serious critics because she did her patriotic and varied show crisply and engagingly. Those who found her banal and hopelessly middlebrow maintained discreet silence.[49]

In 1950, when Seldes published several summary statements, he managed to come up with a balance sheet in the affirmative despite years of criticism directed by him at particular media and their industries. "Those who deplore what mass-produced movies and radio have done to popular taste are wide of the mark," he observed. "Compared to the entertainments they supplanted they are on fairly solid ground." By 1950 a pronounced shift in Seldes' language indicated that he was prepared to acknowledge the advent of mass communication, mass managers of mass media, and the existence of a mass audience.[50] "Mass" suddenly became an almost overused modifier, and a comparison of Seldes' language before and after World War II certainly suggests that in his view it was more appropriate to generalize about *popular* culture prior to the later 1940s, and about *mass* culture thereafter. The two overlapped, of course. The transition cannot be pinned to a date, not even to a decade, perhaps. Nevertheless, a careful reading of critics like Seldes suggests that from the perspective of contemporaries who lived through the process, mass culture emerged and fully took hold almost a generation later than scholars—especially sociologists and historians—have customarily believed.[51]

V

Clearly, a much larger and more monolithic audience existed for entertainment and news during the 1930s and '40s than previously. Why should we delay our recognition of the ripening of a genuinely mass culture until the 1950s and 1960s? There are several reasons, I believe, each of them connected to the emergence and physical (geographical) expansion of television. First, as Seldes noted, as late as the 1950s sports broadcasts were basically local, with very few exceptions such as the World Series in baseball. Moreover, many local stations rejected programs offered to them by the national networks. The South, for example, would simply display a test pattern on TV before it would show programs with a liberal perspective on race relations. The creation of a genuinely continental audience for programs of broad national interest and acceptability did not occur until the 1960s.[52]

Second, and even more significant, as Seldes predicted in 1950, television was destined to become "the primary force in the creation of a unified entertainment industry which will include sports, the theater and the movies, newsreels, radio, night clubs, vaudeville, as well as many minor activities, and will profoundly affect newspapers, magazines, books, the fine arts, and ultimately education. Co-existing within this pyramid of entertainment there will be a highly unified communications industry affecting political life." Although it has not been fulfilled in every respect, that remains one of Seldes' most prescient observations.[53]

Television *has* become—partially for reasons that Seldes could not have anticipated, such as satellites—the most comprehensive, the most integrative, and quite literally the most "massive" and universal of all the mass media. If mass culture did not exactly begin with television at midcentury, it certainly entered a very new and different phase within a decade, just when Gilbert Seldes' career as a cultural critic began to wind down.[54]

At that point in his career, moreover, early in the 1960s, Seldes drew attention to still other ways in which television manifested qualitative differences from all previous forms of popular culture. With film, for example, entertainment remained, in a sense, "somewhat set apart from daily life." Shall we go to the movies tonight? If so, we need a plan. Which one? Where? At what time? When the electronic revolution came to fruition with television, entertainment became completely integrated into the fabric of daily life, rather than just being an option. In addition, unlike film and to a greater degree than radio, Seldes declared that television had become a branch of advertising—not because of the length or frequency or cleverness of the commercials, but because sponsors exercised so much control over which programs appeared and which did not.[55]

If one wants to emphasize incremental persistence and continuity, one way to think about the century that spans the 1890s to the 1990s is in terms of a "national commercial culture," a notion that I borrow from historian Roland Marchand. If, on the other hand, one wants to make distinctions and accentuate change, which I find highly appropriate, then perhaps it is helpful to think about popular culture as the dominant mode during the first half of the twentieth century, and mass culture as the dominant mode during the second half.[56]

What Seldes had to say about television changed over time—as the technology, the industry itself, the power of advertising, and American taste changed. But on two points he did not waver, and neither one should surprise us. Just as he had done with film and radio, Seldes insisted that television must find its own niche, its own distinctive style, technique, and aesthetic, rather than be derivative of any other art form.* As he wrote in 1957, "it will not be movies but uncreativeness that will do television the most harm."[57]

He also remained consistent about a second issue, though he became most adamant on the subject during his years as the founding Dean of the Annenberg School of Communications in Philadelphia, 1959 to 1963. In October 1959 he warned his good friend, Arthur M. Schlesinger, Jr., that he had "just written an ill-tempered attack on all egghead criticism of TV for the Guide." It actually appeared at the end of the year. Seldes criticized intellectuals for blaming on television whatever they did not like about the United States or modern life in general; for blaming all of television's unattractive qualities on commercial sponsors; for being oblivious to such high-quality programs as "Playhouse 90" or "Sunday Showcase"; and for demanding more refined programs without being interested "in raising the total level of entertainment." In fact, he noted, "the amount of highbrow stuff on the air is enormously disproportionate to the tiny number of intellectuals in the country."[58]

Almost two years later Seldes started a long letter to Schlesinger that he never finished. It is interesting because it is autobiographical and adamant and confessional. It begins by conceding that a great many television programs "are pretty awful." Nevertheless, it reaffirmed Seldes' rejection of highbrow elitism, his great bugaboo ever since 1924:

---

*Although Seldes' assertion seems eminently sensible, even the most creative people in charge of the commercial networks usually followed paths of least resistance. Sylvester "Pat" Weaver, the head of television programming at NBC from 1949 until 1953, says that in that period NBC made TV shows (such as "Dragnet") directly from radio scripts and had very little notion of television as a distinctive medium that should innovate its own artistic guidelines. (Weaver, *The Best Seat in the House,* 25.)

I count myself an egghead and always try to identify myself as one before the term is thrown at me. But while I find myself at home with intellectuals in politics, in their general attitude toward society, and toward the sciences, in this one area—the one I know something about—I find the intellectual as wanting as his forerunners in the 1920's were in relation to jazz and the movies. I was accused then of being a traitor, too—of wishing to destroy Bach and Leonardo and the whole of classical European culture in order to exalt ragtime and vaudeville. The situation has changed, it has in many ways changed for the worse because of the greater power of the electronic mass media. But the intellectual has not changed. I wonder if he can.[59]

Twenty-four years earlier, precisely because he seemed to combine a powerful intellect with realism about popular taste, CBS hired Seldes to be its first director of television programs. They did so primarily because in May 1937 he published in *The Atlantic* a lengthy tour de force titled "The 'Errors' of Television" that did not, as the title might suggest, point a finger of blame at the fledgling industry. Rather, it examined a cluster of misconceptions and uncertainties concerning technological, commercial, financial, and programmatic aspects of a medium still in embryo and very much in need of guidance. Although it turned out to be one of the most widely noticed essays that Seldes ever wrote, it concentrated on conveying an impressive amount of fresh information and a fair degree of speculation, but very little in the line of cultural criticism. Only at the end, for instance, did he offer this curious defense of all the poor programs presented on radio: owing to the novelty of that medium, weak programs at least created the habit of listening and thereby built a broadly based audience that then existed to hear the important debates over such issues as Franklin D. Roosevelt's Court-packing plan. He hoped that "a more alert and critical citizenry" would demand more from television and build a broad viewing audience even more swiftly.[60]

Because of that widely noticed essay and his new status at CBS, Seldes received invitations over the next eight years to write speculative pieces about the qualities that television would need in order to succeed and the kinds of programs most likely to be viable. All of these essays enhanced Seldes' visibility and stature as a critic even though they contained little that could properly be called cultural criticism (see Fig. 19). The advent of commercial television was delayed—in part because of World War II and in part because of a kind of catch-22 situation: Without the development of programs there could be no sponsors to pay for broadcast time, but without sponsors committed to program development and the pur-

Fig. 19. Gilbert Seldes and Frank Stanton at CBS (late 1930s–early 1940s). During the 1930s Frank Stanton, president of CBS, told Congress that "a mass media [*sic*] can only achieve its great audience by practicing . . . cultural democracy . . . by giving the majority of the people what they want . . . . We find that most of the people, most of the time, want entertainment from their mass media."

chase of air time, the industry's coming of age would be retarded. For a decade following 1937 not very much happened; so Seldes' television essays tended to speculate, on the basis of film and radio history, about what might work or what ought to be avoided. He often repeated the caveat that "we do not as yet actually know the true nature of television."[61]

Early in 1939 he prepared his first column for *Esquire* concerning television, and voiced the very same concern about eggheads and entertainment that we have just noticed in the early 1960s. Seldes observed that the British didn't get much genuine entertainment on the air because the people in control were excessively devoted to the presentation of uplifting programs. He wondered why the British felt such a need to make the popular arts "ultra-respectable and refined," and he condemned the "supreme indifference of the class that makes British entertainment to the natural demands of the class that has to take it." He hoped that those in charge of broadcasting in the United States would follow quite a different course, though he acknowledged that there were bound to be pronounced differences between systems controlled by government and by commercially oriented free enterprise.[62]

Three months later *Fortune* magazine ran a kind of close-up look at television because it seemed to be on the verge of emerging as a commercial reality. The essay featured one photograph of Seldes (inadvertently looking very much like Humphrey Bogart in profile) and his NBC counterpart, Thomas H. Hutchinson, and then another photo of Seldes' massive studio and workspace above Grand Central Station on 42nd Street. *Fortune* acknowledged that Seldes and Hutchinson had to wrestle with two critical questions—what kinds of programs would the public like best, and what kinds of programs would prompt them to buy sets?—but *Fortune* seemed most fascinated by the physical set-up of CBS at Grand Central:

> an enormous empty room the length of a city block, sixty feet wide, and big enough to hold a circus. At one end rises the white pillbox of the control room with a long, narrow, horizontal slit into which a plate-glass window has yet to be fitted. There is a lot of equipment lying around—two seven-foot racks standing irrelevantly in the middle of the floor and supporting amplifier panels; a flock of big spotlights on tow stands; banks of inside-silvered Birdseye floodlight bulbs on wheeled supports; a camera neatly eviscerated on a table; and wires everywhere.
>
> Such is the spot from which Mr. Seldes labors to bring forth an elephant or a mouse—no one yet knows which.[63]

Some of his most interesting endeavors, in terms of both actual programs and his speculative essays, concerned what we would consider highbrow material, or at least what Russell Lynes later designated as upper-middlebrow. In 1938 he warmed to the one-act play as a form of drama ideally suited for television's constraints of time and cost. He observed that television would have to be creative in transcending the limits of radio drama (if things can be seen, they don't necessarily have to be heard) and the extreme expense of feature films.[64]

In speculating about the role of television in education he tended to minimize its possibilities. When he predicted that "we will not revolutionize education any more than we will revolutionize art or entertainment by a new medium," he did not reckon with the power of such programs as "Sesame Street" and "The Electric Company" to transform pre-school literacy and numeracy. In thinking about television as an educational medium, Seldes tended to emphasize, somewhat narrowly, actuality, factuality, and authenticity—his words—though he nonetheless admitted that at that stage "we are all making guesses."[65]

Eleven years later what had been a nebulous cluster of speculations took firm shape as a concrete set of issues. Educators and intellectuals (not always mutually exclusive groups) began to complain about the mediocre quality of programs and pleaded with the Federal Communications Commission to allocate channels, perhaps as many as one-seventh of the total, exclusively for educational purposes—meaning, of course, an absence of commercial control. Cultural institutions wanted to have their very own channels and offered two basic arguments: first, that television is a medium of "unparalleled virtue" in the field of education, and second that the record of network broadcasting thus far was simply dreadful. The top brass representing commercial TV retaliated with all sorts of gratuitous insults and problematic reasoning, with the result that throughout 1951–52 this debate grew exceedingly lively and Gilbert Seldes became a highly vocal participant.

The networks insisted that reserving channels for cultural institutions would be a waste of resources because those institutions lacked the means actually to establish viable stations and had in the past "betrayed a total incapacity for using mass media." The failure of more than one hundred college radio stations when commercial stations were growing rapidly seemed to clinch the case. The broadcasters called attention to their transmissions from the United Nations, and NBC announced that it would set aside prime evening periods for programs of a cultural nature. The educators responded in FCC hearings by noting a survey taken in New York City in which seven channels, during 560 hours of air time, devoted only 1 percent to public events—all of them carrying a single speech by President Truman.[66]

Seldes responded, in numerous essays, that "exiling" education programs to separate (but not equal) channels was not a wise solution because the major networks would then feel little or no obligation to undertake broadcasts in the public interest. He believed, moreover, that despite its spotty record in terms of quality, commercial television had already "done more to arouse the public to its own interests than radio did in a generation." He also quoted one critic who believed (perhaps feared) that television was actually enjoying its golden age and that the attractive programs might very well vanish, especially if purely educational channels were authorized. He then pulled his arguments together with a reprise (emphasizing democratic systems and values) that seems somewhat specious in retrospect: "If general cultural interests are represented on separate channels, the foundation of a true democratic broadcasting system is undermined. The commercial broadcasters will be under no obligation to vary their programs, to create appetites of many kinds, to interest people at several levels."[67]

Writing four months later, Seldes reaffirmed the substance of his position despite having to acknowledge that in May the National Association of Broadcasters issued a polemic against special cultural channels though "not one word was said about using the regular channels to satisfy the normal cultural needs of the public—nothing!" Despite his shocked disappointment, however, in December Seldes reiterated the argument he had made in March, and perhaps stated it in even stronger terms: "Since I believe the effect of separate channels would be to create arid scholasticism on one side and intellectual vulgarity on the other, I stick to the broadcasters' side of the argument—with some difficulty because they argue so badly." Moreover, Seldes the New Deal partisan who did not fear regulation and the centralization of power in 1938 now believed that "the industry is on firm ground when it repels all efforts to bring the federal government in to judge its accomplishments."[68]

Seldes' position was courageous if unconvincing, and several of the most prominent television critics at the time, such as John Crosby and Jack Gould, strongly favored the existence of special channels devoted to cultural programs. He pleaded once more, true to his convictions, as always, that "culture should not be isolated, it should be an integrated part of commercial broadcasting." Within a few years, however, something caused Seldes to soften his position, perhaps the success of some early educational channels. In 1954, for example, he received a letter from the manager of KUHT in Houston, inviting Seldes to visit and explaining that some 800,000 different people each week watched at least one of the station's programs.[69]

Within a decade, following his deanship at the Annenberg School of Communications, Seldes became a program consultant for National Educational Television, devoting one week per month to his work for NET. Two years later, early in 1966, he wrote an essay of warm praise for Frieda Hennock, a member of the FCC from 1948 until 1955 and the only woman member prior to 1966. Hennock had been the lonely commissioner who pleaded in 1951 that separate channels be set aside for cultural stations. Seldes acknowledged that he had opposed her, explained why (in terms that made more sense than he had fifteen years earlier), and proclaimed that "she is a central figure to whom all of us interested in broadcasting—in *all* broadcasting—owe much. . . . Belatedly for my self-respect, but in time for me to carry on my profession, I became 'a reluctant convert' to that form of television which Miss Hennock had done so much to make possible." Seldes was a proud man, but not too proud; polemical yet reasonable. He could be converted—not often but with candor.[70]

Did his conversion hold? A few years later, working on his memoirs, possibly in 1968, Seldes reaffirmed his belief that *all* television could be educational. A daytime serial (meaning a soap opera) and a special program on relativity would both enlarge the interests of audiences, so long as each one was well done.[71] That contention is entirely consistent with the rationale underlying *The 7 Lively Arts*. It would be facile to say that the more things change, the more they remain the same. In this instance it is important to remember that in 1968 Seldes was primarily writing a memoir of his professional life during the 1920s and '30s. His activities at that time remained the touchstone with which everything else needed to be reconciled, if possible.

VI

Seldes' work on programming for CBS kept him quite busy during the war years. In 1941 Edmund Wilson told Alyse Gregory (Seldes' successor as editor of *The Dial*) that "Seldes works for television and I never see him any more." Seldes sought diligently, for example, to negotiate a contract with Eugene O'Neill, then a recluse at his mountain retreat in Danville, California, for a television adaptation of an O'Neill play. The negotiations failed, not because O'Neill would not allow abridgment but because he wanted far more money than Seldes' budget from CBS would allow.[72]

During 1941–42, however, he successfully arranged for CBS to collaborate with the Metropolitan Museum of Art on a weekly series of programs, as well as specials with the Museum of Modern Art and one program each with several other museums—programs concerning barns and bridges, costumes, and social and political cartoons, along with more traditional forms of art. Seldes proudly told the New York *Sun*'s art critic that these were the first televised previews and live critiques of art exhibitions. He felt pleased that "we have developed a very spontaneous mood and have found that impromptu discussion works very well in television." The success of these programs even prompted Seldes to revise his theory that movement must become essential to TV and that transmitting still pictures would be lethal. "I was so wrong it's incredible," he told columnist Earl Wilson. Following two programs in which Seldes showed masterpieces from the Met he concluded that people would look at still pictures; so long as the images and commentary were clear, the viewing experience could be astonishingly interesting.[73]

Between 1941 and 1945 his duties kept Seldes on the go both inside and outside of his studio. At the ABA Booksellers Convention in May 1942, for instance, he televised a quiz show for booksellers visiting New York City. Late in 1944 CBS began to collaborate with *Mademoiselle* magazine on a monthly piece and thirty-minute program called "Women in Wartime." Critics singled out Seldes, the producer, for special praise: "He set a standard not only for his own staff . . . but for video as a whole."[74]

Despite his successes and growing prominence in the industry, CBS dismissed Seldes as program director later in 1945. Working on his memoirs almost twenty-five years later, Seldes correctly surmised: "I never knew quite why, but I think it was for lack of executive ability, not for lack of imagination in programming." On the following page he mused that he had been hired in 1937 because "I was one of the few critic intellectuals who did not despise the mass media; but I failed disastrously to put my ideas over *on* the masters of the mass media." It was not easy for someone whose vocation had been that of independent cultural critic to become a corporate staff member, even at the executive level. Seldes' temperament was better suited for the role of an outsider than a restless insider. Looking back on his firings at CBS and Paramount, the feisty Seldes recalled "the sense that I had lost the background upon which my shadow was cast." Rarely has a personal statement about the precariousness of professional identity been phrased more poignantly (see Fig. 20).[75]

Seldes soon returned to the role of independent critic, but he never entirely ceased to be a participant. In 1952 he produced a book, *Writing for Television,* that covered the whole field of video scripting—a detailed handbook that drew heavily on his experience as a television producer and writer. It described and explained specific working conditions, provided general guidelines for writing television drama, and emphasized "the most important of all the uses of time—the feeling we communicate that our characters are *living through* time just as they are living in space."[76]

Fig. 20. Gilbert Seldes at a party in Los Angeles in November 1957. Richard Neutra, the architect, is on Seldes' left. They are watching "Viewpoints."

During the 1950s and early 1960s Seldes appeared as a guest on various "talk shows" concerned with cultural matters. Those who appeared with him and interacted with him still recall, as Alistair Cooke told me, "his restless bounce, his boyish vitality and general cheerfulness." In April of 1958 NBC introduced a new series hosted by Seldes, "The Subject Is Jazz," that appeared on Saturday afternoons at five o'clock. It entailed a thirteen-week sequence produced in cooperation with the Educational Television and Radio Center at the University of Michigan. The response of reviewers varied greatly. According to the *New York Times,* the opening program's "handicap was the commentary by Gilbert Seldes, critic, who read from notes and was uncertain both as to what he was going to say and what the program was trying to do." Despite his appearance as a guest, Duke Ellington didn't get much opportunity to express opinions. The following month, however, Jo Coppola, reviewing the series for the New York *Post,* declared that Seldes, "who happens to be a favorite critic of mine, should have a half-hour all to himself. He made some rather provocative statements that seemed to be worthy of much longer discussion." Coppola concluded by noting, however, that she had agreed with some but not all of Seldes' assertions. "And that is the trouble with television commentary. It tickles the mind but leaves it unsatisfied."[77]

Although Seldes rarely responded to his own critics, he did take note of what critics had to say about television in general. Among his papers at the University of Pennsylvania there are clippings that he made of columns written by Jack Gould, John Crosby, Henry Morgan, and Harriet Van Horne, a quartet he referred to as "the professional critics" in his regular "TV and Radio" column in the *Saturday Review*.[78] On one occasion late in 1952 he devoted a column to the mediocre quality of both television *and* its critics. The following July he responded to some dissenting remarks that John Crosby had made in reply to a Seldes column. (Crosby's radio and television criticism was syndicated through the New York *Herald Tribune*.) Seldes' appeal for discrimination in contemplating the responsibilities of a cultural critic now sounded less populistic than usual. "The break between the intellectual and the average intelligent man is not going to be bridged by the intellectual's pretense of having a mind no better trained than that of the sub-average. Nor by pretending that taste and discrimination have no standing."[79]

He returned to that issue three years later in thinking aloud about the potential impact of critics. "We, the small fragment of professional thinkers about the media," he mused, "cannot control the media themselves and probably would make a bad job of it if we had the chance. But by constantly increasing the number of individuals who see what is happening, we multiply the forces of control." He believed that the critical mass of cultural commentators need not be especially large, "but they must have 'social reverberation.' They must have the magic power to stir others." It seems appropriate that at least a few students of television criticism today have seen Seldes in retrospect as a man ahead of his time in calling for socially responsible television criticism during the 1950s.[80]

Because the media increasingly exercised considerable influence over public opinion, Seldes concerned himself from time to time with the issue of media responsibility—the professional ethics of exerting immense power in the civic sector. More often than not, Seldes achieved a greater degree of subtlety, and certainly complexity, than many of his peers. In 1953, for example, he observed that once the broadcasters concede that

[t]he media can raise or lower the public taste, in the very act of satisfying the public demand, they will come closer to their function, which is defined legally as operating in the public interest, and which, morally, does not insist on raising the public taste but demands, as a minimum, that the public be given every opportunity to find its own level of taste by having access to the best as well as to the mean—which in this case, is far from golden.[81]

Six weeks earlier Seldes paused long enough in the midst of an intensely busy schedule of teaching and writing to give an interview to *Variety,* the entertainment trade journal, concentrating on the prospects for television. Some of what he had to say seems predictable, but there were a few surprises. To begin with the former, he wished that TV would "satisfy more of the interests of more of the people" because, in his view, the medium tended to narrow rather than broaden those interests. Television's greatest hope, he believed, lay in its commitment "to reality via its communications function," meaning news broadcasts, special events, and public affairs programs. He continued to regard the televised hearings on organized crime chaired by Senator Estes Kefauver in 1951, which riveted public interest, as "the best thing television has ever done." From a long-term perspective, perhaps, he may have been naive in believing there was little chance of the medium deteriorating into escapism so long as it needed to function "as an eye on the actual world." He ended the interview on a more realistic note, remarking that television "is in a perpetual crisis, hanging between danger and opportunity."[82]

His most arresting comment, perhaps, especially for the year 1953, was that television's greatest effect on American society had been "to reinforce the feeling begun by radio that entertainment is another right," added to such presumed rights as life, liberty, and the pursuit of happiness. Suddenly entertainment no longer had to be "earned, it is continually on tap." Perhaps Seldes felt just a twinge of resentment that for most of *his* lifetime one had to pay, however modestly, for each new episode of entertainment; but now one only had to make the initial purchase of an electronic appliance and it supplied an endless flow of free fun.[83]

By and large, however, Seldes found most of television's genres acceptable if not consistently enjoyable. Although he could be quite acerbic at times, he remained more tolerant of popular taste than most professional critics were. He didn't much like crime programs, particularly if they were accessible to children. Situation comedies he assessed one by one, rather than lumping them all together as a singular category. "You'll

Never Get Rich" seemed vulgar and dumb, for example, but the "Lucy Show" was terrific because he regarded Lucille Ball as a brilliant comedienne. Each of the continuing series about married life—"Ethel and Albert," "Ozzie and Harriet," "The Honeymooners"—had its own distinctive strengths and weaknesses.[84]

By 1954 daytime soap operas had become such a spectacular (and unanticipated) success that Seldes chose to devote six months to a serious, careful survey of their contents and the sociology of their audience. Until 1953–54, when NBC reversed its anti-soap policy because it was losing too many viewers and advertisers, CBS dominated the presentation of soap operas. Once NBC got on the bandwagon, soap operas became an overwhelming presence in the lives of (mainly) American women. The leading character in these programs was invariably a woman, usually a very strong woman. The dominant characteristic of the genre was narrative delay, the kind of suspense about a character or situation that would surely cause the viewer to tune in once again the next day. Seldes also noticed that whereas speed and swift action characterized nighttime TV, daytime soaps moved very deliberately, even ploddingly.[85]

To a much greater degree than usual, Seldes speculated and generalized about the soap opera audience. It consisted overwhelmingly of middle- and lower-class people who admired and envied the upper-middle-class characters in the stories. Viewers tended to be economically dependent women who found the "outside" world somewhat threatening. "They cling to a severe moral code," he believed, "(on which their position as wife and mother is based), but they are anxious about that position and, as housework becomes easier, they worry and wonder whether they are needed." The serials somehow seemed to give them reassurance: the virtuous wife and mother is important; the threatened domestic scene can be saved; right eventually triumphs over wrong. Seldes reported that women believe they learn from the soaps, yet he remained skeptical—in part because women (like men) seemed to make so many foolish errors of judgment, both on the screen and off.* Twelve years later, when Seldes offered his final verdict on the soap opera, it turned out to be more categorically negative. Calling it "by far the most skillful invention of broadcasting," he believed that it ultimately had a

---

*In 1942 a New York psychiatrist had declared that listening to soap operas produced serious medical and health problems for women. See John Fiske, *Understanding Popular Culture* (London, 1989), 93.

corrupting influence, partially because it "blurs the line between the real and the false," and partially because it stimulates "emotional habits which are not wholly desirable."[86]

Although Seldes' analysis of daytime serials was neither profound nor enduring, it is worth noting that while he may have been less epigrammatic than Marshall McLuhan on the same topic, he was considerably more substantive and less enigmatic. Here is the essence of McLuhan on the subject during the early 1950s:

> Horse opera and soap opera . . . embody two of the most important American traditions, the frontier and the home town. But the two traditions are split rather than fused. They show that radical separation between business and society, between action and feeling, office and home, between men and women, which is so characteristic of industrial man. These divisions cannot be mended until their fullest extent is perceived.[87]

Despite the pithiness of Seldes' observations about serial programs and their principal audience, he is ultimately somewhat perplexing when we raise such questions as: should the medium be expected to "level up," or should it be allowed to please the largest common denominator? Do people genuinely want better quality than what they are being offered? Are the designated "culture programs" really all that good? There are several reasons for the apparent inconsistencies in Seldes' responses: first, television developed with almost bewildering speed between 1948 and 1955, and that meant, among other things, astonishing variation in quality from one network to another, from year to year, and even from season to season; second, Seldes came at these issues from different angles in different essays—hence the appearance (if not always the reality) of inconsistency; and third, as with the emergence of the talkies and radio, it took more than a few years for Seldes' compass to settle down and point in a steady direction.

Even so, as late as 1962 Seldes wondered whether television could successfully be both artistic and commercial. Although it seemed possible, he wasn't sanguine. He told the vast readership of *TV Guide* that for a period in its early years television seemed to be little more than an unwieldy combination of average radio and grade B movies. Despite his perception of the negative impact on Hollywood's studio system on television, he wondered whether TV's natural development might have been better nurtured by the film industry than by the broadcast industry;

and then he complained that television had actually become a branch of the advertising industry![88]

During the fourteen years prior to those unfavorable perspectives, Seldes had wavered between hope and dismay. In 1949 a supposedly hopeful essay (judging only by its title) condemned what had emerged until then as being, unhappily, all too predictable. Critics and the informed public alike seemed to be watching, once again, "the traditional development of an American art-enterprise: an incredible ingenuity in the mechanism, great skill in the production techniques—and stale, unrewarding, contrived, and imitative banality for the total result." He saw nothing inevitable about that outcome, however, and argued that television did not have to appeal exclusively to the mass. He believed that it ought to be able to create a comprehensive program schedule that could satisfy multiple taste levels and "combine the two great powers, *actuality* and *imagination*."[89]

Two years later Seldes' prognosis became particularly gloomy. He shared Jack Gould's assessment in the *New York Times* that a "spectacular deluge of new shows and stars is concealing video's first symptoms of artistic and cultural paralysis." Seldes commented that it seemed unprecedented for "senility [to be] setting in at the age of three." And he returned to a distinction that he had made on numerous occasions in writing film criticism—between the delineation of character (desirable) and the mere presentation of personality (meretricious). "What TV can actually carry from the studio into the home is the truth of character. Character, however, is destiny, and our popular arts are content with its false front, which is the fabricated personality."[90]

A few months later, however, he saw an illustrative glimmer of hope: a one-hour adaptation of Fitzgerald's novel *The Last Tycoon,* "so impressive as to revolutionize many people's notions about the *present* possibilities of the medium." Significant improvement or variation in quality did not occur, however, and for several years thereafter Seldes insisted that "people at every level of education, in significant numbers, do imply some dissatisfaction with the programs they are getting, and among these are ten million people, not habitual book readers, not college graduates, who consistently ask for programs of a higher intellectual content." He declared that his data came from studies that had been made for the industry, and blamed broadcasters for using the lame excuse that they were only giving the public what it wanted. "Once they admit that the media can raise or lower the public taste, in the very act of satisfying the public demand, they will come closer to their function, which is defined legally as operating in the public interest, and which . . . demands, as a minimum, that the public be given every opportunity to find its own level of taste by having access to the best as well as to the mean."[91]

During the middle 1950s Seldes remained quite critical of those responsible for determining television entertainment, and in a speech that he gave at Dartmouth in 1955 he noted that the main impetus behind such cultural programs as did appear arose from a fear of competition by the newly emerging educational channels. Some of the commercial network programs were very good, such as "Omnibus," but he cautioned that "they offer more of a cultural scrap book than real education." In 1957 he addressed the issue of cultural stratification directly in a published essay, but now he sounded far more sanguine about what might be achieved in the way of uplift—and that it would be a good thing altogether, even the highbrow element. "If the public begins to hold education in high esteem," he wrote, "we can be sure that in due time networks and sponsors will discover the new commodity and the highbrow program will come into its own." Although that was not exactly a reversal of earlier positions, it represented a fresh emphasis for Seldes. So did his new concern about the existence of a double standard for measuring success:

> The programs we lump together as cultural will then enjoy a prerogative now reserved to commercial programs: the right to make a few mistakes, the chance to recover from errors. At present, if a cultural program isn't at once perfect and successful it vanishes and drags with it half-a-dozen projected programs of the same kind. Failure is blamed on the nature of the program. . . .[92]

Seldes also complained that when a so-called cultural program failed "the blame is placed not on the program, but on culture." He wished that broadcasters would attempt more shows that were "off the beaten path" and would work at them "with as much conviction as they now give to their commercial efforts." At the age of sixty-four, Seldes had finally accepted cultural stratification as an inescapable reality. He never lost his commitment to the goal of cultural democracy, however, and his belief in the need for audiences to be able to make choices—as well as the likelihood that they would choose wisely if they had the opportunity—would be cited and paraphrased for some years to come.[93]

VII

During the 1950s Seldes became increasingly preoccupied by a cluster of related issues: the impact of television on politics; the appropriate way (or ways) for the television industry to handle public controversies; and the propriety of government regulation of television. The most heated discussions of such matters involving Seldes will be treated in Chapter Nine below, but it is appropriate to set the stage for this discussions here, looking mainly at the early 1950s.

When it became apparent in March 1952 that TV would cover (and even commercially sponsor) the presidential nominating conventions of the two major parties and the actual campaign—the first time ever—Seldes wrote fretfully about the commercialization of politics. Had it really become necessary to break the tradition of giving free time for political discussion before and during the conventions? Did everything have to be sponsored? Would important aspects of American public life lose their visibility if no sponsor came forward to purchase air time? Four years later, when the role of television as a major factor in political campaigning had become evident, Seldes wondered aloud whether or not broadcasting should be regarded as a public utility. Up until then broadcasting had been seen as a service properly compelled to operate in the public interest. Although its technological features had been regulated, however, Seldes noted that no commission had been empowered to define standards of programming. Was that a possibility? Broadcasters believed that it was, and the prospect made them very anxious.[94]

In 1951 Seldes expressed adamant agreement with the television industry in opposing any attempt by the federal government to judge the quality of what it produced. He believed that that should be left to the marketplace of ideas and the industry's discretion, even though his faith in the latter was low and would vacillate during the course of the decade. Looking back at what has, in fact, transpired and at Seldes' own growing concern about quality, his stance seems a bit anomalous.[95]

Ever since 1934 the Federal Communications Act required broadcast stations to operate in "the public interest, convenience and necessity." When stations applied for renewal of their franchises every three years they were obliged to report on the extent of their news and public affairs programming. Although the act made it clear that the FCC should not engage in censorship, it has always been the case that the commission does not pay close attention to compliance or even evaluate the merits of the programming that owners reported under the category of public affairs. Over a period of six decades, in fact, no station's license has ever been revoked because of low programming quality. In 1949–50, however, the FCC began to treat broadcasters a little more like newspapers and authorized them to advocate causes if they wished, that is, to take a stand on controversial issues so long as they did not do so in a one-sided way. The networks soon decided that if *they* could take sides, they might just as well sell air time to others for the same purpose. Even Seldes turned up his nose at the commercialization of partisanship concerning matters of public policy and the public interest.[96]

Between 1952 and 1957 these vexed issues would become highly problematic and they embroiled Seldes in some of the harshest and most abrasive conflicts of his entire career. First, how should television handle the McCarthy hearings concerned with communists in the U.S. government and military? Next, how fairly did Edward R. Murrow deal with Senator McCarthy in his sensational "See It Now" exposé? Then, in 1957, when Nikita Khrushchev visited the United States, would television coverage of his speech, interviews, and other activities "bring communist propaganda into American homes"? Seldes approved of the much criticized CBS decision to interview Khrushchev on the air, and he scorned the "nervous mistrust of the American people's ability to distinguish truth from falsehood. . . . What's the use of a Republic, if the people must be patriarchally protected from every mendacity or disturbance? And who's to do the protecting?"[97]

These and other closely related issues will emerge front and center in Chapter Nine. It seems fitting to close this one by calling attention to a fundamental, underlying consistency in Seldes' responses to the actual content of what should be broadcast on radio and television. In a 1950 interview that he gave to *Variety* he explained that he had only one serious complaint to offer against radio broadcasting and he felt compelled to make it because he saw the same problem creeping into television: "too much of it is aimed at one level of intelligence and appreciation." Radio was committing the same error that films had, and now it looked as though TV would follow suit—not building new audiences and attracting diversified clienteles.[98]

He reiterated that plea for variety and choice in a section of *The Great Audience* called "A Pluralistic Universe." Seldes had arrived at Harvard in 1910, the year that William James died; but James' advocacy of pluralism was very much in the air during Seldes' college years and he seemed to rediscover the concept with particular intensity during the 1950s and '60s. In the 1920s and '30s, of course, he had called for a more pluralistic criticism. In 1953 he wrote a major statement and called it "For Pluralistic TV." A monolithic system of broadcasting content, at whatever level, seemed unthinkable. "In the long run," he argued, "it is better for us to have bad entertainment mixed with good than to have one kind of entertainment only, even if it is of high quality. Variety is, in a sense, more important than excellence, because out of variety new forms of excellence can develop."[99]

That had become Seldes' creed as a radio and television critic.

8

In Defense of Americanism

Although writing about film and for radio occupied much of Seldes' time during the 1930s and '40s, along with anticipating what might become of television, there was yet another aspect of his busy life that, in certain key respects, seems to have been something of an aberration. He became, along with some other prominent intellectuals, an intense chauvinist—almost jingoistic at times. He reversed or at least significantly altered positions that he had held for a long time, insisting, for example, that there could be such a thing as "good" propaganda; and he took some stands that would embarrass him years later. As he wrote to a close friend in 1959, referring to 1936–38, "I'm appalled at what I dared to write about in those days."[1]

Unrepresentative of the rest of his career, yet characteristic of the years 1933 to 1945, was his interest in matters of political economy and attendant controversies. When Seldes remarked in 1938 that "it has been my job for twenty years to observe public affairs," he came fairly close to reinventing himself—not if public affairs meant public entertainments, of course, but certainly if it meant, as it ordinarily does, politics, government policies, and ideological postures. It is a bit startling to find Seldes, of all people, proclaiming a longstanding belief that "the average American was indifferent to organization for political purposes," though he did include himself (at least rhetorically) when confessing that "we of the middle class have neglected our political obligations, the habit of thinking about politics has virtually disappeared and we have no standards, no tests for the truth."[2]

The Great Depression, the rise of fascism, and the menacing appeal of communism had changed all of that. So Seldes boldly announced that a serious commitment to the middle class required the active promotion of democracy. Unaccustomed as he may have been to political activism, Seldes clearly embraced it as a writer by 1938 and urged it upon others over the next seven years. An apolitical man had seen the light and swiftly sought to convert readers to a series of stances that he worked through and publicized in three books and numerous essays. He revealed a new sense of urgency in 1938 when he declared, "Unless we—you and I—pay as much attention to public affairs as we do to our private affairs, the time is swiftly coming when our private affairs will cease to exist." Such language coming from Seldes would have been unimaginable a decade (or even a few years) earlier.[3]

As modernism in the arts became less of an imperative than nationalism, Seldes found himself on the same wavelength as men like Van Wyck Brooks, who told Lewis Mumford in the summer of 1935 that "this is still an age for explorers in all things American, and how wonderful to feel that you and I are sailing more or less on the same ship." Seldes took passage aboard a very similar vessel and proclaimed in the *Saturday Evening Post* that his countrymen must go forward "to the America of the future and not to the Europe of the past." After calling attention to recent concessions by H. L. Mencken, Sinclair Lewis, Harold Stearns, Joseph Wood Krutch, Ludwig Lewisohn, and Eugene O'Neill that the United States really wasn't such a terrible place after all, Seldes concluded that "if our writers can make peace with America and can create a past and present and future which have meaning for us, they have still a chance."[4] Seldes had rarely seen eye to eye with Brooks, Mumford, and others previously critical of shallowness in American culture; but for a decade following 1935 they shared a common compass and kept a steady course.[5]

I

We tend to identify a belief in American exceptionalism with cultural provincialism; but during the 1930s the appeal of national distinctiveness led many to strongly emphasize social diversity in the United States, especially ethnic diversity. In November 1933, when Seldes took the train from New York to Chicago in order to visit the Century of Progress exhibition, he commented in a series of newspaper columns on the geographical diversity of the United States.* Five years later, not long before producing "Americans All—Immigrants All" for CBS radio, he reminded readers that from the very outset of colonization "America had been actually a group of nations." Translated over time into social consequences, that meant the middle class was heterogeneous; indeed as he put it boldly in a single-sentence paragraph, "The middle class is the central factor in this pluralistic nation." Translated into political terms, moreover, he added that it wasn't unanimity but *"diversity of opinion which makes a democracy."* He saw great strength in the diversity of the states which in turn prompted "a great variety of experiments."[6]

In 1941 Seldes regarded as offensive the nativism of *The Ground We Stand On,* a book written by John Dos Passos, and warned his college friend that "the 'bedrock habits' of Americans were not formed by Anglo-Saxons but by Jews and Portuguese, Bulgars and Italians and Germans and twenty-one other races." The very meaning of the term American, he continued, "is that it was formed by the action upon one group of all the other groups and vice versa." Less than a year later he cited with approbation William James on social pluralism in the United States as a potential bulwark against totalitarianism. In 1945 Seldes observed that the impact of each immigrant group could be seen in American song, and in a separate essay he saw positive influences in the best American popular singers and their music. When Seldes learned that Italian-American Frank Sinatra would make a cross-country tour talking (and singing) about intolerance, he remarked: "Suppose Sinatra were to say that it is a good thing for America to have a voice like Paul Robeson's *and* one like Crosby's and one like Jolson's; maybe the bobby-sockers [*sic*] who listen will turn out better citizens. . . ."[7]

In *Mainland,* however, Seldes' synoptic view of American civilization published in 1936, he went beyond social and cultural pluralism to invoke the "pluralistic hypothesis" of William James as a means of comprehending American politics. "Kingship and theocracy broke down at the beginning of the American experiment," he wrote, "and the struggle against later efforts to impose a single rule, of the financier or of the State, continues to this day. The American is co-operative enough and he expects the minority to yield to the majority; but he has never entertained

*Eight months later Seldes devoted a column to praise for a new book by Lewis Gannett, *Sweet Land* (1934), that described thirty days of travel across the United States. Seldes' point: too many American intellectuals know Europe better than they know their own land. For a similar emphasis, see Fred J. Ringel, ed., *America as Americans See It* (New York, 1932).

the idea that the majority is privileged to destroy the minority." In the second half of this big book Seldes devoted himself to "connecting our pluralistic experience with our lack of class-consciousness, and placing the traditional American sense of change and variety as the foundation for the natural American way of life."[8]

Ultimately, he believed, Americans turned "naturally to a *pluralistic* conception of the world, resenting the claims of one religion, one state, one political party, or even one economic theory . . . . For our pluralism corresponds to our history and our history not only rejects the idea of a single inevitable way for us to take, but actually suggests that if we take the wrong road we will not necessarily be ruined and if we take the right road it will not lead us to any ultimate solutions or any perfect state." In the years ahead Seldes would increasingly insist upon a pluralistic approach to the explanation of cultural taste—why some people preferred one form of art or entertainment to another, and why tolerance of diversity along with merit were all that mattered, not traditional criteria of cultural priority or respectability.[9]

Between 1932 and 1936, when *Mainland* appeared, Seldes' critical work concentrated on themes that he could elaborate more fully in that substantial book: pluralism, Americanism, the need for historical perspective, faith in the common man, and a defense of democratic values against threats from the left and the right. Seldes' ideas about most of these issues were derivative rather than original, but the writers whose work he turned to tended to be liberal or progressive, such as John Dewey and Charles Beard, and Seldes appropriated their ideas for his own distinctive contexts, mainly in the realm of cultural criticism. Seldes very much admired and identified with the British writer H. G. Wells; radicals regarded Wells as an old-fashioned dreamer, while reactionaries considered him a dangerous visionary.

In the field of education, for example, a subject that Seldes returned to from time to time throughout his life, he was certainly a Deweyan instrumentalist and a pluralist. The principal objective, he declared in 1932, was not to "turn out identical models, but to allow individual development of every child to the greatest possible extent." Although he soon had occasion to wonder whether more discipline than modernists approved might not be prudent, he and his wife sent their two children to Dalton, the "most permissive school then in existence," though not to a radical school in New York City that "indoctrinated youngsters with many opinions I thought sound—but without much of the sense of weighing the evidence." Clear reasoning skills mattered as much to

Seldes as the reception of correct ideas by osmosis, without fully under-standing what made them correct.[10]

As for Americanism in popular culture, a major topic for Seldes after 1937, we find him giving voice to it as early as 1933 when he pleaded with theatre owners to be more nationalistic in what they presented because their impact on public taste could be immense.* "If you choose wisely and mount well," he wrote in a public letter, "you can give the American people a chance to hear American music many times in succes-sion, so that they will no longer be persuaded by propaganda that they must not like anything later than Wagner or anything harder than Puccini."[11] That led directly to more adamant declarations of cultural independence from the Old World, a central theme for Seldes during the mid- and later 1930s. It annoyed him that so many critics on the left, especially communists, looked to Europe in general and the Soviet Union especially for inspiration. Why should the United States become a spiri-tual colony of Europe? he wondered. "As far as we are concerned," he wrote in 1935, "there used to be a sick man of Europe; now there is only a sick Europe. The idea that we must take its medicine, not our own, is not sound." Highly critical of Freudian and Marxian ideas being applied to the United States undiluted and unadapted, he proclaimed both sys-tems of thought "hostile to the American aspiration." Two years later the cosmopolitan Seldes expanded his generalization just on the eve of his most chauvinistic phase as a cultural critic: "I do not see why it is admissible for Europeans to be Europeans and require that Americans should be good Europeans too."[12]

Although Seldes' views were shared by many others at that time, they represented only one point along an ideological spectrum. The absence of anything resembling consensus tended to reinforce Seldes' commitment to the importance of cultural pluralism. In April 1936 *Partisan Review* devoted a widely noticed issue of that journal to "What Is Americanism? A Symposium on Marxism and the American Tradition." A diverse array of ten writers (not including Seldes) had been invited in 1935 to respond to a questionnaire. At its core were the following issues:

> What is your conception of Americanism? Do you think of it as separate
> and opposed to the cultural tradition of Western Europe? . . . Should the

---

*In 1934 Seldes complained that the Pulitzer Prize winners had been poorly chosen. He urged that more attention be given to the spirit of the bequest and that the awards should go to works concerned with the meaning of America—works that revealed "what America was, and is, and stands for." GS, "True to Type," NYEJ, May 18, 1934, p. 21.

values of this American tradition be continued and defended or do they symbolize the brutal struggle for individual riches which some writers . . . have interpreted as the essence of Americanism? . . . In your opinion, what is the relationship between the American tradition and Marxism as an ideological force in the United States, with particular reference to the growth of revolutionary literature in this country? Do you think that our revolutionary literature reflects and integrates the American spirit or is it in conflict with it?[13]

The range of responses was varied and extraordinarily interesting. Theodore Dreiser, for example, believed that a shift from capitalism to socialism was inevitable, and therefore

> if identifying these changes with this powerful emotional force of Americanism will make these changes and processes of adjustment easier for the great mass of people, and correspondingly easier to bring about, then surely the American radical movement should make itself as far as possible free of European associations, and as American as possible in terminology, leadership, and general form.

Newton Arvin, the literary historian and critic, struck a remarkably upbeat chord, stressing continuity and congruence. Only socialism promised to facilitate a genuinely democratic and humane culture; "far from spelling an abrupt break with the American past," he argued, it would be the "only conceivable realization of it." As for the younger American writers of proletarian fiction, drama, and criticism, they represented not some absolute and mythical "Americanism," but rather "what is best and strongest in our inherited national culture."[14]

Robert Herrick, however, a novelist and sometime administrator, took a position quite close to Seldes'. He repudiated both Marxism and fascism and professed a life-long commitment to Americanism, which he defined as a "cultural base differing from that of all other peoples, due to the physical environment, racial inheritances, and historical development of the American people." He felt that many of the noble and salutary qualities of Americanism had been diluted or lost in recent decades, and he saw "predatory" qualities in the national character that distressed him. As a cultural pluralist, however, he did not find the prospect of a homogeneous national literature (predominantly proletarian, for example) at all attractive. Although he admired much of the recent writing concerned with social conditions, he felt certain that it would not be desirable for the United States if its imaginative writers "should be all of one kind or should devote their talents to proselytising for one social pattern or another. The more distinctively 'Marxian' our literature becomes the less actual and distinguished it will be as literature."[15]

Matthew Josephson wrote briefly but realistically. For Marxism to be effectively introduced it would have to be thoroughly adapted to the American environment, moral climate, and historical traditions. He didn't specify how and neglected to indicate by how much that would dilute the ideology. Unlike most of the respondents, Kenneth Burke felt least favorably disposed to anything that smacked of American exceptionalism. Numerous cultural features that many people regarded as distinctive had trans-Atlantic counterparts, as he observed. Regarding personal traits of national character (which his erstwhile associate Gilbert Seldes subscribed to), Burke had this to say: "The tendency to see as the particular essence of Americanism 'the brutal struggle for individual riches' gives me a pain in the pain-receiver. Americans are no greedier than anyone else."[16]

Waldo Frank wrote in a self-promoting and rather pompous manner, concluding with an off-hand dismissal of the shallow pundits who have "reduced revolutionary and cultural criticism to a sort of solipsistic and onanistic activity." William Carlos Williams was tough-minded and forthright in his reply, one that surely did not thrill the editors of *Partisan Review* (even though it did much to diversify their roster). Williams insisted that

> the American tradition is completely opposed to Marxism. America is progressing through difficult mechanistic readjustments which it is confident it can take care of. But Marxism is a static philosophy of a hundred years ago which has not yet kept up—as the democratic spirit has— through the stresses of an actual trial. Marxism to the American spirit is only another phase of force opposed to liberalism.

Williams' unabashed liberalism and commitment to traditional American ideals corresponded closely to Seldes' views, as we shall see. The poet-physician concluded his contribution to the symposium with these words: "My opinion is that our revolutionary literature is merely tolerated by most Americans, that it is definitely in conflict with our deep-seated ideals. I think the very premises of the revolutionary writers prevent an organic integration with the democratic principles upon which the American spirit is founded."[17]

Little more than three years later the editors published a similar symposium, but drew their responses from a different dramatis personae that included Williams (once again) plus Dos Passos, Allen Tate, Harold Rosenberg, Lionel Trilling, Robert Penn Warren, and R. P. Blackmur, a very distinguished coterie of relatively younger critics. One missing person whose solicited response did not appear, however, was James Agee. He found the questions so offensive that he wrote a denunciation of the whole futile exercise which *Partisan Review* declined to print. The two most vexing queries for Agee were these: (1) "Are you conscious, in your own writing, of the existence of a 'usable past'? Is this mostly American?" and (2) "How would you describe the political tendency of American writing as a whole since 1930? How do you feel about it yourself? Are you sympathetic to the current tendency towards what may be called 'literary nationalism'—a renewed emphasis, largely uncritical, on the specifically 'American' elements in our culture?"[18]

The tone and futility of the questions infuriated Agee. Literary nationalism, he believed, was a mindless manifestation of chauvinism. He preferred, instead, that a genuinely global community ought to be established among creative people and that the very notion of a literary tradition should acquire an international aspect. According to F. W. Dupee, two aspects of this *Partisan Review* project were certain to annoy Agee. First, he mistrusted generalizing. "And culture! He hated 'cultural' talk. . . . He was very impatient with the 'culture-fying' of the magazine."[19]

Although Agee and Seldes were temperamentally different in important ways, they shared several perspectives in common. Seldes, too, claimed that he mistrusted facile generalizations, especially if they involved stereotypes extended to an entire society, such as the United States. Like Agee, also, Seldes expressed his faith in the capacity and sound judgment of the average man, and in 1936 he remarked that "the listening public is more interesting and important than those who address them." Two years later he qualified that judgment in a way that made it more applicable to members of a participatory democracy than to all persons in all cultural situations. Ordinary people choose wisely, he explained, when they have a *tradition* of choosing and actually exercising their right to choose.[20]

II

When the *Partisan Review* symposium "What Is Americanism?" appeared in April 1936, Seldes happened to have in press his own responses to most of the items on the *Review*'s questionnaire, a vigorous book titled *Mainland* that appeared in October of that year. Actually, it also offered responses to most of the issues raised by the 1939 queries that so angered Agee. It is a book about the meaning of America and is presented as a declaration of cultural independence. The meaning of America was quite separable from that of Europe, he declared. At times, despite the inclusion of considerable history, Seldes made historical assertions that are simply embarrassing in their innocence. "Can the meaning of America be," he wondered, "that here for the first time came the exploitation of a country instead of the exploitation of the human race, the use of things instead of people, conquest by the hand of man and not by the force of arms?"[21]

Because my own opinion of *Mainland* is not especially favorable, I should acknowledge straightaway that people so diverse as Bernard DeVoto, William Allen White, and Charles A. Beard all responded very positively to it. The book enjoyed considerable impact and added lustre to Seldes' reputation as historian, cultural critic, and now as a political analyst. Perhaps it was in the last of these capacities that Seldes seemed most satisfactory because he emerged as the judicious voice of reason. He reaffirmed democracy and disdained both communism and fascism. He expressed an aversion to absolute individualism as well as total collectivism. He declared that industrial capitalism tended to be exploitative. And he correctly predicted that Americans wouldn't revolt because they mostly shared a middle-class psychology.[22]

As I read it, however (and I have several times), *Mainland* meanders in and out of focus. Seldes invokes topics but fails to develop them. He starts to discuss the Lynds' *Middletown*, for example, but abruptly veers away to something else. Transitions are unclear from time to time. Sections are introduced by quotations whose point is not self-evident and which often are neither pithy nor arresting. The book is more of an *omnium gatherum* than a tour de force: it careens from the history and present state of the film industry to cultural relations between the United States and western Europe to the Soviet Union and its political economy. Nor is it a book in which Seldes sticks to his last. It favors the heartland, "the opening of the western domain" and populating the interior even though that is not the America that Seldes knew best, nor is it the segment of U.S. history that he knew best. Minor anomalies abound. Franklin D. Roosevelt somehow becomes a westerner of sorts simply because he is so pragmatic; and Seldes seeks to preserve the "human liberties which were evolved under Capitalism."[23]

As for structure, Part One is a rambling introduction; Part Two is an historical retrospective with explanatory intent, based upon a strong sense that history is destiny; Part Three consists of five biographical sketches (John Humphrey Noyes, William James, William Jennings Bryan, Irving Berlin, and Henry Ford); Part Four is a critique of communism, fascism, and capitalism that rejects the first two; Part Five is devoted to fascism American style, that is, the philosophy of Agrarianism; and Part Six, ostensibly about the middle class, is really an assessment of New Deal programs and FDR. This is where Seldes makes his pitch for a more humane capitalism and comes across as compassionate, sensible, and specific.

One of the book's central and most persuasive themes is that the United States keeps changing and growing. One of its most attractive qualities also arises from the author's sympathetic linkage of a democratic ethos with that propensity for change. "In my comment on the American critics," Seldes remarked, "I have tried to show that they are really protesting against the special character of America and the inevitable changes brought about when the pleasures once reserved for the few are opened to the multitude." Seldes defended pragmatic reliance upon trial and error as a basis for change and asserted that "criticism of any contemporary taste or habit" should be weighed against the prospect of a more democratic future.[24]

Although *Mainland* is not entirely uncritical—of capitalism as a manipulative economic system, at times, and of Americans for being materialistic and wasteful—it is nevertheless a very upbeat book that is notably understated when the author declares: "I still find some health in American life." For Seldes, American history displayed "a grandeur and a color of romance." Millions of lives have been "buoyed up by hope and made dignified by hard work." Countless men and women have achieved freedom because of opportunities that the United States afforded them. He unabashedly confessed that "life in America has seemed to me rich in texture, perpetually entertaining, almost always agreeable, and full of still unexplored capacities."[25]

The book blended political with cultural criticism because Seldes responded systematically to such American advocates of fascism as Lawrence Dennis and the more numerous supporters of socialism in some form in an effort to explain why neither system offered a viable solution to dilemmas of political economy in the United States. Seldes had been rejecting communism in his newspaper columns and magazine essays ever since 1933. He had scornfully written in 1935 that a sign might very well be posted: *"Communism is the opium of the intellectuals."* In the book he basically argued that communism would not work in the United States because it was inconsistent with the American past: "the hundred and fifty years of our life as a nation have actually created a people and a character essentially non-Communist. The urban cosmopolitan intellectual has been wrong about America because he has been ignorant of American history."[26]

Seldes did offer occasional criticisms of capitalism as it existed in the United States, especially the irresponsible power concentrated in the hands of a few hundred corporations that in turn tended to be controlled by a still smaller group of powerful financiers. Elsewhere in the book, and in other essays, he differentiated between democratic capitalism, "the creator of liberty," and plutocratic capitalism, which was the enemy of liberty. Seldes devoted a section to what he ruefully called the "poverty system" and conveyed a strong sense of concern and compassion for the unfortunate victims of the system in its present form.* He urged that the poverty system be examined just as carefully as the evolution of capitalism, and regretted that "we have diminished poverty just so far as it has been to our advantage to do so; we have done it more by engineering than by idealism. . . ."[27]

Although Seldes acknowledged that he had personally enjoyed certain advantages as a consequence of capitalism, he insisted that he cared far more about the future of middle-class democracy in the United States "than in the preservation of profit for a few people who are probably undermining democracy in America." He believed that some of the most essential liberties that his fellow citizens enjoyed not only were "products of the capitalist system, but are inseparable from it," though not necessarily in its present mode. Throughout the book Seldes sought to refute

---

*I suspect that Seldes' comparatively comfortable life-style during the 1920s and '30s gave him little understanding of welfare capitalism. Despite some medical care, other benefits, and leisure outings, overall conditions for the working class remained poor: low wages, long hours, and seasonal lay-offs. Consequently, as historian Lizabeth Cohen has demonstrated, workers showed their disappointment in welfare capitalism in many ways, especially by 1930. During the Depression the scope of welfare capitalism declined precipitously.

what he called "the general theory that the American system of life has resulted in nothing but tawdriness, childishness, and a dry and withered soul."[28]

Seldes insistently identified with the middle class, advocated its best interests, but lamented (perhaps excessively) that the middle class "is the least conscious of its own situation because each extreme party is trying to identify that middle party with itself." For demagogues, he believed, the question was how best to manipulate the middle class, whereas for democrats like himself the critical issue remained how best to save that class. Seldes prided himself on being a practical man rather than an ideologue, and derived satisfaction from the knowledge that he felt bound to no absolute or rigid system of reform. He called for activism and engagement on the part of Everyman because it was the essence of democracy that "every moment people must create it for themselves."[29]

The book received an extremely warm reception from most reviewers. The *New York Times* called it "prejudiced, argumentative, disorganized, and—brilliant." Bernard DeVoto, who pulled no punches and reveled in the role of caustic critic, described it as "brilliant in its analyses, its characterizations, and its illumination of the present by means of history." Charles A. Beard, who was not even an acquaintance, sent Seldes an appreciative letter. He and his wife Mary agreed with Seldes "that we can escape the dilemma of fascism & Communism and find a worthy middle way if we are true to our heritage and make a wise use of it."[30]

In addition to a number of mixed reviews, much more positive than negative, there were four particularly critical notices that do not, in retrospect, seem at all unfair. Each one has a different emphasis, but taken together they explain why the book, unlike *The 7 Lively Arts,* did not become a classic. *The Nation's* reviewer asserted that it was not useful social criticism and considered as journalism "it is diffuse, verbose, and more irritating than provocative." The reviewer for *Books* found it perplexing because so many particular passages seemed sound, "yet when one tries to put all the parts together he finds himself left with a fascinating Chinese puzzle."[31] Lewis Galantière, in whose Paris apartment Seldes had written *The 7 Lively Arts* in 1923, acknowledged that *Mainland* had stimulated him to think about America "as no other book has ever done," and shared Seldes' belief that the United States had a distinctive civilization because of its idiosyncratic historical development. Nevertheless Galantière complained that Seldes' economic theories seemed obscure and had to be inferred because he failed to lay them out in any kind of programmatic way. Finally, an anonymous reviewer for the IWW lamented that Seldes really did not understand the labor movement and should stick to entertainment where he possessed more sophistication. It was the unfortunate habit of such people "to get all twisted and tangled when they write about unions."[32]

Because Seldes had hitched his polemical wagon to the fortunes of the middle class, and because he was rapidly emerging as a leading spokesman for American exceptionalism, he must have felt especially gratified by an essay that William Allen White contributed to *The Atlantic Monthly* later in 1937. White seems to have shared all of Seldes' predilections, and as the sage of Emporia, Kansas, it particularly pleased White that Seldes took into account the farmer, the villager, and the suburbanite. He also agreed with Seldes that class remained a very fluid phenomenon in American culture. And he may well have attributed to Seldes a more absolute view of exceptionalism than the author of *Mainland* had actually come to in 1936: "he sees America not as an evolutionary offshoot of Europe but as a sport in the social development of humanity. He sees us creating by the evolutionary process a new way of life."[33]

Years later Seldes was capable of remarkable candor and self-criticism. Writing in 1954 he called *Mainland* "lopsided, dogmatic, spoiled by pedantry, and a little isolationist." And in 1963, after cultural historian Cushing Strout looked at *Mainland* as an artifact of the mid-1930s—"it made a biting attack on American intellectuals of the 1920s for their subservience to European models and acclaimed the New Deal for its pluralistic, pragmatic approach"—Seldes told Strout that he had always regarded himself as a cultural internationalist and had to go back and see that "I had specifically said I was prejudiced 'in favor of America and against any international system'—but I still don't feel this made me an isolationist." He did concede, however, that upon re-reading *Mainland* he found the second half, "which justifies your statement, rather heavy going." Nine days later, working on the pertinent section of "As in My Time," he acknowledged the same shortcomings in *Mainland* except to insist that in matters of international relations, as opposed to cultural issues, he had never been an isolationist.[34]

Immediately after William Allen White's generous review of *Mainland* appeared in 1937, Seldes wrote to thank him and to indicate particular interest in White's expressed hope that the worker's cause could be established in "the hearts of the middle classes." Why? Because, Seldes explained, he was then at work on a book with a related but slightly different approach. "I am trying to discover," he explained, "to what degree the interests of the middle classes can be involved with the interests of the corporations, the labor unions, etc." Later that year Seldes asked White for permission to quote from *Forty Years on Main Street;* and early in 1938 Seldes' newest work appeared, *Your Money and Your Life: A Manual for "The Middle Classes."*[35]

The publisher sent William Allen White a complimentary copy and White responded with an endorsement that could be used in promotional ways. Five months later he released a highly favorable review in *The Atlantic,* not at all surprising because White also identified with the middle class and considered himself to be culturally middlebrow. Although *Your Money and Your Life* reiterates some of the ideas presented in *Mainland,* it is less formidable, less dense, and is presented in a lively, accessible middlebrow format. In an interview that Seldes gave soon after the book appeared, he declared that he wrote "for and about people like myself—the middle class." When pressed for a definition he responded: "They are the people who are paid by the week instead of by the year." And, Seldes added, "I am just an average, bewildered citizen."[36]

White's review called attention to Seldes' ongoing distinction between democratic capitalism and finance capitalism: "Mr. Seldes would not declaw the capitalist system or extract the teeth of property owners and profit makers at one fell swoop. He would pare and manicure their claws and file the teeth a bit of the too-predatory instincts now menacing the stability of the social-order, instincts which maintain the middle class in its supremacy." White correctly observed that the book was easy to read but not too elementary to be unimportant. Issues of political economy were addressed clearly but without being oversimplified.[37]

The initial reviews in January 1938 were mixed but positive overall. One called it more stimulating than nourishing because Seldes had "wisely refrained from trying to explain the economic system in detail." Another commented that Seldes was more successful in dissecting the middle-class situation and illuminating its flaws than in showing how it might be improved in practice.[38] Reviews that appeared in journals of opinion during subsequent months tended to summarize the book's contents quite well and rarely dissented in any major way. *Commonweal* urged that the work be widely read because "it makes you conscious of the crisis in which democracy finds itself today." The reviewer for *Social Education* reminded his readers that the middle class had "the real power that makes things go." A complete New Deal wouldn't come overnight, but the middle class could and should look out for its own interests.[39]

That last comment, seemingly innocuous, needs to be contextualized. When Seldes wrote this book during 1937 the economy seemed to be recovering. By the time it actually appeared early in 1938, however, that superficial spurt had given way to recession and many concerned individuals wondered when, if ever, the agony of unemployment and economic stagnation would really end. Appropriately, therefore, *Your Money and Your Life* does express particular concern about poor people, and not only about the middle class (defined as those who earned less than $15,000 per year).* Seldes did concern himself with the "general welfare," and asserted strenuously that each person's economic well-being depended upon that of others in the community or society at large.[40]

In essential ways the book's most basic positions seemed to be consistent with those of *Mainland*. By rejecting socialism in favor of the existing system of political economy, Seldes insisted that he saw "no conflict between a reasonable democracy [preserving individualism] and a vast amount of collective effort." Elaborating upon that, however, and differentiating this book from *Mainland*, was Seldes' new emphasis upon recovering economic health through local organizations rather than national ones or a nationally planned economy. After discussing the pros and cons of governmental centralization in Washington, D.C., Seldes' motto seemed to be: think nationally, but act locally.[41]

Your Money comes across as a somewhat more cynical book than *Mainland*. It warns the reader against the "system," meaning public officials and special interests; and it cautions the reader-as-consumer, especially, that the legal system tended to favor the "producing interests," and that greedy forces (such as big corporations and deceptive advertisers) were determined to get the consumer's money. The tone of *Your Money* differs markedly from the tone of *Mainland*, whose dedication page declares that "it is a book in favor of America and therefore it has to be in favor of uncertainties, it has to be basically pluralistic." The author of *Your Money* remained a pluralist, but he did not care for uncertainties and he wanted the middle class to be inclusive so that class conflict would not result from the inequities of pluralism.[42]

Nearly two decades later, when Seldes reviewed *America as a Civiliza-*

*There seems to have been a convergence of interest in the middle class in 1938. Granville Hicks, a Marxist, published *I Like America* in 1938, a discussion of the American middle class.

tion by Max Lerner, he liked the fact that Lerner's book was upbeat in a restrained way. That tone was more in keeping with his own in *Mainland*.[43] Viewed over the long haul, then, *Your Money and Your Life* may have been more nearly the aberration. Most of Seldes' books were written to affirm something (or things) that he believed in. *Your Money and Your Life,* published after more than eight years of economic depression, conveyed a mood of disquiet atypical of Seldes.

III

When the *Saturday Review of Literature* ran a prominent review of *Your Money* in January 1938, it featured an attractive photograph of Seldes on the cover (see frontispiece) and ran a biographical profile of him that emphasized what a remarkable polymath he had become. It concluded with the flattering speculation that "there is no knowing in what direction his talents will break out next."[44] In part, of course, we only need to remember that in 1938–39 he became intensely busy writing and producing radio programs—whole series, in fact. And he began to ponder the future of television, from its program content to its economic complexities.

As a writer, however, he never ceased to care about the lively arts, and so he continued to celebrate them whenever an opportunity arose. Hence a twenty-first birthday salute to Krazy Kat that connected the lovable genius of that comic strip to the entertainment achievements of Mickey Mouse and Charlie Chaplin. From time to time Seldes succumbed to nostalgia for the literary culture of his young manhood. So in 1939 he devoted one of his *Esquire* essays on the lively arts to the aspiring younger writers of the early 1920s. And in January 1940 he praised Rudy Vallee as "the best showman in the business" and Fanny Brice, the amusing stage and radio comic, for her "genius." From time to time Seldes became genuinely sentimental about the entertainments he had loved during the early interwar years.[45]

Even more striking than these connective lines of continuity in his career, however, were the new developments and turns that appeared late in the 1930s as the political climate changed and Seldes made adjustments in his emphases as a critic. Recall, for example, that during the later 1920s Seldes had neglected to relate the public arts to political exigencies—a lapse that friends would chide him about years later. In 1933, when he became quite interested in the uses of leisure, and saw that increasing federal control of commerce, industry, and finance were inevitable, he flippantly declared that government should keep its hands off anything pertaining to the realm of leisure, which Seldes regarded as a private realm. When a proposal appeared that the U.S. government ought to feature American works of art on postage stamps, Seldes expressed the hope that "art" from pop culture would be featured, ranging from the magazine cover girl and the seed catalogue cover to the cigar store Indian, some Remington scenes of military action, and a few figureheads from old ships. Such selections might "make more cheerful stamp users of all of us."[46]

By 1937 Seldes began to modify his advocacy of the creative artist as an independent entrepreneur in order to defend the legitimacy of such Works Progress Administration undertakings as the Federal Theatre Project, undertakings that had been opposed by critics like George Jean Nathan. In doing so Seldes offered an interesting linkage that was entirely consistent with his commitment to the democratization of culture. "The new patron," he wrote, thereby conflating a set of forces into a singular entity, "the public and its government, will eventually make demands which the artist will have to meet. I foresee the end of estheticism, the end of the soulful superiority of the artist."[47]

Beginning in 1938, however, as the spectre of totalitarianism in several guises became more menacing, Seldes felt increasingly disposed to look at the public arts from a political perspective that, on occasion, became ideologically shrill and even somewhat inconsistent. He presented a flimsy argument, for example, that popular culture could help Americans to resist tyranny: "the triviality of our amusements makes them a solid wall" against which regimentation would inevitably fail. In the sacred name of freedom, moreover, mediocrity seemed preferable to any sort of programmatic action aimed at elevating American taste. Reports of governmental intervention in the arts for ideological purposes in Europe prompted him to say that he preferred the continuation of wretched radio programs "which I can't abide, just to keep people interested in a free radio." Although he had a low opinion of 90 percent of the movies made by Hollywood, he did not want Congress or the President "or any dictatorial successor to both of them, to have the power to improve or destroy what Hollywood makes."[48]

The prospect of war followed by the reality of American participation prompted Seldes to issue a series of statements about the arts that seem, in retrospect, convoluted, vulnerable, or at best, facile. As modernist writers, artists, and composers became increasingly subjective and sometimes obscure, Seldes speculated that dictators had shrewder judgment about how best to communicate effectively with the masses—as though James Joyce, Ezra Pound, or Dimitri Shostakovich pursued their vocations with that objective in mind. Much as Seldes admired such artists (and loathed dictators), he regretted that so many of the former had apparently abandoned the crucial effort to communicate broadly. In 1942 Seldes urged those responsible for the popular arts not to attempt to uplift or improve familiar modes of entertainment "too much" because people might then cease to associate them with pleasure. At a time when morale was low, a sense of genuine freedom and access to traditional pleasures meant a great deal to ordinary Americans.[49]

For more than a decade Seldes had been making a kind of pilgrim's progress toward total commitment to American exceptionalism. It really began late in the 1920s when he criticized expatriates for believing that they absolutely had to go to Europe in order to find themselves as creative artists. At that time Seldes started to emphasize cultural barriers between Americans and Europeans and urged native artists to remain "at home" if they hoped to do their best work. By 1935–36, when he wrote *Mainland,* Seldes clearly felt comfortable with the notion of an American national character. He believed that the dynamics of capitalism were different in the U.S. and stressed "the uniqueness of the democratic experiment in this country."[50] When he chose to elaborate he asserted that "the struggle with the land is the unique factor in our history." More specifically, geographical decentralization seemed to be critical to his reading of that history, which he borrowed directly from Turner and Beard:

> If we could have an animated map of Europe and America, the meaning of the difference between them would leap to the eye, for on the map of Europe we should see the little figures representing human beings moving steadily in from the edges toward a few large centers; and on the map of America, we would see the figures move from coastline toward the frontiers; on one, concentration; on the other, dispersion. (The American coastal centers grow too, but not at the expense of the country to the west.) On the map of England the productive land grows barren; on the map of America the forest becomes fertile; one is an island contracting into a nobleman's park, the other a seacoast expanding into a continent.[51]

It should be noted in passing, however, that Seldes ordinarily thought of himself as a "cultural internationalist," and considering the cosmopolitan range of his knowledge and interests, he really was at that time. When the rejuvenated Monte Carlo Ballet Russe toured the United States in 1933–34 Seldes praised it as the most thrilling cultural presentation he had seen in years. He envisioned dividends, moreover, because George Balanchine, who had directed one of the best offerings, was about to become the director of an American ballet school.[52] Seldes did not object to borrowing the best. But unlike quite a few of his fellow critics in the early and mid-1930s, Seldes did not undertake any sort of sustained comparative study, like Stuart Chase's *Mexico: A Study of Two Americas* (1931), or John Dos Passos' *In All Countries* (1934), or Edmund Wilson's *Travels in Two Democracies* (1936), or similar works by Max Eastman and Waldo Frank. Quite a few of the leading cultural critics during the interwar years found that systematic comparisons served their purposes very well. Although Seldes traveled abroad a fair amount during the 1930s, his references to other cultures remained casual rather than being pursued in depth.

His passion for innovative expressions of American vernacular culture reached its peak between 1938 and 1945. In 1938, for instance, Walker Evans published *American Photographs* in conjunction with an exhibition of his work at the Museum of Modern Art. Seldes, who did not care for either candid or heavily contrived photographs, found Evans' work to be judiciously intermediate and admired it extravagantly. "The significant local detail is never missing; but the universal American feeling is always captured." Seldes did not agree with those who lamented that the United States had become uniform and standardized. "I know that differences persist," he added, "and the people who find monotony in America are those who haven't seen America." Fortunately, Walker Evans had.[53]

Every few years Seldes devoted an essay to the cultural aspects of American song. In this period, predictably, he highlighted songs of the people. In 1939 he announced (rather idiosyncratically) that the United States "has no folk song. . . . You can't count the Negro spirituals because they are not the product of the dominant people." What might explain such a sweeping deficiency? Traditional folk music elsewhere, he believed, developed from dissatisfaction and dissent. The quality of life here was too good to foster authentic folk music. Americans had so much to be grateful for. Less than two years later, however, he produced lavish praise for the "Ballad for Americans," a musical narrative arranged to accompany a radical-patriotic radio broadcast in November 1939. Seldes listened to it in the later spring of 1941 in conjunction with a program about the Bill of Rights and remarked that the innovative format of the

"Ballad" provided an exciting challenge to composers and librettists living in deeply troubled times.[54]

By the summer of 1945 he got around to putting in essay form the central theme of his 1938–39 radio series, "Immigrants All—Americans All." After commenting on the gradual shift in dominant appeal from folk songs to popular songs (thereby contradicting the central theme of his 1939 essay), he warmed to the pluralistic medley of American music. "Follow the course of immigration into the United States," he wrote, "give each new national group a generation to become at home, and you can find the effect of its music in the songs which the whole country was singing." He also acknowledged that during a long and intense war "the songs we sing are not necessarily representative of our national feelings. Patriotism gives us an occasional lift, and songs of parting and of devotion get a kind of value to which neither words nor music entitle them."[55]

The same could also be said of American exceptionalism because in Seldes' case his inclination toward that persuasion reached a peak in 1942–43. In his hortatory book, *Proclaim Liberty!*, Seldes referred repeatedly to "the great complex of our national character." The United States was distinctive because "no other nation . . . has all our habits, because none has had our history." What attributes and advantages had that history produced? Freedom and prosperity, a high standard of living and a truly democratic polity. His chauvinism reached a kind of crescendo in passages of this sort: "At every point in our history the reality had something in it to touch the imagination, the heart, to make one feel how complex and fortunate is the past we carry in us if we are American."[56]

Seldes' intense commitment to the allied cause led him to articulate a sequence of claims that undoubtedly would have embarrassed him in the calmer postwar environment—if he ever re-read his 1942 book, the only one that he published during the entire decade. He believed that American materialism "is not as terrible as it looks," and therefore it should be tolerated. He conveyed the impression, moreover, that no one with any gumption had ever failed in the United States and that economic success was facilitated by an ideal political structure. "The greatest invention of democracy," he boasted, "is the wealth of the people." The nation's genius, in fact, has been invested in the creation of a "well-to-do mass of citizens." The triumph that endured from the nation's birth? A government and favorable conditions that allowed "as many people as possible to make as much money as possible." Never before and never again would Seldes sound quite so much like a bourgeois barker![57]

Could the exigencies of wartime prod this intelligent and sophisticated man to become any more banal than that? It actually got worse before it got better. He pleaded for what he called a positive program of propaganda: "Our government has no more right to deprive us of propaganda than it has to deprive us of pursuit planes or bombers." To that kind of rhetoric Seldes added a few historical howlers. "We have no apologies to make to the immigrant," he declared. "Our law showed them nothing but honor and equity. . . . As a nation we never committed the sin of considering an immigrant as an alien first and then as a man."[58]

He did, in all fairness, include some arresting insights and offer pertinent criticisms. The "normalcy" that Harding proclaimed had been, Seldes observed, a genuine debasement because it destroyed the remaining vestiges of American idealism. When radicals turned against their country they helped to squeeze its culture in a problematic vice because the plutocrats were pressing equally hard from the opposite side. Liberal intellectuals, like himself presumably, found themselves "suspended between the two worlds," so most of them felt deep ambivalence about their native land. Later, in 1940–41, the great debate between internationalists and isolationists became "painful and ludicrous," yet it exemplified the American tradition of contested values in public discourse.[59]

Proclaim Liberty! received glowing reviews from the likes of William Allen White, James Reston, and J. D. Kingsley. More tough-minded assessments came from obscure or anonymous readers. The *Library Journal* predicted accurately that this was an ephemeral book that would nevertheless enjoy a wide and appreciative readership. *The New Yorker* called it a mixed bag containing some sketchy and even naive reasoning and some oversimplified history, but also sound, germinal ideas about strategy, unity, morale, and postwar problems. A critic for the *Christian Science Monitor* observed that Seldes' technique was anything but subtle: "He fairly shrieks . . . 'this is the way to stir up the people.' So the reader is constantly reminded of a circus barker."[60]

IV

The most curious aspect of Seldes' work as a critic during the war years, perhaps, is that he seems to have dichotomized himself into two writers, the one a jingo but the other one his usual judicious and reasonable self. Let us continue for just a moment with the unjustified jingo because *Proclaim Liberty!* is his most expansive manifestation of that character.

The easiest way to follow Seldes through this period is his monthly "department" in *Esquire,* which never missed a beat for thirteen years, much to the publisher's delight. In August 1942 the magazine even devoted a major editorial to his "inexhaustible exhubilance," and concluded that the secret of his success as a cultural critic was really no secret at all. "He has somehow kept, or recaptured, that child-like capacity for astonishment and wonder which the process of intellectualization ordinarily dries up or crowds out."[61]

As early as July 1937 Seldes referred, rather casually, to "the coming war." He did so in a blistering attack upon Alexander Woollcott because one of his Town Crier radio broadcasts tended to "discourage the military mind" in growing boys. Woollcott was, in fact, a pacifist who disliked and distrusted the military mind, a conviction engendered in him by disillusionment from the aftermath of World War I. Seldes deplored the fact that Woollcott "seems to get most excited and most persuasive over the trivial and the second rate." More to the point, it angered Seldes that his rival made the war and America's intervention seem "singularly unimportant." Seldes had not undergone disillusionment, and he remained convinced that the Germans had committed atrocities and that the United States would have been cowardly not to get involved. Seldes felt he clinched his case by pointing out that if only the obtuse Woollcott had read *Road to War, America 1914–1917* by Walter Millis (1935), he would surely have understood why military preparedness was necessary.[62]

Having warned in 1937 that a second world war was inevitable, Seldes virtually ignored the imminence of war itself in his 1939 and 1940 essays for *Esquire.* He offered caustic comments from time to time about the three major dictators, but his monthly "department" didn't start to discuss the war as a cultural phenomenon until December 1941, when he complained about the poor quality of war-inspired caricatures in the United States—they seemed much inferior to the standards set by World War I and Prohibition. Seldes felt strongly that "the cartoon is an editorial for the unlettered, often for the illiterate." Consequently cartoons needed to make a point without being preachy, but also avoid the sort of sterile, composite view favored by syndicated newspapers. Seldes regarded England's Sir David Low as the great cartoonist of the war because of his fierce independence. Although Low worked for Lord Beaverbrook, for example, he included his boss among his satirical targets. In fact, Low could be just as critical of "old" British political gaffes as he could of new German aggression and atrocities. No American cartoonist approached his independence and keen wit.[63]

The next month Seldes devoted a column to his perception of American skepticism concerning the hierarchy of command. Because democratic Americans, in their heart of hearts, regarded military ranks as phony, there would always be gags about the relations between officers and enlisted men. He predicted, moreover, that such skepticism would increase as more and more civilian, temporary officers "take charge of the men." I am not at all sure just how widely Seldes' views on this point were shared, but he blithely seemed to *know* that "the soldier wants to be treated as a citizen except where soldiering, the actual business of warfare, is concerned. He wants to be what he has been called, a citizen-soldier. That was once the definition of militia; it is still the best description of our Army. And our comedy is the proof of it."[64]

The very nature of Seldes' "lively arts" department dictated that most of his essays during the war would assess its impact, one way or another, on modes and styles of entertainment in the United States. In May 1942, for example, he explained that the war had actually provided quite a stimulus for entertainment, because it enhanced the need for escapism and made movies more popular than ever, both on the home front and among the military. Hollywood obliged with lots of comedies, musicals, and a special emphasis on such attractive glamour girls as Betty Grable, Lana Turner, and Carole Landis. Radio may very well have enjoyed the greatest success simply because it easily reached the largest number of people *and* because it combined public affairs information with amusement. He concluded with a speculation indicative of his belief that genuinely mass culture still lay ahead. "The entertainment of the future," he believed, "will try to reach masses of people."[65] When he wrote that, of course, Seldes was deeply involved in planning for the advent of television. That medium, even more than radio, would ultimately bring mass culture fully into the marketplace as a dominant social phenomenon.

By the summer of 1942, following publication of *Proclaim Liberty!*, Seldes had seemingly embraced the role of unabashed jingo. He longed for more patriotic parades because he believed that in wartime the supportive behavior of masses of people caught up in nationalistic enthusiasm was essential. He speculated that "maybe right now people ought to be brought together, physically in one place, to get the companionship and the unity of a crowd feeling one sweeping emotion. Maybe radio could do a tremendous job of calling them together and telling them wonderful things while the parade went by." Just after the war ended Seldes also responded to Paul Gallico's critique of commercials being included in news broadcasts. Seldes defended that pattern on grounds that it was consistent with American cultural values (free enterprise, and so on) and that, realistically, sponsorship was necessary.[66]

Seldes' mood and behavior during the war were not entirely out of character, though, nor did he continuously perform the role of a jingo even though he was more likely than at any other time in his career as a critic to condone the perpetuation of attractive myths. During the 1930s he had advocated, when opportunities arose, the need for lay persons to be historically informed and to discern the differences between authentic history and national myths, however harmless they might be. During the war, however, he observed that even liberal and radical historians had become patriotic revisionists, so he lauded such figures as Frederic Remington and Mr. Dooley because they had transmitted in diverse ways the significance of traditional American symbols, dialogue, and stories. "What we have lost," Seldes lamented, "is the sense of infinite opportunity, of which the West was the last symbol."[67]

One also finds, on occasion, pieces of cultural criticism largely unrelated to the war: a William Safire-like discourse on the swift appearance of new colloquialisms, for instance, many of them originating with sports commentators and the "folksy advertising pluggers"; yet another aimed at those who wrote ads, and mocking caption writers in particular. He noted a sexist difference between matter-of-fact ads aimed at men and cloying, mindless ads for women's clothes. Seldes observed that as women by the millions moved into jobs traditionally held by men, gender distinctions in the workplace would become much less meaningful. It seemed logical to him that "as women meet the same daily problems as men [in the workplace], they will want to be addressed in the same terms as men." There should not be a double standard in advertising and women should be treated with far more respect as consumers.[68]

Throughout the war Seldes prepared the program notes, usually for jazz concerts, held at Carnegie Hall and Town Hall in New York City. He wrote with special appreciation and pride for performers like Bix Beiderbecke and Eddie Condon. But even with activities of this sort the war was neither out of sight nor out of mind. At the bottom of Seldes' program appeared this sentence: "Tonight's concert has been recorded by the War Department for short wave broadcast to United States foreign based troops. . . ."[69]

In 1943 Frederick Lewis Allen commissioned John Dos Passos to write a six-part series for *Harper's* on "The People at War." Seldes did not receive such a highly visible assignment, but he did write scripts, such as "Know Your Ally America," that were used in films made for the U.S. Army by prominent directors who had enlisted. When Frank Capra wrote to thank Seldes for a script in 1944, he remarked that "as true democrats we not only spring from the people but we steal from the people."[70]

The exigencies and ideals of wartime prompted Seldes to behave in all sorts of ways that were uncharacteristic of him—valorizing propaganda only being the most obvious. Essentially, Seldes became politicized, far more than at any other time in his life. He supported Archibald Mac-Leish's initiative to hold town meetings across the country at which there would be discussions of "defense needs, the speed at which local factories are producing, the local boys in service, honor the casualties, and a general discussion of war aims, purposes, etc." In 1944, when Seldes and his wife received in the mail a bizarre, right-wing piece of literature from Congressman Fred E. Busbey of Illinois, they wrote a blistering reply.[71]

Then in 1945, after Archibald MacLeish accepted the new position of Undersecretary of State for Cultural Affairs, Seldes wrote a glowing essay in praise of the appointment because MacLeish "has for years been a radio enthusiast, [and] has turned confidently to the movies. He has a mass job to do and is using *all* means of communication, breaking away from the ancient dignity—and fustiness—which barely recognizes the daily press." As a highbrow sympathetic to popular culture MacLeish seemed the ideal person for this new post; and Seldes felt sanguine that MacLeish would not try to do "what a real Kultur minister must do: alter the thinking of an entire people." Rather, he would use the powers of government with discretion to facilitate cultural expression at all levels rather than shape or dictate cultural policy from on high.[72]

Because MacLeish would be based at the Department of State, his job had more to do with American culture abroad than with the domestic front. Almost anticipating MacLeish's appointment late in 1944, Seldes published an essay providing lavish praise for a new Disney animated film called *Saludos Amigos*. He could thereby show that "good" propaganda would improve relations with our neighbors to the south, and also that governmental impact upon the arts could be benign, thereby allaying two of his longstanding concerns. "People who are absolutely certain that the arts won't flourish under a centralized government," he remarked, "might note that this picture was underwritten by a section of our 'bureaucracy.' . . . Moreover this is a propaganda film.* It introduces cowboys to gauchos and Donald Duck to Joe Carioca; it is a supreme example of constructive political thinking."[73]

Following Franklin D. Roosevelt's death in the spring of 1945, Seldes devoted an interesting essay to the late president's career as a successful popular "artist," singling out for special attention his masterful use of the radio, his effervescence, and his "astounding explanation of economic problems presented with order and clarity, reduced not to the style of the comic strip, but to that of a folk song—a much harder thing to accomplish." Seldes paid FDR the supreme compliment from a cultural critic's perspective: namely, "that he made public affairs a people's interest. And, in a serious sense, he was an artist, a popular artist." It added to Roosevelt's lustre, of course, that he cared and knew about history. From Seldes' perspective, FDR (like MacLeish) seemed to be a highbrow populist. That, of course, is exactly how Seldes really saw himself.[74]

V

In the years following the war criticism changed because the media of communication and entertainment swiftly altered along with the nature and uses of leisure. In Seldes' case political activism and cultural optimism gave way to caution, a mistrust not so much of the media themselves but of the men in charge of them. In 1942 Seldes had been blithely able to write that "the radio, the movies, and popular print are the three tools by which we can create democratic action."[75] After the mid-century mark he remained hopeful but much less optimistic. Why? One major cause was the prevalence, indeed the dominance by the later 1940s, of a type that Seldes called the "anti-intellectual superpatriot." Soon that would mean the House Un-American Activities Committee, Senator Joseph R. McCarthy and his supporters, and a great many powerful people who still controlled Hollywood and the film industry, not to mention men like David Sarnoff of RCA/NBC and William S. Paley of

---

*Historical scholarship has been unenthusiastic about U.S. propaganda during World War II, noting that the government censored photographs that blurred the line between friend and foe or ones suggesting that American authorities were not fully in control. See George H. Roeder, Jr., "Censoring Disorder: American Visual Imagery of World War Two," *Mid-America* 75 (Oct. 1993): 245–67.

CBS. A small taste of things to come, however, occurred just after the war when MacLeish departed the State Department in favor of poetry and drama, only to be replaced by William Benton: onetime advertising agency executive (Benton & Bowles), university administrator, and eventual senator from Connecticut (1949–53). That appointment seemed ominous to Seldes.[76]

The immediate postwar years were not particularly kind to Seldes. Cut loose by CBS, and not long after that from Paramount as well, he languished for several years until his books began to flow again in 1950 and he became a staff writer for the *Saturday Review of Literature,* which once more provided him with a platform.

In the summer of 1945, however, the editors of *Esquire* decided to set him up for a powder-puff, semi-polite battle with George Jean Nathan, a bemused theatre critic Seldes had admired twenty years earlier, but one who now dominated the "theatre" department at *Esquire,* obliging Seldes to assess the *other* lively arts and thereby narrow his scope. Nathan, who had prominent pouchy sacs beneath his eyes, accused Seldes of being blindly enthusiastic about everything, of lacking discrimination. In the realm of radio criticism, Seldes laughed too much at second-rate comedians and admired Bing Crosby excessively, and, a cruel cut, the very thought of television "inspires Gilbert to a boozy rapture."[77]

In point of fact Seldes turned out to be far more prophetic about television than Nathan. But his reply had a little too much of the *ad hominem* (Nathan had not liked *Lysistrata*). Nathan enjoyed undeserved prestige as an acerbic critic, was naively hopeful about the future of live theatre, and spent too much time attacking other critics. "Of critics he expects nothing good and he sees to it that nothing bad is allowed to escape unnoticed."[78]

Because writers and critics invariably require collegial and psychological support, it is instructive to compare Seldes' public ruction with Nathan to an extremely cordial exchange of letters that passed between Lewis Mumford and Van Wyck Brooks during the winter of 1944–45. Here is an extract from Mumford's letter when Brooks had completed three of the five volumes in his cultural history of the United States:

> In your literary history of our country, dear Van Wyck, you have created a new genre; and you can be judged in that performance only by the standards that you yourself have erected. It is history such as we have never had a breath or hint of before; it is a revelation of the sources of spirit such as the critics and philosophers have never taken the pains to explore. You

are writing a sort of Natural History of the American Spirit. . . . But your reputation as a critic, above all as a dissident critic of *America's Coming of Age,* obscures your triumph as a new kind of historian: you are reproached because you do not deal in detail with the books themselves, as subjects for critical evaluation, when the fact is that you have done something infinitely more important by distilling from the books the very flavor, perfume, and colour of America. You have laid our literature open to the sunlight and the air of common day. Henceforth, much that was seemingly buried forever will be accessible; and much that we thought we knew will be forever different, because of what you have revealed of the conditions out of which it grew. The little men will take a whole generation before they will discover your really astonishing originality of conception and treatment; they will be mourning the absence of qualities that have nothing to do with this actual work, that would only cause confusion and distraction if they were present.[79]

Brooks expressed gratitude, of course, but assured Mumford that his work would always "outweigh" Brooks' "if only because it concerns mankind and has nothing of the local or the national about it." Brooks added that he felt very strongly that "anything merely national is doomed and hope in my way I am serving the international."[80]

In a notable essay titled "The Responsibilities of the Critic," written in 1948–49, F. O. Matthiessen took a kind of intermediate position that became a benchmark for many critics during the 1950s. Although Matthiessen's primary concern was American literature, in the wake of World War II he regarded it as a product not merely of the American experience, but of the influence of European literature as well. What mattered most to Matthiessen was the depth that could only be derived from a rich sense of historical context and textual historicity. "Today we can take no tradition for granted," he observed, "we must keep repossessing the past for ourselves if we are not to lose it altogether. . . . The proper balance even for the critic who considers his field to be the present, is to bring to the elucidation of that field as much of the art of the past as he can command."[81]

It needs to be noted that sixteen years before Matthiessen wrote that homily, Seldes had complained that "most Americans aren't conscious of their past at all. Speak of 'the past' to an American and, according to his age, he will think you mean the war with Spain [1898–99], the World War, the coming of Model A or the panic of 1929." Most Americans, unfortunately, seemed to be convinced that their civilization "sprang into being somewhere between 1914 and 1926." The most notable exception among writers, Seldes acknowledged, was Van Wyck Brooks, though Brooks had built his reputation between 1915 and 1925 by condemning the shallowness of American civilization. Because his work became so influential, Seldes wrote, disciples swiftly supplied a "wholesale attack on everything that went on in America since 1850: morals, music, politics, manners, architecture, painting, novels, all were bad." Brooks had not yet experienced his pro-American epiphany.[82]

By contrast, Seldes' Americanism had been visible ever since his essay for the *Saturday Evening Post* in 1927; and his total commitment to the notion of American exceptionalism basically dated from *Mainland* in 1936, the same year that Brooks published *The Flowering of New England,* the first volume in what became his "Makers and Finders" series.

Like most of us, Seldes tended to be more astute in writing about the past than in predicting the future. He explicitly recognized that reality himself on several occasions, and quipped in 1957 that "I fall back on the human privilege (not to be abused by critics) of having a blind spot."[83]

He did, however, observe a particular desire among fellow critics to explain the dynamics of change over time in the popular arts, and offered a colloquial way of conceptualizing what the present does to the past and therefore what to expect in the future. Seldes first offered his "gutter theory of human progress" in 1932; and because his articulation of that theory in 1933 anticipates some key developments of the following chapter (as well as perceptions that were described in the last two), it is appropriate to take note of it here. What he designated as the sewer theory of progress had the following attributes:

> In brief, every new development (in the mechanics of the arts) drains off the worst part of what went before. The early movie, for instance, took away the cheap melodrama from the stage and the early radio has drained off the duller sketches of vaudeville and the less bright side of the comic strip. Television, when it comes, will take over the unbearable side of radio—making radio quite entertaining for a while.[84]

It is not entirely clear from these statements whether Seldes himself subscribed to the sewer theory; but from casual essays that he devoted to the question—what occasions or prompts popular appeal in the lively arts?—he seems to have had a more benign, less negative vision of what actually happens when progress occurs. As he wrote in 1944, to take just one example, "the use of radio for holding general morale at a good level has been successful because all the methods of suspense and shock have been put to the service of information and appeal." A positive and carefully planned advance, if you will, unimpeded by affluvia from the gutter.[85]

Of one thing there can be no doubt. By the later 1940s Gilbert Seldes had long since achieved a well-deserved reputation for creativity, passion, and above all versatility as a critic. It is amusing to look back to a letter that he received from Jersey City in 1934 and printed in his daily column. Here is an extract:

> I have been reading your column for some months now, and with a mounting sense of indignation. I think the scope of your interest is deplorably narrow. What, for example, do you know about small-bore rifle activities in America today? Did you know, for example, that last year the United States won every international contest in which it engaged, knocking the spots out of England, Germany, Australia and East Africa? Now there is something! Or don't you think so? As a matter of fact aiming, the computation of wind drift and elevation, the fine relationship of the physical and mechanical forces in trigger squeeze, delicate appraisals of the effect of temperature on centers of impact; all such things are in as real a sense an art as the way a gifted polo player, a gifted tennis prima donna, or a gifted fencer, plies his mallet, his racket, his rapier—or his adversary.
>
> Now, Mr. Seldes, get religion, and look over the fence of your favorite preserves (enduring books, economics, the pageantry of Recovery, Mae West, Schnozzle Durante, the Silly Symphonies, Art, and NRA). That is all you've thought about in some time now, isn't it, Mr. Seldes? Now, now . . . be honest![86]

Well, fair enough, Seldes *did* favor the kinds of topics cited at the end of that extract, and he did not write about small-bore weapons though he had much to say about big-bore movies and programs on the radio. During the 1950s he became more versatile and expansive than ever, paying attention to all the lively arts and engaging in heated controversies over their use and abuse in the civic culture.

~9

Coming to Terms with Mass Culture

lthough this chapter treats the harvest years of Seldes' career as a cultural critic, the decade of the 1950s, it is necessary to start by dipping back to 1932 when he wrote a semi-serious essay on what he perceived to be a double standard in diverse modes of consumerism. Why had social assumptions developed in such a way that commercial products were not evaluated for the public when they first appeared, yet plays, books, and movies were? Seldes suggested that this made no sense because "we suffer more from the misrepresentation of things we use (and the adulteration of things we eat) than we do from what we see and hear." After speculating about the origins of the critic's profession, and especially the ways that it had changed during the previous century, Seldes expressed the wish that artists and manufacturers might exchange places. "Then we would choose our movies and our radio programs by luck, and have a Coffee Critic and a Mattress Expert to tell us what to buy in the stores."[1]

It is instructive to compare that droll yet provocative observation about the kinds of things that are and are not reviewed with Seldes' comments a quarter of a century later on the critic's vocation. Although advertising and consumerism concerned him even more in the 1950s than they had in 1932, his observations became less whimsical and more clearly focused because of the general presumption that cultural critics reviewed entertainment but not home furnishings and dietary commodi-

315

ties. His comments now were serious, straightforward, and considerably less speculative. "It is part of the duty of the critic to guide the public taste," he wrote in 1956. "I would say that it is also part of the critic's duty to fight against the cynical contempt for the public which corrupts the makers of entertainment."[2]

That mix of roles, mentor to the public regarding the arts along with being an advocate for popular taste—an amalgam that did not always cohere readily—characterized Seldes' mature years as a cultural critic. He now referred to his own field of expertise simply as "public entertainment," and declared that "my profession is to think, or worry, about popular entertainment." When he wrote a monthly column early in the 1950s, "The Lively Arts," for *Park East: The Magazine of New York*, the editor explained that Seldes had devoted a major part of his working life to defending and upholding "the artistic rights of the average man," an accurate indication of his ongoing concern for the democratization of culture, a concern that did not wane during the 1950s and early '60s. He never ceased to pride himself on being an "independent man" and prepared his criticism with the autonomous citizen in mind, not the "herd man."[3]

While Seldes engaged in some acerbic and professionally unpleasant controversies during the 1950s, most notably with fellow critic Dwight Macdonald and with broadcaster Edward R. Murrow, his basic views as a critic converged in many ways with those of F. O. Matthiessen, a man who embodied qualities that, at least in theory, were anathema to Seldes: an academic affiliation, a highbrow perspective, Christian socialism, and a propensity for theorizing about literary culture. Like Seldes, however, Matthiessen emphasized the centrality of change and consequently the importance of historical perspective. In one of his last essays, written in 1949, Matthiessen insisted upon the "inescapable interplay between past and present: that the past is not what is dead, but what is already living; and that the present is continually modifying the past, as the past conditions the present." Seldes would also have agreed with the assertion that "today we can take no tradition for granted, we must keep repossessing the past for ourselves if we are not to lose it altogether."[4]

And then, virtually echoing what Seldes had been saying for decades, Matthiessen acknowledged how difficult, yet how necessary, it was to keep the popular arts of "our technological age" in proper perspective. The consequences of the mass media were becoming steadily more pervasive, "so that we must either channel them to socially valuable ends or be engulfed by them." (If Seldes regretted the proliferation of radio soap operas, he also recognized that that same medium had for almost twenty-five years built up a taste for fine symphonic music among millions of listeners who would not otherwise have encountered it.) The chief art form of their age, moreover, film, served as a "compelling reminder of our immense potentialities and continual corruptions." Seldes would make the same point, in diverse contexts, throughout the 1950s.[5]

Finally, Matthiessen referred to the critic's essential qualities and concerns in pluralistic terms, repeatedly using the word *"awarenesses,"* and he believed quite passionately that the cultural critic could not ignore the political dimensions of his targeted concerns. "The series of awarenesses which I believe the critic must possess lead ineluctably from literature to life, and I do not see how the responsible intellectual in our time can avoid being concerned with politics."[6] The major controversies that engaged Seldes during the 1950s—the nature and future prospects for mass culture, the issue of achieving fairness in interpretive news broadcasting on television—both were knotty political issues that preoccupied him for most of a decade. The imprudent ideological jingo of the war years soon became the judicious conscience of media broadcasting just a few years later—a voice of integrity that willingly challenged the methods of some of the most admired men in print and television journalism.

His institutional and organizational affiliations remained quite modest in the decade that followed 1949. Early in 1952 he contributed essays about film to the *Saturday Review of Literature*. In March he launched a "TV and Radio" contribution to that journal and alternated the two until the spring when he concentrated entirely on TV and radio, a commitment that continued until late in the 1950s when he began to write occasional columns for the vast audience reached by *TV Guide*.

It should be noted that his tone and vocabulary really did not change when he confronted the much larger readership of *TV Guide*. Seldes had long believed that both his style and his message targeted the average American. He did not become overly cerebral for the *Saturday Review,* nor did he pander to the readership of *TV Guide*. To round out the busy life of this cultural pluralist, he also taught literature and communications as an adjunct at Columbia University during the mid-1950s; and in 1956 he started to contribute a weekly column to the *Village Voice*—a commitment that he undertook in order to reach a particular constituency, not for money, because he received none.[7]*

---

*His wife, Alice Hall Seldes, died on January 29, 1954, in Lakeland, Florida, where Seldes had been scheduled to address a gathering. Although he enjoyed the companionship of particular women in the years that followed, he never remarried.

I

From the late 1940s to the close of his career, Seldes wrote almost entirely about film, radio, and television. During the preceding decade, however, he also devoted himself extensively to live entertainment, mainly in his monthly department for *Esquire* called "lively arts." During the years between 1939 and 1946 Seldes sent up his last hurrah for the theatricals, musical revues, and nightclub acts that had been his forte ever since the early 1920s. Although most of these essays had a distinctive charm, few of them added new criteria or fresh concerns to his established identity as a critic. He seemed to alternate between unmitigated praise for the artists he admired (Jerome Kern, especially because of "Ol' Man River"; Rodgers and Hart, most notably for *On Your Toes* and *Pal Joey;* and comedian Jimmy Savo, a pantomimist who did brilliant burlesques of popular songs, usually by presenting sentimental tunes with tragic melancholy)[8] and big disappointments in popular entertainment (most musicals on stage and in film; the phony sentimentalism of popular music; the conservative closed shop being run by the music publishers in ASCAP (Tin Pan Alley); and even much of "hot jazz" because it was music without melody, "performance in which no one cares for the total, and the audience shrieks over solo performances").[9]

A few new developments did prompt warm enthusiasm (invariably accompanied by some sort of caveat): for example, Superman on film; such high-calibre phonograph recordings as John Barrymore's *Hamlet* and John Gielgud's *The Importance of Being Earnest;* and significant western films, such as *The Ox-Bow Incident* and *The Covered Wagon,* which seemed to be appreciated even more in Europe than by American audiences. Because so much of United States history "is one long hearty westward ho!" it puzzled Seldes that so few American literary works dealt seriously with the West.[10]

Despite that deficiency, however, Seldes' observations at home and abroad between 1939 and 1946 kept him convinced that the United States did possess a distinctive national character. After making comparative visits to music halls in England, France, and the U.S., for example, he remained struck by the outstanding qualities of the American show—energy, violence, and speed—which he generalized into stylistic attributes of the society as a whole. "Every nation gets the kind of night life it deserves," he remarked, "and night life is as personal (or national) as government or murder."[11] Seldes had always been partial to the word "violence," by which he did not mean mayhem so much as intense excitement. It is a characteristic that he associated intimately with American proclivities and enthusiasms.

It pleased Seldes that he saw a marked increase in versatility among American artists and entertainers. If John Steinbeck could become involved with film scripts and Theodore Dreiser with radio, and subsequently when radio and film stars did well on television (by no means all, however), these seemed to be signs of good health in the public arts. Seldes liked the idea that the best and the brightest could be creative in more than one field "because if they don't, a lot of second-rate people will grab the controls." He also praised the federal government for providing encouragement that supported creative work in radio and in film documentaries.[12]

Right after the war, however, he wrote a kind of reprise of what had happened to the popular arts during wartime. He was more positive in retrospect, actually, than he had been at the time, and fondly recalled how much fun had been accessible to those who remained on the home front. As for governmental intervention and support, however, his emphasis shifted back to "hands off" by the winter of 1945–46. Having fought a war for freedom, people needed to remember that "one of the choice freedoms we have is to pick our own fun. We'd hate it if some bureau in Washington poked its finger into the editorial office of every pulp magazine and 'oriented' our confession and western magazines so that they conveyed even the noblest of patriotic lessons. We took a lot of propaganda on the air during the war just because we all believed in what the propagandists said—which was that we were fighting to get back to a freer air."[13]

Seldes' concern that government should keep its hands off the popular arts had two principal sources. A less important consideration arose from his ongoing antagonism toward highbrow intellectuals, whose influence upon the arts might increase if government became involved as a producer or sponsor of entertainment. The more important consideration, however, derived from his commitment to cultural democracy and the desirability of pluralism. Because he wanted "the whole country to understand what the value of our mixed heritage is," Seldes insisted with some frequency that variety mattered even more than excellence in the public arts. That postwar emphasis differed somewhat from his 1944 declaration that if the citizen is going to pay more for his entertainment, "he's entitled to get more. . . . He should be able to get more wit and more taste."[14]

From 1944 onward, Seldes became ever more preoccupied with issues of cultural stratification: How much influence highbrows really had in the public arts and how much they ought to have; whether the presumed levels or categories of cultural strata weren't actually so overlapping as to render rigid categories almost meaningless. If the makers of cigarettes and soft drinks had for some years commissioned first-rate painters to do their advertisements, "does it mean that some day we won't have to distinguish between a canvas in a gallery and a picture on a calendar?" Seldes wanted to believe that the future lay with the *vox populi,* and consequently that creative artists could no longer simply please themselves. They would have to please the "gallery."[15]

In 1944 he boldly threw down a gauntlet to the advocates of high culture:

> The time has come to cast a critical eye upon the actual product of the great serious artists, the ones who work in the noble forms, the inheritors of the classic traditions, the symphonic composers and tragic playwrights and painters in oil and the heavy dancers. The time has come to look at them again and ask whether they're holding their own.

Seldes concluded that very little great or enduring art was being produced at the time, which led him swiftly back to his predilection for the vernacular. Could quality and popularity go hand in hand? Perhaps, but only if one took the power to define "quality" out of the hands of highbrows.[16]

By the close of the decade quite a few influential critics were operating on the same wavelength. In 1949, for example, Frederick Lewis Allen, the editor-in-chief of *Harper's,* wrote to Elmer Davis to express appreciation for his essay "on the difference between what has actually happened to America during the past twenty-five years and what you would think had happened if you were dependent upon what the literati wrote."[17]

Early in 1949, however, Russell Lynes, the managing editor of *Harper's* from 1947 until 1967, achieved a kind of notoriety in this whole matter by publishing a widely read essay titled "Highbrow, Lowbrow, Middlebrow," a discussion of taste levels that touched off a national parlor game craze after *Life* magazine carried an epitome of Lynes' cultural analysis accompanied by an amusing chart that suggested standards of taste in *four* categories because middlebrow got subdivided into upper and lower middlebrow. William Barrett, an editor of *Partisan Review,* the paradigmatic highbrow journal, wrote a good-natured letter of protest that indicates quite clearly how self-styled intellectuals felt about such casual caricatures:

"Highbrows" originally coined the terms "middlebrow" and "lowbrow" to apply to cultural products and not to persons. We spoke as critics, not as psychologists. Mr. Lynes's switch makes lively and suggestive reading, but raises many more questions than it can answer. After careful checking, we haven't found any highbrows to fit his description. Maybe we know only a restricted group, but we don't think so.

We think Mr. Lynes is wrong, and one proof is that his analysis leaves him unable to answer a fundamental question: what keeps the highbrows going in American life? The only motives Mr. Lynes acknowledges are snobbery, display of superiority, and conspicuous consumption of learning. We doubt that these motives would be sufficient to keep the highbrow from crumpling before the competitive drives of American life and becoming an extinct species altogether.

Considering the contempt expressed by Gilbert Seldes for so many years toward highbrows, Barrett's rejoinder may help to explain why Seldes was never invited to participate in any of *Partisan Review*'s famous symposia. The erstwhile editor of *The Dial* had become *persona non grata* in the highbrows' sanctum sanctorum.[18]

By 1951 a creative cultural critic, comparatively new on the scene, named Marshall McLuhan, picked up on all of this and commented that Lynes seemed rather alarmed to find an emerging intellectual elite in the United States. He designated Lynes' enterprise a "totalitarian technique of stratification by arbitrary cadres and ranks." Calling attention to *Life*'s widely noticed chart, McLuhan felt certain that twenty million readers had "tied on their mental strait jackets with mingled feelings of disdain, envy, and shame." It was McLuhan's particular (and little noticed) distinction, however, to comment that the basic process did not just involve a "filtering down from high-brow to low-brow arts but equally a nourishing of the esoteric by the popular. The few must depend on the many as much as the many stand to gain from the few." Whereas McLuhan really believed that, Seldes wanted to be able to believe it and devoted considerable attention in the coming decade to attempts at validating McLuhan's symbiotic relationship (without ever mentioning him).[19]

In 1985 Lynes informed an interviewer that he did not consider himself a critic because "the public thinks of a critic as someone who's against everything, and I'm not. I'm amused by a lot of things." It is difficult to say for certain, but I suspect that Lynes was right about the popular perception of critics. Throughout the 1950s quite a few of them lined up to differ with Lynes. McLuhan observed that by proclaiming a set of social and intellectual distinctions in accordance with consumer goods, "the chart ignores and conceals any real basis for such distinctions." When Leo Gurko published a work titled *Heroes, Highbrows, and the Popular Mind* early in 1954, Seldes reviewed it at length, finding Gurko naive for expecting to "close as far as possible the gap between the high and the lowbrow," and unrealistic in believing that contemporary signs pointed to a cultural renaissance in the United States.[20]

Seldes may have been predisposed to disparage Gurko's book because a little more than three years earlier Seldes himself had touched many of the same issues in a book of his own, *The Great Audience*—a book ignored by Gurko—in which Seldes maintained that high culture remained quite a separate taste level, even while he blurred the customary distinctions between folk and popular art: both were readily comprehended, romantic, patriotic, conventionally moral, "and they are held in deep affection by those who are suspicious of the great arts."[21]

Between 1949, when his provocative "brow" essays appeared, and 1954, when *The Tastemakers* was published, Lynes captured much the same kind of attention that Seldes had after 1924 with *The 7 Lively Arts:* a breath of fresh air concerning subjects of broad general interest— popular taste in relation to traditional criteria for the assessment of culture and its hierarchy of merit.

II

By the later 1940s, with the advent of television, Seldes realized that his beloved lively arts of the 1920s were being transformed into something for which a new label emerged: mass media. The shift made Seldes exceedingly apprehensive, and *The Great Audience* took the form of a rather unfriendly look at the impact of film, radio, television, and their social consequences. Much more than Lynes, who concentrated on the ingestion of tangible products rather than the consumption of images and airwaves, Seldes worried about the degradation of taste and the emergence of cultural mediocrity on an unprecedented scale.

The book contains several apparent contradictions because it seemingly alternates between positive and negative conclusions. Although it is quite critical of most Hollywood films, for example, it nonetheless rails against the highbrow tendency to scorn Hollywood (p. 44). That is a genuine contradiction. For another we need only to look to the very first page of text. Seldes admits that he has "somewhat reluctantly been forced to the conclusion that our mass entertainments are, practically speaking, the great creative arts of our time." That sounds cautiously upbeat until one reads the rest of Seldes' paragraph:

> In the traditional sense they are seldom considered as arts and are condemned because they are uncreative. They are machine-made products, they repeat themselves endlessly, using a handful of contrived formulas for plot and stereotyped figures for characters; they are seldom the product of a single powerful imagination but are put together by groups of people who are virtually forbidden to express their own profoundest feelings about the meaning of life. All these things are true, and I can add a more damning indictment still: our mass entertainments are compelled by their own nature to create works that can be promptly forgotten; the work of art as an imperishable object is totally foreign to them. (p. 3)

Once again, as he had in *Mainland* Seldes attacked "finance capital," joining the novelist James T. Farrell and critic Dwight Macdonald in holding that nexus responsible for the development of a vast commercial culture "as a kind of substitute for a genuinely popular, a genuinely democratic culture." Nevertheless he repeatedly affirmed a framework of "democratic capitalism," and kept all of his proposals within a basic capitalist framework because he believed so fully in the "free market in entertainment." Somehow, those people who were responsible for the public arts would have to rescue them, on their own initiative, from the morass into which the arts had fallen. The patient should be allowed to heal himself, or else to go under without governmental intervention. As we shall see, Seldes took what he then regarded as a realistic view of commercial sponsorship; and unlike some of the leading network executives in 1949–50, such as Sylvester Weaver of NBC, Seldes did not condone but did not despair at the dominant role of advertising agencies in determining program content.[22]

Although Seldes certainly was not an egregious Cold Warrior, his growing concern about mass culture came to be wrapped in rhetoric that occasionally reflected the apogee of Cold War anxieties and allegiances early in the 1950s. In asserting that people who produced the popular arts must reverse their direction, he observed that the products presently being created on radio, television, and film led to the shaping of "mass man." They should, instead, "make the popular arts serve free men trying to secure a free society." The political temper that then existed, he felt, reasserted the "American past against the Communist future." Under such circumstances, he cautioned, those responsible for radio programs sentimentalized or glorified the past by using history, reviving stock figures from the past to evoke traditional values, and above all by implying that the future could be based not so much on current needs and problems but on a sanctified past that ought to be perpetuated. The net effect seemed cerebrally stultifying to Seldes. "It requires no effort," he commented. "The receptive listener at home need neither think nor act. He is being kept comfortable, he is being entertained, in an America gone static."[23]

Seldes supplied a succinct and critical summary of the Cold War ideology that American media managed to reinforce with diverse programs. "The fundamental American tradition," he wrote, "is that we came away from the fixed world of Europe to create a dynamic country, with freedom to move, to change, to work; with opportunity to learn; with a chance to rise in the world; with a duty to keep the free spirit of the country free." There it was in capsule form, the media doing everything to reinforce that vision and nothing to question its failures, its casualties, or its human costs.[24]

Turning to the entertainment industries themselves, Seldes observed that movie audiences were steadily declining, especially adults over the age of thirty. Recent research showed that half of the people over thirty did not see even one picture a month. Hollywood had foolishly aimed its products mainly at teenagers with unrealistic tales of immature love. Only when filmmakers stopped evading adult issues, and treated them in a mature way, would the industry recapture the complete clientele that it should serve and actually needed in order to survive. Ultimately, therefore, despite his concern about the emergence of mass culture, Seldes appealed to the entertainment industries to act in their own self-interest by re-establishing contact with large segments of society that they had neglected and thereby achieve an even broader mass audience.[25]

Reviews of *The Great Audience* were quite positive on the whole, praising Seldes for his impressive knowledge of the mechanics of media work as well as their actual products, lauding his clear powers of description and the extraordinary range of his interests as a critic. Hollis Alpert called it a "valid and vital essay," while a reviewer for the *Library Journal* noted an important shift, on Seldes' part, away from his customary view that the audience is always right. As Seldes correctly noted, with the coming of commercialized culture and a substantial increase in the size of the mass, audiences were increasingly passive and unsure of just what they wanted. Writing in the San Francisco *Chronicle,* Joseph Henry Jackson called it "a genuinely important book, one worth the time of all thoughtful readers."[26]

The most astute and substantial review, once again, was written by Edmund Wilson for *The New Yorker*. It began by calling *The Great Audience* a logical sequel to *The 7 Lively Arts,* but immediately noticed differences. The 1924 work had celebrated distinguished artists, whereas the new one had very little to say about individual performers and writers, using them only to illustrate general points. Wilson considered it the most comprehensive and searching book available on mass entertainment in the United States, one that drew conclusions that could not have been foreseen by anyone in 1924:

> This is the first time, so far as I know, that a man of intelligence and taste, with a sound enough education to give him cultural and historical perspective, who has at the same time a practical grasp of the technical and financial aspects of the entertainment business, has set out to attack the whole subject: to describe it, to explain it, to assess it, to assign it to its place in society.

Overall Wilson regarded it as one of those "definitive" works that "sum up and deliver judgment on some phase of human activity—that make us understand what has happened, that establish enduring assumptions, and that remain indispensable landmarks."[27]

Following a superb summary of the book's contents, Wilson registered first a minor and then one major dissent. As for the former, minor yet applicable to a few of Seldes' broad stroke generalizations, Wilson regretted that Seldes didn't know the history of American social and political thought as well as he knew the popular arts. As for the latter, Wilson nailed Seldes because of the major contradiction that he perceived in the book, namely, that Seldes' disdain for a straw-man "intellectual," who supposedly scorns the popular arts, is altogether inconsistent with the bitter complaints of anti-intellectualism that he lodged against radio and the movies. Wilson went on to observe that Seldes himself was an intellectual par excellence:

> His whole appeal to the public is based on the hope—I believe quite justified—that there are still a great many Americans who share his intellectuality and are not satisfied with the programs and the films that the mass media are putting out. His "intellectual" and his "average man" are really demagogic devices, taken over from the very agencies against which he now protests; they have never been anything other than masks to mislead the simple. He shows them up at once when . . . he tells us that "the average man lives at many emotional and intellectual levels."[28]

Wilson closed by ascribing to Seldes an even gloomier view of "American commercialism" than Seldes himself, I believe, intended to convey. Nevertheless, the words that Wilson quoted were written by Seldes: The radio and movies, he concluded, "are the great engines of democratic entertainment and culture," but by imposing more and more uniformity, "they are committed to the destruction of democracy."

Although *The Great Audience* was intended for the so-called general reader, it received very positive reviews from shrewd scholars, ranging from historians like Arthur M. Schlesinger, Jr., to Irwin Edman, a philosopher at Columbia (1918–54) whose books included *Arts and the Man* (1939). Edman drew the same speculative conclusions that Edmund Wilson had, and in doing so called to readers' attention the transformation in cultural criticism that had inevitably followed the transformation of American popular culture during the previous quarter century. Edman recalled for Seldes

> the day a generation ago when your work *The Seven Lively Arts* was required reading for all the young intellectuals including myself. It was sad to find that lively arts organized on a large scale have not turned out to do for the American audience what you and all of us hoped. . . . I could not help feeling that your conclusions on the whole are discouraging. I don't see how commercial pressures from your own evidence are going to be reduced and television especially seems to be aiming at a very low common denominator indeed.[29]

Curiously enough, Seldes' attempt to mitigate the despair of critics even more discouraged than himself brought him into a major controversy that lasted most of the decade. Although it involved Dwight Macdonald as a principal adversary, their quarrel was symptomatic of a much larger debate over the pernicious influence of mass culture, a debate that persisted into the 1960s. During the 1940s Macdonald had written a widely noticed essay (among intellectuals, at least) titled "A Theory of Popular Culture," the first of several that culminated in his famous piece for *Partisan Review* called "Masscult & Midcult" (1960). In *The Great Audience* Seldes referred to the first of these essays, written from a Marxist perspective and blaming the banalities of mass culture on capitalist exploitation. Although Seldes said that Macdonald seemed less doctrinaire than some critics on the left, he summarized Macdonald's views in the following manner: those who dealt in mass culture products cynically manipulated the cultural needs of the people; "they do not satisfy popular taste . . . they exploit it." Therefore, in Macdonald's perspective as well as his own, Seldes found the transformation of culture (and hence criticism) made explicit:

> A generation or so ago the *avant-garde* did not compete, the theater had not degraded itself into being a feeder for the movies, and the movies themselves had a small coterie of artists, including Griffith and Chaplin. Now the theater and the movies are at the same level, and the movies, though better entertainment, are worse art. Since the popular arts feed foolish myths to the people and at the same time draw down the level of the great arts, the exploitation of popular taste becomes a serious threat to democracy.[30]

Seldes then indicated the grounds of his disagreement with Macdonald because the latter found it *inevitable* that mass entertainment under capitalism was "condemned to operate on a quick turnover of the cheapest and shoddiest goods." Seldes saw a glimmer of hope: placed under sufficient pressure to develop new ways to distribute films and develop programs, the manipulators of public taste might change their tactics and offer better pictures and programs. Seldes also differed with Macdonald's belief that expanding capitalism drove a wedge between the artist and the people, forcing them apart and compelling artists to work for a small though appreciative group on the fringe. Seldes believed, by contrast, that the American artist had taken the initiative, often pursuing his or her own interests and needs despite the power of corporate America.[31]

In a 1953 essay offered as "A Theory of Mass Culture," Macdonald struck back. He designated Seldes' approach as the "democratic-liberal proposal" and asserted that *The Great Audience* blamed the low quality of mass culture on the

> stupidity of the Lords of *kitsch,* who underestimate the mental age of the public, the arrogance of the intellectuals, who make the same mistake and so snobbishly refuse to work for mass media like radio, TV and movies, and the passivity of the public itself, which doesn't insist on better Mass Cultural products. This diagnosis seems to be superficial in that it blames everything on subjective moral factors: stupidity, perversity, failure of will. . . . The Lords of *kitsch* sell culture to the masses, it is a debased, trivial culture that avoids both the deep realities (sex, death, failure, tragedy) and also the simple spontaneous pleasures, since the realities would be too real and the pleasures too *lively* to induce what Mr. Seldes calls "the mood of consent": i.e., a narcotised acceptance of Mass Culture and of the commodities it sells as a substitute for the unsettling and unpredictable (hence unsalable) joy, tragedy, wit, change, originality and beauty of real life.[32]

When Seldes published his next book, *The Public Arts* (1956), he differed from Macdonald in three key ways: first, by insisting that the lines of demarcation separating cultural strata were becoming increasingly blurry rather than clearer. Second, by offering a cautionary warning against being too harsh on mass culture: "new things have come to pass," he wrote, recognizing that television had done some rather innovative programming, especially in drama. "We must be sure that the standards of judgment we set up are appropriate to the subject." And third, Macdonald blamed those he deemed pretentious intellectuals— such as Archibald MacLeish, Thornton Wilder, and Stephen Vincent Benét—for the growing appeal of Midcult, whereas Seldes admired such men and blamed corporate entrepreneurs, advertisers, public relations people, and the networks instead. Macdonald's belated public response was simply to include his 1953 rejoinder in the famous 1960 essay for *Partisan Review,* verbatim, and then reprint that long essay in his 1962 collection of essays, *Against the American Grain.*[33]

There is actually more to this contretemps than meets the eye, even though the full story is fundamentally a diversion from our central concern—the great debate during the 1950s over the implications of mass culture in the United States. In the autumn of 1951, barely a year after Seldes published *The Great Audience,* he and Macdonald got into a nasty epistolary bout over what it meant to be a "fellow-traveler" and how you could tell one by his or her words if not behavior. Seldes accused Macdonald of targeting people much too cavalierly as fellow-travelers. "When you say the fellow-travellers ought to be grateful to you because you defend their freedom of speech, I wonder whether it is their freedom of speech you are defending as much as your own freedom to slander." Macdonald acknowledged that if he seemed unfair and McCarthy-like, Seldes seemed to him "politically ignorant." "Look," Macdonald importuned, "I'll be even more careful in the future about this f.t. issue . . . if you'll try to be even less abusive when some one raises the touchy business. Agreed?"[34]

III

The intense concern about mass culture that became so central to discourse among intellectuals during the 1950s was actually anticipated by Gilbert Seldes as early as 1932 when he devoted one of his daily columns to the problem of cultural stratification in general and the swiftly growing impact of radio in particular. He revealed himself less than friendly to proto-mass culture, such as it was in 1932. It bothered Seldes that "The March of Time" did not achieve a broader audience. He acknowledged that many more people listened to "The Rise of the Goldbergs" than to "The March of Time":

> I do not think this speaks well for the intelligence of the community; but the intelligence of the community, and even of its leaders, was betrayed years ago when radio was handed over, bound and sold to advertisers. . . . Radio is safe so long as it is interesting. It is a pity that what interests twenty million people does not interest another, intelligent and significant, two hundred thousand. But newspapers and magazines still exist, and some of them manage to circulate in the millions, too, without entirely losing their intellectual integrity. It only remains for advertisers to find the programs which can interest the millions and not make the minority a little sick.[35]

His point about the control exercised by radio advertising would appear in expanded form eighteen years later in *The Great Audience*. In 1948, moreover, anticipating that book directly, Seldes once again expressed concern about cultural stratification. "Our great entertainment industries," he remarked, "are creating before our eyes a cultural *proletariat:* the intellectually disinherited, the emotionally homeless. . . ." The solution that he advocated? Broadcasters and film makers must recognize the plurality of audiences in a pluralistic society and break up the mass audience into targeted components.[36]

During the later 1940s Theodor W. Adorno and other émigrés from the Frankfurt School did much to launch the discussion of mass culture by attacking it from a leftist perspective as a narcotic that served only to depoliticize the masses as a potentially revolutionary proletariat. In theory, at least, one might expect Seldes to have no use whatever for Adorno, partially because Seldes cared little for European-style abstractions, but even more because Adorno also condemned jazz as animalistic and degrading, and attacked cartoons as violent, vulgar, and even anti-democratic! Although Adorno barely appears in Seldes' firmament, the leading American writer on the lively arts did, at least once, quote with approval from an essay by Adorno on popular music. Bear in mind, however, that during the 1940s Seldes did not care very much for the products of Tin Pan Alley. On that point, at least, he and Adorno could find common ground.[37]

At about the same time, directly following World War II, sociologists like Paul Lazarsfeld and Robert K. Merton issued an array of empirical and theoretical studies in which they described and analyzed phenomena that they designated as mass persuasion and mass communication.[38] Whereas their emphases were far more explanatory and precise from the perspective of social science, by the end of the 1940s journalistic observers began to weigh in with impressionistic essays, largely unfavorable, that sought to evaluate and predict the unwanted consequences of mass culture.

One of the earliest of these writers, yet quite representative, was Milton Klonsky, who published "Along the Midway of Mass Culture" in 1949 in *Partisan Review,* which also printed many other attacks on the newly noticed phenomenon during the 1950s. He observed that the most prominent artifacts of mass culture—comic strips, pulp fiction, radio serials, movies, and pop jazz—were not sudden apparitions from another planet but the direct result of modern technology and changes in public education; in short, they were grounded in a middle-class culture being transformed. Even so, he insisted, "the base forms of mass art have autonomous values and a parallel momentum of their own." Moreover, like Adorno and others from the Frankfurt School, Klonsky feared that mass culture would contribute to authoritarian control (a loss of autonomy for the individual, and so on). Does that sound like high anxiety verging upon unwarranted hysteria? Klonsky's concerns were nonetheless shared by many who held a traditional view of the high arts as both uplifting and liberating. The manifestations of mass culture, he declared, "usurp the functions of traditional art in setting the styles, the manners, the images, the standards and the goals of life for millions, almost as though they were the organs of an unofficial state religion."[39]

In 1952 *Partisan Review* devoted three consecutive issues to a major, ongoing symposium on the broad topic: "Our Country and Our Culture." Looking back many years later, during the 1980s, one of the editors, William Phillips, acknowledged that mass culture had been the central concern prompting the symposium and that most of the contributors, prominent intellectuals, had regarded mass culture as the lethal enemy of traditional culture (a term that they preferred to high or elite culture).[40]

One of the key issues addressed by quite a few of the contributors involved American exceptionalism: Was mass culture significantly different in the United States? Joseph Frank took a widely shared position by arguing that the problem itself was neither new nor peculiarly American. Nevertheless, he noticed a major difference between Europe and America because the "European intellectual minority has no sense of guilt at not being part of mass culture," whereas the democratic ethos in the United States was exceedingly conducive to feelings of guilt. Louis Kronenberger, on the other hand, also spoke for many when he remarked that "the real problem is how to avoid contamination without avoiding contact." The point, of course, was that living in America made it really impossible to avoid contact—especially if the critic wanted to be able to comment in some knowledgeable and original way on mass culture.[41]

William Barrett, a philosopher and associate editor of *Partisan Review,* asserted that the "great new art form which America has contributed to the history of civilization is streamlined mass journalism." Although it existed elsewhere, journalism as a mass art par excellence enjoyed greater prominence and impact in the United States by forcing modifications in the style and format of traditional journalism. The problem of declining discrimination, along with the argument offered by networks and Holly-wood spokesmen that they were only giving the people what they wanted, prompted Arthur Schlesinger, Jr., to declare that "the rise of what Gilbert Seldes has called the Great Audience is one of the awful facts of our modern life."[42]

While Seldes' work was cited, invariably in a positive manner, he did not contribute to that symposium (though in the decade that lay ahead he participated in several others devoted exclusively to mass culture). He found himself in a somewhat awkward position for several reasons. First, and least important, the views he expressed in private tended to be somewhat more severe than those he put in print. In a private letter written in 1952, for example, he referred to "The Great (though tor-pified) Audience."[43]

Second, and much more important, as concerned as he may have been about the qualitative prospects for public entertainment and communica-tions in 1950, he disliked the arrogantly pejorative positions taken by most of those he regarded as arch highbrows. Consequently, he often expressed more hopeful positions during the 1950s and on into the early '60s—not what you could call Pollyana-ish positions, yet he distanced himself from those Cassandras who not only disliked mass culture but regarded it as being beyond redemption. He tended to be more descrip-tive and above all explanatory, whereas the Cassandras felt more com-fortable simply condemning what they saw.

Although his next book, *The Public Arts* (1956), acknowledged that what he had always called the popular arts were becoming "more and more in our time the mass arts," he found much to praise in the skills of people ranging from comedians Jimmy Durante and Jack Benny to news broadcasters like Edward R. Murrow and television programs like "Omnibus." In that book he also made a very strong case that television differed fundamentally from all the other media. Consequently one might infer that mass culture as we understand it (involving super-sophisticated technology and the intensely partisan politics of regulation) really emerged soon after the advent of commercial television.[44]

When he brought out a revised edition of *The 7 Lively Arts* in 1957, Seldes acknowledged that radio had certainly initiated the process through which popular culture was transformed by the mass media in ways that neither Seldes nor anyone else could have conceived in 1924. The complicated challenge of reissuing his classic for readers in the later 1950s elicited this candid confession: When he looked at his most famous book under strikingly altered circumstances, "I was so impressed by the effect of the mass media that I couldn't see in them [the popular arts] precisely those qualities I had originally blamed others for not seeing: their sparkle and snap, their inner life which corresponds to the brighter and better side of American life, their impertinence and good cheer, and above all the strong creative current which in them has found a native, not borrowed, form for itself."[45]

Seldes then conceded that in *The Great Audience* he gave vent to his misgivings about the transformation in public entertainment. Nevertheless, the book's impact was sufficient to place it on course syllabi at many American universities. Feeling in retrospect that it was a "glum book," however, he made it explicitly clear that *The Public Arts* (1956) was meant to achieve a balance. "Getting away from the grim words 'mass media,'" he wrote, "finding a new name for them, connecting their social effects with the pleasures they give—was for me an act of simple justice." He made it apparent that what he preferred to call the public arts (rather than mass media) brought him great delight as well as anxiety and frustration.[46]

Later in the same book Seldes allowed himself to be considerably more critical of the mass media, and called them just that rather than using his new, more neutral euphemism. In June 1959, however, when he participated in a conference on the mass media held at the Tamiment Institute, Seldes seemed to enjoy playing the role of devil's advocate—though never to the point of taking a position that he did not fully believe in. For example, when Leo Rosten, the social critic and film writer, complained that intellectuals projected their own tastes on the masses, who really did not share them, Seldes responded by deflecting the argument in a slightly different direction. The objective shouldn't be to make everyone appreciative of the finer things, he said; but the media were at fault for reducing a pluralistic yet potentially receptive audience to its lowest common denominator. While he felt reluctant to defend "eggheads from the accusation that they are trying to impose their standards on the public," he strongly believed that the public had more diverse interests than the mass media were serving.[47]

When Randall Jarrell, the poet and critic (who had published in 1953 a famous essay titled "The Age of Criticism") lamented the fate of serious artists in an age of stifling mass culture, Seldes felt moved to voice his most vigorous explanation of the cultural transformation that had occurred and its consequences:

All of us here [at the 1959 conference] are aware that a revolution is taking place. It is the shift in power between the print culture and the electronic culture. . . . I haven't any statistical or philosophic basis for this, but I suggest at least as a basis for study that the change in quantity, velocity, and force of our mass media is so great as to really make it a qualitative change; that the mass media cannot any longer be compared with anything that went before.

People have talked here as if a rise in the aesthetic qualities of the mass media would make them perfectly acceptable, and we would all love them. I submit that a nation which is passively accepting works even ten times as good as those we have now, passively accepting them, might still be drugged and become entirely apathetic and remain emotionally immature. The need is not so much for improvement in a single product or for so much criticism of the product that comes from the mass media. We need an audience more active than any audience that has ever before been in the world. . . .

I suggest that we take the producers of the mass media at their word. Let us stop being hostile to them. Let us accept the basic statement that they give the public what the public wants and let us try to make the public want a great deal more.

If we can prove to the purveyors of the media that the public really wants something, then they are, by their own principle, committed to fill that want. My objective therefore is the public, the audience, the individual citizen.

Now I can return, happily, to the basic subject—the traditional role of the artist. The artist goes beneath the surface and finds out the real need of a society, a nation, or a community. That is where I think the artist really returns to the mass media, for it is only through the mass media that he is going to be able to fulfill himself at a time when, whether he regrets it or not, these media are dominant and will remain so.[48]

What I wish to commend here is not so much Seldes' realism, because he may very well have responded with more fatalism than he needed to, but rather his capacity as someone living in the midst of massive cultural change to see it whole and make sensible recommendations for courses of action appropriate to the public at large, the creative artist, and those who controlled the media. At the 1959 Tamiment conference, Seldes performed the role of a discerning critic.[49]

During the early and mid-1950s critics of mass culture were considerably more vocal than its defenders, and probably more numerous. But the latter could be interesting, forceful, and as public spokesmen, by no means inconsiderable. In the 1952 *Partisan Review* symposium, for example, Lionel Trilling called for caution, a wait-and-see attitude. Although mass culture clearly posed a considerable threat to learned culture, he suggested the presence of a "countervailing condition." Unless mass culture simply became irrevocably frozen in its present form, Trilling thought, it could very well improve. How? "It might attract genius and discover that it has an inherent law of development." It might, conceivably, bring good things to large numbers of people. Near the end of the same symposium Max Lerner suggested a silver lining to critics of mass culture: It had been facilitated by the swift growth of mass leisure— which surely meant a distinct improvement in the overall condition of mankind, even if it didn't thrill a smallish group of intellectuals.[50]

As a cultural pluralist, like Seldes, the philosopher Sidney Hook felt that the mere existence of mass culture surely did not preclude or obviate other options in the realm of culture for society as a whole. Therefore mass culture should not be despised by genuine pluralists who valued diversity. Still others, sympathetic to Hook's views, experienced some discomfort at the clear disparity between the democratic stance they aspired to and their tendency toward intolerance of a corrupt or coarse cultural order. That kind of intolerance verged too close to some ugly aspects of totalitarianism (right or left) that they had firmly rejected.

By the time of the Tamiment conference, however, there were cultural critics who did not damn with faint praise (like Lerner), didn't simply hope for the best (like Trilling), and didn't feel deeply ambivalent (like Seldes). By 1959 there were real, live advocates, not just apologists. A prime example is Patrick Hazard, then a young professor of literature at the University of Pennsylvania. He offered what he called a "General Theory" that anticipated the significant swing of the pendulum that took place in the 1960s:

> It is an insufficiently acknowledged virtue of our mass society that it is more permissive to a wider range of aesthetic forms that any other culture in history. Never have the elite arts had, in both relative and absolute numbers, larger and more sophisticated audiences; and it is my impression that the opportunities for both creation and appreciation are rapidly increasing. I suggest that we start reinvesting our critical energies in the new art forms characteristic of mass society.[51]

A few critics, mostly within the academy, took a more detached position during the 1950s and simply tried to comprehend the great transformation that irritated many but had begun to attract enthusiasts like Hazard. Reuel Denney, for example, a sociologist at the University of Chicago who had worked closely with David Riesman on the project that produced *The Lonely Crowd,* published *The Astonished Muse* in 1957, when the whole debate over mass culture reached a crescendo in terms of sheer volume. The stated aim of Denney's book was to stimulate thought and criticism in each area the media affected by "giving it more historical, artistic, and formal analysis than it generally got."

Although Denney failed to make a clear distinction between popular and mass culture, his book tried to do for mass culture what Seldes had done for the lively arts in 1924—make the phenomenon a worthy object of serious critical inquiry. In Denney's case he emphasized the need to explore this proposition; close attention to changes in the form of products, like cars as a hobby, or football games as mass entertainment, can provide an ideal starting point in understanding the mutual effects that producers and consumers have on one another.[52]

Four years later he published an historical essay on "The Discovery of the Popular Culture" that is exceedingly complimentary to Seldes' *The 7 Lively Arts,* "then and now the classic in its field." Although we do not know with assurance how Seldes responded to the article, his pleasure at the warm praise for his seminal book must have been offset by the looseness of Denney's categories of analysis. He casually posited the existence of mass culture in nineteenth-century America, and meandered in bizarre ways when attempting to explain the emergence of mass media in the mid-twentieth century. Here is a sample: "the mass media are a dumping ground for the artistic theories elaborated in the production-minded, late nineteenth century under the labels of realism and naturalism."[53]

Denney, like his colleague David Riesman, participated vigorously in the revival of interest in Alexis de Tocqueville in the United States during the 1950s and '60s. That trend received a major stimulus and became so pervasive in academe, especially, because intellectuals and scholars viewed Tocqueville as a prophet of mass culture and mass society. Tocqueville's concern about the tyranny of the majority and pressures for conformity in a democratic society could be readily transmuted into intellectuals' anxiety about the homogenization of culture with attendant losses of individual creativity and artistic freedom. It is no accident that the great Tocqueville revival of the later 1940s to the mid-1960s coincided exactly with the most self-conscious and vexed phase of the intense debate over the pros and cons of mass culture.[54]

IV

As we have seen, when Seldes wrote *The Public Arts* in 1955–56 he sought to balance his early enthusiasm for what he called the lively arts against his more recent, serious reservations about what had emerged as mass media. Although *The Public Arts* may very well be the clearest and most judicious book that Seldes ever wrote, we get two-thirds of the way through before he explicitly identifies what he calls its thesis (developed in several of his contemporary essays as well), namely, "that only a fragment of the total audience cares *much* for what the broadcasters transmit." His point, which differentiated him from many participants in this conversation, was not that the media failed to satisfy highbrow needs, or that they degraded and diminished high culture, but rather that they failed to satisfy the cultural needs of large numbers of ordinary people. He cited figures from Roper polls showing that only a "tiny fraction" of the listening and viewing public was really satisfied with what it received.[55]

Unlike *The Great Audience,* however, this was a more hopeful, more positive project. Despite his criticisms and his insistence that there was considerable room for improvement in particular ways, Seldes acknowledged that he favored the existing *system* of broadcasting and felt "happy to put up with its shortcomings as long as it preserves its capacity to change." He provided an excellent analysis of television drama: what was good, what was mediocre, and how the whole manner of presentation differed from the live stage. Seldes actually had a very high opinion of TV drama, which at that time was invariably presented live (flubs and all), even though he felt that it had not yet fully realized its own distinctive mode of performance.[56]

Seldes also devoted chapters to major comedians and comedy programs on radio and television, explaining with subtlety and persuasiveness why Jack Benny, Jimmy Durante, Lucille Ball, Sid Caesar, and Imogene Coca were such successful comic geniuses; why Milton Berle was really so dreadful despite his immense popular success; and how Jackie Gleason did have great talent despite Seldes' dislike for his persona and style of presentation. Just when the reader begins to wonder whether a disproportionate amount of space in this book is being devoted to comedy, Seldes makes a compelling case that comedy is inordinately popular in broadcasting, that sponsors favor it over any other type of program, and that "the quantity of comic stuff proliferating on the air may choke off the other normal species of entertainment." Under those circumstances Seldes' in-depth attention to comedy seems altogether appropriate. Besides, as Seldes also noted, comedy left audiences in a "most favorable state for persuasion—the non-critical, gratified mood of consent, the mood most hospitable to the commercial message." Given those realities, the critic's assessment of comedy became no laughing matter. It was extremely serious business.[57]

Central to Seldes' mission in this book was his desire to embrace and connect *all* of the public arts, a desire exemplified by his joint dedication of the book to Edward R. Murrow and Jimmy Durante. As he explained in an almost fulsome tribute to the two men, the fields in which they worked were really parts of the same endeavor, a connection that he had not previously recognized: "the lively arts and the mass media are two aspects of the same phenomenon, which I now call 'the public arts.'"[58]

Seldes repeatedly emphasized throughout the book actual transformations that had occurred in popular culture since the 1920s and the attendant changes in his publicly stated views. Radio, for example, had been transformative for two reasons. By arriving in the privacy of so many million homes it made entertainment universally available and certainly paved the way for mass culture. It was also revolutionary because it turned out to be, in its second decade, so closely tied to commercial imperatives and objectives. As for Seldes' adjustments, by 1956 he moderated his hostility toward educational television and urged that educators be given a fair chance to make their own mistakes and learn from experience. Without quite saying so, he seemed ready to acknowledge that the commercial networks would never offer very much in the way of learning programs, or highbrow stuff, or possibly even middlebrow content.[59]

There were also, perhaps inevitably, some significant elements of continuity with his earlier work. He remained committed to the notion of American exceptionalism, for example, but now in a muted form that arose only a few times in his text. Declaring that the United States had neither classic nor folk arts that were genuinely its own, he insisted that the popular arts in America were indeed indigenous—manifestations of the national character, actually. What he now preferred to call the public arts were so crucial because of their connective nature. They are, he declared, "a cross-section of the classic, the folk, and the fine arts, and you may think of this cross-section as fanning out from a narrow base in the classics, widening in the folk arts, and almost as broad in the field of the popular arts as the field itself."[60]

Although reviewers generally admired the book, they did not view it as a landmark the way they had *The Great Audience* and, long before that, *The 7 Lively Arts.* A few in the San Francisco *Chronicle* and the Chicago Sunday *Tribune,* for example, had nothing but praise. Charles Siepmann, an established authority on the media and chairman of the Communications Department at New York University, observed in the *New York Times Book Review* that despite strong criticism of the media, Seldes persisted in an "optimistic outlook that his own evidence does not always seem to warrant." Writing for the *Herald Tribune Book Review,* Leo Rosten was also complimentary but added that Seldes found himself in "an uncomfortable wrestling match between his own catholicity and his sterner image of the good, the true and the beautiful." Others generally said that whether or not one agreed with all of his points, Seldes was invariably stimulating. A reviewer for *The Atlantic,* Phoebe Adams, admired the clarity of Seldes' diagnosis but found his recommendations "disappointingly vague."[61]

Hollis Alpert began his laudatory assessment with the observation that Seldes "probably can be considered our most responsible critic, not only because he is a sort of watch-dog of the rights and the welfare of the public in the area of communications and entertainment, but because he has done what few critics of his stature have done, the continual assessing, evaluation, and appreciation of our popular arts."[62]

Now that Seldes had reached the age of sixty-three and seemed to many an elder statesman in the field of cultural criticism, the *New York Times Book Review* ran an interview that really emerged as a personal profile, picturing Seldes at ease for the summer in an abandoned post office located behind the dunes of Truro on Cape Cod—without a television set, the medium that he pursued most closely in *The Public Arts*. Consistent with his somewhat wary and caustic mood, Seldes struck a note familiar to writers rejuvenating themselves in the wake of a long project: "Sometime I'd like to do the whole history of the broadcasting industry in photographs and cartoons with long captions." His response to the final question had a flippant tone, yet fair. "I've been carrying on a lover's quarrel with the popular arts for years," he mused. "It's been fun. Nothing like them."[63]

Even as he spoke, two sociologists collaborated to produce a long anthology titled *Mass Culture: The Popular Arts in America,* a volume that achieved, even more effectively than Seldes' *The Public Arts,* a balanced view of virtually every aspect of mass culture. The editors chose seventy-five selections; and because one editor styled himself a strong critic of the popular arts while the other felt far more friendly, the selections range across an evaluative spectrum from hostile to supportive. Macdonald, Adorno, Fiedler, McLuhan, Lazarsfeld, Riesman, Wilson, and Seldes himself were all included, along with many other "usual suspects."

Some of their views seemed odd at the time and even stranger many years later. Dwight Macdonald dated the appearance of mass culture to the early nineteenth century, and sociologist Leo Lowenthal emphasized the centrality of popular culture back in the seventeenth and eighteenth centuries in Europe. Lowenthal's argument was much more carefully grounded in empirical information, but neither man addressed himself to the historian's question, How did we get from one configuration in time to another?, nor did they concern themselves with the obvious issue: If we designate this as "mass" culture in the early nineteenth century, how does it differ from what people subsequently understood to be mass culture by the later 1950s?[64]

Each contributor had the opportunity, of course, to perpetuate his own quirky opinions. So we get Macdonald, for instance, asserting that "mass culture is at best a vulgarized reflection of High Culture" (p. 61), proclaiming that mass culture was considerably older than the middlebrow variant, and casually lumping "popular with mass culture" (p. 63). Needless to say, critics reacted in quite varied ways to such generalizations. Harold Rosenberg, for example, wrote a shrill review for *Dissent*. The whole project seemed to him an exercise in futility. He resented any act of this sort that validated kitsch by providing it with an intellectual rationale. As for critics of mass culture who contaminated themselves by revealing in broad daylight that they *had* views on the subject, Rosenberg explained that he found something "annoying about the mental cast of those who keep handling the goods while denying any appetite for them." Because Rosenberg had nothing but scorn for mass culture, he passionately wanted critics to ignore it totally. Consequently he did not even respect Dwight Macdonald because he paid considerable attention to mass culture, albeit disapproving. Rosenberg was nothing if not pithy, however. "The common argument of the mass-culture intellectuals that they have come not to bathe in the waters but to register the degree of its pollution does not impress me," he insisted. "I believe they play in this stuff because they like it, including those who dislike what they like."[65]

Not surprisingly, though, Seldes felt gratified by the appearance of such a collection, one whose very existence owed much to the discourse he had been promulgating for well over three decades. He proclaimed it "the best book on the subject now available." Seldes conceded that a "small fragment of professional thinkers about the media cannot control the media themselves. . . . But by constantly increasing the number of individuals who see what is happening, we multiply the forces of control." He hoped that the volume, already a book club selection, would be widely read, in part because he wondered whether the very act of reading might not decline a generation hence as television and film reduced the desire to learn from print culture, and the passive reception of visual information had become so much more congenial.[66]

The great debate over mass culture and its impact reached its peak in 1957 with the appearance of *Mass Culture*, yet it has endured ever since because so many of the misperceptions committed at that time persisted for decades, such as the inability or unwillingness to differentiate meaningfully between popular culture and mass culture. Even Rosenberg and White made that error in writing the preface to their book (p. vi); and almost a decade later when historian David M. Potter reviewed the manuscript of a history of American culture, he raised the following issues:

> It attempts to combine a thesis—that popular culture is in relatively good condition, with a survey of almost all aspects of culture. . . . The first chapter really sets the book up as a defense of American popular culture and a reply to the critics of mass society, [yet the author] veers away from

some of the really cogent arguments of the critics of mass culture. It may be that their theory could be taken apart, but there is really very little analysis of their line of reasoning in this manuscript, and very little recognition that things which improve the reproduction of culture products technically—such as the phonograph—do not necessarily enrich the quality of the culture.[67]

By the later 1960s scholars had begun to assess with some detachment the critique of mass culture that flourished only a decade earlier. They recognized that it tended to be "too cerebral" in the sense of being the product of ready-made theory applied to highly vulnerable but moving targets. The difficulty there was that ideological proclivities shaped the ways in which theory was applied: Too many people detested mass and/or popular culture either because they were conservative snobs or because they were leftists who feared that film and television available in gluttonous proportions would de-politicize the masses. The word "nar-cotic" recurs in their rhetoric.* By 1970, the year that Seldes died, we find critics like Leslie Fiedler expressing regret for his own (and his entire generation's) condescension toward popular culture. A transfor-mation of attitudes was largely complete.[68]

V

Seldes' book *The Public Arts* devoted much more space to television than to any other medium, an accurate harbinger of his priorities during the remaining years of his professional career. In a chapter of that book devoted to the relationship between public opinion and television, Seldes casually proposed and offered to practice "a new relationship between critic and broadcaster." The system as it then existed seemed unsatisfac-tory because those in charge of the industry felt aggrieved by the "heavy-weight critics" they regarded as being blind to the virtues and hypersen-sitive to the defects of broadcasting. The critics, for their part, "know that, unless a gross breach of propriety occurs, they cannot arouse public

---

*For the meaning of the frequently used word "narcotic," see Irving Howe, "Notes on Mass Culture," *Politics* 5 (Spring 1948): 120–23. "Mass culture is thus orientated toward a central aspect of industrial society: the depersonalization of the individual. On the one hand, it diverts the worker from his disturbing reduction to semi-robot status by arrang-ing 'relaxing' amusements for him. The need for such amusements explains the ceaseless and hectic quest for novelty in the mass-culture industries."

indignation and are virtually impotent to affect the decisions of broadcasters and sponsors."[69]

Behind that apparently benign and somewhat abstract proposal lay an ongoing issue—a festering sore, in fact—involving Seldes and his good friend Edward R. Murrow, the distinguished newscaster and one of the two men to whom Seldes dedicated *The Public Arts,* the other being Jimmy Durante. To understand the dispute between Seldes and Murrow, which actually persisted from 1954 until 1958, two distinct kinds of contextual information are needed.

First, from the very beginning of television's commercial history in 1947–48, but even prior to that on the radio, it had been extremely unclear whether news broadcasters were only supposed to present facts, or whether they could offer opinions about the facts as well. Elmer Davis, a distinguished news analyst, didn't see any problem because in his view the commentator should not be permitted to deviate from the truth, but should be allowed to offer his judgment concerning motives and meanings.* Edward R. Murrow, however, found the issue much more complicated because he wondered what might happen if a spectacularly successful demagogue won a considerable following on television or radio. Murrow was highly sensitive to the issue of responsibly using a powerful medium, especially when serious political issues were involved.[70]

Seldes, meanwhile—and this is the second segment of contextual information—had for many years been pre-occupied in his own way, for his own reasons, with the vital need for fairness in public presentations concerning disputed issues. As early as 1938 he stated that if a movie house showed some sort of film in favor of capital punishment, it ought to show a film taking the opposite side to substantially the same audience. He also said that it would be criminal "to utter editorial statements while pretending you are a disembodied (and totally disinterested) voice." In 1943, when Seldes worked for CBS, he explained that it was the network's policy "to present both sides of controversial issues as fairly as possible." I have found in Seldes' papers, moreover, that in 1943 he clipped and saved an item from the *New York Times* in which James L.

<hr/>

*On January 25, 1958, the State Historical Society of Wisconsin opened its new Mass Communications History Center with a symposium devoted to mass communications in historical perspective. One of the principal themes was the still controversial "Role of the Commentator," the subject of two papers and a discussion that are available on tape (#155A, 1–5) at the State Historical Society in Madison.

Fly, chairman of the FCC, declared that fair presentation of the news and related issues was an absolute obligation.[71]

In 1952, moreover, when Seldes published a kind of manual called *Writing for Television,* he anticipated the very issues that brought him into conflict with Murrow two years later. Today, he explained, news broadcasters are permitted to take sides on controversial public questions "provided they offer equal opportunity to their opponents." Earlier that year Murrow sent Seldes a warm note of thanks for the critic's cordial congratulations on Murrow's "wise and generous and intelligent" Christmas program for "See It Now."[72]

In January 1954, however, Seldes published an essay about the proper role of commentary in the broadcast of television news. He speculated about whether news anchormen should be free to editorialize, or whether newscasting and commentary ought to be formally compartmentalized. He wondered whether a solution lay in having the weekly discussion programs complement the ideal of an utterly neutral news broadcast—just the facts. After criticizing programs like "Chronoscope" that dealt with controversial topics but offered one-sided opinions, Seldes singled out Murrow's "See It Now" because it either presented both sides of an issue or else called attention to the suppression of ideas within the context of an issue that seemed one-sided in the public arena. Seldes admired Murrow above all others in the business because the latter respected "the decencies of human argument."[73]

Seldes then called attention to a curious discrepancy. Whereas FCC regulators required network productions to provide balanced answers to questions they raised, commercially sponsored programs did not face the same requirement. Seldes insisted that the public interest necessitated news programs that would "insure us against both the massive power of those who can pay for programs and the power of stations afraid to offend the sponsors." He closed by urging that empirical studies be made to learn which kinds of programs were most likely to be one-sided, and where the basic responsibility lay to insure fairness in the public interest. The essay carried a subtitle that served as a virtual warning that Seldes held very strong feelings about the matter: "Can television solve the problems of balanced news reporting which radio has yet to master?"[74]

On March 9, 1954, Murrow devoted "See It Now" to a critical exposé of Senator Joseph R. McCarthy and his demagogic methods. Virtually all liberals applauded it as a huge success and as a demystification from which McCarthy's reputation never really recovered. Murrow, already a kind of hero to many because of his courageous broadcasts from London during World War II, swiftly became the most visible and the most idolized man in public communications. But Gilbert Seldes, ever true to his principles, swallowed hard and, in what became one of his most widely read and controversial columns, charged that Murrow had fundamentally slanted the presentation by selecting only those clips that portrayed McCarthy in the most unfavorable light possible. Few of Seldes' friends and associates, all liberals, agreed with him in this particular instance, and even fewer could understand that for him the requirement of being faithful to one's principles was a matter of basic integrity. Even the editors of the *Saturday Review* appended a note to Seldes' piece acknowledging that "this particular column has caused considerable discussion and debate among the staff."[75]

Seldes began by observing that critics of broadcasting were so impressed by Murrow's coverage and were so sympathetic to his perspective that "they haven't troubled to discuss the thorny problems in the field of communications which the broadcast brought into focus":

> This is a pity, because in the long run it is more important to use our communications systems properly than to destroy McCarthy, and every new development in the handling of controversy in television, particularly, needs to be examined to make sure that the enthusiasm of a crusading liberal hasn't placed new weapons in the hands of demagogues. There are no ground rules yet, no standards of conduct in the newest and most powerful of the mass media; we have to watch it vigilantly.

He then declared that while the formula requiring "equal time" made sense in theory, it really did not work very well in practice, as demonstrated by McCarthy's thirty-minute response on April 6. Why? Because nothing close to equality could really be achieved. The networks have time, resources, and technical expertise totally on their side. Moreover, in an argument that would have been a catch-22 for Murrow if he had taken it to heart, Seldes added that "See It Now" had a decisive advantage in any "equal time" pairing precisely because the program had always "been identified with integrity, with fairness, with a sense of responsibility and justice." Who would take the opposing half-hour seriously except true believers of the viewpoint being challenged? "Because a broadcaster cannot supply equal skill and equal prestige to an adversary, the offer of equal time isn't good enough." Then, to complicate matters even more, Seldes almost seemed to strain in envisioning potential pitfalls. There was also the danger, he believed, that the offer of equal time would be considered as "absolving the attacker from all obligations, so that fair play within a broadcast will not be necessary, since another broadcast may redress whatever imbalances the first creates. We know the force of the first blow: the accusation with which the defense never catches up, the lingering suspicion that smoke must conceal fire."[76]

Seldes felt that all of those negative film clips of McCarthy at his most inane needed to be balanced by clips that showed him at his most effective. Precisely because McCarthy was a powerful and successful demagogue, Seldes argued, it was not "good politics" to present such a menacing person as an "incompetent fool." Beyond that, he believed, negative depictions that ridiculed a public figure needed to be balanced in any program offered as a "report." Seldes suggested that people who "roared with delight" over them should ask themselves how they would have felt if the same technique had been applied to someone they liked, such as Adlai Stevenson? He closed by acknowledging that Murrow's editorial at the end of this program had been eloquent, whereas McCarthy had been rambling, stale, and dull. "I got the impression that the giant Murrow had been fighting a pigmy. Intellectually this may be right; politically I remain as frightened as if I had seen a ghost—the ghost of Hitler, to be specific."[77]

Liberals were generally puzzled by Seldes' concerns about precedent and high principles. The damaging substance of Murrow's achievement seemed easily to outweigh what might happen if, at some future time, the white hats became black hats and the process were reversed.* Murrow, who worried immensely about his future relations with CBS and his sponsor, Alcoa—with good reason, it should be noted, because neither one appreciated controversy—was annoyed and let Seldes know it privately. Other television critics, like Jack Gould, gave Seldes' position a sympathetic hearing while applauding the adverse effects that Murrow's program had on McCarthy's credibility.[78]

In May and July, Seldes devoted columns to the networks' problematic coverage of the McCarthy–Army hearings. He pleaded that the really big issue, the industry's obligations to the public, should be openly discussed on television itself, nationally and locally. He continued to deride CBS and NBC for deciding after two days of the hearings that not enough people were watching to justify the expense, thereby leaving the

---

*James L. Baughman believes that the effect of Murrow's attack on McCarthy has been widely overestimated. See *The Republic of Mass Culture: Journalism, Filmmaking, and Broadcasting in America Since 1941* (Baltimore, 1992), 52.

coverage to ABC and Dumont, both quite minor networks at that time. Seldes and many senators alike speculated whether the hearings had been significantly affected because they had been televised, and the question arose whether broadcasts of this unusual nature should or should not be interrupted by commercial messages. Most of these issues were being raised for the very first time (the Kefauver hearings on organized crime in 1951 were fascinating but far less controversial), and so Seldes' strong conviction on the fairness question seemed much less obvious at the time than it may in retrospect. "If the existence of the audience is having an evil effect, we are up against an 'agonizing reappraisal' of the democratic process; and I would sooner have Congress mend its manners than take away the right of the people to look upon their lawmakers."[79]

When Seldes wrote *The Public Arts* in 1955–56 he devoted two chapters to this episode in which he offered lavish praise for "See It Now" as a series, calling it "the most important program in television," and for Murrow as well, designating him "the conscience of the broadcasting industry." Seldes conceded that after many months of discussion with Murrow and others his views were "somewhat modified," though he did not specify how; and his account of the contretemps softened it somewhat but did not really recant on any matter of principle. Perhaps the most interesting conclusion that Seldes reached—and close readers of his columns could have seen it coming—involved his acceptance of a double standard in terms of public accountability between the press and the electronic media. "The moment a newspaper accepts compulsion [meaning regulation of any sort] it ceases to be part of a free press; whereas the conditions accepted by radio and TV stations spell out the obligations of the broadcaster and the conditional freedom he enjoys." Why conditional? Because the public owned the airwaves and broadcasting was a licensed privilege rather than a right.[80]

Seldes largely devoted the last third of *The Public Arts* to major policy questions concerning broadcasting and the public interest, such as the "right" to editorialize, immunity from censorship, allocation of the ultrahigh frequency channels, the prospects for pay television (largely involving "spectaculars," special athletic events, and so on), and separate channels for educational programs. Ultimately, in sorting out his responses to these matters, Seldes noted that the broadcasters did not feel obligated "in any way to serve the public if they can make more money by not serving it." He then elaborated upon his distinction between the press and television, observing that the press lacked comparable power to expose or conceal an event so consequential as a congressional hearing. If one newspaper committed a sin of omission, another would undoubtedly compensate; "but if no network covers a hearing, vast numbers of people will either know nothing of it or consider it negligible." Therefore, Seldes concluded, "the power so to manipulate our political responses should not be in the hands of commercial broadcasting."[81]

In 1957, having written an effusive dedication to Murrow in *The Public Arts,* Seldes must have believed that the wounds from 1954 were healed, so he asked Murrow to record some passages from a university address he had given at Brandeis. Seldes wanted to use Murrow's remarks, along with others, in a discussion manual for the mass media provided by the Fund for Adult Education. Murrow ignored the request for six months; Seldes not only renewed it but warned Murrow that yet another "totally ill-informed and uncalled for attack" was imminent! It was brief and it essentially repeated what Seldes had said in *The Public Arts:* That Murrow's "Person to Person" show was banal and "indicates a low and contemptuous estimate of human values." He did not comprehend how the same person could also produce such a distinguished program as "See It Now."[82]

That sharp barb infuriated Murrow, who wrote a curt reply declining to make the recording, calling Seldes' language "intemperate," and indicating that "[Seldes] attributed motives to my colleagues and myself that went far beyond the bounds of legitimate criticism." Some of Murrow's staff sent angry letters to Seldes, which he answered by saying that Krishna Menon, the Indian statesman, was the only impressive or interesting person to appear on the program and that "every guest I've myself known has been from 25 to 50% less of a human being, a total person, than I've known him or her to be." In brief, Murrow somehow trivialized the distinguished guests he interviewed.[83] If Seldes' critique of "Person to Person" seems curious or strained, keep in mind the goals and seriousness of purpose that characterized his own CBS radio series, "Americans at Work," in 1938.

On March 8 Seldes gave over his TV and Radio column in the *Saturday Review* to an angry letter in defense of Murrow written by Morris Ernst, a prominent lawyer and writer on such issues as censorship. Seldes held his ground and insisted that the kinds of interviews conducted on "Person to Person" invariably descended into trivia and thereby diminished the guest. Moreover, the program tended to emphasize the guest's home and possessions. "The average personality on this program is not individualized. The questions do not lead to their hearts or their minds or their selves. They lead to exhibiting goods and gadgets."[84]

Meanwhile the private exchange of notes and letters became lamentably unpleasant. Seldes told Murrow that because he had criticized the formula of "Person to Person" Murrow had said in "a semi-public place, in front of a group of people including men with whom I work and with whom I couldn't work if my integrity was in doubt, that you couldn't be sure what use I would make of your recording. . . . Your implication was that I was dishonorable. It seems to me that, between us, I have the better right to be aggrieved." Murrow, in turn, insisted that they terminate the correspondence "since I doubt that it will be of any major interest to historians and suspect that it reflects no considerable credit upon either of us."[85]

Thus ended a relationship that Seldes valued with a man he greatly admired. In this instance, Seldes seems to have been his own worst enemy. It would be a charitable explanation that his health had been poor since the previous July. Perhaps he had been feeling out of sorts for some months. Perhaps, once again, his compulsion to be candid got the better of him. When Seldes published *The New Mass Media* he included a capsule summary of the Murrow–McCarthy episode from 1954 in a manner unrepentant and unfavorable to Murrow. It seems ironic that Seldes responded to Hemingway's many egregious slaps by turning the other cheek; yet for some reason he could not do so with Murrow. There is no apparent or plausible explanation.[86]

VI

The most constant variable in Seldes' career, perhaps, was change along with his own recurrent emphasis upon the absolute centrality of change in American culture. Back in 1927 he had criticized foreign observers for being insensitive to the rapidity of change in the United States. When he wrote *Mainland* in 1936 he also highlighted the "traditional American sense of change," more particularly changes that accompanied the democratization of culture in the United States. In the years following World War II he recognized that changes in the nature of leisure affected the entertainment media—and therefore cultural criticism.[87]

When he published *The Great Audience* in 1950, Seldes fully realized how much his views of the popular arts had altered since the 1920s and '30s in response to new and unanticipated circumstances. Writing in 1956 about the revolution in broadcasting then under way, he referred to the "uneasy, in-between stage through which we are passing." He ended *The Public Arts* with a homily: If Americans recognized that those arts were a precipitant as well as a symptom of social change then they had both a right and a duty to give direction to change. Working on his memoir in 1967 he acknowledged in the very first paragraph of one segment that "I changed my own ideas."[88]

Perhaps that sensitivity to change enabled Seldes to spot cultural trends in the making, something that he often did casually in ephemeral essays. In 1940, for example, he complained that ordinary people read poetry less and less because poetry was becoming increasingly obscure. The idea that he offered there in an underdeveloped way would be articulated much more fully by Stuart Hall and his associates in 1965: Namely, that one of the unfortunate attributes of modern culture had been "the progressive alienation of high art from popular art. Few art forms are able to hold both elements together: and popular art has developed a history and a topography of its own, separate from high and experimental art."[89] Similarly, another of his 1940 essays, this one concerned with phony photographs in newspapers and magazines and (unexplained) re-enactments in newsreels, anticipated by more than two decades key elements in Daniel J. Boorstin's book *The Image: A Guide to Pseudo-Events in America.*[90]

When William Attwood returned to the United States in 1954 after nine years abroad as a foreign correspondent, he and his wife wanted to rediscover the United States. They drove more than 10,000 miles through twenty-eight states, spanning vast distances from Boston to Los Angeles and Portland, Oregon, to Palm Beach, Florida. Their most dominant impression? That the country remained the most exciting in the world and that "it is changing faster than even Americans suspect." Their secondary impression sensed the onset of mass culture, primarily generated by physical mobility, a greater amount of leisure time than ever before, and television. "Americans are getting to be more like each other."[91]

Curiously, however, the Attwoods' contact with people at the grass roots caused them to draw optimistic conclusions somewhat at odds with those of the cultural critics active during the mid-1950s. The Attwoods believed, without citing a single source, that "even the intellectuals admit that TV is stimulating new interests [they did not specify what]. As viewers become more selective (and they are), programs will improve." Their positive assertions about television turn out, with the benefit of hindsight, to have been wrong in the long run. But with respect to the decade of the 1950s they may very well have been more accurate than Seldes and his skeptical fellow critics.[92]

Serious studies of television during the 1950s show a surprisingly high level of programming, which eventually gave rise to the designation "golden age of television" for the 1950s. We now know that many television executives and producers wanted to elevate the level of mass culture, encouraged experimentation, and actually achieved more diverse and more unusual programming than there would be for years to come. Erik Barnouw observed that "things were happening in television." He felt a "sense of exploration and achievement." Producers strongly preferred the vitality of live programs, for example, to the sterility of filmed ones.[93]

If historians of television are correct, then Dwight Macdonald and other harsh critics of the electronic media surely overreacted during the early and mid-1950s. The cautious hopefulness that Gilbert Seldes expressed in *The Public Arts* in 1956 appears to have been more judicious, a better informed and more realistic assessment of what was actually happening in the studios and on the screen during the '50s.

In one other respect, however, the Attwoods' optimism would be challenged by cultural critics in the years ahead. The Attwoods proclaimed that "culture is busting out all over," and they cited as evidence that in town after town they found "amateur drama societies, symphony orchestras, art groups and sculpture classes—nearly all of them postwar developments."[94] That upbeat assessment by journalists and travelers persisted into the early 1960s, when it was noticed and challenged by serious cultural critics, people Seldes would have considered highbrows who regarded the Attwoods' judgment as wide of the mark in quantitative as well as qualitative terms.

Harold C. Schonberg, music critic for the *New York Times,* produced a typical blast in which he denounced the so-called national "cultural explosion" as specious. After dismissing the validity of figures commonly cited to demonstrate book sales, program hours of concert music on the radio, and purchases of serious recorded music, he leveled his most lethal fire at the claim that seventy-some new cultural centers had emerged or were in progress. Schonberg's own investigations had shown that "any city erecting a building—any building—can call it a cultural center and have it accepted as such no matter if the project has as much to do with culture as Yogi Berra has to do with Einstein's physics." From Schonberg's perspective, national boosters who bragged that American culture was booming did a grave disservice to serious cultural needs and aspirations in the United States. In key respects he was correct, of course, but his disdain for non-professional activities at the grass-roots level revealed that highbrow standards of measurement remained very much in evidence early in the 1960s.[95]

After forty years, Gilbert Seldes' critical campaigns had won many battles but not the war. He would devote his final decade to education at several levels, to setting the record straight about shifts in the cultural climate of opinion between the wars, and, by no means least, to sifting through the conflicting claims being made about consumerism and the commercialization of culture in the United States.

10

Commerce, Communications, and Criticism

Although Seldes produced no major works during the final decade of his career, he wrote a number of extended essays that epitomized and emended his enduring concerns with the mass media and public entertainment. There is a sense in which his professional life unraveled during the 1960s: He did not complete a projected work on the social consequences of advertising; he underwent a challenging but sometimes difficult period as founding dean of the Annenberg School of Communications at Penn; and when interruptions and ill-health did not dog him, he wrestled intensely with a memoir that he never pulled together, an attempt at coming to terms with his major endeavors and the cultural transformations he had witnessed.

Although none of these enterprises achieved success, each of them is instructive because it illuminates rapid patterns of social change that many contemporaries responded to with ambivalence and ultimately found elusive from a judgmental perspective. What to make of a consumer culture that had come to dominate all aspects of American life? How best to comprehend modernism and the cultural innovations that flourished at all levels during the interwar decades? Although Seldes understood perfectly well that his great preoccupations of the later period—mass communications, public relations, and advertising—were closely connected, he did not articulate the links quite so forcefully as the galaxy of critics half a generation younger than himself, who often tended to be more cynical, more tough-minded perhaps, but also less judicious at times. Writing about advertising and entertainment, for example, Marshall McLuhan declared that theirs was the first age in which shrewd people "have made it a full-time business to get inside the collective public mind. To get inside in order to manipulate, exploit, control is the object now. . . . So many minds are engaged in bringing about this condition of public helplessness."[1]

Responding to the same troubling nexus seven years later, Raymond Williams was even more succinct. "The whole powerful array of mass cultural institutions has one keystone," he remarked: "money from advertising." As early as the 1950s Williams worried about the commercialized character of mass culture, and recognized that to change what was vulgar about mass culture one would have to alter the role played by advertising. On the American side of this pan-Atlantic assessment it is symptomatic that *Fortune* magazine commissioned young Alvin Toffler to prepare an essay that appeared as "The Quantity of Culture" in 1961 and subsequently, in expanded form, as a book titled *The Culture Consumers* (1964).[2]

The nexus that critics like Williams, Toffler, and Seldes responded to during the 1950s and '60s was not new; but it certainly had expanded, and observers believed that its consequences had increased profoundly. A revolution began early in the 1890s when Samuel S. McClure and Frank A. Munsey lowered the prices of their flossy magazines to fifteen and ten cents respectively in order to attract a much larger readership. Other publishers swiftly followed their example, and they all assumed that increased profits would result from the higher volume of advertising that a much enhanced circulation would attract.[3]

Seventy years later, however, because of the revolution in electronic communications and the emergence of a truly mass culture, issues of power and responsibility came to be raised in ways that no one could have envisioned at the close of the nineteenth century. When President John F. Kennedy addressed the National Association of Broadcasters in 1961, he surprised them by acknowledging the immense consequences of their enterprise. "The flow of ideas, the capacity to make informed choices, the ability to criticize, all the assumptions on which political democracy rests," he told them, "depend largely upon communication. And you are the guardians of the most powerful and effective means of communication ever designed."[4]

During these very years, 1959 to 1963, Seldes served as founding dean of the Annenberg School of Communications in Philadelphia. His major essays at that time dealt with such broad topics as "The Public Interest" and ethical standards in the world of broadcasting. He commanded immense respect, ultimately signified by his election in 1963 to the American Academy of Arts and Letters; and his longstanding concern with the media, consumerism, and public entertainment caused many to regard him as sui generis among critics. The chairman of the English Department at New York University acknowledged in 1965 that he himself lacked special expertise on the mass media, broadly conceived: "But who, save Gilbert Seldes, could be so designated?" He then added that "a pluralistic critic should have pluralistic interests," a desideratum that Seldes exemplified and supported 100 percent.[5]

Meanwhile, soon after completing *The Public Arts* in 1956, Seldes began to work on an extended reconsideration of the arts and related cultural endeavors, such as criticism, in the United States during the 1920s and '30s. But first the deanship and then a series of medical problems in the mid-1960s made sustained work on that project difficult when not impossible. Emotional hurdles also stood in the way. As he explained to two very old friends in 1962, even before his health collapsed (1964 to 1967), "although it isn't really a memoir it deals with the past and many people long dead and I find it painful to write."[6]

He completed a detailed prospectus by the autumn of 1964, and at the time of his death six years later he had written or dictated dozens of segments concerning people, episodes, and developments to which he had borne witness. The segments, along with what Seldes had to say about them, are important for several reasons: partially for the additional light that they shed on cultural activities in the United States during the interwar years; also because of the curious changes of heart that he underwent concerning some key figures from that fascinating time; but above all, perhaps, because of Seldes' personal struggle with memory. Toward the end he came to recognize that it may well have been the most elusive and unreliable medium that he tried to deal with in an entire lifetime devoted to observing and understanding media.

Memory turned out to be the most capricious, the most vulnerable, and the most problematic. As he told one close friend in 1968, "I am dismayed at my failing memory," a comment that he also made to beloved associates of long standing, like Marianne Moore, and to more recent antagonists with whom he sought reconciliation, like Dwight Macdonald. Memory became the most frustrating nemesis of old age.[7]

I

To Seldes' credit it should be acknowledged that he gave serious attention to the role of advertising and consumerism in American life more than a generation before it became common practice for cultural critics to do so. On the not so creditable side, however, it also has to be conceded that his responses were not notably consistent, a pattern that cannot simply be explained away by calling attention to the changing nature of advertising itself. We have already seen just how critical Seldes could be of radio commercials early in the 1930s and again two decades later.[8] He complained especially about hard-sell advertisements, and in 1937 he devoted an *Esquire* essay to the problem of immature advertising: "All of the things which men and women enjoy after the first flush and heyday of their youth are still associated in the advertisements with the 'teens or at a pinch with the early twenties." Unlike later critics of rampant commercialism in the United States, who tended to fire casual broadsides, Seldes usually got down to nitty-gritty-issues:

> One of these days American business will have to reconcile itself to the fact that it is selling to the middle-aged and that a considerable number of the middle-aged may be put off buying a lipstick or a roadster if it is constantly advertised as peculiarly suitable to the bright lads and even brighter hoydens of about seventeen. The age limit in the advertisements will have to rise. We are all willing to cut off five years or perhaps ten, but what we want to see in the advertisements are men and women not too overwhelmingly different from ourselves.[9]

Nevertheless, there is yet another aspect to Seldes' perspective on the stimuli to a consumer culture. In 1932 he called attention to the positive role of advertising agencies in guiding industrial artists and designers to be creative and produce attractive products. In that same year he also stated that ads in the United States were more subtle than in Europe. The latter usually confined themselves to statements of fact, whereas American advertisers had mastered the art of association: washing soap for clothes being linked with women going to a matinee, a soft drink in the hands of a suave man emphasized leisure and refreshment rather than any specific qualities of the beverage, and so forth.[10]

As we have also seen, Seldes became annoyed when critics were excessively caustic about commercialism on the radio; and in 1933 he emphasized the need for consumerism if the economy were to recover. As he put it in a daily column, his tongue only partially in his cheek, "no one has a right to be born unless he (or she) is prepared to take on a proper share of the universal burden—which is to spend money. What this world needs is a good consumer." And yet, five years later he informed middle-class Americans—perhaps because he believed that economic recovery was at hand—that they had been "tricked and cajoled and seduced and persuaded by the advertising manufacturers to select your purchases by following the advertisements. Your great power today is actually your spending power—your right to choose the objects which you are buying."[11]

Following World War II it became especially compelling for culture critics, journalists like Vance Packard, pop sociologists, and some novelists to decry the pernicious influence of advertising in American society.[12] Seldes devoted a chapter of *The Great Audience* (1950) to advertisements on radio and television, along with scattered remarks elsewhere in the book. Although highly critical in many respects (ads were tasteless, repetitious, insulting to the intelligence, made misleading claims, and so on), Seldes explained the crucial role of advertising agencies more clearly than anyone else had done, and even saw a silver lining. Once the networks had sold their quota of time to sponsors, those with time slots still remaining open devoted their energies to developing quality programs that could be showcased and serve as models of innovation. By 1951, as Seldes turned his attention increasingly to ads on television, he regarded the animated cartoon ad as a fairly benign improvement—almost entertaining—such as the singing and dancing commercials created by Lucky Strike cigarettes.[13]

By 1952, having listened to and watched a vast number of commercials, Seldes decided to write a book on the subject, called "The Motives of Advertising." Although he never completed the project, the essays that he did produce are interesting because of their fresh perspective and personal touch. They are more thoughtful than the customary attacks written by cultural purists. Seldes began a 1954 essay by establishing his primary credential to be a critic in this new field. "I am a professional in the most important branch of the advertising business—which is, of course, the receiving end. I have read more ads and listened to more commercials than any copy writer has composed."[14]

Rather than offering the customary blanket criticism, he became interested in assessing and measuring effective strategies. Consequently he argued that too much advertising was aimed at attracting new consumers, while too little was directed at the present clientele. It seemed a mistake, in Seldes' view, to concentrate upon the patrons of competitors.

Why? The major risk involved in aiming excessive hype at the potential customer was "*un*selling the regular customer who is satisfied with the primary quality of the product, but doesn't get—and is painfully aware of not getting—all that the advertising appears to promise." That sense of being let down or disappointed made the regular customer vulnerable to the seductions of rival brands. "He needs to be immunized—by being reminded of his satisfactions."[15]

In a related essay, written at about the same time, Seldes anticipated the work of scholars like Michael Schudson by taking a serious look at the history and sociology of advertising. He found it unfortunate that while advertising used the mass media and provided the principal support for some of the most important ones, advertising itself was not then considered a medium of communication. He suggested that just as most printed ads actually constituted a form of information, television commercials were (or ought to be) a form of entertainment. That meant, according to Seldes, that successful commercials would have to meet the aesthetic standards and the social expectations of sound entertainment. Striking a positive note, he asserted that some of the best commercials did exactly that.[16]

An acutely felt ambivalence about advertising had characterized Seldes' interest in the volatile phenomenon ever since it "took off" during the 1920s. Recognizing its immense importance in 1925, he called advertising a "fascinating manifestation of American impulses, as expressive of certain things about us as any art we possess; and nothing gives the tempo of American life more definitely than the speed with which advertising changes its appeal and its direction." While that certainly validated more than three subsequent decades of intense interest on his part, Seldes emerged as a trenchant critic from the outset. "Cajolery has changed to a subtle seduction," he remarked, "as in the class-advertising which hardly describes the product at all but concentrates on the superior social qualities of its patrons." He speculated that perhaps a high standard of living had made American advertising undemocratic in the sense that it catered to the wealthy and made less affluent people into consumers whose desires exceeded their means.[17]

By 1957 Seldes acknowledged that he wouldn't complete the book he meant to write about "the advertising arts"; yet his interest in the subject persisted for several more years. In June 1957 he wrote a guarded though positive review of Vance Packard's new work, *The Hidden Persuaders,* a description of psychological tactics being used by manufacturers "to assault the purchaser's purse." Seldes made it clear, however, that while

Packard had belatedly discovered what social psychologists call motivational research, Seldes himself had spent almost a year working on a promotional project for a daytime serial along with Dr. Ernest Dichter, who almost certainly had invented the concept of M.R. Seldes particularly welcomed findings by Packard that reinforced his own, such as the judgment made by some TV sponsors that "too good a program, too funny or too exciting, is bad for sales because the audience talks during the commercial" or is for some reason not readily disposed to accept it. The serious use of social psychology by sponsors scared Seldes for reasons that can be related to his concern about Murrow's failure to be perfectly fair in his McCarthy program: potential manipulation of the unwary or unwitting viewer. As Seldes put it in his evaluation of Packard's book: "the deeper the [promotional] research goes, the more effective the methods become—and when you couple these with the still unplumbed effectiveness of our new mass media, you may approach the robot-state."[18]

Even though Seldes had explicitly abandoned his book on "The Motives of Advertising" by 1957, he still found the subject irresistibly important and interesting. In 1957–58 he published a series of three essays in *Tide,* a trade journal in the advertising field that started in 1927 and was eventually absorbed by *Printer's Ink.* Appropriately enough, his overall theme was the criticism of advertising copy from the perspective of sound communication (as opposed to a strict reckoning by sales).

Responding to some negative reactions to his previous pieces in *Tide,* Seldes observed that the advertising business wished to be immune from criticism and got strangely upset "when a little does get into print." He called attention to a danger that highly professionalized copywriters faced: inadvertently writing for colleagues in the business rather than for ordinary consumers. But in comparing advertising with his biggest interest by the later 1950s, television, Seldes lessened the sting of his criticism. He acknowledged that advertising certainly wasn't the only form of communication that commonly defeated itself by "starting the mind of the recipient off in the wrong direction." That seems to have been a common failing of television drama, for instance.[19]

In his last book Seldes declared that no evidence demonstrated that large numbers of people actually disliked television commercials. In fact, he even saw reason to believe that many commercials were accepted because they were amusing or instructive. The notion that commercials were anathema to civilized society came from a small minority of worrisome intellectuals. A few years later, however, he strongly supported one politician's battle against the interruption of news by commercials. What could be more irritating than the following, the third interruption in a fifteen-minute newscast: "A great lady died today. More on that after this message." Even then, however, the *manner* of the interruption seems to have been more offensive than the inevitability of sponsorship itself. Seldes indicated that the newscaster might have said: "Lady Astor died today. I'll give you the highlights of her career after this message." That would have been at least tolerable, he believed.[20]

Even though Seldes tended to be more forgiving about the offensive sins of advertising than most cultural critics, it bothered him nonetheless that the industry seemed to be so impervious to constructive criticism, a tendency that he referred to as the "immunity" of advertising, which became the overall title for his 1958 series of essays in *Tide*. It infuriated him that the advertising trade persisted in making this assumption: "If the campaign is a success, it's the advertising; if it's a failure, it's the product."

At the Tamiment conference on "Mass Culture and Mass Media," held in June 1959, Seldes met Patrick Hazard, a young faculty member in English, journalism, and cultural studies at the University of Pennsylvania who scorned the highbrows for being so uppity about advertising. A few months later, when Seldes set up shop as dean of the Annenberg School of Communications there, Hazard became one of his most engaged faculty members, and it seems likely that Hazard's views reinforced Seldes' disposition to be critical yet realistic about the necessity for generous commercial sponsorship if television was going to fulfill its potential by offering first-rate programs.[21]

II

Early in 1959, when Seldes learned that Walter Annenberg had decided to endow a school of communications at Penn, he swiftly devoted an essay in the *Saturday Review* to praising the timeliness of this academic innovation. Without seeking to flatter anyone—though perhaps hoping for a last hurrah—he noted that the Annenberg name "is connected with both the press and television, and the augury is a good one because we are in the critical stage of the shift between print and electronics as the prime medium of disseminating information, carrying on debate, and providing diversion." He expressed the hope that graduates of such a school, and the broad range of people they affected, would behave more wisely as a result of what they had learned. He made that wish more specific with a sentence revealing an element of subjectivity: he connected the cultural transformation so central to his own later years with a designation that he must now have envisioned as reputable—responsible aesthete. "So far as communications deals with the mass arts," he commented, "this means that a school must help to create a new kind of man who might be called a responsible aesthete."[22]

Apparently the timeliness of that piece got him the job as dean—after Edward R. Murrow declined. Seldes' decision to accept an appointment as professor of journalism along with the deanship at Annenberg (initially designated as director) did not mark quite such a radical departure in his career as it might at first seem. It is certainly true that he had, on occasion, made uncomplimentary remarks about academic scholars. But between the mid-1930s and the later 1950s he had accepted invitations to visit colleges and universities as a lecturer, mainly in New England and the Middle West. And from 1954 until 1956 he had enjoyed teaching various courses in Columbia University's School of General Studies. There is a press release from Columbia located in Seldes' papers with a quotation that he highlighted in pencil: "Although in college courses we do a reasonably good job of preparing people to live intelligently in a world of books, the theatre, concerts, and museums, we have not given our students similar bases for understanding and judging the products of films, radio, and television." That is exactly the need he filled at Columbia, of course, and those would also be his priorities at the Annenberg School —especially television. (In 1958 Walter Annenberg, the publisher of *TV Guide*, had actually wanted to call it a school of tele-communication.)[23]

During the mid- and later 1950s he had also taught classes on an ad hoc basis at a television school located on West 57th Street. Moreover, several acquaintances had described him over the years as being professorial in manner. Seldes was more often debonair than didactic, I believe, but he always cared deeply about education. Starting in 1965, when he went to Truro for the summer he took a number of young people under his wing and provided them with a kind of group tutorial each Sunday on American literature and culture, primarily from the 1920s and '30s. These sessions came to be so lively and well attended that by the end of the decade Seldes speculated about the prospect of his informal pedagogical experiment becoming a model, that it could be replicated "in the parks of large cities and on the beaches of metropolitan areas." Although it may sound naive to us, Seldes believed that genuine cerebral excitement might actually serve to forestall or counteract the youthful rebelliousness and disorderly behavior of the later 1960s.[24]

One other contextual aspect should be noticed in seeking to understand how a life-long independent critic could become a dean at a major university. The sociologist Lewis Coser offered this comment in 1965: "One of the most important observations that can be made about unattached intellectuals in contemporary America is that there are so few of them." Why? Coser pointed to the demise of avant-garde culture and radical ideology, on the one hand, and the expansive rise of academe since World War II on the other. New institutes and schools flourished, many of them not affiliated with traditional scholarly disciplines and requiring faculty as well as administrators with "hands on" experience in the so-called real world. As someone who had spent forty-five years in journalism, publishing, radio, film, and television, Seldes seemed ideally suited to head the new Annenberg School, whose curriculum would emphasize broadcasting in general and television in particular. His authorship of *Writing for Television* in 1952 was also a strong credential. By coincidence, moreover, at just about that time Seldes urged Harvard to create a department, a school, or at least a professorial chair in the field of communications. It chose not to, but Penn's initiative in 1959 approximated what Seldes had envisioned for Harvard half a dozen years earlier. He accepted happily.[25]

The arrangements involved in establishing the Annenberg School were haphazard in certain respects. Many important matters, ranging from curriculum to the configuration of faculty appointments, had not been fully worked out, and Seldes did not actually receive his contract until several months after he began work. By April 1960 he pleaded with the university's top administrators for more adequate remuneration because his duties had severely reduced the amount of time available to him for free-lance writing. Equally serious, the modest size of the school's staff made it necessary to narrow its focus promptly in order to avoid being spread too thin. Consequently the performing arts were virtually eliminated from the program at the outset.[26]

A different sort of pressure constrained the new Annenberg School in quite another way, one frequently encountered by new programs of this sort with a vocational mission: achieving academic respectability in the eyes of the rest of the university. Seldes had wanted journalism to be a central component of the curriculum, but the English Department behaved as a kind of watch-dog to make sure that Seldes and his staff wouldn't demean the integrity of journalism from a serious calling into a mere vocational trade. A year after Seldes retired he conveyed his personal feelings on these matters to his successor, including his sense of isolation from related professional programs at Penn. "I think we have managed to get over the initial suspicions of the academic integrity of communications as a subject and of ourselves as a School," he wrote, "but much can be done to involve the School with the major graduate schools."[27]

Seldes' long-range vision for the school included four elements. First, an historical approach to the media emphasizing their origins and development. Second, conveying a critical stance toward all of the media, in which young professionals learned to evaluate how well they fulfilled their functions and purposes. Third, establishing workshops to convey an understanding of the actual mechanics of the media (how to use a television camera, how to make a program, and so on). Fourth, researching the social impact of communications media. Overall, Seldes viewed his program as the counterpart of a law or business school. He hoped to develop well-informed and responsible young people who would enter and elevate standards in the appropriate industries. He fully expected that the school's alumni would significantly improve the media. The school opened in September 1959 with an entering class of thirty. Full enrollment was projected to be 120.[28]

From time to time in those early years the faculty considered undertaking new initiatives, such as offering a course for professionals already employed in communications fields, offering them a conspectus of new theories and concepts in the field as a whole along with supplementary briefings in more specialized areas. Seldes and his colleagues considered weekend seminars, lasting perhaps for three long afternoons during the course of a month. As he remarked in 1964, however, "we were so intent on establishing our foundations" that the steering group postponed these innovative but logical initiatives.[29]

Charles Lee, one of Seldes' closest associates in that group, remembers him vividly: "A fascinating, exuberant man. Congenial. Brilliant. A wonderful raconteur. An enthusiastic teacher and colleague. . . . He was helpful, not just friendly but virtually paternal; he taught me lessons in enthusiasm, industry, courage, humor, and gallantry." (Lee and other faculty members often stopped by Seldes' apartment late in the day for a drink and lively conversation.) Lee taught a seminar built around prominent figures in the media. There would be a lecture by the guest followed by a question-and-answer session attended by Seldes, the school's entire student body, and interested members of the public. Walter Annenberg himself even attended the inaugural session and proclaimed it "very interesting" even though Lee had advised him that the group would be "dealing with tendencies to monopoly in or excesses of power in media control."[30]

Annenberg's interest and presence were frequently problematic for Seldes, and after a year or so the two men did not get along particularly well. Annenberg took an active role on the school's board of trustees and liked the board to meet in the conference room of his newspaper, the Philadelphia *Inquirer.* The school had actually been endowed in honor of his father, Moses Annenberg, a hard-driving publisher. Coincidentally, back in 1938 George Seldes devoted a chapter to Moses Annenberg in his book called *Lords of the Press.* He noted that the father had made millions of dollars from the New York *Morning Telegraph,* the *Daily Racing Form, Running Horse,* the Miami Beach *Tribune, Radio Guide,* and the Nation Wide News Service, Inc. He also earned considerable sums from the publication of *Screen Guide, Official Detective Stories,* and other pulp literature. When he purchased the *Inquirer* for $15 million, it added to his aura as a man of legendary shrewdness when it came to matters of circulation and promotion. The *Inquirer* became the first newspaper in the United States, however, to be cited by the National Labor Relations Board for unfair labor practices. Annenberg had refused to obey the law that required corporations to deal collectively with their employees, which in this instance meant the Philadelphia branch of the Newspaper Guild.[31]

If Moses was an authoritarian union-buster, his son could be equally tough and intervened in school affairs at the most trivial levels. When a young reporter for the *Daily Pennsylvanian* who had sparked a student protest against elimination of a liberal radio program from station WFIL applied for a scholarship at the Annenberg School, Walter indicated that he did not want the student to receive any of *his* money. Seldes got the young man a scholarship directly from the university provost, bypassing Annenberg's attempt at partisan control. In a memoir that Seldes dictated in 1965, he recalled that Annenberg and his wife were ill-at-ease when they gave parties for the school. Seldes noted that "he was displeased with me because I said all of us were determined to make ours the best damn school of its kind in the country—I had said 'damn' in front of his mother."[32]

Seldes concluded this memoir with ruminations on Annenberg's temperament and how others perceived him:

Even those who suffered most at the corporate hands felt pity for Walter. There seemed in him a capacity for ease and for pleasure which was constantly checked. The whole miserable business of the School rose from an incapacity to give freely—the School had not only to be a memorial to the Father whom Walter had not loved—it had also to remain a piece of property of the family and the corporation.[33]

Always a versatile and independent critic, Seldes' strengths did not include rigorous administrative skills. And he came to the university too late in life to function as an astute academic politician. Nevertheless, the Annenberg School did get off to a successful start under Seldes' leadership, and he could be fearlessly combative in contretemps with media giants, even using personal conflicts as a way of promoting the potential influence of the school and its students.* Owing to the prestige of his deanship, he served in 1961–62 as chairman of the Conference on the Public Interest, a group that included the heads of communications schools and departments all over the United States. Late in 1961, as chairman of that conference, Seldes transmitted a report to Newton N. Minow, controversial head of the FCC, urging the appointment of a public defender to serve as a watchdog on behalf of viewer and listener interests.[34]

In the February 2, 1962, issue of *Time* a book review of Daniel Aaron's *Writers on the Left* identified Seldes as having been hostile to capitalism during the 1930s, and suggested that he might even have been a communist fellow-traveler. That so infuriated Seldes that he sent a three-page refutation directly to Henry R. Luce, summarizing the positions he had in fact taken during the Depression, and insisting that he had been "specifically enthusiastic about the possibilities of an intelligently conceived democratic capitalism." His publications had been unmistakably "against the idea that some form of Marxist communism . . . would necessarily supplant the capitalist system." After chiding Luce's staff at some length for irresponsible journalism, Seldes got around to using his new institutional affiliation as the basis for a threat of retaliation. The threat is interesting not because it might have intimidated Luce and his associates; surely it did not. Rather, it is interesting because it suggests

*At a retirement ceremony held on May 20, 1963, in Philadelphia, numerous speakers referred to Seldes' abundant energy, verbal fluency, and "indestructible optimism." They called him a professional gadfly, a caustic curmudgeon, and a "loveable son of a bitch." (Two reels of tape, MSP.)

that Seldes, a life-long free-lance and relatively powerless person except for his "pen," briefly relished being in a situation where he at least had the appearance of institutional leverage.

"I would like to believe myself immune to whatever harm *Time* may have done me," he explained. "But I am interested in something else":

> You and your associates are powers in the field which I have studied and which I now, being possibly a "sociologist," observe as a teacher. I am the responsible head of a graduate school of a university and my first obliga-tion is to my students. I have to help them to discover the true nature of mass communications in America. I have to guide them, if they need to be guided, to discovering those practices which make for success.

Seldes closed with a challenge. He felt obliged to explain to his students how careless and shameless *Time*'s editorial practices were. He therefore invited Luce to personally visit the Annenberg School in order to correct the dreadful impression its students would have "of the service *Time* renders to the dignity of mass communications in America."[35]

Luce had his fact-checkers dig out some very damaging quotations from *Americana,* the ephemeral monthly with which Seldes had briefly been associated as an editor in 1932–33. Although Seldes most likely had not written it, he could be tainted by association with this sentence from the very first issue of *Americana:* "We are Americans who believe that our civilization exudes a miasmic stench and that we had better prepare to give it a decent but rapid burial." Luce gently explained to Seldes that, in his view, the tone of *Time*'s book review "was one of generous under-standing of how troubled people in a troubled-time did indeed think that capitalism was finished." Luce closed by politely declining Seldes' invitation—as one reasonable critic to another:

> It is kind of you to invite me to talk at the Annenberg School of Communi-cations. I am sorry my schedule does not permit that just now, but in any case I would not want to appear there in the posture of "correcting" you. I do not worry about anything that may be said about TIME by a fair-minded and perceptive critic. Believe me, that is the kind of critic TIME also seeks to be.[36]

It is germane, perhaps, that Seldes revised a second edition of his last book at this time, and titled it *The New Mass Media: Challenge to a Free Society.* Once again he conveyed a strong sense of difference between print journalism and television broadcasting, and the book concentrated almost entirely on television. At one point, however, Seldes made a comment that epitomized his fracas with Henry R. Luce. "The critic who is not the enemy of the mass media," he wrote, "but is the enemy of the uses to which they are often put is bound to meet skillful and statistically formidable arguments."[37]

Although this book speculated whether television might not eventually overwhelm the printed word, Seldes sought to maintain an optimistic tone overall, affirming that Americans still had the capacity to control the mass media before those industries totally gained the upper hand. He joined many other critics in wondering whether the mass media functioned in ways that encouraged social conformity, but Seldes argued that "in matters of taste, and in matters of opinion leading to action, the mass media can produce changes of no great depth, but are particularly effective in corroborating tastes and opinions which already exist." The media tended to reinforce existing patterns of taste, in other words, keeping them static rather than producing significantly new patterns.[38]

Of greater concern to Seldes was the tendency for television to make all of the programs shown during prime viewing hours acceptable to children and adults alike, thereby offering only light entertainment options to mature people who wanted and deserved greater variety. It would be unfortunate to have the adolescent and the grown-up "fixed in a limited zone of intellectual development and of emotional maturity." Nevertheless, Seldes also persisted in his customary fear of coercion where matters of taste were concerned. He pleaded with well-educated people to be sensitive to the rights of others, "especially the right to have the kind of entertainment that they like, without interference." That meant that critics and intellectuals must not "approach the problem of altering the nature of the mass media in a dictatorial spirit." He even added a notably benign touch: "we are unlikely to be effective if we begin with contempt for the product and a sense of superiority to those who enjoy it." Was Seldes being unrealistic in his effort not to be condescending? Perhaps, but he believed that a more critical and demanding audience could be achieved by paying far more attention to the mass media in school programs and curricula. That might also have been naive on his part, but it has to be conceded that his suggestion has not been acted upon in a systematic way.[39]

Despite the benign concessions to popular taste and freedom of choice noted above, Seldes ultimately recognized that serious critics and those in charge of the media had fundamental differences on the most vital issues raised by the coming of mass culture. Leaders from the media insisted that what they did was comparable to any other form of business enterprise, and that their influence would always be counteracted by the prestige and effectiveness of other institutions. Therefore, unless it could be demonstrated that the media did demonstrable harm, it violated the spirit of civil freedom to interfere with them. The extreme view in opposition to that one, of course, was that the mass media comprised, in Seldes' words, "a new and revolutionary phenomenon, that their power is incalculably greater than the combined power of all other institutions," and that the media possessed not only the power but even a "need to undermine all these others."[40]

Seldes then produced an interesting and useful exercise, a systematic comparison of the hypothetical views of media managers and cultural critics concerning eight key issues. Although he also had film and radio in mind, his primary concern was the astonishing ascendancy of television after only fifteen years. Seldes' theoretical dialogue needs to be seen in its entirety.[41]

"Are the ultimate needs of the public met by satisfying the day-to-day wants of large audiences?"

Managers	*Critics*
Within reason, yes. The obligations of the mass media are to meet the daily wants of large majorities, and it would be improper to devote their powers to satisfying negligible minorities.	Not necessarily. The day-to-day wants do not necessarily represent deep-seated desires. Satisfaction of superficial wants may be actually against the ultimate good of the public.

The individual members of the audience have many wants, differing in degree of intensity. Are the ones satisfied by the mass media the only ones worth satisfying?

Managers	*Critics*
They are the only ones held in common by enough people to justify using the mass media. They are basic and legitimate. No known want is left unsatisfied, and it would be unfair to sacrifice the wants of the majority in order to follow the dictates of the superior few.	The satisfactions desired intensely by considerable minorities exist in the majority, also, in lesser degree. It is desirable to let people become aware of more satisfactions in life, and this can be done by giving them a chance to experience what the minorities already know.

Does satisfying the common wants tend to make all others less acute?

Managers	*Critics*
Not necessarily. Other attractive ways of satisfying these other wants exist.	Inevitably. The latent appetite has no chance to be active if others are constantly fed. Desires difficult to fulfill can atrophy if unused.

Should the mass media make a deliberate effort to bring to the surface other wants and desires?

Managers	*Critics*
Only those they can satisfy (which they often do, as in the case of classical music). Beyond that point, this is a function of our schools, churches, and other institutions.	Only those which are socially desirable—not such wants as lie below the threshold now accepted as a minimum (*e.g.,* desire for morbid thrills). Those lying above the present levels should be encouraged.

Within the framework of private enterprise, is there any obligation to offer entertainment which is not popular enough to guarantee a profit?

Managers	*Critics*
No. There is, however, an obligation to provide vital information (in broadcasting).	Yes. Profit is made on the whole schedule (of pictures or programs) and it is not necessary to show a book-profit on each item separately.

On whom does the obligation rest to provide for the wants of considerable minorities?

Managers	*Critics*
On those who find it to their advantage to do so. On the state (or other community-unit) if a public benefit is involved, as in higher education.	On those who have access to the majority and profit by it— *i.e.,* on the mass media.

Who is to prevent the presentation of entertainment of low intellectual or moral character if such entertainment turns out to be profitable?

Managers	*Critics*
Public opinion as represented by the police power (not by prior censorship). By the workings of the competitive system, the offending material will turn out to be unprofitable.	Public opinion acting at random unless this proves ineffective— when it must be organized and spurred to action.

In the special case of children, who is to prevent exposure to excitements, diversions from schoolwork, and subject matter they are too young to evaluate properly?

Managers	Critics
The parents. To compel the producer to do so would reduce the mass media to an infantile level.	Primarily the parents. But pictures should be publicly graded as suitable and unsuitable, and programs not for children should not be broadcast at inappropriate hours.

Seldes then made it clear that two divergent views of law and public policy were at odds in this face-off. Media people adhered to a strictly legal notion of rights, whereas critics insisted that the mass media were "affected with a public interest" and consequently should be accountable to public pressure. Seldes felt, once again, that a debate on the very meaning of the democratic process was at stake—but with several very curious inversions:

> The critic, deploring the low quality of what the public accepts, is called anti-democratic. The producer who says the people are not capable of understanding anything better is called a friend of democracy. But the critic is the one who believes that the public has an infinite capacity to grow in maturity and intelligence, which is the foundation of faith in democracy. And any producer whose daily operations are predicated on a low estimate of his audience is, in reality, the enemy of the people.[42]

Seldes concluded that spurious friends of the people, in this instance, had perverted the meaning of democracy to suit their own interests—as he put it, "the concept of a people incapable of progress except in income and the gadgets they buy with their income. It is against this concept that the critic of the media, consciously or not, aligns himself." He concluded by offering a bold and clear definition of what he meant by "standards" and the criterion that he proposed for distinguishing between what is socially (as well as culturally) good or bad. Seldes wanted his definitional standard to be applied across the board to all aspects of the mass media, and he felt so strongly about it that he italicized all but the negative portion: "*whatever engages more of the interests of the individual, whatever tends to enlarge his understanding of life, whatever makes him able to use more of his faculties and to "live more abundantly" is good;* and whatever limits, restricts, and diminishes is bad."[43]

In March 1963, near the close of his career as dean of the Annenberg School, Seldes received the Alfred I. du Pont Award in Radio and Television. He had to sing for his supper at the foundation's annual awards dinner held in Washington, D.C., and chose as his topic "The Public Interest" even though he acknowledged at the outset that such a thing was exceedingly difficult to define. He referred to it as the "undefined phrase in the law under which broadcasting operates." Rather than offer a definition of his own, Seldes asserted that the major question, really, was not *how* to define the public interest but *who* would be privileged to define it.[44]

Despite that shrewd observation, Seldes was now past seventy years of age and on the verge of ill health. His address did not unfold with wondrous clarity and it raised more questions than it resolved. He did observe, however, that in de facto ways the public interest got defined overtly on a daily basis by the extremely small number of individuals who put programs on the air, and that it got "defined passively by the enormous number of people" who obligingly accepted the limited range of choices open to them. Once again Seldes expressed his fear that the potential for an elite to direct or alter public taste in entertainment threatened to divide the public culture into two camps, and that doing so would "give a free hand to those calculators of common denominators who always seek the lowest."[45]

Essentially, Seldes found himself somewhat stuck in this swan song because he genuinely doubted whether the media managers would do the right thing: namely, diversify their programming, level up rather than down, and offer on individual channels the careful array that the BBC segregated onto three distinct program levels. Yet at the same time his philosophical roots precluded governmental intervention as a solution to the problem of program mediocrity. As he put it in an unpublished document written around the same time as his du Pont award address: Seldes had been raised as an anarchist; consequently "thinking about the need for *control* of both social forms and mechanical invention, I would rather not face the part Government . . . would play."[46]

The address did, however, serve as a kind of summation at three score and ten. He explicitly acknowledged his witness to an extraordinary transformation: What he had once called, with affection, the lively arts were now "rather grimly known as the mass media." Because the United States was so pluralistic a society, creative "mechanisms" were required to deal with such diverse educational phenomena as the media, sermons, advertising, and political campaigns. He concluded with an eloquent appeal for Americans to exercise the power required to shape and control their own cultural institutions, however complex, that had emerged.[47]

Although Seldes did not try to make this honorific moment of recognition prescriptive, detailed, or some kind of formula for cultural reconciliation, he did at least anticipate several major emphases that subsequently became prominent in contemporary cultural criticism: namely, that ideological orthodoxies would not help to illuminate or elevate the public arts, and that culture itself as well as the evaluation of culture must not become prisoners of technology.[48]

III

During the 1960s, when Seldes became a respected elder statesman among professional critics, his interests did not narrow and he continued to express his views on diverse topics in assorted ways. When illness laid him low, he had his beloved Skye terrier, Bobby, for companionship; and he played endless games of Canfield (a form of solitaire) while contemplating some subject that he wanted to write or broadcast about (see Fig. 21).

His occasional radio pieces remained clever. In April 1963, for example, he chose to talk about the artist living through rapid change and hence the need for people to constantly rethink their image of the artist. That was his essential point, but he hooked the reader at the outset by demonstrating what a difference the analyst's choice of phrasing could make. Whereas he would probably offend most of his audience if he said that "the artist is the most reactionary of all men," he might endear himself by saying that the artist, "of all men, preserves all that is most valuable in our heritage and enables us to use it in creating the present and the future."[49] The power of carefully chosen words!

His enthusiasm for jazz, especially what he had always called cerebral jazz, endured. On January 24, 1963, Seldes appeared on an NBC special, "The World of Benny Goodman," occasioned by Goodman's enormously successful tour of the Soviet Union. Seldes wore a suit and an elegant polka dot tie. He was the most formally dressed of those interviewed about Goodman. (Others included Aaron Copland, Sol Hurok, Willis Conover, and Dave Brubeck.) He comes across on the video as an elder statesman who speaks deliberately but vigorously, using his folded glasses as a baton to punctuate his carefully chosen words. Seldes' hair is thinning and wispy. His forehead is prominent, his eyelids appear heavy.

Fig. 21. Gilbert Seldes (ca. 1960).

Creases run down from the corners of his mouth. He speaks with assurance, with total belief in his views.

Seldes admired Goodman and his big band jazz because he was "exporting America's most original and expressive art form." He applauded Goodman because he was balanced and judicious in his approach to jazz. "He's not a maniac. He's not a wild man." He didn't go to extremes. And then a touch of Cold War anti-communism: I hope no one will think that they sent us their ballet and we sent them Goodman, so we're chums, because "Chums isn't good enough." On this occasion, much more than most, the politics of culture peeked through. What was most memorable about Seldes' testimony on that program, however, was the sheer joy that he derived from talking about good jazz. "It's not that it's respectable," he insisted, "it's *good*."[50]

Other passions persisted through the mid-1960s, whenever his health was conducive to enthusiasm. Having achieved the status of critic-as-senior citizen helped him to feel perfectly comfortable being officious. So when the Irish-American novelist Edwin O'Connor published *I Was Dancing* in 1964, Seldes felt quite at ease mingling warm compliments concerning immigrant accents with advice on how the plot might have been structured more effectively. (O'Connor was part of Seldes' Cape Cod summer circle.) In 1966 he lauded Ralph Nader and *The Nation* for their brave battle with General Motors on behalf of driver safety—first telephoning the editor, Carey McWilliams, to convey his enthusiasm and then following with a public letter of commendation for acting in the public service.[51]

Seldes' penultimate appearance in print took the form of an invited contribution to a special issue, concerning "Ethics in America," of the *Annals* of the American Academy of Political and Social Science. He wrote the essay in 1965, when his health remained precarious, and it lacks sharp focus and a compelling argument. Even so, it is in this piece of Ave! Vale! (Hail and Farewell) that Seldes produced the sentence that justifies our engagement with his career as a whole. Once again, presciently, he italicized the entire statement: *"In my own lifetime I have witnessed more changes in the modes of communication than occurred in all recorded history before."*[52]

It is in this essay, moreover, that he provided historical context and hence an element of perspective for those critics and intellectuals distressed by the coming of mass culture. The very structure of mass entertainment and the lowering of cultural standards were not new phenomena, he noted. Print had been the first medium that could be readily reproduced. Films were duplicated for broad distribution because theaters demanded new films and profits could be maximized more swiftly for the backers and producers if many people saw a given movie in multiple locations. The new element in radio and television, however, was that the entertainment did not get paid for directly by those who observed it. Consequently the entertainment being presented sought approval not merely for itself, but for a commodity—the sponsor's product. In *that* sense, the electronic media marked a major qualitative change compared with print and film. The electronic media were, to a much greater degree, critically engaged in the seductions of consumerism. Seldes performed a signal service by making that point particularly clear.[53]

Seldes retraced, albeit with fresh language, the critic's dilemma in a democratic society: how to justify telling millions of people that according to some cerebral or perhaps idiosyncratic criteria, programs that they were prepared to like really did not deserve their attention. That led him to the imperative and hortatory conclusion of his essay: that the mass media tended to reduce all viewers to the same level of intelligence and the same zone of emotional maturity. The media's greatest crime was that they induced inertia and diverted people from the harsh realities of life. In a sense, Seldes had now accepted the mass culture-as-narcotic argument of the mass culture critics on the left who had been so vocal back in the 1950s. That is why he pleaded for a "thousandfold multiplication of the number of *independent, thinking* men and women" in American society.[54]

Seldes had always been, if anything, independent-minded. That quality of autonomous judgment is what he wanted to see vastly increased in 1966. People were too easily satisfied with what the media offered them, and too little of that offering stimulated engaged intelligence or criticism. At the end of his public career, Seldes simply wanted the great audience to be more discerning. In a very practical sense, to paraphrase Carl Becker, he yearned for Everyman to be his own critic. That would have meant, surely, the genuine democratization of cultural criticism.

Because Seldes had been a cultural populist for so long, and because he so passionately wanted to believe that the patient (a.k.a. media management) *could* cure himself, he never drew the kinds of profoundly pessimistic conclusions that we find in his contemporary, the poet and critic Randall Jarrell. The contrast between them is instructive, and Jarrell's despair is indeed representative of those who found *nothing* but mediocrity in the mass media. Jarrell contrasted the realm of high or serious culture, where creativity endured, with the morass of mass culture where planned obsolescence and sheer trendiness made everything evanescent. As he phrased it, "most of the information people have in common is something that four or five years from now they will not even remember having known."[55]

The cultural revolution that Jarrell believed *he* had witnessed was characterized by a distinctive product that he designated in 1958 as Instant Literature. Advertising seemed doubly culpable to Jarrell because it was both a manifestation as well as a symptom of Instant Literature. One of the most frightening things about his own time, Jarrell concluded, was that "much of the body of common knowledge that educated people (and many uneducated people) once had, has disappeared or is rapidly disappearing." Because Instant Literature was equally ephemeral, if not more so, Jarrell surveyed a bleak and barren landscape indeed.[56]

Seldes, by comparison, could be almost as critical yet considerably more hopeful. The only common ground that he and Jarrell genuinely shared involved their mutual certainty that American culture had perpetually been in transition. Even on that point, however, Jarrell's assessment was gloomier than Seldes'. "The American present is very different from the American past," Jarrell wrote, "so different that our awareness of the extent of the changes has been repressed."[57]

Seldes would not have agreed because he had devoted three decades to charting and explaining those changes. Moreover, if Jarrell *seems* more realistic and less naive in his critique, it needs to be noticed that he resented the way people were compelled to buy things that they did not need or really even want. Yet he simply blamed the media without ever pointing a finger at capitalism as a system. Although Seldes never proposed to overthrow capitalism entirely, he freely conceded its most pernicious shortcomings and connected them in an explanatory way to the most glaring banalities of mass culture. Although Seldes may have been the greater optimist, he was also, surely, the greater realist.

Early in 1970, less than a week following the death of Bertrand Russell, the contemporary philosopher most admired by Seldes, he sent a letter to the *New York Times* calling attention, with strong approval, to the closing page of Russell's autobiography. "I have lived in the pursuit of a vision both personal and social," he wrote. "Personal: to care for what is noble . . . beautiful . . . gentle. Social: to see in imagination the society that is to be created. Here hate and greed and envy die because there is nothing to nourish them."[58] Seldes felt touched by the grandeur of Russell's vision, not merely because he admired him, but because for more than a decade Seldes, too, had been seeking to sum up and come to terms with the meaning of his life.

11

"I Am by Now Accustomed
to Flashbacks"

I n 1956, soon after Fred Allen died, Clifton Fadiman devoted one of his "Conversation" programs on NBC radio to a discussion he had recorded (but never previously played) in which he and Seldes interviewed Allen, a comedian they both very much admired. At one point in the program Fadiman turned to Seldes and asked him whether he would live his life differently if he had the opportunity. "You've done half a dozen things," Fadiman noted. "Do you regret having done any of them in the sense that you feel you've wasted your time and would rather have filled your time with some other kind of work?" Later in the broadcast Seldes remarked that many immigrants had come to the United States saying, "I will take a chance and I will start again"; but Seldes did not yearn for a different career—only for wiser financial management. Had he been more frugal in the fat years he would have been better situated "to do the work I most wanted to do if I hadn't been under pressure to go and make money."[1]

Also in 1956, Seldes began planning a book-length memoir that progressed through several stages in his mind. In 1964 he commented in a memorandum to himself that he had intended to "trace the connection between the movements of thought and feeling in the 1920's and the movements in the following decades." He recently sharpened the focus, however, to search for a more particular historical connection. He wanted to write about the intellectuals, the aesthetes, and the expatriates he had known during the 1920s "and then to see whether their fundamental attitudes of mind did—or didn't—lead to a kind of communism which was, in a sense, halted during the great reconciliation between the intellectual and the politician . . . under FDR."[2] If that sounds like a problematic line to pursue, particularly because Seldes already assumed that a connection *did* exist, other stimuli prompted him to keep at the project simply in order to set the record straight about issues that mattered to him personally.

Ever since the later 1950s he had received letters of inquiry from scholars writing books about events and people he had known, and quite a few of those books appeared between 1958 and 1966. He found most of them flawed on matters of fact, or else surprising because of their peculiar emphases.[3] So he wanted to set the record straight from the perspective of a participant. He explained repeatedly that motives interested him especially, an elusive element that is usually difficult to document and that historians are often likely to get wrong—or at least, not quite right. Besides, when Frederick Hoffman's book on *The Twenties* only quoted from two minor essays that Seldes printed in *The New Republic,* but never so much as mentioned *The 7 Lively Arts,* Seldes began to wonder whether he had left no enduring legacy.

Between the queries he received, the eventual publications themselves, and the reviews of them, Seldes lamented to Edmund Wilson in 1965 that he seemed to be "living totally in the past." Wilson himself had undergone a similar experience in 1951 when his mother's death required him to spend two weeks at her home in Red Bank, New Jersey, perusing remnants of the past. He worked back through family history along with his own "partly-forgotten early life, and though interesting, it got to be too much for me, at moments rather suffocating and sickening—all the more as I was working at the time on a book of my old articles of the twenties and thirties, which also made me relive the past. . . . The result is that I'm feeling as I never have before that I belong to a past era from which I'm not sure I'm capable of emerging, and I see myself in relation to the rest of the world as a probably rather mouldering than mellow old codger from the frivolous twenties who looks back on a world they can never know. . . ."[4]

For Seldes, however, there was a whole configuration of obstacles, beyond his bouts of ill health in the mid-1960s, that conspired to prevent his completion of "As in My Time."[5] First, just as he didn't "diary" during World War I, neither did he maintain a well-organized file of his own writings, printed or unpublished. Unlike Edmund Wilson, Seldes didn't keep a journal and didn't anthologize himself from time to time. As he once wrote to Fitzgerald, "I have an ingrained dislike of all books not written to be books, but collected from scattering magazine pieces." Seldes never gathered his fugitive pieces into any sort of "reader" or book format.[6]

Second, as a complicating obstacle though not an insuperable one, Seldes changed his opinions about assorted issues and individuals over the course of his career. Once upon a time, for example, he had admired Ralph Waldo Emerson, George Santayana, and Richard Wagner; but by the 1960s all three had slipped from their esteemed places in Seldes' pantheon.[7]

Third, despite his genuine belief that history mattered, Seldes had customarily—his 1965 lament to Wilson notwithstanding—tended by temperament to live in the present, to contemplate cultural change and comment upon it. As he phrased it in one of the dozens of memoranda that he drafted in preparation for his memoir, "I've been, most of my professional life, a defender of the present. Partly this must be the consequence of my attachment to the popular arts which were, when I began, under attack." Or, as he phrased it elsewhere in the same memo, he really wanted to know "whether it is useful to find out why we are in our present state. . . . What happened to all the possibilities of a decent world?"[8]

Fourth, Seldes' memory did not serve him well during the 1960s. His dictated memoranda contain numerous factual errors, lapses involving names and dates. In 1962 he could not recall Josephine Baker's name; he could not remember that Marcel Duchamp had painted *Nude Descending a Staircase,* the most controversial painting exhibited at the Armory Show in 1913. He conflated works by Frederick Jackson Turner and Vernon L. Parrington into a single title that he blithely called *The Frontier in American Civilization.* The awkwardness in dealing with "As In My Time" if he had finished the book is epitomized by a sentence that Seldes wrote in 1933: "It was like telling a man that his memories were mistaken. . . ." To make the situation even more poignant, Seldes knew that his aging memory often failed him and commented accordingly to friends.[9]

In February 1964 he recorded wistfully in one of his memoranda, "I am by now accustomed to flashbacks." But almost four years later he explained to a close friend that he couldn't get himself to a library to check on desperately needed materials, and couldn't afford to hire a researcher. The project seemed virtually paralyzed, yet the tumultuous events of 1968 made him feel that he really ought to reconceptualize it. He told Robert M. Hutchins, head of the Center for the Study of Democratic Institutions in Santa Barbara, "the events of the last year have altered the configuration of the book I am writing. It is still about the men and movements I observed in the 1920's and 1930's—but I suspect it is more gloomy now—as concerning why we [liberals?] failed."[10]

Many members (and hangers-on) of the "lost generation" did eventually write memoirs of one kind or another. A student of this genre, if it can be called that, has perceived a dominant pattern or trajectory that moves, in mood, from exhaltation to deflation, from youthful rebellion to brooding let-down.[11] Seldes had a different experience. Although he knew many of the expatriates quite well, he never became one. Instead of undergoing some sort of psychic decline after the 1920s, moreover, he hit his stride with the great success of *Lysistrata* early in the 1930s.

Consequently the process of coming to terms with his life took a different course for Seldes. In addition to the examined self, an inevitable ingredient, he wanted to give considerable attention to what he called "ideas and movements." If he devoted some time and space to self-vindication, he also concerned himself with such provocative but difficult issues as defining the qualities characteristic of an intellectual; how immigrants become Americans; and how greater rapport might be achieved between practitioners of the humanities and the natural sciences. Consequently, Seldes' attempt at autobiography may have been a failure, but it was neither self-indulgent nor an apologia for an unfulfilled career as a critic. Rather, it reflected the same restless curiosity that had propelled him throughout his life. Even in his mid-seventies, Gilbert Seldes continued to grow.

I

Looking back to his education at Harvard, Seldes quite shrewdly realized that he eventually became an intellectual disciple of William James, exemplified especially by his admiration for James' book of lectures, *A Pluralistic Universe* (1909). Because James died in 1910, however, the year that Seldes entered college, he did not "discover" James immediately and therefore passed through aesthetic and moralistic phases under the tutelage of Santayana in philosophy and Babbitt in literature. James was fundamentally "a democrat," Seldes recalled, and James believed that magazines like *McClure's, Collier's,* and others like them "constituted a real popular university, a new educational power" and he said that "knowing a good man when you see one" is one of the functions of higher education. I am sure I would have found him irresistible and in a way he would have saved me from many imbecilities. But I feel, in a way, that it was necessary for me to find my own devious way. . . . But it was as well for me to see the scenery the others provided and to arrive at my destination, which was more Jamesian than that of either Babbitt or Santayana, after my submission and reaction to them.

In retrospect Santayana seemed important because he reinforced Seldes' instinctive skepticism, "even to the point of being skeptical of the philosophy he taught."[12]

In a separate segment that Seldes devoted to James and *A Pluralistic Universe,* he wondered why he hadn't said more about James and used James' ideas as a basis for thematic integration when he wrote *Mainland* in 1935–36. He acknowledged that James' pluralism seemed so crucial to him in the mid-1960s because he needed to make sense of the extreme diversity in his interests: "that I could find pleasure in the movies, involvement in Joyce, and a hundred other satisfactions in earning a living, voting for popular or unpopular candidates, [etc.]. . . ."[13]

He closed this inconclusive segment by reaffirming his own pluralism in the face of his most single-minded protagonists of the 1950s and 1960s, James Marston Fitch, the architectural critic at Columbia "with his dogmatism about the original work [versus reproductions] to Dwight MacD with his demand for an elite to destroy his midcult. The antagonism toward whatever is diffused and made easy of access [to the general public], the fear of corruption when vast numbers begin to like what once was appreciated only by the few—are to me symptoms of insecurity."[14] Outright and categorical rejection of mass culture irritated Seldes.

The more urgently he looked for continuity in his cumulative enterprise, the more intensively he sought "the connection between my lively arts work and my interest in and books about the character of the United States," the more closely he read and rethought William James' philosophical pluralism. When his concern about nuclear holocaust became especially great during the later 1960s, Seldes hoped that somehow the mass media could be used to bridge the gap between divergent social strata so that scientists, in particular, might sensitize ordinary people to the grave risks created by the arms race. He hoped that the popular arts could, in a sense, serve as "common ground" for disparate sectors of a pluralistic society. "I want to use the popular arts," he wrote, "not only to bring a reconciliation between the intellectual and the people, but to give the intellectual a chance to make people aware of the appalling danger in which our whole civilization lies."[15]

Seldes' commitment to pluralism during his mature years also had the effect of reinforcing his life-long enthusiasm for vaudeville because that medium of entertainment had been so helpful in promoting the careers of ethnic performers. In a very real sense, vaudeville did for Jews and Italians what athletics did later for African Americans: It humanized them in the eyes of others as well as popularized them. They seemed less like alien demons and more like engaging hyphenated Americans who could make you laugh (and cry) at their awkward attempts at assimilation. At vaudeville performances many children had "their first encounters with the Jew, the German, the Irish, the Italian. No one who lived through that time and was at all conscious of religion or nationality can forget the strange ambiguity of these presentations." The negative aspect of all this diversity, Seldes quickly acknowledged, was the perpetuation of ethnic and racial stereotypes. He felt that the Negro suffered most severely from that perpetuation. Otherwise, Seldes believed, the presentation of ethnic caricatures did not mean that any immigrant group was being ridiculed or defamed. I do not agree; but that was Seldes' perception, as well as many others', during the 1960s.[16]

Between 1965 and 1967, especially, Seldes was recurrently intrigued with the whole process by which immigrants became Americanized. He felt that in unprecedented ways what had most distinguished the United States during the nineteenth century "was the freedom of its people to cross frontiers, both real and imaginary—to break down barriers." (The two exceptions, he swiftly noted, were not exactly immigrants: the Negro and the Native American, the Indian.) In the three segments on this subject that he dictated for "As in My Time," Seldes constantly recurred to the unique American circumstances and how congenial they were to James' social philosophy. "I see a climate favorable to movement," Seldes declared. "I see the essential pluralism of William James and see in him what he saw in Bergson, the importance of becoming what you were not."[17]

In an explicitly autobiographical paragraph, Seldes viewed his own career as a process of "becoming," which really meant crossing boundaries and somehow reconciling antimonies:

I crossed several barriers in my time—and am naturally influenced by them. I was born a Jew (in the technical sense—I was never brought up to be one) and married an Episcopalian—it was easy because we were both indifferent; I combined my work on the Dial with my work on the Lively Arts; my main preoccupation now, apart from writing this book, is an attempt to integrate the sciences and the arts as parts of the humanities— and I am not sure that politics and economics are not equal sharers.

He then proceeded to generalize from his personal experience to the entire history of entertainment in the United States.[18]

Without ever mentioning the social philosopher Horace Kallen and his concept of cultural pluralism (first articulated in 1915), Seldes actually shared many of Kallen's basic views: that immigrants who became Americans did not lose all of their native customs and attributes; that immigrants were not passive products who were only acted upon— rather, they helped to determine their own destinies; and that in the process their presence altered the America that the next generation of immigrants entered. They were participants, and here Seldes' sense of American exceptionalism remained very much alive: "this was the only country of which this could be said."[19]

Seldes prepared two segments for "As in My Time" that were germane to this theme: one being an in-depth look at Paul Robeson's artistry and the prejudice that he encountered for ideological as well as racial reasons, and the second being an affirmation of his general thesis (stated above) connected with an admission that it did not apply in the case of African Americans. The act of becoming an American, he observed in 1965, "which I place at the centre of our character and history—was in principal and by custom made available to all immigrants (although we did exclude the Chinese *by law* for a time). It was never a possibility for the Negro—and the Negro was never an immigrant." Seldes then weakened the veracity of his historical overview by declaring that white aesthetes and intellectuals who went to Harlem to party during the 1920s were essentially color blind: "while we were not propagandists [for racial tolerance and integration]—at that moment we simply weren't aware of the need of propaganda—we all had arrived at the stage of not being conscious of color."[20]

Both personally and intellectually, it mattered a great deal to Seldes that William Allen White of Emporia, Kansas, not only liked him but approved of his ideas. To Seldes, White seemed an archetypal American: middle-class, white, Protestant, and from a small community in the Midwest. "I felt," Seldes mused, "that he represented the essential America and he felt that I understood him. In that sense, the act of becoming American had proved itself in me—and his recognition was essential."

No wonder White liked *Mainland.* It celebrated all of the virtues that White was believed to epitomize.[21]

When Seldes re-read *Mainland* in 1963 as part of this whole exercise in intellectual retrospection, his notes paid considerably more attention to the process of becoming American than to the ideological liberalism and defense of humane capitalism that had seemed so central to the book's construction in 1936. The other interesting linkage that he undertook in this dictated text involved the making of Americans and the popular arts. At first Seldes protested that he really wasn't pressing a specious connection:

> I am not trying to force my professional life (in the popular arts) into the framework of this book ["As in My Time"]. The two may fit snugly together—and may not. I have never felt any wrench—any separation— because all the popular arts and eventually the mass media have seemed to me natural American phenomena. Yet the connection may be close. And not without a tragic irony. For in my time the popular arts were invigorated by immigrants and first-generation people. . . .

Nineteenth- and early twentieth-century America, which Seldes now idealized in some respects, offered careers open to talent, and also offered that most benign of all opportunities, becoming American.[22]

What, in the meanwhile, did Americans of older stock do while the newcomers were being acclimated? They conquered the continent, made the nation a unified whole, and (some, at least) made the first escape to Europe. The earliest expatriates came from old, established families. They were also, according to a candid Seldes, "amused and offended by the vulgarity of one group or the quaintness of another; there was even then some resentment about jobs being taken away." Seldes had considerably more to say, and of an astute nature, when he described the actual process of becoming American. He could also be naive on the subject of the nativist response. He could comfortably relate to the catchy, uncomplicated notion of "Americans All—Immigrants All." A singular or monolithic mental outlook virtually defied his comprehension. He was, after all, a self-described pluralist.[23]

II

By the beginning of 1968, having just turned seventy-five, Seldes dictated a segment concerning *The 7 Lively Arts* and subsequent work that he had done of that sort. He started by expressing a sense that what he had written about American history and character actually gave him greater satisfaction. He then paused reflectively, however, and declared: "I am, after all, a critic, and should be able to discriminate. I certainly should be able to do this about other writers; my difficulty is that it is myself about whose work I am more or less prejudiced." He then added, by way of explaining his curious preference for *The Stammering Century* over *The 7 Lively Arts,* that "the life—or the life-history of America—is of more interest to me now than the portion of it with which I was actively engaged."[24]

He indicated that he had never claimed to have "discovered" popular culture, "only that it was worthy of intelligent criticism." Nor had he sought to improve or "upgrade" the lively arts because they had already achieved so much merit. He disliked highbrows who acted superior just because they went to the opera, irrespective of the opera's intrinsic quality. Similarly, it bothered him that David Garrick and Sarah Bernhardt had both appeared in dreadful productions, yet attracted throngs at the box office. Seldes simply wanted rigorous standards of criticism applied at all cultural levels. Looking back, he mused,

> I think there was some justification of the idea that I was a fanatic and a crusader; it didn't seem so to me at the time. To myself I appeared . . . a moderate of the most violent sort; I wasn't against the fine arts, I was only against "high-class-trash" as, indeed, I was against low-class-trash.

Decades later it meant a great deal to Seldes that Paul Lazarsfeld and Arthur M. Schlesinger, Jr., both testified that Seldes' books had successfully "placed the popular arts on the agenda of intellectual discussion."[25]

In a segment written or dictated three years earlier, Seldes observed that during the 1920s iconoclastic critics (like Mencken and himself) tended to be well received, and then added, on a more personal note, that most of the people he attacked had been other critics and journalists.[26] That was true of men like Ernest Boyd and H. L. Mencken, of course, but Seldes also crossed swords from time to time with creative writers, such as Hemingway and Joseph Hergesheimer. As we observed much earlier, long after Hemingway made it publicly clear that he loathed Seldes, the latter continued to praise the novelist's work when he felt that it deserved commendation, which meant almost always.[27] More often than not, Seldes had the ability to separate personal conflicts from ones involving public taste and judgment. That, surely, was one of his notable strengths.

When Hemingway's posthumous *A Moveable Feast,* with Malcolm Cowley serving as conduit, came from the grave to haunt Seldes in 1964, it did prompt Seldes to tell Carlos Baker, Hemingway's biographer, that he resented *A Moveable Feast* because Hemingway had assassinated Seldes' character in such a snide manner.[28] I am reminded of a wonderful note that Marianne Moore wrote to Archibald MacLeish in which she spoke of being "menaced by footpads of the pen." Hemingway, dead or alive, became exactly that to Seldes, and in 1967 he admitted to Moore that Hemingway's bile still bothered and perhaps helped to diminish him. His letter to Moore is exceedingly poignant. "I catch you on television," he wrote, "and you, like everyone else connected with The Dial, win prizes—everyone except me." After mentioning his ill health during the previous eighteen months, Seldes acknowledged that "one of the misfortunes of my illnesses has been lapses of memory. From that, too, I am recovering." Nevertheless, these years of precarious memory were precisely the years when he tried desperately to bring his memoir to completion.[29]

Seldes cannot be accused of paranoia where Hemingway was concerned. Gerald Murphy, a much admired friend of both men, but considerably closer to Hemingway, indicated privately as early as 1932 that Hemingway's personal relationships were immensely complicated and easily turned poisonous. After *A Moveable Feast* appeared, Murphy expressed deep sadness. "What a strange kind of bitterness," he wrote, "or rather accusitoriness. . . . What shocking ethics! . . . What an indictment. Poor Hadley!"[30]

Despite his negative reviews of F. Scott Fitzgerald's earliest work, Seldes and that moody novelist became fast friends, a relationship that grew even stronger after 1933 when Hemingway and Fitzgerald ceased to be close. By the mid-1960s, a generation after his death, Fitzgerald reemerged as something of a cult figure, and Seldes found that he rose in the esteem of young people when they discovered he had known Fitzgerald not just casually but well. Seldes recorded in 1965 his feeling that "people were far more interested in the tragic character than in the gifted novelist." After mulling over assessments that Edmund Wilson had made of Fitzgerald's early fiction, Seldes remarked with much insight that "it is the later relationship between Scott and our society that interests me more: was Scott destroyed by the quality of American life? His talent was not diminished and while he did not move in the direction Wilson thought desirable, into writing about the Middle West, he became a far better writer than seemed possible for the man presumably spoiled by early success."[31]

Seldes' memoir of Fitzgerald is one of the longest and most speculative segments that he wrote for "As in My Time." At the point where he ruminates about the relationship between Fitzgerald's Roman Catholic childhood in the Midwest and the kind of writer he became, Seldes paused to recover, for comparative insight, some notion of his own sensibility in Philadelphia on the eve of college, when he felt destined to become a writer but was extremely uncertain just what kind of a writer he might turn out to be:

> I can guess at something in Scott from something I remember of myself just before I went to college. I had the feeling that I would never know the world, the great world. I was going to high school in Philadelphia at the time; I've noted, I think, that in my last year there (1909–10) Ernest Lacy introduced me to Nietzsche and even before that, in Pittsburgh and in Philadelphia, I knew I was the one student for whom teachers of English predicted a future as "a writer." (It meant a novelist to me, then.) Yet I had the sense of a great world outside with which I would not have any connection. I do not think this lasted very long, but I can be sure the sense was sharp and painful; I can be sure because in 1965 I can remember [back in 1908 or 1909] walking across the Girard Avenue Bridge [in Philadelphia], on my way to school, and thinking my life was closed in. I have to place as a parallel to what I think happened to Scott, his sense of being a middle-class Mid-Westerner, my sense which was not oppressive, of being a Jew—although being an atheistic-anarchistic youngster born of non-believing Jews in Philadelphia in 1909 was not a peculiarly burdensome fate. I suspect that what happened to me was an acute self-consciousness in the two or three years preceding, of the advent of puberty, the sudden opening of some kind of splendor in the contemporary literary-intellectual world (the time of Huneker, the beginning of Mencken) perhaps the sense that New York was central to all brilliance.[32]

Seldes felt that it revealed a great deal about Fitzgerald's personality that he had announced at one point in France that he would not return to the United States until he had become famous—as Fitzgerald put it, until he was sure that there would be a brass band to meet the boat. Although Seldes himself was certainly ambitious, he invested himself in more modest expectations. When he and Amanda returned in 1926, they were utterly broke and were met only by his father.

Although Seldes was very much a man of the 1920s, and an integral part of the American literary "scene" during that decade, one attitude in particular set him apart from so many of his prominent contemporaries. Writing about Fitzgerald, Sinclair Lewis, and others, Seldes recalled in the later 1960s that "the superior person, the artist, thought that he was fighting a battle . . . against the entrenched mediocrity of the middle class." That message, not subtly rendered, pervaded Lewis' *Main Street* and *Babbitt;* but because Seldes did not share that anti-middle class bias, he never felt any particular admiration or affection for Sinclair Lewis.[33]

At a time when iconoclasm became all the vogue among American writers, Seldes emerged as something of an oddity. He didn't debunk historical heroes and he didn't deride middle-class mediocrity. Instead, he scored the highbrow along with intellectual snobbery. Doing so helped to make Seldes' reputation, in a very real sense, but it also marked him as being somewhat out of step. At a time when fashion dictated that intellectuals should have superior taste, Seldes thrived by proclaiming that what had been perceived as inferior was, in fact, superior at its best and fun, at the very least, when it wasn't in fact fabulous. Seldes made a singular name for himself by turning the traditional priorities of intellectual critics upside down.

III

Among all the segments that Seldes wrote for "As in My Time," the most interesting concern such questions as: Who is an intellectual? What qualities define an intellectual? and above all, Why have most intellectuals, especially critics, been so obtuse about appreciating popular culture? From February 1965 until the summer of 1967, especially, those questions concerned Seldes and became the focal point of his project. Consequently we need to retrace his thoughts with some care, despite elements of repetition and inconsistency. Both of those qualities, when they occur, can be quite revealing.

Let's begin with a lengthy text that Seldes dictated or most likely typed himself in February 1965:

> Coming to terms with my own terms is a nuisance. But if I can make specific my bill of complaints, I must be accurate about those whom I accuse. . . .
>
> I've used the term "intellectuals" and find it loose or worse. It is only a minor consolation that I did not use "the treason of the intellectuals" as a

comprehensive title for the first part of *Mainland*—only as a subhead—because I was improperly altering the sense of Benda's phrase. . . .

But I look at the list of my targets: Mencken, Nathan, Sinclair Lewis, Ludwig Lewisohn, Dreiser, Sherwood Anderson, O'Neill—they all occur right at the start, and how many of them were in any serious sense intellectuals?

Among the others, I'd say that Mumford, Van Wyck Brooks, Edmund Wilson, perhaps Parrington were by training and the use they made of their minds, intellectuals. Of all the people I quoted Santayana was the only philosopher, the only one who was an intellectual in the Continental sense. . . .

It is, indeed, a good mark for us that in the 1920's the hostile critics got so good a reception. Or, it can be said, the country was so prosperous it didn't mind a bit of fun at its expense.

But for my purpose, I must be specific.

Mencken influenced the minds of thousands of young people when they were in or recently out of college. In that sense, he took part in creating the climate of the time—in relation to ideas, to the arts, and to society. As far as ideas and the arts were concerned, he had an effect on the intellectual climate—here using intellectual in its looser sense.

If he had had a more subtle mind—without losing the vigor of his utterance—would the generation he most influenced have been better able to meet its dilemmas? I am not sure.

In the period I am at this moment discussing, I was considered an intellectual. I was connected with The Dial, Vanity Fair, The New Republic—what could be more highbrow than that?

It strikes me as an oddity, now, that Vanity Fair (with which I never had any official position) was probably closer to what I represented than any of the others.

In that list, I have omitted The Saturday Evening Post to which I began contributing after my return from Europe, in 1926. . . . I was the Post's intellectual just as I was The New Republic's relatively light-minded critic of the popular arts. I use this phrasing instead of "I was The New Republic's lowbrow" because I was not a lowbrow and the NR was not condescending to the popular arts by using me.[34]

In yet another segment Seldes observed that hostility to the popular arts had two basic sources: snobbery and fear. The first could best be exemplified by people who didn't want to do what millions of other people were doing at the very same time, such as watch television. The second he illustrated with the case of T. S. Eliot and other elitists who admired earlier moments of cultural renaissance when the achievements of a talented few were chiefly responsible. What is feared, according to Seldes, "is the destruction of all that is noble and beautiful in mortal life presumably because these things are so fragile, they cannot even bear being admired by the multitude. In the sanctuary of the arts, it is understood, not only the altar, but the church itself is for the high-priests."[35]

At certain junctures Seldes' self-awareness and candor become disarming. Here is an extract from 1965:

> From time to time, as I write these drafts, I get a sense of self-righteousness—of my superiority to the people who didn't see what I saw, who held to old prejudices long after I'd exposed them . . . and so on. It isn't easy for me to correct this although I know that the tone is wrong. I have to separate the two interests: the popular arts and the nature of American society—or, more accurately, the acceptance of the popular arts and the acceptance of one's duty to the society in which he lives.

He then acknowledged that for most of his professional career he had been regrettably non-political, as indifferent to the "stream of events" as most of the highbrows of whom he disapproved. Without absolving himself of responsibility for being so indifferent to serious public issues, Seldes pointed more than once to his temperamental disposition to be a non-joiner and his mistrust of cause-based movements.[36]

Between July 4 and 17, 1967, Seldes returned to several of these concerns, along with related ones, in a ten-page text that began: "I am not competent to write a morphology of the intellectual Americans' attitude to popular arts and entertainment." Why? Because more historical and sociological perspective than he felt capable of supplying were needed. And because he had been a participant in the whole process and admitted that he remained partial to his own ideas. He did, however, offer a capsule history that contains an element of explanatory power:

> Before the coming of [the] highspeed press and what is called "universal literacy," the popular arts were oral—the singer, the minstrel show, the theatre, the evangelist, the Chautauqua lecturer, and so on, and the intellectual's attitude was indifference to the point that one wonders whether he knew what was going on; and at the other extreme, the entertainments which began with the dime novel and the comic strip, and then movies and broadcasting, transforming the popular arts into the mass media, have created a sort of panic among the intellectuals, fearful that the arts they cherish will somehow not survive.

Once again, Seldes emphasized fear in attempting to explain highbrow elitism.[37]

Toward those like the Victorian Matthew Arnold and his disciples, who mostly cherished the perpetuation of high culture more than the responsibility for educating large numbers of ordinary people, Seldes expressed only scorn. That led him to a reprise of his 1963 disagreement with James Marston Fitch, a professor of architecture at Columbia who had insisted that nothing could compare with being in the actual presence of an original work of art. Reproduction and duplication of art and music for the masses didn't measure up. Seldes once again rebutted Fitch with the argument that ever since the 1920s conditions had changed because art and music could be reproduced so faithfully in portfolios and on phonograph records—thereby making high culture as well as the avant-garde accessible to large numbers of people to a degree never before imagined. Hence it became one of Seldes' causes to combat the pernicious view that "diffusion somehow lowers the value of the original or the pleasure one can take in it."[38]

Seldes' public reply to Fitch in 1963 had been more acute and provocative. To Fitch's declaration that "the industrial duplicate or facsimile cannot, under any circumstances, be the qualitative equal of its prototype," Seldes answered that he simply had too much "confidence in the fine arts to believe that they are jeopardized inevitably by the mass media." Fitch had also, however, objected to Seldes' notion of the "public arts" because he believed that the mass media were primarily received privately by a "new kind of audience that is public only in a statistical sense." That is, Fitch insisted that television, film, and radio tended to *segment* audiences into small, un-communicative clusters rather than to mass them into vast groups of interactive viewers or auditors. To that Seldes offered a somewhat capitulatory reply, namely, that "an off-Broadway play witnessed by 200 persons is a public event and a televised *Hamlet* seen by 5,000,000 is private" because it is watched by individuals and small groups in private homes.[39]

Near the close of a long, meandering segment dictated in 1967 for "As in My Time," Seldes fired salvos at Dwight Macdonald, both for his elitist view of cultural stratification and for his earlier, misguided Marxism. Whereas in the original version of "Masscult & Midcult" (1944) Macdonald had favored "an attempt to integrate the masses into high culture," in the 1953 version he lost confidence in that possibility and moved toward "a contrary attempt to define two cultures, one for the masses and the other for the classes." In the ultimate version (1960),

Macdonald viewed the second as the "only practical solution." What had happened in less than two decades to change Macdonald's mind? In words the latter never saw, Seldes speculated that initially it might have been "a lingering memory of his devotion to the proletariat that led Mr. Macdonald to admit the possibility of integrating the masses; it was to be a one-way movement, to be sure—the high culture had nothing to learn from popular arts and the masses were to be weaned from their pleasures."[40]

Although I am persuaded that Macdonald's highbrow elitism was more offensive to Seldes than his Marxism, Seldes observed in a segment devoted to communism and the intellectuals that "to have been a real Marxist, that is to have understood Marx and to have joined the Bolshevik movement in spirit and applied it to the U.S. wasn't particularly sensible."[41] It didn't fit with American realities.

Late in 1965 Seldes dictated a loosely constructed ten-page installment in which he asked rhetorically, halfway through, whether his attitude toward the intellectual had changed since the 1920s, or since he wrote *Mainland* in 1935–36. Because the civil rights movement so pre-occupied him at the time, Seldes responded with the assertion that he had never known an "intellectual racist . . . nor one prejudiced against any religious group." On the debit side, however, he said that almost no intellectuals felt any pressing need to "enlighten their fellow countrymen. Nor the need to know what their country-men were desperately in want of." From Seldes' perspective the intellectuals had chosen to ignore American social realities because "the surfaces were so mangy." Nor could he recall any intellectual taking pleasure in the freedom gained by immigrants to become Americans. If the intellectuals had not been overt nativists, neither were they enthusiastic cultural pluralists. They did not notably welcome newcomers.[42] (Seldes failed to specify that among his contemporaries quite a few of the leading intellectuals were themselves newcomers.)

Every so often, however, a kind of confessional candor interrupted this venting of Seldes' pique. He conceded that for a long time he was very much a part of the cohesive entity that he designated as the intellectuals —"even after, I suppose, I began to be interested in the lively arts and later in American history." Perhaps he scolded them, he thought, because they had failed to do what he too was unable to do—be activists in the civic sector. In a separate text, an undated single sheet that reads like a rough synopsis of what his book ideally ought to cover, Seldes simply listed a whole cluster of prominent writers, including Edmund Wilson, Donald Ogden Stewart, Robert Sherwood, John Dos Passos, T. S. Eliot, and others, "who illustrate dramatically the relation between the artist-critic-intellectual and political action or non-action."[43]

Intellectuals who had moved across the ideological spectrum from left to right puzzled Seldes, perhaps because he had never been drawn to ideological extremes and had remained, fairly consistently, a bourgeois liberal. Among those he considered recanters, his old friend John Dos Passos remained the most baffling and "disagreeable." Dos Passos' rediscovery of Jeffersonian democracy seemed notably inconsistent with his open conservatism as a writer for William F. Buckley's *National Review.* John Chamberlain also remained an enigma to Seldes for the same reason, and he devoted a relatively brief segment of "As in My Time" to an attempted explanation, historical and personal, of the hegira these disillusioned men undertook between the 1930s and the 1960s. Seldes did not find Marxism personally congenial, but he did regard it as intellectually challenging. Reactionary conservatism, however, he found intellectually vacuous and repugnant.[44]

Seldes' sense of his political distance from Dos Passos did not prevent him from writing long, intimate, nostalgic letters to him during the later 1960s. In one of them he observed that he had known some affluent businessmen who were admirable people, especially owners of department stores (Edgar Kaufmann, Jesse Straus, and Stanley Marcus), men quite unlike the unhappy, alcoholic tycoons who appeared in Dos Passos' fiction during the later 1920s and '30s.[45]

Looking back at the variegated pieces of his memoir, near the end of the 1960s, Seldes wondered whether he had been too categorical in his assessments and too judgmental with the benefit of hindsight (see Fig. 22). "I have joined the worst representatives of the capitalist system with their worst enemies," he conceded. "This is perhaps a proof that I knew what Frick and Morgan were about." As for the judgmental aspect, he felt torn between moralism and realism. "What troubles me," he noted, "is that the United States seems not to have lived up to its commitment. And just as I would like to name an individual or a class as guilty, I would like to set a date—the date on which we took the wrong turn. And this is sheer folly."[46]

Engaged in retrospective contemplation at the close of his life, however, Seldes believed that he had been absolutely correct in calling the intellectuals "to account," as he phrased it; but by then he felt even more fully aware of "the calamities [unspecified] for which they are partly responsible." Their great sins had to do with snobbery and self-interest. "Almost all were foolishly prejudiced in favor of their own class." And

Fig. 22. Gilbert Seldes (late 1960s).

the periods when they managed any sort of empathy for ordinary people were all too brief and ineffectual. At the end of his long career, this prominent public intellectual had little to say of a positive nature about intellectuals as a social "class" in the United States.[47]

IV

Seldes unabashedly admired a sizable constellation of truly extraordinary individuals. They included philosophers like Bertrand Russell and George Santayana (reservations about the latter arose later on), scientists like Albert Einstein and especially J. Robert Oppenheimer, creative artists like James Joyce and Pablo Picasso, politicians like Abraham Lincoln and Franklin D. Roosevelt, critics like Edmund Wilson and Clive Bell, performers like Charlie Chaplin and Jimmy Durante, musicians ranging from Irving Berlin to Toscanini, and such diverse entertainers as Al Jolson, Fanny Brice, and Paul Robeson.

He came to know Oppenheimer at a private luncheon in Princeton on November 18, 1960. Seldes had long been fascinated by Oppenheimer, and left the luncheon in awe of the politically controversial physicist, not because he had been controversial but because he was such a polymath, as comfortable with ancient Greek poetry as he was with high energy physics.[48] Two aspects of Seldes' charming account of that occasion are noteworthy, the first because of what it reveals about the importance to Seldes of effective communication. He told Oppenheimer that his personal motto came from a small book written by the physicist Erwin Schrödinger, *What Is Man?* In translation the motto read: "If you cannot, in the long run, tell everyone what you are doing, what you are doing is worthless." Oppenheimer's shrewdness became apparent in his reply: "If you cannot, in the long run, *hope* to tell everyone . . ."[49]

The second aspect Seldes repeated to several people on various occasions during the 1960s. It was a matter of some regret and embarrassment to him that he was "analphabetic" when it came to the natural sciences. The major technological advances made during the '60s prompted his curiosity, however, and moved him to adopt as a cause the need to "integrate the sciences and the arts as parts of the humanities." As he explained in 1966 to his old friend from *The Dial* days, Dr. J. Sibley Watson, "I am interested in preventing the further propagation of the idea that the sciences and the humanities are hostile to one another. . . . I insist that they are not inevitably hostile and that each needs the other to be useful to the time or place or society in which they exist."[50]

In 1959, as it happened, C. P. Snow, a science don in Cambridge, England, had stirred immense interest on both sides of the Atlantic with the publication of his Rede Lecture under the title *The Two Cultures and the Scientific Revolution,* a plea on behalf of scientific literacy by nonscientists. Although Seldes surely had read it and must have been familiar with its accusatory tone of intellectual inertia in the world beyond the scientific community, he never mentioned Snow's widely discussed book in the letters and memoranda that he devoted to this very issue between 1965 and 1969. As early as 1962 Seldes and Arthur Schlesinger, Jr., shared a concern that the Soviet Union threatened to move ahead of the United States in science and technology. But almost without exception, Seldes' ruminations in this area were non-political and non-ideological in nature. He made an emphatic statement of his views to Schlesinger early in 1968:

The sciences are as fundamental parts of the humanities as the fine arts. Four or five years ago J. Bronowski and I had the idea of an academy based on this principle (which is implicit in his *Science and Human Values*) and my only contribution was that one cannot speak of "the humanities and science"—you can speak of "the fine arts and the sciences" (or science).[51]

In 1964 Seldes had indeed talked with Bronowski about the creation of some sort of institute or academy where the principal objective would aim at resolving the artificial "hostilities between the arts and the sciences (the differences are real)."[52] Although the two represented distinct modes of intellectual enterprise, reading books like *The Double Helix* by James D. Watson readily persuaded Seldes that physical science certainly did include a highly humanistic dimension. His concerns on that account were germane to this period of intense retrospection precisely because science had been so utterly lacking in his formal education, especially at Harvard, and consequently "in my experience of life." He recalled the following with some embarrassment in 1969:

> When I quoted Bertrand Russell in *Mainland* in 1936 I agreed with him that "when one views the XIXth century in perspective, it is clear that Science is its only claim to distinction" but I am afraid I knew little of Science then and was merely using Russell in the course of my quarrel with aestheticism and the complacency that went with it.

Seldes felt gratified in 1969 when Harvard, "maybe for the first time," began "fighting for a program for science." I suspect that by then Seldes was more than a little out of touch with the Harvard curriculum; but the depth of his concern that science should be a vital component in American education was genuine and directly linked to his strong sense of inadequacy about his own intellectual preparation.[53]

Seldes had been aware of the California Institute of Technology ever since 1930 when Albert Einstein began winter visits there and enhanced its visibility to the general public.[54] During the mid-1960s, after Seldes found that his cultural views about science converged with Bronowski's, he had some desultory contacts with people at Caltech (Albert R. Hibbs, a senior staff scientist at the Jet Propulsion Laboratory who ran the "Exploring" series for NBC, 1961–65, and Rose Kemp, a staff member in the Institute's administration who dealt with television, film, and radio) about what he called his "ideas of crossing-over and intersections" between the sciences and the humanities.[55]

For a while Seldes, Kemp, and Hibbs discussed plans for a major conference on "Scientific Progress and Human Values" to be held in October 1966 in honor of the seventy-fifth anniversary of Caltech's founding. Consideration was given by the conference organizers to the possible preparation of a documentary film germane to the theme of this distinguished occasion. Consequently, Seldes prepared a four-page overview (which he described as a "philosophical summary") for such a documentary. Although the film never came to fruition, the prospectus offered an interesting distillation of his thoughts on "Science and Society," which is the working title that he gave to the documentary enterprise. This would have been Seldes' vehicle for enhancing lay comprehension of the social impact of science. He hoped to connect what science, and the technologies based upon them, "have done to answer the needs of society and in the process have altered these needs."[56]

The purpose of the documentary, he added, should go beyond making people aware of what science had done for them. "We want more people to share in the concerns of science," he wrote, "to feel that they can, to an extent, help to determine the direction in which society is moving to understanding the part played by science." The documentary would have covered three principal topics: space, communications, and health. Understandably, Seldes' views on the content for the section devoted to communications are the most thoughtful, and in fact, really constitute his last formally stated views on that subject broadly conceived. He wanted to focus on changes in the organization of social institutions brought about by changes in the means of communication.

Seldes believed that all of the major changes involving communications since the introduction of printing from movable type had occurred during the previous seventy-five years, that is, almost exactly during his own lifetime. The primary theme that he wanted to develop in this section (following the work of Harold Innis, which he very much admired), was that "every major change in the chief mode of communication is followed by a major change in the structure of society."[57]

He recognized that connections between communications and space had been spectacular, and noted "the annihilation of time in transmission" as well as the importance of communications in education, facilitating new instruments of teaching and "new ways of diverting the human mind." Closely related was the major social transformation, long so important to Seldes, "which changed entertainment from an occasional reward to a constantly available thing—looked upon as a natural right."[58]

In the concluding section of his prospectus Seldes carefully sought to call attention to the delicate balance between the new excitement and power provided by science and the frightening hazards that it introduced. He felt, above all, that the documentary he had schematized with two Caltech associates would be "immune to the charge of fraudulent optimism because we have connected Science with the problems which it has itself created and those it has not sufficiently devoted itself to." With the exception of Lewis Mumford, perhaps, Seldes seems to have been several decades ahead of most of his peers in cultural criticism. Only in 1991 did Andrew Ross publish a manifesto that called upon fellow critics to abandon their technophobia and help explore the ways in which science was shaping the popular imagination. Like Seldes, Ross has urged cultural critics to broaden themselves and become fully engaged in debates that might shape a common future.[59]

V

As late as 1969 Seldes continued to feel that intellectuals (meaning critics, creative writers, and humanistic scholars, apparently) were fundamentally hostile to science, a circumstance he described as silly and alarming. By that time, however, he was seventy-six, and his customarily contentious self had given way to the more mellow mood of a retired warrior, living modestly in a small apartment four floors below that of his daughter, Marian Seldes, the accomplished actress who devotedly looked after him in his last years (see Fig. 23).[60]

His mellowness even prompted him to recant or question views that he had passionately adhered to for decades. In one updated memorandum, for instance, he wrote that the comic strip, "far more popular than political cartooning, was perhaps the most despised of the vulgar arts, and though I still believe that all of these should be subjected to criticism, I have myself lost interest. The effort of looking at them is beyond me and, with one exception, I do not think that the strips of the past were as good as I thought them to be." The exception, of course, was Herriman's Krazy Kat.

In yet another undated memorandum Seldes recanted, to a greater degree even, his longstanding affirmation of American exceptionalism. In this instance his reversal can be explained, I believe, by the disputes, disappointments, violence, and embarrassments that afflicted the United States during the mid- and later 1960s:

Fig. 23. Gilbert Seldes with his daughter Marian (ca. 1969) at his apartment, 125 East 57th Street, New York.

The problem that I do not want to face is that, in a way, there never was any difference between the history of the United States and virtually all previous history. Granted that something unique exists in every nation and granted that in many respects what happened in America was similar to what happened elsewhere, it still could not be said of any country that it was "the last great hope" of mankind.

What we now come up against is, to many minds, an exaggeration of the evils from which we had thought ourselves immune. We did not invent violence in labor disputes nor organized crime nor assassination.[61]

And in a third memorandum written for a close friend early in 1968, we find his explicit recognition of the vacillation that we have noted concerning just how extensive a role the government ought to have in matters involving communications and cultural policy. "Perhaps the trouble is that I was brought up as an anarchist and now, thinking about the need for *control* of both social forms and mechanical invention, I would rather not face the part Government (in whatever country, however constituted) would play."[62]

Composing a segment for "As in My Time" in 1965, Seldes noted his disappointment early in the decade because television had "created no new form—as radio did in the daytime serial and elsewhere"; but writing in about 1969 he declared that "nothing could be more astonishing than the contrast between the deplorable daytime serial of thirty years ago [meaning radio] and what it is now. It is, on TV, almost sophisticated." He also wondered whether his feelings about "the intellectual" (meaning highbrow?) had changed since the 1920s. Or since 1936 when he published *Mainland*.[63]

Seldes apparently believed that "As in My Time" would be published, if not in his lifetime then posthumously. At one point he speculated about what reviewers "will find in mine—particularly the vulnerable spots." He revealed a perspective on the immigrant's role in American culture that is at variance with what he had felt during the 1930s and '40s. He flatly declared that he did not want his book "to be taken as a glorification of the immigrant—what the country offered to the immigrant was greater than what he brought—although much of what it offered . . . was created by other immigrants."[64] Should we consider that chauvinism, realism, or pessimism? Seldes had always taken great pride in the immigrants' contribution and made bitter remarks about the nativism that closed the Golden Door between 1921 and 1924. Here, too, he seems to have had a change of heart late in the 1960s—prompted, perhaps, by a sense of melancholy because the disintegration of a once rich public culture in the Untied States so distressed him.

Many of Seldes' contemporaries, such as Archibald MacLeish, also felt distressed and depressed by the condition of American life in the later 1960s. He was hardly unique in that regard. Nor did ill health alone prevent him from converting all of these segments and fragments into a publishable manuscript, though his health problems certainly did not help. Ultimately, I believe the heart of the problem was an intellectual one—an inability to demonstrate conclusively what he long envisioned as the central point of the book. To comprehend that point fully it helps to take note of a letter that he wrote to Robert M. Hutchins late in 1963: he had returned to his enduring concern, "the relation between the scholar intellectual and the destiny of democratic institutions in America."[65]

Less than four months later he specified the linkage that he hoped to be able to demonstrate and highlight in his book. What was the meaningful connection, the causal relationship, between the life of the mind in the United States during the two quite different decades when Seldes felt most vital, the 1920s and '30s? Once again, retrospective intellectual integrity may have overcome him. "I do not like to force connections," he confessed. Yet he wanted to show the nature of the 1920s as he had known and understood the decade, through the people I knew—and this was bound to be a study of the intellectuals, the aesthetes, and the expatriates—and then to see whether their fundamental attitude of mind did—or didn't—lead to a kind of communism which was, in a sense, halted during the great reconciliation between the intellectual and the politician . . . under FDR.[66]

Seldes found it plausible that such a connection did exist. But he agonized and worried about all sorts of uncontrollable variables, yet ignored others that have since been emphasized by students of American culture during the 1930s.[67]

A few years later, when Seldes was ineffectually spinning his wheels with "As in My Time," he made one final attempt to summarize his basic point. It really was, in a sense, the grail that he could not find because it was not the life that he personally had lived. Rather, it was a life that he had observed and rejected:

> I want to show—without forcing events and people to prove my point— that the initiative must be taken by men of intelligence who can avoid the errors of the past. Schematized—and shockingly simplified, I feel that
> > the aesthetes of the '20's who were unable to find any satisfaction in American life, prepared the way for the radical of the 30's who could not find in the American tradition a framework for change and progress in American society
> and together these have made easier the work of the demagogue and the reactionary.[68]

While it is easy to agree with Seldes' guiding imperative, namely, that intelligent people should avoid the errors of the past, it is not at all clear who he had in mind as the demagogues and reactionaries of the 1960s. George Wallace and Barry Goldwater? Perhaps, but Seldes doesn't say. As for the radicals of the 1930s who had been or reacted against the aesthetes a decade previous, there might have been a few, such as Dwight Macdonald and Matthew Josephson, but the causal relationship remains undeveloped in Seldes' schematization, and works such as Daniel Aaron's *Writers on the Left: Episodes in American Literary Communism* (1961) indicate that very few among his dramatis personae had been aesthetes during the 1920s.*

---

*Consider, for example, such prominent radical writers of the 1930s as Granville Hicks, V. F. Calverton, James T. Farrell, and Clifford Odets, all of them born around 1900–1904. Some became members of the Communist Party and others were non-Communist radicals. But *none* of them had been aesthetes or expatriates during the 1920s.

In the last analysis, it may well have been the problematic nature of Seldes' thesis that prevented him from bringing his manuscript to a state where others might have seen it through to publication after his death. What I find most intriguing is that the connection Seldes wanted to establish, but couldn't, would have provided a vindication of his own preferences and choices—although he never said so explicitly. He had disapproved of the aesthetes in certain ways during the 1920s and his *Mainland* (1936) shows just how clearly he disagreed with those who could not find "in the American tradition a framework for change and progress in American society." Seldes could and did. Had he been able to complete "As in My Time," it might have validated the major choices that he made and the initiatives that he took as a critic and historian during the interwar years.

The very last obstacle, perhaps, lay in his own disillusionment with the quality of American life during the mid- and later 1960s. That disillusionment surely gave him pause, and caused him to have second thoughts about the American tradition as a basis for change and progress in American society. Those he disagreed with during the Depression decade may have been dead wrong, but perhaps Seldes himself had not been exactly right either. Functioning as a self-aware yet subjective historian and trying to write a memoir that would have explanatory power in more broadly historical terms led him into a cul-de-sac and hence a particular kind of literary paralysis. By 1968 he no longer referred to his second hat, the historian's hat. "I am, after all, a critic," he wrote in 1968. Historical inquiry had not eluded him; but the power of historical explanation, in this instance, had.

VI

During 1967, when Seldes must have suspected that he would not finish "As in My Time," he undertook two small projects to satisfy himself and perhaps amuse his friends. The first he called "E. & O.E.," meaning "errors and omissions excepted," a phrase printed on the bottom of accounting bills that his father had sent from his pharmacy. The pamphlet consisted mainly of short pieces, reviews, and points of view that he had written earlier and wanted to reiterate. Some of them insisted upon vindication concerning issues where he believed that he had been maligned—such as the circumstances surrounding T. S. Eliot's receipt of *The Dial*'s annual award in 1922, or whether Seldes had deliberately chosen to omit Eliot's notes to "The Waste Land" when he published it in November of that year.[69]

"E. & O.E." was a literary reckoning, not so different, at least temperamentally, from the reckonings with his wobbly finances that Seldes made on occasion. In addition, he composed two broadsides that he circulated to friends. The first one, sent out in March 1968, he called "A Calendar of Inventions." In fact it was a miscellany of ruminations on topics that concerned him at the time, such as the following:

> I hope that scientists, statesmen, intellectuals, and all creative artists will not persist in the isolation of their disciplines; I want them to be together at least in their speculations about the future—since I think for the first time—the future is open to them. I would myself be unhappy in an authoritarian state setting up the calendar of social change.[70]

The next broadside, titled "In Others' Words," consisted of twenty-six quotations from people whose wisdom Seldes had admired over a span of more than six decades, including Whitman, Santayana, Durante, Spinoza, Russell, Eliot, Shaw, Bronowski, and J. Robert Oppenheimer.[71]

The reactions to "E. & O.E." that Seldes received from very old friends, like Edmund Wilson and Kenneth Burke, enlivened his spirits, and he took pleasure in playfully responding to their queries and corrections, mostly relating to minor points about pieces written many years earlier.[72]

In Broadside #3 Seldes included a translation from Spinoza's Latin sentence: "Of all things free man thinks about, death is the least," an observation that he quoted to Burke at Thanksgiving in 1969 by way of explaining why Seldes held a lower opinion of Malcom Cowley's work than Burke did. Clearly, in Seldes' opinion Cowley had written too much by way of self-vindication and, perhaps, to insure that his own perspective on the so-called "lost generation" would endure.

Two comments seem worthy of note in conclusion. When James Sibley Watson wrote to acknowledge Broadside #3, Seldes replied: "The motto is still, when you make a mistake, make it BIG."[73] In his last years, especially, Seldes had been notably candid about views that he wished to recant, in whole or in part. And he frankly acknowledged, as well, those things he wished he had done differently along with those that he still affirmed because they had given shape and meaning to his life.

The final comment to be noted Seldes actually wrote in 1934 at the age of forty-one. It is not so much a comment on his own demise as it is on those of people like Ernest Hemingway, Sinclair Lewis, and Dorothy Parker, each of whom had enormous self-destructive propensities, and each of whom Seldes found talented as artists but mean-spirited and unattractive as people. Seldes had written this sentence in his 1934 rebuttal to Hemingway on behalf of the recently deceased Ring Lardner: ". . . nine-tenths of us die undistinguished deaths and the others make ungodly messes of our deaths as we do of our lives."[74]

Hemingway blew half of his head off with a shotgun blast in 1961. Seldes died more peacefully of heart failure in his apartment, attended by his daughter Marian, just after midnight on September 29, 1970. A long obituary in the *New York Times* summarized his career fully though not altogether accurately. Others that followed during the next fortnight all emphasized the importance of *The 7 Lively Arts* and Seldes' lavish praise for Chaplin, Jolson, jazz, Krazy Kat, and the rest of his enthusiasms, "all of which," *Time* noted, "enraged serious critics of the day and titillated Seldes' many fans."[75]

One of the latter, a critic for the New York *Morning Telegraph* named Leo Mishkin, published a warm appreciation rather than a conventional obituary. "He was my teacher," Mishkin began, "as he was also for thousands of others just coming of age back in the mid-1920s":

Not in the sense of standing up in front of a classroom and lecturing, or correcting examinations. . . . But outside of school one of the requirements we all had was to read The Dial (at the time he was the editor). . . . And when "The Seven Lively Arts" was published in 1924 we knew instinctively that a new age, a new appreciation of the arts, indeed a new horizon had opened up for us all. . . . [His enthusiasms] will endure as long as the mass of Americans look for relaxation and rewards in the mass entertainment media. It was Gilbert Seldes who set the whole nation on that road. His name remains a monument to his influence.[76]

George Jean Nathan, a contemporary of Seldes who also specialized in popular culture and particularly in theatre criticism, quipped in 1923 that he was "constitutionally given to enthusiasm about nothing."[77] As Seldes showed just one year later, he was Nathan's temperamental opposite. To the extent that enthusiasm is more attractive than cynicism, Seldes emerges as one of the most engaging cultural critics of his time. To the extent that an excess of enthusiasm leaves one open to being second-guessed, Seldes also remains one of the most vulnerable critics of his time—yet one of the most versatile and instructive as well.

Abbreviations

AAAPSS	*Annals* of the American Academy of Political and Social Science
AIMT	"As in My Time," Seldes' unpublished autobiographical memoir
ALUV	Alderman Library, University of Virginia, Charlottesville
AMS, JR.	Arthur M. Schlesinger, Jr.
BLYU	Beinecke Library, Yale University
BPL	Boston Public Library, Department of Rare Books and Manuscripts
CURBML	Columbia University, Rare Book and Manuscript Library
GS	Gilbert Seldes
HLHU	Houghton Library, Harvard University
HRHUT	Harry Ransom Humanities Research Center, University of Texas at Austin
JFKL	John F. Kennedy Presidential Library, South Boston, Massachusetts

JR	Judith Randorf
MDLC	Manuscript Division, Library of Congress, Washington, D.C.
MS	Marian Seldes
MSP	Marian Seldes Papers (an extensive collection of Gilbert Seldes' correspondence, journals, clippings, notes, and memoirs)
NL	The Newberry Library, Chicago
NR	The New Republic
NYEJ	New York *Evening Journal*
NYPL	New York Public Library
NYPL-BR	New York Public Library for the Performing Arts, Lincoln Center, New York, Billy Rose Theatre Collection
NYT	*New York Times*
PR	*Partisan Review*
PUL	Princeton University Libraries
RGM	Rosenbach Gallery and Museum, Philadelphia, Pennsylvania
SEP	*Saturday Evening Post*
SLYU	Sterling Library, Yale University
SUL	Stanford University Libraries, Special Collections
UML	University of Michigan Library
UPSC	University of Pennsylvania Libraries, Special Collections Department
VF	*Vanity Fair*

Among Seldes' papers in his daughter's possession there are many segments of "As in My Time" in typescript. They are mostly eight- to fifteen-page transcripts of recollections and reflections that he dictated. Most of them are dated, but some are not. Only a few have headings or titles. Almost all of them, however, are marked by a letter code that looks like an acronym but, with the exception of SEP (for *Saturday Evening Post*) are not.

I have cited these in the notes in the following manner: GS (for Seldes), his code letters for the particular segment, arabic numerals for the appropriate pages, the date if there is one, and finally AIMT, MSP.

Notes

Introduction

1. GS, "Public Entertainment and the Subversion of Ethical Standards," AAAPSS no. 363 (Jan. 1966): 91; GS, "Surfaces," NR 45 (Feb. 17, 1926): 357–58. For Ralph Ellison's agreement with Seldes concerning the "swiftness of change" in the United States, see his speech accepting the National Book Award for *Invisible Man*, quoted in Daniel Aaron, *American Notes: Selected Essays* (Boston, 1994), 76.

2. Tape recording of a talk that Seldes gave in a class taught by Professor Charles Lee, May 1963, MSP.

3. Uncoded segment, Feb. 26, 1964, AIMT, MSP. Seldes' obituary in the Washington *Post* included an interview with Alistair Cooke, who commented that after World War II, when the popular arts that Seldes had exuberantly defended "turned into the mass media, he had troubled second thoughts, which he never lost, about a glut of entertainment, and the uses the media were discovering in reporting and exploiting violence." (*Post*, Oct. 1, 1970, p. C8.)

4. GS, WID-1/2, Feb. 1968, AIMT, MSP; GS, "How They Brought the Bad News," *Esquire* 16 (Nov. 1941): 166; GS, "No Timing Whatever," *Esquire* 11 (March 1939): 66, 166; GS, "The Accent of Truth," *Esquire* 26 (July 1946): 107–8.

5. GS, "New York Chronicle," *Criterion* 4 (Oct. 1926): 734; GS, "Complaint Against Critics: They Tell You What You Are and Where To Get Off," SEP 201 (June 1, 1929): 18; GS, "Don't Tread on Me!," *Esquire* 9 (Feb. 1938): 75, 126; GS, "What To Do for Money," *Esquire* 10 (Oct. 1938): 76, 124–25. Seldes' complaint about the quality of "critical ability" in the United States during the interwar years was echoed more stridently by his contemporary Harold E. Stearns in *The Confessions of a Harvard Man: The Street I Know Revisited* (Santa Barbara, 1984), 157–58.

6. See John Henry Raleigh, *Matthew Arnold and American Culture* (Berkeley, 1957); Arnold T. Schwab, *James Gibbons Huneker: Critic of the Seven Arts* (Stanford, 1963); Casey Nelson Blake, *Beloved Community: The Cultural Criticism of Randolph Bourne, Van Wyck Brooks, Waldo Frank, and Lewis Mumford* (Chapel Hill, 1990).

7. Carl N. Degler, *In Search of Human Nature: The Decline and Revival of Darwinism in American Social Thought* (New York, 1991), 90, 93, 95, 98; GS, SLAM-2, 1967, AIMT, MSP.

8. GS, "The Artist at Home," NR 42 (May 20, 1925): 341.

9. See Henry F. May, *The End of American Innocence: A Study of the First Years of Our Own Time, 1912–1917* (New York, 1959), 237, 296–97; Joan Shelley Rubin, "Between Culture and Consumption: The Mediations of the Middlebrow," in Richard W. Fox and T. J. Jackson Lears, eds., *The Power of Culture: Critical Essays in American History* (Chicago, 1993), 163–64; I. A. Richards, *Practical Criticism: A Study of Literary Judgment* (London, 1929), 3; John W. Aldridge, "Remembering Criticism," *American Scholar* 62 (Autumn 1993): 585.

10. GS, "The Beginnings of Popularity," in C. S. Marsh, ed., *Educational Broadcasting 1936* (Chicago, 1937), 337; GS, "The Errors of Television," *Atlantic* 159 (May 1937): 531–41; GS, "Omissions and Errors," *TV Guide*, July 28, 1962, p. 2; GS to Joe?, [1967?], MSP. ("I find that I outlined the course the movies might-should take five years before they did. . . .")

11. For some thoughtful definitions of what cultural studies means today, see Cary Nelson, "Always Already Cultural Studies: Two Conferences and a Manifesto," *Journal of the Midwest Modern Language Association* 24 (Spring 1991): 24–38, but esp. 30–38. The journal *Cultural Studies* has been published since 1987.

12. William Crary Brownell, *Democratic Distinction in America* (New York, 1927), 41; GS, "Beginnings of Popularity," 338. For an important revisionist statement concerning middlebrow literati and the democratization of culture beginning in the 1920s, see Rubin, "Between Culture and Consumption," 167 and passim.

13. GS, "Are Critics Necessary?," *TV Guide*, May 6, 1961, p. 23; GS, *The New Mass Media: Challenge to a Free Society* (1957; Washington, D.C., 1968).

14. See note 2 above and Sacvan Bercovitch, *The Rites of Assent: Transformation in the Symbolic Construction of America* (New York, 1993), 22.

15. GS, "True to Type," NYEJ, Jan. 8. 1932, p. 19; GS, "The Incomparable Bing," *Esquire* 21 (Feb. 1944): 38.

16. GS to AMS, Jr., Dec. 18, 1965, Schlesinger Papers, JFKL. See also GS, "Pick 'em Where You Find 'em," *Esquire* 1 (Feb. 1934): 70, 123, one of the most autobiographical pieces Seldes ever wrote.

17. GS, "Cakes and Ale Return to Favour," VF 21 (May 1924): 108; Florence Low, "An Enemy of the 'Bogus': Gilbert Seldes and *The Seven Lively Arts*" (M. A. thesis, Southern Illinois University, 1968), 56; John K. Hutchens, "One Thing and Another," SRL 52 (April 5, 1969): 36–38, a biographical piece built upon an interview with Seldes at seventy-six.

18. Marian Seldes to the author, Jan. 30, 1991.

19. GS, "The Lively Arts," *Park East* (June 1951).

20. For Seldes' acknowledgment of this in 1953 and 1957, see Chapter Seven, pp. 251–52, 279 below; and see Edward A. Purcell, Jr., *The Crisis of Democratic Theory: Scientific Naturalism & the Problem of Value* (Lexington, Ky., 1973), chs. 7–8, 11, 13–14.

Chapter 1. A Portrait of the Critic As a Young Man

1. For a valuable monograph on this cohort, see Leslie Fishbein, *Rebels in Bohemia: The Radicals of the Masses, 1911–1917* (Chapel Hill, 1982).

2. The most useful explication of intra-generational distinctions for this period is a book about European intellectuals by Robert Wohl, *The Generation of 1914* (Cambridge, Mass., 1979), esp. the Introduction and ch. 6.

3. George Seldes, *Witness to a Century: Encounters with the Noted, the Notorious, and the Three SOBs* (New York, 1987), 7–8.

4. GS, "No Decameron?," *Publisher's Weekly* 128 (Oct. 19, 1935): 1460. Seldes wrote the following in a 1932 newspaper column: "Although I was one of those uncomfortable little boys who are always reading and have to be booted out to play and get their health, I do not remember what I read until I was about twelve, when, in the natural course of events, I went through 'Uncle Tom's Cabin' . . . and ruined my eyes on 'David Copperfield.'" Concerning anything before that, he explained, he remembered nothing and could not say what had formed his mind or his style. His childhood, he declared, was a blur. GS, "True to Type," NYEJ, Sept. 13, 1932, p. 17.

5. GS to JR, March 8, 1910, MSP. The entire extract is underlined in the original. Because Seldes underlined so extensively for emphasis in his letters, ca. 1909–14, the practice loses much of its desired intensity. I have taken the liberty of not using italics where he underlined unless there is some other indication of special importance to him in the passage.

6. GS, "The House of Esau," *Nation* 113 (Oct. 5, 1921): 374; GS to JR, [Feb. 1923?], MSP. The book he refers to is *The 7 Lively Arts* (1924).

7. GS to Wilson, Dec. 10, 1968, Wilson Papers, BLYU. Final ellipses are by GS.

8. George Seldes, *Witness to a Century*, 3; GS to JR, Dec. 14, [1916?], MSP.

9. GS to AMS, Jr., Nov. 10, 1964, in response to Schlesinger's draft of a biographical preface to a softcover reprint of Seldes' *The Stammering Century* (New York, 1928), a history of perfectionist reform movements in nineteenth-century America. (The exchange located in the AMS, Jr. Papers, JFKL.) For context see Charles J. Rooney, Jr., *Dreams and Visions: A Study of American Utopias, 1865–1917* (Westport, Conn., 1985).

10. George Seldes, *Witness to a Century*, 3–7; George Seldes, *Tell the Truth and Run* (New York, 1953), vii–xvii; GS to John Dos Passos, Feb. 28, 1966, Dos Passos Papers, ALUV.

11. See Fishbein, *Rebels in Bohemia*, 7–8. It may or may not be noteworthy that, like Seldes, Van Wyck Brooks and Randolph Bourne also grew up in New Jersey. In the late nineteenth century the cultural seedbed of the United States seemed to be gradually shifting away from New England.

12. GS to Ralph Thompson, Oct. 7, 1936, Thompson Papers, NYPL; Seldes, *Tell the Truth and Run*, xviii–xix.

13. GS to Arthur E. Morgan, Sept. 5, 1939, HLHU. Morgan (1878–1975) wrote *Edward Bellamy* (1944) and *Nowhere Was Somewhere: How History Makes Utopias and Utopias Make History* (1946).

14. Seldes, *Tell the Truth and Run*, xvi, xxi–xxii; GS, "The Changing Temper at Harvard," *The Forum* 52 (Oct. 1914): 523. Scofield Thayer, a Harvard contemporary of Seldes and one of *The Dial*'s two affluent angels during Seldes' tenure as editor, was most concerned about the "Imaginative Individual . . . the Marooned Individual." See Nicholas Joost, *Years of Transition: The Dial, 1912–1920* (Barre, Mass., 1967), 273.

15. See GS, "Poets Can Learn from Acrobats," *Esquire* 13 (May 1940): 140; GS, *The New Mass Media; Challenge to a Free Society* (1957; Washington, D.C., 1968), 17–18.

16. GS to JR, [Dec. 1909?], MSP.

17. May, *The End of American Innocence: A Study of the First Years of Our Own Time, 1912–1917* (New York, 1959), 20; a copy of "Public Morals" in MSP.

18. GS to JR, April 21, 1911, MSP.

19. GS to JR, [early 1910], MSP. Fifty-eight years later he recalled that one evening in April 1910 "I was on top of a bus (not enclosed in that era) and saw Mark Twain in his white suit taking a stroll on lower fifth avenue. I am sure he was pleased to see me. . . ." GS to Edmund Wilson, Dec. 10, 1968, Wilson Papers, BLYU.

20. GS to Vincent Starrett, April 18, 1917, HRHUT; in 1948 Seldes received an invitation to join the Arthur Machen Society (fewer than fifty members); GS to Starrett, Oct. 27, 1964, PUL; and see Wesley D. Sweetser, *Arthur Machen* (New York, 1964), and Michael Murphy, ed., *Starrett vs. Machen: A Record of Discovery and Correspondence* (St. Louis, 1977).

21. Three letters from GS to Mackenzie, undated but clearly from 1912, 1913, and 1916 in HRHUT. See also Andro Linklater, *Compton Mackenzie: A Life* (London, 1987), 110–20. Seldes offered praise tempered by pretentious qualifications for Mackenzie in an essay about contemporary American and British fiction, "They Order This Matter Better," *Harvard Monthly* 57 (Jan. 1914): 105–7.

22. GS, "The American Novel II: Chaos and Lightening," *Harvard Monthly* 56 (March 1913); GS, "Form and the Novel," *Bookman* 70 (Oct. 1929): 128; GS journal, entries for Jan. 19 and 22, 1912, MSP. There is a charming account of Santayana's last lecture at Harvard (Jan. 22, 1912) in GS to Edmund Wilson, March 21, [1946 or 1947?], Wilson Papers, BLYU.

23. May, *End of American Innocence* 62, 219–20. Seldes met Lippmann at a Boston club on November 2, 1911, and apparently took an instant dislike to the 1910 graduate. Seldes described his reaction in a word: "awful." GS diary, MSP.

24. GS to George Seldes, Jan 26, [1912?], MSP.

25. GS, "Changing Temper at Harvard," 527.

26. Mencken's first choice had been the precocious but unreliable Harold Stearns (class of 1913); but Stearns failed to produce "and in the end I had to get Gilbert Seldes to do it." Mencken, *My Life as Author and Editor* (New York, 1992), 397.

27. GS, "Harvard," *The Smart Set* 67 (Feb. 1922): 60–61. Six years later Seldes noted with amusement that in 1885 Santayana and William Randolph Hearst had been on the *Lampoon* together, along with Ernest Lawrence Thayer, the future author of *Casey at the Bat*, a mock heroic poem first published on June 3, 1888, in the *San Francisco Examiner*, published by Hearst. GS, "Harvard," *College Humor* 17 (Dec. 1928): 116.

28. Sherman Paul, *Edmund Wilson: A Study of Literary Vocation in Our Time* (Urbana, 1965), 14–25; David Castronovo, *Edmund Wilson* (New York, 1984), 6–9.

29. George Seldes, *Witness to a Century*, 38–39. Seldes' middle name came from Disraeli's novel *Vivian Grey* (1826). Actually, Seldes used "Vivian" for almost another ten years. I do not know why he dropped it early in the 1920s. George received five B's in 1912–13; Gilbert got five A's. Years later, in 1967, Gilbert referred to college as "my Nietzschean days," apparently because Copeland "slipped me the undercover Nietzsche."

30. George Seldes to the author, Sept. 27, 1990; interview with George Seldes at Hartland-4-Corners, Vermont, July 12, 1991. For some of his more important books about international affairs, see *World Panorama, 1918–1933* (Boston, 1933), *Iron, Blood, and Profits: An Exposure of the World-Wide Munitions Racket* (New York, 1934), *Sawdust Caesar: The Untold Story of Mussolini and Fascism* (New York, 1935).

31. Putnam, Conn., *Observer*, June 12, 1929; reprinted in Tulsa, Okla., Sept. 7, 1930, clippings in MSP.

32. Quoted in Fishbein, *Rebels in Bohemia*, 182.

33. G. H. and G. V. Seldes, "The Press and the Reporter," *The Forum* 52 (Nov. 1914): 722, 723.

34. Ibid., 725. For later echoes, see George Seldes, *Freedom of the Press* (Indianapolis, 1935) and GS, *Proclaim Liberty!* (New York, 1942).

35. GS, "Changing Temper at Harvard," 527.

36. Ibid., 528–29.

37. Ibid., 524.

38. See Steven Biel, *Independent Intellectuals in the United States, 1910–1945* (New York, 1992), 40.

39. GS, *The Public Arts* (New York, 1956), 192; GS to JR, Feb. 15, 1910, and Jan. 6, 1912, MSP.

40. Seldes had no prior experience or training in music. His musical tastes would evolve from classical to a strong preference for jazz and popular tunes by the later 1920s. He never cared very much for grand opera, and his inclinations in classical music changed. He admired Wagner's music a great deal in 1910, for example, but not at all in later years.

41. GS to JR, Oct. 1, 1916, MSP. Seldes' columns were distributed by the Edward Marshall Syndicate.

42. GS, "The United States and the World," *The Living Age* 292 (Jan. 13 and Feb. 3, 1917): 114–15, 304, 308; GS to *The New Yorker*, [1963?], clipping in MSP. See also GS, "A New Literature of Peace," *The Dial* 62 (Jan. 25, 1917): 61–64.

43. George Seldes, *Tell the Truth and Run*, 28; unpub. memoir by George Seldes, undated, MSP.

44. GS, "Tramps—Are We?—Abroad," SEP 204 (June 11, 1932): 65; GS to JR, Jan. 24, March 4, 1917, MSP.

45. GS to JR, [Dec. 1917], MSP.

46. GS to JR, Dec. 20, 1916, MSP.

47. GS to JR, May 10, 1912, [April 11, 1914?]. Most of Seldes' collegiate writing appeared in *The Harvard Monthly* during 1913 and 1914. His topics included the American novel, Henri Bergson, the spirit of the Renaissance, Syndicalism as a gospel of violence, and Boston's Drama League.

48. GS to JR, Sept. 20 and fall 1916, early Jan., May 7, June 21, and July 16, 1917, MSP.

49. GS to JR, Oct. 18, 1916, March [22?], 1917, MSP.

50. GS to JR, Jan. 24, 1917, and undated [spring 1917?], [June 1917], MSP.

51. GS to JR, [Aug. 1917], MSP.

52. GS, "Making Books as Plentiful at Home as They Were at the Front," *Collier's* 65 (May 15, 1920): 76–77.

53. GS, "Emancipated," *Forum* 51 (June 1914): 899–910. Seldes first explored the same theme and situation in a playlet about "modern people" and their "modern views." GS, "Marionettes: A Modern Fantasy," *Harvard Monthly* 57 (Jan. 1914): 124–29.

54. GS to JR, Aug. 22, [1917?], MSP.

55. John Carver Edwards, "Atlanta's Prodigal Daughter: The Turbulent Life of Jane Anderson as Expatriate and Nazi Propagandist," *Atlanta Historical Journal* 28 (Summer 1984): 23–41, adapted as ch. 2 in Edwards, *Berlin Calling: American Broadcasters in Service to the Third Reich* (New York, 1991), 41–56; Zdzislaw Najder, *Joseph Conrad: A Chronicle* (New Brunswick, N.J., 1983), 411–13, 419–21; Fredrick R. Karl, *Joseph Conrad: The Three Lives* (New York, 1979), 162–63, 784–85, 790–91.

56. Joan Givner, *Katherine Anne Porter: A Life* (New York, 1982), 114–15, 120.

57. Ibid., 121–22; George Seldes, *Witness to a Century* 54–55, says that Gilbert and Jane were engaged in 1919.

58. Quoted in Givner, *Porter*, 121–22, from Porter, "American Critics Discredit Fetish of Foreign Artists."

59. "Lady Haw-Haw," *Time* 39 (Jan. 19, 1942): 30; Edwards, *Berlin Calling*, 51–56.

60. May, *End of American Innocence*, 336–37; Fishbein, *Rebels in Bohemia* 50, 52–53; James Oppenheim, "The Story of the *Seven Arts*," *American Mercury* 20 (June 1930): 156–64, esp. 157, 164.

61. See Joan Shelley Rubin, *The Making of Middlebrow Culture* (Chapel Hill, 1992), 290–99. Dorothy Parker, like Seldes, was born in 1893, wrote criticism, short stories, and became a central figure in the Algonquin circle. Seldes *seems* to have been oblivious to her existence even though, of course, he could not have been.

62. GS, "That Was Woollcott Speaking," *Esquire* 8 (July 1937): 79, 122. Seldes was infuriated by a radio broadcast in which Woollcott purported to explain to young people "who will do the fighting in the next war," how the United States got into the Great War, "what it was like and who was responsible." From Seldes' perspective, based heavily on the writings of Walter Millis, Woollcott was dead wrong.

63. See Harold Stearns, *The Confessions of a Harvard Man: The Street I Know Revisited*, Hugh Ford, ed. (Santa Barbara, 1984), 176. Stearns observed of the postwar mood swing by writers and critics that "seriousness was the one thing we wanted as little to do with as possible—hadn't we had our tragic full measure of it for too long."

64. William H. Nolte, ed., *Mencken's Smart Set Criticism* (Washington, D.C., 1987), 204.

Chapter 2. On Being an Editor and Becoming a Critic

1. GS to George, Nov. 16, [1921?], MSP. When artist Reginald Marsh painted an overture curtain for the "Greenwich Village Follies" in 1922, he crowded his scene of Village life with portraits of newly emerged literati and critics who were becoming young celebrities. In a truck whizzing across Seventh Avenue on the curtain were Wilson, Bishop, Seldes, Dos Passos, and Fitzgerald. At the center of the curtain, diving into the fountain at Washington Square, was the dazzling Zelda Fitzgerald. See Nancy Milford, *Zelda: A Biography* (New York, 1970), 96–97.

2. GS, "True to Type," NYEJ, Sept. 17, 1932, p. 15. For an illustration of Scofield Thayer's American chauvinism, see his letter to Alfred Stieglitz, Nov. 12, 1923, in Nicholas Joost, *Scofield Thayer and The Dial* (Carbondale, Ill., 1964), 59 n. 87.

3. See Thomas S. Hines, *Richard Neutra and the Search for Modern Architecture: A Biography and History* (New York, 1982); Daniel J. Singal, *The War Within: From Victorian to Modernist Thought in the South, 1919–1945* (Chapel Hill, 1982).

4. GS, "Nineties—Twenties—Thirties," *Dial* 73 (Nov. 1922): 574–78; GS, "An Enquiry into the Present State of Letters," *Dial* 83 (Nov. 1927): 436.

5. Joost, *Thayer and The Dial*, 3–4, 24–26.

6. Ibid., 4–8.

7. Ibid., 16–18.

8. "Announcement," *The Dial* 78 (June 1925): 532.

9. Joost, *Thayer and The Dial*, 175–76; *The Dial* 71 (June 1921): 63–68.

10. GS, "True to Type," NYEJ, Dec. 6, 1932, p. 16; Joost, *Thayer and The Dial*, 112, 117, 119.

11. Thayer, "Announcement," *The Dial* 78 (Jan. 1925): 90; Joost, *Thayer and The Dial*, 171; William Wasserstrom, *The Time of the Dial* (Syracuse, 1963), 100–101, 128.

12. Alyse Gregory, *The Day Is Gone* (New York, 1948), 210–11; Joost, *Thayer and The Dial*, 76–83; GS to Amy Lowell, May 26 and June 3, 1922, Lowell Papers, HLHU.

13. Joost, *Thayer and The Dial*, 196.

14. GS, "True to Type," NYEJ, Aug. 3, 1932, p. 17; Joost, *Thayer and The Dial*, 6.

15. Donald L. Miller, *Lewis Mumford: A Life* (New York, 1989), 112; Sophia Mumford to the author, Dec. 6, 1992.

16. See Casey Nelson Blake, *Beloved Community: The Cultural Criticism of Randolph Bourne, Van Wyck Brooks, Waldo Frank, and Lewis Mumford* (Chapel Hill, 1990), 235–38. For Seldes' defense of aestheticism, see GS, "Notes and Queries," NR 44 (Oct. 21, 1925): 231.

17. *Time* 1 (March 3, 1923): 12; Ralph G. Martin, *Henry and Clare: An Intimate Portrait of the Luces* (New York, 1991), 85, 97.

18. *Secession* no. 1 (Spring 1922): 22–24. For a running commentary on *Secession* and its motives, see John Tyree Fain and Thomas D. Young, eds., *The Literary Correspondence of Donald Davidson and Allen Tate* (Athens, Ga., 1974), 8, 10, 17, 19–20. There are scattered references to *Secession* in relation to *The Dial*.

19. Burke to Cowley, May 5, 1922, in Paul Jay, ed., *The Selected Correspondence of Kenneth Burke and Malcolm Cowley, 1915–1981* (New York, 1988), 118–19.

20. See Joost, *Thayer and The Dial*, 246–47.

21. See GS to Edmund Wilson, Aug. 15 and Oct. 24, 1922, Wilson Papers, BLYU; GS to Nock, May 23, 1922, Dial/Thayer Papers, series 1, box 6, BLYU; GS to Mary Maguire Colum, [1922?], Berg Collection, NYPL.

22. Henry S. Canby to GS, Aug. 29, 1922, Dial/Thayer Papers, box 6, BLYU. For the best treatment of Canby and the development of "middlebrow" cultural taste, see Joan Shelley Rubin, *The Making of Middlebrow Culture* (Chapel Hill, 1992), 110–47.

23. Joost, *Thayer and The Dial*, 239; GS to Edmund Wilson, [May or June 1922?], Wilson Papers, BLYU; Clive Bell, *Old Friends: Personal Recollections* (London, 1956).

24. GS to Edmund Wilson, [1922?], Wilson Papers, PUL. Seldes wrote the following to J. S. Watson on July 25, 1922 (Dial/Thayer Papers, box 7, BLYU): "Frederick Booth got very sore at my suggestion that he shorten the story and has refused to send it in. I hope he does not commit suicide with my letter on his person."

25. The sad and sordid story of Hemingway's hatred for Seldes has never been fully told. The best account appears in Nicholas Joost, *Ernest Hemingway and the Little Magazines: The Paris Years* (Barre, Mass., 1968), 130–31, 152–54, 160–64; Joost, *Thayer and The Dial*, 60. It may seem strange that Dorothy Parker's name hardly ever surfaces in Seldes' career. They were exact contemporaries (her dates are 1893–1967); she took over the theatre column for *Vanity Fair* while Seldes wrote a comparable column for *The Dial*; and she wrote a lot for the *Saturday Evening Post* late in the 1920s when Seldes did also. Her central role at the Algonquin and her malicious rumor-mongering on Hemingway's behalf in 1929–30 suggest why Seldes and Parker had no relationship. In 1933, however, when she published a collection of stories, *After Such Pleasures*, he slyly praised her in his daily column. "I wish there were no Dorothy Parker legend," he wrote. "Almost in spite of the pleasure I get when I see her once a year or so, I could wish that I had never met her, so that when she published a book, discussion would be about the book only, not about the person or the legend. The book itself is enough." GS, "True to Type," NYEJ, Oct. 24, 1933, p. 17.

26. Joost, *Hemingway and the Little Magazines*, 165.

27. Hemingway, *The Sun Also Rises* (New York, 1926), 121–29; James R. Mellow, *Hemingway: A Life Without Consequences* (Boston, 1992), 311–12. Although Mellow is sympathetic to Hemingway in general, he finds Seldes utterly blameless for the thirty-

seven-year quarrel, and chides Hemingway for being so churlish. For Seldes' repetitious use of "irony and pity" see GS, *The 7 Lively Arts*, 2nd ed. (New York, 1957), 25 (in connection with Charlie Chaplin), and 211, 212, 217 (in connection with George Herriman's Krazy Kat). Hemingway had read Seldes' book very carefully. The preoccupation with "irony and pity" surfaces once again in GS, *An Hour with the Movies and the Talkies* (Philadelphia, 1929), 71.

28. Hemingway to Pound, Feb. 10, 1924, in Carlos Baker, ed., *Ernest Hemingway: Selected Letters, 1917–1961* (New York, 1981), 111; Mellow, *Hemingway*, 257. Following Wilson's fundamentally favorable "Dry-Points" review in *The Dial* (August 1924), Hemingway submitted a story that Gregory rejected on December 4. He then sent in one of his major early stories in January 1925. Thayer wanted to accept it but Watson and Marianne Moore voted no and carried the day. It should also be noted that Hemingway stories that later came to be regarded as classics were rejected by Mencken and Nathan at the *American Mercury*

29. Parker is quoted in the editor's footnote to a nasty letter that Hemingway sent to Seldes on December 30, 1929 ("Aren't all the magazines of culture now defunct?"). Baker, ed., *Hemingway: Selected Letters*, 318; and Hemingway to Arnold Gingrich, Nov. 16, 1934, in ibid., 411.

30. Nicholas Joost to GS, Feb. 16, 1965, and GS to Joost, Feb. 18, 1965, MSP. For the most definitive repudiation of Hemingway's accusations against Seldes, see Carlos Baker, *Ernest Hemingway: A Life Story* (New York, 1969), 613.

31. GS to Moore, [early Dec. 1926], Dial/Thayer Papers, box 6, BLYU; an undated clipping (1929) from the New York *Graphic*, ibid.

32. GS, "True to Type," NYEJ, Sept. 24, 1932, p. 14; GS to Nicholas Joost, Feb. 18, 1965, MSP. The text of *A Moveable Feast* was read and approved for publication by Malcolm Cowley, a long-time friend of Hemingway. This and other comparable episodes strongly suggest that Cowley also did not care for Seldes. See William Wasserstrom, "Hemingway, the *Dial*, and Ernest Walsh," *South Atlantic Quarterly* 65 (Spring 1966): 171–77, esp. 173.

33. GS to Watson, June 26, 1922, Dial/Thayer Papers, box 7, BLYU. For the circumstances under which Hemingway first met George Seldes in 1922 at Genoa, when Seldes was head of the *Chicago Tribune's* Central European Bureau, see Mellow, *Hemingway*, 180.

34. Lawrence Langner, *The Magic Curtain: The Story of a Life in Two Fields, Theatre and Invention, by the Founder of the Theatre Guild* (New York, 1951), 71; Ellen Thayer to GS, April 21, 1927, Dial/Thayer Papers, box 6, BLYU; GS to Thayer, [ca. April 22/23, 1927], ibid. Gordon Hutner, "The Dynamics of Erasure: Anti-Semitism and the Example of Ludwig Lewisohn," *Prospects* 16 (1991): 391–404, the Brande quotation on p. 397.

35. Anderson to Roger Sergel, [Dec. 18, 1923?], in Howard Mumford Jones and Walter B. Rideout, eds., *Letters of Sherwood Anderson* (Boston, 1953), 117; MacLeish to Bishop, July 30, 1924, in R. H. Winnick, ed., *Letters of Archibald MacLeish, 1907 to 1982* (Boston, 1983), 142. For a notable instance of philo-Semitism by an old-line critic, see James Gibbons Huneker, "My Friends the Jews," in Huneker, *Steeplejack*, 2 vols. (New York, 1920), I: 162–72, esp. 164.

36. GS, "The House of Esau," *The Nation* 113 (Oct. 5, 1921): 374; Robert C. Benchley, "The Negro Revues," *Life* (Aug. 10, 1922): 18. Seldes used the phrase "nigger show" (meaning an all-black minstrel show) casually, and allowed it to stand in the 1957 second edition of *The 7 Lively Arts*, 148. On p. 73 of the 1957 edition, however, he interpolated the following: "In the paragraph below a phrase occurs which I should not use now and I haven't been too sure about leaving it in. I think it is fair to say that the words "nigger

mammy" could have been used without giving offense in 1924. To use it now, in a new work, would be gratuitously insulting, but it is not insulting to say that it had been used. I hope the change in our vocabulary means that a change in feeling has occurred, because it is of small value to suppress a word and keep the thought. The substitutes for the offensive word thought up by racist Southerners seem to me abominable."

37. Pound to Quinn, Oct. 9, 1920, in Timothy Materer, ed., *The Selected Letters of Ezra Pound to John Quinn, 1915–1924* (Durham, N.C., 1991), 194–95; GS to the editor of *The Literary Review*, Nov. 27, 1922, Dial/Thayer Papers, box 6, BLYU; George Seldes, *Witness to a Century* (New York, 1987), 262. In March 1920 Quinn had persuaded Thayer and Seldes to hire Pound as Paris correspondent for *The Dial*.

38. Eliot, *After Strange Gods: A Primer of Modern Heresy* (London, 1934), 19–20; Eliot to Pound, Oct. 22, 1922, and Eliot to Seldes, Dec. 1, 1922, in Valerie Eliot, ed., *The Letters of T. S. Eliot* (San Diego, 1988), I: 586, 604–5; Eliot to Seldes, Nov. 12, 1922, MSP.

39. See Joost, *Thayer and The Dial*, 60–72 and passim.

40. Ibid., 161; GS to Wilson, Feb. 24, 1965, Wilson Papers, BLYU; GS to Richard Poirier, March 20, 1965, MSP; also a ten-page typescript to Hiram Liveright dictated by Seldes in his later years, sometime after 1965, concerning Seldes' relationship with Eliot and publication of "The Waste Land," MSP. Seldes acknowledged in this text that many of the details from 1922 eluded him.

41. Eliot, ed., *Letters of T. S. Eliot*, I: 359, 501, 515.

42. Ibid., 571, 586; Seldes to Sibley Watson, Aug. 31, 1922, Dial/Thayer Papers, box 7, BLYU; Peter Ackroyd, *T. S. Eliot: A Life* (New York, 1984), 126–27. Seldes alerted Watson that "the notes, by the way, are exceedingly interesting and add much to the poem, but don't become interested in them because we simply cannot have them."

43. Eliot to Seldes, Dec. 27, 1922, MSP; Daniel H. Woodward, "Notes on the Publishing History and Text of the Waste Land," *Papers of the Bibliographical Society of America* 58 (3rd quarter 1964): 258, Wasserstrom, *The Time of the Dial*, 104.

44. GS to Sibley Watson, June 1, 1966, and March 24, 1968, Berg Collection, NYPL. Seldes rehashed the matter once again with Watson in the final months of his life, March 3, 1970, ibid.

45. GS to Anderson, Oct. 26, Nov. 10, 1921, March 9 and 16, 1922, Anderson Papers, NL.

46. GS, unpaginated typescript that begins, "This Is about Sherwood Anderson," p. 3, MSP. It is worth noting that as a writer Anderson felt indebted to Van Wyck Brooks, a critic with whom Seldes agreed on very little. For a more sympathetic treatment, see T. J. Jackson Lears, "Sherwood Anderson: Looking for the White Spot," in Richard Wightman Fox and Lears, eds., *The Power of Culture: Critical Essays in American History* (Chicago, 1993), 13–37, esp. 34–37.

47. GS, "About Anderson," pp. 4–5. Similarly, Seldes and John Dos Passos, who met at Harvard, remained lifelong friends; but Seldes' response to *Manhattan Transfer* was "cold." GS to Sibley Watson, Jan. 16, 1926, Dial/Thayer Papers, box 7, BLYU.

48. Spingarn, "The Younger Generation: A New Manifesto," *The Freeman* 5 (June 7, 1922): 296–98. This essay is reprinted in Spingarn, *Creative Criticism and Other Essays*, 2nd ed. (New York, 1931), 109–22. Early in 1922 Brander Matthews, Columbia's conservative literary historian and critic, reviewed Harold Stearns' new manifesto, *America and the Young Intellectuals* (1921), and titled his piece "America and the Juvenile Highbrows," *NYT Book Review*, Jan. 29, 1922, p. 8. The title tells all.

49. Elena Wilson, ed., *Letters on Literature and Politics, 1912–1972* [by Edmund Wilson] (New York, 1977), 88; GS to Spingarn, July 25, 1922, Spingarn Papers, NYPL. Spingarn lived at a country home called Troutbeck near Amenia, New York, a town just

west of the Connecticut border in the Berkshire foothills. Lewis Mumford summered in one of the cottages at Troutbeck and later purchased a permanent home in Amenia.

50. Joost, *Thayer and The Dial*, 119; G. A. M. Janssens, *The American Literary Review: A Critical History, 1920–1950* (The Hague, 1968), 89.

51. Nicholas Joost, *Years of Transition: The Dial, 1912–1920* (Barre, Mass, 1967), 270; Brooks, *Days of the Phoenix: The Nineteen-Twenties I Remember* (New York, 1957), 66; Edmund Wilson, *The Thirties: From Notebooks and Diaries of the Period*, Leon Edel, ed. (New York, 1980), 356–57.

52. Boyd, "Aesthete: Model 1924," in John K. Hutchens, ed., *The American Twenties: A Literary Panorama* (Philadelphia, 1922), 353–60, reprinted from *The American Mercury* (Jan. 1924); Cowley, *Exile's Return: A Literary Odyssey of the 1920s* (1934; New York, 1951), 190–91.

53. Cowley, *Exile's Return*, 193–94.

54. Autobiographical typescript marked GSS—11, June 12, [1968?], MSP. For Seldes' approving linkage between the aesthete and wit and "feeling," see GS, "Notes and Queries," NR 44 (Oct. 21, 1925): 231.

55. GS to James Sibley Watson, July 17, 1922, Dial/Thayer Papers, box 7, BLYU; GS to Wilson, Feb. 24, 1965, Wilson Papers, BLYU.

56. Joost, *Thayer and The Dial*, 40, 43–44, 46, 105–9; J. S. Watson to GS, [later 1922], Dial/Thayer Papers, box 7, BLYU; Lowell to GS, Aug. 26, Nov. 23, 1921, Lowell Papers, HLHU. In May 1922 Seldes wrote a laudatory essay about Lowell for *Vanity Fair*, for which she communicated her warm appreciation.

57. GS to J. S. Watson, May 26, 1922, Dial/Thayer Papers, box 7, BLYU; Max Beerbohm to GS, Jan. 23, 1923, HRHUT; GS to S. N. Behrman, Feb. 8 and 28, 1960, HRHUT; GS to Norman Foerster, Aug. 10, 1922, Foerster Papers, SUL; GS to Raymond Mortimer, Jan. 5, 1922, PUL.

58. Anon. to Sibley Watson, April 6, 1922, Dial/Thayer Papers, box 7, BLYU; and see *The Dial* generally for 1920 to 1923, but especially April 1920, October 1921, January and May 1923. For the personal impact of Nietzsche, see ch. 1, note 29 above.

59. GS, "Claude Bovary," *The Dial* 73 (Oct. 1922): 438. For an extensive statement of critical principles made in 1924 by Henry Seidel Canby when the *Saturday Review of Literature* emerged, see Norman Cousins, *Present Tense: An American Editor's Odyssey* (New York, 1967), 7.

60. "American Letter," Dante, Va., October 1922, *The Dial* 73 (Nov. 1922): 555–58, quotation at 557–58.

61. GS, "The Theatre," *The Dial* 71 (Nov. and Dec. 1921): 620–21, 724–25, quotation at 724.

62. Benchley, "Destroy the Audience!," *Life* 78 (Dec. 22, 1921): 18.

63. See GS, "The Theatre," *The Dial* 76 (Jan. 1924): 98–99; GS to George Seldes, April 3, [1922], MSP.

64. GS to Sylvia Beach, Sept. 14, Nov. 10, Dec. 12, 1921, PUL; J. S. Watson to GS, June 6, 1922, and GS to Watson, June 12, 1922, Dial/Thayer Papers, box 7, BLYU; Jeffrey Potter, *Men, Money & Magic: The Story of Dorothy Schiff* (New York, 1976), 63.

65. GS to Mary Colum, [late spring 1922], Berg Collection, NYPL; GS to Van Doren, Dial/Thayer Papers, box 6, BLYU; GS to H. S. Canby, Aug. 30, 1922, ibid.

66. GS, "Ulysses," *The Nation* 115 (Aug. 30, 1922): 211–12. When the *Little Review* was censored by U.S. authorities for publishing segments of *Ulysses*, Thayer and Watson were notably supportive, especially in view of the criticism that had been directed at *The Dial* by the *Little Review*. Joost, *Thayer and The Dial*, 81, 102.

67. GS to Sibley Watson, [May 27, 1970], MSP; GS to Joyce, [Jan. 1923], MSP. Late in

1933, when Judge John M. Woolsey approved the admission of *Ulysses* to the United States, Bennett Cerf and Random House promptly decided to publish it. Seldes celebrated this reversal with as much enthusiasm as he applauded the end of Prohibition. See GS, "True to Type," NYEJ, Dec. 9, 1933, p. 11.

68. "The New Order of Critical Values," VF 18 (April 1922): 40–41.

69. On April 7, 1922, Seldes wrote to Mencken (in Baltimore): "I don't see why you should have paid for my dinner and drink, but I will do worse for you some day." That "day" came two weeks later. On November 9, 1923, Seldes closed a brief note to Mencken from *The Dial*, referring to the new *American Mercury*: "I palpitate to see your magazine." Mencken Papers, NYPL.

70. Fitzgerald, "Echoes of the Jazz Age" (Nov. 1931), in Edmund Wilson, ed., *The Crack-Up* (New York, 1945), 14; GS, "True to Type," May 31 and June 13, 1932, NYEJ, pp. 17, 13, quotation from June 13.

71. "Sganarelle" [GS], "A Competent Critic," *The Dial* 68 (Jan. 1920): 107–12. Joost incorrectly identifies Watson as "Sganarelle."

72. Cynthia Ozick, "It Take a Great Deal of History to Produce a Little Literature," PR 60 (1993, no. 2): 195; Wilson, "On Being Bibliographed" (1943), in Wilson, *Classics and Commercials: A Literary Chronicle of the Forties* (New York, 1950), 112.

73. James Gibbons Huneker, "Criticism," in Huneker, *Steeplejack*, II: 122–27, esp. 123. See also Huneker, *Americans in the Arts, 1890–1920* (New York, 1985), 295–308, 403–41.

74. GS, "T. S. Eliot," *Nation* 115 (Dec. 6, 1922): 614–16.

75. D.H., "Should Drama Critics Be Guinea Pigs of the Theatre?," *Life* 80 (Oct. 5, 1922): 20.

76. George Jean Nathan, "The Code of a Critic," from *The World in Falseface* (New York, 1923), reprinted in Hutchens, ed., *The American Twenties*, 365–66.

77. Wasserstrom, *Time of the Dial*, 92; Joost, *Thayer and The Dial*, 201, 207; "Comment," *The Dial* 72 (Feb. 1922): 234.

78. GS, "Manners Maketh Man," *The Freeman* 5 (April 12, 1922): 115–16.

79. Matthew Josephson, "Made in America," *Broom* 2 (June 1922): 266–70, quotation at 270; Philippe Soupault, "The 'U.S.A.' Cinema," *Broom* 5 (Sept. 1923): 68, 69.

80. Loeb to GS, Sept. 15, 1922, and GS to Loeb, Oct. 10, 1922, PUL; Joost, *Thayer and The Dial*, 201.

81. GS to Mrs. J. Warren Ritchey, Sept. 6, 1922, Dial/Thayer Papers, box 6, BLYU; GS to J. S. Watson, Sept. 13, 1922, ibid., box 7; GS to J. P. Bishop, [ca. Sept. 27, 1922], Bishop Papers, PUL. Seldes and Bishop had become close friends by 1922, and for several years thereafter Seldes shared his intimate feelings and aspirations with Bishop in an affectionate correspondence.

82. GS to Leo A. Pollock, Nov. 10, 1922, Dial/Thayer Papers, box 6, BLYU; Joost, *Thayer and The Dial*, 211. Unlike so many of his contemporaries, who suffered at one time or another from serious nervous or mental breakdowns—T. S. Eliot (1922), Van Wyck Brooks (1925–1929), Edmund Wilson (1929), Dwight Macdonald (1953)—Seldes never did, though his correspondence suggests that at times he felt quite fragile.

83. GS to George Seldes, Oct. 11, 1922, Dial/Thayer Papers, box 6, BLYU; GS to Frank Crowninshield, Dec. 8, 1922, ibid.

84. Joost, *Thayer and The Dial*, 167; Cummings to William Slater Brown, Aug. 12, 1923, in F. W. Dupee and George Stade, eds., *Selected Letters of E. E. Cummings* (New York, 1969), 74. Seldes tried to reconstruct the episode in a very long and fascinating letter to Dos Passos, Feb. 28, 1966, Dos Passos Papers (#5950aa), box 4, ALUV. Charles Norman provided an account, disputed by Seldes regarding some details, in *E. E. Cummings: The Magic-Maker* (New York, 1964), 138–40.

85. GS to George Seldes, [late May and early June 1923], MSP. Seldes expressed a strong preference at this time for Paris over London as an affordable place to get work done and enjoy life. Moving from his personal perspective to a much broader view, one scholar has recently observed that between 1918 and 1941 the reputation of London as a grand icon and central place of British national identity declined precipitously. See Stephen Daniels, *Fields of Vision: Landscape Imagery and National Identity in England and the United States* (Princeton, 1993), 32. But cf. Noel Annan, *Our Age: English Intellectuals Between the World Wars—A Group Portrait* (New York, 1990).

86. Joost, *Thayer and The Dial*, 125–27, 212–13, 232; GS to Bishop, [late 1923 or early 1924], MSP.

87. GS to John Quinn, Dec. 12, 1923, Dial/Thayer Papers, box 6, BLYU; GS to Eileen Creelman, Dec. 14, 1923, ibid.

88. Janssens, *American Literary Review: A Critical History*, 71–72.

89. Ibid., 53, 58. See also Gaye L. Brown, ed., *The Dial: Arts and Letters in the 1920s* (Worcester, Mass., 1981).

90. GS, "New York Chronicle," *Criterion* 4 (Jan. 1926): 175.

91. GS, "Lively Arts," *Park East* (April 1951): 43–44. See also Marianne Moore, "The Dial," *Life and Letters Today* 27/28 (Dec. 1940 and Jan. 1941): 175–83 and 3–9; and Moore, "*The Dial*: A Retrospect," in *Predilections* (New York, 1955), 103–14.

92. See GS to Edmund Nehls, Aug. 12, 1956, HRHUT; GS to Nathan Halper, May 26, 1965, Halper Papers, CUSCBL. For examples of Seldes' input see Nehls, ed., *D. H. Lawrence: A Composite Biography*, 3 vols. (Madison, Wis., 1957–59), and Halper, *The Early James Joyce* (New York, 1973).

93. Burke, "Gilbert Seldes," *Proceedings of the American Academy of Arts and Letters* 2nd ser., no. 21 (New York, 1971): 95–97.

Chapter 3. The Lively Arts and Cultural Criticism Revitalized

1. See Florence Low, "An Enemy of the 'Bogus': Gilbert Seldes and *The Seven Lively Arts*" (M. A. thesis, Southern Illinois Univ., 1968), 22; GS to Edmund Wilson, May 2, [1923], Wilson Papers, BLYU; GS, "The Cult of the Second-Rate," VF 23 (Oct. 1924): 68.

2. GS, *The 7 Lively Arts*, 2nd ed. (New York, 1957), 108.

3. Ibid., 303, 304.

4. Ibid., 242, 304.

5. Ibid., 81, 300.

6. William H. Nolte, ed., *H. L. Mencken's Smart Set Criticism* (Washington, D.C., 1987), 204; Arnold T. Schwab, *James Gibbons Huneker: Critic of the Seven Arts* (Stanford, 1963); Huneker, *Unicorns* (New York, 1917), 218–27; Steven Biel, *Independent Intellectuals in the United States, 1910–1945* (New York, 1992), 58–59.

7. GS, *7 Lively Arts*, 3, 8.

8. Nicholas Joost, *Years of Transition: The Dial, 1912–1920* (Barre, Mass., 1967), 273–74; GS, *7 Lively Arts*, 49.

9. Santayana to Brooks, May 22, 1927, in Daniel Cory, ed., *The Letters of George Santayana* (London, 1955), 225–26.

10. Lloyd Goodrich, *Reginald Marsh* (New York, 1972); Marilyn Cohen, *Reginald Marsh's New York* (New York, 1983); Vadim Uraneff, "Commedia dell'arte and American Vaudeville," *Theatre Arts Magazine* 7 (Oct. 1923): 318–28.

11. GS to Walter Haviland, Dec. 18, 1922, Dial/Thayer Papers, box 6, BLYU; GS, "The Damned Effrontery of the Two-a-Day," VF 19 (Oct. 1922): 51, 102.

12. GS to Canby, Nov. 3, 1922, Dial/Thayer Papers, box 6, BLYU.

13. GS to Edmund Wilson, [Jan. 1923], Wilson Papers, BLYU; GS, "The One Man Show," VF 21 (Aug. 1923): 74.

14. See Brooks, *Three Essays on America* (New York, 1934), 17–19, 177, 182–83, and passim; Lawrence W. Levine, *Highbrow/Lowbrow: The Emergence of Cultural Hierarchy in America* (Cambridge, Mass., 1988); Casey Nelson Blake, *Beloved Community: The Cultural Criticism of Randolph Bourne, Van Wyck Brooks, Waldo Frank, & Lewis Mumford* (Chapel Hill, 1990), 115–117, 136, 138–39, 160.

15. See Daniel T. Rodgers, *The Work Ethic in Industrial America 1850–1920* (Chicago, 1978), 91.

16. Quoted in Carl N. Degler, *In Search of Human Nature: The Decline and Revival of Darwinism in American Social Thought* (New York, 1991), 54.

17. Levering, "If Shakespeare Had Written for Broadway," *Puck* 60 (Dec. 26, 1906): 6.

18. *Life*, Aug. 10, 1922, p. 1.

19. GS, *7 Lively Arts*, 295–96. In the 1957 second edition Seldes acknowledged that in 1923–24 he hadn't *"placed* the popular arts in relation to either the fine arts or the folk arts" (ibid., 81).

20. GS to AMS, Jr., [1961?], Schlesinger Papers, JFKL; George Seldes, "A Brother Looks at a Writer," *The World* (Tulsa, Okla.), Sept 7, 1930, clipping in MSP; George Seldes, *Witness to a Century* (New York, 1987), 282.

21. GS, *7 Lively Arts*, 292–94.

22. Ibid., 294–95.

23. Robert Redding, *Starring Robert Benchley: "Those Magnificent Movie Shorts"* (Albuquerque, 1973), 81–82; Benchley, "Drama," *Life*, June 19, 1924, p. 20. For Seldes' praise of Benchley's satire of business and businessmen in *Of All Things* (1921), see *The Dial* 72 (Jan. 1922): 95.

24. GS, *7 Lively Arts*, 11, 186. In the privacy of reminiscence during his seventies, Seldes tended to *contrast* rather than try to combine high and popular culture. On February 27, 1964, he dictated the following: "One of the charming evenings of my life was when I came home and found two letters—one from T. S. Eliot and the other from Paul Whiteman [the jazz band leader]. That must have been in the early 1920's." (Uncoded typescript, p. 10, AIMT, MSP.)

25. Crowninshield to Seldes, May 13, 1924, MSP.

26. See GS, *7 Lively Arts*, 63, 245, and passim.

27. Ibid., 272.

28. GS to Edmund Wilson, [late June 1923?], Wilson Papers, BLYU.

29. Margery Longley, Louis Silverstein, and Samuel Tower, *America's Taste, 1851–1959: The Cultural Events of a Century Reported by Contemporary Observers in the Pages of the New York Times* (New York, 1960).

30. GS, "Cakes and Ale Return to Favour," VF 22 (May 1924): 49, 108.

31. GS, *7 Lively Arts*, 133–34, 263–65.

32. Ibid., 194; GS to Norman Hapgood, Nov. 25, 1922, Dial/Thayer Papers, box 6, BLYU; examples of the personalized greetings will be found in the Edmund Wilson Papers, BLYU.

33. GS to Frank Crowninshield, July 28, 1922, Dial/Thayer Papers, box 6, BLYU. In 1944, when Seldes learned that E. E. Cummings intended to publish a book-length anthology of Krazy Kat "strips," he offered to lend Cummings "my ancient and incom

plete collection of these masterpieces." The copy of that volume (New York, 1946) in the Berg Collection, NYPL, has inserted an extract of what Seldes wrote about Krazy Kat in *The 7 Lively Arts*.

34. GS, *7 Lively Arts*, 66, 153–63; Low, "An Enemy of the 'Bogus,'" 83.

35. Low, "An Enemy of the 'Bogus,'" 81; GS, "Toujours Jazz," *The Dial* 75 (Aug. 1923): 151–66; GS to Berlin, Oct. 3, 1923, Dial/Thayer Papers, box 6, BLYU.

36. GS, "Some Premature Reviews of Our First Jazz Opera," VF 23 (March 1925): 42, 94; GS, *7 Lively Arts*, 95–98, 145–46.

37. GS, "An African Legend in Choreography," VF 21 (Dec. 1923): 73, 92; GS, *7 Lively Arts*, 145–52, esp. 147, 151–52. During the spring of 1922, when Seldes schematized the essay for *Vanity Fair* that became "The Darktown Strutters on Broadway" in *The 7 Lively Arts*, he wrote the following to Edmund Wilson: "For the first time the negro shows would be treated with sympathetic cynicism (they really aren't good shows, mostly) and . . . for the first time in my series the featured persona would be a dead man, the great and immortal Jim Europe." (Undated, Wilson Papers, BLYU.)

38. GS, *7 Lively Arts*, 181–82.

39. Ibid., 7.

40. Wilson, "The Theatre," *The Dial* 75 (Nov. 1923): 514; Edmund Wilson, *Letters on Literature and Politics, 1912–1972*, Elena Wilson, ed. (New York, 1977), 94, 114, 117; Wilson's review is conveniently reprinted in *The Shores of Light: A Literary Chronicle of the Twenties and Thirties* (New York, 1952), 156–64. Seldes pulled no punches in a review of *The Undertaker's Garland* by Bishop and Wilson (1922) in *The Dial* 73 (Nov. 1922): 574–78.

41. Wilson, *The American Earthquake: A Documentary of the Twenties and Thirties* (Garden City, N.Y., 1958), esp. 15–94. On March 17, 1968, Seldes observed that when Wilson dropped "my subject" there was no one else who knew what they knew who had any interest in it. WID-13, AIMT, MSP.

42. Wilson, *Letters on Literature and Politics*, 127; Wilson, *The Twenties: From Notebooks and Diaries of the Period*, Leon Edel, ed. (New York, 1975), 231–32. In 1935 Wilson made a brief reference to "the usual Seldes cocktail crowd" and in 1941 he remarked that "Seldes works for television and I never see him any more." That would change in the 1950s and '60s.

43. Wilson, *Shores of Light*, 230. The whole essay runs from 229–47.

44. Ibid., 237. A response from "An Observer" appeared in NR 47 (July 28, 1926): 283.

45. GS to Wilson, Aug. 10 [1926], Wilson Papers, BLYU; GS to the editors of *The New Republic*, ibid. There is a sense in which one admires in Wilson, and in Seldes as well, the qualities for which Wilson so appreciated Francis Parkman: "the avoidance of generalization, the description of the events always in concrete detail. The larger tendencies are shown by a chronicle of individualized persons and actions." Wilson, *The Sixties: The Last Journal, 1960–1972*, Lewis M. Dabney, ed. (New York, 1993), 178.

46. NYT, April 27, 1924, p. 6; *N.Y. Herald Tribune*, Apr. 27, 1924, p. 25; NR, April 30, 1924; *Atlantic*, July 1924; *Outlook*, Nov. 19, 1924, p. 466. See also *Theatre Arts Monthly*, Aug. 1924, p. 574.

47. *N.Y. Evening Post*, May 24, 1924; *Springfield Republican*, May 7, 1924, p. 10; *The Dial* 77 (Sept. 1924): 244–50; *The Independent* 112 (May 10, 1924): 260; Boyd, *Portraits: Real and Imaginary* (New York, 1924), 21–22.

48. Eliot to GS, June 12, 1924, MSP; *The Criterion* 3 (Oct. 1924): 148–50.

49. *transatlantic review* 2 (July 1924): 128–29. Galantière had come from Chicago and served as Paris Secretary for the International Chamber of Commerce.

50. Anon., "And Out of America," ibid., 102–3. Seldes did, in fact, seek material

from prominent European dada-ists, especially Tristan Tzara, for publication in *Vanity Fair* and *The Dial*. See Frank Crowninshield to GS, May 13, 1924, MSP.

51. See Carlos Baker, *Ernest Hemingway: A Life Story* (New York, 1969), 128, 587–88.

52. GS, "Art and 'Artiness,'" *Arts and Decoration* 21 (June 1924): 13.

53. GS to the Editor of *The Independent* 113 (Aug. 16, 1924): 112.

54. GS, *The Public Arts* (New York, 1956), 288–91, esp. 288.

55. Fitzgerald to Perkins, [ca. June 1, 1925], in Andrew Turnbull, ed., *The Letters of F. Scott Fitzgerald* (New York, 1963), 185.

56. Hemingway to Pound, ca. May 2, 1924, in Carlos Baker, ed., *Ernest Hemingway: Selected Letters, 1917–1961* (New York, 1981), 114.

57. GS to Judith Randorf, [spring 1924], MSP.

58. GS, "True to Type," NYEJ, Oct. 26, 1932, p. 17.

59. GS to William Goldhurst, Nov. 10, 1962, Fitzgerald Papers, PUL; Wilson to John Peale Bishop, Jan. 15, 1924, in Wilson, *Letters on Literature and Politics,* 119; GS, "Spring Flight," *The Dial* 79 (Aug. 1925): 162–64.

60. Bishop to Fitzgerald, June 9, 1925, in Matthew J. Bruccoli and Margaret M. Duggan, eds., *Correspondence of F. Scott Fitzgerald* (New York, 1980), 167, and Seldes to Fitzgerald, May 26, 1925, in ibid., 164–65; Fitzgerald to Perkins, ca. July 1, 1925, in Turnbull, ed., *Letters of Fitzgerald,* 191; Fitzgerald to Seldes, [July 1925], ibid., 485; letters from Fitzgerald to Seldes, [July and Aug. 1925], MSP.

61. Thomas Daniel Young, ed., *Conversations with Malcolm Cowley* (Jackson, Miss., 1986), 10; GS, "Lively Arts," *Park East* (April 1951): 43.

62. Hemingway to Perkins, April 21, 1928, in Baker, ed., *Hemingway: Selected Letters,* 276; Hemingway to Fitzgerald, Sept. 4, 1929, and May 28, 1934, ibid., 305, 408.

63. GS, "Dance on the Yellow Sands," NR 47 (June 16, 1926): 112–13.

64. GS, DJ-3 (Nov. 1958), AIMT, MSP; Lucien Bluphocks [GS], "How To Be Frightfully Foreign," VF 22 (Aug. 1924): 55; GS, "Europe Unvisited," NR 43 (June 3, 1925): 46–47; GS, "Thompson's Panorama, the Woolworth Building, and Do It Now," VF 23 (Dec. 1924): 39, 108.

65. Frank, "The Artist in Our Jungle" (1925), in Frank, *In the American Jungle* [1925–1936] (1937; Freeport, N.Y., 1968), 149, 153.

66. GS letter, NR 43 (Aug. 5, 1925): 294. Seldes recapped and perpetuated this rather minor difference in emphasis in his "New York Chronicle" for *The Criterion* 4 (Jan. 1926): 177.

67. GS, "Certain Enthusiasm," NR 44 (Nov. 11, 1925): 306–7; GS, "A Few Lessons in English," NR 45 (Dec. 2, 1925): 44–45; GS, "Tariff and Character," NR 49 (Nov. 24, 1926): 19–20.

68. GS, "Thompson's Panorama and Do It Now," 39, 108; GS, "Dainty Cubes of Ice," NR 48 (Nov. 17, 1926): 376–77.

69. GS, "The Living Christ," NR 43 (June 24, 1925): 127; GS, "Service," NR 43 (July 15, 1925): 207–8; GS, "Salvation and 5 Percent," NR 44 (Sept. 9, 1925): 70; GS, "A Note on Advertising," NR 43 (July 8, 1925): 180. For a satirical piece on the get-tough, ruthless American male in business and politics, see GS, "The Hysteria of the He-Man," *Arts & Decoration* 23 (May 1925): 36. In a Veblen-esque way, Seldes suggested that "there might be a week in each year . . . in which everything went wrong, from clocks to telephones— and the holiday from perfection would be good for us."

70. GS, "Henry Ford's English," NR 44 (Sept. 23, 1925): 125–26; GS, "Three for a Quarter," NR 43 (July 29, 1925): 261–62.

71. GS, "The Singular—Although Dual—Eminence of Ring Lardner," VF 24 (July 1925): 45, 94; Jonathan Yardley, *Ring: A Biography of Ring Lardner* (New York, 1977), 286.

72. GS, "The Singular Eminence of Lardner," 45, 94. Burton Rascoe, a contemporary critic (1892–1957) and competitive rival of Seldes, thought less well of Lardner and declared (in 1924) that "Seldes misunderstands Lardner's genius when he suggests that Lardner go to school to Mr. Dooley." Rascoe, *A Bookman's Daybook* (New York, 1929), 249.

73. GS, "George M. Cohan: The Song and Dance Man," VF 21 (March 1924): 59, 82; GS, "Jazz and Ballad," NR 43 (Aug. 5, 1925): 293–94; GS, "Jerome Kern," NR 48 (Oct. 20, 1926): 244–45.

74. GS, "The Famous Touch of Nature," VF 21 (Feb. 1924): 40, 74.

75. GS, "This Little Girl," NR 43 (June 17, 1925): 99; GS, "Shake Your Feet," NR 44 (Nov. 4, 1925): 283–84; GS, "Three Clowns," NR 45 (Jan. 20, 1926): 243–44. Predictably, Seldes observed that comic strips are "outside the official canon of the arts; and that may be why they are so refreshing." GS, "Some Sour Commentators," NR 43 (June 10, 1925): 74.

76. Burns Mantle, ed., *The Best Plays of 1925–26* (New York, 1926), 518–19.

77. Fitzgerald to GS, [Feb. 1926?], MSP; undated memo in AIMT, MSP.

78. GS to JR, [Sept. 1926], MSP; GS, 7 *Lively Arts*, 241–43; Low, "An Enemy of the 'Bogus,'" 115–16. Harold Stearns recorded in his memoir that columnists were emerging in 1912–1913. See Stearns, *Confessions of a Harvard Man: The Street I Know Revisited* (Santa Barbara, 1984), 76.

79. There is a characteristic postcard that Amanda Seldes sent to John Dos Passos on May 17, 1925: "Dos we crave your company next Sat. night at our Great Drunken House Warming Party at 32 Beekman Place. Be sure to come." Dos Passos Papers, #5950-ae, box 1, ALUV.

80. GS, "What Happened to Jazz: Rejected Corner Stones," SEP 199 (Jan. 22, 1927): 25, 102, 107; GS, *Mainland* (New York, 1936), 120–21.

81. William Crary Brownell, *Democratic Distinction in America* (New York, 1927); John Henry Raleigh, *Matthew Arnold and American Culture* (Berkeley, 1957), 123; Percy Holmes Boynton, *More Contemporary Americans* (Chicago, 1927), ch. 10.

82. See, for example, Harold E. Stearns, *America: A Re-appraisal* (New York, 1937), esp. chs. 12–14; Russell Lynes, *The Lively Audience: A Social History of the Visual and Performing Arts in America, 1890–1950* (New York, 1985).

83. Kurt London, *The Seven Soviet Arts* (New Haven, 1938). Stuart Hall and Paddy Whannel published *The Popular Arts* in 1964, finally doing for Britain what Seldes had done for the United States four decades earlier. They mention Seldes exactly once, glancingly, and fail to acknowledge his primacy in the field. Their book is basically a sophisticated guide for teachers.

84. Neal Gabler, *An Empire of Their Own: How the Jews Invented Hollywood* (New York, 1989), 410; GS, "Perspective on Popularity," *Esquire* 22 (Dec. 1944): 174.

85. Irwin Edman to GS, Feb. 19, 1951, Edman Papers, CURBML; Amory, NYT *Book Review*, Oct. 27, 1957; Denney, "Discovery of the Popular Culture," in Robert E. Spiller and Eric Larrabee, eds., *American Perspectives: The National Self-Image in the Twentieth Century* (Cambridge, Mass., 1961), 167; and Denney, *The Astonished Muse*, 2nd ed. (New Brunswick, N.J., 1989), xxix, xxxii.

86. Eric Gillett, "Illuminating the Light Side," (London) *Daily Telegraph and Morning Post*, Aug. 19, 1960, p. 17; Larrabee to Seldes, March 9, 1965, MSP; Paul Buhle, ed., *Popular Culture in America* (Minneapolis, 1987), xvi. For a very recent cultural critic engaged in serious dialogue with Seldes, see Stanley Aronowitz, *Roll Over Beethoven: The Return of Cultural Strife* (Hanover, N.H., 1993), 180–81, and ch. 2 in general.

87. WID-2 and WID-6, AIMT, MSP.

88. GS to Florence Low, Dec. 7, 1967, quoted in Low, "An Enemy of the 'Bogus,'" 39; 17-page typescript, AIMT, MSP.

89. GS, "The Great Theatre Hoax of 1914," VF 22 (March 1924): 39, 94.

90. GS, "American Noises: How to Make Them, and Why," VF 22 (June 1924): 59, 86. Seldes made a similar comparison in *Esquire* 3 (May 1935): 82.

91. GS, "Nietzsche After an Interval," NR 43 (Aug. 12, 1925): 320–21; GS, "True to Type," NYEJ, Jan. 26, 1932, p. 15.

92. GS, "True to Type" ("After a Decade Writer Reverts to Hobby"), NYEJ, June 14, 1932, p. 17.

93. Ibid.

Chapter 4. "It Was a Good Time for Magazine Writers"

1. GS, *The 7 Lively Arts* (New York, 1924), 316–17; GS, "Thompson's Panorama, the Woolworth Building, and Do It Now," VF 22 (Dec. 1924): 108.

2. GS, "Outlaws from Parnassus," SEP 200 (Nov. 5, 1927): 186; GS, "Imported Goods Only," SEP 200 (Feb. 11, 1928): 141.

3. See GS, *The Future of Drinking* (Boston, 1930); DeVoto, *The Hour* (Boston, 1951).

4. See Wallace Stegner, *The Uneasy Chair: A Biography of Bernard DeVoto* (Garden City, N.Y., 1974), 98, 184; George C. Homans, *Coming to My Senses: The Autobiography of a Sociologist* (New Brunswick, N.J., 1984), 88–89.

5. Mumford to Brooks, Dec. 12, 1956, in Robert E. Spiller, ed., *The Van Wyck Brooks-Lewis Mumford Letters: The Record of a Literary Friendship, 1921–1963* (New York, 1970), 406.

6. Biel, *Independent Intellectuals in the United States, 1910–1945* (New York, 1992), 40. Like Casey Nelson Blake in *Beloved Community*, Biel believes that "a new community came together in the United States" (p. 2). I would suggest that more than one community of critics existed, or perhaps that there were overlapping communities. Benchley and Seldes got along extremely well, for example, but Benchley remained an integral part of the Algonquin circle, which had a mutually negative relationship with Seldes and others. Overall, the amount of back-biting, intense rivalry, and transient relationships should not be minimized.

7. Richard Kluger, *The Paper: The Life and Death of the New York Herald Tribune* (New York, 1986), 256–59; and esp. William R. Taylor, "Walter Lippmann in *Vanity Fair*," in Taylor, *In Pursuit of Gotham: Culture and Commerce in New York* (New York, 1992), 109–18. Some writers incorrectly assume that the *New York Times* introduced the Op-Ed page on September 21, 1970.

8. GS, "The Menace of the Un-Kept Press," VF 22 (July 1924): 28. See also GS, "Ted Cook," NR 59 (May 29, 1929): 45–46, about a columnist whose work was vital to the success of the New York *American*.

9. Seldes, *Witness to a Century* (New York, 1987), 228, 288; Wilson, "Thoughts on Being Bibliographed" (1943), in *Classics and Commercials: A Literary Chronicle of the Forties* (New York, 1950), 112.

10. GS, SEP-1 (Feb. 11, 1965), AIMT, MSP.

11. Benét to MacLeish, [Nov. 7, 1939], MacLeish Papers, box 3, MDLC.

12. GS, GF-4 (Nov. 17, 1964), AIMT, MSP.

13. See GS, "Rx for Revolution," SEP 199 (May 21, 1927): 22–23, 62, 64; GS, "The Hatchet and the White Ribbon," SEP 199 (June 4, 1927): 24–25, 137–38, on temperance

and the WCTU; GS, "Jonathan Edwards," *The Dial* 84 (Jan. 1928): 37–46; GS, "Open Your Mouth and Shut Your Eyes," *North American Review* 225 (April 1928): 425–34, on food fads and Christian calisthenics. For a follow-up to *Stammering Century* concerning the amusing history of dress reform in the United States, see GS, "Dress and Undress," *The Mentor* 17 (Nov. 1929): 13–15, 56, 58, 60. "No woman reformer," Seldes declared, "ever sketched a pretty dress."

14. Furnas, *My Life in Writing: Memoirs of a Maverick* (New York, 1989), 153.

15. GS, GF-1 (Nov. 17, 1964), AIMT, MSP.

16. Wilson, "The Critic Who Does Not Exist" (Feb. 1928), in Lewis M. Dabney, ed., *The Portable Edmund Wilson* (New York, 1983), 138–40. Just at this time, when Dwight Macdonald was an undergraduate at Yale, he became interested in cultural criticism and formed opinions about what critics should do and be. See Michael Wreszin, *A Rebel in Defense of Tradition: The Life and Politics of Dwight Macdonald* (New York, 1994), 13–14.

17. Boynton, *More Contemporary Americans* (Chicago, 1927), ch. 1, "Winds of Criticism," 15, 18–19. See also ch. 10, "Democracy and Public Taste"; Eliot is quoted in John Henry Raleigh, *Matthew Arnold and American Culture* (Berkeley, 1957), 202–3.

18. Munson, "The Young Critics of the Nineteen-Twenties," *The Bookman* 70 (Dec. 1929): 370. Burton Rascoe had warned in 1924 that not everyone took kindly to "young" as a modifier—that, indeed, it could be a "term of reproach" to some because it had connotations of immaturity "and therefore insignificance." "What Are Intellectuals?" (June 19, 1924), in Rascoe, *A Bookman's Daybook* (New York, 1929), 263.

19. GS, "Irving Berlin," NR 57 (Dec. 12, 1928): 100–102.

20. Fitzgerald to Bishop, [Jan. or Feb. 1929], in Edmund Wilson, ed., *The Crack-Up: F. Scott Fitzgerald* (New York, 1956), 275; Hemingway, "Chroniques III: And to the United States," *transatlantic review* 1 (May 1924): 355.

21. Matthiessen, "New Standards in American Criticism," *Yale Review* 18 (March 1929): 603–5; Wilson to Tate, May 20, 1929, Dabney, ed., *Portable Wilson*, 565–66.

22. GS, "Outlaws from Parnassus," SEP 200 (Nov. 5, 1927): 35, 181–82, 185–86. For Seldes' ongoing interest in industrial design, see Chapter Three, pp. 111–12 above and Chapter Five, p. 199 and n. 94.

23. GS, "Imported Goods Only," SEP 200 (Feb. 11, 1928): 25, 137–38, 141. For another blast at foreign visitors who unfairly accused the United States of materialism, see GS, "The Air Industry—Hot," SEP 200 (May 5, 1928): 33, 93, 96, 98.

24. GS, "Les Americains Toujours Pressés," SEP 200 (Oct. 22, 1927): 41, 96.

25. GS, *The Stammering Century* (New York, 1928), 5, 141.

26. GS, "The Cassandras of Europe," SEP 199 (March 5, 1927): 31, 119–20; GS, "Captious Columbuses," SEP 199 (June 11, 1927): 70, 72.

27. GS, "Thompson's Panorama, the Woolworth Building, and Do It Now," 39; GS, "Tramps—Are We?—Abroad," SEP 204 (June 11, 1932): 21, 64–66.

28. GS, "Uneasy Chameleons," SEP 199 (Jan. 1, 1927): 21, 78, 81–82. Seldes had not been sympathetic to the "Lost Generation" since he frolicked on its fringes in 1923 and 1924. By 1930 he had shed all sympathy for its members and said so in an essay that, somehow, slid elusively out of focus. See GS, "Finding the Lost Generation," SEP 203 (Aug. 30, 1930): 21, 69–70.

29. GS, "Background and High-lights," NR 57 (Dec. 26, 1928): 165–66.

30. GS, "The Artist at Home," NR 42 (May 20, 1925): 341.

31. Ibid. For a variation on this theme, see GS, "Surfaces," NR 45 (Feb. 17, 1926): 357–58.

32. GS, "True to Type," [subtitled "Fresh Eyes Wanted to See Charms of America"], NYEJ, Jan. 30, 1933, p. 13.

33. GS, "Fred Stone and W. C. Fields," VF 21 (April 1924): 88. For simultaneous second thoughts by Sinclair Lewis concerning his attack upon the quality of life on Main Street in Gopher Prairie, see Lewis, "Main Street's Been Paved," *The Nation* 119 (Sept. 10, 1924): 255–60. The essence of the piece is a dialogue between Lewis and a doctor (in Gopher Prairie) who calls Lewis a parlor socialist and a highbrow, and indirectly accuses him of stereotyping. Lewis admits, "I was confused by his snatching away my chance to be superior by being superior to me."

34. GS, "Captious Columbuses," SEP 199 (June 11, 1927): 31, 70, 72, quotation at 74.

35. GS, "The Boob Haters," SEP 200 (Oct. 1, 1927): 43, 44.

36. Ibid.

37. GS, "A Super-American Credo," SEP 201 (July 21, 1928): 23, 45–46.

38. GS, "New York Chronicle," *Criterion* 4 (Jan. 1926): 176; GS, *Stammering Century*, xi–xiii.

39. GS, "True to Type," NYEJ, March 16, 1932, p. 17; ibid., July 1, 1932, p. 13.

40. GS, "An ABC of GJN," *Esquire* 24 (Nov. 1945): 77; GS, "Lively Arts," *Park East* (April 1951): 44; GS to Wilson, Jan. 17, 1968, Wilson Papers, BLYU.

41. GS, "Captious Columbuses," SEP 199 (June 11, 1927): 72.

42. GS, "Debunking the Debunkers," N.Y. *Herald Tribune*, Sunday Magazine, Oct. 21 and 28, 1928, pp. 1–3, 12–13, 16; GS, "True to Type," NYEJ, Feb. 24, 1932, p. 17. During the late 'teens and early 1920s even such a moderate liberal as Frederick Lewis Allen wrote cynically about business mores in the United States. See Darwin Payne, *The Man of Only Yesterday: Frederick Lewis Allen* (New York, 1975), 38.

43. GS, "The New Wagon," SEP 202 (Dec. 21, 1929): 21, 56; GS, *Future of Drinking*; *Outlook*, July 16, 1930; NYT, July 27, 1930, IV, p. 9. See also *Bookman*, August 1930; Boston *Transcript*, Nov. 15, 1930.

44. Bluphocks, "The Ultimate Fat-Head, the Most Important Man in the World," VF 23 (Feb. 1925): 48; GS, "Satire, Death of . . . ", NR 49 (Jan. 5, 1927): 193; GS, "Man Ray and Metropolis," NR 50 (March 30, 1927): 170–71. Seldes first lamented the paucity of satire in U.S. magazine fiction in a book review that he published in *The Dial* 73 (July 1922): 106–7.

45. GS, "Captious Columbuses," SEP 199 (June 11, 1927): 70; GS, "An Ocean of Lemonade," SEP 199 (May 7, 1927): 177.

46. GS to Miss Thayer (*Dial*), ca. April 22, 1927, Dial/Thayer Papers, box 6, BLYU; GS to Wilson, Aug. 26, 1927, and [Aug. 9, 1928], Wilson Papers, BLYU. In 1932 Seldes called the Beards' *Rise of American Civilization* "the best history of America for the general reader ever written." NYEJ, Oct. 8, 1932, p. 14.

47. Lovett in NR 56 (Sept. 19, 1928): 129–30; Rourke in N.Y. *Herald Tribune*, Dec. 9, 1928, p. 5.

48. Adams in *Bookman*, Nov. 1928; Curti in the Springfield *Republican*, Nov. 11, 1928; Riley in SRL, Dec. 8, 1928, p. 455. For other highly positive reviews, see Boston *Transcript*, Sept. 15, 1928; N.Y. *Evening Post*, Oct. 20, 1928; *North American Review*, Nov. 1928. For "fan mail," see Joseph Jastrow to GS, Sept. 10 and Dec. 6, 1928, MSP.

49. A. N. W. in *Outlook*, Dec. 12, 1928, p. 1331; Solow in *The Nation*, Sept. 26, 1928; and Charles W. Thompson in NYT, Sept. 16, 1928, sec. IV, p. 3.

50. GS to AMS, Jr., Aug. 25 and Oct. 18, 1964, Schlesinger Papers, JFKL. The same collection contains a draft of Schlesinger's preface sent to Seldes with a covering letter, Nov. 9, 1964; and Seldes' reply, dated Nov. 10, 1964. A five-page draft of Seldes' own introduction to the new edition, sent to Schlesinger on Oct. 10, 1964, is in MSP.

51. GS, *Stammering Century*, 202–4, 249, 255, 268.

52. Ibid., 11–35, but esp. 16.

53. For examples, see Lucien Bluphocks, "'Twas Brill-ig and the Slithy Freuds," VF 18 (July 1922): 59, 106; GS, "Back from Utopia," SEP 202 (July 13, 1929): 137; GS, *Future of Drinking*, 79, 105, 157. In 1921 Scofield Thayer went to Vienna to be psychoanalyzed by Sigmund Freud. Seldes remained skeptical whether it ultimately made any difference for Thayer.

54. See GS, *Stammering Century*, xvi, xviii, 118, 256, 316, 405, quotation at 407.

55. Ibid., 16, 166, 411; AMS, Jr., to GS, June 15, 1956, MSP.

56. GS, "The Empty Triumph of the Liberal Mind," VF 23.(Sept. 1924): 52, 92. In a 1927 review of a biography of Tom Paine, Seldes said that on the one hand, in a time when fundamentalism was pervasive, one yearned for an iconoclastic deist like Paine. On the other hand, his efforts as a pamphleteer seemed to have been futile—perhaps an object lesson for aspiring reformers. See GS, "The Old Disbeliever," NR 52 (Sept. 21, 1957): 124–25.

57. GS, "The Prejudices of Liberalism," SEP 200 (March 17, 1928): 29, 145–46, 149; GS, "The Background of Bigotry," NR 55 (July 11, 1928): 200–201; GS, "The Appetite of Tyranny," SEP 202 (March 22, 1930): 25, 154, 157. For the wider tendency to link liberalism with individualism around 1930, see Daniel Aaron, *American Notes: Selected Essays* (Boston, 1994), 26.

58. See Trilling, *The Liberal Imagination: Essays on Literature and Society* (1950: Garden City, N.Y., 1953), 215; GS, "Good Theatre," *The Atlantic* 161 (Jan. 1938): 82–85, quotation at 85; GS, ONE-3 (Feb. 14, 1965), AIMT, MSP.

59. GS, SSVV (May 28, 1968), 1–2, AIMT, MSP. Despite Seldes' personalized sense of guilt, there does seem to be something generational at work here. Kenneth Burke, Seldes' assistant and successor at *The Dial*, believed that art and the artist must take priority over politics. See his obituary, NYT, Nov. 21, 1993, p. A-21.

60. *Harvard Class of 1914: Fiftieth Anniversary Report* (Cambridge, Mass. 1964), 480–81. Seldes covered much of this in a lengthy letter to Fred Cook, a journalist with *The Nation*, Dec. 26, 1962, MSP. "The Sacco-Vanzetti case has for long been an absorption of mine—perhaps because I wasn't aware of it until late in the day and did nothing when I could have at least spoken."

61. GS, "The Complex of Radicalism," SEP 200 (Nov. 19, 1927): 35, 182, 185–86, 189, esp. 182; GS, *Stammering Century*, 201; GS, "The Better Americans," SEP 201 (April 20, 1929): 90.

62. GS, "True to Type," NYEJ, Jan. 9, 1932, p. 9; GS, *Mainland* (New York, 1936), 123, 129.

63. SEP (Feb. 11, 1965), AIMT, MSP.

64. See Jan Cohn, *Creating America: George Horace Lorimer and the Saturday Evening Post* (Pittsburgh, 1989), 165, and for Lorimer's affection for the American businessman, see 170–71, 198–99, 267. For a fierce critique of Lorimer, "this great literary Fascist," see Upton Sinclair, *Money Writes!* (New York, 1927), 67.

65. SEP (Feb. 11, 1965), AIMT, MSP. To some authors the good pay did not compensate for the routine of producing imaginative literature on a precise schedule. By the fall of 1933, for example, F. Scott Fitzgerald dreaded "the possibility of being condemned to go back to *The Saturday Evening Post* grind . . . . " Quoted in Robert Sklar, *F. Scott Fitzgerald: The Last Laocoön* (New York, 1967), 298..

66. GS, "What Happened to Jazz: Rejected Corner Stones," SEP 199 (Jan. 22, 1927): 25, 102, 107.

67. GS, "Jimmie Is Exhubilant," NR 57 (Jan. 16, 1929): 247–48; GS, "Tad," NR 58 (May 15, 1929): 358–60; GS, "Summer Shows," NR 59 (July 24, 1929): 262–63; GS, "Mr. Carroll's Vanities," NR 63 (Aug. 13, 1930): 370–71.

68. GS, "Musicals, Imp. & Dom. [sic]," NR 60 (Nov. 20, 1929): 375–76; GS, "Big, Little and Good Shows," NR 64 (Nov. 5, 1930): 323–24; GS, "Torch Songs," NR 65 (Nov. 19, 1930): 19–20; GS, "Fat Ladies," NR 70 (March 30, 1932): 182–83. Malcolm Cowley's assistant at *The New Republic* in 1932, Otis Ferguson, sounds like a Seldes clone. He hated highbrow culture and loved jazz, movies, and radio. See Alfred Kazin, *Starting Out in the Thirties* (Boston, 1965), 29–30.

69. GS, "Pictures and Landscapes," NR 47 (June 2, 1926): 61; GS, "The Art Bogy," SEP 201 (Jan. 12, 1929): 33, 129.

70. Ibid., 130. In 1927 Seldes was hired by Ivy Lee, the principal public relations man for John D. Rockefeller, to ghost-write an autobiographical book about his profession and his life. (Lee had become jealous of the eminence achieved by Edward L. Bernays in the field of public relations.) Seldes lasted four months at a salary of $250 per week.

71. GS, "The Business Bogeyman," SEP 202 (Sept. 28, 1929): 29, 147–48. In 1934 Seldes proclaimed that the *American Mercury* had finally abandoned its relentless attack on the American businessman as a philistine. See GS, "True to Type," NYEJ, May 2, 1934, p. 21. "I do not doubt the limitations of the American businessman," he wrote, "but I am pretty sure that the limitations of his critics are more serious."

72. GS, "Open Your Mouth and Shut Your Eyes," *North American Review* 225 (April 1928): 425–34, esp. 433. In 1926, however, Seldes had lamented the internationalization of French cuisine! GS, "The Federation of the World," NR 47 (July 21, 1926): 253–54. His general point? When cultural habits distinctive to a nation are exported, the "native thing perishes."

73. GS, "The Machine Wreckers," SEP 200 (July 23, 1927): 27, 149–50, 153, quotation at 150. Five years later Seldes wrote with unqualified enthusiasm about the functional benefits and *beauty* of industrial design. See GS, "Industrial Design," SEP 204 (May 28, 1932): 34, 36.

74. GS, "Provincialism and Charm," VF 24 (June 1925): 69–70.

75. GS, "The City's Giddy Whirl," SEP 202 (May 31, 1930): 43–44, 133–34.

76. For context see Ralph Borsodi, *Flight from the City: The Story of a New Way to Family Security* (New York, 1933).

77. GS, "Park Avenue Voodoo," SEP 201 (Nov. 24, 1928): 23, 121–22; GS, "Diaghileff," NR 60 (Sept. 11, 1929): 97–98; GS, "Found Money," *The Mentor* 22 (Nov. 1930): 11–13.

78. GS, "Diplomat's Delight: Detective and Mystery Stories, Good and Bad, Passed in Review," *Bookman* 66 (Sept. 1927): 91–93.

79. N.Y. *Herald Tribune*, March 27, 1927, sec. 7, p. 25; *Bookman* 65 (March 1927): 105.

80. Foster Johns, *The Victory Murders* (London, 1927).

81. NYT, March 6, 1927, p. 6; Benchley in N.Y. *Herald Tribune*, March 27, 1927, p. 25; *World*, Aug. 21, 1927, p. 7; Hammett in SRL 3 (May 21, 1927): 846.

82. Foster Johns, *The Square Emerald* (New York, 1928); N.Y. *Herald Tribune*, March 25, 1928, p. 12; Boston *Transcript*, April 18, 1928, p. 4.

83. GS, "Back from Utopia," SEP 201 (June 29, 1929): 6–7, 131, 133, 137; SEP 202 (July 6, 13, and 20, 1929): 18–19, 46, 50; 20–21, 133, 134, 137; 33–35, 162, 165, 170.

84. GS, *The Wings of the Eagle* (Boston, 1929); NYT, Oct. 27, 1929, p. 7; N.Y. *Evening Post*, Oct. 19, 1929, p. 12; N.Y. *Herald Tribune*, Oct. 20, 1929, p. 14; *Bookman*, Nov. 1929; *Nation*, Dec. 25, 1929; *Outlook*, Oct. 16, 1929; NR, Jan. 1, 1930.

85. GS, "Van Dine and His Public," NR 59 (June 19, 1929): 125–26; GS, "Form and the Novel," *Bookman* 70 (Oct. 1929): 128–31. See also GS, "The Art of the Novel," *The Dial* 72 (March 1922): 318–22.

86. See Richard S. Kennedy, *A Biography of E. E. Cummings* (New York, 1980), 294–96; Charles Norman, *E. E. Cummings: The Magic-Maker* (New York, 1964), ch. 10.

87. GS, "Introduction," to *him AND the CRITICS: a collection of opinions on e e cummings' play at the provincetown playhouse* [New York, 1928], 2–4.

88. Nicholas Joost, *Scofield Thayer and the Dial* (Carbondale, Ill., 1964), 130.

89. GS, "The Better Americans," SEP 201 (April 20, 1929): 29, 90, 93; GS, "The Federation of the World," NR 47 (July 21, 1926): 253–54.

90. GS, "The Censor," SEP 202 (Sept. 21, 1929): 16, 150, 153; GS, "The Appetite of Tyranny," SEP 202 (March 22, 1930): 25, 154, 157.

91. Brownell, *Democratic Distinction*, 20; Wilson to Tate, May 20, 1929, Dabney, ed., *The Portable Edmund Wilson*, 565–66.

92. Wilson to Seldes, March 6, 1929, in Edmund Wilson, *Letters on Literature and Politics, 1912–1972*, Elena Wilson, ed. (New York, 1977), 161; GS, "The City's Giddy Whirl," SEP 202 (May 31, 1930): 134.

93. Wilson, "A Weekend at Ellerslie," in *The Shores of Light: A Literary Chronicle of the Twenties and Thirties* (New York, 1952), 378.

94. Ibid., 383; James R. Mellow, *Invented Lives: F. Scott and Zelda Fitzgerald* (Boston, 1984), 309–12.

95. Seldes to Wilson, [March 1928], Wilson Papers, BLYU; Fitzgerald to John Lardner, Sept. 20, 1933, in Andrew Turnbull, ed., *The Letters of F. Scott Fitzgerald* (New York, 1963), 506.

96. GS, "True to Type," NYEJ, Feb. 20, 1932, p. 16; ibid., July 11, 1932, p. 13.

97. See GS, "Mr. Jeeves' Gentleman," *Esquire* 2 (Aug. 1934): 65; GS, "To Hell, in a Word, with Art," ibid. 5 (Jan. 1936): 94; GS, "So They Got a Plot," ibid. 9 (May 1938): 78, 138; GS, "Good-bye to a Friend," ibid. 10 (July 1938): 72, 135.

Chapter 5. Accessible Culture for Depressed Times

1. See Daniel Aaron, *Writers on the Left: Episodes in American Literary Communism* (New York, 1961).

2. Warren Susman, "The Culture of the Thirties," in Susman, *Culture as History: The Transformation of American Society in the Twentieth Century* (New York, 1984), 151–53, 164–65, 179–80, 192–94; Lawrence W. Levine, "American Culture and the Great Depression," in Levine, *The Unpredictable Past: Explorations in American Cultural History* (New York, 1993), 208; Richard H. Pells, *Radical Visions and American Dreams: Culture and Social Thought in the Depression Years* (New York, 1973); and Irving Howe, "The Thirties in Retrospect," in Ralph F. Bogardus and Fred Hobson, eds., *Literature at the Barricades: The American Writer in the 1930s* (University, Ala., 1982), 27.

3. GS, "The America of the Intellectuals," SEP 207 (March 9, 1935): 11, 94, 96, 98; GS, "From Chicken Shack to Casino," *Esquire* 9 (March 1938): 75, 135.

4. GS, "True to Type," NYEJ, May 7, 1932, p. 8; ibid., Nov. 5, 1932, p. 15.

5. Ibid., Nov. 22, 1932, p. 13.

6. Sinclair, *Money Writes!* (New York, 1927), ch. 27.

7. GS, "True to Type," NYEJ, May 8, 1933, p. 13.

8. GS, "True to Type," NYEJ, Jan. 30, 1932, p. 10; ibid, Sept. 30, 1932, p. 17.

9. GS, *Aristophanes' Lysistrata: A New Version* (New York, 1930), xi.

10. GS to Bel Geddes, April 29 and May 8, 1930, HRHUT.

11. Atkinson review, NYT, April 29, 1930, p. 30. According to Burns Mantle, "at its first performances [in Philadelphia], the less elastically minded of the Quakers who saw

Lysistrata gasped quite audibly; but because of its superior social backing and its frankness of presentation, the revival soon became a social as well as a theatrical event, achieving a sort of prideful home-town success that kept it out of New York for several weeks." Mantle, ed., *The Best Plays of 1929–30* (New York, 1930), 5.

12. Brown, N.Y. *Post*, May 10, 1930; Richard Lockridge, N.Y. *Sun*, May 5, 1930, p. 20; H. T. P., Boston *Evening Transcript*, May 26, 1930; Atkinson, NYT, June 1, 1930, sec. 8, p. 1. All clippings found in the Harvard Theatre Collection, Pusey Library.

13. Atkinson, NYT, June 6, 1930, p. 20; Hammond, N.Y. *Herald Tribune*, June 15, 1930, sec. 8, p. 1. As the successful run built momentum, the *Tribune* devoted a column to a backstage peek at the performers in *Lysistrata* (Nov. 30, 1930). Clippings in the Harvard Theatre Collection.

14. Atkinson, NYT, June 6, 1930, p. 20; anon., "Los Angeles: Lawless but Pure," 2 pp. from unknown magazine (Feb. 1932), clipping in the Harvard Theatre Collection.

15. GS to F. Scott Fitzgerald, July 29, [1930], MSP; GS to T. S. Eliot, April 6, 1932, MSP.

16. *Plays of the Moscow Art Theatre Musical Studio* (New York, 1925); Rosamond Gilder, "Each in His Own Way," *Theatre Arts* 30 (Dec. 1946): 697. E. E. Cummings sent Seldes a critical letter about "Lysistrata-the-second" some time late in 1946. Here is the central portion:

Unless wiser men than myself are very vastly deceived,the Greeks(whatever they weren't)were —&,I should like to observe, still are for those lucky mortals who haven't yet tumbled into some barbarism—a luminous mature complex & rarely developed people

to interpret this rarely developed as primitive,this complex as simple,this mature as infantile,& this luminous as black,may constitute(for our mutual friend Jimmie Light)a pleasing tour de force

for me,it's an obscenity typical of the Ultra-epoch Of Superconfusion;id est a gruesomely perverse(=cruel)obscenity—the negro race being,per se & in its own right,A 1.

The letter is incorrectly dated as [1940?] in F. W. Dupee and George Stade, eds., *Selected Letters of E. E. Cummings* (New York, 1969), 155–56.

17. In 1969–70, when the Limited Editions Club brought out a new printing of *Lysistrata*, Seldes remarked that it had had "the longest run in the American theatre of any classic drama up to its time—I think till now, but am not sure." Helen Macy to GS, Aug. 29, 1967, and GS to Helen Macy, Jan. 7, 1970, MSP.

18. George S. Kaufman to GS, Oct. 22, 1929, MSP; GS to Dorothy Lockhart, April 13, 1931, Lockhart Papers, box 2, NYPL.

19. GS to Lockhart, April 13, 1931, ibid.

20. Ibid., and GS's three pages of explanation which accompanied the 53-page text to Lockhart in Philadelphia. See also GS, "The Theatre," *The Dial* 84 (June 1928): 528–30.

21. *The Love of Three Oranges*, typescript in Lockhart Papers, box 2.

22. GS, "True to Type," NYEJ, Oct. 19, 1932, p. 17.

23. Ibid., Nov. 21, 1932, p. 17.

24. Ibid., Feb. 7, 1933, p. 13.

25. Ibid., April 11 and 27, 1933, pp. 15, 28; GS, "Hammerstein the Extravagant," *Harper's* 165 (July 1932): 187–97; GS, "The Great Glorifier," *New Yorker*, May 31, 1993,

pp. 60–61, reprinted from 1931; GS, "Credit to Mr. Wiman," *Esquire* 10 (Nov. 1938): 84, 148.

26. GS, *The Years of the Locust (America, 1929–1932)* (Boston, 1933), 66; GS, "Music Plays Rule Broadway Theatres," *D'A'C News* (April 1932): 42, 44.

27. GS, "Torch Songs," NR 65 (Nov. 19, 1930): 19–20; GS, "Fat Ladies," NR 70 (March 30, 1932): 182–83; GS, "The Blackout Fades Out," *Esquire* 1 (April 1934): 65, 148; GS, "Extremely Foreign Affairs," *Esquire* 5 (April 1936): 52, 165; GS, "Notable Plays . . . and Popular Art," *Scribner's* 100 (Dec. 1936): 77–79; GS, "Good Theatre," *Atlantic* 161 (Jan. 1938): 82–85.

28. GS, "True to Type," NYEJ, March 3, 1933, p. 21. Seldes did note in his column, however, that *Lysistrata* had been seen by at least a quarter of a million people. "If it was immoral," he remarked, "at least one per cent of this number should have been caught in some overt act. . . ." Ibid., Jan. 14, 1932, p. 17. He also concluded his preface to *Lysistrata* in book form by warning against the prospect and the inanity of censorship (p. xiii).

29. GS, "True to Type," NYEJ, March 14, 1933, p. 15; ibid., April 15, 1933, p. 18. For the public controversy involving a complex work titled "Civic Virtue," see Michele H. Bogart, *Public Sculpture and the Civic Ideal in New York City, 1890–1930* (Chicago, 1989), 259–70.

30. GS, "True to Type," NYEJ, July 5, 1933, p. 15; GS, *The Movies Come from America* (New York, 1937), 55; GS, "No Decameron?," *Publisher's Weekly* 128 (Oct. 19, 1935): 1459–60.

31. GS, "True to Type," NYEJ, July 26, 1932, p. 13.

32. Ibid., Sept. 6, 1932, p. 14; ibid., Dec. 17, 1932, p. 15; GS, "Over the Tops," SEP 208 (April 25, 1936): 85.

33. GS, "Sugar and Spice and Not So Nice," *Esquire* 1 (March 1934): 60; GS, "The Movies in Peril," *Scribner's* 97 (Feb. 1935): 83–84. See also GS, "The Theatre," *The Dial* 84 (June 1928): 528, 531–32.

34. GS, "True to Type," NYEJ, Jan. 26, 1933, p. 15; GS, "'Dear Null'—and Void," *Esquire* 7 (Feb. 1937): 87, 205–6; GS, "The State of the World," *Esquire* 23 (March 1945): 66.

35. GS, "True to Type," NYEJ, Feb. 11, 1932, p. 23.

36. GS, "The Boob Haters," SEP 200 (Oct. 1, 1927): 44; and see GS, "Park Avenue Voodoo," SEP 201 (Nov. 24, 1928): 23, 121–22; GS, "The Masculine Revolt," *Scribner's* 95 (April 1934): 279–82.

37. GS, "True to Type," NYEJ, Nov. 8, 1932, p. 5HB; ibid., Nov. 10, 1932, p. 15. See also GS, "American Humor," in Fred J. Ringel, ed., *America as Americans See It* (New York, 1932), 342–60.

38. GS, "I am Dying, Little Egypt," *Esquire* 1 (Autumn 1933): 40.

39. GS, "Mr. Jeeves' Gentleman," *Esquire* 2 (Aug. 1934): 65; GS, "The Master of Them All," *Esquire* 14 (Dec. 1940): 150, 152, 154; GS, "So They Got a Plot," *Esquire* 9 (May 1938): 78, 138. "There is a dandy statistical report," he concluded sarcastically, "on the need for housing in America which might be handled in the style of Puccini."

40. GS, "An Old Masterpiece," *Esquire* 2 (June 1934): 74; GS, "Good-bye to a Friend," *Esquire* 10 (July 1938): 72, 135.

41. GS, "The Gershwin Case," *Esquire* 2 (Oct. 1934): 108, 130.

42. GS, "The Park Avenue Hill-billies," *Esquire* 3 (April 1935): 79.

43. GS, "The Gershwin Case," *Esquire* 2 (Oct. 1934): 108; GS, "No More Swing?," *Scribner's* 100 (Nov. 1936): 70.

44. GS, "True to Type," NYEJ, April 18, 1933, p. 26; ibid., Feb. 2, 1933, p. 15. He

published a critique of a hostile biography of Warren G. Harding that defended the dead president not on substantive grounds but because Seldes disliked iconoclasts. See ibid., Jan. 16, 1932, p. 7.

45. GS, "True to Type," NYEJ, Nov. 9, 1932, p. 15; ibid., April 25, 1933, p. 26; ibid., Nov. 28, 1932, p. 15.

46. GS, "True to Type," NYEJ, Nov. 30, 1932, p. 17; Brooks to Mumford, April 8, 1936, in Robert E. Spiller, ed., *The Van Wyck Brooks-Lewis Mumford Letters: The Record of a Literary Friendship, 1921–1963* (New York, 1970), 132.

47. GS, "True to Type," NYEJ, March 1, 1932, p. 15; ibid., March 22, 1932, p. 17. Two years later Seldes attacked Woollcott's new book, *While Rome Burns*, declaring that Woollcott "writes in one of the most annoying styles on record and is a sucker for the second-rate. . . . He knows that he is trivial." GS, "True to Type," NYEJ, March 13, 1934, p. 13.

48. GS, "True to Type," NYEJ, May 24, 1932, p. 19; GS, "Men Are Funny," *Esquire* 1 (May 1934): 48, 121. Cf. Susan Ware, *Still Missing: Amelia Earhart and the Search for Modern Feminism* (New York, 1993).

49. GS, "True to Type," NYEJ, May 11, 1933, p. 17; ibid., April 5, 1933, p. 4.

50. GS, "True to Type," NYEJ, March 18, 1933, p. 14.

51. See Darwin Payne, *The Man of Only Yesterday: Frederick Lewis Allen* (New York, 1975), 87–88, 91–92, 99, 100, 116–18, 140, 153, 158.

52. GS, "True to Type," NYEJ, June 25, 1932, p. 14; ibid., Nov. 11, 1932, p. 19.

53. GS, "True to Type," NYEJ, May 29, 1933, p. 10.

54. GS, "Lie Down and Die," *Esquire* 6 (Sept. 1936): 88, 122. In 1934 he devoted a column to the persistent reality of failure, especially among utopian communities in the U.S. See GS, "True to Type," NYEJ, March 10, 1934, p. 10.

55. GS to Vincent Starrett, April 18, 1917, Starrett Papers, HRHUT; Wesley D. Sweetser, *Arthur Machen* (New York, 1964), 37–40. On June 26, 1936, Seldes told Scott Fitzgerald, "I have an ingrained dislike of all books not written to be books, but collected from scattering magazine pieces." Matthew J. Bruccoli and Margaret M. Duggan, eds., *The Correspondence of F. Scott Fitzgerald* (New York, 1980), 436.

56. Payne, *Man of Only Yesterday*, 107, 132–33, 136, 192–93.

57. Jan Cohn, *Creating America: George Horace Lorimer and the Saturday Evening Post* (Pittsburgh, 1989), 176.

58. GS to Samuel Putnam, Nov. 15, 1932, Putnam Papers, PUL; GS, *The Years of the Locust* (Boston, 1933), 47–48; GS to Henry Luce, Feb. 13, 1962, MSP.

59. The American Antiquarian Society and the New York Public Library have complete sets.

60. See the issues for Dec. 1932, p. 2; Jan. 1933, p. 2; March 1933, p. 2; and April 1933, p. 2.

61. GS, "True to Type," NYEJ, June 2, 1932, p. 13; ibid., June 7, 1932, p. 13; ibid., June 22, 1932, p. 13; ibid., July 27, 1932, p. 13.

62. GS, *Against Revolution* (New York, 1932), quotations at 6, 7, 8, 12, 15, 25.

63. Alfred Dashiell to GS, April 20 and 29, May 2 and 25, 1932, Scribner's Papers, PUL; GS to Dashiell, April 22 and 30, May 19 and 30, ibid. Seldes reiterated much of this in "True to Type," NYEJ, Feb. 3, 1933, p. 15. For indications that many people shared Seldes' outlook, see Howe, "The Thirties in Retrospect," in Bogardus and Hobson, eds., *Literature at the Barricades*, 27.

64. GS, "Have Americans Lost Their Nerve?," *Scribner's* 92 (Sept. 1932): 149–52; Edmund Wilson, *Letters on Literature and Politics, 1912–1972*, Elena Wilson, ed. (New York, 1977), 222–24.

65. GS, *The Years of the Locust (America, 1929–1932)* (Boston, 1933), 6, 11, 15, 19, 61, 153, 156, 239.

66. Ibid., 22, 43–44, 331–34. Seldes finished this project during the heated 1932 presidential campaign. He rejected the efficacy, appropriateness, and meaningfulness of the phrase "New Deal." Seldes didn't believe that it would catch on as a slogan. (Ibid., 259.) He also doubted whether Prohibition would be repealed within ten years! ("True to Type," NYEJ, Dec. 7, 1932, p. 17.)

67. NYT, Feb. 5, 1933, p. 3; N.Y. *Evening Post*, Feb. 4, 1933, p. 7; N.Y. *Herald Tribune*, "Books," Feb. 5, 1933, p. 6; *Nation*, Feb. 15, 1933; *Christian Science Monitor*, Feb. 18, 1933, p. 6; NR, April 12, 1933, p. 254.

68. SRL 10 (Feb. 4, 1933): 409–10; *Forum* 89 (March 1933): v; *Current History* 38 (April 1933): iv; *Commonweal* 17 (April 12, 1933): 668; *Survey Graphic* 22 (June 1933): 328–29; GS to Morley, Feb. 27, 1933, Morley Papers, HRHUT.

69. Roosevelt, "Inaugural Address," March 4, 1933, in Samuel I. Rosenman, ed., *The Public Papers and Addresses of Franklin D. Roosevelt* (New York, 1938), III: 11; GS to AMS, Jr., Feb. 2, 1968, Schlesinger Papers, JFKL.

70. Wilson, "Thoughts on Being Bibliographed," in Wilson, *Classics and Commercials: A Literary Chronicle of the Forties* (New York, 1950), 107–9; Alfred Kazin, *Starting Out in the Thirties* (Boston, 1965), 9.

71. On the distinction between intellectual and highbrow, see GS, "Post-Mortem," *Americana* (April 1933): 8. By contrast, George Horace Lorimer made no distinction and had an intense distaste for both intellectuals and highbrows. See Cohn, *Lorimer and the Saturday Evening Post*, 241. For a brief time in 1935–36 the *Post* attempted to highlight its anti-intellectual position by means of a regular book review department called "The Literary Lowbrow."

72. GS, "The America of the Intellectuals," SEP 207 (March 9, 1935): 10–11, 96–99; Tate to GS, March 8, 1935, Tate Papers, PUL.

73. GS to Tate, March 16 and April 26, 1935, ibid., Tate to GS, April 29, 1935, ibid. For the enduring friendship, see GS to Tate, Jan. 7, 1964, Feb. 5, [1964?], and Oct. 23, 1965, ibid.

74. Goldman to GS, Jan. 14, 1932, MSP. And see Goldman to GS, April 24, 1935, MSP.

75. GS to Tate, March 16, 1935, Tate Papers, PUL.

76. GS, "The Worst People in the World," *Esquire* 6 (Nov. 1936): 108, 131. For an earlier and much tamer essay on "the position of the artist in times like ours," see GS, "True to Type,"NYEJ, May 12, 1933, p. 17.

77. GS, "Melancholy in the Comics," *Esquire* 2 (Sept. 1934): 78, 107; GS, "The Halfway Winkle," *Esquire* 3 (May 1935): 82. For the recurrence of this pattern in Seldes' criticism, see Chapter Three, note 90 above.

78. Fitzgerald to John Lardner, Sept. 20, 1933, in Andrew Turnbull, ed., *The Letters of F. Scott Fitzgerald* (New York, 1963), 505–6; Jonathan Yardley, *Ring: A Biography of Ring Lardner* (New York, 1977), 286, 378–79.

79. Fitzgerald to Perkins, Oct. 7, 1933, in Turnbull, ed., *Letters of Fitzgerald*, 235; George Seldes, *Witness to a Century* (New York, 1987), 61. An extensive correspondence between Gilbert Seldes and Perkins (1933–34) will be found in the Perkins Papers, a section of the Scribner's Papers, PUL.

80. GS to Perkins, Jan. 16, 1934, Perkins Papers, PUL; Perkins to GS, Dec. 5, 1933, ibid.

81. GS, "Is Sport an Art or an Orgy?," *Esquire* 2 (Dec. 1934): 71, 144; GS, "The Horse without a Heart," *Esquire* 8 (Oct. 1937): 104, 167, 168, quotation at 167.

82. Fitzgerald to Seldes, Feb. 2, 1934, in Matthew Bruccoli and Margaret M. Dug-

gan, eds., *Correspondence of F. Scott Fitzgerald* (New York, 1980), 327–28, 365–67; Donald Elder, *Ring Lardner* (Garden City, N.Y., 1956), 287; Fitzgerald to Seldes, May 31, 1934, MSP; Lardner, *First and Last* (New York, 1934), v.

83. Yardley, *Ring Lardner*, 379. Seldes devoted a column to his Lardner anthology when it appeared, and observed that anyone who wrote for a newspaper would appreciate "the astounding high level of Lardner's output. Of course the slaves who write a column every day will snort and note the fact that Lardner wrote only once a week; but they will also remember that many people who write once a month come nowhere near the heights which Lardner so easily attained." GS, "True to Type," NYEJ, June 8, 1934, p. 21.

84. Hemingway, "Defense of Dirty Words," *Esquire* 2 (Sept. 1934): 19; GS, "Was Ring Lardner a Humorist?," *Esquire* 2 (July 1934): 44. Although it ultimately comes down to a question of personal taste, Hemingway's complaint had some basis in fact. The essays about radio that Lardner wrote in the last years of his life *did* express disdain for risqué material and "suggestive" songs. See Seldes, ed., *The Portable Ring Lardner* (New York, 1946), 659–81.

85. GS, "The Prize-fighter and the Bull," *Esquire* 2 (Nov. 1934): 52.

86. Ibid., 173; GS, "Is Sport an Art or an Orgy?," 71.

87. Hemingway, "Notes on Life and Letters: Or a Manuscript Found in a Bottle," *Esquire* 3 (Jan. 1935): 21; George Seldes to GS, [1969], MSP.

88. Wilson, "Letter to the Russians about Hemingway," in Wilson, *The Shores of Light: A Literary Chronicle of the Twenties and Thirties* (New York, 1952), 621; the card from Amanda to Wilson, postmarked Dec. 30, 1935, is in the Wilson Papers, BLYU.

89. GS, "The Man Who Went to Pieces Entirely," *Harper's* 170 (Jan. 1935): 250–52; GS, "Lachaise: Sculptor of Repose," NR 54 (April 4, 1928): 219–20. Seldes said that he admired Lachaise because he did not pander to the intelligentsia (his work lacked humanitarian and story interest), and followed no trendy aesthetic doctrine. Lachaise's work also seemed very American to Seldes because "he can set, against a multitude of racing circumstances, a single fact in complete repose."

90. See Payne, *The Man of Only Yesterday*, 124–25.

91. GS, "True to Type," NYEJ, Sept. 3, 1932, p. 15; ibid., June 20, 1934, p. 17; GS, *The 7 Lively Arts* (New York, 1924), 123. For attitudes toward the middle class of cultural critics prior to Seldes, from Matthew Arnold to Stuart Pratt Sherman, see John Henry Raleigh, *Matthew Arnold and American Culture* (Berkeley, 1957), 164–65, 248–49, and Frederick J. Hoffman, *The Twenties* (New York, 1962), ch. 7, "Critiques of the Middle Class."

92. GS to Sarton, April 5, 1935, Sarton Papers, HLHU; GS, "They Did It for Money," SEP 208 (Oct. 12, 1935): 16–17, 94, 98, esp. 17. Unlike many of Seldes' essays for the *Post*, this one is notably learned, chock-full of historical information. For an anticipation, see GS, "Found Money," *The Mentor* 22 (Nov. 1930): 11–13, 56–58.

93. GS, "True to Type," NYEJ, July 28, 1932, p. 13.

94. GS, "Wanna Buy a Truck?," *Esquire* 4 (Aug. 1935): 86, 131; GS, "Retreat from the Undecorated Age," *Esquire* 15 (April 1941): 72, 144, 146. In the second of these essays Seldes actually conveyed a certain nostalgia for nineteenth-century excess in decoration and design, a time when everything didn't have to have a function to justify its existence.

95. GS, "Bing Crosby, Marcel Proust . . . and Others," *Scribner's* 100 (Oct. 1936): 78.

96. Ibid., 78–79. For a consistent anticipation, see GS, "Pictures and Landscapes," NR 47 (June 2, 1926): 61.

97. This "reckoning" is untitled and dated March 3, 1969, MSP.

98. GS, "No More Swing?," *Scribner's* 100 (Nov. 1936): 70; Melvin P. Ely, *The*

Adventures of Amos 'n' Andy: A Social History of an American Phenomenon (New York, 1992), 97; GS, "What Makes Men Dance?," *Esquire* 7 (May 1937): 106, 194. For the modest yet notable increase in performances with all-black casts during the 1930s, see Thomas Bender, *New York Intellect: A History of Intellectual Life in New York City, from 1750 to the Beginnings of Our Own Time* (New York, 1987), 327, and Ann Douglas, *Terrible Honesty: Mongrel Manhattan in the 1920s* (New York, 1995), 78, 80.

99. GS, "True to Type," NYEJ, May 18, 1932, p. 17. By the mid-1920s *The Dial* indicated its partiality for African-American cultural expression. Marianne Moore told Seldes on Nov. 5, 1926, that the editors had decided not to review a new biography of George Washington, but to do a long, combined review of *Seventy Negro Spirituals* and *The Second Book of Negro Spirituals*. She was also determined to include Alain Locke's *The New Negro*. (Dial/Thayer Papers, box 6, BLYU.)

100. Atkinson, NYT, Nov. 30, 1939, p. 24; Watts, N.Y. *Herald Tribune*, Nov. 30, 1939; John Mason Brown, N.Y. *Post*, Nov. 30, 1939; Whipple, N.Y. *World-Telegram*, Nov. 30, 1939; Coleman, N.Y. *Daily Mirror*, Nov. 30, 1939; Anderson, N.Y. *Journal-American*, Nov. 30, 1939; *Daily Worker*, Nov. 30, 1939, all from a Seldes clipping file, NYPL-BR.

101. Abel, *Variety*, Dec. 6, 1939; *Time* 34 (Dec. 11, 1939): 50; Euphemia Van Rensselaer Wyatt, *Catholic World* 140 (Jan. 1940): 471; Gilder, "Broadway in Review," *Theatre Arts* 24 (Feb. 1940): 93. Detailed confirmation of these difficulties also comes from Franklin Heller, first assistant stage manager for *Swingin' the Dream*, and an admirer of Seldes. Heller to the author, April 14, 1994.

102. GS, "True to Type," NYEJ, May 20, 1933, p. 15.

103. Eliot to GS, Aug. 11, 1924, MSP.

104. Greenberg, "Avant-Garde and Kitsch" (1939), in Greenberg, *The Collected Essays and Criticism*, vol. 1, *Perceptions and Judgments, 1939–1944*, John O'Brian, ed. (Chicago, 1986), 5–22.

105. Payne, *The Man of Only Yesterday*, 38. Allen's appeal first appeared in NR 10 (March 31, 1917): 264–65. For a significantly elaborated update of Allen's analysis, see Malcolm L. Willey and Stuart A. Rice, "The Agencies of Mass Impression," in Wesley C. Mitchell, ed., *Recent Social Trends in the United States: Report of the President's Research Committee on Social Trends* (New York, 1933), I: 203–17.

106. Between October 23 and December 18, 1935, Margaret Marshall and Mary McCarthy wrote a four-part series for *The Nation* called "Our Critics, Right or Wrong." Because it concentrated on literary criticism, Seldes was not mentioned. "Criticism in America during the past ten years," they wrote, "has on the whole worked for the misunderstanding of works of art and the debasement of taste. The tony critics as well as the hack book reviewers have contributed to this anarchy of standards." *Nation* 141 (Oct. 23, 1935): 472.

Chapter 6. "The Movies Come from America"

1. GS, *An Hour with the Movies and the Talkies* (Philadelphia, 1929), 54–55; GS, "Films Across the Sea," NR 55 (May 30, 1928): 46–47; GS, "Some Current Talkies," NR 59 (June 12, 1929): 97–99; GS, "Some Russian Films," NR 59 (July 3, 1929): 179–80.

2. GS, "True to Type," NYEJ, Sept. 1, 1932, p. 12; GS, "The Little Things," *Esquire* 24 (Dec. 1945): 147.

3. GS, *An Hour with the Movies*, 15, 26, 48–49, 79, 108, 111, 139; GS, *The Movies Come from America* (New York, 1937), 5, 21.

4. GS, *Movies Come from America*, 20; Florence Low, "An Enemy of 'the Bogus': Gilbert Seldes and *The Seven Lively Arts*" (M.A. thesis, Southern Illinois University, 1968), 61–62; Charles Champlin, *Back There When the Past Was: A Small-Town Boyhood* (Syracuse, 1989), 95.

5. GS, "Over the Tops," SEP 208 (April 25, 1936): 21; GS, *Movies Come from America*, 9; GS, "Who Wants a Noble Movie?," *Esquire* 18 (Dec. 1942): 215.

6. GS, *An Hour with the Movies*, 95, 100–101. For a less friendly view of film critics, see GS, "Outline of a Preface," NR 51 (May 25, 1927): 18–19.

7. GS, "Tintypes and Tenderness," *Esquire* 6 (Oct. 1936): 98, 115.

8. GS, "And Twice as Natural," *Esquire* 14 (Nov. 1940): 84, 156; GS, "What Every Woman Hater Knows," *Esquire* 17 (June 1942): 54, 164.

9. GS, "Christ in the Movies," NR 50 (May 4, 1927): 298–99.

10. GS, "Theory about 'Talkies,'" NR 55 (Aug. 8, 1928): 305–6.

11. Greene, *The Pleasure Dome: The Collected Film Criticism, 1935–40* (London, 1972), 1.

12. GS, "The Famous Touch of Nature," VF 21 (Feb. 1924): 40, 76. See also GS ["Vivian Shaw"], "The Old Fashioned Menace of the Screen," VF 21 (March 1924): 40; GS, "Fred Stone and W. C. Fields," VF 21 (April 1924): 42, 88.

13. GS ["Vivian Shaw"], "Moving Pictures," *The Dial* 74 (Jan. 1923): 111–12; GS, "The Path of the Movies," *Nation* 120 (April 29, 1925): 498, 500; GS, "Some Elaborate Pictures," *Nation* 120 (May 27, 1925): 607; GS, "The Plot and the Picture," NR 44 (Sept. 16, 1925): 97–98.

14. GS, "The Plot and the Picture," 97–98; GS, "A Letter to the International Film Art Guild," NR 44 (Nov. 18, 1925): 332–33; GS, "'Art' in the Movies," *Nation* 121 (July 29, 1925): 148. In 1927 Seldes praised art films, but a decade later he expressed skepticism about the potential impact of the art film because it now seemed too "aesthetic" for general appreciation and commercial success. See *Movies Come from America*, 99.

15. GS, "Moving Pictures," *The Dial* 74 (Jan. 1923): 112. For Seldes' ongoing fascination with *Dr. Caligari*, see GS, *An Hour with the Movies*, 102–4. For Seldes on the technical differences between U.S. and foreign film-making, see GS, "The Movie Director," NR 43 (May 27, 1925): 19–20.

16. GS, "Again We View-with-Alarm: The Moving Picture," VF 24 (April 1925): 57; GS, "Back to the B's Boys?," *Esquire* 25 (April 1946): 94, 177–78.

17. GS, "The Quicksands of the Movies," *Atlantic* 158 (Oct. 1936): 422. For other critical statements spanning a twenty-five-year period, see GS, "Progress in the Movies," NR 51 (July 27, 1927): 255–56; GS, "The Movies," *Americana* 1 (May 1933): 18; GS, "John Huston in Darkest Africa," SRL 35 (Feb. 23, 1952): 29.

18. GS, "Some Movie Disproportions," NR 49 (Dec. 29, 1926): 161; GS to Edmund Wilson, [spring 1927], Wilson Papers, BLYU; GS, *An Hour with the Movies*, 33, 73, 96.

19. GS, *An Hour with the Movies*, 102–3. He elaborated on these views in "The People and the Arts," *Scribner's* 101 (Feb. 1937): 79.

20. GS, *An Hour with the Movies*, 29–30.

21. For reviews of *An Hour with the Movies*, see *Outlook* 153 (Oct. 2, 1929): 189, and NR 61 (Dec. 18, 1929): 118–19. GS to Gessner, May 12, 1965, MSP; and Gessner's essay in Gyorgy Kepes, ed., *The Nature and Art of Motion* (New York, 1965), 158–67 ("Seven Faces of Time: An Aesthetic for Cinema").

22. GS, "The Movies Commit Suicide," *Harper's* 157 (Nov. 1928): 706–12, esp. 711–12.

23. GS, *An Hour with the Movies*, 123–25, 138–39, 153–54; GS, "Some Amateur Movies," NR 58 (March 6, 1929): 71–72; GS, "Talkies' Progress," *Harper's* 159 (Sept. 1929): 454–61; GS, "The Mobile Camera," NR 60 (Oct. 30, 1929): 298–99.

24. GS, "Musicals, Plain and Fancy," NR 61 (Feb. 12, 1930): 327–28; GS, "Newsreels and Pictures," NR 66 (March 11, 1931): 96.

25. GS, *Movies Come from America*, 89; GS, "From Griffith to Garbo," SRL 18 (May 21, 1938): 13.

26. GS, "The Movies in Peril," *Scribner's* 97 (Feb. 1935): 86; GS, "Suggestion for Hollywood," *Esquire* 14 (Aug. 1940): 71, 165; fragment of an undated newspaper column, Seldes clipping folder, NYPL-BR.

27. GS, *Proclaim Liberty!* (New York, 1942), 157.

28. Raymond Fielding, *The March of Time, 1935–1951* (New York, 1978), esp. ch. 4 and pp. 4, 12.

29. GS, *Writing for Television* (Garden City, N.Y., 1952).

30. GS to Gilbert K. Chesterton, Sept. 11, 1922, Dial/Thayer Papers, box 6, BLYU; GS to Wilson, [Sept. 1931?], Wilson Papers, BLYU; Wilson to Sinclair, Oct. 2, 1931, in Wilson, *Letters on Literature and Politics, 1912–1972*, Elena Wilson, ed. (New York, 1977), 216; GS "True to Type," NYEJ, Jan. 26, 1933, p. 15.

31. GS, "True to Type," NYEJ, June 20, 1934, p. 17; GS, "Also Selected Short Subjects," *Esquire* 4 (Oct. 1935): 86; William Stott, *Documentary Expression and Thirties America* (New York, 1973).

32. GS to Dr. Arthur E. Morgan, Sept. 5, 1939, Morgan Papers, HLHU. In 1933, or thereabouts, Seldes planned several film projects that did not come to fruition: a scenic tour of New York and a movie version of Sherwood Anderson's story "I'm a Fool." GS to Anderson, Aug. 26, [1933?], Anderson Papers, NL.

33. GS, "Also Selected Short Subjects," *Esquire* 4 (Oct. 1935): 86.

34. GS, "Good Theatre," *Atlantic* 161 (Jan. 1938): 82; clipping from the N.Y. *Post*, Feb. 14, 1938, MSP.

35. GS, "Pictures and Politics," *Esquire* 15 (May 1941): 87, 103. The central issue that Seldes contemplated in this essay might be formulated as follows: If a symphony orchestra were to be shown performing on television, the director had to consider what to show on the screen as an alternative to watching the orchestra itself. Watching an orchestra on television had to be different from attending a concert hall. A diverse range of images seemed essential.

36. GS, "True to Type," NYEJ, Aug. 15, 1932, p. 13; GS, "Tintypes and Tenderness," *Esquire* 6 (Oct. 1936): 98; GS, "Pictures and Politics," *Esquire* 15 (May 1941): 103.

37. GS, "The Movies in Peril," *Scribner's* 97 (Feb. 1935): 81–86.

38. J. C. Furnas, "Searching for Hamlet in Pictures," N.Y. *Herald Tribune*, Feb. 17 and March 3, 1935, clippings in MSP. For partial agreement *and* lively divergence from Seldes on these and related matters, see Mortimer J. Adler, *Art and Prudence: A Study in Practical Philosophy* (New York, 1937), 578–81.

39. GS, "The Movies in Peril," *Scribner's* 97 (Feb. 1935): 81–86; GS, "Stand Up and Kick," *Today*, March 23, 1935, p. 19; GS, "Is It Thrifty To Be Smart?," *Esquire* 7 (Jan. 1937): 95.

40. GS, "The Number One Blight," *Esquire* 9 (Jan. 1938): 91, 193; GS, "The Two-Thirds Masterpiece," *Esquire* 15 (March 1941): 89, 175–76.

41. GS, "Chaplin and Some Others," *Nation* 121 (Nov. 11, 1925): 549–50; GS, "A Chaplin Masterpiece," NR 66 (Feb. 25, 1931): 46–47; GS, "Production No. 5," *Esquire* 4 (Nov. 1935): 94.

42. GS, "The Best Pictures of Last Tuesday," *Esquire* 10 (Aug. 1938): 72, 90; GS, *The Public Arts* (New York, 1956), 17.

43. GS, "Mr. Cagney Is Tough Enough," *Esquire* 9 (June 1938): 93, 177.

44. GS, "Disney and Others," NR 71 (June 8, 1932): 101–2; GS, "No Art, Mr. Disney?," *Esquire* 8 (Sept. 1937): 91, 171–72, quotation at 172.

45. GS, "The Goblins Catch Up," *Esquire* 14 (July 1940): 92.

46. Ibid., 166. There is no reason to believe that Seldes had seen an essay by Walter Benjamin (published in German in 1936) that came to be famous several decades later. See Benjamin, *Illuminations*, Hannah Arendt, ed. (New York, 1968), 217–51.

47. GS, "Lively Arts," *Park East* (Sept. 1951): 42–43.

48. GS to JR, May 7, 1917, MSP; GS, "Some Movie Notes," NR 65 (Dec. 10, 1930): 103; GS, "Mr. Abbott and Mr. Costello," *Esquire* 13 (April 1940): 80, 156, 157; GS, "Sam Goldwyn and the Movies," *Esquire* 24 (Sept. 1945): 60, 151–52.

49. GS, "The Movies in Peril," *Scribner's* 97 (Feb. 1935): 85–86; GS, "The Itsy-Bitsy Actors," *Esquire* 3 (Jan. 1935): 56, 128; GS, "The Quicksands of the Movies," *Atlantic* 158 (Oct. 1936): 426–27; GS, "Oh, Rare Miss Bergman," *Esquire* 22 (Oct. 1944): 84, 161.

50. GS, "The Natives Return," *Esquire* 15 (June 1941): 68, 169–70; GS, "Hollywood Goldfish Bowl," *Esquire* 17 (March 1942): 58, 114; GS, "Radio Boy Makes Good," *Esquire* 16 (Aug. 1941): 57, 111.

51. GS, "Good Old Sex Appeal," NR 46 (April 21, 1926): 275–76; GS, "The Other Side of It: A Premature Post-Mortem," *Century* 118 (July 1929): 297–302.

52. GS, *Movies Come from America*, 34; GS, "The Quicksands of the Movies," *Atlantic* 158 (Oct. 1936): 430–31.

53. GS, *Movies Come from America*, 35.

54. GS, "Two Great Women," *Esquire* 4 (July 1935): 86, 143; GS, "What Happened to Love?," *Esquire* 12 (Dec. 1939): 163, 164, 166.

55. GS, "Cosmetically Sealed," *Esquire* 4 (Dec. 1935): 86; GS, "The Juvenile Leads," *Esquire* 7 (April 1937): 99, 133–34; GS, "Tots Save the Show," *Esquire* 13 (Feb. 1940): 75, 99. In 1932 Seldes wrote about a fascinating human drama: Charlie Chaplin's appearance in a California court asking that his two sons be kept out of the movie business. Otherwise, he feared, they would never quite be treated as autonomous people in their own right. GS, "True to Type," NYEJ, Aug. 31, 1932, p. 17.

56. GS, "People and the Arts," *Scribner's* 101 (June 1937): 62, 64.

57. GS, "Some Movie Disproportions," NR 49 (Dec. 29, 1926): 161–62; GS, *An Hour with the Movies*, 123; GS, *Movies Come from America*, 57, 113. See also Victoria de Grazia, "Mass Culture and Sovereignty: The American Challenge to European Cinemas, 1920–1960," *Journal of Modern History* 61 (March 1989): 53–87.

58. GS, *Movies Come from America*, 98; GS, "The Quicksands of the Movies," *Atlantic* 158 (Oct. 1936): 424; GS, "People and the Arts," *Scribner's* 101 (March 1937): 70.

59. *Times* (London) Literary Supplement, Oct. 23, 1937, p. 784; *Manchester Guardian*, Oct. 19, 1937, p. 7. On Nov. 12, 1937, Seldes wrote a letter in response to the *Guardian's* review because he objected to a note of national chauvinism (copy in MSP).

60. Springfield *Republican*, Nov. 27, 1937, p. 6; *Books*, Dec. 19, 1937, p. 2; Leyda, *Theatre Arts Monthly* 21 (Dec. 1937): 987–88.

61. Lennox Grey, "Communication and the Arts," in Lyman Bryson, ed., *The Communication of Ideas* (New York, 1948), 138; GS, "Are the Foreign Films Better?," *Atlantic* 184 (Sept. 1949): 49–52; Charles Brackett (of Paramount Pictures) to GS, Sept. 1, 1949, MSP, in response to the essay in *Atlantic*.

62. In 1950, when Seldes published *The Great Audience*, he received a warmly appreciative note from one of his Hollywood friends: "I wish you had been able to stick out here. That is, in a way I do. I recognize the desert around me." Irving Pichel to GS, Nov. 9, 1950, Seldes Papers, UPSC.

63. Robert Sklar, *F. Scott Fitzgerald: The Last Laocoön* (New York, 1967), 333–34; Fitzgerald to Murphy, Sept. 14, 1940, in F. Scott Fitzgerald, *The Crack-Up*, Edmund Wilson, ed. (New York, 1945), 281–82. See also Tom Dardis, *Some Time in the Sun* (New York, 1976).

64. GS, "The Vandals of Hollywood," SRL 14 (Oct. 17, 1936): 14; GS, "No More Swing?," *Scribner's* 100 (Nov. 1936): 72.

65. GS, "The Vandals of Hollywood," 3, 13, 14.

66. GS, "True to Type," NYEJ, Nov. 25, 1932, p. 19.

67. GS, "The Movies Go Literary," *Esquire* 11 (May 1939): 108, 179.

68. GS, "Who's Running Away?," *Esquire* 13 (June 1940): 92, 156; GS, "Stand Up and Kick," *Today*, March 23, 1935, pp. 6–7, 18–19. From February until May 1937, Seldes wrote "The People and the Arts" column for *Scribner's Magazine*. Starting in June 1937 it became the "Screen and Radio" column. Many of his cultural complaints about film also applied elsewhere in the popular arts.

69. GS, "The Abstract Movie," NR 48 (Sept. 15, 1926): 95–96; GS, "Man Ray and Metropolis," NR 50 (March 30, 1927): 170–71; GS, "Camera Angles," NR 50 (March 9, 1927): 72–73; GS, "'Chang': A Great Picture," NR 50 (May 11, 1927): 332–33; GS, "A Fine American Movie," NR 54 (March 7, 1928): 98–99; GS, "The Movies Commit Suicide," *Harper's* 157 (Nov. 1928): 708.

70. See Townsend Ludington, *John Dos Passos: A Twentieth Century Odyssey* (New York, 1980), 270, 356–57; Laurence Bergreen, *James Agee: A Life* (New York, 1984), 213–14; Dardis, *Some Time in the Sun*, 218–51; J. A. Ward, *American Silences: The Realism of James Agee, Walker Evans, and Edward Hopper* (Baton Rouge, 1985), 87–89.

71. The clipping is in MSP. For James Agee's collected film criticism, see *Agee on Film: Reviews and Comments*, 2 vols. (New York, 1958–60), and Peter H. Ohlin, *Agee* (New York, 1966), ch. 3, "Film Criticism."

72. GS, "Disney and Others," NR 71 (June 8, 1932): 101–2. See Paul Gleye, *The Architecture of Los Angeles* (Los Angeles, 1981), 104–7; Ralph Sexton, *American Theaters of Today* (New York, 1927); David Naylor, *American Picture Palaces: The Architecture of Fantasy* (New York, 1981): Lary May, "Making the American Way: Moderne Theatres, Audiences, and the Film Industry, 1929–1945," *Prospects* 12 (1987): 89, 101–2.

73. David and Evelyn T. Riesman, "Movies and Audiences," in Riesman, *Individualism Reconsidered and Other Essays* (Glencoe, Ill., 1954), 194.

74. Ibid., 194–95.

75. Ibid., 195.

76. I am indebted to Hal S. Barron of Harvey Mudd College for the opportunity to read a chapter (from his work-in-progress on consumerism in rural America) titled "Eating Not the Bread of Idleness: The Rural North and Consumer Culture in the 1920s," 26–28.

77. See Richard Randall, *Censorship of the Movies: The Social and Political Control of a Mass Medium* (Madison, 1968); Leornard J. Leff and Jerold L. Simmons, *The Dame in the Kimono: Hollywood Censorship and the Production Code from the 1920s to the 1960s* (New York, 1990); Seldes, *The New Mass Media* (1957; Washington, D.C., 1968), 71.

78. GS, *An Hour with the Movies and the Talkies*, 115.

79. GS, "Naked and Uninteresting," *Americana* 1 (Feb. 1933): 9.

80. Ibid. Later in 1933 Seldes devoted two of his daily columns to nudism, which he found silly and unattractive, yet believed certainly should be permitted. GS, "True to Type," NYEJ, Dec. 20 and 30, 1933, pp. 19 and 11.

81. GS, *Movies Come from America*, 54–55.

82. Greene, *The Pleasure Dome: The Collected Film Criticism*, 269.

83. GS, "Should the Movies Tell?," *Esquire* 23 (Jan. 1945): 105, 122; GS, "Are the Foreign Films Better?," 49–52.

84. The eighth paragraph of Brown's essay very clearly mocks Seldes' early encomia for Chaplin: "The intellectuals . . . found him to be an artist. They began to talk about the poetry of his pantomime. About the perfection of his technique. About his sense of timing. About his style. About the Commedia dell'Arte in relation to him. About the tragedian lurking in the pie-slinger," and so on. John Mason Brown, "Seeing Things," SRL 30 (May 3, 1947): 24–27; GS to Norman Cousins, n.d., Brown Papers, HLHU; Chaplin to Seldes, Feb. 14, 1950, MSP. The delay in Chaplin's response was caused by Seldes' defense of "M. Verdoux" in *The Great Audience* (New York, 1950), 35. Chaplin responded to that.

85. GS, "Pressures and Pictures," *Nation* 172 (Feb. 3 and 10, 1951): 104–6, 132–34. For a good summary of the issues and the controversy, see Hollis Alpert, "Love, Fagin, and the Censors," SRL 34 (Jan. 27, 1951): 28–29. *The Saturday Review* shared Seldes' scorn for the formal censorship as well as informal pressure brought to bear against *The Miracle*.

86. GS, "Pressures and Pictures," *Nation* 172 (Feb. 10, 1951): 132–34.

87. GS, "A Short Angry View of Film Censorship," *Theatre Arts* 35 (Aug. 1951): 56–57.

88. Ibid.

89. Ibid.

90. Ibid., 57; GS, *Great Audience*, 31. His most extended discussion of censorship and the Code appears in ibid., 64–81.

91. GS, "Chaplin's Triumph of Comedy," *Esquire* 15 (Jan. 1941): 72, 134–36.

92. GS, "Terror in the Newsreels," *Esquire* 19 (May 1943): 88, 162.

93. Ibid., 88. For general context, see Thomas Doherty, *Projections of War: Hollywood, American Culture, and World War II* (New York, 1993).

94. GS, "Short Hooray for Hollywood," *Esquire* 19 (June 1943): 85, 151; GS, "In Motion Pictures It's Timing," *Esquire* 21 (June 1944): 90, 177, extended his infatuation with *Casablanca*.

95. GS, "An Actor Who Knows When To Fight," *Esquire* 20 (Oct. 1943): 86. For a scathing attack on Hollywood and its myth-making propensities, written late in the 1940s from a British perspective, see Hortense Powdermaker, *Hollywood the Dream Factory: An Anthropologist Looks at the Movie-Makers* (Boston, 1951).

96. GS, "A Note on Television," NR 69 (Dec. 2, 1931): 71–72; GS, *Movies Come from America*, 15, 112–13.

97. GS, "Can Hollywood Take Over Television?," *Atlantic* 186 (Oct. 1950): 51–53; GS, *Great Audience*, 160, 169–73.

98. GS, "Lively Arts," *Park East* (Oct. 1951): 42; GS, *New Mass Media*, 7. See also Laurence Bergreen, *As Thousands Cheer: The Life of Irving Berlin* (New York, 1990), 501, and Christopher Anderson, *Hollywood TV: The Studio System in the Fifties* (Austin, Tex., 1994).

Chapter 7. Radio and Television

1. *The Dartmouth*, March 2, 1955, p. 1; Clara S. Logan to GS, Feb. 21, 1952, Seldes Papers, box 2, UPSC; GS, *Previews of Entertainment* (New York, 1952).

2. GS, "True to Type," NYEJ, Feb. 16, 1933, p. 17, and Dec. 7, 1933, p. 25.

3. Ibid., GS, "Some Radio Entertainers," NR 67 (May 20, 1931): 19–20; GS, "True to Type," NYEJ, June 15, 1932, p. 13; GS, "Male and Female and Radio," *Esquire* 1 (Jan. 1934): 35; GS, "Professor, I'm Through," *Esquire* 3 (Feb. 1935): 64.

4. GS, "Male and Female and Radio," 35; GS, "Stand Up and Kick," *Today*, March 23, 1935, p. 18; GS, "TV and Radio," SRL 40 (March 2, 1957): 27.

5. GS, "Phony Takes All," *Esquire* 8 (Dec. 1937): 137, 243; GS, "The Great American Handshake," SRL 35 (Oct. 18, 1952): 32.

6. GS, "Before It's Too Late," *Esquire* 5 (March 1936): 72; GS, "True to Type," NYEJ, April 21, 1933, p. 32.

7. GS, "Listening In," NR 50 (March 23, 1927): 140–41; GS, "True to Type," NYEJ, Jan. 29, 1934, p. 13. In a rather technical essay in which he speculated about the prospects for FM and other possibilities in radio, Seldes anticipated the development of FAX by almost fifty years. See GS, "Radio for the Future," *Atlantic* 167 (April 1941): 453–61.

8. Clayton R. Koppes, "The Social Destiny of the Radio: Hope and Disillusionment in the 1920s," *South Atlantic Quarterly* 68 (Summer 1969): 363–76. For confirmation of disillusionment from Seldes' point of view, see GS, "No More Swing?," *Scribner's* 100 (Nov. 1936): 70. For Seldes on radio and the decline of reading among children, see GS, "No Decameron?," *Publisher's Weekly* 128 (Oct. 19, 1935): 1459–60. "The great enemy of children's reading, just now, is the radio. And the only way publishers will conquer, is by combining with the radio. . . . Why haven't good children's books been radio-dramatized?"

9. Malcolm M. Willey and Stuart A. Rice, "The Agencies of Communication," in Wesley C. Mitchell, ed., *Recent Social Trends in the United States: Report of the President's Research Committee on Social Trends* (New York, 1933), 211.

10. GS, "True to Type," NYEJ, Jan. 10, 1933, p. 17; ibid., Feb. 21, 1933, p. 13. In 1947 an admirer who had just read *Only Yesterday* wrote the following to Frederick Lewis Allen: "Is not radio the most powerful force for education & the most influential molder of public opinion in mankind's history?" Allen wrote in the margin: "Maybe, but not by 1930." Ted Powell to F. L. Allen, Dec. 28, 1947, Allen Papers, box 3, MDLC.

11. This identical comment will be found in GS, "True to Type," NYEJ, April 21, 1933, p. 32; GS, *The Years of the Locust (America, 1929–1932)* (Boston, 1933), 29; GS, "Funniest Thing about Radio," *Esquire* 5 (May 1936): 93; GS, *The Great Audience* (New York, 1950), 106–7.

12. GS, *Great Audience*, 163, 197.

13. GS, "True to Type," NYEJ, Jan. 5, 1933, p. 13, and Sept. 17, 1933, p. 17; GS, "Funniest Thing about the Radio," 93; GS, "Stuff the Little Children," *Esquire* 6 (Aug. 1936): 97, 167; GS, "The Case for the Commercial," *Esquire* 24 (Oct. 1945): 77, 78, 160.

14. GS, *Proclaim Liberty!* (New York, 1942), 160; GS, *Great Audience*, 132 and passim. See also Alexander Woollcott to Archibald MacLeish, Dec. 16, 1941, and MacLeish to Woollcott, Dec. 22, 1941, MacLeish Papers, box 23, MDLC. MacLeish, then Librarian of Congress, read the Bill of Rights script written by Norman Corwin.

15. Hal S. Barron, "Eating Not the Bread of Idleness: The Rural North and Consumer Culture in the 1920s," work-in-progress, Nov. 1993.

16. GS, "True to Type," NYEJ, Aug. 11, 1933, p. 14.

17. GS, "The Beginnings of Popularity," in C. S. Marsh, ed., *Educational Broadcasting 1936* (Chicago, 1937), 340.

18. GS, *Great Audience*, 113; GS, "People and the Arts," *Scribner's* 101 (June 1937): 61–62; GS, four-page dictated typescript about the expatriates, March 8, [1964?], MSP. MacLeish responded promptly on May 27, 1937, that Seldes' review "seems to me to

represent the possible relation between a critic and an experimenting writer about as beautifully as anything that has happened in recent years" (MSP).

19. GS, "Professor, I'm Through," *Esquire* 3 (Feb. 1935): 64, 114; GS, "Einstein, Kip, and Stoop," *Esquire* 25 (May 1946): 89 ff; for the perspective that Seldes did not share, see Joy Elmer Morgan, "A National Culture—By-Product or Objective of National Planning?," in Tracy F. Tyler, ed., *Radio as a Cultural Agency* (Washington, D.C., 1934), 23–32.

20. GS, "An Earful of Fun," *Americana* 1 (March 1933): 14.

21. GS, "Apology to Crooners," *Esquire* 7 (June 1937): 103, 168.

22. GS, "Serenade to Fred Allen," *Esquire* 20 (Sept. 1943): 72, 147. See also GS, "Stand Up and Kick," *Today* March 23, 1935, pp. 7, 18.

23. GS, "Actor for a Night," *Esquire* 25 (June 1946): 107–8.

24. Ibid., GS, *The Public Arts* (New York, 1956), 153–56. Seldes also published an essay complaining that artificial or induced audience laughter was lethal to successful radio comedy. See GS, "How to Laugh on the Air," *Esquire* 23 (May 1945): 88, 156.

25. Clippings from the New York *Post*, July 29, 1937, and NYT, Aug. 1, 1937, MSP.

26. Seldes had enjoyed a cordial correspondence with White since the summer of 1937 when White wrote a warm review of Seldes' *Mainland* for *The Atlantic Monthly*. See Chapter Eight below. At the same time, brother George Seldes also indicated his great admiration for White. See his book *Lords of the Press* (New York, 1938), 272.

27. GS to William Allen White, June 22, 1938, White Papers, series C, box 290, MDLC.

28. White to GS, July 14, 1938, ibid; GS to White, July 19 and 27, Aug. 16, 1938, ibid. See also Sally F. Griffith, "Mass Media Come to the Small Town: The *Emporia Gazette* in the 1920s," in Catherine L. Covert and John D. Stevens, eds., *Mass Media Between the Wars: Perceptions of Cultural Tension, 1918–1941* (Syracuse, 1984), 141–55.

29. A transcript of this broadcast dated Nov. 27, 1938, is enclosed with a letter from GS to Gertrude Stein, Feb. 3, 1939, Stein Papers, BLYU. Stein was also mentioned in the broadcast. Interestingly enough, six years earlier Seldes had speculated in a column about the possible outcome of libel and slander suits involving cultural issues. "True to Type," NYEJ, Nov. 12, 1932, p. 6.

30. Corwin to the author, Feb. 12, 1992.

31. GS, "How to Laugh on the Air," 88, 156. In 1950 Seldes called Corwin "the political conscience of the broadcasting industry," a designation that he applied a few years later to Edward R. Murrow. GS, *Great Audience*, 120.

32. GS, "How to Laugh on the Air," 88, 156; Mumford to Brooks, May 26, 1942, and Brooks to Mumford, May 31, 1942, in Robert E. Spiller, ed., *The Van Wyck Brooks-Lewis Mumford Letters: The Record of a Literary Friendship, 1921–1963* (New York, 1970), 211, 213.

33. Darwin Payne, *The Man of Only Yesterday: Frederick Lewis Allen* (New York, 1975), 268–70. During the mid-1930s Sylvester "Pat" Weaver produced a successful series for CBS on moments of crisis in American history. See Weaver, *The Best Seat in the House: The Golden Years of Radio and Television* (New York, 1994), 27.

34. Seldes to Nevins, April 25, 1938, Nevins Papers, CURBML.

35. Seldes to Nevins, April 28 and Sept. 9, 1938, Nevins Papers, CURBML.

36. The scripts for "Living History" are in the collection of CBS radio scripts, box 28, MDLC. *Variety* reviewed the series on June 22, 1938, noted that multiple modes of narrative were used, suggested an occasional lack of smoothness in shifting from one to the next, and wondered whether Seldes tried to "cover too much historical ground" in each broadcast.

37. GS to Nevins, [late summer 1938], Nevins Papers, CURBML.

38. Ibid. Seldes' series very likely provided the inspiration for one written by Archibald MacLeish, "The American Story," that NBC broadcast on Saturday evenings, 7 to 7:30, in 1944. MacLeish wanted "to use radio to give wide circulation to the basic human, first-hand accounts which are far and away the best of historical reading, and which are usually known only to the historians." MacLeish to Edward Weeks, March 16, 1944, MacLeish Papers, box 23, MDLC.

39. The scripts and related materials for "Americans All—Immigrants All" are in the CBS radio scripts, box 32, MDLC.

40. Ibid.; and see GS, "Experiment in Broadcasting," *Esquire* 11 (Jan. 1939): 78, 130; GS, *Proclaim Liberty!*, 102–3.

41. The manual was published by the Federal Radio Education Committee in cooperation with the U.S. Office of Education in Washington. Seldes' copy and his memo are in MSP.

42. Scraps of material from "The Lively Arts" will be found with other Seldes material among the CBS radio scripts, boxes 28 to 32, MDLC; Joan Shelley Rubin, *The Making of Middlebrow Culture* (Chapel Hill, 1992), 326; Clifton Fadiman to the author, Nov. 6, 1992. Fadiman recalled Seldes "with pleasure" because of his appearances on "Conversation," "always with distinction."

43. GS, "Listening In," NR 50 (March 23, 1927): 140; GS, "Professor, I'm Through," 64; GS, "Stand Up and Kick," 6. Lawrence W. Levine has made a forceful argument that the audiences for popular culture were *not* passive. He does not, however, address the fact that so many contemporaries, and *especially* cultural critics, like Seldes, perceived an increasing amount of passivity in American audiences. See Levine, "The Folklore of Industrial Society: Popular Culture and Its Audiences," *American Historical Review* 97 (Dec. 1992): 1369–99, esp. 1373. For Seldes' emphasis upon the growth of audience passivity in the 1950s, see Chapter Nine, p. 340, and Chapter Ten, pp. 371, 375, below.

44. GS, *Mainland* (New York, 1936), 38; GS, *Proclaim Liberty!*, 150. During his last years, 1931–33, Ring Lardner wrote essay-reviews about radio entertainment—mostly to amuse himself. See GS, ed., *The Portable Ring Lardner* (New York, 1946), 659–81. "To get as many as two people to agree on any radio program as perfect is impossible," he remarked (p. 678).

45. GS, "The People and the Arts," *Scribner's* 101 (March 1937): 69–70. In support of Seldes' view, see Joseph Horowitz, *Understanding Toscanini: How He Became an American Culture-God and Helped Create a New Audience for Old Music* (New York, 1987).

46. GS, "The Mike-Swallowers," *Esquire* 6 (Dec. 1936): 100, 250. I am grateful to Professor Roland Marchand for the opportunity to read his fascinating essay on "'Sweet Voices from the Rank and File': Major Bowes, the Amateur Hour, and New Ventures in the Mode of Participation" (draft dated July 1989).

47. GS, "The Mike-Swallowers," 250; MacLeish to Seldes, Dec. 8, 1941, and April 21, 1942, MacLeish Papers, box 20, MDLC.

48. DeVoto to Davis, July 21, 1940, Davis Papers, box 1, MDLC; Edward R. Murrow to Davis, Sept. 15, 1940, ibid.; GS, *Great Audience*, 8, 151–52; GS to Davis, April 7, 1953, Davis Papers, box 3.

49. The McBride Papers, boxes 1–2, MDLC, include a lot of fan mail along with information about her many programs over a twenty-three-year span; John Farrar to Robert E. Kintner, April 24, 1953, McBride Papers, box 1, MDLC. See also her autobiographical *Out of the Air* (Garden City, N.Y., 1960).

50. GS, "Nickelodeon to Television," *Maclean's Magazine*, Jan. 1, 1950, pp. 12–13, 44; GS, *Great Audience*, 4–6. On pp. 108–9, however, Seldes declared that "radio seldom

reaches the vast majority; it is a mass-minority medium." He never adequately clarified the distinction, and I am inclined to believe that his tentativeness is itself an indication that understanding of the arrival of mass culture was incomplete at mid-century.

51. See, e.g., Paul F. Lazarsfeld, *Radio and the Printed Page* (New York, 1940); Warren Susman, "The Culture of the Thirties," in Susman, *Culture as History: The Transformation of American Society in the Twentieth Century* (New York, 1984), 160; Lary May, "Making the American Way: Moderne Theatres, Audiences, and the Film Industry, 1929–1945," *Prospects* 12 (1987): 89–124.

52. See GS, *The 7 Lively Arts*, 2nd ed. (New York, 1957), 10; GS, *Great Audience,* 164, 170; Payne, *Frederick Lewis Allen*; 221; Robert H. Stock (President of Tele-Scripts, Inc.) to David Frederick, Aug. 30, 1949, Frederick Lewis Allen Papers, box 4, MDLC.

53. GS, *Great Audience*, 161; GS, "Television in Print," *Nation* 184 (March 9, 1957): 217–18.

54. See, among others, Cecelia Tichi, *Electronic Hearth: Creating an American Television Culture* (New York, 1991); J. Fred MacDonald, *One Nation Under Television: The Rise and Decline of Network TV* (New York, 1990); Mark Crispin Miller, *Boxed In: The Culture of TV* (Evanston, 1988); Shanto Iyengar and Donald R. Kinder, *News That Matters: Television and American Opinion* (Chicago, 1987); Hal Himmelstein, *Television: Myth and the American Mind* (New York, 1984); Todd Gitlin, *Inside Prime Time* (New York, 1983).

55. GS, *The New Mass Media: Challenge to a Free Society* (Washington, D.C., 1968), 12; GS, "We Might Still Create an Art of Television," *TV Guide*, April 7, 1962, pp. 11, 13–14.

56. Marchand uses the phrase in his essay "Major Bowes, the Amateur Hour, and New Ventures in the Mode of Participation," p. 4. Historian Kathy Peiss used the same phrase in conversation with me in 1993. Lizabeth Cohen emphasizes the emergence of what she calls mass culture in Chicago during the 1920s. But she does not attempt to demonstrate that it was a *nationwide* mass culture of the sort that emerged after the 1950s. The numerous radio stations that proliferated in Chicago until the later 1930s, for example, were unaffiliated local stations with a limited range. See Cohen, *Making a New Deal: Industrial Workers in Chicago, 1919–1939* (New York, 1990), ch. 3, esp. 129, 132–38, 326–29. For a perspective that emphasizes discontinuity and change, see Richard Wightman Fox and T. J. Jackson Lears, eds., *The Culture of Consumption: Critical Essays in American History, 1880–1980* (New York, 1983).

57. GS, "Television," *Nation* 182 (May 26, 1956): 457–58; GS, "TV and Radio," SRL 40 (Jan. 19, 1957): 50.

58. GS to Schlesinger, Oct. 4, 1959, Schlesinger Papers, JFKL; GS, "The Petulant Highbrow and TV," *TV Guide*, Jan. 2, 1960, pp. 17–19.

59. GS to Schlesinger, autumn 1961, MSP. For a similar statement by Seldes, see his memorandum concerning Robert M. Hutchins, Feb. 24, 1963 (bh-1), AIMT, MSP. It chastises Hutchins as well as Eric Goldman for their elitist views of what television ought to be doing.

60. GS, "The 'Errors' of Television," *Atlantic* 159 (May 1937): 531–41. When CBS issued a press release on September 16, 1937, proudly announcing his appointment, the network noted that Seldes had witnessed his first television experiments in 1927, and that his extensive writings on film and radio meant that he had considerable experience with all of the entertainment mediums that would be incorporated into television. CBS noted Seldes' pride in the fact that he had written about jazz for *The Dial* and about Spengler's philosophy for the *Saturday Evening Post*. He had also prophesied that Mae West would be a major film star six years before she went to Hollywood. And finally, he wrote the program notes and helped to select the songs for the first concert performances of George

Gershwin and Paul Whiteman. CBS clearly felt that it had achieved a coup by hiring Seldes.

61. See GS, "The Nature of Television Programs," AAAPSS no. 213 (Jan. 1941): 138–44, quotation at 139.

62. GS, "Uplift by Wireless," *Esquire* 11 (Feb. 1939): 51, 137.

63. "Television II: 'Fade In Camera One!,'" *Fortune* 19 (May 1939): 72.

64. GS, "The One-Act Play and Television," in William Kozlenko, ed., *The One-Act Play Today: A Discussion of the Technique, Scope and History of the Contemporary Short Drama* (New York, 1938), 129–36.

65. GS, "Television in Education," *Education* 60 (June 1940): 653–55.

66. GS, "A Siberia for Culture?," *Printer's Ink* no. 234 (March 9, 1951): 33–35, 56–57.

67. Ibid., esp. 56. Seldes was at least consistent in his invocation of the democratic consideration. During the summer he responded negatively to a proposal for pay-per-view television ("coin in the slot"), on egalitarian grounds: The wealthy would be able to watch programs that the poor would miss. See GS, "Lively Arts," *Park East* (Aug. 1951): 21.

68. GS, "Lively Arts," *Park East* (July 1951), 38; GS, "Benton Bill Puts TV on Defensive—Again," *Printer's Ink* no. 237 (Dec. 7, 1951): 43–45.

69. GS, "Benton Bill Puts TV on Defensive," 44; John C. Schwarzwalder to GS, Sept. 14, 1954, Seldes Papers, box 2, UPSC. Preparing his book *Writing for Television* (Garden City, N.Y., 1952), Seldes declared that it was too early to establish technical criteria for educational programs because the educators themselves had not yet defined their objectives (197–98).

70. GS to AMS, Jr., Jan. 11, 1964, JFKL; GS to Gale Research Co., Feb. 29, 1964, MSP; GS, "A Deep Bow to the Lady Commissioner," *Channel 13/WNDT Program Guide* (Feb. 1966), 1–6.

71. GS, WID-9, AIMT, MSP.

72. Wilson to Gregory, 1941, in Wilson, *Letters on Literature and Politics, 1912–1972,* Elena Wilson, ed. (New York, 1977), 115; O'Neill to Seldes, undated but early 1940s, O'Neill Papers, BLYU. See GS, "Long Day's Journey into Night," SRL 39 (Feb. 25, 1956): 15–16.

73. GS to Henry McBride, Feb. 16 and March 2, 1942, McBride Papers, series I, box 11, BLYU; Earl Wilson, "Television Gets a Big Fan Mail," New York *Post*, July 12, 1941, clipping in Seldes folder, NYPL-BR; GS, "Television and the Museums," *Magazine of Art* 37 (May 1944): 178–79.

74. Unidentified news clipping, April 25, 1945, Seldes Papers, box 1, UPSC.

75. The first two quotations are from WID-10 and WID-11, March 9, 1968, AIMT, and the third from SEP, undated, AIMT, MSP.

76. GS, *Writing for Television* (Garden City, N.Y., 1952), esp. 38–39. During Seldes' deanship at the Annenberg School, 1959–63, practical training in all aspects of television production was at the core of the curriculum.

77. "Jazz Series Debut," NYT, April 7, 1958, p. 45; Coppola, "Subject Is Jazz," New York *Post*, May 28, 1958, p. 54.

78. On December 1, 1948, Jack Gould, radio and television critic for the *New York Times*, sent an extraordinary letter to Mary Margaret McBride. He reassured her that he and the *Times* were not hostile to her, but that the criteria that made for a felicitous radio program did not translate into a successful television production (McBride Papers, box 1, MDLC).

79. GS, "A Time for Anger?," SRL 35 (Nov. 8, 1952): 34; GS, "Trash Is Where You Find It," SRL 36 (July 25, 1953): 29–30. In 1952 Seldes wrote an effusive review of John

Crosby's collected radio and television journalism, titled *Out of the Blue*, in SRL 35 (Nov. 29, 1952): 36.

80. GS, "Taste, Mediocrity, and Everyman," SRL 40 (May 11, 1957): 46; Bruce E. Gronbeck, "The Academic Practice of Television Criticism," *Quarterly Journal of Speech* 74 (Aug. 1988): 334–47.

81. GS, "Radio, TV and the Common Man," SRL 36 (Aug. 29, 1953): 11–12, 39–41, quotation at 41. On October 9, 1941, Edward L. Bernays wrote a letter to Frederick Lewis Allen, who had just become editor-in-chief of *Harper's*, emphasizing that magazine editors tended to underestimate "the tremendous power they have in molding public opinion." (Allen Papers, box 2, MDLC.)

82. John Horn, "TV in Perpetual Crisis," *Variety*, July 15, 1953, p. 24; GS, "Whither TV?," *Printer's Ink* no. 235 (April 20, 1951): 33–35.

83. Horn, "TV in Perpetual Crisis"; Seldes emphatically reaffirmed this point in "Some Impressions of Television," *Journal of Social Issues* 18, no. 2 (1962): 30–31.

84. GS, "A Clinical Analysis of TV," NYT *Magazine*, Nov. 28, 1954, pp. 13, 55–56, 59–60; GS, "Rich You Will Get," SRL 38 (Dec. 31, 1955): 27; GS, "The Lucy Show," 1b-1 and 2, AIMT, MSP; GS, "Domestic Life in the Forty-ninth State," SRL 36 (Aug. 22, 1953): 28–29.

85. GS, "New Bubbles for Soap Opera," NYT *Magazine*, Sept. 12, 1954, pp. 25, 38, 42, 44.

86. Ibid., esp. 44. (Some of this material on soap operas appeared once again in GS, *The Public Arts* (New York, 1956), 106–7.) GS, "Public Entertainment and the Subversion of Ethical Standards," AAAPSS no. 363 (Jan. 1966): 93. In 1962 Seldes reported that about five years earlier Paul Lazarsfeld said the following to him: "'You have moved from esthetics to sociology'—a move of which I was hardly conscious." GS, "Some Impressions of Television," 29.

87. McLuhan, *The Mechanical Bride: Folklore of Industrial Man* (New York, 1951), 157. Hugh Dickinson considered Seldes the "most discerning critic" of soap operas. See "Soap Opera Down the Drain," *America* 94 (Oct. 29, 1955): 127–30.

88. GS, "We Might Still Create an Art of Television," *TV Guide*, April 7, 1962, pp. 11, 13–14. For a scholarly monograph with historical perspective and a more positive view of the film industry's impact on television, see Christopher Anderson, *Hollywood TV: The Studio System in the Fifties* (Austin, Tex., 1994).

89. GS, "Television: The Golden Hope," *Atlantic* 183 (March 1949): 34–37, an essay filled with data indicative of early trends.

90. GS, "The Lively Arts," *Park East* (Feb. 1951): 36, 51. Seldes had warned against precisely this tendency while television was in its infancy and he worked for CBS. See GS, "The Nature of Television Programs," AAAPSS no. 213 (Jan. 1941): 142.

91. GS, "The Lively Arts," *Park East* (May 1951): 26, 35; GS, "Radio, TV and the Common Man," SRL 36 (Aug. 29, 1953): 39–41.

92. "The Lexicon of a New Folklore," SRL 37 (Jan. 2, 1954): 10; *The Dartmouth*, March 2, 1955, p. 1, clipping in MSP; GS, "Culture, Blessed Word," SRL 40 (April 6, 1957): 28.

93. GS, "Such Popularity," SRL 40 (Feb. 16, 1957): 27; Gifford Phillips et al., *The Arts in a Democratic Society* (Santa Barbara, 1966), 7.

94. GS, "Politics—Televised and Sponsored," SRL 35 (March 15, 1952): 30–31; GS, "TV and the Voter," SRL 35 (Dec. 6, 1952): 17–19, 57–59; GS, "The More the Media," SRL 37 (Nov. 27, 1954): 29–30; GS, "Question Reversed," SRL 39 (Aug. 18, 1956): 30.

95. GS, "Benton Bill Puts TV on Defensive—*Again*," *Printer's Ink* no. 237 (Dec. 7, 1951): 45.

96. GS, *Great Audience*, 157–59. See also Robert W. McChesney, "Conflict, Not Consensus: The Debate Over Broadcast Communication Policy, 1930–35," in William S. Solomon and Robert W. McChesney, eds., *Ruthless Criticism: New Perspectives in U.S. Communication History* (Minneapolis, 1993), 222–58.

97. GS, "Television and the Hearings—An Interim Report," typescript of a radio broadcast made in 1952 or 1953, MSP; GS, "Bad Manners and Good Rules," SRL 40 (March 16, 1957): 28; GS, "America and the Face of N. Khrushchev," SRL 40 (June 29, 1957): 20; GS, "Invitation to Serfdom," SRL 43 (Oct. 22, 1960): 20.

98. "Seldes Sez He's Radio's Best Friend, Only It Doesn't Build New Audiences," *Variety*, Jan. 18, 1950; GS, *Great Audience*, 214, 229–31. Lyman Bryson, a CBS Counselor on Public Affairs and a friend of Seldes, had articulated a similar position in 1947. See Bryson, "A Highbrow Experiment," NYT, Nov. 9, 1947, sec. 2, p. 9.

99. GS, *Great Audience*, 229–32; GS, "For Pluralistic TV," SRL 36 (Sept. 19, 1953): 31–32. He made the same point in "Nickelodeon to Television," *Maclean's Magazine*, Jan. 1, 1950, p. 44.

Chapter 8. In Defense of Americanism

1. GS to AMS, Jr., Oct. 4, 1959, Schlesinger Papers, JFKL.

2. GS, *Your Money and Your Life: A Manual for "The Middle Classes"* (New York, 1938), 10, 14, 289, 321.

3. Ibid., 337–39, 344. Although Edmund Wilson was mildly attracted to socialism early in the 1930s, Daniel Aaron has written of Wilson that "the personal affairs of his family and friends, as well as his own, preoccupied him more than unemployment and the New Deal." Aaron, "Edmund Wilson's Political Decade," in Ralph F. Bogardus and Fred Hobson, eds., *Literature at the Barricades: The American Writer in the 1930s* (University, Ala., 1982), 186. By contrast, Mary McCarthy, Wilson's third wife, was intensely politicized during the mid- and later 1930s. See Carol Brightman, *Writing Dangerously: Mary McCarthy and Her World* (San Diego, 1992), chs. 8–10.

4. Brooks to Mumford, Aug. 4, 1935, in Robert E. Spiller, ed., *The Van Wyck Brooks-Lewis Mumford Letters: The Record of a Literary Friendship, 1921–1963* (New York, 1970), 115; GS, "The America of the Intellectuals," SEP 207 (March 9, 1935): 99.

5. Seldes offered special praise for Mumford's *Technics and Civilization* in GS, "True to Type," NYEJ, April 28, 1934, p. 15. For highly charged statements of nationalism in art and culture at that time, see J. Benjamin Townsend, ed., *Charles Burchfield's Journals: The Poetry of Place* (Albany, 1993), 466, 634; Alfred Kazin, *Starting Out in the Thirties* (Boston, 1965), 134, 136.

6. GS, "True to Type," NYEJ, Nov. 2, 1933, p. 17; ibid., Nov. 3, 1933, p. 27; ibid., Nov. 4, 1933, p. 11; ibid., Nov. 10, 1933, p. 27; GS, *Your Money and Your Life*, 233–34, 329–32, 344.

7. GS to Dos Passos, Oct. 7, 1941, quoted in Townsend Ludington, *John Dos Passos: A Twentieth Century Odyssey* (New York, 1980), 407; GS, *Proclaim Liberty!* (New York, 1942), 97; GS, "The State of the World," *Esquire* 23 (March 1945): 66; GS, "The Songs America Sings," *Esquire* 24 (July 1945): 57. See also GS, "The Great American Face," *Esquire* 20 (July 1943): 80.

8. GS, *Mainland* (New York, 1936), 195–96, 198, 242.

9. Ibid., 242. The same volume also contains echoes of Seldes' belief that the movies were symbolic of a "pluralistic universe" (97) and proclaimed that Franklin Delano

Roosevelt was surely a pluralist in politics (402). See GS, "First Aid to Producers," *Esquire* 10 (Sept. 1938): 89, 134.

10. GS, "True to Type," NYEJ, March 12, 1932, p. 7; ibid., Sept. 8, 1933, p. 21; GSS-7/8 (June 10, 1967), AIMT, MSP. In 1955, when Congress held hearings on the effect of television and comic books on teenagers, especially in connection with casual presentations of violence, Seldes took a particularly strong interest.

11. GS, "An Open Letter to Roxy [S. L. Rothafel]," *Modern Music* 10 (Nov. 1933): 7. Throughout the 1920s and '30s it was the declared aim of George Horace Lorimer of the *Saturday Evening Post* "to work for national unity under our common banner of Americanism." See Jan Cohn, *Creating America: George Horace Lorimer and the Saturday Evening Post* (Pittsburgh, 1989), 217.

12. GS, "America of the Intellectuals," 10, 94, 96; GS, "To Hell, in a Word, with Art," *Esquire* 5 (Jan. 1936): 94; GS, "The People and the Arts," *Scribner's* 101 (March 1937): 70. Seldes had been a bit more judicious in 1933 when he devoted a newspaper column to the subject of patriotism and self-criticism in the American theatre. Satirical musicals by Irving Berlin and Moss Hart were acceptable because they made fun of individuals rather than U.S. culture as a whole. As for Eugene O'Neill, "he didn't make the mistake of thinking that Americans were unique in their bestial stupidities." GS, "True to Type," NYEJ, Oct. 6, 1933, p. 27.

13. PR 3 (April 1936): 3.

14. Ibid., 3–4.

15. Ibid., 7–8. Seldes' views were very close to Herrick's. Seldes regarded most radicals in the United States (but not in the Soviet Union) as disagreeable complainers. See "True to Type," NYEJ, Feb. 2, 1934, p. 21, and May 8, 1934, p. 19.

16. PR 3 (April 1936): 8–9.

17. Ibid., 13–14. Norman Corwin, the pioneer in poetic documentaries for the radio, also felt a need to explain what he meant by liberalism. See R. LeRoy Bannerman, *Norman Corwin and Radio: The Golden Years* (University, Ala., 1986), 219–20.

18. "The Situation in American Writing: Seven Questions," PR 6 (Summer 1939): 25–51, and (Fall 1939): 103–23.

19. Genevieve Moreau, *The Restless Journey of James Agee* (New York, 1977), 172–73; Laurence Bergreen, *James Agee: A Life* (New York, 1984), 229–30. Agee simply took the critique that PR rejected and inserted it into *Let Us Now Praise Famous Men* (Boston, 1941), 349–57.

20. GS, "The Alien Menace of Sex," *Esquire* 6 (July 1936): 83; GS, "The Beginnings of Popularity," in C. S. Marsh, ed., *Educational Broadcasting 1936* (Chicago, 1937), 341, 343; GS, *Your Money and Your Life*, 322.

21. GS, *Mainland*, 6, 8, 75, 104, 420, quotation at 104.

22. Ibid., 157–58, 253–54, 262. In many respects *Mainland* directly anticipated *Your Money and Your Life* (1938).

23. GS, *Mainland*, 7, 121–23, 140–41, 174–76, 403, 415.

24. Ibid., 240, 249, 323–24. In *Proclaim Liberty!* (1942) Seldes declared that acceptance of change had been fundamental in American history and that Americans had made a tradition of change (p. 25).

25. *Mainland*, 142, 274, 323, 347.

26. GS, "True to Type," NYEJ, Nov. 29, 1933, p. 15; GS, "America of the Intellectuals," 98–99; GS, *Mainland*, 123, 150, 325–54, 361.

27. GS, "True to Type," NYEJ, May 21, 1934, p. 9, "the concentration of [economic] power" is unhealthy and unfair; GS, *Mainland*, 276, 298–99, 313, 442; GS, *Your Money and Your Life*, 261.

28. GS, *Mainland*, 7, 273–74, 276–77.

29. Ibid., 35, 136, 323, 353–54, 385, 419, 425. He reiterated these views in capsule form when he wrote his twenty-fifth anniversary class report for Harvard College in 1939; and strong echoes also occur in *The Great Audience* (New York, 1950), 6, 87, 104. See *Harvard College of 1914: Twenty-fifth Anniversary Report* (Cambridge, Mass., 1939), 701–3.

30. Francis Brown in NYT *Book Review*, Oct. 4, 1936, p. 1; DeVoto, "Civilization in the U.S.A.," SRL 14 (Oct. 3, 1936): 7; Beard to Seldes, Oct. 10, [1936], MSP. DeVoto declared that "it is courageous and exhilarating, it is hard and firm, it is in great part unassailable."

31. James Rorty, *Nation* 143 (Oct. 10, 1936): 423; E. S. Bates, *Books*, Nov. 8, 1936, p. 17.

32. Galantière, "Radical—American Style," *North American Review* 242 (Winter 1936–37): 241–57; "Tabby," "Literary Illusions about the I.W.W.," *One Big Union Monthly* (Feb. 1937): 33–34.

33. White, "The Challenge to the Middle Class," *Atlantic* 160 (Aug. 1937): 200.

34. GS, "Critique and Accompaniment," SRL 37 (March 20, 1954): 15; Strout, *The American Image of the Old World* (New York, 1963), 197, 201; GS to Strout, Nov. 20, 1963, MSP; TE-G-1 (Nov. 29, 1963), AIMT, MSP.

35. GS to White, July 22, Dec. 3 and 21, 1937, White Papers, series C, box 270, MDLC.

36. GS to White, Jan. 26, 1938, ibid., box 290; Joan Shelley Rubin, *The Making of Middlebrow Culture* (Chapel Hill, 1992), 143; New York *Daily Mirror*, Feb. 27, 1938, clipping in MSP.

37. White, "Your Money and Your Life," *Atlantic* 161 (June 1938): "The Bookshelf" section, unpaginated.

38. David C. Coyle, "A Middle Way for America," SRL 17 (Jan. 15, 1938): 5; William MacDonald, NYT *Book Review*, Jan. 16, 1938, p. 17; R. M. B., *Christian Science Monitor*, Jan. 25, 1938, p. 20.

39. NR, Feb. 2, 1938, p. 376; E. S. Bates in *Books*, March 20, 1938, p. 11; Friedrich Baerwald in *Commonweal*, April 29, 1938, p. 22; Paul Lewinson, *Social Education* 2 (Sept. 1938): 443.

40. GS, *Your Money and Your Life*, 249.

41. Ibid., 230–32, 292, 295–96, 310–11.

42. Ibid., chs. 9–10, pp. 238, 259; GS, *Mainland*, v. V. I. Lenine in *Mainland* became Nikolai Lenin in *Your Money!*.

43. SRL 40 (Nov. 30, 1957): 14–15.

44. SRL 17 (Jan. 15, 1938): 19.

45. GS, "The Kat Comes of Age," *Esquire* 4 (Sept. 1935): 103; GS, "Could Those Boys Write?," *Esquire* 12 (Nov. 1939): 75, 147, 148; GS, "After All These Years," *Esquire* 13 (Jan. 1940): 70, 165.

46. GS, "True to Type," NYEJ, Aug. 15, 1933, p. 17; ibid., Nov. 22, 1933, p. 19; ibid., Dec. 6, 1933, p. 23. For his neglect of political relationships during the 1920s, see Chapter Four, pp. 144–45 above.

47. GS, "The People and the Arts," *Scribner's* 101 (Feb. 1937): 80.

48. GS, "Don't Tread on Me!," *Esquire* 9 (Feb. 1938): 75, 126. Seldes would have strongly approved of an exhibition titled "Assault on the Arts: Culture and Politics in Nazi Germany," held at the New York Public Library, Feb. 27 to May 28, 1993.

49. GS, "Are People Critics?," *Esquire* 9 (April 1938): 70, 208; GS, "Restatement About Liberty," *Esquire* 17 (April 1942): 63, 130.

50. GS, "Have Americans Lost Their Nerve?," *Scribner's* 92 (Sept. 1932): 149–50; GS, *Mainland*, 278, 415.

51. GS, *Mainland*, 279, 283–84. Here, and even more in *Proclaim Liberty!* (New York, 1942), 136–37, Seldes anticipated the central argument of George Wilson Pierson, *The Moving American* (New York, 1973).

52. GS to Cushing Strout, Nov. 20, 1963, MSP; GS, "True to Type," NYEJ, Dec. 26, 1933, p. 17.

53. GS, "No Soul in the Photograph," *Esquire* 10 (Dec. 1938): 121, 242. It could easily be argued that Evans ought to be regarded as an important twentieth-century cultural critic. See James Guimond, *American Photography and the American Dream* (Chapel Hill, 1991), 130–31.

54. GS, "The Cost of a Song," *Esquire* 12 (Aug. 1939): 65, 102; GS, "Songs for Times of Jeopardy," *Esquire* 16 (July 1941): 65, 174.

55. GS, "The Songs America Sings," *Esquire* 24 (July 1945): 57.

56. GS, *Proclaim Liberty!*, 38, 54, 70–71, 122, 132, 155, 192; and for echoes see GS, "Apple Trees and Jerks on Jeeps," *Esquire* 18 (Oct. 1942): 60, 95.

57. GS, *Proclaim Liberty!*, 50, 150, 196. Back in 1934 Seldes insisted that too little attention had been paid to the highly instructive history of failure in the United States. "True to Type," NYEJ, March 10, 1934, p. 10.

58. GS, *Proclaim Liberty!*, 63, 120. Three years later Seldes repeated his belief that there could be "good" propaganda and that government can sponsor popular culture with positive effects. See GS, "MacLeish: Minister of Culture," *Esquire* 23 (June 1945): 103. Seldes was hardly alone or unusual in holding these views. See Clayton R. Koppes, *Hollywood Goes to War: How Politics, Profits, and Propaganda Shaped World War II Movies* (New York, 1987).

59. *Proclaim Liberty!*, 48, 52–53, 55, 60. Looking back to the 1930s Irving Howe, not even the most radical of dissenters in that decade, remarked that "liberalism seemed tired, pusillanimous, given to small repairs where an entire new structure was needed." Howe, "The Thirties in Retrospect," in Bogardus and Hobson, eds., *Literature at the Barricades*, 15.

60. White in *Books*, June 14, 1942, p. 5; Reston in SRL 25 (July 4, 1942): 8; Kingsley in NR 107 (Aug. 17, 1942): 204; *Library Journal* 67 (May 15, 1942): 476; *New Yorker* 18 (June 6, 1942): 64; R. H. M. in *Christian Science Monitor*, July 16, 1942, p. 20.

61. Editorial, "The Inexhaustible Exhubilance of Gilbert Seldes," *Esquire* 20 (Aug. 1943): 6.

62. GS, "That Was Woollcott Speaking," *Esquire* 8 (July 1937): 79, 122; Samuel Hopkins Adams, *Alexander Woollcott: His Life and His World* (New York, 1945), 257, 323.

63. GS, "Cartoonists' Ups and Downs," *Esquire* 16 (Dec. 1941): 143, 281.

64. GS, "Anything for a Laugh," *Esquire* 17 (Jan. 1942): 98, 194.

65. GS, "There's Gold in Them Camps," *Esquire* 17 (May 1942): 64, 171. There is an extraordinary memorandum from Seldes to two colleagues at CBS, Coulter and Taylor, Dec. 17, 1942, that pleads for more effective use of radio for purposes of wartime propaganda (MSP). Norman Corwin certainly concurred in this judgment. See his "Radio and Morale," SRL 25 (July 4, 1942): 6.

66. GS, "No More Parades?," *Esquire* 18 (July 1942): 62, 179; GS, "The Case for the Commercial," *Esquire* 24 (Oct. 1945): 77, 78, 159. Gallico's critique had appeared in *Esquire* in May.

67. GS, "True to Type," NYEJ, Feb. 27, 1933, p. 17; ibid., Sept. 25, 1933, p. 17; GS, "The Gibson Girl for Me," *Esquire* 19 (Feb. 1943): 49, 149.

68. GS, "What Cooks with Slang," *Esquire* 17 (Feb. 1942): 68, 113; GS, "The Fall of the Flattering Word," *Esquire* 19 (March 1943): 68, 118.

69. Copies of these programs in MSP.

70. Darwin Payne, *The Man of Only Yesterday: Frederick Lewis Allen* (New York, 1975), 169–71; Capra to Seldes, March 24, 1944, MSP. Seldes worked on scripts for Capra's unit during World War II, along with John Huston, William Saroyan, Lillian Hellman, John Cheever, Janet Flanner, Irwin Shaw, William L. Shirer, and John Gunther.

71. MacLeish to GS, April 21, 1942, MacLeish Papers, box 20, MDLC; Alice Hall and Gilbert Seldes to Hon. Fred E. Busbey, Nov. 20, 1944, MSP.

72. GS, "MacLeish: Minister of Culture," *Esquire* 23 (June 1945): 103.

73. GS, "Eight 21-Gun Salutes," *Esquire* 19 (April 1943): 73, 151.

74. GS, "The Most Popular Man in the World," *Esquire* 24 (Aug. 1945): 61.

75. GS, *Proclaim Liberty!*, 166.

76. GS, "Life on the Tinsel Standard," SRL 33 (Oct. 28, 1950): 9–19; Pat Weaver, *The Best Seat in the House: The Golden Years of Radio and Television* (New York, 1994), 167–68, 177–78, 238–44; Sally Bedell Smith, *In All His Glory: The Life of William S. Paley* (New York, 1990); GS, "Notes and Queries," *Esquire* 25 (March 1946): 78.

77. GS, "New York Chronicle," *Criterion* 4 (Jan. 1926): 175; GS expressed his disagreements politely in "Mr. Nathan and the Movies," NR 52 (Nov. 9, 1927): 313–14, and more aggressively in "Open Letter to George Jean Nathan," *Esquire* 18 (Aug. 1942): 60, 112. Then see Nathan, "First Nights & Passing Judgments," *Esquire* 24 (Sept. 1945): 84, 136.

78. GS, "An ABC of GJN," *Esquire* 24 (Nov. 1945): 77–78.

79. Mumford to Brooks, Dec. 22, 1944, in Spiller, ed., *The Brooks-Mumford Letters*, 267.

80. Brooks to Mumford, Jan. 12, 1945, ibid., 269. On the relationship between nationalism and cultural criticism, see also ibid., 218–20.

81. Matthiessen, *The Responsibilities of the Critic: Essays and Reviews*, John Rackliffe, ed. (New York, 1952), 7; Frederick C. Stern, *F. O. Matthiessen: Christian Socialist as Critic* (Chapel Hill, 1981), 238.

82. GS, "True to Type," NYEJ, Oct. 30, 1933, p. 17.

83. GS, *The 7 Lively Arts*, 2nd ed. (New York, 1957), 168.

84. GS, "True to Type," NYEJ, July 20, 1932, p. 13; ibid., Sept. 29, 1933, p. 17.

85. GS, "Over the Tops," SEP 208 (April 25, 1936): 20–21, 83–85, 88, where he commented that "we know very little about the process of creating popularity"; and GS, "Perspective on Popularity," *Esquire* 22 (Dec. 1944): 174, 176.

86. GS, "True to Type," NYEJ, Jan. 31, 1934, p. 15.

Chapter 9. Coming to Terms with Mass Culture

1. GS, "True to Type," NYEJ, Feb. 3, 1932, p. 17. In a 1934 newspaper column Seldes speculated about American habits and taste twenty years hence. He wondered what "ideas, habits, customs as well as what works of art would persist through the great reconstruction of society which must go on during the next generation." GS, "True to Type," NYEJ, Feb. 1, 1934, p. 17.

2. GS, *The Public Arts* (New York, 1956), 293–94.

3. Ibid., 142; GS, "We Might Still Create an Art of Television," *TV Guide*, April 7, 1962, pp. 11, 13–14.

4. Matthiessen, *The Responsibilities of the Critic: Essays and Reviews*, John Rackliffe, ed. (New York, 1952), 6–7.

5. Ibid., 8–9.

6. Ibid., 10.

7. He gave a five-week summer course of lectures on "Television—A Critique" for the American Theatre Wing; continued his radio-essay series on "The Lively Arts"; and worked on a new book that would update *The 7 Lively Arts* to include the television era. That fall he launched his fifteen-week courses at the New School for Social Research, one a series of lectures on television and the other a workshop on writing.

8. GS, "Composer with a Light Touch," *Esquire* 14 (Oct. 1940): 85, 156; GS, "This Can't Be Corn," *Esquire* 16 (Oct. 1941): 51, 160; GS, "The Vagaries of Jimmy Savo," *Esquire* 22 (Nov. 1944): 93.

9. GS, "Lament for Music Makers," *Esquire* 20 (Dec. 1943): 173–74; GS, "Sing Us a New Song," *Esquire* 21 (Jan. 1944): 88; GS, "My Neck Out on Swing," *Esquire* 22 (July 1944): 69, 156; GS, "So You've Written a Song," *Esquire* 22 (Aug. 1944): 89, 141.

10. GS, "Preliminary Report on Superman," *Esquire* 18 (Nov. 1942): 63; GS, "The Talking Machine-Sensational!," *Esquire* 20 (Nov. 1943): 72; GS, "The Eternal Western," *Esquire* 25 (Feb. 1946): 101.

11. GS, "Fun for One and All," *Esquire* 12 (Oct. 1939): 65, 146.

12. GS, "Big Names Take Over," *Esquire* 16 (Sept. 1941): 65, 156, 157.

13. GS, "Nice Clean Post-Atomic Fun," *Esquire* 25 (Jan. 1946): 107–8.

14. Ibid., 108; GS, "Evolution of the Night Club," *Esquire* 22 (Sept 1944): 66; GS, "Lively Arts," *Park East* (Jan. 1951): 35.

15. GS, "Miss West and Mr. Proust," *Esquire* 23 (April 1945): 75.

16. GS, "Great Big Beautiful Thoughts," *Esquire* 21 (May 1944): 92, 156.

17. Allen to Davis, Aug. 12, 1949, Davis Papers, box 2, MDLC. By 1942, however, Allen felt considerable anxiety that *Harper's* had become too commercial and out of touch with the cutting edge in ideas. Darwin Payne, *The Man of Only Yesterday: Frederick Lewis Allen* (New York, 1975), 189.

18. Lynes, *Confessions of a Dilettante* (New York, 1966), 119–38, an essay much expanded in Lynes, *The Tastemakers* (New York, 1954); Barrett's letter in *Harper's* 198 (April 1949): 14.

19. McLuhan, *The Mechanical Bride* (New York, 1951), 58–59.

20. Lynes' obituary, NYT, Sept. 16, 1991, p. B12; McLuhan, *Mechanical Bride*, 59; GS, "Lexicon of a New Folklore," SRL 37 (Jan. 2, 1954): 10.

21. GS, *The Great Audience* (New York, 1950), 258.

22. Ibid., 4, 6, 260; GS, *The Public Arts* (New York, 1956), 175; Pat Weaver, *The Best Seat in the House: The Golden Years of Radio and Television* (New York, 1994), 179–82, 189–91. For Seldes' shifting views on the effects of advertising, see Chapter Seven, pp. 250–51 above.

23. GS, *Great Audience*, 6, 268–69, 287–89, 293–94.

24. Ibid., 269.

25. Ibid., 9–88, passim.

26. SRL 33 (Dec. 16, 1950): 11–12, 26; *Library Journal* 75 (Nov. 15, 1950): 2014; San Francisco *Chronicle*, Nov. 17, 1950, p. 16. See also N.Y. *Herald Tribune* Book Review, Nov. 19, 1950, p. 8; *Christian Science Monitor*, magazine section, Dec. 9, 1950, p. 9; NYT, Dec. 31, 1950, p. 9; *Theatre Arts* 34 (Dec. 1950): 2, 4–5.

27. Wilson, "Gilbert Seldes and the Popular Arts," *New Yorker* 26 (Oct. 28, 1950): 107.

28. Ibid., 110, 112.

29. Edman to GS, Feb. 19, 1951, Edman Papers, CURBML; GS to AMS, Jr., Feb. 5,

1951, Schlesinger Papers, JFKL. Schlesinger had reviewed the book in *The Reporter* 4, (Feb. 6, 1951): 36–38.

30. Macdonald, "A Theory of Popular Culture," *Politics* 1 (Feb. 1944): 20–23; GS, *Great Audience*, 261–62.

31. GS, *Great Audience*, 263–64. Michael Wreszin believes that in 1953 Macdonald decided to be a cultural critic with an adversarial stance, rather than remain a radical writer primarily concerned with politics. See *A Rebel in Defense of Tradition: The Life and Politics of Dwight Macdonald* (New York, 1994), 295, 304, 306, 390–91.

32. Macdonald, "A Theory of Mass Culture," *Diogenes* no. 3 (Summer 1953): 1–17, quotation at 16.

33. GS, *Public Arts*, 104, 295; Macdonald, *Against the American Grain: Essays on the Effects of Mass Culture* (New York, 1962), 3–75.

34. GS to Macdonald, Sept. 4, 1951, Macdonald Papers, box 45, SLYU; Macdonald to GS, Oct. 3, 1951, ibid.

35. GS, "True to Type," NYEJ, March 2, 1932, p. 19. See also GS, *Proclaim Liberty!* (New York, 1942), 157, where he seems to connect the emergence of mass culture with radio's coming of age in the later 1930s.

36. GS, "How Dense Is the Mass?," *Atlantic* 182 (Nov. 1948): 25, 27. William Phillips was unsympathetic to the notion of cultural pluralism. See Neil Jumonville, *Critical Crossings: The New York Intellectuals in Postwar America* (Berkeley, 1991), 170–71.

37. See Theodor Adorno, "Cultural Criticism and Society," in Peter Davison et al., eds., *Literary Taste, Culture and Mass Communication*, vol. 1, *Culture and Mass Culture* (Cambridge, 1978), 107–22; Adorno, *Prisms* (London, 1967); GS, "This Can't Be Corn," 51, 160, in which Seldes quotes at length from Adorno, *Memorandum: Music in Radio* (Princeton Radio Research Project, 1938).

38. Robert K. Merton, Marjorie Fiske, and Alberta Curtis, *Mass Persuasion* (New York, 1946); Paul Lazarsfeld and Robert K. Merton, "Mass Communication, Popular Taste, and Organized Social Action," in Lyman Bryson, ed., *The Communication of Ideas: A Series of Addresses* (New York, 1948), 95–118; Leon Bramson, *The Political Context of Sociology* (Princeton, 1961), 96.

39. Milton Klonsky, "Along the Midway of Mass Culture," *The New Partisan Review Reader, 1945–53* (New York, 1953), 344–60. Klonsky's belief that "the base forms of popular culture have an autonomous system of values indifferent to the standards of artistic criticism" was quite alien to Seldes (p. 357).

40. William Phillips, "Our Country and Our Culture" (1984), in Phillips, ed., *Partisan Review: The Fiftieth Anniversary Edition* (New York, 1984), 290–91. See also Philip Rahv, *Essays on Literature and Politics, 1932–1972*, Arabel J. Porter and Andrew J. Drosin, eds. (Boston, 1978), 333–34.

41. Frank and Kronenberger in PR 19 (July 1952): 432–33, 442.

42. Barrett in ibid., 422–23; Schlesinger in ibid. (Sept. 1952), 572. Neil Jumonville is especially perceptive on the issue of mass culture in a society that professed democratic values. He also argues quite plausibly that in their published memoirs many of these critics minimized the importance of the debate over mass culture because the protests of the 1960s displaced that debate and received disproportionate space. See *Critical Crossings: The New York Intellectuals in Postwar America* (Berkeley, 1991), 232–34.

43. GS to Richard C. Boys, May 3, 1952, Boys Papers, UML.

44. GS, *Public Arts*, 268, 295.

45. GS, *The 7 Lively Arts*, 2nd ed. (New York, 1957), 10.

46. Ibid., 10–11.

47. Ibid., 242; Seldes' comments appear in a panel discussion in Norman Jacobs, ed., *Culture for the Millions: Mass Media in Modern Society* (Boston, 1964), 170–71.

48. Ibid., 179–80. For a position comparable to Jarrell's taken by a prominent writer who had engaged Seldes in dialogue during the 1930s, see Allen Tate, "The Man of Letters in the Modern World" (1952), in Tate, *Essays of Four Decades* (Chicago, 1968): ". . . all languages are being debased by the techniques of mass control" (p. 3).

49. Some of the other participants were Leo Lowenthal, Edward Shils, and Oscar Handlin. The latter two told me in 1993 that they had little memory of Seldes at the conference. *Sic transit gloria* Seldes!

50. Trilling in "Our Country and Our Culture," PR 19 (May 1952): 322; Lerner in ibid. (Sept. 1952): 584. For a brief overview of the great debate concerning mass culture during the 1950s, see Jumonville, *Critical Crossings*, chap. 4, esp. pp. 151–58, 171–75, 184–85.

51. Hazard, "A General Theory," in Jacobs, ed., *Culture for the Millions*, 157.

52. Reuel Denney, *The Astonished Muse* (Chicago, 1957). Denis Brogan also failed to differentiate between popular and mass culture in "The Problem of High Culture and Mass Culture," *Diogenes* no. 5 (Winter 1954): 1–15, a reply to Dwight Macdonald.

53. Denney, "The Discovery of the Popular Culture," in Robert E. Spiller and Eric Larrabee, eds., *American Perspectives: The National Self-Image in the Twentieth Century* (Cambridge, Mass., 1961), 154–77.

54. Jeffrey Hyson, "Habits of the Historians: The Tocqueville Revival in American Historiography" (research paper, Department of History, Cornell University, 1993), 10; Abraham S. Eisenstadt, ed., *Reconsidering Tocqueville's Democracy in America* (New Brunswick, N.J., 1988).

55. GS, *Public Arts*, 205–6.

56. Ibid., 209, 186, 192.

57. Ibid., 176–77 and chs. 14–20 generally.

58. Ibid., v–viii, 287.

59. Ibid., 1, 66, 275.

60. Ibid., 284–87.

61. San Francisco *Chronicle*, June 27, 1956, p. 27; Chicago Sunday *Tribune*, July 8, 1956, p. 4; Siepmann in NYT *Book Review*, July 1, 1956, p. 3; Rosten in N.Y. *Herald Tribune*, July 15, 1956, p. 5; *Christian Science Monitor*, July 5, 1956, p. 13; *Atlantic* 198 (Aug. 1956): 83–84.

62. Alpert, SRL 39 (July 21, 1956): 24.

63. NYT *Book Review*, July 8, 1956, p. 19.

64. Bernard Rosenberg and David Manning White, eds., *Mass Culture: The Popular Arts in America* (New York, 1957), esp. 46–97. See also Leo Lowenthal, *Literature, Popular Culture, and Society* (Palo Alto, 1961), ch. 1, "Popular Culture in Perspective," and ch. 4, "The Triumph of Mass Idols."

65. Harold Rosenberg, "Pop Culture: Kitsch Criticism," in Rosenberg, *The Tradition of the New* (New York, 1965), 260–63; this review first appeared in *Dissent* 5 (Winter 1958): 14–19. Firing away at Dwight Macdonald, Rosenberg repeatedly misspelled his name: "MacDonald's taste for kitsch is largely negative, but it is genuine, at least genuine enough to yield him the time to become familiar with it. . . . What is true about MacDonald is true about most of the writers on mass culture. Popular art is their meat" (pp. 262–63).

66. GS, "Taste, Mediocrity, and Everyman," SRL 40 (May 11, 1957): 46.

67. David Potter to Norman Holmes Pearson [1965], Potter Papers, box 1, SUL. The

work that Potter referred to, titled "The Shaping of American Culture" was written by a Yale Ph.D. in American Studies (1953) but never published.

68. See Jack Behar, "On Rod Serling, James Agee, and Popular Culture," in Patrick Hazard, ed., *TV as Art: Some Essays in Criticism* (Champaign, Ill., 1966), 51–52; Fiedler's Introduction to George Lippard, *The Monks of Monk Hall* (New York, 1970); and Michael Denning, "The End of Mass Culture," *International Labor and Working-Class History* no. 37 (Spring 1990): 4–18.

69. GS, *Public Arts*, 211.

70. Ibid., 215. Seldes admired Elmer Davis immensely as a defender of the public interest. See GS' review of Davis' book, *But We Were Born Free*, in SRL 37 (Feb. 13, 1954): 13–14. Davis, like Seldes, was deeply concerned about the intellectual's relation to his society.

71. GS, "What to Do for Money," *Esquire* 10 (Oct. 1938): 76, 124–25; GS letter to NR 109 (Dec. 13, 1943): 854; NYT, Sept. 14, 1943, p. 25, the clippings in Seldes Papers, box 1, UPSC.

72. GS, *Writing for Television* (Garden City, N.Y., 1952), 199; Murrow to GS, March 28, 1952, Murrow Papers, microfilm reel 16, MDLC.

73. GS, "The News on Television," NR 130 (Jan. 18, 1954): 7–9.

74. Ibid.

75. Robert Metz, *CBS: Reflections in a Bloodshot Eye* (New York, 1975), 288; GS, "Murrow, McCarthy and the Empty Formula," SRL 37 (April 25, 1954): 26–27.

76. GS, "Murrow, McCarthy and the Empty Formula," 26–27.

77. Ibid., 26–27. For a view quite similar to Seldes', see Oscar and Lilian Handlin, *Liberty and Equality, 1920–1994* (New York, 1994), 184–85. On Labor Day in 1963 NBC presented a three-hour special on civil rights, "The American Revolution of '63." Twice the length of any previous public affairs program, it scrupulously examined both sides of the issue, that is, why southerners felt as they did about immediate integration of all public facilities. See Robert Donovan and Ray Scherer, *Unsilent Revolution: Television News and American Public Life, 1948–1991* (Washington, D.C., 1992), 18.

78. Daniel J. Leab, "See It Now: A Legend Reassessed," in John E. O'Connor, ed., *American History/American Television: Interpreting the Video Past* (New York, 1983), 20–21. In his autobiography George Seldes praised Murrow's broadcast and called it fair. He never mentioned his brother's critique of the program. See Seldes, *Witness to a Century: Encounters with the Noted, the Notorious, and the Three SOBs* (New York, 1987), 372.

79. GS, "TV and the Hearings—An Interim Report," SRL 37 (May 29, 1954): 24; GS, "TV and the Hearings: Unfinished Business," ibid. (July 10, 1954): 27–28.

80. GS, *Public Arts*, 210, 212, 218, 220–24, 226–27. Earlier in the same book (pp. 118–20) Seldes criticized Murrow's "Person to Person" as a lightweight endeavor, citing the impropriety of subjecting a famous person to "spurious chuckles and jocose banalities."

81. Ibid., 232, 237, 270.

82. GS to Murrow, June 7 and July 5, 1957, and Jan. 30, 1958, Murrow Papers, reel 16, MDLC; GS, "Notes from a Wheel-chair," SRL 41 (Feb. 8, 1958): 29.

83. GS to Messrs. Aaron and Zousmer, Feb. 28, 1958, Murrow Papers, reel 16, MDLC.

84. GS, "Mr. Ernst Objects," SRL 41 (March 8, 1958): 44–45. Seldes was not alone in regarding "Person to Person" as a meretricious, shallow program. See A. M. Sperber, *Murrow: His Life and Times* (New York, 1986), 424–26, 518, 575–78.

85. Murrow to GS, Feb. 25 and March 5, 1958, Murrow Papers, reel 16, MDLC; GS to Murrow, Feb. 27 and March 1, 1958, ibid. In October 1958 Murrow publicly denounced commercial television! See Baughman, *Republic of Mass Culture*, 93–94.

86. GS, *The New Mass Media* (1957; Washington, D.C., 1968), 38. As late as 1969 Seldes continued to write letters to critics, editors, and producers pleading that equal time be given to controversial or unpopular views. Having come from a context of philosophical anarchism, perhaps it is no surprise that Seldes ended up a staunch civil libertarian.

87. See Chapter Four, p. 132 above; Chapter Eight, pp. 288, 295 above; and GS, *The Public Arts*, 303.

88. GS, *Great Audience*, 233; GS, *Public Arts*, 231, 303; GS, SLAM (July 4, 1967), AIMT, MSP.

89. GS, "Poets Can Learn from Acrobats," *Esquire* 13 (May 1940): 139; Stuart Hall and Paddy Whannel, *The Popular Arts* (New York, 1965), 84.

90. GS, "Mr. Garner and Thelma Oonk," *Esquire* 14 (Sept. 1940): 79, 161; Boorstin, *The Image: A Guide to Pseudo-Events in America* (New York, 1962).

91. William Attwood, "A New Look at America," *Look* (July 12, 1955): 48–54.

92. Ibid., 48.

93. See James L. Baughman, "Television in the 'Golden Age': An Entrepreneurial Experiment," *The Historian* 47 (Feb. 1985): 175–95. For a revisionist look at the 1950s, however, see William Boddy, *Fifties Television: The Industry and Its Critics* (Champaign, Ill., 1991).

94. Attwood, "A New Look at America," 50.

95. Harold C. Schonberg, "The National 'Culture Explosion' is Phony," SEP 236 (July 13, 1963): 10. See also Wreszin, *The Life and Politics of Dwight Macdonald*, 390, for Macdonald's skepticism that a cultural renaissance was afoot in the later 1950s and early 1960s. For Macdonald's careful articulation of an intermediate position between Attwood and Schonberg, see "Masscult & Midcult," 58–61.

Chapter 10. Commerce, Communications, and Criticism

1. McLuhan, *The Mechanical Bride: Folklore of Industrial Man* (New York, 1951), v.

2. Williams, "Culture Is Ordinary" (1958) in his *Resources of Hope* (London, 1989), 17. During the early 1960s there seems to have been a convergence of interest by a small number of writers on both sides of the Atlantic in the relationship between advertising and mass communication. See James D. Halloran (University of Leicester), *Control or Consent? A Study of the Challenge of Mass Communication* (London, 1963), ch. 3, "Advertising."

3. See Darwin Payne, *The Man of Only Yesterday: Frederick Lewis Allen* (New York, 1975), 27–28.

4. Quoted in Erik Barnouw, *Tube of Plenty: The Evolution of American Television*, 2nd ed. (New York, 1990), 299.

5. Oscar Cargill, *Toward a Pluralistic Criticism* (Carbondale, Ill., 1965), 193.

6. GS to Sara and Gerald Murphy, July 29, 1962, MSP.

7. GS to AMS, Jr., Dec. 9, 1968, Schlesinger Papers, JFKL; GS to Marianne Moore, April 18, 1967, Moore Papers, RGM; GS to Dwight Macdonald, May 15, 1968, Macdonald Papers, box 45, SLYU.

8. See Chapter Seven, pp. 250–51, and Chapter Nine, pp. 323, 329, above. His explicit interest in advertising can be traced back to an essay that appeared in VF (Feb. 1925).

9. GS, "Rabbi ben Advertise," *Esquire* 7 (March 1937): 85, 137. For a representative illustration of the generalized attack on mass culture and consumerism, very different

from Seldes' approach, see Randall Jarrell, *A Sad Heart at the Supermarket: Essays & Fables* (New York, 1962), 64–89.

10. GS, "Industrial Design," SEP 204 (May 28, 1932): 34; GS, "True to Type," NYEJ, March 31, 1932, p. 21. During the 1920s and '30s people (mostly men) moved readily from careers in journalism to advertising and public relations. Many men interested in one found the other unavoidable. See Michael Kirkhorn, "This Curious Existence: Journalistic Identity in the Interwar Period," in Catherine L. Covert and John D. Stevens, eds., *Mass Media Between the Wars: Perceptions of Cultural Tension, 1918–1941* (Syracuse, 1984), 131–32, 136, 138.

11. GS, "True to Type," NYEJ, Aug. 2 and 3, 1933, pp. 18, 18; GS, *Your Money and Your Life: A Manual for "The Middle Classes"* (New York, 1938), 70.

12. Lori A. Strauss, "The Anti-Advertising Bias in 20th-Century Literature," *Journal of American Culture* 16 (Spring 1993): 81–85. In 1953–54 Packard undertook his examination of advertising that resulted in *The Hidden Persuaders* (1957) at a time when advertising became so potent that, he believed, it interfered with his journalistic freedom. His personal experiences intensified his anger against agencies that were shaping mass culture. See Daniel Horowitz, *Vance Packard and American Social Criticism* (Chapel Hill, 1994), 98–99.

13. GS, *The Great Audience* (New York, 1950), 132, 192–201; GS, "Lively Arts," *Park East* (Sept. 1951): 43; GS, "Three—Count'em—Three," *Atlantic* 189 (May 1952): 85–86. Seldes devoted the final chapter of *Writing for Television* (Garden City, 1952) to "The Commercial."

14. GS, "Stop Un-selling Present Customers!" *Printer's Ink*, April 23, 1954, p. 37.

15. Ibid., p. 39.

16. GS, "Change Your Brand To-day," 19-page typescript, Seldes Papers, box 1, UPSC.

17. GS, "A Note on Advertising," NR 43 (July 8, 1925): 180. See Stuart Ewen, "Advertising and the Development of Consumer Society," in Ian Angus and Sut Jhally, eds., *Cultural Politics in Contemporary America* (New York, 1989), 82–95.

18. GS, "What Makes the Customer Tick?," SRL 40 (June 1, 1957): 29–30.

19. GS, "Much Less Noise, Please," *Tide*, April 11, 1958, pp. 23–25.

20. GS, *The New Mass Media: Challenge to a Free Society*, 2nd ed. (1957; Washington, D.C., 1968), 7; GS to Governor Leroy Collins, [1964?], MSP.

21. It could not have been sheer coincidence that in 1959 a sharp dispute erupted among scholarly historians interested in the history of advertising over whether or not a pioneering book written as a Ph.D. dissertation at Yale under David M. Potter leaned too heavily and naively on the advertising industry's "self-portrait." *The Responsibilities of American Advertising: Private Control and Public Influence, 1920–1940* (1958) by Otis Pease was reviewed in the *American Historical Review* 64 (Jan. 1959): 467, by Irvin G. Wyllie of the University of Wisconsin. A sharp exchange of letters between Potter and Wyllie appeared in ibid. (July 1959): 1085–86. See also Pease to Potter, Feb. 15, 1959, Potter Papers, box 3, SUL. Pease had toned down overt criticism of the industry in his original manuscript, on Potter's advice, "to let the material rather than my editorial comment on it carry the burden of the message." It amused Pease somewhat that liberal colleagues expressed disappointment that he had "pulled my punches," and then, "as if to confirm this image of timidity, I have received long and rather complimentary letters from several older advertising men . . . on the 'fairness' I had shown to advertising 'during its adolescence,' as one of them put it."

22. GS, "A Light in the Sky," SR 42 (Jan. 24, 1959): 26–27.

23. Donald L. Clark to GS, Nov. 12, 1954, Seldes Papers, box 2, UPSC; the Columbia

press release in ibid. Columbia seems to have contemplated the creation of an Institute of Communication, a graduate program, though nothing came of it at that time.

24. Seldes left several accounts of his informal outdoor seminar on Cape Cod, one dated Sept. 20–21, 1965 (I-P-L), AIMT, MSP; another undated but clearly written in 1969/70 for AMS, Jr., ibid.; and see Harold Taylor to GS, June 10, 1969, MSP.

25. Lewis Coser, *Men of Ideas* (New York, 1965), 263; *Harvard Class of 1914: Fiftieth Anniversary Report* (Cambridge, Mass., 1964), 481.

26. GS to George Gerbner, Sept. 20 and Nov. 8, 1965, Gerbner Papers, xeroxed for the author in 1992; GS to Loren Eisley, April 1, 1960, MSP.

27. GS to George Gerbner, June 6, 1964, Gerbner Papers. A one-year hiatus occurred after Seldes retired in 1963. Gerbner, who succeeded him as dean on July 1, 1964, was a professor of communications at Penn, editor of the *Journal of Communication*, and author of *Mass Communications and Popular Conceptions of Education: A Cross-Cultural Study* (Urbana, 1964).

28. Telephone conversation with Professor Charles Lee, July 14, 1993. Lee had been a professor of English at Penn and a participant in the faculty planning committee for the Annenberg School. He became a crucial member of Seldes' informal advisory group and managed a lot of daily detail as well as the school's budget. Lee also published light poetry and served as a cultural critic on WFLN-FM, Philadelphia's "arts" station at that time. See Charles Lee, *Love, Life, & Laughter* (Newton Square, Pa., 1990), 58 and 85 for occasional poems about Seldes.

29. GS to George Gerbner, June 6, 1964, Gerbner Papers.

30. Charles Lee to the author, June 24, 1993.

31. Seldes, *Lords of the Press* (New York, 1938), 240–41.

32. GS to George Gerbner, Nov. 8, 1965, Gerbner Papers; Charles Lee to the author, July 2, 1993; GS, IVL-10 (Feb. 22, 1965), AIMT, MSP.

33. GS, IVL-11 (Feb. 22, 1965), AIMT, MSP.

34. *Variety*, Dec. 13, 1961, p. 2.

35. GS to Luce, Feb. 13, 1962, MSP. Ironically, almost three decades earlier Seldes had been extremely complimentary to *Time* as a valuable source of information. See GS, *The Years of the Locust (America, 1929–1932)* (Boston, 1933), 72n.

36. Luce to GS, March 3, 1962, MSP.

37. GS, *New Mass Media*, 38–39, quotation at 67.

38. Ibid., 45, 51.

39. Ibid., 30–31, 97.

40. Ibid., 64, 66.

41. Ibid., 64–65.

42. Ibid., 66.

43. Ibid., 66–67.

44. GS, "The Public Interest" (Lexington, Va., 1963), 11-page pamphlet, 4.

45. Ibid., 7–8. Later in 1963 a journalist wrote an essay about Robert M. Hutchins and the Center for the Study of Democratic Institutions, located in Santa Barbara, California. At one point Hutchins turned to a senior staff member and said: "You've been spending most of your time on the media of mass communication. I haven't heard a new syllable or a new idea in mass communication since 1947." (John Bainbridge, "Our Footloose Correspondents," *New Yorker*, Nov. 9, 1963, p. 128.) Seldes, apparently, read the essay and felt very hurt.

46. Untitled, undated two-page typescript that begins, "Some time in the 1930s . . . ." MSP.

47. GS, "The Public Interest," 3, 6, 10, 11. In a single sheet of "biographical data"

that Seldes wrote early in the 1960s he reiterated his self-definition: "a pamphleteer and propagandist whose profession it is to worry in public about the effects of those entertainments he once called "Lively" and are now somewhat grimly called 'the mass media.'" (MSP.)

48. See Paul Buhle, ed., *Popular Culture in America* (Minneapolis, 1987); Neil Postman, *Technopoly: The Surrender of Culture to Technology* (New York, 1992).

49. Rough script, "Adam's Rib," dated April 7 [1963?], MSP.

50. "The Work of Benny Goodman," cassette T78:0078, Museum of Broadcasting, New York, N.Y. The vitality of popular culture in Germany during the later 1920s owed a great deal to jazz and the populist ideal of utilitarian art. From 1923 until 1933 the Bauhaus had its own jazz band, a clear indication of how central jazz really was as a source of cultural renewal in all of the arts. Seldes seems to have had no interest in German popular culture, either then or later, although he did pay attention to films made in Germany prior to about 1935.

51. GS to Edwin O'Connor [1964], Ms. Am 1600 (242), BPL; GS to Carey McWilliams, March 23, 1966, MSP.

52. GS, "Public Entertainment and the Subversion of Ethical Standards," AAAPSS no. 363 (Jan. 1966): 91.

53. Ibid., 92.

54. Ibid., 87, 94, See also Kevin Brownlow, *Behind the Mask of Innocence* (New York, 1990), 370, for an observation made by Seldes in 1964 about democratic and undemocratic revolutions.

55. Jarrell, *A Sad Heart at the Supermarket*, 73–75.

56. Jarrell, "The Taste of the Age," SEP (July 26, 1958), in Jarrell, *Kipling, Auden & Co.: Essays and Reviews, 1935–1964* (New York, 1980), 293, 295, 298–99.

57. Jarrell, *A Sad Heart at the Supermarket*, 86.

58. GS, letter to the editor, "Russell's Greatness," NYT, Feb. 8, 1970, sec. 4, p. 13.

Chapter 11. "I Am by Now Accustomed to Flashbacks"

1. The script of "Conversation" for March 22, 1956, pp. 5, 15, in BPL. There is also a document in Seldes' papers dated June 7, 1966, in which he recounts episodes of his financial imprudence, along with a letter of complaint to the American Express Co., dated Sept. 17, 1965, about a bothersome billing, MSP. In a memo for his own use dated Feb. 26, 1964, Seldes confessed on the first page of twelve that his current interest "is that the money-nexus is not as detestable as it has been made out to be." He then described his conversations over the years with Bertrand Russell, Stravinsky, Cocteau, and Sherwood Anderson concerning the importance of money (MSP).

2. GS, uncoded memorandum, Feb. 26, 1964, pp. 10–11, AIMT, MSP.

3. See, as examples, Charles Norman, *E. E. Cummings: The Magic-Maker* (New York, 1958); Frederick J. Hoffman, *The Twenties: American Writing in the Postwar Decade* (New York, 1962); S. Cushing Strout, *The American Image of the Old World* (New York, 1963); and Nicholas Joost, *Scofield Thayer and the Dial* (Carbondale, Ill., 1964).

4. GS to Wilson, Feb. 24, 1965, Wilson Papers, BLYU; Wilson to John Dos Passos, Nov. 27, 1951, Dos Passos Papers, box 5 (#5950-AA), ALUV.

5. Although Seldes very much admired Mark Sullivan's multi-volume *Our Times* (1926–35), there is no evidence that he wanted to echo that title. Seldes surely remembered that Ernest Hemingway called his first book *in our time* (Paris, 1924), a miscellany

of stories and vignettes; but he would not have wanted to echo Hemingway, I believe, not even as an ironic gesture.

6. GS to F. Scott Fitzgerald, June 26 [1936], in Matthew J. Bruccoli and Margaret M. Duggan, eds., *Correspondence of F. Scott Fitzgerald* (New York, 1980), 436.

7. GS to JR, March 8, 1910, MSP; GS to Christopher Farley, May 21, 1969, MSP.

8. GS, RFM 1–4 (Dec. 24, 1964), AIMT, MSP.

9. GS, *The Years of the Locust (America, 1929–1933)* (Boston, 1933), 45; GS to Edmund Wilson, Dec. 10, 1968, Wilson Papers, BLYU.

10. GS, untitled memo dated Feb. 26, 1964, p. 5, MSP; GS to AMS, Jr., Jan. 16, 1968, MSP; GS to Robert M. Hutchins, Nov. 16, 1968, MSP.

11. See Marc Dolan, "The (Hi)story of Their Lives: Mythic Autobiography and 'The Lost Generation,'" *Journal of American Studies* 27 (April 1993): 35–56.

12. GS, GSS-9/13 (June 11–12,?), AIMT, MSP.

13. GS, APU-1/6 (Nov. 28, 1964), AIMT, MSP.

14. Ibid.

15. GS, DG-1, undated, AIMT, MSP. Seldes devoted one segment of AIMT to a memoir of his public and private debates with physicist Edward Teller, the foremost advocate of the H-bomb as a deterrent to war. See GS, AOT-1/3 (Feb. 23, 1965), AIMT, MSP.

16. GS, CCC-1/7, (Nov. 30, 1965), AIMT, MSP.

17. GS, untitled two-page memo (April 25, 1967), AMS, Jr., Papers, JFKL. For this process from the perspective of an intellectual and social historian, see Stow Persons, "The Americanization of the Immigrant," in David F. Bowers, ed., *Foreign Influences in American Life* (Princeton, 1944), 39–56.

18. GS, untitled two-page memo cited in note 17.

19. GS, TRU-1/5 (Oct. 2, 1967), AIMT, MSP.

20. GS, HK-1/3 (Dec. 21, 1965), AIMT, MSP.

21. GS, EMP-1/2 (n.d.), AIMT, MSP.

22. GS, TE-G-1/2 (Nov. 29, 1963), AIMT, MSP.

23. Ibid.

24. GS, WID-1 (Feb. 20, 1968), AIMT, MSP.

25. Ibid., WID-2/11.

26. GS, BOC-1 (Feb. 11, 1965), AIMT, MSP.

27. See Chapter Two, pp. 55–56 above; and *Esquire* 8 (July 1937): 79.

28. GS to Carlos Baker, March 3, 1966, MSP.

29. Moore to Archibald MacLeish, Oct. 15, 1954, MacLeish Papers, box 16, MDLC; GS to Moore, April 18, 1967, Moore Papers, RGM.

30. Gerald Murphy to Archibald MacLeish, Sept 8, 1932, and May 30, 1964, Mac-Leish Papers, box 16, MDLC.

31. GS, FNSF-1/5 (Nov. 26, 1965), AIMT, MSP.

32. Ibid., 7/8.

33. GS, SA-4 (n.d., later 1960s), AIMT, MSP.

34. GS, BOC-1/2 (Feb. 11, 1965), AIMT, MSP.

35. From an undated text marked EE, MSP. In another undated (but late 1966) document titled only *Book*, Seldes ascribed the intellectuals' scorn for the popular arts to "insecurity" and contempt for ordinary life.

36. GS, PSV-1/2 (Feb. 25, 1965), AIMT, MSP. For Seldes' strong sense of himself as a "non-joining" non-participant in causes, see the handwritten ON-3 (item #17), AIMT, MSP.

37. GS, SLAM-1 (July 4, 1967), AIMT, MSP.

38. Ibid., SLAM-2/3. It is not likely that by 1967 Seldes had seen the English translation of Walter Benjamin's 1936 essay "The Work of Art in the Age of Mechanical Reproduction," in Benjamin, *Illuminations*, Hannah Arendt, ed. (New York, 1968), 217–51.

39. James Marston Fitch, "The Form of Plenty," *Columbia University Forum* 6 (Summer 1963): 4–9; Seldes' reply is in ibid. (Fall 1963): 43.

40. GS, SLAM-9/10, AIMT, MSP. For Seldes' final point of reference, see Macdonald, "Masscult & Midcult," in Macdonald, *Against the American Grain* (New York, 1962), 3–75. On pp. 64–65 Macdonald admits his surprise that British radicals found his critique of mass culture snobbish and elitist. This essay first appeared in PR (Spring 1960). For an acerbic exchange of notes, see Macdonald to GS, Aug. 14, 1967, and GS to Macdonald, [Aug. 1967?], both in Macdonald Papers, box 45, SLYU.

41. GS, "Communism and the Intellectuals, 1925–1935" (Feb. 15, 1969), AIMT, MSP.

42. GS, ENI-5/7 (Nov. 19, 1965), AIMT, MSP.

43. Ibid., 7/8; undated page with a cover sheet titled Proletarian writers and case histories, MSP.

44. GS, TX-1/2 (Jan. 17, 1965), AIMT, MSP. For an admirable book on exactly this subject, see John P. Diggins, *Up from Communism: Conservative Odysseys in American Intellectual History* (New York, 1975).

45. GS to Dos Passos, Feb. 28, 1966, Dos Passos Papers (#5950-aa), box 4, ALUV.

46. GS, FIN (undated), AIMT, MSP.

47. Ibid.

48. Seldes left a detailed account of this meeting, along with his worshipful feelings about Oppenheimer in general, in a 12-page document, uncoded but dated Feb. 26, 1964, for AIMT, MSP (pp. 6–9).

49. Ibid., 9. Seldes actually conflated two small books by Schrödinger, *What Is Life? The Physical Aspects of the Living Cell* (Cambridge, Eng., 1944) and *Science and Humanism: Physics in Our Time* (Cambridge, 1951). The quotation appears in the latter, 8–9.

50. GS to Watson, June 2, 1966, Seldes Papers, Berg Collection, NYPL.

51. AMS, Jr., to GS, Sept. 1, 1962, MSP; GS to AMS, Jr., Feb. 2, 1968, Schlesinger Papers, JFKL.

52. GS to Robert M. Hutchins, [1964?], MSP. It is clear that Seldes had at some point read and been influenced by Erwin Schrödinger, *Science and Humanism*, a 68-page lecture.

53. GS, A-SCI (Aug. 5, 1968), AIMT, MSP; GS, uncoded memorandum (Feb. 12, 1969), AIMT, MSP. Seldes enjoyed conversations and correspondence with Buckminster Fuller about "design science." See Fuller to GS, July 24, 1969, MSP.

54. GS, NYEJ, Feb. 3, 1933, p. 15; and for Seldes' interest in bringing natural science to the general public, see ibid., Jan. 6, 1933, p. 18.

55. GS, TOJ-1/2 (Jan. 21, 1966), AIMT, MSP.

56. GS, "Science and Society," [1966?], four-page typescript with "Caltech" scrawled across the top, MSP. Albert R. Hibbs achieved prominence explaining science and technology to the general public, first for NBC (1961–65) and then on WCET in Los Angeles (1965–69).

57. Ibid. See Harold A. Innis, *Empire and Communications* (Oxford, 1950) and *The Bias of Communication* (Toronto, 1951), two works that influenced Seldes and many others.

58. GS, "Science and Society," [1966?], MSP.

59. See Thomas P. and Agatha C. Hughes, eds., *Lewis Mumford: Public Intellectual* (New York, 1990), 43–65, 152–63, 181–232; Andrew Ross, *Strange Weather: Culture, Science, and Technology in the Age of Limits* (New York, 1991).

60. For the intellectuals' hostility to science, see GS, uncoded memorandum, Feb. 12, 1969, AIMT, MSP. See Marian Seldes, *The Bright Lights: A Theatre Life* (Boston, 1978).

61. GS, FIN 1/2 (n.d.), AIMT, MSP.

62. GS to AMS, Jr., two-page memo (n.d.), Schlesinger Papers, JFKL. This same statement appeared in GS, "Broadside #1," privately printed and sent to friends in March 1968.

63. GS, ENI-5, AIMT, MSP; GS, untitled and undated memo (item D), AIMT, MSP.

64. GS, ENI-10, AIMT, MSP.

65. GS to R. M. Hutchins, Nov. 11, 1963, MSP. For an instructive example of disillusionment by a very different sort of cultural critic who lamented the passing of modernism, see Clement Greenberg, "Where is the Avant-Garde?" (1967), in Greenberg, *The Collected Essays and Criticism*, vol. 4, *Modernism with a Vengeance, 1957–1969* (Chicago, 1993), 259–65. For MacLeish and others see Michael Kammen, *Mystic Chords of Memory: The Transformation of Tradition in American Culture* (New York, 1991), 619.

66. GS, uncoded 12-page memorandum, Feb. 26, 1964, AIMT, MSP. Seldes concluded the memorandum (p. 12) with this historical observation and connection. In 1921–24, when the U.S. severely tightened access for immigrants "we were warning people not to try to become new men in a new world, [so] we stopped being the NEW WORLD. In 1917—for the first time in our history—a revolution occurred which had different aims from our revolution. For the first time in our history, people turned their backs on us and looked elsewhere for a new concept of a good life."

67. See Richard H. Pells, *Radical Visions and American Dreams: Culture and Social Thought in the Depression Years* (New York, 1973); Lawrence W. Levine, *The Unpredictable Past: Explorations in American Cultural History* (New York, 1993), 206–30; Warren I. Susman, *Culture as History: The Transformation of American Society in the Twentieth Century* (New York, 1984), 150–83.

68. GS, uncoded and undated one-page manuscript, AIMT, MSP. Seldes had actually been contemplating such a connection ever since 1934. See GS, "True to Type," NYEJ, June 13, 1934, p. 17. Oddly enough, even as Seldes wrote this passage a young American scholar prepared a book that agreed with his position to some degree yet recognized the complexity and diversity of such intellectual trajectories. See James B. Gilbert, *Writers and Partisans: A History of Literary Radicalism in the United States* (New York, 1968), 59–65, esp. 61.

69. For the reasons why his relationship with Eliot continued to bother him well into the 1960s, see GS to Richard Poirier, March 20, 1965, MSP; GS to James Sibley Watson, Jr., June 1, 1966, and March 3, 1970, Berg Collection, NYPL.

70. I am grateful to Marian Seldes for lending me originals of the two broadsides.

71. He called this Broadside #3, and ended it with a note in italics: *"Broadside #2 has been postponed. It is called* The Arrogance of the Artist."

72. GS to Wilson, Feb. 21, 1968, Wilson Papers, BLYU; GS to Burke, Nov. 1968, MSP.

73. GS to Watson, [June 1970], Berg Collection, NYPL.

74. GS, "In Defense of Dirty Words," *Esquire* 2 (Nov. 1934): 173.

75. NYT, Sept. 30, 1970, p. 46; *Time*, Oct. 12, 1970, p. 62; *Newsweek*, Oct. 12, 1970, p. 84.

76. Mishkin, "Seldes Heralded a New Age," N.Y. *Morning Telegraph*, Oct. 1, 1970, clipping in MSP.

77. Nathan, *The World in Falseface* (New York, 1923), x.

Acknowledgments

This project would not have been possible without the cooperation of Gilbert Seldes' children, Marian and Timothy. They made available to me a very considerable amount of unpublished material that remains in their possession: letters to and from their father, his early journals, newspaper clippings, ephemera, and above all the very substantial manuscript of his unpublished autobiographical memoir. (Many important segments of that memoir are undated. They were mainly dictated into a machine and some obvious inaccuracies in the typed transcripts are the result of a transcriber's misunderstanding of what Seldes said.)

Marian and Tim were equally generous with their time, patiently answering questions that often must have seemed either tedious or else, quite literally, curious. In return they have been amazingly restrained in not pressing *me* with questions about how I intended to deal with one thing or another. And they have given me permission to quote from everything that Gilbert Seldes wrote, manuscripts as well as printed matter. I have no doubt that they are likely to dissent from some (perhaps even many) of the observations and criticisms that pervade this book. I am deeply appreciative that they have respected my independence as a scholar.

Letters to and from Seldes also exist in the papers of many of his contemporaries. I am obliged to curators and archivists at numerous institutions where I worked; and also to those who expedited my requests for photocopies to be sent by mail. A complete record of those institutions will be found in the list of abbreviations that precedes the notes.

For granting me permission to quote extracts from unpublished correspondence, I am deeply grateful and acknowledge the following: The Sherwood Anderson Papers, The Newberry Library, Chicago, and Harold Ober Associates Incorporated, Copyright © 1953 by Eleanor Copenhaver Anderson, Copyright renewed 1978 by Eleanor Copenhaver Anderson; Thomas Benét and Brandt & Brandt Literary Agents, Inc., for permission to publish an unpublished letter written by Stephen Vincent Benét; Mrs. Elizabeth H. Dos Passos for permission to quote from the papers of John Dos Passos; the Irwin Edman Papers, Rare Book and Manuscript Library, Columbia University, New York; for letters written by T. S. Eliot, Copyright Mrs. Valerie Eliot of London; permission from Scribner, an imprint of Simon & Schuster, Inc., for an extract from *F. Scott Fitzgerald: A Life in Letters*, edited by Matthew J. Bruccoli, copyright © 1994 by the Trustees u/a dated 7/3/75, created by Frances Scott Fitzgerald Smith; for an extract from F. Scott Fitzgerald, *The Crack-Up*, copyright 1945 by New Directions Publishing Corporation, reprinted by permission of New Directions; for letters written by Emma Goldman, David Ballantine of Bearsville, New York; Houghton Mifflin Co. for an excerpt from *The Letters of Archibald MacLeish, 1907–1982*, edited by R. H. Winnick, copyright © 1983 by the Estate of Archibald MacLeish and by R. H. Winnick; the Marianne Moore Papers, The Rosenbach Museum and Library, Philadelphia; for Lewis Mumford, Robert Wojtowicz, Old Dominion University, Norfolk, Virginia; for a letter written by Gerald Murphy, Honoria Murphy Donnelly of East Hampton, New York; for Ezra Pound letters, Timothy Materer, ed., *The Selected Letters of Ezra Pound to John Quinn, 1915–1924* (Durham, N.C.: Duke University Press, 1991), reprinted with permission; for Allen Tate, the Manuscripts Division, Department of Rare Books and Special Collections, Princeton University Libraries; Farrar, Straus & Giroux, Inc. for excerpts from *Letters on Literature and Politics, 1912–1972* by Edmund Wilson. Copyright © 1957, 1974, 1977 by Elena Wilson, Executrix of the Estate of Edmund Wilson; and an excerpt from *The Shores of Light* by Edmund Wilson. Copyright © by Edmund Wilson. Copyright renewed © 1980 by Helen Miranda Wilson. Reprinted by permission of Farrar, Straus & Giroux, Inc.

I also enjoyed notable cooperation from Professor George Gerbner, who succeeded Seldes as Dean of the Annenberg School of Communications at the University of Pennsylvania; Professor Charles Lee, who served on the faculty there during Seldes' deanship and worked closely with him on curriculum as well as administrative matters; Gilbert's older brother, George Seldes, a distinguished and venerable journalist who gave me a delightful interview in July 1991 at his home in Hartland-4-Corners, Vermont; and Norman Corwin, who provided immensely helpful conversations in March 1994 at his home in Los Angeles.

This book was initially composed during 1993–94 when I served as the Times Mirror Foundation Research Professor of American Studies at the Huntington Library, Art Collections, and Botanical Gardens in San Marino, California. I cannot imagine a more serene and congenial setting for scholarly work, and I will long remember the cooperation that I received there from Robert A. Skotheim, the President; Jane Hill, Assistant to the Director of Research; David Brigham, Research Associate in Art and American Studies; Alan Taylor of the University of California, Davis, a Fellow in residence during my tenure; Peggy Bernal, Publications Director; Evie Cutting, Special Events Coordinator; but, above all, Robert C. Ritchie, the Huntington's splendid and wry Director of Research, who really made it all not merely possible, but thoroughly pleasurable as well.

During 1992–93 I had conscientious help with my research at Cornell from Christopher Martin, John J. Jeziorski, and Maura Flood. Julie S. Copenhagen of Cornell's Inter-Library Loan Services expedited numerous requests. Victoria Bernal and Yvonne Sims put my archaic manuscript on disks and patiently endured numerous rounds of revision. Jennifer Lawrence and Arthur Cameron Smith proof-read meticulously and helped to locate out-of-the-way books. Janice Whittleton did the photocopying with dispatch and good cheer.

At Oxford University Press I have enjoyed warm support and wise counsel from Senior Vice-President Sheldon Meyer, and efficient help from his assistant, Brandon Trissler. Andrew Albanese and Joellyn M. Ausanka thoughtfully supervised the production process, and Stephanie Sakson handled the line editing with extraordinary promptness, care, and consideration.

Robert Dawidoff, Richard Polenberg, Joan Shelley Rubin, and Jill Watts read the manuscript and offered invaluable suggestions for improvement. And Carol Kammen, as always, looked after me, looked over the manuscript, and overlooked the inconvenience of relocation from hearth and home for eight months. Once again, her support has made it all worthwhile. Happily we not only escaped the Northeast's horrendous winter of 1993–94, but Carol even managed to miss the unsettling Los Angeles earthquake of January 17, 1994, and most of its 8,000 aftershocks. That's family planning at its finest.

Above Cayuga's Waters   M.K.
June 1995

Index

Aaron, Daniel, 365, 401
ABC network, 345–46
Adams, Franklin P., 124, 184, 264
Adams, Henry, 132
Adams, James Truslow, 141, 180
Addams, Jane, 89
Adorno, Theodor, 12, 329, 339
advertising: changing nature of, 356; and class issues, 358; and democracy, 358; as entertainment, 358; in Europe, 356; history and sociology of, 358; "immunity" of, 360; Jarrell on, 375–76; McLuhan on, 354; in magazines, 354; and mass culture, 322, 329; Packard on, 357, 358–59; as "pernicious" influence, 357; psychology of, 358–59; Seldes posing in, *197;* Seldes' interest in, 47, 112, 198–99, 248, 249, 250–51, 308, 315, 356, 357–59; Seldes' unfinished work about, 353; Williams (Raymond) on, 354;

and women, 308. *See also* commercials
aesthetes, 11, 64–65, 212, 215, 224, 237, 361, 383, 401, 402
aesthetic criticism, 67, 396
Against the American Grain (Macdonald), 328
Against Revolution (Seldes), 185–86
"The Age of Criticism" (Jarrell), 333
Agee, James, 4, 232–33, 292
Agrarianism, 189–90, 294
Aiken, Conrad, 76, 103–4, 155
alcohol, 37, 139–40, *197. See also* Prohibition
Algonquin circle, 24, 39, 42, 69, 80, 92, 136, 140
"The All-Star Literary Vaudeville" (Wilson), 100–102
Allen, Fred, 253, 254, 377
Allen, Frederick Lewis, 180–81, 183, 208, 258, 264, 309, 320
Alliance, New Jersey, 17, 20, 21–22